MCSE CORE ELECTIVE EXAMS

IN A NUTSHELL

Other networking resources from O'Reilly

Related titles

MCSE Core Required
  Exams in a Nutshell
Active Directory
Active Directory
  Cookbook™
Securing Windows Server
  2003

Learning Windows Server
  2003
Windows Server
  Cookbook™
Windows Server 2003
  Security Cookbook™
Windows XP Cookbook™

Networking Resource Center

networking.oreilly.com is a complete catalog of O'Reilly's books on networking technologies.

Conferences

O'Reilly brings diverse innovators together to nurture the ideas that spark revolutionary industries. We specialize in documenting the latest tools and systems, translating the innovator's knowledge into useful skills for those in the trenches. Visit *conferences.oreilly.com* for our upcoming events.

Safari Bookshelf (*safari.oreilly.com*) is the premier online reference library for programmers and IT professionals. Conduct searches across more than 1,000 books. Subscribers can zero in on answers to time-critical questions in a matter of seconds. Read the books on your Bookshelf from cover to cover or simply flip to the page you need. Try it today for free.

MCSE CORE ELECTIVE EXAMS
IN A NUTSHELL

Pawan K. Bhardwaj and Roger A. Grimes

O'REILLY®

Beijing · Cambridge · Farnham · Köln · Paris · Sebastopol · Taipei · Tokyo

MCSE Core Elective Exams in a Nutshell
by Pawan K. Bhardwaj and Roger A. Grimes

Published by O'Reilly Media, Inc., 1005 Gravenstein Highway North, Sebastopol, CA 95472.

O'Reilly books may be purchased for educational, business, or sales promotional use. Online editions are also available for most titles (*safari.oreilly.com*). For more information, contact our corporate/institutional sales department: (800) 998-9938 or *corporate@oreilly.com*.

Editor: Jeff Pepper
Production Editor: Mary Brady
Copyeditor: Mary Brady
Proofreader: Lydia Onofrei

Indexer: John Bickelhaupt
Cover Designer: Karen Montgomery
Interior Designer: David Futato
Illustrators: Robert Romano and Jessamyn Read

Printing History:

October 2006:   First Edition.

 This book uses RepKover™, a durable and flexible lay-flat binding.

ISBN-10: 0-596-10229-1
ISBN-13: 978-0-596-10229-6
[C]

*To my late father, Sudershan Bhardwaj,
who passed away during the writing of
this book.*

—Pawan Bhardwaj

*To my friends, co-workers, and mentors
at The Training Camp, who helped me to
become a better MCSE instructor*

—Roger Grimes

Table of Contents

Part II. Exam 70-297

Part III. Exam 70-298

Preface

Welcome to *MCSE: The Core Elective Exams in a Nutshell*. We designed this book for IT professionals who want to complete their Microsoft certifications. Microsoft offers multiple certification tracks for various levels of IT professionals. As a systems administrator or an engineer, the tracks you will be most interested in are:

Microsoft Certified Professional (MCP)
> This is an entry level certification track. To become an MCP, you need to pass only one current Microsoft certification exam.

Microsoft Certified Systems Administrator (MCSA)
> This is an intermediate certification track for experienced administrators. To become an MCSA, you must pass three core exams and one elective exam.

Microsoft Certified Systems Engineer (MCSE)
> This is an advanced certification track for experienced administrators with strong engineering backgrounds. To become an MCSE, you must pass five core exams and two elective exams. One of the elective exams covers a client operating system, and the other exam covers one design exam.

Taken appropriately, the certification tracks can measure the progress of your IT career from a beginner to a professional level. For those who are already experienced, the certification tracks can be a measure of your progress through the process of getting your professional credentials. Regardless of your certification plans, the exam we recommend studying for and taking is the *Exam 70-270: Installing, Configuring and Administering Microsoft Windows XP Professional*. This exam is covered in this book. When you pass this, you will get your MCP credentials.

After you become an MCP, you should aim for getting the MCSA credential, and then the MCSE credential. To become an MCSA, you will need to pass two core exams from the MCSE track. These exams are *Exam 70-290: Managing and Maintaining a Windows Server 2003 Environment* and *Exam 70-291: Implementing,*

Managing and Maintaining a Windows Server 2003 Network Infrastructure. These are also part of the MCSE track. Our companion book, *MCSE: The Core Exams In A Nutshell,* by William Stanek (O'Reilly) covers all four core exams for the MCSE track.

After you have passed four core exams and the client exam, you will need to take one of the design exams. Although this book covers two design exams, you will need to take only one to complete your MCSE certification track. The design exams covered in this book are *Exam 70-297: Designing a Microsoft Windows Server 2003 Active Directory and Network Infrastructure* and *Exam 70-298: Designing Security for Microsoft Windows Server 2003 Network.*

If you are a current MCSA on Windows 2000, you need to pass Exam 70-292 to upgrade your certification to Windows Server 2003. If you are a current MCSE on Windows 2000, you need to pass Exams 70-292 and 70-296 to upgrade your certification to Windows Server 2003. These exams are designed to cover the delta (changes) between Windows 2000 and Windows Server 2003.

The focus of this book is on providing the core knowledge to prepare you for the current certification exams, which include performance-based testing through simulation. Use this book as part of your final preparation—not as your only preparation—for the exams. Think of this as the notes you'd have written down if you were to highlight and then record every essential nugget of information related to the skills being measured in Exams 70-270, 70-297, and 70-298.

Basically, we have boiled down the required knowledge to its core. Thus, rather than presenting 500 to 700 pages for each exam, there are approximately 150 pages for each. With this in mind, the best way to use this book is as part of your final review. So after you've acquired sufficient hands-on expertise and studied all the relevant texts, grab this and study it cover to cover as part of your final exam cram.

 Unless you have access to a very complete test environment, we recommend employing some type of virtual machine technology as part of your exam preparation. Microsoft offers Virtual PC and Virtual Server. Virtual PC lets you configure desktops and servers and run them in a virtual network environment. Virtual Server builds on Virtual PC and offers better resource usage and extended APIs for automated deployment and management.

Conventions Used in This Book

Each part within this book corresponds to a single Microsoft exam and consists of the following sections:

Exam Overview
 Provides a brief introduction to the exam's topic, a list of objectives, and a cross reference to where the objectives are covered.

Study Guide
> Provides a comprehensive study guide for the skills being measured on the exam. You should read through and study this section extensively. If you encounter topics you haven't practiced with and studied extensively prior to reading this text, you should do more hands-on work with the related area of study and refer to an expanded discussion in a relevant text. Once you've built the real-world know-how and developed the essential background needed to succeed, you can resume your studies and move forward.

Prep and Practice
> Provides exercises to supplement your studies, highlights from all the topics covered for the exam, and practice questions to help test your knowledge. Sample questions are followed by answers with explanations where necessary.

The following font conventions are used in this book:

Constant width
> Used for code terms, command-line text, command-line options, and values that should be typed literally.

Italics
> Used for URLs, variables, filenames, and to introduce new terms.

 Notes are used to provide additional information or highlight a specific point.

 Warnings are used to provide details about potential problems.

Other Study Resources

No single magic bullet for passing the Microsoft Certification exams exists. Your current knowledge will largely determine your success with this study guide and on the exams. If you encounter topics you haven't practiced with and studied extensively prior to reading this text, you need further preparation. Get the practical hands-on know-how and knowledge before continuing.

Throughout your preparations for certification, we recommend that you regularly visit Microsoft's web site Certification page (*http://www.microsoft.com/certification/*). The related pages will help you keep up to date with the certification process and any changes that may occur.

A wide variety of Microsoft Certification study guides, training classes, and learning resources are available. Regardless of whether these materials say they are for MCPs, MCSAs, or MCSEs, the materials should relate to specific exams. The exams are the same regardless of the certification track.

Also, a large number of practice tests and exam simulations are available on the Web both for purchase and for free. These tests, like this book, are useful as part of your exam preparation.

How to Contact Us

We have worked with the good folks at O'Reilly to test and verify the information in this book to the best of our ability, but you may find that features have changed (or even that we have made mistakes!). To make this book better, please let us know about any errors you find, as well as your suggestions for future editions, by writing to:

O'Reilly Media, Inc.
1005 Gravenstein Highway North
Sebastopol, CA 95472
800-998-9938 (in the United States or Canada)
707-829-0515 (international/local)
707-829-0104 (fax)

O'Reilly has a web page for this book, which lists errata, examples, and any additional information. You can access this page at:

http://www.oreilly.com/catalog/mcseceeian

You can also send us messages electronically. To be put on the mailing list or request a catalog, send email to:

info@oreilly.com

To ask technical questions, to comment on the book, or more information about the authors, please send email to:

bookquestions@oreilly.com

For more information about O'Reilly, please visit:

http://www.oreilly.com

Safari® Enabled

 When you see a Safari® Enabled icon on the cover of your favorite technology book, it means the book is available online through the O'Reilly Network Safari Bookshelf.

Safari offers a solution that's better than e-books. It's a virtual library that lets you easily search thousands of top tech books, cut and paste code samples, download chapters, and find quick answers when you need the most accurate, current information. Try it for free at *http://safari.oreilly.com*.

Acknowledgments

We are grateful to our technical editors, Rodney Buike and Erik Eckel, for working their way through the book to expose errors and omissions. They worked hard to make sure that the book is technically complete. Jeff Pepper proved to be very instrumental in pioneering the entire project with great enthusiasm. John Vacca read every page of the book for grammatical mistakes. Finally, special thanks to Mary Brady for a very fine editing job.

Exam 70-270:
Installing, Configuring, and Administering Microsoft Windows XP Professional

Exam 70-270 Overview

Exam 70-270: Installing, Configuring, and Administering Microsoft Windows XP Professional is Microsoft's entry-level exam for MCSE and MCSA in Windows 2003 and Windows 2000 tracks. The main emphasis of this exam is the use of the Windows XP Professional operating system as a network client for Windows Server 2003 and Windows 2000 Server. The exam focuses on your skills to install, configure, administer, and troubleshoot the Windows XP Professional operating system in a medium- or large-scale organization. better

This exam is required if you have not passed Windows 2000 Professional as a client exam for the MCSE Windows 2000 track, or if you have just started your journey toward achieving MCSA or MCSE certification. In the latter case, this should be your first exam, because the knowledge you will gain by studying for it will be very helpful when you prepare for the Windows Server 2003 exams. By just passing this, you become a Microsoft Certified Professional (MCP).

This exam has recently been upgraded to include features of the Windows XP Professional Service Pack 2. Some of these features include Security Center and enhancements to Internet Explorer 6. Security Center runs as a background service and includes Windows Firewall, Automatic Updates, and Virus Protection. Internet Explorer now includes a pop-up blocker and an information bar.

In order to be prepared for Exam 70-270, Microsoft recommends that you have at least one year's worth of hands-on experience with installing, configuring, and troubleshooting a desktop operating system in a network environment with 250 or more users. It is a good idea to have studied a Windows XP Professional self-paced exam study guide or taken a training course.

Some of the problem areas that you should concentrate on while studying include installation, upgrading from previous operating systems, unattended installations using automation, administration and troubleshooting access to resources, optimizing the performance of various system and hardware components, configuring the desktop environment, and configuring network services.

Exam 70-270 is one of the two available client operating system exams required for MCSA or MCSE. The other exam is *70-210: Installing, Configuring and Administering Microsoft Windows 2000 Professional*. You need to pass only one of these exams in order to start your MCSA or MCSE certification process. When you pass this exam, you also get the MCP credential. Since Windows XP Professional replaced Windows 2000 Professional and is likely the most widely used client operating system, you should consider taking this exam instead of the Windows 2000 Professional exam.

Areas of Study for Exam 70-270

Installing Microsoft Windows XP Professional

- Perform and troubleshoot an attended installation of Windows XP Professional.
- Perform and troubleshoot an unattended installation of Windows XP Professional.
  — Install Windows XP Professional by using Remote Installation Services (RIS).
  — Install Windows XP Professional by using the System Preparation tool.
  — Create unattended answer files by using Setup Manager to automate the installation of Windows XP Professional.
- Upgrade from previous versions of Windows to Windows XP Professional.
  — Prepare a computer to meet upgrade requirements.
  — Migrate existing users' environments to a new installation.
- Perform post-installation updates and product activation.
- Troubleshoot failed installations.

See "Installing Microsoft Windows XP Professional" on page 16.

Implementing and Conducting Administration of Resources

- Monitor, manage, and troubleshoot access to files and folders.
  — Configure, manage, and troubleshoot file compression.
  — Control access to files and folders by using permissions.
  — Optimize access to files and folders.
- Manage and troubleshoot access to shared folders.
  — Create and remove shared folders.
  — Control access to shared folders by using permissions.
  — Manage and troubleshoot web server resources.
- Connect to local and network print devices.
  — Manage printers and print jobs.
  — Control access to printers by using permissions.
  — Connect to an Internet printer.
  — Connect to a local print device.
- Configure and manage filesystems.
  — Convert from one filesystem to another.
  — Configure NTFS, FAT32 or FAT filesystems.
- Manage and troubleshoot access to and synchronization of offline files.

See "Implementing and Conducting Administration of Resources" on page 38.

Implementing, Managing, Monitoring, and Troubleshooting Hardware Devices and Drivers

- Implement, manage, and troubleshoot disk devices.
  - — Install, configure, and manage DVD and CD-ROM devices.
  - — Monitor and configure disks.
  - — Monitor, configure, and troubleshoot volumes.
  - — Monitor and configure removable media, such as tape devices.
- Implement, manage, and troubleshoot display devices.
  - — Configure multiple-display support.
  - — Install, configure, and troubleshoot a video adapter.
- Configure Advanced Configuration Power Interface (ACPI).
- Implement, manage, and troubleshoot I/O devices.
  - — Monitor, configure, and troubleshoot input and output (I/O) devices such as printers, scanners, multimedia devices, mice, keyboards, and smart card readers.
  - — Monitor, configure, and troubleshoot multimedia hardware such as cameras.
  - — Monitor, configure, and manage modems.
  - — Monitor, configure, and manage Infrared Data Association (IrDA) devices.
  - — Monitor, configure, and manage wireless devices.
  - — Monitor, configure, and manage universal serial bus (USB) device.
  - — Monitor, configure, and manage handheld devices.
  - — Monitor, configure, and manage network adapters.
- Manage and troubleshoot drivers and driver signing.
- Monitor and configure multiprocessor computers.

See "Implementing and Conducting Administration of Resources" on page 38.

Monitoring and Optimizing System Performance and Reliability

- Monitor, optimize, and troubleshoot performance of Windows XP Professional desktop.
  - — Optimize and troubleshoot memory performance.
  - — Optimize and troubleshoot processor utilization.
  - — Optimize and troubleshoot disk performance.
  - — Optimize and troubleshoot application performance.
  - — Configure, manage, and troubleshoot Scheduled Tasks.
- Manage, monitor, and optimize system performance for mobile users.

- Restore and backup the operating system, System State data, and user data.
  - Recover System State data and user data by using Windows Backup.
  - Troubleshoot system resources by starting in Safe Mode.
  - Recover System State data and user data by using Recovery Console.

See "System Performance and Reliability" on page 80.

Configuring and Troubleshooting the Desktop Environment

- Configure and manage user profiles and desktop settings.
- Configure support for multiple languages or locations.
  - Enable multiple-language support.
  - Configure multiple-language support for users.
  - Configure local settings.
  - Configure Windows XP Professional for multiple locations.
- Manage applications by using Windows Installer packages.

See "Configuring and Troubleshooting the Desktop Environment" on page 97.

Implementing, Managing, and Troubleshooting Network Protocols and Services

- Configure and troubleshoot the Transmission Control Protocol/Internet Protocol (TCP/IP) protocol.
- Connect to computers using dial-up networking.
  - Connect to computers by using a virtual private networking (VPN) connection.
  - Create a dial-up connection to connect to a remote access server.
  - Connect to the Internet by using dial-up networking.
  - Configure and troubleshoot Internet Connection Sharing (ICS).
- Connect to resources by using Internet Explorer.
- Configure, manage, and implement Internet Information Services (IIS).
- Configure, manage, and troubleshoot Remote Desktop and Remote Assistance.
- Configure, manage, and troubleshoot an Internet Connection Firewall (ICF).

See "Implementing, Managing, and Troubleshooting Network Protocols and Services" on page 105.

Configuring, Managing, and Troubleshooting Security

- Configure, manage, and troubleshoot Encrypting File System (EFS).
- Configure, manage, and troubleshoot a security configuration and local security policy.

- Configure, manage, and troubleshoot local user and group accounts.
  - — Configure, manage, and troubleshoot auditing.
  - — Configure, manage, and troubleshoot account settings.
  - — Configure, manage, and troubleshoot account policy.
  - — Configure, manage, and troubleshoot user and group rights.
  - — Troubleshoot cached credentials.
- Configure, manage, and troubleshoot Internet Explorer security settings.

See "Configuring, Managing, and Troubleshooting Security" on page 123.

2

Exam 70-270 Study Guide

This chapter provides a study guide for *Exam 70-270: Installing, Configuring, and Administering Microsoft Windows XP Professional*. Many sections in this chapter cover the various objectives of the exam. Each of these sections identifies the exam objective, provides an overview of the objective, and then discusses the key details that you should grasp before taking the exam.

An overview of each of the objectives sections in this chapter follows:

Windows XP Basics
This section does not relate directly to any exam objectives but is included here to review some basics of the operating system, different versions of Windows XP, an overview of workgroups and domains, and enhancements in the SP2.

Installing Microsoft Windows XP Professional
This section describes the essential tasks that you must complete for a successful installation of Windows XP Professional, and various installation methods. It also covers upgrading the previous operating system, automating the installation process, and troubleshooting a failed installation. The startup process, boot options, and registry are also part of this section.

Implementing and Conducting Administration of Resources
This section describes implementing and troubleshooting filesystems and shared folders, and controlling access to files and folders with NTFS and share permissions. Also covered is administration of local and network printers.

Managing Hardware Devices and Drivers
This section describes installation, configuration, and troubleshooting of hardware devices such as disks and display devices, and I/O devices such as scanners, modems, USB devices, and network adapters. Managing driver-signing options for supported devices is also discussed.

Managing User and Group Accounts
   This section covers creating and maintaining local user and group accounts.

Optimizing System Performance and Reliability
   This section describes methods to optimize the system performance by managing components such as memory, processor, and disks. Objectives also cover identifying system bottlenecks, backup, and recovery planning.

Configuring and Troubleshooting Desktop Environment
   This section describes user profiles, display and desktop settings, multiple-language support, and other basic operating system settings in order to optimize the user desktop environment.

Implementing, Managing, and Troubleshooting Network Protocols and Services
   This section includes configuration and troubleshooting of TCP/IP protocol, dial-up remote access connections, Internet Connection Sharing (ICS), Internet Connection Firewall (ICF), and Internet Information Services (IIS). Also covered are Remote Desktop and Remote Assistance.

Configuring, Managing, and Troubleshooting Security
   This section includes discussion of local user and group account management, user rights, auditing, and configuration of local security policy. Encrypting File System (EFS) is also discussed in this section.

This chapter contains several exercises that you will need to complete as part of your preparation. We recommend a computer with the following minimum hardware configuration:

- A PC with an Intel 233 MHz or faster processor (350 MHz recommended) with a CD-ROM or DVD drive and a mouse
- A minimum of 256 MB RAM (512 MB recommended)
- A least 2 GB of free hard disk space
- A Super VGA or higher-resolution monitor

In addition to this, you will need access to a Windows Server to complete exercises in the networking section. A Windows 2000 Server will serve the purpose, but Windows Server 2003 would be a better choice. Needless to say, you will also need an active Internet connection.

 The exercises included in this study guide should be part of your preparation for the exam. Do not perform any exercises in a production environment but instead create a test environment with the recommended hardware.

Windows XP Basics

Windows XP is the next major client operating system introduced by Microsoft after Windows 2000 Professional. Windows XP can work as a standalone operating system at home or in a small office, or as a client operating system in a large enterprise network. The current version of Windows XP comes preinstalled with Service Pack 2 and is also called Windows XP SP2. We will discuss the following basic information in this section:

- Windows XP editions
- Major enhancements in SP2
- Workgroups and domains

Windows XP Editions

This section discusses various editions of Windows XP and the difference in features included with each of them. Each edition of Windows XP is designed for specific purposes and specific types of users.

Windows XP Professional edition

Windows XP Professional edition is designed to work as a client operating system in networked environments comprised of Windows Server domains, although it can also be used as a standalone desktop operating system at home or as part of a small workgroup. The majority of small business users prefer using Windows XP Professional because its features are designed to optimize desktop performance, reliability, and system and file security.

The 70-270 exam is also based on Windows XP's Professional edition and hence is the subject of this study guide. All references in this study guide refer to Windows XP Professional edition.

Windows XP Home edition

As is evident from the name, the Windows XP Home edition is meant primarily for home or small office use. It has very limited networking capabilities but is fully optimized for ease of operation—that is, it avoids the nuisances of complex configurations, which are usually required for networked client computers. This edition has the following limitations as compared with Windows XP Professional:

- It supports only one processor (CPU), whereas the Professional Edition supports up to two processors.
- It does not support mass deployments using Remote Installation Services (RIS), which is an integral part of Windows XP Professional edition.
- The computer cannot join a domain (but you can create a workgroup of computers running Windows XP Home edition).
- It supports only simple file sharing among the workgroup computers, unlike NTFS file permissions in Windows XP Professional. This is due to the fact that the NTFS filesystem is not supported.
- It does not support use of Dynamic disks and file security using Encrypting File System (EFS); EFS is not included.
- It does not support printing permissions. If you share a printer, everyone in the workgroup can print to your printer.
- Internet Information Services (IIS) is not included; however, a part of Windows XP Professional edition. Home edition supports Remote Desktop client but cannot be used as a Remote Desktop server.

Windows XP Media Center edition

Windows XP Media Center edition runs on new personal computers designed as Media Center PCs. This operating system is optimized to let you experience digital entertainment such as music, TV, home videos, movies, and radio. It is considered a PC as well as a home entertainment center. Media Center PCs use special hardware and are not meant to be part of a corporate network. The current version is Windows XP Media Center 2005.

Windows XP Tablet PC edition

Windows XP Tablet PC edition is as powerful as Windows XP Professional edition, but it is meant basically for mobile computing. It includes features such as touch screen interface, pen input, and speech and handwriting recognition. While users can take full advantage of Windows XP Professional features, software developers can utilize the Tablet PC edition's features to create new applications.

Windows XP Professional 64-Bit edition

The 64-bit edition of Windows XP Professional is a high-performance operating system designed to meet the requirements of applications such as video editing and composing, 3-D animations, scientific and mechanical designs, and analysis. These applications usually require powerful processing and large amounts of system memory. This edition can run on up to 16 GB of RAM as compared to 4 GB of RAM supported by the 32-bit edition of Windows XP Professional. The 64-bit edition runs only on 64-bit processors.

Major Enhancements in Service Pack 2

Service Pack 2 (SP2) is now integrated with Windows XP Professional and is known as Windows XP Professional SP2. Some of the major enhancements to the operating system include a Security Center, improved Automatic Updates, an improved software firewall (now known as Windows Firewall), a more secure Internet Explorer (new Pop-up Blocker), and enhanced default security for the operating system in general.

 Recent updates to Exam 70-270 cover new features included in Service Pack 2. You should pay attention to these new features such as Windows Firewall, Security Center, and enhancements to Internet Explorer.

If you want to know whether your Windows XP installation includes SP2, perform one of the following actions:

- Run the command Winver.exe from the Run dialog box in the Start menu. This opens the About Windows dialog box, which tells you about the currently installed operating system and service packs (if any), as shown in Figure 2-1.

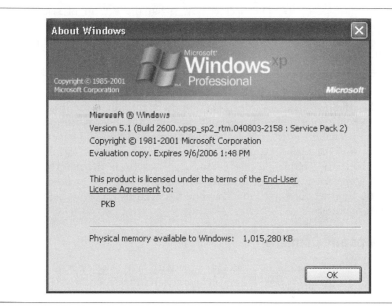

Figure 2-1. Examining the installed version of Windows XP

- Right-click My Computer from the Start menu and click Properties. This opens the General tab of the System properties menu; you can view the name of the operating system and service packs if installed.

Security Center

This new feature is added to the operating system once you install SP2. The Security Center runs as a background service and is mainly responsible for checking the status of Windows Firewall, Automatic Updates, and Virus Protection. If any of these services is disabled, not running, or not updated, a notification pops up in the Windows system tray within the Taskbar, and you can fine-tune the security settings of the operating system. You can also fine-tune settings for an application by double-clicking its icon in the system tray.

Windows Firewall

The previously installed Internet Connection Firewall (ICF) is updated to Windows Firewall when you install SP2. When configured, it will drop all traffic unless the traffic meets specific conditions. The Windows Firewall is enabled by default on all networked Windows XP computers, whereas ICF was enabled only when the ICF service was started.

Automatic Updates

The Automatic Updates feature in Windows XP enables the computer to automatically check for critical updates on the Windows Update web site, download the updates, and apply them in the background. After installing SP2, all critical updates including Service Packs are downloaded. These encompass support for

Microsoft Office products. The user is now given the option of selecting the update and rescheduling its installation. There is no need to accept any End User License Agreement (EULA). You can also prioritize the download of updates if more than one update is available at the same time.

Internet Explorer

Most of the updates included in SP2 for Internet Explorer 6 focus on security. There is a new information bar that is used as a common area to inform you about blocked pop-up windows and blocked ActiveX controls. You still have the option of disabling this bar and returning to your previous settings to display pop-up messages. You can enable or disable the pop-ups from the information bar settings. If some software needs another add-on software file to download and install using Internet Explorer, you are shown a security warning before any of these actions take place.

Workgroups and Domains

There are two basic types of networks possible with Windows operating systems. The first is *workgroups* or *peer-to-peer networks,* and the second is *domains*. In a workgroup, each computer is independently responsible for controlling its resources, which include user accounts, files, folders, and printers. In a domain, a Windows 2000 Server or a Windows Server 2003 computer is designated as a domain controller and holds a centralized database. This database, known as *Active Directory*, stores all the information about the user accounts and shared resources in the network. More details about workgroups and domains are given in the following sections.

Workgroups

A workgroup, or peer-to-peer network, is a simple grouping of computers running Windows XP Professional (or a mix of Windows XP Professional and Windows 2000 Professional) computers. There can also be computers running non-Microsoft operating systems such as Mac OS or Unix. You will see workgroups in very small offices where the number of computers is usually less than 10—this is where Microsoft draws a line between workgroups and domains. Each computer is independent of the others and is controlled by the principal user of that computer, who makes his own decision about sharing resources and controlling the level of access. This information is stored in the local hard disk and is known as a Local Security Database.

Advantages. The advantages of workgroups lie in the ease of operation as compared to domain-based networks. Because there are no servers, there is also no need for an administrator, which helps keep the cost of operation low. This simply means that each user is the administrator of her own computer, managing the user accounts, resource sharing, and security. This is known as *decentralized administration*. Workgroups are simple in design and are easy to implement.

Disadvantages. The disadvantages of workgroups start appearing as soon as the number of computers starts to grow. Since there is no centralized administration, the management of shared resources and security becomes troublesome. You have to visit each computer to configure, manage, and troubleshoot shared resources and security settings. Any changes to user accounts must be done at the local computer, and anyone who wants to log on to a computer must be sitting at that computer.

Domains

A domain is a logical grouping of computers that share a single centralized database located on a server known as *domain controller*. The database, known as Active Directory, holds all the information about user accounts, security, and shared resources in the network. Domains are also known as server-based networks. The server or the domain controller is essentially a computer running the Windows Server 2003 (or Windows 2000 Server) operating system. All of the Windows XP Professional (or Windows 2000 Professional) computers that are part of the domain are known as client computers.

When Windows XP Professional computers join a domain, they usually do not share files, folders, or printers. This functionality is provided and controlled by the domain controller. The domain administrator is responsible for managing the network resources and can control user accounts and resource sharing, and access security from the server computer for the entire domain.

Advantages. The main benefit of the domain-based networks is the centralization of administration. Since all of the information about users, computers, and shared resources is located in a single location, users need not have a username and password on each client computer, but instead can use a single username and password to log on to the entire domain. Administrators can control access to resources based on user information in the Active Directory. Sharing resources such as files, folders, and printers becomes easy, as permissions are set at the domain level and not on each individual client computer. This is particularly useful when there are thousands of client computers in the network. In other words, domain-based networks offer the benefit of scalability.

Disadvantages. The only disadvantage of domain-based networks is the cost of operating, which includes the cost of servers and of hiring a dedicated system administrator. But given the advantages of domains in medium- to large-scale networks, this disadvantage usually turns into an advantage as servers and administrators actually streamline the network operations and contribute to the success of the business.

Types of computers in a Windows Server 2003 network

If you have a small workgroup or a peer network, all the computers will probably be running Windows XP Professional. Each computer is called a peer computer. The same peer computers will be called clients when they join a Windows Server

2003 domain. A Windows Server 2003-based network domain would include the following three types of computers:

Domain controllers
Domain controllers are servers running the Windows Server 2003 operating system. Each domain controller holds a copy of the Active Directory database. Users in the network have only one user account, which they use to log on to any computer in the network. When a user logs on to the domain, his credentials are checked against the Active Directory. A successful logon also gives the user access to domain resources based on his credentials. When there is more than one domain controller in the network, all domain controllers take part in the periodic *replication* of Active Directory information in order to keep the database information up to date. Remember that there is no local security database in the domain controller.

Member servers
Server computers running the Windows Server 2003 (or Windows 2000 Server) operating system that are part of the domain but are not domain controllers are known as member servers. Member servers are usually meant for hosting shared applications and resources such as files, folders, and printers. Remember that member servers do not store the Active Directory database.

Client computers
Computers running the Windows XP Professional (or Windows 2000 Professional) operating system that are also part of a domain are known as client computers, or simply clients. Clients provide a working environment for end users. They have accounts in the domain and can access its shared resources.

Installing Microsoft Windows XP Professional

This section explains various installation scenarios, methods of installation, and deployment of the Windows XP Professional operating system. The installation process of Windows XP Professional on a single computer is fairly simple, but when it comes to large-scale deployment, you should prepare well in advance. This includes becoming familiar with unattended installation methods and correct use of answer files. In this section, you will also learn about post-installation procedures, updating the operating system, and troubleshooting failed installations. The section is divided into the following subsections:

- Planning before installation
- Installation methods
- Performing installation
- Upgrading from previous operating systems
- Automating the installation
- Product activation
- Post-installation updates
- Troubleshooting failed installations

Planning Before Installation

Before you start installing Windows XP Professional, you should check your computer's hardware, make a decision regarding disk partitions, select the file-system that you will be using, and determine whether the computer will join a workgroup or a domain. These considerations are explained in the following discussion.

Hardware requirements

Before starting the actual installation process, make sure your computer meets the minimum hardware requirements. Usually, the hardware is selected based on the requirements of the user and the job at hand. Although many new computers will surpass these requirements, older computers will need to be checked against these.

> You must memorize the minimum hardware required for a success-ful installation of the Windows XP Professional operating system. At the very least, remember that you should have a 233 MHz processor, 64 MB RAM, and 1.5 GB free hard disk space.

The minimum hardware requirements for Intel-based computers are shown in Table 2-1.

Table 2-1. Windows XP Professional hardware requirements

Item	Minimum required	Recommended
CPU	Pentium 233 MHz.	Pentium II 350 MHz. or faster
RAM	64 MB	128MB (4GB maximum supported)
Hard disk space	1.5 GB free	2GB free
Display	VGA adapter and monitor	Super VGA (SVGA) monitor and PnP monitor
Network interface	Not necessary (required if installing over the network)	Any network adapter (required if installing over the network)
CD-ROM	12X (not required if installing over the network)	Faster speed CD-ROM and a DVD-ROM drive

In addition to this, you would need a mouse and a keyboard. When you have met the minimum hardware requirements, you should check that all of these items are compatible with the Windows XP Professional operating system. Verify that the hardware is listed in Windows Catalog, which is available on the microsoft.com web site. Windows Catalog was previously known as Hardware Compatibility List (HCL).

Disk partitions and filesystems

One of the most important decisions to make when installing Windows XP Professional concerns disk partitions. A *partition* is a logical section of the hard disk where the system can store data. When you start installing Windows XP Professional, the setup program lets you install the operating system on an existing hard disk partition, or create a new partition. Whether you decide to use the existing hard disk partition or create a new partition, all data previously stored on the disk partition will be lost.

Microsoft recommends that you create only one partition during installation, which should be used for installing the operating system. Create other partitions after the installation is complete. In case you are dual booting the system with Windows XP Professional and another operating system, you should install each operating system in a separate disk partition.

After deciding on hard disk partitions, you also need to decide which filesystem to use for the installation. Windows XP Professional supports three types of filesystems:

File Allocation Table (FAT)
> FAT was implemented in DOS operating systems. The main limitation of FAT is that it supports only eight-character filenames with three-character extensions. The maximum partition size in FAT is 2 GB in Windows 95, Windows 98, and Windows ME. In Windows NT 4.0, Windows 2000, and Windows XP, the maximum supported FAT partition size is 4 GB.

FAT32
> FAT32 is an improved version of FAT (but not compatible with FAT!) and is supported in Windows 95 (OSR2) and later operating systems. Major benefits include more reliable storage than FAT and an extended disk partition size of up to 2 TB (Terabytes). In addition to Windows XP, Windows 2000, Windows ME, and Windows 95, OSR2 also supports the FAT32 filesystem. Windows 2000 does not support the FAT32 filesystem.

NT File System (NTFS)
> NTFS is the preferred filesystem for Windows XP Professional, Windows Server 2003, Windows 2000, and Windows NT operating systems. This filesystem has many improvements over the older FAT and FAT32 filesystems. These improvements include support for long filenames and disk partitions of up to 16 EB (Exabytes). Following are some other benefits of using NTFS:
>
> - It supports file- and folder-level security. The administrator can control access to files and folders by setting permissions.
>
> - The NTFS Encrypting File System (EFS) enables administrators and file or folder owners to encrypt the data on the hard disk to restrict access to unauthorized persons.
>
> - It supports disk quotas in which the administrator can limit the use of disk space on per-user basis.
>
> - It supports files larger than 4 GB in size and provides file compression so that more data can be stored on the hard disk.
>
> - It supports Dynamic disks, remote storage, and mounting of volumes in Windows XP Professional.

Here are some guidelines for choosing a filesystem before you start installing Windows XP Professional:

- If you are dual booting Windows XP Professional with an older operating system that does not support NTFS (DOS/Windows 95/Windows 98/Windows ME), select a FAT or FAT32 filesystem. This is because these older operating systems cannot read files stored on NTFS volumes.

- NTFS has many advantages over FAT and FAT32. Microsoft recommends that unless you have a very specific reason to use FAT/FAT32, you should only use NTFS with Windows XP Professional. This enables you to take advantage of the advanced filesystem capabilities of NTFS, which include file-level security, data encryption, disk compression, remote storage, and disk quotas. Moreover, NTFS is a much more efficient and reliable filesystem than FAT/FAT32.

Converting from FAT or FAT32 to NTFS. Windows XP Professional includes a command-line utility *CONVERT.EXE* that converts FAT or FAT32 partitions to NTFS without loosing any existing data on the partition. To use this command, click Start → Run and type cmd in the dialog box. This opens the Windows Command Prompt. Here is an example of how the Convert command should be used to convert partition D of the hard disk from FAT/FAT32 to NTFS:

```
convert D: /FS:NTFS
```

If the partition you are converting is a system volume, the conversion is done after the system restarts. Remember that you can convert from FAT or FAT32 to NTFS at any time during or after the installation without losing any data. This conversion is a one-way process. You cannot convert from NTFS back to FAT/FAT32 without losing data.

Joining a workgroup or domain

When the initial preparations are done, you will need to determine whether the computer will be part of a workgroup or a domain. If the computer will join an existing workgroup, you will need to find out the name of the workgroup. Alternatively, you can create a new workgroup when you install the networking components of the operating system.

If the computer will join an existing domain, you will need to acquire the following information from the domain administrator:

- The DNS name of the domain, which is usually in the format *mydomain.com*.

- A computer account in the domain. An administrator should create this account before you start the installation process. If you have been given the "Add Workstations to Domain" right, you can also create the computer account yourself during installation.

- An available domain controller to validate your credentials and a DNS server to resolve names during installation.

Installation Methods

Windows XP Professional can be installed using several methods, but our discussion is focused on the following two:

- Attended installation from the setup CD-ROM or from setup files stored on a shared network folder.
- Unattended installation using Answer Files and Setup Manager, Remote Installation Service (RIS), or the Disk Duplication method.

The installation methods are explained in the following discussion.

Performing the Installation

Windows XP Professional comes on a single CD-ROM with a product key that will be used during the installation. Installation from a CD-ROM is fairly simple. If your computer Basic Input Output System (BIOS) supports booting from the CD-ROM, simply insert the Windows XP Professional CD in the CD-ROM drive and start the computer. If you are starting the installation from an existing operating system such as Windows 98, Windows NT 4.0, or Windows 2000 Professional, the setup will start automatically if the auto execute feature is enabled.

Installation of Windows XP Professional can also be started using the winnt.exe or winnt32.exe command located in the /i386 directory of the Windows XP Professional CD-ROM. This is the preferred method when installing over the network.

The setup process starts in text mode, during which the hard disk is prepared and certain installation files are copied to the hard disk. Setup then enters the GUI phase, in which the user is prompted for information about the computer, username, password, etc. This is followed by a network phase, in which the setup program collects information about networking components in order to communicate over the network. The installation finally completes when the setup program copies final files to the hard disk and restarts the computer. Each of these phases is explained in the following discussion.

> Whether you should use winnt.exe or winnt32.exe is a popular exam question. Remember that winnt.exe is used to launch the installation when you are starting the computer using DOS or a boot disk. winnt32.exe is used from within the Windows 98, Windows NT, Windows 2000 Professional, or Windows XP Home edition command prompt. It is normally used to upgrade an existing Windows operating system.

Text mode

The text mode phase of the installation loads the initial setup files to the computer memory, creates hard disk partitions, and then copies setup files to the hard disk. The following steps explain the text mode of the installation process:

1. If the computer BIOS supports booting from the CD-ROM, you can start the text mode by inserting the Windows XP Professional CD-ROM into the CD-ROM drive. When you restart the computer, the text mode portion of installation begins.

2. If you are already running an operating system, simply insert the CD-ROM and choose whether you want to upgrade the previous operating system or perform a clean installation from the Welcome screen.

3. If you wish to install any third-party device drivers, press F6.

4. Installation continues with copying initial setup files into memory. A Welcome screen appears. Press Enter to continue.

5. Press the F8 key to accept the Licensing Agreement.

6. In the Disk Partitioning section, select the disk partition you wish to use for Windows XP Professional. Press C to create a new partition or press D to delete an existing partition.

7. The setup program checks the selected partition for errors and formats the partition with the selected filesystem. Setup then copies necessary files to the hard disk partition.

8. The computer restarts and enters the GUI phase as explained in the next section.

GUI mode

After the computer restarts, the setup wizard starts. This is known as the *GUI phase* or *GUI mode*. Follow the steps given here to proceed with the installation:

1. Press Enter to continue installation. During this time, setup detects and installs various devices and drivers. It takes several minutes before the next screen is displayed.

2. The "Regional and Language Options" screen appears. Make your selections appropriately and click Next.

3. In the Personalize Your Software page, fill in the correct information and click Next. Enter the correct 25-digit Product Key and click Next.

4. In the "Computer Name and Administrator Password" screen, enter a name for the computer, and then enter the password that you wish to assign to the computer's local administrator. Click Next.

5. In the "Date and Time" screen, check the date and, if required, correct it, along with the time and time zone settings. Click Next.

6. The setup now enters the Network phase. Networking components are detected and installed. Choose Typical if you wish to proceed with automatic configuration; otherwise, choose Custom. *Typical* networking components include Client for Microsoft Networks, File and Print Sharing for Microsoft Networks, and TCP/IP protocol with automatic IP addressing. Click Next.

7. The "Workgroup or Computer Domain name" screen appears next. If you select a domain name, you will be asked about the domain administrator's username and password. Enter the correct information and click Next.

8. Setup continues with the installation process. Several files are copied to the hard disk. This may take anywhere between 15 to 60 minutes.

9. Setup completes the installation by installing the Start menu items, registers the various components you selected, saves your configuration to the registry, removes temporary installation files, and restarts the computer.

When the computer restarts, the Welcome screen appears if you chose to join a workgroup. If you chose to join a domain during installation, the "Logon to Windows" screen appears instead.

Installing over the Network

When installing Windows XP Professional over the network, the installation files are stored on a network file server known as the Distribution server. These are the same files that are located in the /i386 folder of the CD-ROM. The setup process is started using either the winnt.exe or winnt32.exe command depending on the operating system currently in use. Refer to Table 2-4 later in this chapter, which lists supported upgrade paths.

The following are some essential steps that you must take before starting the installation process:

1. Locate the distribution server and correct path in order to connect to the shared folder.

2. Create a FAT partition on the computer where you want to install Windows XP Professional.

3. Install necessary network client software in order to enable the computer to connect to the distribution software. If the computer does not have an operating system, you can use a boot floppy disk that contains network client software to communicate on the network.

Once these steps are complete, you can start the installation as follows:

1. Start the computer either by using the currently installed operating system or from the network client boot disk.

2. Connect to the shared folder (/i386) on the distribution server.

3. Start the installation by running the winnt.exe or winnt32.exe from the command prompt.

   - If you are using MS-DOS or Windows 3.x versions, run winnt.exe to start the installation process.

   - If you are currently using Windows 95, Windows 98, Windows ME, Windows NT 4.0, or Windows 2000 Professional operating systems, run winnt32.exe to start the installation. The rest of the installation process is similar to the one explained earlier in this chapter.

 If you just want to check whether your computer can be upgraded to Windows XP Professional, use the winnt32.exe /checkupgradeonly command.

Both `winnt.exe` and `winnt32.exe` utilities include a number of parameters that can be used to install Windows XP Professional in a desired way. Tables 2-2 and 2-3 describe some of the commonly used parameters for the `winnt.exe` and `winnt32.exe` commands, respectively.

Table 2-2. Winnt.exe parameters

Parameter	Function
`/r[folder]`	Copies and saves an optional folder. The folder is saved after installation.
`/rx[:folder]`	Copies an optional folder. The folder is deleted after installation.
`/s[:sourcepath]`	Specifies the location of source files in the format *server**share**[path]*.
`/t[:tempdrive]`	Specifies the temp drive to contain installation files. By default, the drive with most available space is selected.
`/u[:answer file]`	Specifies an answer file in case the installation is unattended. This parameter must be used with the `/s` parameter.
`/udf:id[,UDF_file]`	Specifies the identifiers that setup uses to see how a uniqueness database file (UDF) modifies the answer file. The parameters given in the UDF file override the parameters given in the answer file. If you do not specify a UDF file, you are prompted to insert a disk containing the *$UNIQUE$.UDB* file.

Table 2-3. Winnt32.exe parameters

Parameter	Function
`/checkupgradeonly`	Checks the computer only if it can be upgraded to Windows XP Professional.
`/cmd:command_line`	Specifies a command that should be run immediately after restarting the computer, when the text phase is complete.
`/cmdcons`	Installs Recovery Console as a startup option.
`/copydir:foldername`	Creates an additional folder with the *%systemroot%* folder.
`/debug[level] [:filename]`	Creates a debug file at the specified level from 0 to 4. The default level is 2; it collects information about setup warnings. The default debug file is *C:\Winnt32.log*.
`/dudisable`	Disables dynamic updates during installation.
`/makelocalsource`	Specifies that setup should copy all installation files to the local hard drive.
`/noreboot`	Executes another command before restarting the computer when the text phase is complete.
`/s:sourcepath`	Specifies the location of source files for a Windows XP Professional installation.
`/syspart:[driveletter]`	Copies the installation files to the specified drive and makes it active. This parameter must be used with the `/tempdrive` parameter and works only on computers running Windows NT 4.0, Windows 2000, and Windows XP Professional.
`/tempdrive:driveletter`	Copies installation files to the temporary drive mentioned in the above entry and installs the operating system on that drive.
`/udf:id[,UDF_file]`	Specifies the identifiers that setup uses to see how a uniqueness database file (UDF) modifies the answer file. The parameters given in the UDF file override the parameters given in the answer file. If you do not specify a UDF file, you are prompted to insert a disk containing the *$UNIQUE$.UDB* file.

Table 2-3. Winnt32.exe parameters (continued)

Parameter	Function
/unattend	Upgrades the previous versions of Windows 98, Windows ME, Windows NT 4.0, and Windows 2000 without any user input. Also downloads dynamic updates during installation and includes them in the installation files. Copies all user settings from the previously used version of Windows.
/unattend[num]:[answerfile]	Performs a fresh installation of Windows XP Professional in unattended mode using the specified answer file. The num option specifies the time that must lapse between the copying of files and the restart of the computer. Dynamic updates are downloaded and included in installation files.

Upgrading from Previous Operating Systems

Windows XP Professional can upgrade previous versions of Windows desktop operating systems. Before performing an upgrade, you must check that the hardware meets the minimum requirements of the new operating system. You should also make sure that the current operating system can be upgraded directly to Windows XP Professional. The following sections explain the upgrade process.

Checking hardware compatibility

The Windows XP Professional setup program includes an option to test whether the current computer hardware and software meets the requirements for upgrading the operating system. Although this program runs automatically when you run the upgrade process, running it beforehand helps you identify the components that need to be upgraded in order to run the upgrade successfully.

Insert the Windows XP Professional CD-ROM in the CD-ROM drive and run the following command (located in the /i386 folder):

```
winnt32 /checkupgradeonly
```

It takes a while before the system completes the test and displays the compatibility report. You can save the report as a text file if you wish to analyze it later.

Upgrade paths

Most of the recent Windows desktop operating systems can be upgraded directly to Windows XP Professional. For some older versions, such as Windows NT 3.1, Windows 95, and Windows NT 3.5, you must first upgrade to a compatible operating system and then perform a second upgrade. Table 2-4 summarizes upgrade paths for various older desktop operating systems.

Table 2-4. Windows XP Professional upgrade paths

Previous operating system	Upgrade
Windows NT 3.1, 3.5, 3.51	Upgrade to Windows NT 4.0 Workstation first, then upgrade to Windows XP Professional.
Windows 95	Upgrade to Windows 98 first, then upgrade to Windows XP Professional.
Windows 98	Directly upgrade to Windows XP Professional.

Table 2-4. Windows XP Professional upgrade paths (continued)

Previous operating system	Upgrade
Windows ME	Directly upgrade to Windows XP Professional.
Windows NT 4.0 Workstation	Directly upgrade to Windows XP Professional.
Windows 2000 Professional with SP4	Directly upgrade to Windows XP Professional.
Windows XP Home	Directly upgrade to Windows XP Professional.

Although Microsoft provides a number of options to upgrade older operating systems to Windows XP Professional, it also recommends that instead of performing a two-step upgrade, it is always better to perform a clean installation. Choose upgrades only if you wish to keep your old files and settings in the new operating system.

You should memorize the above table, as questions on upgrading generally make their way into Exam 70-270. Also make it a point to figure out a tricky question in which you would be asked to upgrade a previous server operating system (Windows NT 4.0 Server or Windows 2000 Server) to Windows XP Professional. Remember that only client operating systems can be upgraded to Windows XP Professional.

Upgrading from Windows 98

Upgrading from Windows 98 requires you to first create a computer account in the domain. Remember that Windows 98 computers cannot have a domain account, but Windows XP Professional computers need one. This is not required if your computer is part of a workgroup.

You can start the upgrade process by inserting the Windows XP Professional CD-ROM and selecting Install Windows XP from the Welcome screen. Windows XP Professional will retain most of the system's settings after the upgrade is complete. If the CD-ROM does not start automatically, you can launch the setup program by clicking Start → Run and typing d:\setup.exe, assuming that drive D: is your CD-ROM drive.

If you want to customize the upgrade process, you can run the winnt32.exe utility from the *i386* folder on the CD-ROM and specify additional switches. If D is the drive letter of your CD-ROM drive, run the following command from the command prompt using appropriate switches:

```
d:\i386\winnt32.exe
```

The upgrade process conducts a compatibility test and displays the results. If the computer is compatible with Windows XP Professional, the process requires very little user input.

Upgrading from Windows NT 4.0 and Windows 2000 Professional

Since Windows NT 4.0 and Windows 2000 Professional computers already have accounts in the domain, the process is fairly simple and similar to upgrading from

Windows 98. After you make sure that your computer's hardware and software is compatible with Windows XP Professional, just insert the installation CD in the CD-ROM drive. Select Install Windows XP from the Welcome screen.

If your computer does not automatically start the Windows XP Professional CD, you can start the installation by running the setup.exe command from the Start menu, which in turn runs the winnt32.exe command. If you want to customize the upgrade process, you should use the following command with appropriate switches:

```
d:\i386\winnt32.exe
```

You are shown a "Welcome to Windows" screen and are asked to choose the Installation Type. Select Upgrade from the drop-down menu and click Enter.

Automating the Installation

Windows XP Professional installations can be automated in the following three ways:

Using Setup Manager (Setupmgr.exe)
Use this to create answer files for unattended installations. These answer files are used with winnt.exe or winnt32.exe to automate the installation process.

Using the System Preparation (Sysprep.exe)
Use this tool to create images of a computer running Windows XP Professional and deploying these images on multiple computers. This method is also known as the Disk Duplication Method.

Using Remote Installation Service (RIS)
This runs on a Windows Server 2003 computer in a domain. This service requires that Active Directory and DNS services are available during the installation.

Setupmgr.exe and *Sysprep.exe* along with their help files are located in the *\Support\ Tools* folder on the Windows XP Professional setup CD-ROM. These files must be extracted from the *\Support\Tools\Deploy.cab* file to the local hard drive.

Unattended installation using Setup Manager

Windows Setup Manager (*Setupmgr.exe*) is a GUI-based utility that makes it easy to create or modify answer files quickly for unattended installations. The answer file is usually named *unattend.txt*. Setup Manager is an alternative to creating an answer file manually. This utility provides three options for various installation options and then creates the answer file. You can create answer files for unattended installations, for Sysprep Installations, or for RIS-based installations.

The User Interaction page is shown in Figure 2-2. This gives you the following five options for selecting the user interaction level during the installation process:

User Controlled
This allows you to specify the default choices for installation options. The user can accept or change the answers you provide in the answer file.

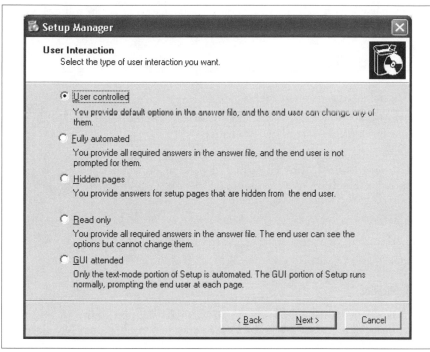

Figure 2-2. User Interaction in Setup Manager

Fully automated

The installation is performed without the intervention of the user, and all answers are provided automatically. The user cannot see or modify any answers.

Hide pages

This shows the user only those pages for which the answer file does not provide any options. Other pages are hidden from the user so that she cannot make any changes.

Read only

The user can see the pages that are not hidden but cannot change any options selected by the answer file.

GUI attended

Only the text mode is automated and runs without user intervention. The GUI phase of the installation proceeds as normal.

After selecting an option, you are prompted for the distribution folder in which Windows XP Professional files are stored. Further pages prompt you for appropriate installation options such as License Agreement, Software Customization, and the Product key pages. When this is complete, the Setup Manager prompts you for the Computer name and Administrator password and asks whether the Administrator's password should be encrypted. After this, the networking components are configured for the answer file. These include network settings, the domain name, and how the computer account will be created in the domain.

The setup manager finally shows the completion page and that the following three files have been created:

Unattend.txt –
   The answer file

Unattend.udb –
   The uniqueness database file

Unattend.bat –
   The batch file that starts the installation

When the answer file is ready, you can start the installation using either the winnt.exe or the winnt32.exe command, depending on which operating system is currently installed on the computer. From an MS-DOS or Windows 3.x computer, use the following command:

```
winnt.exe [/s:SourcePath] [/u:AnswerFile] [/udf:ID [,UDB_File]]
```

From other client operating systems, use this command:

```
winnt32.exe [/unattend[num]:[AnswerFile] [/udf:ID [,UDB_File]]
```

Disk duplication

The disk duplication method uses the System Preparation utility to prepare a master image of an existing Windows XP Professional installation. This image can then be copied to other computers with identical hardware. The Sysprep utility removes the computer-specific information from the image. This method can only be used when all of the computers have identical hardware, and you can perform a clean installation. Upgrading the previous operating system is not supported by the Sysprep utility.

The computer used for this purpose is known as the master or reference computer and can have any number of applications installed besides the Windows XP Professional operating system. Once you have configured the master computer correctly, you can run the Sysprep utility to prepare an image of the hard disk.

The Sysprep utility can be run in its default mode by simply double-clicking the filename. Some of the optional parameters available with this utility are listed in Table 2-5.

Table 2-5. Sysprep parameters

Parameter	Function
/quite	The user is not prompted for any input.
/nosidgen	The utility does not generate any SID after the reboot.
/pnp	Forces the Setup to detect PnP devices on destination computers.
/reboot	Restarts the master computer after Sysprep is complete.
/noreboot	Shuts down the computer without rebooting.
/forceshutdown	Forces the computer to complete shutdown.

A third-party utility must then be used to perform an actual disk imaging. The Sysprep utility also creates a mini-setup wizard that runs on destination computers. The users start this mini-setup wizard, which prompts them for computer-specific details such as the computer name and the administrator's password. This information can also be provided in an answer file created using Setup Manager, as explained in the previous section.

Remote Installation Service (RIS)

Remote Installation Service (RIS) runs on a Windows Server 2003 Server or Windows 2000 Server computer and provides the best option for Windows XP Professional deployment in large organizations. The RIS server acts as a disk-image server and hosts many disk images for various client configurations. The computers must be part of an Active Directory network and domain controller, and DNS and DHCP services must be running at the time of installation.

The RIS server can be configured to download a preconfigured image to the RIS client computer or to let the client select an image from available disk images. RIS supports two types of images: CD-based images and RIPrep images. The CD-based image uses the Windows XP Professional CD-ROM and an answer file to complete the installation. The RIPrep image contains the Windows XP Professional operating system along with other applications.

In order to use RIS for Windows XP Professional deployment, the following conditions must be met:

- DNS service must be running on the network, as the RIS server depends on DNS service to locate directory service and client computer accounts.
- DHCP service must be available on client computers to get an initial IP address.
- Active Directory service must be available so that the Windows XP Professional clients can locate the RIS servers.

 The three main services required for using Remote Installation Service for large-scale deployments of Windows XP Professional are DNS, DHCP, and the Active Directory. If any of these services is not available, RIS installation cannot work.

The RIS client computers must conform to NetPC specification or should have a network adapter that supports the *Preboot eXecution Environment (PXE)* standard for booting from the network. These specifications allow a client computer to boot from the network even if no operating system is installed. Another option is to use a RIS boot disk that can be created by the RIS service itself. This utility is known as *Remote Boot Disk Generator (rbfg.exe)* and supports several standard network adapters. The user account that is used to start the installation must be granted Log On As Batch Job rights in the Active Directory domain.

Product Activation

The retail and evaluation copies of Windows XP Professional must be activated within 30 days of installation. Activation is not required if you are using a copy of Windows XP Professional that is part of a volume licensing plan. When you log on to Windows for the first time after installation, you are prompted to activate the product; if you choose to defer the activation, Windows XP continues to remind you. After 30 days, the Windows XP Professional ceases to work and does not allow you to log on to the system.

Windows Product Activation (WPA), which requires each copy to have a valid 25-character product key, performs this activation. During installation this key is used to generate a 20-character product ID (PID). Microsoft uses these keys to register your copy of Windows XP Professional in order to prevent software piracy.

Post-Installation Updates

Once the Windows XP Professional installation is complete, you will need to keep it updated by installing the latest critical updates and service packs available from the Microsoft web site. Windows Update is an online service designed to keep your system updated. It automatically scans your system and downloads and installs critical software and security updates on your computer. The URL for the Microsoft Windows Updates web site is *http://www.microsoft.com/windowsupdate* and can be accessed using Internet Explorer or any other web browser. You can perform an Express Install, and if you are running Windows XP Professional SP2, you are not required to accept the End User License Agreement (EULA).

Automatic Updates

Windows XP Professional also includes Automatic Updates. Complete the following steps in order to access and configure Automatic Updates as shown in Figure 2-3.

1. Click Start → Control Panel.
2. Click System in the Control Panel window.
3. Click the Automatic Updates tab in the System Properties page.
4. Configure how you want the Automatic Updates to download and install on your computer.
5. Click OK to close the System Properties dialog box.

Windows Software Update Services

Windows Software Update Services (WSUS) runs on a Windows Server 2003 or Windows 2000 Server computer. This service centralizes the selection and deployment of software updates in a network environment. The SUS server synchronizes its contents with the Windows Updates site and schedules them to be installed on client computers. The installation can be done automatically or manually. Group Policy settings in a Windows 2003 domain usually control how these software updates are distributed to client computers.

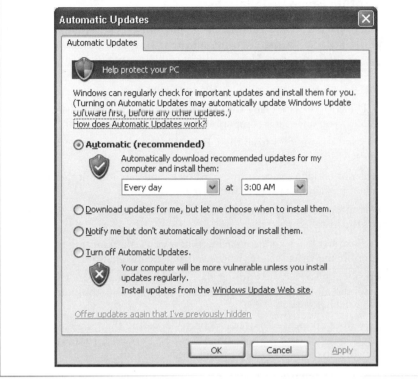

Figure 2-3. Automatic Updates

Service packs

Service packs are collections of several updates into a single file commonly known as *update.exe*. They also include new features added to the operating system after its release. Service packs are free of charge if downloaded from the Microsoft web site. As previously discussed in this chapter in the section "Major Enhancements in Service Pack 2," you can use the winver.exe utility to check whether your computer has the latest service pack installed.

You can start the installation of a service pack by typing update.exe from the command prompt. Several switches are available to customize the installation process. You can get help in running the installation of service pack by typing update.exe /? at any time. If you choose to back up the files during installation, you can also uninstall the service pack from the Control Panel, using the Add/ Remove Programs utility.

Slipstreaming

When the installation of a service pack is combined with the installation of the operating system, the method is called *Integrated Installation* or *Slipstreaming*. The service pack is applied to the distribution files in the shared network folder on the distribution server. All new installations then include the service pack. Service packs that are installed in this way cannot be uninstalled.

Troubleshooting Failed Installations

In order to perform a trouble-free installation, you must make sure that you fully understand the installation requirements and that you have chosen the correct installation type and method. Most of the installation problems are minor in nature and can be addressed by taking simple steps. The most commonly faced problems—and their solutions—include the following:

- If the CD-ROM you are using for installation does not work, use a different CD-ROM. If you have an incompatible CD-ROM drive, replace it.
- If Setup cannot copy files from the CD-ROM, you might have insufficient or defective RAM.
- If there is not enough space on the hard disk, you can add another hard disk or format the existing hard disk and recreate partitions.
- If the setup stops during text mode, check that Windows XP Professional supports the installed hard disk.
- If a virus scanner gives an error saying that a virus is attempting to infect the BIOS, disable the virus scanner before starting the installation.
- If a dependency service fails during the GUI phase, make sure that the network adapter and its settings are correct and that the computer name is unique on the network.
- If Setup cannot connect to a domain controller, verify that you have supplied the correct name of the domain, that the DNS service is running, and that your network adapter can communicate on the network.

You can overcome or remove many installation problems by running the compatibility tests (winnt32 /checkupgradeonly). You should remove any unsupported devices and uninstall applications and disable virus scanners.

Windows XP Professional installation generates logfiles that can be reviewed to troubleshoot the installation problems. These files are text files and are stored in the *C:\Windows* folder by default. The following two files are most commonly used for resolving installation problems.

Setupact.log
> This is also known as Action Log and contains all the actions taken by the setup program. This file also contains the errors that are generated and written to the Error Log file.

Setuperr.log
> This file is known as the Error Log file and contains all the errors generated by the setup program during installation. In cases of trouble-free installations, the file is empty.

Windows XP Startup Process

Windows XP Professional files are located in the local hard disk and loaded in a fixed sequence each time the system is started. This section explains different steps in the startup process and how you can modify it by changing certain parameters in the *Boot.ini* file.

Pre-Boot Sequence

When the computer is started, it performs a *pre-boot sequence*, which is comprised of the following steps:

1. A Power-On Self Test (POST) is performed to check that the minimum hardware to start the operating system exists on the computer. These components include physical memory (RAM), video, and the keyboard. In case the computer BIOS supports Plug and Play (PnP), the configuration of PnP-compatible hardware devices is performed.

2. The computer locates a boot device. An appropriate boot device, which can be a hard disk, floppy disk, or CD-ROM depending on the BIOS configuration, is selected. The *Master Boot Record* (MBR) is loaded from the selected boot device. The MBR in turn loads the NTLDR file from the default partition on the boot device. In case the computer has a Small Computer System Interface (SCSI) device as the boot device and doesn't have its own BIOS, the *NTBOOTDD.SYS* file is loaded.

Boot Sequence

NTLDR takes charge of the process from here onward and performs the following steps:

1. In the initial boot loader phase, NTLDR switches the processor to 32-bit flat memory mode. It loads the filesystems driver to access the FAT, FAT32, or NTFS partitions, depending on which boot device is being used.

2. NTLDR reads the *Boot.ini* file and selects an operating system. If multiple operating systems are installed on the computer, the *Boot.ini* file prompts the user to select an operating system. If the MS-DOS operating system is selected, NTLDR loads the boot sector from the *BOOTSECT.DOS* file. In case Windows XP is the only operating system installed, it is loaded by default and the operating system selection screen does not appear.

3. NTLDR calls on the *NTDETECT.COM* file to perform hardware detection. *NTDETECT.COM* detects some of the hardware and displays error messages if any hardware problems exist. If the computer has more than one hardware profile, the user is given the choice to select an appropriate profile.

Kernel Load and Initialization

The Kernel Load phase begins and performs the following steps:

1. NTLDR calls on the *NTOSKRNL.EXE* file, which is the Windows XP Kernel. This changes the screen color from black to blue. The Kernel loads another module known as the hardware abstraction layer, HAL.DLL.

2. The Kernel initializes by creating a registry key known as HKEY_LOCAL_MACHINE\HARDWARE. This key contains information about the hardware device on the computer based on the results of *NTDETECT.COM*.

3. The Kernel creates a Clone Control Set by copying the control set in the HKEY_LOCAL_MACHINE\SYSTEM\Select subkey of the registry.

4. The Kernel loads low-level device drivers and filesystems. The device drivers initialize as they are loaded. The user mode subsystem is loaded, and the computer display changes to the GUI mode.

5. Once the Kernel has loaded and is initialized, the services are started and initialize system services.

Logon Process

The Logon Process starts as soon as the Winlogon service is started. The Local Security Authority (Lass.exe) displays the logon screen. The Service Control Manager scans the HKEY_LOCAL_MACHINE\SYSTEM\CurrentControlSet\ Services subkey to look for services that should start automatically.

After you log on successfully to the system, the operating system copies the Clone Control Set to the Last Known Good Control Set.

 Although it is very unlikely that you will be asked to specify the Windows XP startup process or its order, you must be familiar with the names of files used during this process and the function of each file. The *Boot.ini* file and ARC paths are especially important in this section.

Files Used in the Startup Process

Several files are critical for the Windows XP Professional operating system to start successfully. While some of these files are stored in the root of the system partition, others are located in the System32 subfolder in the drive in which you installed the operating system. This is known as *%systemroot%*. These startup files are listed in Table 2-6.

Table 2-6. Windows XP Professional startup files

Filename	Startup phase	Location
NTLDR	Pre-boot and Boot	System Partition Root (usually C:\ drive)
BOOT.INI	Boot	System Partition Root (usually C:\ drive)
BOOTSECT.DOS	Boot (used if MS-DOS is used)	System Partition Root (usually C:\ drive)
NTDETECT.SYS	Boot	System Partition Root (usually C:\ drive)
NTBOOTDD.SYS	Boot (used if a SCSI device is used to boot)	System Partition Root (usually C:\ drive)
NTOSKRNL.EXE	%systemroot%\System32	Kernel load
HAL.DLL	%systemroot%\System32	Kernel load
SYSTEM	%systemroot%\System32	Kernel initialization

The BOOT.INI File

When you start the Windows XP Professional operating system on a computer with multiple operating systems, a boot loader screen is displayed where you can select the operating system that you wish to start. This is made possible by the *BOOT.INI* file that is initially loaded by the NTLDR file.

A typical *BOOT.INI* file for a computer with Windows XP Professional and Windows 2000 Professional reads like the following:

```
[boot loader]
timeout=30
default=multi (0) disk (0) rdisk (0) partition (1) \WINDOWS
[operating systems]
multi (0) disk (0) rdisk (0) partition (1) \WINDOWS="Microsoft Windows XP
Professional" /fastdetect
multi (0) disk (0) rdisk (1) partition (2) \WINNT="Microsoft Windows 2000
Professional" /fastdetect
```

The *BOOT.INI* file is a read-only file that is comprised of the following two sections: Boot Loader and Operating Systems.

The *Boot Loader* section contains the following parameters:

timeout
> The timeout is the minimum number of seconds that should lapse before the default operating system is selected. A value of −1 causes the boot loader to wait indefinitely.

default
> The default is used as the default operating system when no selection is made. This is one of the entries in the Operating Systems section.

The *Operating Systems* section contains Advanced RISC Computing (ARC) paths that direct the boot loader to the correct boot partition where the selected operating system is installed. The format for ARC entries is as follows:

```
multi (0) disk (0) rdisk (0) partition (1) \WINDOWS="Microsoft Windows XP
Professional"
```

multi (x) *or* scsi (x)
> This entry identifies the adapter to which the hard disk is connected. This value is always multi for most IDE and SCSI adapters—except for some SCSI drives without on-board BIOS. The number in parentheses identifies the loading order of the adapter. The starting number is 0.

disk (x)
> This entry is used only for SCSI ID for SCSI adapters with an *scsi* entry. The entry is always 0 if you use multi.

rdisk (x)
> This number identifies the disk and is ignored for *scsi* entries.

partition (x)
> This parameter identifies the partition of the hard disk that contains the selected operating system. Remember that partition numbers always start from 1.

Directory or Folder
> This entry specifies the path within the partition where the operating system files are located. Usually, it is *\WINDOWS* for Windows XP Professional and *\WINNT* for Windows NT 4.0 and Windows 2000 Professional.

Description

This entry is within quotes and describes the operating system that will be loaded. The description is displayed in the Boot Loader menu.

Optional parameters for BOOT.INI

The following optional parameters can be added to the entries in the Operating System section of the *BOOT.INI* file:

/basevideo

This parameter forces Windows XP Professional to use the VGA mode instead of using the installed video adapter. The VGA mode entry in the default *BOOT.INI* file uses this mode.

/fastdetect=ports

This option disables scanning for a serial mouse connected to the serial ports. If you do not specify a port, it disables detection of devices on all serial ports (COM ports).

/maxmem:number

This option forces the operating system to use a specified amount of physical memory.

/noguiboot

This option will skip the Graphical Boot Status screen.

/sos

This option is used to specify verbose mode for device drivers. All device drivers are displayed as they are loaded.

Modifying the BOOT.INI file. You should not modify the *BOOT.INI* file directly under normal circumstances. If you need to change the way boot options are displayed, you can complete the following steps, which in turn modify the *BOOT.INI* file:

1. Click Start → Control Panel to open the Control Panel. If using the classic menu, click Start → Settings → Control Panel.

2. Open the System utility.

3. Click the Advanced tab to open the Advanced Properties dialog box.

4. Click the Startup And Recovery Settings button.

5. In the System Startup section, select the operating system from the Default Operating System drop-down menu.

6. Enter the number of seconds the boot option should be displayed in "Time in order to display list of operating systems" spinner box.

7. Click OK twice to close the windows.

The file is located in the system boot partition that is usually the C: drive of your computer. Since the file is hidden and has read-only attributes by default, you will need to configure Windows Explorer to show hidden files and then change file attributes to clear the Read Only check box. You can open the file by using Notepad or Word Pad, make your changes, and then save the file. It is usually a good idea to save a backup copy of this file before you edit it.

You can also modify the file attributes from the command line as follows:

```
attrib -s -r -h boot.ini
```

Microsoft recommends that you should normally make changes to the Boot Options menu from the Control Panel.

Windows Registry

The Windows Registry is a collection of system configuration settings in a hierarchical datafile. The configuration data includes the operating system settings, user specific settings, application data, hardware components, and all installed device drivers. The hierarchy is organized into keys and subkeys, each of which can have one or more values. The value can be a text identifier, string, binary, word, multiple string, or expandable string.

There are five main subtrees in the Registry hierarchy, as shown in Figure 2-4 and described next.

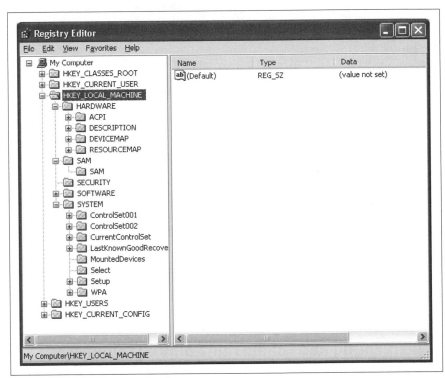

Figure 2-4. Windows Registry subtrees

HKEY_CLASSES_ROOT
    This subtree mainly stores Object Linking and Embedding (OLE) data and file associations. File associations are used to link the files with the programs used to run them based on their extensions.

HKEY_CURRENT_USER

This subtree contains data about the currently logged on user, that is taken from her user profile.

HKEY_LOCAL_MACHINE

This subtree contains all the hardware-specific configuration data for the machine, which essentially includes operating system configuration and hardware devices and drivers. The operating system, applications, device drivers, and system startup read this data. This data is the same for every user of the computer.

HKEY_USERS

This subtree contains a default set of settings as well as data for each user profile. The information for a particular user is copied to the HKEY_CURRENT_USER when a user logs on to the computer.

HKEY_CURRENT_CONFIG

This subtree contains data about the currently loaded hardware profile. Certain applications and device drivers use this data for dynamic configuration information.

Registry Editor

Under extreme circumstances when you require changes to the Registry, you should first make a backup copy of the existing Registry files. The Registry Editor (regedit.exe *or* regedt32.exe) program is located in the *%SystemRoot%\System* folder. It can either be run from the command prompt or from the Run option in the Start menu.

With most of the systems settings and configurations made easy using the Windows Wizards, you will hardly need to edit the Registry directly. Unless you do not have another way to configure your system, you should not edit the Registry to change any configuration values. Improperly editing the Registry may render your system unable to boot or generate unexpected errors.

You must have advanced-level knowledge of the Windows XP operating system and Registry keys in order to configure the Registry correctly. If you are unsure of your actions, do not attempt to edit the Registry. Otherwise, you may damage the operating system and may have to reinstall it.

Implementing and Conducting Administration of Resources

Windows XP Professional resources essentially include files, folders, and printers. You are expected to have a good understanding of managing and controlling access to these resources. Access to files and folders is controlled through NTFS permissions and shared permissions. You should know how to set permissions for files and folders and how these permissions change when these files and folders are copied or moved. The second part of this section deals with local and network print devices (printers), print permissions, and managing print jobs.

This section is further divided into the following two subsections:

- "Configuring and Managing Access to Files and Folders"
- "Configuring and Managing Print Devices"

Configuring and Managing Access to Files and Folders

Windows XP Professional manages file and folder permissions on disk drives formatted with NTFS. FAT and FAT32 do not support file permissions. Each file or folder on an NTFS volume has an associated *Access Control List* (ACL), which controls the level of access that should be granted to users or groups.

NTFS file permissions

The standard NTFS file permissions that can be assigned to users and groups are listed in Table 2-7.

Table 2-7. NTFS file permissions

Permission	Description
Read	Read the file and its attributes, permissions, and ownership.
Read and Execute	Run the file; access granted by the Read permission.
Write	Overwrite the file, change file attributes, and view permissions and ownership. This permission also allows a user to create new files.
Modify	Modify and delete the file; access granted by the Write and the Read and Execute permissions.
Full Control	All actions permitted by other NTFS permissions; in addition, this allows the user to change permissions and take ownership.

NTFS folder permissions

The standard NTFS folder permissions that can be assigned to users and groups are listed in Table 2-8.

Table 2-8. NTFS folder permissions

Permission	Description
Read	View the folder's files and subfolders as well as its attributes and permissions.
List Folder Contents	View the names of files and subfolders.
Read and Execute	Move through folders and subfolders. It has other permissions granted by the Read and the List Folder Contents permissions.
Write	Create new files and subfolders within the folder and change folder attributes.
Modify	Delete the folder; other permissions granted by the Read and the Execute and Write permissions.
Full Control	Change permissions, delete files and subfolders, and take ownership. Includes all other NTFS folder permissions.

The above permissions can be set to Allow or Deny any user or group. Permissions can also be assigned individually or as preset combinations, such as the Full Control permission that includes all other permissions. The Deny permission, on the other hand, denies all access to the file or folder.

 If you do not see the Security tab on properties of a file or folder in Windows Explorer, the volume is not an NTFS volume but a FAT or FAT32 volume. Remember that FAT and FAT32 do not support NTFS security. Another reason for a missing Security tab is that Simple File Sharing might be enabled on the computer.

Effective permissions

Windows XP Professional also allows you to set multiple permissions for a single user when the user is a member of multiple groups. In this case, the effective permissions are a combination of all permissions. It is also notable that individual file permissions override the permissions granted on the parent folder. Permissions can also be inherited from the parent folder. By default, the permissions assigned to a folder propagate to files and subfolders unless inheritance is specifically blocked.

Assigning NTFS permissions

By default, administrators and owners of the file and folder get Full Control permissions. Permissions can be assigned to users and groups from the Security tab of the file or folder properties, as shown in Figure 2-5.

Follow the procedure given here to assign permissions to a user or group:

1. Right-click a folder and select Properties from the menu.
2. Click the Security tab in the Properties dialog box.
3. Click the Add button to add a user or group.
4. Select a user or group from the "Select Users and Groups" dialog box and click OK.
5. Click the "Allow or Deny" checkbox for appropriate permissions. Click OK.

Special permissions and inheritance

The Advanced button in the Security tab of the file or folder properties dialog box opens up the Advances Security Settings dialog box. This dialog box has another Permissions tab that is used to assign special permissions on the object and control how permission inheritance works. By default, permissions assigned to the parent folder propagate to all files and subfolders. To change this setting, clear the "Inherit From Parent The Permission Entries That Apply to Child Objects" checkbox. This opens up another dialog box with the following options:

Copy
> Copy the permissions previously applied from the parent to the child and then deny subsequent permission inheritance from the parent.

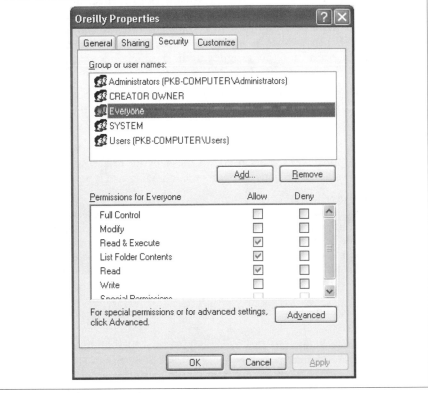

Figure 2-5. Configuring NTFS permissions

Remove
> Remove the permissions previously applied from the parent to the child and then retain only the permissions assigned here. If you select this option, you must immediately assign yourself appropriate permissions because this option removes all permissions from the file or folder.

Cancel
> Cancel and close the dialog box.

Copying and moving files and folders

Files and folders in Windows XP Professional are copied and moved using Windows Explorer. When files and folders are copied or moved, their associated permissions might not be copied or moved with them.

- If a file or folder is *copied* within the same NTFS volume or across different NTFS volumes, it is treated as a new file and the permissions are assigned to the destination folder. You must have Write permission on the destination folder to perform the copy operation. If the destination volume is FAT or FAT32, the file permissions are lost.

- If a file or folder is *moved* within the same NTFS volume, it retains its original permissions. You must have Write permission on the destination volume and Modify permission on the original volume in order to complete the move operation. When the file or folder is moved from one NTFS volume to another, the permissions are assigned to the destination folder. If the destination volume is FAT or FAT32, the NTFS permissions are lost.

In either of these cases, the user performing the copy or move operation becomes the owner of the file or folder on the destination NTFS volume.

Shared folders

Folders are shared to allow other users on the network to access your files and folders. Windows XP Professional supports the following two types of file sharing.

Simple File Sharing
> Allows users on the workgroup to share files and folders without any complex configuration of permissions. With Simple File Sharing, everyone on the network has the same level of access to the shared file or folder. You can disable Simple File Sharing and configure normal Shared Folder permissions. Simple File Sharing is not available when the computer is a member of a domain. It can be disabled from the Windows Explorer by using the Tools menu. Click Folder Options and, in the View tab, clear the Use Simple File Sharing (Recommended) button located in the Advanced Settings list.

Folder Sharing
> Configured on computers that are members of a domain. Once shared, you can configure shared permissions in addition to the NTFS permissions already set on the shared folders. You should be the owner of the folder, and a member of the Administrators or the Power Users groups in order to share the folder. Also, users who are given Create Permanent Shared Objects rights can also configure shares on Windows XP Professional computers.

Follow the steps below to share a folder:

1. Open Windows Explorer and right-click the folder you want to share.
2. Click Properties to open the Properties dialog box.
3. Click the Sharing tab.
4. Click the "Share this Folder" button and specify a share name.
5. Set the number of users that can access the shared folder.

In order to enable the users to access the folder with different names, you can repeat these steps. This allows you to create different shares for the same folder. The share name can be up to 80 characters long, but you should try to keep it shorter in order to let older Windows operating systems access the share. The Permissions tab allows you to set Shared Folder permissions as shown in Figure 2-6.

In addition to the normal shared folders that you can manually create from Windows Explorer, the operating system also creates some hidden shares. These are called *Administrative Shares,* and their names end with a dollar sign ($). Examples of such shares are Admin$, Print$, C$, D$, IPC$, etc. Network users cannot locate these shares using their computer browsers. You can also create hidden shares by appending the $ sign to the share name.

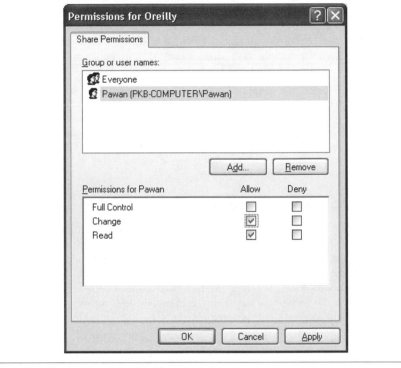

Figure 2-6. Configuring Shared Folder permissions

Exam 70-270
Study Guide

Shared Folder permissions

Shared Folder permissions are used to control access to the shared folders. These permissions can only be assigned to folders and not individual files. Shared Folder permissions are not effective if someone logs on locally and tries to access the folder. On FAT and FAT32 volumes, the only way to control access to resources is through Shared Folder permissions.

By default, the system assigns Read permission to the Everyone group when a folder is shared. You should remove this permission for security reasons and configure your own customized permissions. The standard Shared Folder permissions are listed in Table 2-9.

Table 2-9. Shared Folder permissions

Permission	Description
Read	View the folder name and attributes, view and execute files, and change folders within the shared folder.
Change	Add files to the folders, create subfolders, change data in files, delete files and folders, and change file attributes. Also allows the actions that can be performed by the Read permission.
Full Control	Take ownership and change permissions of the folder, subfolders, and files within the shared folder. In addition, all permissions are assigned by the Read and Change permissions.

Each of the permissions in Table 2-9 can be set to Allow or Deny. The Deny setting should be used very carefully. Usually, it is best to configure permissions based on user groups instead of individual users, unless you have a specific reason to do so. When assigning shared permissions, you should follow the Principle of Least Privilege. This principle says that a user should be given only as many permissions as is required to perform the job.

 Shared Folder permissions and NTFS permissions work together, but these are two separate sets of access controls. Remember that Shared Folder permissions are not effective when someone is logged on locally to the Windows XP Professional computer. NTFS permissions work both for locally logged-on users and users accessing the share across the network.

Using Computer Management to manage shared folders

Shared folders in Windows XP Professional can also be managed from the Computer Management console. This utility allows you to view shared folders, create new shared folders, stop sharing a folder, and manage users connected to any shared folder. Right-click the My Computer icon on the desktop and click Manage. This opens the Computer Management console. Click Shared Folders under the System Tools to view the shared folders on the computer. The following steps explain how you can use this console to manage shared folders:

- Double-click the Shared Folders node to expand it, and then click the Shares node. The shares currently configured on the computer are shown in the Details pane.
- Right-click the Shares node and click New File Share to create a new shared folder. This will also allow you to set Share permissions on the new shared folder.
- Right-click any share in the Details pane and click Stop Sharing.
- Click the Sessions folder in the left pane to view a list of connected users. Right-click the Sessions folder and click Disconnect All Sessions to disconnect all users from the computer.
- To disconnect a single user, right-click the name in the Details pane and click Close Session.
- To view files opened by connected users, click the Open Files folder in the left pane.

Combining NTFS and Share permissions

While you can configure NTFS permissions on every file and folder on an NTFS volume, you can assign Shared Folders permissions only on FAT and FAT32 volumes. When NTFS as well as Shared Folder permissions are configured on a particular folder, you should be able to calculate effective permissions on the folder for a particular user or group. Users must have NTFS permissions on a shared folder in addition to the Shared Folder permissions in order to access the folder or any files within the shared folder.

The following steps explain how you can calculate effective permissions when both NTFS and Shared Folder permissions are configured:

1. Calculate the effective NTFS permissions for the user on the folder. This is the sum of all NTFS permissions assigned through group memberships.

2. Calculate the effective Shared Folder permissions assigned through group memberships.

3. Determine the most restrictive of the NTFS and Share permissions. This will apply to the user.

Offline files and folders

Offline files and folders allow you to continue working on your documents even when you are not connected to the network. This is a handy feature for mobile users, as the documents are cached in the local hard disk and can be accessed at any place. When the network is available again, these documents can be synchronized with the copy of the document stored on the network file server.

In order to work with offline files and folders on your computer, make sure that Fast User Switching is disabled. For computers that are members of a domain, this feature is disabled by default. Fast User Switching can be disabled from the User Accounts utility in the Control Panel. When this is done, open the Folders Options from the Tools menu in My Computer. Click the Offline Files tab and check the Enable Offline Files and "Synchronize all offline files before logging off" options as shown in Figure 2-7.

In order to make files and folders available offline, complete the following steps:

1. Right-click the shared folder that you want to make available offline and click Make Available Offline.

2. Click Next in the Offline Files Wizard.

3. Select the "Automatically Synchronize The Offline Files When I Log On and Log Off My Computer" checkbox. Click Next.

To make shared files and folders available offline from your computer, you must first configure your computer to allow offline caching of documents. Open the Properties of the shared folder from Windows Explorer, select the Sharing tab, and click Caching. In the next dialog box, select "Allow Caching of Files In This Shared Folder." You can then select one of the following three caching options:

Manual Caching of Documents
> This option allows users to manually specify the files that should be made available offline. This is the default option.

Automatic Caching of Documents
> With this option selected, any file the user opens is automatically cached in the user's local hard disk.

Automatic Caching of Documents and Programs
> This is similar to the earlier option but in addition can cache applications files.

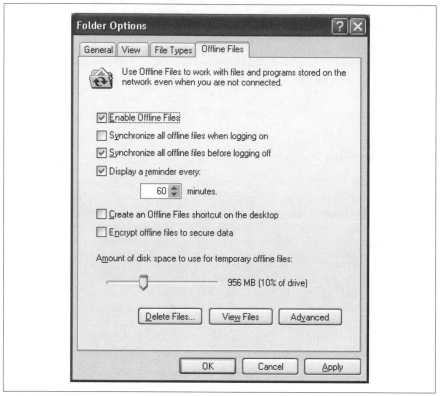

Figure 2-7. Offline files and folders

Synchronization Manager

Synchronization of offline files is done automatically by default when a user logs off. The Synchronization Manager allows you to manually configure synchronization settings. The Synchronization Manager can be accessed in one of these two ways:

- Click Start → All Programs → Accessories → Synchronize.
- Open Windows Explorer, click Tools, and select Synchronize.

Either of these options will open the "Items to Synchronize" window. The Synchronize button will force synchronization of all cached files with their versions on the network file server. The Setup button allows you to manually configure the synchronization. There are three sets of options to choose from: The Logon/Logoff tab allows you to specify whether you want to synchronize at logon, logoff, or both. The On Idle tab allows you to perform synchronization automatically when your computer is connected to the network but you are not using it. The Scheduled tab opens the Schedule Synchronization Wizard, in which you can configure the time when the synchronization should take place. With each of the three options, you can also specify the documents that you want to synchronize.

Configuring and Managing Print Devices

Windows XP Professional includes comprehensive support for configuring and sharing printers across the entire network. Print devices installed on the computer can be viewed and configured from the Printers and Faxes utility in the Control Panel. In the previous versions of Windows, the actual printing device was known as print device, and the term *Printer* was used to describe the software that controlled the printing process. This terminology has changed in Windows XP Professional. Before going into the details of configuring printers, you should have a good understanding of the following terminology associated with the printing process:

Logical printer

A logical printer is the software component that links to the printing device and is used to configure the device. This component controls how the jobs are sent to the printing device.

Printer

The printer is the actual printing device that produces hard copies of the document. A local printer is the one that is connected to a local port on the computer or on the print server. A network printer is the one that is connected directly to a network port.

Printer port

The printer port is the software interface that enables the computer to communicate with the printer. LPT1, COM, and USB, etc. are some examples of ports that can be configured as printer ports.

Print job

The print job is the document that is sent to the printer. The computer stores the print jobs in a queue until they are printed. The print job can be cancelled or paused while it stays in the queue.

Print server

The print server is the computer that receives, processes, and controls the print jobs sent by client computers and servers.

Printer driver

The printer driver is the software that accompanies the printer in order to enable Windows XP Professional to convert the print jobs into a format that the printer can understand. Each printer has an associated printer driver.

The computer that is configured as a print server must have sufficient hard disk space and a large amount of physical memory (RAM) in order to process print jobs sent by the client computers. A computer running Windows XP Professional allows only 10 concurrent connects and may not be suitable to serve as a print server in a large organization. It supports printing from NetWare and Macintosh clients but does not support printing from Unix clients. A Windows Server 2003 is best suited for such organizations, as it supports large number of concurrent connects and can take print jobs from Unix, Macintosh, and NetWare clients.

Installing and configuring printers

New printers are added from the Printers and Faxes utility in the Control Panel. When you right-click the printers, the Add Printer Wizard walks you though various pages that collect information about the printer and then installs the printer driver. You can configure the new printer as a local printer or as a network printer, depending on where the printer is actually connected, by specifying the printer port. You can select one of the preconfigured ports on the computer, such as LPT1, or you can create a new port. When you select the "Create a New Port" button, you can specify the type of port that you want to use. This is where you can configure a printer connected directly to the network.

Finally, you are prompted to specify whether you want to share the printer. When you share a printer, you will need to configure clients so that users can locate and send print jobs to the new printer. All client computers will need a printer driver in order to print to the shared printer. Windows XP Professional will automatically download printer drivers for Windows 2000, Windows NT 4.0, Windows ME, Windows 98, and Windows 95 clients. Other operating systems that will print using the LPR port will need Unix printer drivers.

Adding Print Services for Unix. Before Unix clients can print to the printer, you will need to install Print Services for Unix. This can be done as follows:

1. Open the Control Panel and click Network Connections.
2. Click the Advanced menu.
3. Click Optional Networking Components. This opens the Windows Optional Networking Components Wizard dialog box.
4. Highlight "Other Network File and Print Services" and click the Details button.
5. Click "Print Services for Unix," and then click OK.
6. Close all dialog boxes when the installation is complete.

After Print Services for Unix is installed, you should create an LPR port. The following steps explain how you can add an LPR port for facilitating printing from Unix clients:

1. Click Start → Printers and Faxes. This opens the "Printers and Faxes" window.
2. Click Add A Printer. This starts the Add Printer Wizard dialog box.
3. On the "Local or Network Printer" page, click "Local Printer Attached to this Computer."
4. Clear the "Automatically Detect and Install my Plug And Play Printer" checkbox, and then click Next.
5. In the Select A Printer Port page, click Create A New Port.
6. From the "Type of Port" drop-down list, select LPR Port. Click Next, and then complete the configuration appropriately.

Once installed, the properties of the printer can be accessed by right-clicking the printer icon. This is shown in the Figure 2-8.

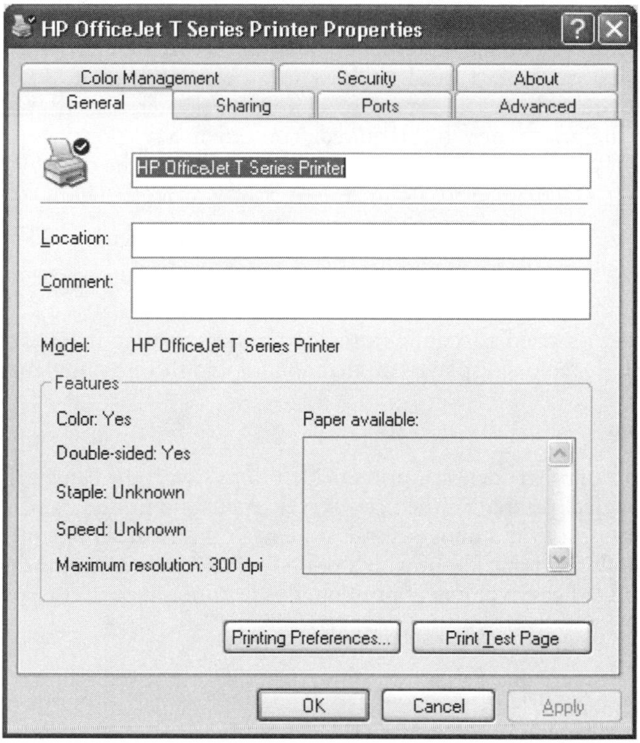

Figure 2-8. Printer properties

Printer properties vary from one printer to another, but almost all printers have the following common properties:

General
This page has options for specifying the printer location, setting printing preferences, and printing a test page.

Sharing
This page allows you to share the printer (or stop sharing, if currently shared), specify the share name, and install additional printer drivers for clients.

Ports
This page allows you to configure the port that is connected to the printer. You can add or delete a port and enable Printer Pooling. *Printer Pooling* is used for load sharing when you have multiple identical printers connected to the same port.

Security
This page allows you to set access permissions for both local and network users who send print jobs to the printer. Printer permissions are explained later in this section.

Advanced

The Advanced properties let you configure availability of the printer, printer priority, and spooling options. *Printer priority* is defined when you have configured multiple logical printers for the same printer. Printer priority enables you to prioritize print jobs sent to the printer. On this page, you can update the printer driver, if required. You can also set printing defaults, set a separator page, and specify which print processor is to be used by the printer.

Device Settings

This page enables you to configure device-specific settings. These settings differ from one device to another.

Color Management

This page is used to configure color options so that there is consistency between the colors displayed on the monitor and those printed on paper.

Printer pooling

Installing two or more identical printers (or printers with the same printer driver) as a single logical printer on the print server can create printer pools. This helps share the printing load among several printers. A user can send print jobs to the printer without worrying about which printer will actually print his document. In networks with a heavy volume of printing, this feature is very useful.

Follow the steps given here to create a printer pool:

1. In the "Printers and Faxes" window, right-click an installed printer and then click Properties.
2. Click the Ports tab in the Printer Properties page.
3. Select each port to which additional identical printers are connected, then click OK.

Printer priorities

Besides printer pooling, you can create multiple logical printers for the same printer in Windows XP Professional. Although the physical printer is the same, different users see the printer as a different print device. You can then set priorities for each logical printer so that users with high-priority print jobs can print before other users. Printer priorities range from 1 to 99, with 99 being the highest priority.

To enable printer priority, first create additional printers, selecting the same port for each additional printer. Open the Properties of each printer and click the Advanced tab. Specify the printer priority and click OK. You can then assign permissions for each logical printer to users or groups.

 Printer pooling and printer priorities must be understood in detail to answer questions in Exam 70-270. Make sure that you have a strong grasp of how to create printer pools and configure printer priorities.

Print Permissions

Print Permissions allows you to control the level of access that users or groups can have to the printers. With properly configured permissions, you can control who can print to the printer, who can manage documents, and who can install or configure printers. Available print permissions in Windows XP Professional are shown in Figure 2-9 and listed in Table 2-10.

Exam 70-270
Study Guide

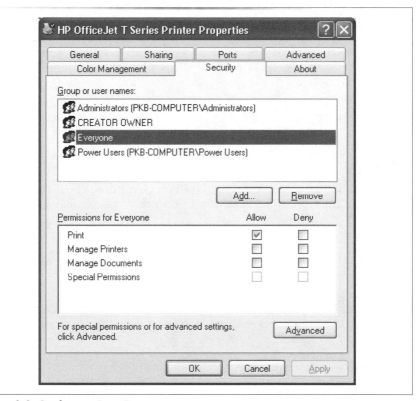

Figure 2-9. Configuring Print Permissions

Table 2-10. Windows XP Professional Print Permissions

Permission	Description
Print	Print documents, as well as pause, resume, and cancel a user's own documents.
Manage Documents	Pause, resume, and cancel all users' documents. Also provides Print permissions.
Manage Printers	Share a printer, change permissions, delete a printer, cancel all documents. All actions are permitted by the Print and the Manage Documents permissions.

Printer permissions are assigned from the Security tab of the Printer Properties dialog box. Permissions can be set to Allow or Deny. By default, Windows XP Professional assigns Print permission to the Everyone group, and the Administrators group gets the Full Control permission. You should remove the permissions for the Everyone group and assign permissions based on user groups if security is a concern in your organization.

Managing printers and print jobs

The Manage Printers permissions allow a user to manage everyday tasks related to printers. These tasks, including pausing a printer, resuming printing, and canceling all documents sent to the printer, are necessary if there is a problem with the printer.

When a printer is having a problem that you do not think can be quickly fixed, you can redirect the print jobs in the print queue to a different printer. This is called *Printer Redirecting*. Follow the steps given here to redirect print jobs to a different printer:

1. In the "Printers and Faxes" window, right-click the printer and click Properties.
2. Click the Ports tab and click Add Port.
3. In the Available Port Types list, click the Local Port button, and then click New Port.
4. Enter the name of the new port in the Port Name dialog box. For example, you can enter the UNC name for a new port in the format *PrintServer*\ *PrinterName*.
5. Click OK to close the Port Name dialog box. Close all windows.

Remember that you must redirect all documents in the print queue to an alternative printer. It is not possible to redirect individual documents.

Print jobs or documents sent to the printer can be managed from the print queue. Double-click a printer in the "Printers and Faxes" window to access the print queue. The Document menu gives you options to pause, resume, restart, cancel, or view the properties of a print job.

Connecting to an Internet printer

Windows XP Printers can also be accessed and managed using a web browser. You must have Internet Information Service (IIS) installed on the print server before you can make the printer available from a web browser. Once this is done, anyone with proper permissions can manage the printer or print documents.

To access a printer using a web browser, type `http://PrintServer/PrinterName`.

To view a list of all available shared printers on a print server, type `http://PrintServer/printers`.

Managing Disks and Data Storage

Hard disks are the primary data storage devices used in computers. Hard disks are treated as fixed storage devices and are connected to IDE or SCSI interfaces. USB disks, CD-ROMS, and DVDs are called *removable storage media*. Windows XP Professional supports two types of hard disks for data storage: *Basic disks* and *Dynamic disks*. The following sections explain Basic and Dynamic disks and the types of volumes that can be created on each type of disk.

Basic disks

Basic disks are the traditional type of disk used in computer systems. Windows XP Professional initializes all disks as Basic unless they are converted to Dynamic using the Disk Management utility. The disks are divided into one or more *partitions*—each of which can be a logical storage unit accessible by a drive letter. Windows XP Professional stores partition information in a partition table that is not a part of the operating system and can be accessed from any operating system besides Windows. Partitions in Basic disks can be *Primary* or *Extended*.

Primary partition
> Each Basic disk can have up to four Primary partitions or three Primary and one Extended partition. One of the Primary partitions is marked as the *Active partition* and is used to boot the system. There can be only one active partition on a computer. The Primary partition is formatted using one of the file systems: FAT, FAT32, or NTFS.

Extended partition
> An Extended partition is created on unallocated space on the hard disk. You then create logical drives on this partition and assign them drive letters. Extended partitions cannot be formatted with any filesystem, and they cannot be assigned drive letters.

Logical partition
> Logical partitions are created inside the Extended partitions. Logical drives cannot be marked as active and cannot be used to boot the system. These partitions are used to organize files and folders on the hard disk.

Dynamic disks

Dynamic disks are the disks that are specifically converted from Basic disks using the Disk Management utility. Dynamic disks treat the entire disk as a single partition. You can create volumes on the disk to organize your files and folders. Dynamic disks are not supported on notebook computers. Dynamic volumes can be extended on single or multiple Dynamic disks and offer fault tolerance features. You can create Simple, Spanned, and Striped volumes on Dynamic disks as explained in the following list.

Simple volume
> A *Simple volume* contains space from all or part of a single Dynamic disk. It is similar to a partition on a Basic disk. Simple volumes can be formatted with FAT, FAT32, or NTFS filesystems.

Spanned volume
> A *Spanned volume* is a dynamic volume that contains space from a single or multiple Dynamic disks. You can add unallocated space from 2 to 32 Dynamic disks to create a large Spanned volume. Each disk can be of any size. Windows XP writes data to the first disk until it is full and then continues on the remaining disks. One big disadvantage of Spanned volume is that failure of a single disk can bring down the entire volume, causing all data to be lost. This implies that Spanned volumes are not fault-tolerant.

Striped volume

A *Striped volume* combines space from 2 to 32 Dynamic disks to make a single dynamic volume. Spanned volumes offer better performance and more-efficient use of disk space. Data is stored on Spanned volumes in stripes (chunks of 64 KB) on each disk in turns so that each disk has equal amount of disk space. It is recommended that all disks in a Striped volume be of equal size, but this is not a requirement. You can create a Striped volume on disks with unequal space, but this results in wasting space on larger disks as the Striped volume utilizes only space equal to the smallest disk in the volume from each disk. Striped volumes cannot be extended and are not fault-tolerant. If one of the disks in a Striped volume fails, all data is lost.

 Dynamic disks also support fault-tolerant volumes such as RAID-1 (Mirrored Volume) and RAID-5, but these are not supported on Windows XP Professional. If you still want to configure fault-tolerant volumes on Windows XP, you will have to rely on third-party utilities or deploy hardware RAID solutions. Windows 2000 Server and Windows Server 2003 support software-based RAID-1 and RAID-5 fault-tolerant volumes.

Disk management

Disk management tasks are performed using the Disk Management utility found within the Computer Management console. Right-click the Windows My Computer icon (typically found on the desktop and also accessible from the Start menu) and select Manage in order to open the Computer Management console. The Disk Management tool is located beneath the Storage folder. When you open the Disk Management tool, Windows presents a graphical view of a system's installed disks. Disks are marked as Basic or Dynamic. Disk Management reveals additional information, including a disk's health status, filesystem, type, and capacity.

Creating partitions. To create a partition, right-click a disk and click Create Partition. The New Partition Wizard allows you to create a Primary partition, an Extended Partition or a logical drive. If the disk does not already have any partitions, you can also configure it as a Dynamic disk. Once configured as a Dynamic disk, you can right-click the Dynamic disk to create Dynamic volumes.

Once you create a partition, you can format it with the FAT, FAT32, or NTFS filesystem. Right-click the partition and select Format. Existing volumes can also be formatted from Windows Explorer. This destroys all data on the partition. The Format option also allows you to assign a volume label and a drive letter to the partition.

Converting from Basic disk to Dynamic disk. To convert a Basic disk to Dynamic, you must have at least 1 MB of free space at the end of the disk, and the sector size must not be larger than 512 bytes. Right-click the disk and select Convert To Dynamic Disk. This action does not cause any loss of data. If the Convert To Dynamic Disk option is not available, either the disk is already a Dynamic disk or you are trying to convert the disk on a portable computer. Remember that Dynamic disks are not supported on portable computers. This option is also not available on removable disks such as CD-ROMS, floppy drives, and ZIP drives.

Converting from Dynamic disk to Basic disk. Converting a disk from Basic to Dynamic is a one-way process. Conversion from Dynamic disk back to a Basic disk destroys all data on the disk. You must first back up all the data on the disk before attempting to perform this conversion. To convert a disk back to Basic, right-click the disk in Disk Management and select Convert To Basic Disk.

Conversion from Basic disk to Dynamic disk is a one-way process. If you want to revert a disk back to Basic from Dynamic, you must backup all data on the disk before starting the conversion. This reverse process causes loss of all data on the disk.

Creating a Simple volume. A Simple volume contains an area on a single Dynamic disk. Follow the steps given here to create a Simple volume:

1. Right-click an unallocated space on the Dynamic disk and select New Volume.

2. In the New Volume Wizard, select Simple from the Volume Types options and click Next.

3. In the Select Disks page, type the size of the volume in MB and click Next.

4. Select a drive letter in the "Assign Drive Letter or Path" page. You can also enter a path to a mounted volume. Click Next.

5. Select a filesystem to format the volume in the Format Volume page. Click Next. Click Finish to complete the process.

Creating a Spanned volume. Spanned volumes can contain from 2 to 32 Dynamic disks. To create a Spanned volume, right-click an unallocated space on the Dynamic disk and select New Volume. In the New Volume Wizard page, select Spanned. You can also extend an existing Simple volume or a Spanned volume if you have unallocated space on other Dynamic disks. Select the Extend Volume option to extend a Spanned volume.

Creating a Striped volume. In order to create a Striped volume, you must have free or unallocated space on at least two disks. You can add up to 32 identical disks. Right-click unallocated space on the first Dynamic disk and select New Volume. Select Striped from the New Volume Wizard Page. Follow the onscreen instructions to complete the process. Remember that you cannot extend a Striped volume.

Creating a Mounted volume. Volume Mount Points are used to extend available disk space without actually extending the size of the volume. Although you can mount a volume on an existing FAT/FAT32 or NTFS, the volume that you wish to mount must be formatted with NTFS. The following steps illustrate how a Mounted volume is created.

1. Open Windows Explorer and create a folder on a NTFS volume. This folder will serve as your Volume Mount Point. Close Windows Explorer.

2. Open Disk Management from within the Computer Management console.

3. Right-click the volume where you want to mount the volume. Select Change Drive Letter Or Path.

4. In the "Add Drive Letter or Path" dialog box, click the "Mount in the Following Empty Folder" option, and type the name of the folder you previously created with Windows Explorer. Click OK.

Using DISKPART to manage disks. DiskPart is a command-line utility that is used to manage disks and volumes. When you run the `diskpart.exe` command from the command prompt, the DiskPart interpreter starts and the prompt changes to `DISKPART>`. You can type `Help` at the `DISKPART>` prompt to get a list of all available commands to manage disks. The only facility not available with DiskPart is the ability to format volumes. You must use the `format.exe` command to format disks and partitions.

Disk quotas

Disk quotas are used to limit usage of disk space by allocating limited space on a per-user basis. Disk quotas are supported only on volumes formatted with NTFS. You can allocate disk space for users, warn them when the quota threshold is reached, allow or deny disk space over the quota limit, and log quota entries. Figure 2-10 shows the Quota tab of the New Volume Properties page. The following steps explain how identical quotas can be configured for all users on an NTFS volume.

1. Right-click an NTFS volume and open its properties.

2. Click the Quota tab. If the Quota tab is not available, the volume is not an NTFS volume.

3. Select the Enable Quota Management checkbox.

4. Click the "Limit Disk Space to" button and enter the size of the quota in KB, MB, or GB. Enter a value for Set Warning Level To.

5. Click appropriate options in the Event Log Entries checkboxes.

The Quota Entries button allows you to configure different quota settings for different users. Remember that disk quotas can only be set on a per-user basis and not on a group basis. The Quota Entries button opens the Quota Entries window. Click Quota → New Quota Entry to add users and set their quota limits.

 If you do not see the Quota button in the disk or volume Properties dialog box, the disk or volume is not formatted with NTFS. You should be a member of the Administrators group to manage disk quotas. Disk quotas do not take into account compression when disk space is calculated for a user. File and folder ownership is taken into account while calculating quotas.

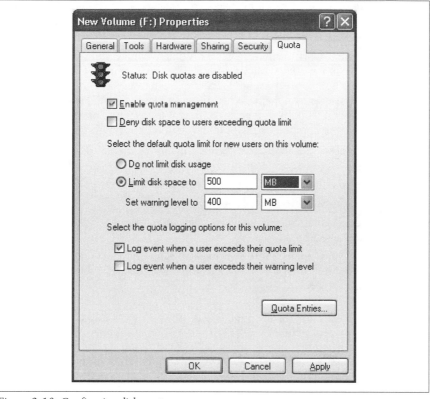

Exam 70-270
Study Guide

Figure 2-10. Configuring disk quotas

Data compression

File compression is used to conserve disk space by compression of files and folders. The files are stored in a compressed form and are uncompressed automatically when a user opens them. This allows you to store more data on a disk or volume. Windows XP Professional supports two types of compression:

- Compressed Folders
- NTFS Compression

Compressed Folders is a new feature in Windows XP Professional that keeps the folders and files within it in a compressed state. Any new files added to the folder are automatically compressed. It is not possible to compress individual files using this feature, but if the same file is copied to the compressed folder, it gets compressed. Folder Compression works on both NTFS and FAT volumes, and you can even compress encrypted folders—a feature that is not available with NTFS compression.

To use Folder Compression, open Windows Explorer. Navigate to the drive or folder where you want to create a compressed folder and highlight it. Right-click an empty area and click New, and then select Compressed (zipped) Folder. This creates a new compressed folder. Alternatively, you can select the drive or folder, click New from the File menu, and select Compressed (zipped) Folder. Any files that you move to this folder will be automatically compressed. The compressed folder is shown as a zipped item in Windows Explorer.

NTFS Compression works only on NTFS volumes. Unlike Compressed Folders, NTFS Compression works with individual files but cannot be used with file encryption. Files compressed using NTFS compression are automatically uncompressed when a user opens them. When the user closes the file, it is compressed again. NTFS Compression is also enabled from Windows Explorer. The following steps explain how to compress a file or folder with NTFS compression.

1. Open Windows Explorer and locate the file or folder that you wish to compress.

2. Right-click the file or folder and click Properties.

3. Click the Advanced tab in the Properties window.

4. In the Advanced Attributes window, click the "Compress Contents to Save Disk Space" checkbox.

5. Click OK. This opens the Confirm Attribute Changes dialog box. Select whether you want to apply changes to this folder or to the folder, subfolders, and files. Click OK.

 Remember the main differences between NTFS Compression and Folder Compression. NFTS Compression works only on NTFS volumes, can compress individual files and folders, and cannot be used together with Encryption. Folder Compression works on both FAT and NTFS volumes, works only on folders, and can be used even if files are encrypted.

Another compression feature called *Disk Compression* allows you to set NTFS compression on an entire disk. Right-click a disk drive or volume in Windows Explorer and click Properties. You will notice the "Compress Drive to Save Disk Space" checkbox in the bottom part of the General tab. Check this box to enable compression for the entire volume or disk.

Copying and moving files

NTFS compression in Windows XP follows a certain set of rules that governs the compression state of the files when they are copied or moved from their original location. The following list explains these rules:

* When a file is copied to another folder with the same NTFS volume, or copied to another NTFS volume, it inherits the compression state of the destination folder.

* When a file or folder is moved from one folder to another folder on the same NTFS volume, it retains its compression state. When it is moved from one NTFS volume to another NTFS volume, it inherits the compression state of the destination folder.

- When a compressed file or folder is copied or moved to a FAT volume, including a floppy disk, it loses its compression state and is automatically uncompressed.

Encrypted File System (EFS)

The *Encrypting File System* (EFS) is a security feature that protects files and folders from unauthorized access. It uses public key cryptography to encrypt the documents and only the users who have the private key, which is granted at logon, can access the document. Encryption is enabled from the Advanced page of file or folder properties. You can also use the cipher command in Windows XP Professional to encrypt or decrypt files or folders. Encryption is transparent to any authorized user who has permissions to access the file. The file is automatically decrypted when the authorized user opens it and is encrypted again when it is closed.

The following steps explain how to encrypt files or folders:

1. Open Windows Explorer and locate the file or folder that you want to encrypt.
2. Right-click the file or folder and click Properties.
3. Click the Advanced tab to open the Advanced Attributed page.
4. Click the Encrypt Files To Secure Data checkbox located at the bottom of the page.
5. Click OK. The Confirm Attribute Changes dialog box will open. Select whether you want to "Apply Changes to This Folder Only" or "Apply changes to This Folder, Files and Subfolders."
6. Click OK.

Decryption is done in the same way as encryption. Open the Advanced Properties of the file or folder and clear the checkbox for "Encrypt Contents to Secure Data". Remember that NTFS Compression and Encryption are mutually exclusive. You cannot encrypt a file or folder that is already compressed using NTFS Compression. You must uncompress the file or folder before you can encrypt it.

The cipher command is also used to encrypt or decrypt files and folders. In its basic form, the command is used as follows:

```
cipher [/e] [/d] [/s:FolderName]
```

The parameter /e is used to encrypt, and /d is used to decrypt. The /s parameter specifies the folder where the encryption should be performed. Typing cipher /? displays help for the command.

Maintaining disks

Windows XP Professional includes three basic utilities to maintain disks. These are *Disk Defragmenter*, *Check Disk*, and *Disk Cleanup*. Each of these utilities is explained in the following sections.

Disk Defragmenter. Hard disks become fragmented when some applications are installed or after a large number of files are moved or deleted. *Fragmentation* refers to the state of a hard disk when it no longer has contiguous space available to store new files or folders. The Disk Defragmenter utility can analyze hard disks and defragment them to free up contiguous space. This helps improve the efficiency of the disk. Disk Defragmenter works on FAT, FAT32, and NTFS volumes.

There are several ways to access the Disk Defragmenter:

- Click Start → All Programs → Accessories → System Tools → Disk Defragmenter.
- Open Windows Explorer and open the Properties of disk or volume. Select the Tools tab. Click Defragment Now to open Disk Defragmenter.
- Right-click My Computer and click Manage in order to open Computer Management. The Disk Defragmenter is located under the Storage folder.

The Disk Defragmenter window is shown in Figure 2-11.

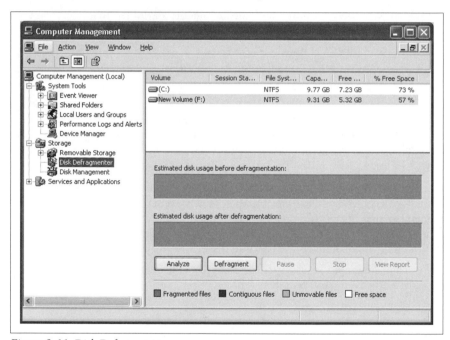

Figure 2-11. Disk Defragmenter

At the top of the window, you can select the disk or volume that you wish to analyze or defragment. The condition of the disk is displayed in four different colors. Red indicates fragmented files, blue indicates files that are not fragmented, green indicates system files, and white indicates free space on the disk.

In Figure 2-11, the two buttons, Analyze and Defragment, have the following effects:

Analyze

   When you click the Analyze button, the utility analyzes the entire disk and displays the results in the graphical form in the Analysis band.

Defragment

   When you click the Defragment button, the utility starts to defragment the disk. The disk is automatically analyzed before it is defragmented.

Check Disk. The Check Disk utility checks hard disks for filesystem errors and scans and attempts to recover bad sectors on the disk. As with the Disk Defragmenter, Check Disk can also be accessed in a number of ways. An equivalent command-line utility known as chkdsk.exe is also available for this purpose. There are two options available with the Check Disk utility:

Automatically Fix File System Errors

   This option allows you to scan the disk for filesystem errors and fix them automatically. All files and applications should be closed before the system can perform this action.

Scan For and Attempt Recovery of Bad Sectors

   This option allows you to scan and fix bad sectors on the hard disk. All files and applications should be closed before the system can perform this action. If you check this option, you need not check the Automatically Fix File System Errors option because all those actions are included in this utility.

In case any files are open or any application is running when you start the Check Disk utility, you are prompted to schedule the operation to start at a later time.

The Check Disk utility can also be started from the command prompt with the chkdsk.exe command. A number of switches are available with this command. You can type chkdsk /? in order to get help on syntax and switches.

Disk Cleanup. The Disk Cleanup utility is used to free up disk space by deleting temporary files and folders from the disk or volume. This utility is also available from either Windows Explorer or from System Tools under Accessories in the All Programs menu. Disk Cleanup essentially gives you options to delete several types of files. These files include:

- Program files downloaded from the Internet, including ActiveX controls and Java Applets.

- Temporary Internet files to clear the computer cache. These files are stored in the Temporary Internet Files folder.

- Temporary Files located in the Temp folder.

- Files stored in the Recycle Bin.

 Disk Defragmenter, Check Disk, and Disk Cleanup are three main utilities for maintaining disks. Each is used for different purposes, and you must know which utility is the best to use for a given situation.

Removable media

Floppy disks, CD-ROMS, DVDs, and tape drives are termed as *removable media* in Windows XP Professional. Most of the CD-ROM drives and DVD drives are Plug and Play (PnP) devices and are automatically configured by the operating system. You can manually configure these devices from the Device Manager that is accessible from the Computer Management console under the Storage folder. You should verify that the device you are installing is compatible with Windows XP Professional before you install it.

Removable Storage organizes removable media in *media pools* that in turn groups the media based on their usage and sharing by applications. Removable media is installed and configured using the normal hardware installations methods. The Removable Storage utility under the Storage folder in Computer Management allows you to control access to media and insert or eject media as required. External removable media does not use the Removable Media utility included with Windows XP Professional.

Managing Hardware Devices and Drivers

As with previous versions of Windows, Windows XP Professional also supports Plug and Play (PnP) and non-Plug and Play devices. Most of the time, the supported hardware is automatically detected and installed if an appropriate device driver is available. The computer BIOS also supports PnP. Other non-PnP devices can be installed using the Add Hardware Wizard. This section includes discussions on installation and configuration of hardware devices, device drivers, the Advanced Configuration and Power Interface (ACPI), and other input/output (I/O) devices. Display devices and drivers are also part of this section. Networking devices such as the network interface card (NIC) and modems are covered in "Implementing, Managing, and Troubleshooting Network Protocols and Services," later in this chapter.

Device Manager

The Device Manager utility is used to manage hardware devices and drivers in Windows XP Professional. This utility can be accessed in one of the following ways:

- From the Computer Management console, the Device Manager is located under the System Tools folder.
- From the Start menu, click Start Control Panel System. The Device Manager is located within the Hardware tab and is shown in Figure 2-12.

When you install any PnP device and start the computer, the device is automatically detected by the operating system. The New Hardware Found Wizard installs an appropriate driver for the device. In case the device is PnP-compatible but is not detected by the operating system, you can still install the device using the Add Hardware Wizard.

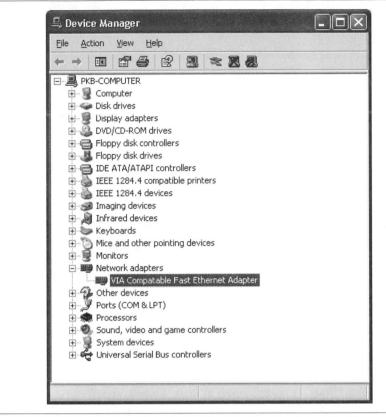

Figure 2-12. Device Manager in Windows XP Professional

Installing a non-PnP device

To install a non-PnP device, you must first determine what kind of resources are required by the device. The resources refer to input/output (I/O) port, Direct Memory Address (DMA), Interrupt Request (IRQ), and memory range. You should consult the documentation accompanying the device. Turn off the computer and install the hardware. Start the computer and open Device Manager. The new device would be listed as an unknown or unidentified device with a question mark. Right-click the device and open its Properties window to install appropriate device drivers. Once the device driver is installed, the Device Manager will show the device as normal.

Hardware resources

Each hardware device, whether it is a PnP or a non-PnP, requires some system resources to operate in the desired way. With PnP devices, the operating system automatically assigns these resources when installing the device. With some older PnP and non-PnP devices, you will need to assign these resources manually using the Device Manager. The most common resources are explained in the following list.

Interrupt Request (IRQ)

Hardware devices use IRQs to send requests or messages to the microprocessor in order to draw its attention. There are a total of 16 available IRQ numbers ranging from 0 to 15.

Input/output (I/O) port

The I/O port is the section of memory that is used by the device to communicate with the operating system.

Direct Memory Access (DMA)

Hardware devices use DMA channels to directly access the memory without going through the microprocessor. DMA channel numbers range from 0 to 7.

Memory

Certain hardware devices reserve a chunk of system memory for their exclusive use. When reserved, other devices and the operating system cannot access that memory space.

Device Manager is used to determine the hardware resource assignment to various devices in the computer. Open Device Manager from within the Computer Management console. From the View menu, select Resources By Connection. The Device Manager shows a list of all hardware resources in use by devices. You can also determine which resources are available for other devices, if needed.

System Information. Another method to determine hardware resources is to access the System Information from the Start menu. Click Start → All Programs → Accessories → System Tools, and then select System Information. There is a separate folder for Hardware Resources within the System Information. You can view hardware conflicts, IRQ, DMA, Memory, and other resources in use by different devices and software applications. System Information is a very useful utility for troubleshooting.

Driver Signing

The Driver Signing feature in Windows XP Professional ensures that only those drivers are installed that are verified by Windows Hardware Quality Labs (WHQL). These drivers carry a digital signature that verifies that the driver has been tested and approved, by Microsoft or the vendor, to work with the operating system. Windows XP keeps all signed device drivers in a compressed file named *Driver.cab*, which is copied to the *\%Systemroot%\DriverCache\i386* folder during installation.

Windows XP includes three options to control how the system responds when a user attempts to install an unsigned device driver. The three options are configured from the Hardware tab of System Properties in the Control Panel.

The following driver signing options can be configured:

Ignore
> This option allows you to install any unsigned device driver.

Warn
> This is the default setting and displays a warning message when you attempt to install an unsigned device driver. You are given the option to cancel or continue with the installation.

Block
> This option will block installation of any unsigned device driver.

If you are a member of the Administrators group, you can click the Make This Action The System Default checkbox so that no other user can install an unsigned device driver on the computer.

Windows XP Professional includes another utility known as *Signature Verification* to verify that the installed device drivers have digital signatures. This utility can be run from the command prompt by typing sigverif.exe, and displays the results of the analysis on screen or in a logfile.

Installing, uninstalling, and updating device drivers

Device drivers are managed from the Drivers tab of the Device Properties dialog box. To access this box, open the Device Manager as explained previously and locate the device. Right-click and then click Properties to open the device's properties. Click the Driver tab to open the details of the currently installed device driver as shown in Figure 2-13.

This dialog box allows you to perform the following actions:

Driver Details
> Click this button to view the details of the currently installed driver. Details include the vendor's name and the location of the driver files.

Update Driver
> Click this button if you wish to update a device driver with a more recent version. You can also reinstall a driver if the previous installation did not work for some reason. This action is not required for PnP devices, as the operating system will automatically install a correct device driver.

Roll Back Driver
> Click this button if you find that the newly installed updated driver does not work and you would like to revert to the previously working device driver. This feature works only when you have updated the driver and not for a fresh installation. You cannot roll back a device driver for printers.

Uninstall
> Click this button when you wish to remove a device from the computer. Sometimes when a driver does not work at all, you may wish to completely uninstall it before installing a new or updated driver.

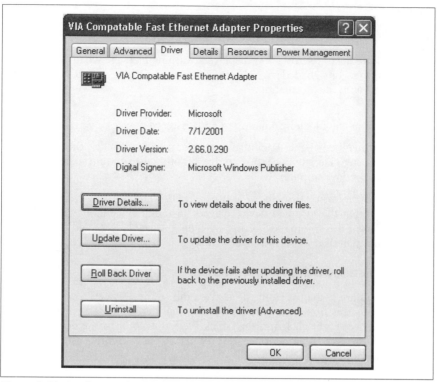

Figure 2-13. Configuring device drivers

 The Roll Back Driver option is a useful utility when a new device driver is not functioning as expected. Unfortunately, this option is not available for printer drivers.

Hardware profiles

Hardware profiles are used when you have different hardware configurations in your computer and wish to enable certain devices at some times and disable them at other times. For example, if you have two network adapters in your computer and wish to use one of them when connected to one network and use the other when connected to another network, you can create two separate hardware profiles to save the networking configuration of the computer. In one of the hardware profiles, you will enable one of the network adapters and disable the other; in the second hardware profile, you will enable the second network adapter and disable the first. Windows XP Professional includes features that dynamically change hardware settings, which leaves you with little to do with hardware profiles. Hardware profiles might be useful when you are faced with configuration of some older hardware.

The following procedure explains how to create a hardware profile for a system that currently has only one hardware profile:

1. Open the Control Panel from the Start menu.

2. Click the System applet and click the Hardware tab.

3. Click the Hardware Profiles button to open the Hardware Profiles dialog box. You will notice that the only profile listed in this dialog box is Profile1, marked as current.

4. Click the Copy button to make a copy of Profile1. Type a name for the new profile. Click OK.

5. Click the new profile from the Available Hardware Profiles and click the Properties button to open the properties of the new profile.

6. Make your selections appropriately and click OK to return to the Hardware Profiles dialog box.

7. Enter a time value in seconds that the operating system will wait for you to select an appropriate profile during the boot process. You can also have Windows wait indefinitely until you select the hardware Profile by clicking the "Wait Until I Select a Hardware Profile" button.

Once you have created the new hardware profile, you can boot the system by selecting the new hardware profile and make appropriate configuration changes.

Display devices

Display properties are configured from the Displays utility in the Control Panel. This utility allows you to configure Windows themes, your desktop, screen-savers, and appearance and screen resolution settings. Besides this, the Settings tab allows you to configure color quality, adapter settings, monitor types, and multiple monitor configurations. Display configurations are also discussed later in this chapter in the section "Configuring and Troubleshooting the Desktop Environment."

Multiple monitors

Windows XP Professional can be configured to extend your display space to include up to 10 monitors simultaneously. All display devices must be Peripheral Connect Interface (PCI)-compatible or Accelerated Graphics Port 9AGP-compatible in order to configure the operating system to support multiple monitors. If the computer has an integrated video adapter built into the motherboard, it must also support multiple displays and is treated as a secondary display adapter. You should take the following actions in order to configure multiple displays:

Install multiple monitors
Install one or more PCI or AGP video adapters in the empty slots on your computer. Connect each monitor to each of the adapters. Turn on the computer and let the operating system detect the new adapters. Open the Display utility in the Control Panel. Select one of the additional monitors and click the Extend My Windows Desktop Onto This Monitor checkbox. Repeat these steps for each monitor.

Configure the Display on multiple monitors

Open the Display utility in Control Panel. Click the Settings tab. Click the primary monitor and set Color Quality and Screen Resolution. Then click the second monitor and click the Extend My Windows Desktop Onto This Monitor checkbox. Set the Color Quality and Screen Resolution for the second monitor. Repeat these steps for each additional monitor.

You should use identical monitors when configuring your display for multiple monitors. This means that each monitor should be of the same size and should be able to display the same color quality and screen resolution.

Input/output (I/O) devices

Windows XP Professional supports most of the common Plug and Play (PnP) I/O devices. These devices include keyboards, mice, scanners, cameras, printers, faxes, and several other items. Most of the newer PnP devices are automatically detected and installed by the operating system, and you most likely will not need to configure them. Following is a list of the most commonly used I/O devices:

USB devices

With the Universal Serial Bus (USB), you can attach up to 127 devices to the computer. It is fully PnP-compatible. Most USB devices support *hot plugging*, which means that you can connect or disconnect a USB device to the computer while it is powered on.

Keyboard

Most of the newer keyboards are generally PnP devices and are connected to either the PS2 or the USB port of the computer. Wireless keyboards are also becoming very popular these days. Some of the settings that you can configure with the keyboards include setting the character repeat rate and character repeat delay in the Speed tab.

Mouse

Like the keyboard, a mouse is also a PnP device, and it is connected to either a USB or PS2 port on the computer. Newer wireless mice that communicate with the system using a wireless USB hub are also available. You can configure mouse settings such as switching left and right buttons, choice of pointers, and the wheel.

Scanner and camera

Most scanners and cameras are PnP devices that usually connect to the USB port of the computer. Once installed, Windows XP automatically detects the device and installs the appropriate device driver. You can also manually install the device using the "Scanners and Cameras" utility in the Control Panel. The Add An Imaging Device Wizard walks you through various steps to correctly configure the device.

Smart card readers

Smart cards are credit-card-sized devices that are generally used to store personal information or authentication credentials such as public or private keys. Smart cards need a smart card reader, a device driver, and a smart card service running on the Windows XP Professional computer before they can communicate with the computer.

IrDA wireless devices

IrDA stands for InfraRed Data Association. Most internal IrDA-compatible devices are installed automatically during the installation of the Windows XP operating system. Other IrDA devices must be installed using the Add Hardware Wizard utility in the Control Panel. When installed, a separate Wireless Link utility appears in the Control Panel.

Handheld devices

Handheld devices are connected to the computer using either the USB port or the IrDA standard. Each handheld device needs software to enable it to communicate with the Windows XP Professional operating system.

Managing Power Options

Windows XP Professional manages power consumed by different parts of the system using its power management features. The Power Options utility in the Control Panel allows you to configure different power schemes to turn the monitor and the hard disk on or off after a specified idle time has lapsed. You can put the system in standby mode, configure hibernate options, and configure the Uninterruptible Power Supply (UPS) settings.

Windows XP Professional also supports Advanced Power Management (APM) and the Advanced Power Configuration Interface. But before you can utilize any of the power options, you must make sure that your computer hardware, including the system BIOS, supports these features. To configure Power Options, open the Control Panel from the Start menu and click Power Options. The Power Options Properties window is shown in Figure 2-14.

Power schemes. You can configure when the power to the monitor and the hard disk of the computer should be turned off after a specified idle time has lapsed, and when the system should be put in standby mode. Table 2-11 lists several power schemes that are available.

Table 2-11. Power schemes available in Windows XP Professional

Power scheme	Used for	Turn off monitor	Turn off hard disk
Home/Office Desk	Desktops	After 20 minutes	Never
Portable/Laptop	Portable/laptop	After 15 minutes	After 30 minutes
Presentation	Desktop/laptop	Never	Never
Always On	Personal servers	After 20 minutes	Never
Minimal Power Management	Desktops	After 15 minutes	Never
Max Battery	Portable/laptop	After 15 minutes	Never

The Minimal Power management power scheme disables some of the power management features of the operating system, such as the Hibernate mode.

In case none of the power schemes are suitable for your requirements, you can modify one of the built-in power schemes to fit your needs. The following steps explain how you can create a new power scheme:

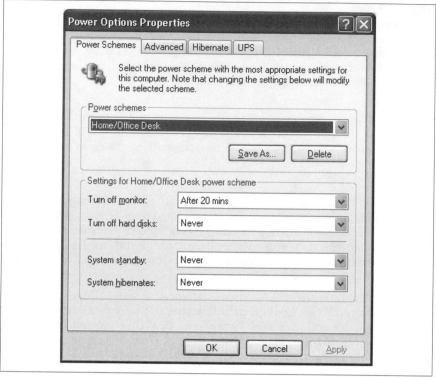

Figure 2-14. Power Options

1. From the drop-down menu, select the power scheme that closely matches your requirements.
2. Make changes to the Turn Off Monitor, Turn Off Hard Disk, and Standby Power settings.
3. Either click OK to change the existing power scheme, or click the Save As button and enter a name for the new scheme.
4. Click OK.

Advanced Power Options. The Advanced tab of the Power Options always includes the following two options:

Always Show Icon On The Taskbar
Shows an icon in the notification area of the task bar to display the current status of the computer's power, and provides instant access to power management features.

Prompt For Password When Computer Resumes From Standby
Is a security feature that allows only the authorized user to work on the computer after it resumes from the standby mode.

On portable computers, there are other options in the Advanced tab. You can configure settings for the Power button, opening or closing the portable display (lid), and the Sleep button.

Advanced Power Management (APM). The Advanced Power Management (APM) tab is available in the Power Options utility on only those computers that are not compatible with the Advanced Power Configuration Interface (APCI). If your computer has an APCI-compliant BIOS, Windows XP automatically enables Advanced Power Management and disables the APM tab. Otherwise, you can enable APM support from the APM tab by clicking the Enable APM Support checkbox.

 There are several power options included in Windows XP Professional. Most of these options are useful only when you are working on a portable/laptop computer. If you don't have access to a portable computer, you should explore all the options in this utility to get good grip on available configuration options.

Hibernate mode. In the *Stand By mode*, Windows XP Professional turns off power to the monitor, the hard disk, and most of the peripherals. When you move the mouse or press a key on the keyboard, the system returns to normal. *Hibernate mode* differs from Stand By mode in that the operating system saves the information currently in the memory to the hard disk and then shuts down the system. When you turn on the system again from Hibernate mode, you are returned to the state where you left the system idle. Any programs and applications that were running when the system went into Hibernate mode are restarted.

To configure the Hibernate settings of your computer, open the Power Options utility from the Control Panel and click the Hibernate tab. Click the Enable Hibernate Mode checkbox. The main advantage of Hibernate mode over Stand By mode is that the computer is not dependent on any power source because Hibernate mode completely shuts down the system.

Uninterruptible Power Supply (UPS). The *Uninterruptible Power Supply (UPS)* protects the computer from sudden power outages, power surges, and brown outs, as well as helps save your currently open and unsaved documents when the system's power supply fails. The UPS tab in the Power Options utility opens the UPS Configuration dialog box, where you can configure various settings such as notifications, critical alarm, and whether you want to shut down the system and the UPS. Some UPS systems come with their own software, and you should always make sure that the UPS system you are buying is compatible with Windows XP Professional.

Managing User and Group Accounts

User accounts allow a person to log on to the local computer or to the domain and access local or network resources. Access to resources is normally managed using groups of users or Groups. Windows XP Professional supports two types of user accounts.

Local user accounts

Local user accounts are created and maintained at the local computer. This type of account grants local logon access to a user and allows access to the resources on that computer only. The local user accounts are maintained in the local hard disk of the computer and in the Local Security Database. Local user accounts are recommended only on those Windows XP Professional computers that are not part of a domain. Domains do not recognize local user accounts, and hence you should not create local user accounts if a computer is part of a domain.

Domain user accounts

Domain user accounts are created in the *Active Directory* database and are stored on the *domain controller*. You should have at least one computer in the network running Windows Server 2003 or Windows 2000 server running Active Directory services in order to create a domain. If there is more than one domain controller in the network, the account information is replicated to all domain controllers along with other Active Directory data.

Users with a domain account can log on to any computer on the network as well as access resources anywhere on the network. When you log on to the domain using your Windows XP computer, your credentials (username and password) are passed on to the domain controller for authentication. The domain controller generates an authentication token that is valid in the entire network. This token allows you to access any resources on the network where you have sufficient permissions. The authentication token remains valid as long as you do not log off from the network.

 The focus of this section and Exam 70-270 is local user and group accounts. It is unlikely that you will be asked about user or group accounts that exist only in a domain. For example, computer accounts are used only in domains.

Managing User Accounts

When your computer is a part of a workgroup, you will need to create and maintain local user accounts on your computer. This enables other users to connect to your computer and access shared resources such as files, folders, and printers.

Built-in user accounts

When you install Windows XP Professional, the operating system creates certain user accounts. These are known as *built-in local user accounts* and are created automatically and cannot be deleted. You can, however, rename or disable them. The following built-in user accounts are created:

Administrator

This account is used to manage the computer and the operating system. It has full control of all the devices and resources on the located computer. All administrative tasks, such as creating and managing user accounts, installing and uninstalling devices, and configuring shared resources, are performed using this account.

Guest

Users who do not need access to the computer on a regular basis use the built-in Guest account. This account is disabled by default.

HelpAssistant

This account is enabled automatically when a user logs on using *Remote Assistance* and disabled when the user logs off. Remote Assistance is discussed later in this chapter in the section "Implementing, Managing, and Troubleshooting Network Protocols and Services."

InitialUser

This account is created for the registered user of the operating system and made a member of the Administrators group when Windows XP Professional is installed and used for activating the product with Microsoft.

SUPPORT_xxxxxx

This account is known as the "Help and Support Service Account" and is used by Microsoft when you request help from within the Help And Support Center. The number *xxxxxx* is randomly generated by the operating system during installation.

Creating new user accounts

If there are several users who need access to resources on your computer, you will need to create a separate account for each user. This needs a little planning so that usernames in the workgroup are unique and so that a strong Password Policy is enforced. This ensures that only authorized persons will gain access to shared resources on your computer and that no outsider is able to guess a weak password.

Before you proceed to create new user accounts on your computer, complete the following two tasks:

* Disable the guest account if it is not already disabled.
* Rename the Administrator account and assign it a strong password to prevent unauthorized access to your computer.

Follow thee guidelines when you create new user accounts:

* User logon names should be unique in the workgroup. No two users should have the same username.
* You can have up to 20 characters in the username, including uppercase letters, lowercase letters, and numbers. Usernames are not case-sensitive.
* There are some characters that cannot be used in usernames. These are: " / \ [ ] ; : | = + < > ? and *.
* Implement a policy of using strong passwords and ask users to change their passwords regularly.
* Passwords can contain up to 128 characters, but a minimum of 8 is recommended.
* Let the users manage their own passwords. It is also possible for you, the administrator, to assign and manage passwords for all users.

Local user accounts are created and managed for a Windows XP Professional workgroup computer from the User Accounts utility in the Control Panel, or from the "Local Users and Groups" utility in the Computer Management console, which has two separate folders, one for Users and the other for Groups. You can use this console to create, delete, enable, and disable user accounts and group accounts.

The Computer Management console is shown in Figure 2-15. The following steps explain how to create a new user account from the Local Users and Groups utility using the Computer Management console.

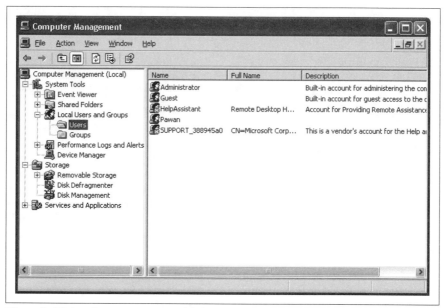

Figure 2-15. Local users are managed from Computer Management

1. Click Start → All Programs → Administrative Tools → Computer Management. You can also access the Computer Management console by right-clicking the My Computer icon on the desktop and selecting Manage.

2. In the Computer Management window, click the plus sign (+) beside the System Tools folder to expand it.

3. Click the + sign beside the "Local Users and Groups" folder to view the Users and Groups subfolders.

4. Right-click Users and click New User.

5. Type the username, full name, and description of the user in the appropriate boxes.

6. Type an initial password for the user in the Password box and retype it in the Confirm Password box.

7. Ensure that the User Must Change Password At Next Logon checkbox is selected.

8. Click Create. This creates a user account for your computer.

User account options

When you create or modify a user account, you will notice four different options for the account. These options are as follows:

User Must Change Password At Next Logon
> This option is selected by default. Use this option so that the user can select her password when she logs on for the first time. This ensures that only the user knows her password.

User Cannot Change Password
> Select this option if you as an administrator want to control the user's password. This option is useful when multiple users share the same user account. Note that this option is disabled (unavailable) if you have already selected the User Must Change Password At Next Logon option.

Password Never Expires
> This option is normally used for service accounts. It is not available if you have already selected the User Must Change Password At Next Logon option.

Account Is Disabled
> Use this option to temporarily disable a user account. For example, if a user leaves the company or is on a long leave, you should disable his account to prevent unauthorized access to the computer.

Modifying or deleting a user account

When a user account is created, you can view the new account in the Details pane of the Computer Management console along with other existing user accounts. You can right-click an account and click Properties to open the properties window for the user account. Modifications to the account can be made from this window.

To delete a user account, simply right-click the account and select Delete. This opens a new dialog box that warns you that all permissions and rights associated with the user account will be lost. Click Yes to confirm the deletion of the account.

 Microsoft recommends that you should disable a user account instead of deleting it. Disabling a user account retains all desktop settings as well as permissions and rights associated with the account. Deleting the account permanently deletes the account and all settings. If a user leaves the company, disable her account, modify it, and assign it to another user.

The User Accounts tool

The *User Accounts* tool is located in the Control panel and provides an easy and user-friendly way to manage user accounts on the Windows XP Professional computer. You can perform the following tasks from the "Pick a Task" portion of the tool when you are logged on as an administrator or as a member of the Administrators group. The bottom portion of the User Accounts screen shows current user accounts, and you can pick any account and modify its properties.

Change An Account

This option allows you to modify or delete an existing local user account. Modifications that you can make include changing the username, creating, changing or removing the password, changing the display picture, and setting up the account to use a .NET Passport.

Create An Account

You can create new user accounts by clicking the Create An Account option. The onscreen dialog boxes prompt you for information about the username and account type. You can choose between *Computer Administrator* or *Limited Account*.

Change The Way User Logs On Or Off

By default, all users log on locally to the system using *Fast User Switching*. Fast User Switching allows another user to log on without first logging off the current user or closing his programs. The second option, "*Use the Welcome Screen*," allows the user to access the system using the Windows XP welcome screen instead of prompting her for a username or password.

Configuring properties of user accounts

When you access the properties of a user account from within the Computer Management console, you are allowed to configure several properties of the account. The following three tabs are available from the User Account Properties window:

General

This tab allows you to modify all the settings of the user account except the username and its description. In addition, you can unlock a locked account by clearing the "Account is Locked Out" checkbox. This checkbox is disabled if the account is not locked.

Member Of

This tab allows you to add the account to a group or remove it from a group.

Profile

This tab allows you to specify a path for the user's profile, his logon script, and the home folder. You can also specify which drives should be connected when the user logs on.

Home folder

Users can store their documents in their *home folders*, which are folders on the local computer or on a shared network drive. This is in addition to the My Documents folder that Windows XP creates for each user account on the computer. Specify the path of the user's home folder on the Profile tab of the User Account Properties dialog box, using the Universal Naming Convention (UNC). Normally all home folders are named after the usernames for simplicity and ease of administration. For example, if the home folder were located in a shared folder named *SharedFolder* on a file server named *FileServer*, the UNC path for the folder would be *FileServer**SharedFolder*\%*UserName*%.

Logon script

A *logon script* is a file that is used to configure desktop settings for the user and is assigned to the user account. The logon script is run whenever the user logs on to the computer.

User profile

Windows XP Professional creates a user profile for each user when she logs on to the system for the first time. The user profile contains settings such as desktop configuration, application configurations, Windows Settings, and other personal documents. The user profiles on local computers are stored as a subfolder named after the username in the Documents And Settings folder. Any changes made to the desktop settings and other Windows Settings are automatically saved to the user profile when the user logs off. No matter how many persons log on locally to the computer, each user gets his personal desktop environment and other settings that are retrieved from the user profiles folder.

 Make sure that you understand various configuration options for user accounts. Explore all the tabs of the user account properties and experiment with different settings.

Managing Group Accounts

Although workgroups generally do not exceed 10 or 12 computers, it is very difficult to manage user accounts and access to resources on each computer. The problem escalates when multiple users share the same computers. Windows XP Professional supports local and domain user groups to simplify the management of user accounts and assigning access permissions and rights to groups instead of individual users. All you have to do is to simply add the user accounts to appropriate groups, and the access permissions assigned to the group are automatically assigned to the users. When the computer is a member of a domain, groups are implemented at the domain level. Only local groups are available in a workgroup environment. Exam 70-270 focuses only on local groups.

Built-in local groups

Several built-in groups are automatically created when you install Windows XP Professional. As with built-in user accounts, these built-in groups cannot be deleted, but some of their properties can be modified. The following types of groups are created by default:

Administrators
    The members of this group have full control over the system. The built-in *Administrator* user account is a member of this group by default. If the computer is a member of domain, the *Domain Admins* group is added as a member of this group.

Guest

Members of this group can perform only those tasks and access only those resources for which they are specifically granted permissions. The built-in Guest account is a member of this group by default. Guests cannot save changes to their desktop settings. If the computer is a member of a domain, the *Domain Guests* group is added to this group.

Backup Operators

Members of this group can use the *Windows Backup* utility (ntbackup.exe) to back up and restore data on the computer.

Power Users

Members of this group can create and modify user accounts, install devices, and manage sharing of resources such as files, folders, and printers on the local computer.

Replicator

This group is used to support file replication on the computer.

Users

By default, all local users are added to this group as soon as their accounts are created. Members can perform only those tasks and access only those resources for which they are specifically granted permissions. If the computer is a member of a domain, the Domain Users group is also added to this group.

Built-in system groups

System groups do not specifically include any members by default. The membership dynamically changes based on system requirements. These groups are not visible in the Computer Management console when you add or modify group accounts. These groups appear only when you access the resources to assign or modify permissions. The following built-in local groups are available by default:

Authenticated Users

This group represents all user accounts on the local computer. If the computer is a member of a domain, this group represents all user accounts in the domain Active Directory database.

Everyone

This group represents all users who have access to the computer.

Creator Owner

This group represents the user who creates or takes ownership of a resource. If a member of the Administrators group creates the resource, the Administrators group becomes the Creator Owner.

Network

This group represents any user who is not logged on locally but connected to the computer from the network and is accessing a shared resource.

Interactive

This group represents any user who is logged on locally to the computer.

Anonymous Logon
> This group represents any user who does not have a user account and cannot be authenticated by the computer.

Dialup
> This group represents users who are connected to the computer using dial-up networking.

Creating a local group

As is evident from the name, a local group is created on the local computer, and its members can access resources located only on the local computer. Groups are created so that you can easily administer resource sharing and permissions. Figure 2-16 shows the Computer Management console with the available built-in local groups. Before you start creating a local group, check the built-in groups to see whether any of these groups can fulfill your requirements. If not, you can create a new local group as explained in the following steps:

1. Right-click My Computer on the Desktop and click Manage. This opens the Computer Management console.
2. Click the + sign beside System Tools to expand the node.
3. Click the + sign beside "Local Users and Groups" to expand the node.
4. Right-click the Groups node and click New Group. This opens the New Group dialog box.
5. Type a name for the local group and enter a description for the group.
6. Click the Add button to add members to this group.
7. Click Create to complete the creation of a new local group.

If your computer is a member of a domain, check with your Domain Administrator to avoid duplicating group names that already exist in the domain.

Modifying group membership

1. Right-click My Computer on the Desktop and click Manage. This opens the Computer Management console.
2. Click the + sign beside System Tools to expand the node.
3. Click the + sign beside "Local Users and Groups" to expand the node.
4. Click the Groups node and select the group you wish to modify in the details pane.
5. Right-click the group and click Properties. This opens the Group Properties dialog box.
6. Click Add to add a new member to the group, and then follow instructions.
7. Select a member and click Remove to remove a user from the group.

An alternative to adding members to groups is to access the user account properties and add the user to appropriate groups from the Member Of tab. This feature is useful when you wish to add the user account to multiple groups.

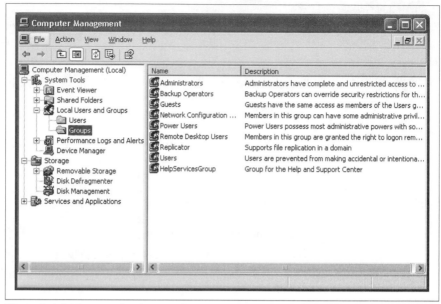

Figure 2-16. Managing local groups from Computer Management

Deleting a group

You can delete a group from the Computer management console in the same way as you create a new group. Locate the group you want to delete from within the "Local Users and Groups" node. Right-click the group from the Details pane of the Groups node. Click Delete from the Context menu.

Deleting a group does not delete any user accounts or permissions associated with individual user accounts. This action deletes only permissions and rights associated with the group.

System Performance and Reliability

Once the operating system is installed and configured, you need to keep it up and running. Maintenance tasks include monitoring and fine-tuning the system performance, backing up and restoring data, and troubleshooting several types of problems as they occur. Windows XP Professional includes several tools to accomplish these tasks. This section covers several tools and utilities helpful in maintaining the system that are explained in the following subsections.

Task Manager

The Task Manager utility provides a means to monitor applications, processes, system performance, and networking from a single window. You can start programs, stop any running processes, and get an overview of systems network utilization. The Task Manager is different from the Performance Monitor because you can get instant real-time information about the performance and usage of system resources. You can access the Task Manager in any of the following ways:

- Press the CTRL-ALT-DELETE keys together and select Task Manager.
- Right-click the Task Bar and select Task Manager.
- Press the CTRL-SHIFT-ESC keys at the same time to directly open Task Manager.

The Task Manager window is shown in Figure 2-17.

Figure 2-17. Windows XP Professional Task Manager

The Task Manager window is divided into four different tabs: Applications, Processes, Performance, and Networking.

Applications
    The Task Manager shows the Applications tab by default. This window displays applications currently running on the system. You can click any of the applications and then click the End Task button to terminate the application. The Switch To button brings the selected application to the foreground.

Processes
    The Processes tab displays all the processes running on the system, including the system processes. By default, the windows display only the name of the process, the name of the user running the process, CPU usage, memory

usage, and the assigned session ID. You can change the number of items displayed in this window. Click the View menu and select the columns you want to add to the display. Some other columns that you can add are Base Priority, Non-Paged Pool, Paged Pool, Page Faults, Peak Memory Usage, and Thread Count.

Base priority

Base priority refers to the way the operating system allocates CPU time to various processes. Most of the processes can run well with a Normal base priority. You can, however change the base priority of a process. Available base priorities include: Realtime, High, Above Normal, Normal, Below Normal, and Low. To set a new base priority for a process, right-click the process, click Set Priority, and choose from one of the priority levels.

Processor affinity

Windows XP Professional Edition supports up to two microprocessors. When two microprocessors are installed in the computer, you can assign a particular process to a particular microprocessor. This is called *processor affinity*. The process will always use the dedicated microprocessor instead of switching between the two installed processors. In a dual CPU computer, the CPUs are assigned numbers such as 0 and 1. To set processor affinity for a process, right-click the process and click Set Affinity. Select one of the two CPUs.

Performance

The Performance tab of the Task Manager displays a real-time graphical view of the system performance. Following are various sections included in this window:

CPU Usage

This section displays the percentage of time the CPU is busy. A continuously high percentage indicates an overloaded processor.

CPU Usage History

This section is useful when you want to monitor a specific process activity over a period of time. The display updates depending on what Update Speed is used. Higher Update Speed means that the display would be updated more frequently.

PF Usage

PF stands for Paging File, or virtual memory. The amount of virtual memory used is displayed in megabytes (MB).

Page File Usage History

This shows the amount of virtual memory (paging file) used over a period of time. You can set the Update Speed for this display also.

Handles, Threads, and Processes

These numbers indicate total object handles, total running threads used by all processes, and total active processes.

Physical Memory

These numbers indicate the amount of total available physical memory (RAM) installed on the computer, memory available to the processes, and the amount of memory utilized by the file cache.

Commit Charge

These numbers indicate the total amount of virtual memory used by all processes, the limit of the memory that can be committed (allocated) to the processes, and the peak usage in the current session.

Kernel Memory

These numbers indicate the total amount of paged and nonpaged memory. The paged pool and nonpaged pool is also shown here individually. Paged pool is the data in RAM that the operating system writes to the page file to free up memory for other processes.

Networking

The Networking tab shows an overview of real-time network performance and utilization. A list of installed network adapters, their link speed, network utilization, and current status is displayed by default in the lower panel. The graph adjusts dynamically depending on the percentage of network utilization for each network adapter.

When monitoring network utilization, keep in mind the following:

- The amount of network utilization for a standard Ethernet connection is from 60 to 80 percent.

- The amount of network utilization for wireless networks is from 30 to 40 percent.

You can add or remove items in the display from the View menu.

Performance Console

The Performance console (Figure 2-18) consists of two tools to monitor system performance: System Monitor, and Performance Logs and Alerts. System Performance is used to monitor real-time performance of system components such as CPU, memory, disks, network, etc. The "Performance Logs and Alerts" tool allows you to collect performance data over a period of time, save it for later analysis, and generate alerts if a performance threshold is reached. You can monitor your own computer or a remote computer. You can access the Performance console from Administrative Tools located in the Control Panel.

The main difference between Task Manager and Performance console is that the Task Manager gives you an instant view of the system performance while the Performance console allows you to collect performance data over a period of time so that you can analyze it.

System Monitor

The System Monitor snap-in allows you to view real-time performance data on a local or remote computer. You can configure the System Monitor to display the data as a graph, histogram, or report. The data is collected based on what *objects*, *counters*, and *instances* have been selected for monitoring.

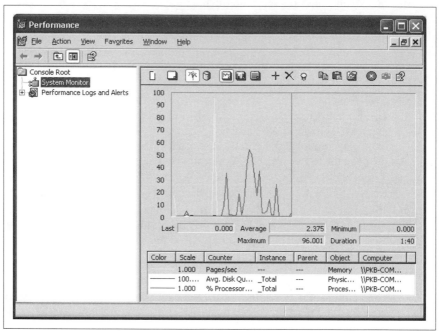

Figure 2-18. System Monitor in Performance console

Object
> An object refers to a major hardware or software component of the system, such as CPU, memory, hard disk, etc. Windows XP Professional includes several objects that can be monitored. Each object in turn consists of several counters.

Counter
> A counter is a particular aspect of the object. For example, the Processor object can have counters such as *%Processor Time*, *Interrupts/Sec*, *%User Time*, etc.

Instance
> Each occurrence of an object is considered an instance. If there is one processor in the computer, there is only one instance of the Processor object. For a dual-processor computer, there will be two instances. Similarly, a computer with two hard disks will have two instances for the Physical Disk object.

Adding counters to System Monitor

To add counters to the System Monitor, you can right-click an empty area on the display and then click Add Counter. This opens the Add Counters window, in which you can select from a list of available objects and counters for each object and instance of the object. The following is a partial list of useful counters that you should monitor regularly:

Processor: %Processor Time
> This counter measures the overall usage of the processor. This value should remain under 80 percent. If the value is consistently above 90 percent, you should consider upgrading the processor or adding a second processor to the computer.

System: Processor Queue Length
> This counter indicates the number of threads in the queue waiting for processor time. A number larger than two indicates a system bottleneck.

Memory: Available Bytes
> This counter shows the amount of physical memory available. A consistently low number indicates a memory bottleneck.

Memory: Pages/Sec
> This counter indicates whether the system is frequently reading from or writing to the paging file. A number more than 20 suggests that the system is running out of physical memory.

Paging File: %Usage
> This counter indicates what percentage of the paging file is in use.

Physical Disk: %Disk Time
> This counter is a measure of the amount of time the disk keeps busy serving read/write requests. If the number is consistently over 50 percent, the disk is too slow and should be replaced with a faster disk.

Physical Disk: Avg. Disk Queue Length
> This counter indicates the number of requests waiting for the disk. A number larger than 2 means that the disk is too slow and should be replaced with a faster disk.

Logical Disk: %Free Space
> This counter is the ratio of available free space to the total space on the logical disk.

> You must be aware of the main objects and counters generally monitored in the System Monitor snap-in. In addition, make sure that you know the performance thresholds for each of these counters.

Performance Logs and Alerts

The "Performance Logs and Alerts" tool is used to collect performance data for later analysis. You can also configure performance alerts to keep an eye on the performance counters and take appropriate action.

There are three parts of the "Performance Logs and Alerts" tool:

Counter Logs
> This tool is used to log performance activity for the selected counters at regular intervals and over a period of time. The data is saved as a text file and can be analyzed at a later time.

Trace Logs

This tool is used to log activity for selected counters when a particular event happens.

Alerts

This tool allows you to configure administrative alerts (send messages) when a set threshold is reached for a selected counter.

Performance Logs can be configured from the console similarly to the way that you configure the System Monitor. Just add objects and associated counters for which you wish to collect performance information. As shown in Figure 2-19, you can add objects and counters in the General tab of the New Log properties window. The following steps explain the procedure:

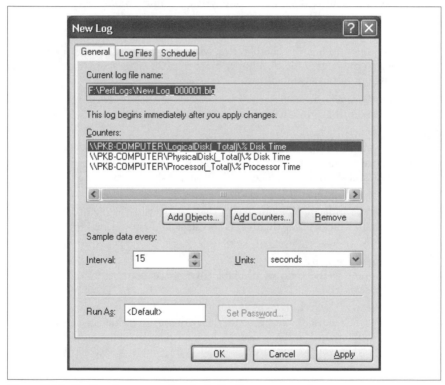

Figure 2-19. Configuring counter logs in the Performance console

1. Right-click Counter Logs in the Performance window.
2. Click New Log Settings, enter the name for the logfile, and click OK.
3. In the General tab, add counters in the same way you would for System Monitor. Enter a value for the Sampling Interval.
4. In the Log Files tab, change the name and location of the logfile that will be generated by this log.
5. In the Schedule tab, make necessary changes to the start and stop times.
6. Click OK to save your log settings.

Alerts can also be configured in a similar way. When configuring alerts, you are given the following four options when the configured threshold for the selected counters is reached:

- Log an entry in the Application Event Log
- Send a Network Message
- Start a Performance Log
- Run a Program

The last option, "Run a Program," is generally used to run a script file that would send an email message to the network administrator so that she could take an appropriate action to address the performance problem.

Event Viewer

The Event Viewer console displays error messages, warnings, and other information about system activities. It is also used to view the contents of logfiles and includes tools to search particular events from the logs. Event Viewer is essentially a troubleshooting tool included with Windows XP Professional.

You can open the Event Viewer console by clicking Start Menu → Control Panel → Administrative Tools utility. By default, the console displays the following three types of logs:

Application log
> This log contains errors, warnings, or other information generated by application programs. The amount and type of information depends on how the program is developed to write events to the Event Viewer. If an application crashes, you can check the Application Event log to find details on what actually caused the event.

Security log
> This log contains errors, warnings, and information about security events and security problems such as incorrect logons that are included here by default. If auditing has been enabled on the system, two additional logs are available: Audit Success and Audit Failure. If you suspect someone is trying to get unauthorized access to the computer, you should check the logon failure events.

System log
> This log contains errors, warnings, and information about system events such as system startup and shutdown, services, and devices and drivers. If any of the system events are configured for auditing, they appear in the System log.

Log filters

Log filtering is used to search for specific events and is included in the Event Viewer. To view specific events, select "Filter or Find" from the View menu. You can filter events by event type, event source, category, event ID, user, or computer.

Maintaining Event logs

The properties of Event logs can be configured to change the way Event logs are saved. The default size of the logfiles is 512 KB, but you can set the size anywhere from 64 KB to 4 GB. Three options are available:

Overwrite Events As Needed
Older events are deleted automatically to make space for newer events.

Overwrite Events Older Than X Days
Events older than the specified number of days are deleted.

Do Not Overwrite Events (Clear Logs Manually)
The logs stop recording newer events when the logfile becomes full. You must delete the logs manually.

Task Scheduler

The Scheduled Tasks utility in Windows XP Professional is used to schedule applications, utilities, and scripts to run at a predetermined time. This feature is very helpful in maintenance and run programs when the systems are not otherwise busy in other processes. You can access this utility in the Control Panel.

New tasks can be scheduled by running the Scheduled Task Wizard from within the Scheduled Task utility in the Control Panel. Double-click the icon to start the wizard. The wizard has the following configuration options to schedule a new task:

Application
This allows you to schedule a built-in application, batch file, or script to run at the preconfigured time.

Name
This is the description of the application.

Perform This Task
This configures how often the task is to be run. You can choose from these options: Daily, Weekly, Monthly, One time only, When I Log On, and When My Computer Starts.

Start Time And Start Date
This option enters the start time and date for the application to run.

User Name And Password
This option holds the user credentials that should be used to run a scheduled task.

Advanced Properties
This option allows you to configure additional options. These include changing the user credentials, running the task in a recurring manner, and other security-related settings.

After you have added the new task, the same appears as an icon in the Scheduled Tasks window. To view the task and its properties or to change any settings, right-click it and select Properties.

Managing Services

Most of the services start even when the user has not logged on to the system and keep running in the background. Services keep running whether or not any user is logged on to the system. Some services depend on other services and thus create service dependencies. The Services console in the Administrative Tools utility Control Panel allows you to manage services. You can start, stop, pause, or resume any service, control the startup type, or configure how the system should behave if any service fails.

The Services Console (Figure 2-20) provides an excellent means of system maintenance. You can access the Services console in any of the following ways:

- From the Services icon under Administrative Tools in the Control Panel.
- From the Computer Management console. The Services node is located under Services And Applications.
- By creating a custom Microsoft Management Console (MMC) by adding the Services snap-in.

Exam 70-270 Study Guide

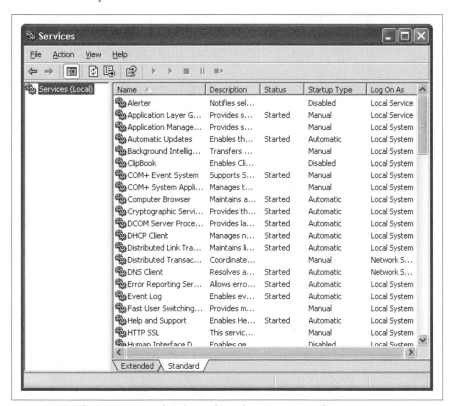

Figure 2-20. The Services console is located in Administrative Tools

To access the properties pages of any service, right-click the service and click Properties. The following configuration tabs are available:

General

The General tab of the Services properties dialog box displays the name of the service and the path of the executable file that is run to start the service. You can configure the startup type of the service as follows:

Automatic

The service starts when the system is started.

Manual

The service remains enabled but must be started manually from the Services console.

Disabled

The service is disabled. It does not start automatically or manually until it is enabled. It is a normal practice to disable unused services in the system in order to improve system performance.

The lower half of the window shows the current status of the service that can be started, stopped, or paused. You can also manually start a stopped service, stop a running service, pause a running service, or resume a paused service from the buttons provided for each purpose.

Log On

This tab displays the service account that is used to run the service. Services that are started automatically by the operating system at startup use the Local System Account. Some services use the Network System account. Other services can be configured to use one of the user accounts specially created for the service. Unless you know the details of the service account, you should not change the Logon type of any service.

Recovery

The Recovery tab includes options that the system is given when the selected service fails. If any of the services fail, the other services dependent on the failed service also fail and an event is recorded in the system log. You can configure the system response on first, second, and subsequent service failures in one of the following ways:

Take No Action

The system ignores the failure of the service. This is the system default.

Restart The Service

The system will attempt to restart the service automatically.

Run A Program

You can configure a program to run when the service fails. This program is specified in the Run Program section of the window. This can be an executable program or a command-line script.

Restart The Computer

The computer will reboot if this option is selected. This option should be selected as a last resort.

You can also reset the Fail count after a certain number of days as well as have the system wait for a certain amount of time in minutes before it attempts to restart the service.

Make a note of the four options you get in the Recovery tab of the Service properties dialog box. Each of these options can be configured for first, second, and subsequent failure.

Dependencies

The Dependencies tab shows what other services are dependent on the selected service and on which other services the selected service is dependent.

Backing Up and Restoring Data

The Windows XP backup wizard is located under the Start menu. Click Start → All Programs → Accessories → System Tools → Backup. You can also launch the Backup Wizard by running ntbackup.exe from the Run dialog box. This utility runs in two modes: Wizard Mode and Advanced Mode. The three main options in the backup utility include Backup Wizard, Restore Wizard, and Automated System Recovery Wizard.

You must be a member of the Administrators group or the Backup Operators group in order to back up and restore data. Users can back up and restore their own files and folders. Any users who have the Read, Read and Execute, Modify, and Full Control permissions can also back up files and folders on which they have such permissions. To restore files and folders, users should have Write, Modify, or Full Control permissions. The "Backup Files and Directories" user right also allows users to perform backups while "Restore Files and Directories" allows them to perform restores.

Backup files and folders

Windows Backup can back up data to a backup file located on hard drives or tape drives, or to a network share. Windows XP Professional does not support backing up data directly to CD-ROM or DVD drives. Click on the Backup tab to select the files and folders that you wish to back up, as shown in Figure 2-21. You can select individual files, folders, System State, and/or files from a network share. The *System State* includes boot files, registry, and the COM+ Class Registration database. You can select the destination of backup data and the filename that has a *.bkf* extension.

The Backup Utility in Windows XP Professional does not support directly backing up on CD-ROM and DVD drives, but you can make a backup on the hard disk and then burn the data onto any of these drives. Also, if you wish to include System State data in the backup job, you must perform the backup on the local computer.

The following types of backups are supported in Windows XP Professional:

Normal

Also known as Full Backup. This option backs up all selected files and folders irrespective of when the files were last modified. This operation clears the

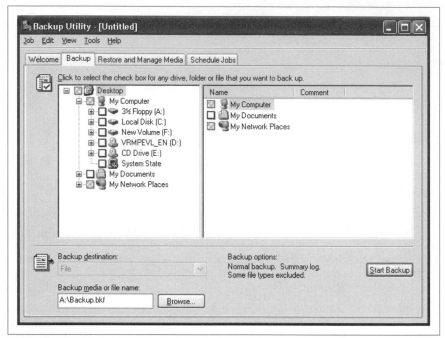

Figure 2-21. Windows Backup Utility

backup *Archive Bit* or *markers*. This bit indicates whether the files were modified since the last backup.

Copy

This is similar to the Normal backup, but it does not clear the Archive Bit.

Incremental

This backs up all files and folders that have changed since the last Normal backup indicated by the Archive Bits. This is the fastest type of backup, and the Archive Bits are cleared after the backup operation is complete. When restoring data, you must use the last Normal backup tape and all Incremental backups performed after that.

Differential

This backs up all selected files and folders that have changed since the last Normal backup. This type of backup does not clear the Archive Bits. To restore data from Differential backups, you need the last Normal backup and the Differential backup tapes.

Daily

This backs up all files and folders changed during the current date. This type of backup neither uses the Archive Bits nor clears them.

Scheduling backup jobs

You can schedule backup jobs in order to run them in unattended modes. The Schedule Jobs tab in the Backup Utility is used to create one or more backup jobs to occur on a regular basis. The Task Scheduler service must be running on the computer where you wish to perform the unattended scheduled backup jobs. Click the Add Job button to add a backup job. A Backup wizard guides you through the process of creating one or more backup jobs.

Restoring data

Backed-up data can be restored from the Restore tab of the Backup Utility. You can specify the location of backed-up files and the destination where the files should be restored. The Restore File To drop-down menu provides the following three options for restoring data:

Original Location
> When this option is selected, the files are replaced by the backup versions in their original location.

Alternate Location
> When this option is selected, the files and folders are copied to a separate location on the hard disk and the original folder hierarchy is maintained.

Single Folder
> When this option is selected, the files are copied to a single folder on the hard disk, but the original folder hierarchy is lost.

When you restore files that already exist on the hard disk of the computer, you may select how the files will replace the original files as follows:

Leave Existing Files
> This is the default and recommended method so that files are not accidentally replaced.

Replace Existing Files If They Are Older Than The Backup Files
> Replaces the original files only if the backed-up files are newer than the original files on hard disk.

Replace Existing Files
> Always replaces all original files on the hard disk with files from backup.

Windows Advanced Boot Options

Some of the Windows startup problems can be resolved using the Advanced Boot Options during the startup phase. The most commonly used advanced options include Safe Mode, Last Known Good Configuration and Recovery Console. When Windows XP Professional fails to complete the boot process, you can access any of these options by pressing the F8 key immediately after the Power-On Self Test (POST) is complete. Windows XP has three different Safe Mode options:

Safe Mode
> In the Safe Mode, Windows XP loads with minimum basic system services and device drivers sufficient to boot the operating system. These components include keyboard, mouse, hard disks, and VGA monitor, as well as the other most essential system services. All other services and user profiles are ignored. In Safe Mode, Windows starts with a black screen with "Safe Mode"

appearing on all four corners. A dialog box informs you that Windows is running in diagnostics mode. Safe Mode provides access to all system and device configuration options so that you can enable or disable components one by one and try to pinpoint the system component that is preventing the system from loading normally.

Safe Mode With Networking
Safe Mode With Networking is similar to Safe Mode, except that networking devices, drivers, and services are also initialized.

Safe Mode With Command Prompt
Safe Mode With Command Prompt loads the command interpreter just as in MS-DOS, instead of loading the graphical user interface (GUI).

If the startup problem is not resolved using the Safe Mode, you can try using the Last Known Good Configuration, discussed next.

Last Known Good Configuration

The Last Known Good Configuration option loads the last used system configuration that worked well. It is quite possible that the system was working well when you installed a new device driver to replace the older driver and the system did not start after that. The Last Known Good Configuration allows you to return to the previous working configuration. This option is normally helpful in cases where you have made changes to the system configuration.

Windows XP saves two types of configurations in the Registry:

Default
The Default Configuration is saved to the Registry when you shut down the system.

Last Known Good
The Last Known Good Configuration is saved when you log on to the system. If Windows detects that your last startup attempt was unsuccessful, it automatically loads the Last Known Good Configuration.

The Last Known Good Configuration will not be useful if you have already logged on to the system with incorrect configuration. This option must be used before a successful logon happens.

You can manually load the Last Known Good Configuration by selecting it from the Advanced Boot Options menu if you suspect that some configuration change is causing trouble. Windows restores the system to its previous working configuration by removing the culprit services or drives from the system. But remember that this option must be used before you log on to the system. If you have logged on to the system even once, the current problematic configuration is saved to as the Last Known Good Configuration.

Recovery Console

The Recovery Console is useful in resolving system startup problems when the Safe Modes and Last Known Good Configurations do not work. The Recovery Console allows you to repair critical system files that might have been corrupted by copying original files from the Windows XP Professional setup CD-ROM. You can also enable or disable services that you think might be causing the problem.

The Recovery Console can either be started from the Windows XP Professional setup CD-ROM or be installed as one of the Advanced Boot Options as explained in the following sections.

Starting Recovery Console from Windows XP setup CD-ROM

1. Insert the Windows XP setup CD-ROM in the CD-ROM drive. Make sure that the computer BIOS is set to start from the CD-ROM. Restart the computer.

2. Press Enter when the Setup Notification message appears.

3. At the Welcome screen, Press R to repair a Windows XP installation using the Recovery Console.

4. In case there is more than one Windows XP installation on the computer, type the installation number corresponding to the installation that you wish to repair, and press Enter.

5. Press C at the Windows XP Recovery Console screen to start the Recovery Console.

6. Type the Administrator password when prompted and press Enter. This password must be the password of the Local Administrator.

7. The Recovery Console displays a command prompt.

You can type help and press Enter at any time to get a list of available commands. Type exit and press Enter to close the Recovery Console and restart the system.

Installing Recovery Console as Advanced Boot Options

1. Insert the Windows XP setup CD-ROM in the CD-ROM drive while running Windows XP Professional.

2. Select NO when you are prompted to upgrade to Windows XP Professional.

3. Click Start → Run to open the Run dialog box. Type cmd and press Enter to open the command prompt.

4. At the command prompt, type the following command, replacing the word *drive* with the drive letter of your CD-ROM drive:

    drive:\i386\winnnt32.exe /cmdcons

5. Restart the computer.

The Recovery Console appears as one of the options in the Advanced Boot Options menu when you press F8 during the startup process. You must press F8 immediately after POST is complete but before the GUI phase has started.

Make sure that you understand how to install the Recovery Console and the correct procedure to use it.

Table 2-12 lists some of the commonly used commands available in the Recovery Console.

Table 2-12. Commands available in Recovery Console

Command	Function
Attrib	Change the attributes of a file or folder. Options include − to clear the attribute and + to set the attribute. Select c for compression, h for hidden file, r for read-only, and s for system attribute.
Chdir or cd	Change the current working directory or folder.
Chkdsk	Check a disk for errors.
Cls	Clear the screen display.
Copy	Copy a file. Remember that you cannot copy a file to a floppy disk; you may copy from a floppy or a CD-ROM to hard disk.
Delete or Del	Delete one or more files.
Dir	Display the contents of a folder and its subfolders.
Disable	Disable a service.
Diskpart	Create or delete partitions on the hard disk.
Enable	Enable a disabled service.
Exit	Exit the Recovery Console and restart the computer.
Expand	Expand a compressed file in a .cab folder and copy to a specified location on hard disk.
Fdisk	Manage partitions on hard disk.
Fixboot	Write a new boot sector on the system partition.
Fixmbr	Repair the master boot record on the system partition.
Format	Format a hard disk with FAT, FAT32, or NTFS. NTFS is used if no filesystem is specified.
Help	Display a list of all commands available in the Recovery Console.
Logon	Log on to the operating system.
Listsvc	Display a list of services.
Map	Display drive letter mappings.
Mkdir	Create a new directory (folder).
Rmdir	Delete a directory (folder).
Rename or Ren	Rename a single file.
Systemroot	Change the current working directory to *%systemroot%* folder.

Enabling and disabling services using Recovery Console

1. At the Recovery Console prompt, type listsvc and press Enter. A list of services and drivers is displayed along with their startup types and other information.
2. To disable a device driver, type the following and press Enter:

        disable *drivername*

3. To enable a driver, type the following and press Enter:

```
enable drivername startup_type
```

4. The service startup can be specified in one of the following ways:
   - *service_boot_start*
   - *service_system_start*
   - *service_auto_start*
   - *service_demand_start*

Automated System Recovery

The Automated System Recovery (ASR) Wizard is located in the Backup Utility. This utility is used to restore the system when there is a major failure. Click the ASR Wizard on the Backup Utility window to prepare an ASR backup for the computer. You will need a blank floppy disk and a full backup of the system partition of the computer. This backup can be taken on a tape drive or on a network file server.

The following procedure explains how the ASR Wizard can be used to back up critical system components:

1. Click Start → Programs → Accessories → System Tools → Backup.
2. Click the ASR Wizard from the Backup Utility window. This opens the ASR Wizard dialog box. Click Next.
3. Select the Backup Media Type and the "Backup Media or Filename" checkbox. Click Next.
4. Check the information on the Completing The Automated System Recovery Preparation Wizard page. If correct, click Finish.
5. It takes the system about an hour or so to back up the system files. You are prompted to insert a blank floppy disk.
6. The backup completes writing to the floppy disk and presents an option to view the report.
7. Click Close to close the backup process and then close the Backup Utility window.

When you need to restore the system using the Automated System Recovery, you can use the floppy disk to restore the system partition of the computer. You must also restore critical system files that you backed up on the tape drive or a network file share. Other applications and data can be restored using regular backup sets.

Configuring and Troubleshooting the Desktop Environment

This section is about configuring your system to meet your needs, whether it be your desktop, user profiles, or language selection.

Desktop Settings

Each user of a Windows XP Professional computer can customize her desktop settings based on personal preferences. All settings are stored in the Registry of the Windows XP computer. Desktop settings primarily include display settings, desktop preferences, power management options, and configuration of shortcut menus on the desktop. Out of these, we have already discussed power management options in the "Managing Hardware Devices and Drivers" section. Most of the user-defined settings are stored in user profiles that are discussed later in this section.

Configuring Display Properties

Since every user has different preferences on how his desktop should appear, the Windows XP Professional operating system offers various settings for configuring the desktop settings, such as background color, themes, screensavers, color quality, and screen resolution. These settings can be configured from the Display Properties dialog box.

To change your display settings, right-click an empty area on the desktop and select Properties. The Display Properties dialog box that appears is shown in Figure 2-22. The tabs in this dialog box are explained in the following list.

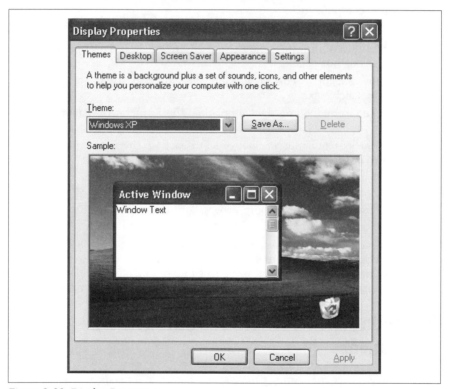

Figure 2-22. Display Properties

Themes
    The Themes tab enables you to personalize your Windows XP computer by setting desktop background, sounds, and icon types on your personal prefer-

ences. The Themes tab allows you to choose one of several built-in themes or to modify any of these themes and save them.

Desktop

The Desktop tab enables you to choose a background and color for the desktop. The Desktop Items button opens another dialog box, where you can select icons that should be displayed on the desktop. You can change the icons or restore the icons to the system defaults. This dialog box also has the Desktop Cleanup options, to clean up the desktop instantly or to schedule a cleanup to run every 60 days.

Screen Saver

The Screen Saver tab allows you to configure a screensaver to run on the computer screen when the computer is not in use. By default, the screensaver runs after the system is idle for 10 minutes, but you can change this time. If your computer contains some confidential data and you do not want security for the system, you can set a password to bring the computer out of the screensaver mode.

Appearance

The Appearance tab has several settings to configure different windows, color schemes, button styles, and font sizes. There is an Effects button that configures several settings such as transition effects for menus and tool tips, using large icons, shadows under menus, displaying window items while dragging, etc.

Settings

The Settings tab includes configuration options such as screen resolution and color quality. This tab also includes a troubleshooting button as well as a button for advanced setting options for each display adapter. The settings in this tab are discussed next.

Configuring display settings

Display settings such as screen resolution and color quality are configured from the Settings tab of the Display Properties dialog box. Here are the main options available in this tab:

Screen Resolution

The Screen Resolution tab shows the currently configured resolution for the monitor attached to the display adapter shown in the Display list. The default resolution for most display adapters is usually 800×600 pixels. More resolution means more information can be displayed on the monitor. When you increase or decrease the resolution and click OK, Windows shows the display in its new resolution for 15 seconds, and you can check whether the new resolution is suitable for you. If you do not accept the new resolution setting from the displayed dialog box, Windows will automatically reconfigure the resolution to the previous setting.

Color Quality

The Color Quality tab shows currently configured color depth for the monitor attached to the display adapter shown in the Display list. You can set the color quality to the highest level supported by the adapter and the monitor.

Identify
> The Identify tab is used in a multiple monitor configuration to display large characters on the selected monitor.

Troubleshoot
> Clicking the Troubleshooting tab opens the Video Display Troubleshooter to help you resolve problems with video displays.

Advanced
> The Advanced tab opens advanced properties for the display adapter listed in the Display list. Different settings in the Advanced dialog box allow you to configure and troubleshoot the selected display adapter.

User Profiles

Users profiles control the user's desktop environment. Each user on a Windows XP Professional computer has an associated user profile that stores her settings for the desktop configuration and application preferences. Windows XP Professional supports three types of user profiles

Local user profile
> The local user profile is created, stored, and available only on the computer where it is created. This user profile is created on every computer where the user logs on.

Roaming user profile
> The roaming user profile is stored in a shared folder on a network file server and is available to the user on any computer where he logs on.

Mandatory user profile
> The mandatory user profile is primarily a roaming user profile stored in a shared folder on the network file server, but it differs in that the user is not allowed to make changes to this profile.

> You need not memorize what folders are stored in user profiles, but you must understand the difference between different types of profiles such as the local, roaming, and mandatory profiles.

Built-in user profiles

User profiles are stored by default on the local computer in the Documents And Settings folder in the *%SystemRoot%* drive. All user profiles are stored locally by default. There are two types of built-in local user profiles:

Default User Profile
> This profile is used to create a new user profile for a user who logs on to the computer for the first time. The settings in the Default User Profile, which is stored in the *Documents And Settings\Default User* folder, are modified and stored under the user's name.

All Users Profile
> This profile contains settings that apply to all users of the computer. When a user logs on to the system, Windows combines the settings of the All Users

Profile with the profile of the user and makes them available to the user until the time she is logged on to the system. Any changes made to the profile by the user are not saved. The All Users Profile is stored in the *Documents And Settings\All Users* folder.

Files and folders stored in user profiles

Each user has a profile associated with her user account. The user profile contains several desktop settings as well as personal preferences for the applications. Some of the common items stored in user profiles are listed in Table 2-13.

Table 2-13. Files and folders stored in user profiles

Item	Description
Application Data	This hidden folder contains configuration information about applications.
Internet Cookies	This folder contains cookies used by Internet web sites. Web sites use cookies to store users' preferences and personal information on the local hard disk.
Desktop	This folder contains files, folders, and desktop shortcuts that the user creates on her Windows XP desktop.
Favorites	This folder stores a user's shortcuts to favorite locations in Windows Explorer or Internet Explorer.
Local Settings	This hidden folder contains application data, history, and temporary files. Temporary Internet files are also stored here.
My Documents	This is the folder that appears in the Start menu. Most of users' documents are stored in My Documents by default.
My Recent Documents	This folder contains shortcuts to recently opened documents. This is also available from the Start menu.
Start Menu	This folder contains the shortcuts to programs that appear in the Start menu.
NTUSER.DAT	This is a part of the Registry that is specific to a particular user. It contains Windows Task Bar and Explorer settings as well as changes made to the configuration of Control Panel and Accessories settings.

Managing local user profiles

User profiles are created, deleted, and modified from the User Profiles utility in the Control Panel as shown in Figure 2-23.

To access the User Profiles dialog box, follow the steps given here:

1. Open the Control Panel from the Start menu.
2. Double-click System to open the System Properties dialog box.
3. Click the Advanced tab and click the User Profiles Settings button.

You can perform the following actions from the User Profiles dialog box:

Change Type
> This button allows you to change the type of the user profile from local to roaming.

Delete
> This button allows you to delete the selected user profile.

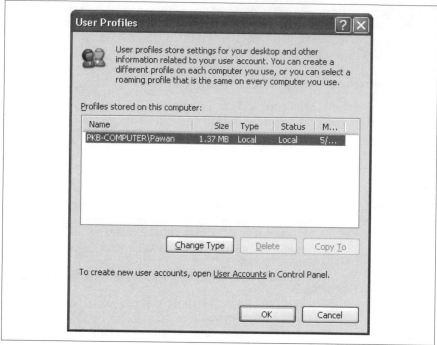

Figure 2-23. User Profiles

Copy To

> This button is used to copy the selected user profile. A copied user profile can be assigned to another user. The Copy To button stores a copy of the profile in a specified location. You can locate the profile later and specify the users in the Permitted To Use dialog box to assign the profile to other users.

Supporting Multiple Languages and Locations

The Regional And Language Options utility in the Control Panel is designed to configure a Windows XP Professional system to support multiple languages, multiple locations, and regional settings such as currency, measurement units, date and time format, and more.

Configuring multiple languages

The following steps explain how you can configure the computer to support multiple languages:

1. Open the Control Panel and double-click the Regional And Language Options utility.
2. In the Regional And Language Options window, click the Languages tab.
3. Click Details in the Text Services And Input Languages box.
4. Click Add in the Installed Services box to open the Add Input Language dialog box.

5. Select a language from the drop-down menu and click Close.

6. Notice that two languages are not displayed in the Text Services And Input Languages dialog box.

7. Click OK twice to close all dialog boxes.

Configuring multiple locations

The following steps explain how you can configure the computer to support multiple locations:

1. Open the Control Panel and double-click the Regional And Language Options utility.

2. The Regional Options page is displayed by default in the Regional And Language Options window.

3. Open the drop-down menu in the Standards And Formats area to select a suitable format.

4. Open the drop-down menu in the Location area and select a country or region from the list.

5. You may click Customize if you need to make further changes to these settings.

6. Clock OK to close the dialog boxes.

Managing Applications with Windows Installer Packages

Windows Installer works in conjunction with installation packages to simplify installation of applications on desktop computers. Each installation package is a file with an *.msi* extension, known as an installation database, that contains all the information that Windows Installer requires to install or to uninstall the application. Windows Installer allows you to easily uninstall or roll back an installation if the installation does not complete due to some problem.

Windows Installer works by advertising the availability of an application or applications without actually installing it on the user's computer. The user sees only the interfaces for launching the application. When activated, the interface loads and installs the application.

Application advertising works in the following two ways:

Assigning
> When assigned, the application appears to the user as if it is installed on his system and is available as one of the Start menu items. When the user attempts to open the application, it is installed on the user's computer.

Publishing
> Windows Installer applications are published in the Active Directory. A user can locate and install the application from the Control Panel by using the Add or Remove Programs.

Files And Settings Transfer Wizard

The Files And Settings Transfer (FAST) Wizard is used to transfer user settings and datafiles from an old computer to a new installation of Windows XP Professional. Users can get the feel and look of their old settings when this wizard is used to migrate their desktop preferences from old computers. At the same time, administrators do not have to configure each user's desktop on newly installed computers.

In order to use the FAST Wizard, you must have both the old and new computers available. The data is transferred from the old computer to the new one using either a *null modem cable* or the *serial ports (COM port)*. The null modem cable is also a kind of serial cable. The parallel port and the parallel cable cannot be used for this purpose. Other methods to transfer files and settings include using removable disks and copying data to a network share.

To transfer settings and files from an old computer to a new computer using the FAST Wizard, complete the following steps:

1. Click Start → All Programs → Accessories → System Tools → Files And Settings Transfer Wizard. This starts the FAST Wizard.

2. Click Next, and the wizard displays the What Computer Is This page. Select Old Computer and click Next.

3. Click Unblock in the Windows Security Alert page if you are using Windows XP Professional with SP2.

4. Select an appropriate option in the Select The Transfer Method page. These options are Direct Cable, Home or Small Office Network, Floppy Drive or Other Removable Media, and Other. Click Next.

5. You are prompted to configure the option you selected in the previous step. Click Next when you are done.

6. The What Do You Want To Transfer page appears. You can choose from Settings Only, Files Only, and Both Files And Settings. You can also click Let Me Select A Custom List Of Files And Settings When I Click Next. Click your selection and click Next.

7. The Collection In Progress Page appears. Click Finish when this process is complete.

8. Go to the new computer, run the FAST Wizard, and repeat the above steps. Select New Computer when prompted.

 The FAST Wizard is used for transferring settings and data from one computer to another while the User State Migration Tool is used in the Active Directory network for large-scale deployments.

User State Migration Tool

The User State Migration Tool (USMT) helps administrators in an Active Directory domain transfer files and settings for large number of users from old computers to new computers. This tool offers the same functionality as the FAST Wizard but with the added advantage of working for a large number of users instead of a single user. Two executable files are associated with USMT:

ScanState.exe and *LoadState.exe*. The *ScanState.exe* file gathers information about user data and settings and the *LoadState.exe* file transfers the data and settings to the new computer. USMT works only on fresh installations of Windows XP Professional and does not work on upgraded computers.

Implementing, Managing, and Troubleshooting Network Protocols and Services

Windows XP Professional is intended to be a network client operating system. It has strong support for Transmission Control Protocol/Internet Protocol (TCP/IP) and services related to this protocol such as Dynamic Host Configuration Protocol (DHCP) and Domain Name System (DNS). It works as an Active Directory client in Windows 2000 and Windows 2003 Server environments. TCP/IP is supported in local area networks, network file and print services, and remote access dial-up connections. TCP/IP enables the computer to access the Internet and related services. This section covers TCP/IP basics, configuring TCP/IP, DNS, and DHCP client services on a Windows XP Professional computer. Dial-up connections, remote access, and Internet connectivity are also part of this section.

TCP/IP Protocol

TCP/IP is a suite of protocols that is widely used on the Internet. TCP/IP is the default networking protocol in Windows XP Professional computers. You can configure the Windows XP Professional computer to either use a static (manually assigned) TCP/IP configuration or dynamically obtain this configuration from a DHCP server. In either case, the computer must have unique *IP Address* to communicate on the network.

IP address

The *IP address* is a unique address used to identify a computer or a host on the network. This address is made up of 32-bit numbers written in dotted decimal notation in the *w.x.y.z* format. Each 8 bits are known as an *octet* or a *byte*. A part of the IP address is known as the *network address* or *network ID,* and the rest of it is known as the *Host Address* or *Host ID*. These parts are based on the *class* of IP addresses used on the network. All computers on a particular network must have the same number as the network address, whereas the host address must be unique on the entire network. A second address known as the *subnet mask* is used to help identify the part of the network where the host is located.

IP addresses are assigned and controlled by an organization called Internet Assigned Numbers Authority (IANA). Table 2-14 summarizes the main classes of IP addresses, known as *classful IP address* ranges.

Table 2-14. IP address classes

Class	Range of first byte	Number of networks	Hosts per network	Default subnet mask
A	1–126	126	16,777,214	255.0.0.0
B	128–191	16,384	65,534	255.255.0.0

Table 2-14. IP address classes (continued)

Class	Range of first byte	Number of networks	Hosts per network	Default subnet mask
C	192–223	2,097,150	254	255.255.255.0
D	224–239	N/A	N/A	N/A
E	240–255	N/A	N/A	N/A

The first byte identifies the class of IP addresses used in the network. For example, a host with an IP address of 92.137.0.10 is using a class A IP address, and a host with an IP address of 192.170.200.10 is using a class C IP address. A special address of 127.0.0.1 is used as a *loopback* address for troubleshooting the TCP/IP configuration of the computer.

The IP addresses in the A, B, and C classes are available for public companies and can be assigned by an Internet Service Provider (ISP). The class D and class E addresses are reserved for special usage. Every IP address is accompanied by a subnet mask. The subnet mask is a 32-bit binary number that distinguishes the network ID from the host ID. Its digits are set to 1 and 0, where 1 represents the network portion of the address and 0 represents the host portion. Apart from the IP addresses, the hosts on a network also have a general alphanumeric hostname or Fully Qualified Domain Name (FQDN) in the format *mycomputer.mycompany.com*. Each hostname corresponds to an IP address, and the DNS is used to translate the IP address of a host to its IP address.

 The Windows Internet Name Service (WINS) is used to resolve computer names (NetBIOS names) to their respective IP addresses, while the DNS is used to resolve FQDNs.

Following are the main configuration options when configuring TCP/IP on a computer connected to a TCP/IP network:

IP Address
A 32-bit IP address. This address must be unique in the network.

Subnet Mask
A 32-bit number that distinguishes the network ID from the host ID in the IP address.

Default Gateway
The IP address of the router or the gateway when there are more than one segment of the network. A router allows your computer to communicate to a remote network.

When the network is using FQDNs, you will also need to configure the IP address of the DNS server in order to translate the IP addresses to hostnames.

Private IP addresses

Private IP addressing is used when your computer network is not connected to the Internet or if it is located behind a proxy server or a firewall. IANA has set aside a range of IP addresses in each of A, B, and C address classes that can be used by private organizations for their internal IP addressing. These addresses are listed in Table 2-15.

Table 2-15. Private IP address ranges

Class	Start address	End address	Subnet mask
A	10.0.0.0	10.255.255.255	255.0.0.0
B	172.16.0.0	172.31.255.255	255.240.0.0
C	192.168.0.0	192.255.255	255.255.0.0

You should not use any of the given private IP addresses if your network is directly connected to the Internet. These addresses ensure that your network is either completely isolated from the Internet or that it is located behind a firewall or a proxy server.

Automatic Private IP Addressing (APIPA)

Usually the IP address is either statically assigned to a computer or assigned through the DHCP server. In its default configuration, a Windows XP Professional computer will dynamically obtain its IP address configuration from a DHCP server. When the DHCP server is not available for some reason, the computer can assign itself an IP address automatically. This feature is enabled by default on all Windows XP computers. The automatically assigned address is in the range 169.254.0.0 to 169.254.255.255. With this address, the computer can connect only to the local network and cannot access any remote networks, as only the IP address and subnet mask are assigned.

A computer assigned with APIPA keeps on trying to locate a DHCP server every five minutes in order to obtain a genuine IP address. You can disable the APIPA feature by using the Alternate Configuration. This alternate configuration will be used in case the computer is not able to connect to a DHCP server on startup.

Local Area Network Connections

When you install a network adapter, a Local Area Connection icon appears in the Network Connections window in the "Network and Internet Connections" window inside the Control Panel. You can view and configure the properties of this adapter by right-clicking this icon. Different icon symbols indicate different types of connections. Dial-up connections are indicated by a phone and modem symbol, LAN and High Speed Internet connections appear as small pictures, and disabled or disconnected connections appear as dimmed pictures. A lock sign shows a connection behind a Windows firewall.

In this window, you can perform the following actions:

- View the status of the Local Area Connection and enable or disable it.
- View or modify the properties of a Local Area Connection by right-clicking the icon and selecting Properties.
- Rename the Local Area Connection.

- Bridge a Local Area Connection to connect two network segments when there is more than one network adapter.
- Install network components such as Clients, Protocols, and Services on the computer.
- Repair a Local Area Connection when it stops functioning.

Creating a new connection

You can launch the New Connection Wizard by clicking Create A New Connection from the left pane of the Network Connections window. The wizard allows you to create and configure the following types of connections, as shown in Figure 2-24.

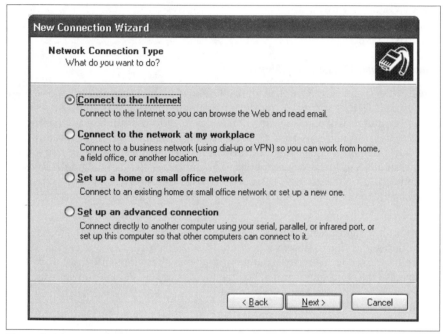

Figure 2-24. New Connection Wizard

Connect to the Internet
    This is for connecting to the Internet, browsing for email, and surfing the Web.

Connect to a network at my workplace
    This is for connecting to the business network using a dial-up or virtual Private Network (VPN) connection so that you can work from home, a field office, or another location.

Set up a home or small office network
    This is for connecting to an existing small office network.

Set up an advanced connection
This is for connecting directly to another computer using a serial, parallel, or infrared port, or setting up this computer so that other computers can connect to it.

Configuring network components

Networking components such as Clients, Protocols, and Services can be installed, uninstalled, and configured from the Properties dialog box of a Local Area Connection. The following networking components are installed, enabled, or disabled, from the Properties dialog box of a Local Area Connection.

Configuring a static IP address

By default, a Windows XP computer is configured to obtain an IP address automatically from a DHCP server. In some cases, it may be necessary to assign this address manually. The following steps explain how you can assign a static IP address to a Windows XP computer:

1. Click Start → Control Panel. In the Control Panel window, click Network Connections.
2. Double-click Local Area Connection to open its Properties dialog box.
3. Click Internet Protocol (TCP/IP), but make sure that you do not clear the checkbox.
4. Click Properties to open the General properties dialog box (Figure 2-25).
5. Click "Use the following IP address" and enter the IP address, subnet mask, and default gateway, if any. Make sure that the IP address you enter is not in use by any other computer on the network.
6. Click OK twice to close the Internet Protocol (TCP/IP) properties and Local Area Connection dialog boxes.
7. Click Close to close the Network And Internet Connections dialog box.

Configuring DNS server addresses

The DNS is used to resolve (translate) FQDNs such as *mycomputer.mycompany. com* to their corresponding IP addresses. Every Windows XP Professional computer runs a DNS client service that is known as a *DNS Resolver*. You can configure a Windows XP Professional client computer to obtain the DNS server address automatically, or it can be specified manually. In its default setting, the computer is configured to obtain the DNS server address automatically through the DHCP server. You can assign the IP addresses of a Preferred DNS server and an Alternate DNS server. To assign the static IP addresses of the DNS servers, click "Use the following DNS server addresses" and enter the IP addresses of the Preferred DNS server and the Alternate DNS server.

In case you have multiple DNS servers in the network, you can specify additional DNS server addresses also. Click the Advanced button to open the Advanced properties dialog box, and click the DNS tab. Click the Add button to specify IP addresses of additional DNS servers or the Remove button to remove any of the

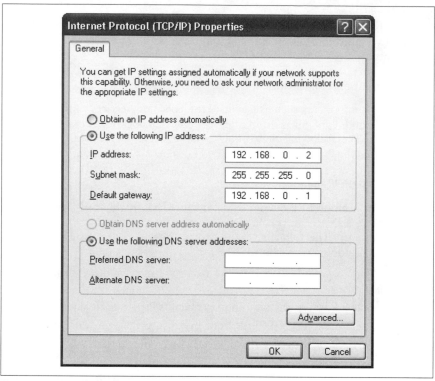

Figure 2-25. Configuring static IP address

already specified DNS server addresses. You can also change the order of DNS servers using the Up and Down buttons.

DNS suffixes and DNS registration

In the Advanced properties dialog box, you can change the way your computer's DNS queries will be handled by the DNS server. For resolving unqualified names (names that are not FQDN), the DNS client service that is running on the Windows XP Professional computer adds certain suffixes to the unqualified names to make them FQDN. These settings need not be done manually when you are using a DHCP server. The following options are available as shown in Figure 2-26.

Append primary and connection specific DNS suffixes
  This option along with the "Append parent suffixes of the primary DNS suffix" option is selected by default. The DNS Resolver appends the primary domain name to the computer name and also appends the DNS name specified in each connection's TCP/IP properties.

Append these DNS suffixes (in order)
  When this option is selected, you can specify the DNS suffixes and the order that they will be appended to unqualified names.

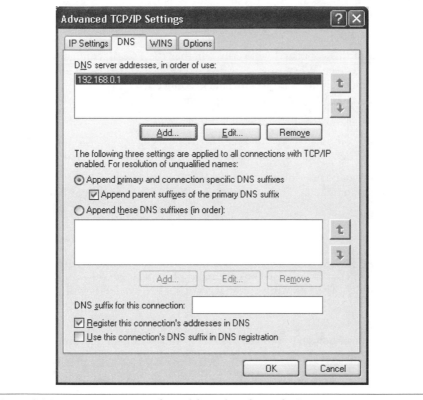

Figure 2-26. DNS settings are configured from the Advanced TCP/IP properties

Register this connection's addresses in DNS
    When this option is selected, the computer will dynamically register its full computer name and IP address in the DNS server database.

Use this connection's DNS suffix in DNS registration
    When this option is selected, the computer can use dynamic updates to register its IP address and the domain names of each connection in the DNS database.

TCP/IP Troubleshooting Utilities

TCP/IP connectivity problems can be resolved using a number of built-in troubleshooting utilities. Depending on the nature of the problem, any or all of these utilities can be used to pinpoint the source of the problem. These utilities include Ping, Ipconfig, Tracert, Pathping, and Net View.

Ping

Ping is used to check connectivity between two hosts on the network. If you are not able to connect to a remote computer, you should ping the local loopback IP address first. The local loopback IP address is 127.0.0.1. Run the following command from the command prompt:

```
ping 127.0.0.1
```

The output of this command will verify whether the TCP/IP configuration of the computer is correct. When this is verified, you should ping the IP address of the remote computer. For example, to check connectivity to a computer with IP address 192.168.0.10, type the following command:

```
ping 192.168.0.10
```

If the remote computer is on a different network segment, you should ping the IP address of the default gateway or the router that connects to the remote network.

The Ping command uses Internet Control Message Protocol (ICMP). The Ping to a remote computer can fail if the computer is behind a firewall that blocks ICMP messages.

Ipconfig

The Ipconfig command is used to verify the TCP/IP configuration of the local computer. Type ipconfig /? at the command prompt to list the options available with this utility. The following optional switches are available with the Ipconfig utility:

ipconfig /all
> This option shows the complete TCP/IP configuration of the computer.

ipconfig /release
> This option releases the TCP/IP configuration obtained automatically from the DHCP server.

ipconfig /renew
> This option renews the TCP/IP configuration from the DHCP server.

ipconfig /displaydns
> This option displays the contents of the DNS cache on the local computer.

ipconfig /flushdns
> This option clears the DNS cache on the local computer.

ipconfig /registerdns
> This option first renews the TCP/IP configuration from the DHCP server and then registers this information with the DNS server.

ipconfig /setclassid
> This option sets the user class for the local computer when the DHCP server supplies the TCP/IP configuration based on user classes.

Remember that the ipconfig command is always used from the command prompt. You can run it from the Run dialog box in the Start menu, but you will not be able to view the results.

Tracert

Tracert stands for trace route. Tracert is helpful in locating where the network packets stop on their way to the destination computer. Tracert is also used from the command prompt along with the IP address of the destination computer. For example, if you are not able to connect to a host with IP address 192.168.0.10, use the following command:

```
tracert 192.168.0.10
```

The output of this command will indicate where the connection is broken on the way.

Pathping

The Pathping command is similar to the Tracert command but it shows exactly where the network packets are being lost on their way to the destination computer. While Tracert is used to identify the point where the connection is broken, Pathping is used to determine where data packets are lost. It is a combination of the Ping and Tracert commands. This command is used at the command prompt as follows:

```
pathping 192.168.0.10
```

Net View

The Net View command is also used to test connectivity between two computers. This utility is primarily used to display file and print shares on a remote computer. You will need proper credentials to successfully use this command. The following example explains how this command can be used to view shares on a computer with an IP address 192.168.0.10:

```
net view \\192.168.0.10
```

Repairing a connection

When a local area connection (LAN) stops working, the Repair utility is very useful to reconfigure the TCP/IP properties of the connection. To access the Repair utility for a LAN connection, right-click the LAN connection and click Repair. The following actions are performed by this utility:

- An attempt is made to renew the IP configuration from the DHCP server. This action is equivalent to using the ipconfig /renew command.
- The Address Resolution Protocol (ARP) cache on the local computer is cleared. This action is similar to using the arp -d command.
- The NetBIOS name cache is reloaded and the NetBIOS name update is sent. This action is equivalent to using the nbtstat -R and nbtstat -RR commands.
- The DNS cache on the local computer is cleared. This action is equivalent to using the ipconfig /flushdns command.
- The computer's DNS name is registered again with the DNS server. This action is equivalent to using the ipconfig /registerdns command.
- For wireless connections, the IEEE 802.1x authentication is restarted.

Another way to access the Repair button is from the LAN icon in the notification area of the Task Bar. Right-click the icon and click Status. In the Local Area Connection Status dialog box, click the Support tab. The Repair button is located in the lower-righthand corner.

 Make sure that you understand the difference between the Tracert and Pathping commands. Tracert is used to check where the connection is broken, while Pathping is used to check where data packets are being lost on the way.

Dial-up Networking

Dial-up connections are used to connect to the Internet or to the Remote Access Servers at your workplace. These connections use the public switched telephone network (PSTN) to carry data from one place to another. The dialing computer uses a modem, an ISDN adapter, or a DSL modem. These modems are configured from the Phone And Modem Options in the Control Panel. The actual connection is configured from the Local Area Connections dialog box in the Internet And Network Connections window in the Control Panel.

Dial-out connection

To create a dial-up connection, right-click the empty area in the Local Area Connections window and click Create A New Connection. Dial-up connection appears as a separate icon in this window. Right-click the icon to view or modify the properties of the dial-up connection. The properties dialog box of the dial-up connection is shown in Figure 2-27, and the tabs are described in the following list:

General
> This tab allows you to configure the modem properties and one or more phone numbers used to dial up to a remote network. You can specify the dialing rules, such as area code, number to access outside phone line, and calling card information.

Options
> This tab allows you to specify dialing and redialing options. Windows prompts for logon name and password.

Security
> This tab allows you to configure authentication settings used to connect to the remote server.

Networking
> This tab allows you to view the type of remote server you are trying to connect to.

Advanced
> This tab allows you to configure Windows Firewall and Internet Connection Sharing (ICS). These are covered next.

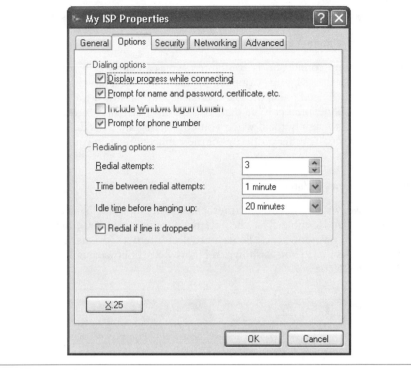

Figure 2-27. Dial-up connection properties

Dial-in connection

In order to configure a Windows XP Professional computer to accept incoming dial-up connections, create a new connection from the LAN Connections window and then select Set Up An Advanced Connection. In the Advanced Connection Options window, select the Accept Incoming Connections option and click Next. The dialog boxes that follow allow you to configure these properties:

Devices For Incoming Connections
    This page allows you to configure one of the dial-up devices to accept incoming connections and configure its properties, including data bits, parity, modulation type, and the number of stop bits.

Incoming Virtual Private Network (VPN) Connection
    This page allows you to set up an incoming VPN connection to this computer.

User Permissions And Callback
    This page is used to set user permissions and callback options for the incoming connection. You can specify the users that are allowed to connect and configure permissions for them. For each user, you can also enable callback options and specify the callback number.

Networking Software

This page allows you to select networking software for the connection.

Connecting to the Internet using a dial-up connection

When the dial-up connection is configured, you can connect to the Internet by double-clicking the Dial-up Connection icon in the Network Connections window. You will need to supply the username and password for the connection as well as the phone number to be dial. You can also save these credentials so that you don't have to supply them when you connect again. This dialog box allows you to view or modify other properties of the connection when you click the Properties button.

Configuring Internet Explorer

There are two ways to configure Internet Explorer options. You can open the Control Panel and double-click the Internet Options icon or, from within the Internet Explorer window, click Tools and select Internet Options. This opens the Internet Options dialog box as shown in Figure 2-28. Following is a description of the tabs in the dialog box.

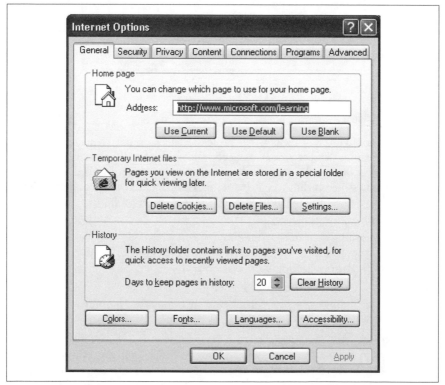

Figure 2-28. Use Internet Options in the Control Panel to configure Internet properties

General

This tab allows you to set the home page for Internet Explorer, delete cookies, delete temporary Internet files, and configure settings for temporary Internet files. You can also configure colors, fonts, language, and accessibility options from this tab.

Security

This tab allows you to configure security zones for web sites. Four different levels of security zones can be configured: Internet, Local Intranet, Trusted Sites, and Restricted Sites. Besides this, you can set four different security levels: High, Medium, Medium-Low, and Low. ActiveX controls are also enabled or disabled from this page.

Privacy

This tab allows you to configure how the computer will handle cookies and pop ups. Cookies are temporary Internet files stored on your computer's hard disk by various web sites; they contain personal preferences and personal information. You can also enable the Pop-up Blocker from the Privacy tab and configure its settings. You can configure the Internet Explorer to block or accept all cookies or set different levels for storing cookies on the local computer.

Content

The Recreational Software Advisory Council on the Internet (RSACi) rates contents of web sites. The Content tab of Internet properties allows access to the content advisor so that you can control what web sites will be visited and what content is allowed to be downloaded and displayed on your computer.

Connections

This tab allows you to view, modify, add, or delete dial-up and VPN connections used to connect to the Internet. The LAN Settings button opens another window in which you can configure the computer to detect settings automatically or use a proxy server for an Internet connection.

Programs

This tab allows you to view and configure the programs that Windows will use for Internet services, such as HTML editor, email, newsgroups, Internet chat, calendar, and contact lists.

Advanced

This tab allows you to configure additional settings for Accessibility, Browsing, Multimedia, Printing, and Security.

Internet Information Server

Internet Information Server (IIS) is a part of the built-in Windows Components but is not installed by default. IIS allows you to create your own web site and to publish information on the Internet. Internet users connect to your site using Internet Explorer or other web browsers and access the information that you publish. You can install IIS by clicking the "Add or Remove Programs" utility in the Control Panel and then selecting Windows. The following steps explain how you can install IIS on a Windows XP Professional computer.

1. Click Start → Control Panel to open the Control Panel window.
2. Click "Add or Remove Programs."
3. In "Add or Remove Programs," click "Add or Remove Windows Components" (on the lefthand panel).
4. The Windows Components Wizard starts.
5. Click the checkbox for Internet Information Server (IIS) and click Next.
6. If you wish to install the File Transfer Protocol (FTP) Service (which is not installed by default), click Details and then click the checkbox for FTP service. Click OK.
7. IIS is installed and its components are configured to default settings.
8. Click Finish to complete the installation of IIS. Click Close to close the "Add or Remove Programs" window.
9. Close the Control Panel window.

When IIS is installed, the IIS snap-in is installed as part of the Administrative Tools in the Control Panel. Open the IIS snap-in to configure or manage IIS services and web sites on your computer. The IIS console is shown in Figure 2-29.

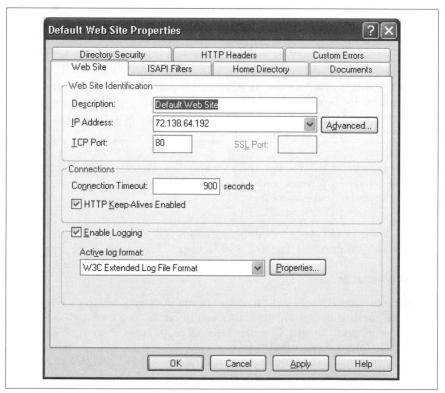

Figure 2-29. Properties of Default Web Site are managed from the IIS snap-in

Right-click the default web site in the IIS snap-in and click Properties in order to open the Properties dialog box of the web site. This is where you will manage most of the aspects of your site. You can change the location of your home directory from the Home Directory tab. Home Directory can be a shared folder on your computer, or another computer, or a Uniform Resource Locator (URL) to another web site.

If the web site contains files or folders located on another computer, you can create virtual directories. Right-click the web site in the IIS snap-in, click New, and select Virtual Directory. This starts the Virtual Directory Wizard, which guides you through the process of creating a new Virtual Directory for the web site.

Internet Connection Sharing

Internet Connection Sharing (ICS) is a simple and cost-effective way to share a single connection to the Internet among several computers on a small network. When configured, the computer hosting the Internet connection acts as a gateway between workgroup computers and the Internet. Other computers obtain their IP addresses automatically from the ICS host that serves as a DHCP server. The DHCP service allocates IP addresses in the 192.168.0.1 address range with a subnet mask of 255.255.255.0. The ICS host always assigns itself an IP address of 192.168.0.1 with a subnet mask of 255.255.255.0.

To enable ICS, make sure that the computer hosting the ICS is connected to the Internet and that all other computers are connected to this computer. Click the Allow Other Network Users To Connect Through This Computer's Internet Connection option, located in the Advanced tab of the Properties dialog box of the network connection.

While ICS comes with a simple solution for Internet connectivity for a small workgroup, it also has several limitations:

- ICS can be used only in a workgroup environment. Although workgroups hardly have any servers, if you have any Windows 2000 or Windows 2003 servers configured as domain controller, a DHCP server, or a DNS server in this workgroup, ICS will not work.

- Computers are always assigned IP addresses in the range 192.168.0.2 to 192.168.0.254. Any statically configured computer that is not within this IP address range will not be able to connect to the Internet.

- If any computer's statically assigned IP address conflicts with the IP address allocated by the ICS host, the connection will cause problems due to duplicate IP addresses.

- You must bridge LAN connections if there are two or more adapters and LAN connections on the same computer.

Windows Firewall

Windows Firewall was previously known as Internet Connection Firewall. This firewall is automatically installed and enabled by default when Windows XP Professional Service Pack 2 is installed on the computer. You can, however, disable the Windows Firewall, if you do not want to keep it enabled. Microsoft recommends that you keep the Windows Firewall enabled, since it is the basic protection from the Internet sources that may harm your computer. A green shield in the notification area of the Task Bar indicates that the firewall is enabled, while a red shield indicates that it is off.

When SP2 is installed, a new icon labeled Windows Security Center appears in the Control Panel. You can configure Internet Options, Automatic Updates, and Windows Firewall by opening the Windows Security Center. You must be a member of the Administrators group in order to make changes to the Windows Firewall settings. The Windows Firewall dialog box is shown in Figure 2-30. The tabs in the dialog box are described next.

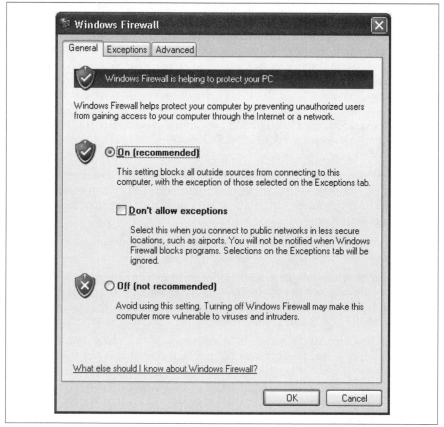

Figure 2-30. Windows Firewall

General

This tab allows you to enable or disable the Windows Firewall. By default, the Windows Firewall is enabled on all network connections including dial-up and Internet connections. The Advanced tab can be used to enable or disable the Windows Firewall for specific connections.

Exceptions

This tab allows you to create exceptions for the Windows Firewall by specifying specific applications and ports from which trafficc should be allowed. By default, all network traffic is blocked by the Windows Firewall when it is enabled. Common exceptions include ActiveSync Applications, Connection Manager, File And Printer Sharing, Remote Desktop, and Remote Access. You can add or remove programs and ports from the Exceptions tab.

Advanced

This tab allows you to enable or disable the Windows Firewall for particular connections and configure security logging and ICMP settings. The security logging settings allow you to collect network traffic activities in a logfile. The Security Logging is not enabled by default. The ICMP settings allow you to configure settings so that the computer responds to certain troubleshooting utilities such as Network Monitor.

Remote Desktop

Remote Desktop (see Figure 2-31) allows you to get access to a remote computer and control it from your own computer. This feature is very helpful in troubleshooting operating system and application problems when it is not possible to personally visit the remote computer. Remote Desktop works on LAN connections as well as over the Internet. You can get full control over the desktop of the remote computer and run programs or configure it as if you were sitting locally on that computer.

The following requirements must be met before establishing a Remote Desktop connection:

- The remote computer must be connected to the LAN or to the Internet and be running the Windows XP Professional or another Windows operating system that supports Remote Desktop.

- Terminal Services must be running on the Windows XP computers since Remote Desktop uses this service.

- The user who wants to connect to the remote computer using Remote Desktop must be a member of the Remote Desktop Users group or the Administrators group on the remote computer.

The Remote Desktop connection for the computer hosting the connection is configured from the Remote tab of the System Properties dialog box in the Control Panel. In order to configure a computer to accept the incoming Remote Desktop connection, the following steps must be completed:

1. Right-click My Computer and select Properties in order to open the System Properties dialog box.

2. Click the Remote tab.

3. Click the Allow Users To Connect Remotely To This Computer checkbox.

4. Click the Select Remote Users button to add the users who will be allowed to connect remotely to this computer.

5. Click OK to close the System Properties dialog box.

To connect to a remote computer using Remote Desktop, complete the following steps as shown in Figure 2-31.

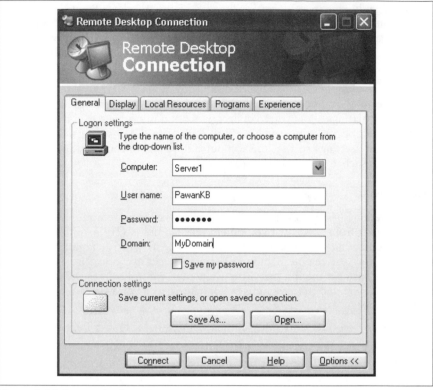

Figure 2-31. Remote Desktop Connection

1. Click Start → All Programs → Accessories → Communications → Remote Desktop Connection. This opens the Remote Desktop Connection dialog box.

2. In the General tab, enter the name or IP address of the remote computer, as well as its username, password, and domain name. You can choose to save the password if you want.

3. Click Connect.

4. When prompted, enter the username and password again.

5. If you save the username and password, you can click the Options button so that next time you do not have to enter all this information again.

In order to end the Remote Desktop session and disconnect from the remote computer, you can simply close the Remote Desktop window or simply log off from the remote computer. You can also disconnect by clicking Disconnect from the Start menu.

Remote Assistance

Remote Assistance helps users get help from expert users when they are facing a problem in troubleshooting the operating system or applications. The user first sends an *invitation* to the expert user or *helper* over the network connection, and the helper must accept the invitation before the session can start. When the connection is established, the helper can take shared control of the user's computer with the user's permission. This allows the helper to send and receive files to the remote user. Like Remote Desktop, Remote Assistance also helps in troubleshooting when it is not possible to personally visit the user's computer.

The Remote Assistance connection is started from the Help And Support Center located in the Start menu. The following steps must be completed in order to successfully establish a Remote Assistance connection:

1. Click Help And Support Center from the Start menu.
2. Click Invite A Friend To Connect To Your Computer Using Remote Assistance located under Ask For Assistance.
3. Select Invite Someone To Help You.
4. The invitation can be sent using any of the following methods: via Windows Messenger, as an email attachment, or by saving the invitation as a file on a shared folder on a network file server.
5. Specify the name, message, invitation expiration date, and password to establish the connection when prompted.
6. Click Send Invitation.

The expert user or helper must accept the invitation in order to complete the process and establish a connection. Depending on the method used by the user to send the invitation, the helper must open the invitation. The user sending the invitation is then notified that the invitation has been accepted. The user must click Yes in the Remote Assistance dialog box to finally establish the connection.

The user sending the invitation is presented with a User Console while the expert or helper is presented with a Helper Console. Both the user and the helper can send and receive files as well as chat to resolve the problem for which the user wants assistance. The Disconnect button is used to end the Remote Assistance session.

Configuring, Managing, and Troubleshooting Security

The Security Options included with the Windows XP Professional operating system are managed in several ways, including local security policies, assignment of user and group rights, NTFS file and folder permissions, account policies, the Encrypting File System (EFS), and auditing. We already discussed the NTFS permissions and encrypting filesystem in the section "Implementing and Conducting Administration of Resources." In this section, we will look at local security policies such as account policies, user rights, and auditing.

Local Security Policy

The Local Security Policy applies only to that Windows XP Professional computer on which it is defined. This policy allows the administrators to control various local security aspects of the local system, such as account policies, user rights, Security Options, and audit policies. The Local Security Policy can be accessed from the Administrative Tools folder in the Control Panel as shown in Figure 2-32.

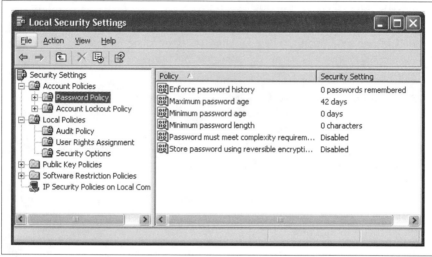

Figure 2-32. Local Security Policy console in Windows XP Professional

Account Policies

Account policies determine the Password and Account Lockout Policies that are enforced on a Windows XP Professional computer. The Password Policies determine how passwords are created and managed on the computer. The Account Lockout Policies determine how accounts are locked out or unlocked in case an unauthorized person is trying to get access to the computer using someone else's user account.

Password Policy

Password Policies determine how passwords are created and maintained on the computer. The Password Policies are explained in the following list:

Enforce password history
> This value indicates the number of passwords that are kept in history or remembered by the operating system so that the user cannot reuse old passwords. The default value is 0, meaning that no password history is kept. You can specify a value between 0 and 24. This forces the user to create a new password every time the password is changed.

Maximum password age

This value indicates the maximum number of days a user can keep his current password and forces the user to change the password when the specified number of days have passed. If a value of 0 is specified, the password will never expire, and the users will not be required to change the password. The default value is 42 days, but you can specify any value from 0 to 999 days.

Minimum password age

This value indicates the number of days that must pass before a user can change his password and prevents frequent change of passwords. A value of 0 days means that the user can change his password any time; this value should not be used when you have enforced password history. The default value is 42 days, but you can specify any value from 0 to 999 days. The value of minimum password age must be less than the value of maximum password age.

Minimum password length

This value indicates the minimum number of characters required for the password. You can specify any value from 0 to 14 characters. Usually administrators keep this value at seven characters. A value of 0 characters means that a password is not required.

Passwords must meet complexity requirements

This option can either be enabled or disabled but is disabled by default. When enabled, the complexity requirements mean that the passwords must be at least six characters long and must contain upper- and lowercase letters, numbers, and special characters. The passwords cannot contain the user's account name or full name. The password must also comply with the "Enforce password history" settings.

Store passwords using reversible encryption for all users in the domain

This option can either be enabled or disabled but is disabled by default. When enabled, this option stores passwords for all users of the domain in reversible encryption. You can use this option only when your computer is a member of a domain. Enabling this option weakens password security and should only be enabled when a specific application requires it.

Account Lockout Policy

The Account Lockout Policies are explained in the following list:

Account Lockout Duration

This value indicates the number of minutes the account will be locked out. You can specify any value between 0 and 99,999 minutes. A value of 0 minutes means that the account will be locked out indefinitely and an administrator must unlock the account.

Account Lockout Threshold

This value indicates the number of invalid or bad logon attempts permitted before the account is locked out. You can specify any value between 0 and 999 for this setting. A value of 0 means that the account will never be locked out and unlimited invalid logon attempts will be permitted. You should not use a value of 0 if security is a concern in your organization.

Reset Lockout Counter After

This value in minutes indicates the time after which the account lockout counter will be reset. You can specify any value between 1 and 99,999 minutes.

 You should memorize the default values of different password and account policy settings. Also remember how the accounts can be locked out indefinitely and how someone can be allowed unlimited invalid logon attempts without locking out the account.

Local Policies

The Local Policies node contains Security Options, User Rights, and Audit Policies. These policies are discussed in the following sections.

Security options

The Security options are located under the Local Policies node of the Local Security Policies. These options are divided into categories such as accounts, audit, devices, domain controller, domain member, interactive logon, Microsoft network client, network access, network security, Recovery Console, shutdown, system security, and system objects. Some of the commonly used Security Options are listed in Table 2-16.

Table 2-16. Commonly used Security Options

Security Option	Description
Accounts: Administrator Account Status	Enables or disables the Administrator account. This setting does not apply when the system is running in safe mode.
Accounts: Guest Account Status	Enables or disables the Guest account.
Accounts: Rename Administrator Account	When enabled, you must specify a different account name for use with the Administrator account.
Accounts: Rename Guest Account	When enabled, you must specify a different account name for use with the Guest account.
Audit: Audit The Use of Backup And Restore Privilege	Works in conjunction with the Audit Privilege Use. When both policies are enabled, an entry is written when files are backed up or restored.
Devices: Prevent Users From Installing Printer Drivers	Allows members of only Administrators and Power Users groups to install printer drivers. When disabled, any user can install printer drivers when adding printers.
Devices: Restrict CD-ROM Access To Locally Logged On User Only	When enabled, the CD-ROM drive cannot be accessed simultaneously by a locally logged on user and network user. When disabled, simultaneous CD-ROM access is allowed to the local user and remote user.
Devices: Restrict Floppy Access To Locally Logged On User Only	When enabled, the floppy drive cannot be accessed simultaneously by a locally logged-on user and network user. When disabled, simultaneous floppy drive access is allowed to the local user and remote user.

Table 2-16. Commonly used Security Options (continued)

Security Option	Description
Devices: Unsigned Driver Installation Behavior	When enabled, this determines what happens when someone attempts to install an unsigned device driver. You can set the policy to Block, Warn, or Allow installation of unsigned device drivers.
Interactive Logon: Do Not Display Last User Name	Prevents the Log On To Windows dialog box from displaying the name of the user who was logged on to the system.
Interactive Logon: Do Not Require CTRL-ALT-DEL	When enabled, a user does not need to press the CTRL-ALT-DEL key combination in order to log on to the system.
Network Access: Let Everyone Permissions Apply To Anonymous Users	When enabled, the permissions applied to the Everyone group also apply to the users who log on Anonymously.
Network Access: Shares That Can Be Accessed Anonymously	Creates a list of network shares that can be accessed by users who log on anonymously.
Recovery Console: Allow Automatic Administrative Logon	Determines whether the administrator is required to enter a password when using the Recovery Console. When enabled, the Recovery Console does not prompt for the Administrator's password.
Shutdown: Allow System To Be Shut Down Without Having To Log On	When this policy is enabled, the Shut Down option becomes available at the Windows Log On screen. You don't have to log on to the system in order to shut it down.

User rights

User rights help simplify the administration of the system and resources by assigning responsibilities to users and groups. User rights are divided into two main categories: privileges and user rights.

Privileges. *Privileges* are user rights that are assigned to users or groups in order to complete specific tasks. These user rights apply to the system as a whole instead of a particular object. Some of the most commonly used privileges are listed in Table 2-17.

Table 2-17. Privileges on Windows XP Professional computers

Privilege	Description	Assigned by default to
Act As Part Of Operating System	When enabled, allows a process to log on like a normal user account. Processes that need this privilege use the LocalSystem account.	None
Add Workstations To Domain	Allows a user to add workstations to a domain.	Only applicable on Domain Controllers and is defined in the Default Domain Controller Policy
Backup Files And Directories	Allows a user to backup files and folders even if she does not have permissions.	Administrators and Backup Operators groups
Change The System Time	Allows a user to change the system time.	Administrators, Power Users, groups, LocalSystem and NetworkService accounts

Table 2-17. Privileges on Windows XP Professional computers (continued)

Privilege	Description	Assigned by default to
Force Shut Down A Remote System	Allows a user to shut down a computer remotely.	Administrators
Load And Unload Device Drivers	Allows users to install or uninstall PnP device drivers. It does not affect non-PnP device drivers.	Administrators
Manage Auditing And Security Log	Allows a user to specify which objects should be audited. Also allows users to manage security logs.	Administrators
Remove Computer From Docking Station	Allows a user to remove a portable computer from the docking station.	Administrators, Power Users, and Users groups
Restore Files And Directories	Allows users to restore files and folders from backup tapes or other media even if they do not have permissions on destination folders.	Administrators and Backup Operators groups
Shut Down The System	Allows a user to shut down the Windows XP Professional computer.	Administrators, Power Users, Backup Operators, and Users groups
Take Ownership Of Files Or Other Objects	Allows a user to take ownership of files, folders, printers, registry keys, and other system objects such as processes and threads.	Administrators

Logon rights. *Logon rights* are user rights that are assigned to a particular user account or group account in order to control the way users log on to the system. Some of the most commonly exercised logon rights are listed in Table 2-18.

Table 2-18. Logon rights on Windows XP Professional computer

Logon right	Description	Assigned by default to
Access This Computer From Network	Allows users to connect to the system from the network.	Administrators, Backup Operators, Power Users, Users, and Everyone groups
Deny Access To This Computer From The Network	Prevents users from connecting to the system from the network.	None
Log On As A Batch Job	Allows users to log on to the system as a batch job.	Administrators group and Anonymous users when IIS is installed on the system
Deny Log On As A Batch Job	Prevents users from logging on to the system as a batch job.	None
Log On As A Service	Allows a user, computer, or service to log on to the system as a service. Services are usually configured to run with LocalSystem, LocalService, or NetworkService accounts.	None
Deny Log On As A Service	Prevents a user, computer, or service from logging on to the system as a service.	None
Log On Locally	Allows a user to log on to the system locally or interactively.	Administrators, Backup Operators, Account Operators, Print Operators, and Server Operators groups

Logon right	Description	Assigned by default to
Deny Log On Locally	Prevents a user from logging on to the system locally or interactively.	None
Allow Log On Through Terminal Services	Allows users to log on to the system through terminal services. Remote Desktop runs as part of the terminal services.	Administrators and Remote Desktop Users groups
Deny Allow Log On Through Terminal Services	Prevents users from logging on to the system through terminal services.	None

You need not memorize all the user privileges or logon rights for Exam 70-270, but you must explore all the options in the Local Security Policy and understand the function of each so that if you face a simulation question, you can easily configure a security policy for the given situation.

Audit Policy

Audit Policy is used to track the success or failure events of user actions as well as provide access to objects on a Windows XP Professional computer. Auditing becomes necessary when you suspect that unauthorized persons are attempting to log on to the system or some unauthorized users are attempting to access resources for which they are not granted access. Auditing is essentially a three-step process:

1. Setting the Audit Policy

   You must set the Audit Policy in the Local Security Policy. If this policy is not enabled for success or failure, no events are recorded in the security logs.

2. Enabling auditing of resources

   Auditing is not enabled by default. You must enable auditing of the specific resources, such as files, folders, and printers, for success and failure events. Other events that can be audited include logon and logoff, start and shut down of the computer, and management of user accounts.

3. Viewing the security log

   When auditing is enabled on resources and the audit policy is set on Windows XP Professional, the success or failure events are written to security logfiles. These events can be viewed from the Security logs in the Event Viewer console.

Setting the Audit Policy

Audit Policy is located in the Local Security Policy under the Local Policies node. Table 2-19 lists the events for which audit policies are available.

Table 2-19. Types of events available for auditing

Event	Description
Account Logon	Audits success and failure events related to users logging on or off the computer.
Account Management	Deals with events related to enabling, disabling, renaming, creation, deletion, or modification of user or group accounts, and resetting passwords.
Directory Service Access	Audits events related to directory service access but is undefined for Windows XP computers.
Audit Logon Events	Deals with events related to logging on and off on the computer and includes events related to running logon scripts and accessing user profiles.
Audit Object Access	Deals with events related to access of files, folders, printers, and other resources.
Policy Change	Deals with events related to change in Security Options, user rights assignment, and audit policies.
Privilege Use	Deals with events related to use of user rights.
Process Tracking	Deals with events related to an action performed by an application or program, as well as indirect object access.
System Events	Deals with events related to system events such as starting or shutting down a computer. Also includes security-related events.

Enabling auditing of resources

Once the Audit Policy is set in the Local Security policy, you must decide which resources should be audited and enable auditing on these resources. The following steps must be completed in order to audit file or folder access:

1. Open Windows Explorer and locate the file or folder for which you want to configure auditing.
2. Right-click the folder and click Properties.
3. Click the Security tab in the Properties dialog box of the folder.
4. Click the Advanced button to open the Advanced Security Settings dialog box of the folder.
5. Click the Auditing tab as shown in Figure 2-33.
6. Click the Add button to open the Auditing Entry for the folder.
7. In the Auditing Entry for the Folder dialog box, select the user for which you want to configure auditing. Notice that the auditing applies by default to the current folder, subfolders, and files.
8. Click the checkbox under Successful or Failed events for the access type you need to audit.
9. Click OK to return to the Advanced Security Settings dialog box.
10. Close all dialog boxes one by one.

Security Templates

Security Templates are predefined security policies that can be applied to an individual Windows XP Professional computer. These templates are meant to simplify the job of an administrator and are based on different computer roles. The administrator can choose one of the several available built-in Security Templates and

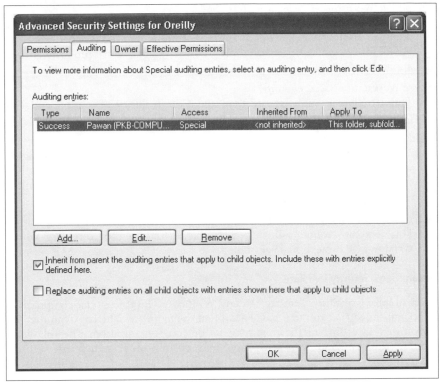

Figure 2-33. *Auditing is enabled from Advanced Security Settings*

apply that template to a Windows XP Professional system. The administrators would usually choose a template that closely matches the role of a computer in the network and make a copy of the template. This copy is then modified to reflect exact security requirements of the organization and applied to Windows XP Professional computers. The security policies are either applied individually to each computer or simultaneously to all systems through Group Policies. Group Policies are discusses later in this section.

To access Security Templates, open Windows Explorer and locate the *%System-Root%\Security\Templates* folder. This folder contains the files for Security Templates. Some of the Security Templates applicable for Windows XP Professional are as follows:

Default Setup Security (Setup Security.inf)
>This template contains the security settings applied to the system during the installation of Windows XP Professional. If you make a lot of changes to security settings, you can return the system to default security by applying this template.

Compatible Workstation (Compatws.inf)

This template contains more security than the Default Setup Security template and allows all users to run applications that are certified with the Windows Logon program. Only Power Users can run uncertified applications.

Secure Workstation (Securews.inf)

This template is more secure than the Compatible Workstation and can prevent certain applications from running properly on the system.

Highly Secure Workstation (Hisecws.inf)

This template contains security settings that are meant to create a highly secure working environment. This template provides the maximum level of security for authentication, encryption, and applications. All communications on the network must be digitally signed.

System Root Security (Rootsec.inf)

This template contains default permissions for the root directory where Windows XP Professional is installed.

Customizing a Security Template

To customize a Security Template to any Windows XP Professional computer, it is recommended that you first make a copy of the template. The copy can then be customized according to the requirements or your organization. The following exercise explains how you can copy and customize a predefined Security Template:

1. Click Start → Run. Type mmc and click OK in the Run dialog box. This opens an empty Microsoft Management Console (MMC).

2. In the empty console, click Add/Remove Snap-in from the File menu.

3. In the Add Stand Alone Snap-ins dialog box, click Security Templates and click Add.

4. Click Close and then click OK. The Security Templates are displayed as shown in Figure 2-34.

5. Right-click the template that you want to customize and click Save As.

6. Enter a name for the copy of the template in the Save As dialog box and click OK. A new template is added to the displayed window.

7. Expand the new template and locate the policies that you wish to modify.

Applying a Security Template

The following exercise explains how you can apply a predefined Security Template to an individual computer:

1. Click Start → Run. Type mmc and click OK in the Run dialog box to open an empty Microsoft Management Console (MMC).

2. In the blank console, click Add/Remove Snap-in from the File menu.

3. In the Add Stand Alone Snap-ins dialog box, click Security Configuration And Analysis and click Add.

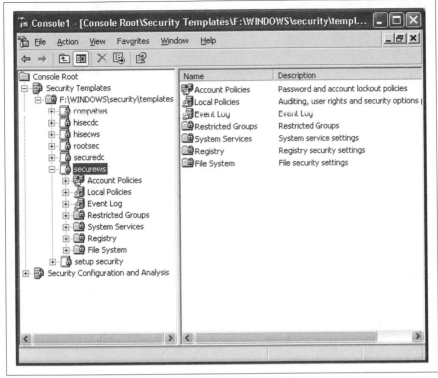

Figure 2-34. Security templates in Windows XP Professional

4. Click Close and then click OK.
5. Right-click Security Configuration And Analysis and click Open Database.
6. Type the name of the database in the Open Database dialog box and click Open.
7. The Import Template dialog box appears. Click the new Security Template you just customized and click Open.
8. To analyze the current security settings of the computer with the settings in the template, right-click Security Configuration And Analysis and click Analyze Computer Now.
9. To apply the security settings in the template to the computer, right-click Security Configuration And Analysis and click Configure Computer Now.

Group Policies

Group Policies are used to apply uniform security settings to computers that are part of a domain. Computers with similar roles are grouped together, and a Security Template is created for these computers. This template is then applied to all similar computers using the Group Policy. Apart from the security settings discussed earlier in "Local Security Policy," the Group Policy is also used to install software and software updates, configure Remote Installation Service on desktop computers, and redirect folders on a network location.

Multiple Group Policies

It is possible to apply multiple Group Policies from multiple sources to a computer based on specific computer roles. When multiple Group Policies are applied, they are processed in the following order:

- Local Group Policy Objects (LGPOs) are processed first and applied.
- Group Policy Objects (GPO) linked to the site are applied next. Settings in this policy that conflict with LGPOs override settings in the LGPOs.
- GPOs linked to the domain are applied next. These GPOs override any conflicting settings in the previously applied group policies.
- GPOs linked to the Organizational Unit (OU) that contains the computer are applied next. These GPOs override any conflicting settings applied previously by other GPOs. If the computer is a member of multiple OUs, the GPO linked to the highest-level OU is applied first.

Resultant Set Of Policy

When multiple Group Policies are applied to a Windows XP Professional computer from different sources such as Local, Site, Domain, or Organizational Units, it is possible to check which is the resulting policy and where it is coming from. The Resultant Set Of Policy (RSoP) tool makes it easy for administrators to analyze the effective group policy on a computer. The RSoP tool is available as a standalone snap-in in the Microsoft Management Console (MMC). The RSoP tool works in the following two modes:

Planning Mode
> This mode allows you to query a group policy in order to simulate the effects of a group policy before you actually apply it. This mode works only on computers that are members of a domain.

Logging Mode
> This mode lets you examine the security settings effective on the computer resulting from multiple group policies.

3

Exam 70-270 Prep and Practice

The material in this chapter is designed to help you prepare and practice for *Exam 70-270: Installing, Configuring and Administering Microsoft Windows XP Professional*. The chapter is organized into four sections:

Preparing for Exam 70-270
This section provides an overview of the types of questions on the exam. Reviewing this section will help you understand how the actual exam works.

Exam 70-270 Suggested Exercises
This section provides a numbered list of exercises that you can follow to gain experience in the exam's subject areas. Performing the exercises in this section will help ensure you have hands-on experience with all areas of the exam.

Exam 70-270 Highlighters Index
This section compiles the facts within the exam's subject areas that you are most likely to need another look at—in other words, the areas of study that you might have highlighted while reading the Study Guide. Studying the highlights is useful as a final review before the exam.

Exam 70-270 Practice Questions
This section includes a comprehensive set of practice questions to assess your knowledge of the exam. The questions are similar to the exam format. After you've reviewed the Study Guide, performed the Suggested Exercises, and studied the Highlighters Index, read the questions and see whether you can answer them correctly.

Before you take Exam 70-270, review the exam overview, perform the suggested exercises, and go through the practice questions provided. Many online sites provide practice tests for the exam. Duplicating the depth and scope of these practice exams in a printed book isn't possible. You should visit Microsoft's Certification site for pointers to online practice tests (*http://www.microsoft.com/ learning/mcpexams/prepare/practicetests.asp*).

Preparing for Exam 70-270

Exam 70-270 is a computer-generated exam. The exam is timed, and the amount of time that remains on the exam is displayed by an onscreen timer clock. Most questions on the exam are multiple-choice. Multiple-choice questions are one of the following:

Multiple-choice, single answer
> A radio button allows you to select a single answer only.

Multiple-choice, multiple answer
> A checkbox allows you to select multiple answers. Usually the number of correct answers is indicated in the question itself.

Typically, the test environment will have Previous/Next and Mark For Review options. You can navigate through the test using the Previous and Next buttons. You can also click the Mark For Review checkbox to flag a question to review later. A Calculator button is available at the bottom of the screen.

Other formats for questions are used as well, including:

List prioritization
> You should pick the choices that answer the question and arrange the list in a specified order. Lists initially appear on the right side; therefore, you have to click on << ADD to add them in the correct order to the list on the left side. For example, you might have to list the steps for creating a local user from the Computer Management console.

Hot area
> You should also indicate the correct answer by clicking on one or more areas of the screen or dialog box that is provided with the question. For example, you might be asked to click on an appropriate tab on the Display Properties to configure screen resolution.

Select and place
> Using drag-and-drop, pick answers from a given set of choices and place them in an appropriate spot in a dialog box or diagram. For example, you might be asked to select local users or groups who have the rights to backup files and folders.

Active screen
> You should use the dialog box provided to configure the options correctly or perform the required procedure. For example, you may be asked to click on an appropriate option from the local policies in order to configure the Account Lockout Policy.

Simulation
> You should also use the simulated desktop environment provided to perform a specific task or for troubleshooting. For example, you might be asked to configure a static IP address for a given network adapter.

With the exception of multiple-choice, single-answer questions, all of the other questions can have multiple answers or multiple required procedures to obtain full credit. If all of the expected answers or procedures are not performed, you will only get partial credit for the answer. This is usually indicated in the question itself.

While many of the questions on Exam 70-270 are multiple-choice, hot area, select and place, and active screen, simulation type questions are being used increasingly to ensure the testing process more accurately reflects actual hands-on knowledge, rather than memorization. Individuals with adequate hands-on experience who have reviewed the study guide, performed the practice exercises, memorized the essentials, and taken the practice tests should do well. Individuals who lack this hands-on experience and have not prepared appropriately will find the exam hard to pass.

Exam 70-270 Suggested Exercises

Exam 70-270 requires that you have good hands-on experience with the Windows XP Professional operating system. You should be familiar with the various tasks related to installing, configuring, and administering the operating system, as well as troubleshooting tools and techniques. You will also need to review the Study Guide and pay close attention to the areas that are new and/or you feel uncomfortable with. Practice is always the key to passing Microsoft exams. The more you practice, the more comfortable you will feel with the exam.

This section includes exercises from all of the areas covered in the exam. You should perform all of these exercises to gain hands-on experience with the Windows XP Professional operating system. Although it is possible to perform most of the exercises by installing Windows XP Professional on a single computer, we suggest that you create a network consisting of at least two computers. One of these computers should be a Windows Server 2003 domain controller, and the second should be your Windows XP Professional client computer. This setup will be particularly helpful when you install the operating system over the network and perform exercises in the networking section.

In addition to performing the following suggested exercises, you should also be familiar with all of the administrative tools included in Windows XP Professional, as well as the various methods to access these tools. For example, you can access the Computer Management console from either the My Computer icon on the desktop or from the Administrative Tools in the Control Panel.

 It is recommended that you do not perform any of the suggested exercises in your organization or in any running computer network. Create a test environment consisting of two computers for completing these exercises.

Attended Installation of Windows XP Professional

1. Make sure that the computer selected for installation meets the minimum hardware requirements.

2. Perform an attended installation of Windows XP Professional.

3. Select an appropriate disk for installation and choose NTFS as the filesystem for formatting during installation.

4. Join a workgroup during the networking phase of installation.

Upgrade a Previous Operating System

1. Make sure that the previous operating system can be directly upgraded to Windows XP Professional.

2. Check hardware compatibility by using the `winnt32.exe /checkupgradeonly` command.

3. Start the upgrade installation from the welcome screen when you insert the Windows XP Professional setup CD-ROM.

4. If the upgrade does not start automatically, start the installation by using either the `winnt.exe` or `winnt32.exe` command.

Using Setup Manager for Unattended Installation

1. Extract the setup tools from the Windows XP Professional setup CD-ROM from the \Support\Tools\Deploy.cab file.

2. Start the Setup Manager to create an answer file for unattended installation.

3. Select the Fully Automated option from the User Interaction Level page.

4. Check the three files created by the Setup Manager.

5. Perform an unattended installation using answer files.

Using Sysprep to Prepare System for Disk Duplication

1. Prepare a reference computer by installing Windows XP Professional and some applications.

2. Run `Sysprep.exe` from the Run dialog box from the Start menu to prepare an image of the reference computer.

3. Use a third-party disk-imaging utility to duplicate the disk.

Using Automatic Updates

1. Open the System utility in the Control Panel.

2. Launch the Automatic Updates dialog box.

3. Configure Automatic Updates in order to download the updates. Automatic Updates also allows you to choose when to install the updates.

Configuring NTFS Folder Permissions

1. Make sure Simple File Sharing is turned off on the computer.

2. Open Windows Explorer and locate a folder where you want to set the NTFS permissions.

3. Open the Properties dialog box of the folder and click on the Security tab.

4. Add a user or a group from the Select Users And Groups dialog box.

5. Click the "Allow or Deny" checkbox for one or more selected folder permissions.

Sharing a Folder on the Network

1. Make sure Simple File Sharing is turned off on the computer.

2. Open Windows Explorer and locate a folder that you want to share.

3. Right-click on the folder and select Sharing And Security from the context menu.

4. Click on Share This Folder and enter a share name.

5. Select the number of users that can access the shared folder.

6. Click on the Permissions tab to set share permissions.

7. Remove the Allow Read permission for the Everyone group.

8. Add a user or a group from the Select Users And Groups dialog box.

9. Click the Allow checkbox for one or more selected share permissions.

Managing Shares from Computer Management

1. Open the Computer Management console from the My Computer icon on the desktop.

2. Right-click on the Shares node and click on New Share to create a new share.

3. Right-click a previously created share in the Details pane and click on Stop Sharing.

4. Recreate the share for the folder that you just stopped sharing.

Configuring Offline Folders

1. Make sure that Fast User Switching is disabled on the computer.

2. Open the Properties dialog box of a shared folder in Windows Explorer.

3. Click on the Sharing tab and click on Caching.

4. In the Caching Settings dialog box, select "Allow Caching of Files In This Shared Folder."

5. From the Settings drop-down menu, select "Automatic Caching of Documents."

Configuring Printer Sharing

1. Open the Printers And Faxes window from the Start menu.

2. Right-click on an installed printer and open the Properties dialog box.

3. Click on the Sharing tab to share the printer.

4. Set the share permissions for the printer.

Managing Print Jobs

1. Locate a large Word document from Windows Explorer, open it, and send it to the printer.
2. Open the Printers And Faxes window from the Start menu.
3. Double-click on the printer to view the document being printed.
4. Select the document, click Document from the menu, and click Pause. Note that the printing stops.
5. Click Document again from the menu and then click on Resume. Check to make sure that the document starts printing again.

Managing Disks and Volumes

1. Open Computer Management and click on the Disk Management node.
2. Examine different disks and volumes on the computer.
3. Check the disk type and how the volumes are formatted.
4. Examine the volume where the system files reside.
5. If any of the disks have unallocated space, create and format a new volume using NTFS.
6. Allocate a drive letter to the new volume.
7. Mount the new volume to an empty NTFS folder on another volume.

Convert a Basic Disk to Dynamic

1. Convert a Basic disk to Dynamic.
2. Create a volume on the newly created Dynamic disk.
3. If possible, expand the Dynamic volume.
4. Create a Spanned or Striped volume.

Using the Diskpart Utility

1. Open the command prompt and run the diskpart.exe command.
2. List the current disks on the computer when the diskpart> interpreter is displayed.
3. Select a disk and list its volumes.

Configuring Disk Quotas

1. Open the properties of an NTFS volume and click the Quota tab.
2. Select the Enable Quota Management checkbox.
3. Select Limit Disk Space and specify a quota of 500 MB.
4. Set the warning level to 400 MB.
5. Click on the Quota Entries button and add users to configure disk quotas.

Configuring Data Compression

1. Open Windows Explorer and locate the folder you wish to compress.
2. Open the Properties dialog box of the folder and click Advanced.
3. In the Advanced Attributes dialog box, click the "Compress Contents To Save the disk Space" checkbox.
4. Click OK in the Confirm Attribute Changes dialog box.

Using Check Disk

1. Open Windows Explorer and open the properties of a disk or volume.
2. Click on the Tools tab and then click Check Now.
3. Select "Scan For And Attempt Recovery of Bad Sectors."

Defragment a Disk

1. Open the Computer Management Console from My Computer or from Administrative Tools in the Control Panel.
2. Click the Disk Defragmenter node under the Storage folder.
3. Select a disk or volume and click on Defragment.

Examining Currently Installed Hardware Devices

1. Open the Device Manager and examine the hardware components installed on the computer.
2. Click on a network adapter and check whether its driver is digitally signed.
3. Click the View menu and select View Resources By Type.

Configuring Driver Signing Options

1. Configure the driver-signing options so that a warning is displayed when someone attempts to install an unsigned device driver.
2. Select Make This Action The System Default.
3. Verify the driver signatures by using the sigverif.exe utility from the command prompt.

Troubleshooting Hardware Devices

1. Open Device Manager and examine the installed network adapter for possible resource conflicts.
2. Start the Hardware Troubleshooter.
3. Examine the options available for troubleshooting.

Configuring Power Options

1. Open the Power Options utility in the Control Panel.
2. Select a power scheme from the available options.

3. Make changes to Turn Off Monitor, Turn Off Hard Disk, and Standby Power Settings.
4. Save the new power scheme with a new name.

Creating New Local Users

1. Open the Computer Management console and click on the Local Users And Groups node.
2. Examine the existing local users under the Users node.
3. Create a few new local users and configure their properties (such as logon hours).

Creating New Local Groups

1. Open the Computer Management console and click on the Local Users And Groups node.
2. Examine the existing local groups under the Groups node.
3. Create a new local group and add users to this group.
4. Verify from the properties of the user account that the membership is listed there.

Using the User Accounts Tool

1. Open the User Accounts tool in the Control Panel.
2. Select an account and modify it.
3. Create a new user account by selecting the Limited account or the Administrator account.
4. Turn on and turn off the Fast User Switching.

Using Task Manager

1. Open the Task Manager from the Task Bar.
2. Examine the current processor and memory usage on the computer.
3. Click on the Processes tab and determine a process with maximum CPU usage.
4. Determine the amount of total virtual memory on the system.
5. Examine the percentage of network utilization from the Networking tab.

Using Performance Console

1. Open the Performance console from Administrative Tools.
2. Open the System Monitor and add processor, memory, and the physical and logical disk counters to the display.
3. Configure performance logging to monitor the processor, memory, and physical and logical disk counters according to a schedule.

4. Configure an alert for when CPU utilization is 90 percent or over and the amount of free disk space is less than 20 percent.

5. Configure an alert when CPU utilization is 90 percent or over, and the amount of free disk space is less than 20 percent.

Managing System Services

1. Open the Services utility from the Administrative Tools in the Control Panel.
2. Examine the services that are configured to start automatically.
3. Right-click on the Automatic Updates service and open its properties.
4. Pause the service and then resume it.
5. Check the dependencies of this service from the Dependencies tab.
6. Open the Recovery tab and configure the system response for the first failure by clicking Restart The Service.

Backing up and Restoring Data

1. Configure Windows Backup to back up drive C: of the computer.
2. Configure a schedule for a weekly backup.
3. Perform a test restore by restoring from the backup on an Alternate Location, and then examine the folder hierarchy.
4. Perform a test restore by restoring from the backup on a Single Folder, and then examine the folder hierarchy.

Examining Advanced Boot Options

1. Restart the computer.
2. Press F8 during the startup process to invoke the Advanced Boot menu.
3. Examine the available boot options.
4. Start the computer in Safe mode.

Using the Recovery Console

1. Install the Recovery Console from the Windows XP Professional setup CD-ROM.
2. Restart the computer and verify that the Recovery Console is available as one of the options in the Advanced Boot menu.
3. Select the Recovery Console from the menu.
4. Display a list of available commands in the Recovery Console.
5. Display a list of services running on the computer.
6. Exit the Recovery Console mode.

Using the Automated System Recovery Wizard

1. Open the Windows Backup utility in Advanced mode and then select the Automated System Recovery Wizard.
2. Select the backup media type and a filename for the backup, and then examine the information displayed by the wizard.
3. Wait for the system to complete the process and prompt for a floppy disk.
4. Mark the floppy disk as ASR Disk and keep it safe.

Configuring Display Properties

1. Open the display properties from the desktop.
2. Examine the available themes and screensavers.
3. Configure the color schemes and font sizes from the Appearance tab.
4. Set the color quality to a high 32 bits and the screen resolution to 1024×768 pixels from the Settings tab.
5. Launch the troubleshooter to explore the troubleshooting options for the display adapter.

Configuring Multiple Locations and Languages

1. Open the Regional And Language Options in the Control Panel.
2. Select any additional country or region, standards, and text formatting in the Regional Options page.
3. Add one more language in the Languages page.
4. Verify that the two languages are displayed in the "Text Services and Input Languages" dialog box.

Configuring User Profiles

1. Open the System properties from the Control Panel and click the Advanced tab.
2. Open the User Profiles dialog box and examine the existing profiles.
3. Create a new user account.
4. Log on and log off with the new user account.
5. Log on and log off with your credentials.
6. Open the User Profiles dialog box again and examine the profile of the new user.
7. Delete the profile of the new user.

Creating a New Network Connection

1. Use the New Connection Wizard.
2. Create a connection to connect to the Internet.

3. Verify that the new connection appears in the Local Area Connection window.

4. Disable the new connection. Enable it and examine its properties.

Configuring a Static IP Address

1. Open the properties of the Local Area Connection.

2. Open the TCP/IP properties of the network adapter.

3. Click on the Use The Following IP Address button.

4. Configure the static IP address, subnet mask, and default gateway for the network adapter.

5. Click on the Advanced tab and examine the DNS properties.

6. Verify that the default DNS settings are configured for the network adapter.

Using TCP/IP Troubleshooting Utilities

1. Verify the TCP/IP configuration of the computer by using the Ping command and the 127.0.0.1 IP address.

2. Use the Ping command to verify connectivity to another computer, if available.

3. Disconnect the network cable and use the Ping command again. Check the results.

4. Reconnect the network cable.

5. Use the Tracert command to check the network path to an Internet web site.

6. Use the Pathping command to check the network path to an Internet web site.

7. Examine the difference between the outputs of the Tracert and the Pathping commands.

Configuring Internet Options

1. Open the Internet Options from the Control Panel with Internet Explorer.

2. Set the home page to *http://www.oreilly.com/*.

3. Set the History to the 10 last-visited web sites.

4. Configure a security level for the Local Intranet zone.

5. Enable the Content Advisor.

6. Examine the different configuration options in the Advanced tab.

Configuring Remote Desktop

1. Open the System properties from the Control Panel and click on the Remote tab.

2. Click "Allow Users to Connect Remotely To This Computer."

3. Select users who are allowed to make a remote desktop connection to this computer.

Accessing the Local Security Policy Snap-in

1. Open an empty Microsoft Management Console (MMC).
2. Click Add/Remove Snap-in.
3. Add the Local Security Policy snap-in from the displayed standalone snap-ins.

Password Policy

1. Examine the current settings in the Password Policy.
2. Enable the Password History policy and configure it to six passwords.
3. Enable the Maximum Password Age policy and configure it to 30 days.
4. Enable the Minimum Password Length and set it to eight characters.
5. Enable the Passwords Must Meet Complexity Requirements option.

Account Lockout Policy

1. Examine the current settings in the Account Lockout Policy.
2. Enable the Account Lockout Duration policy and set it to 10 minutes.
3. Enable the Account Lockout Threshold policy and set it to four passwords.

Configuring the Security Options and User Rights

1. Examine the various Security Options available for configuration.
2. Rename the Administrator account.
3. Disable the Guest account.
4. Enable the "Devices: Restrict CD-ROM Access to Locally Logged On Users Only" policy.
5. Assign the Load And Unload Device Drivers to a user or group.
6. Enable the "Take Ownership of Files And other Objects" checkbox and add users or groups.

Enabling the Audit Policy

1. Examine the various Security Options available for configuration.
2. Enable the "Audit Logon Events for Success" events.
3. Enable the "Audit Object Access for Success and Failure" events.
4. Enable the "System Events for Failure" events.

Using Security Templates

1. Add the Security Templates snap-in to an empty MMC.
2. Select the *compatws.inf* template and save it as a different file.
3. Expand the new template file.
4. Make changes to the Password Policy, Account Lockout Policy, Security Options, and the User Rights and Audit Policy.

Analyzing System Security and Applying a Security Template

1. Add the Security Configuration And Analysis snap-in to an empty MMC.
2. Import the previously created Security Template.
3. Analyze the current security settings of the computer with those configured in the template.
4. Apply the new Security Template to the computer.

Exam 70-270 Highlighters Index

In this section, we've attempted to compile the facts, within the exam's subject areas, that you are most likely to use, as well as provide another look at the areas of study that you might have highlighted while reading the Study Guide. The title of each highlighted element corresponds to the heading title in the Exam 70-270 Study Guide. This way, if you have a question about a highlighted area, you can refer back to the corresponding section in the Study Guide. For the most part, the entries under a heading are organized as term lists, to present a Windows XP Professional feature, a component, or a configuration tool. The terms and key details for each feature, component, or configuration tool are then listed.

Installing Microsoft Windows XP Professional

This subsection covers the summary of highlights from the "Installing Microsoft Windows XP Professional" section of the Exam 70-270 Study Guide.

Minimum hardware requirements
Make sure the computer meets the minimum hardware requirements as given in Table 3-1.

Table 3-1. Windows XP Professional hardware requirements

Item	Minimum required	Recommended
CPU	Pentium 233 MHz.	Pentium II 300 MHz or faster
RAM	64 MB	128 MB (4 GB maximum supported)
Hard disk space	1.5 GB Free	2 GB
Display	VGA adapter and monitor	Super VGA (SVGA) monitor and PnP monitor
Network interface	Not necessary (required if installing over the network)	Any network adapter (required if installing over the network)
CD-ROM	12X (not required if installing over the network)	Faster-speed CD-ROM and a DVD-ROM drive

Disk partitions and filesystems
• You can create a partition before starting the installation or during it.
• You should create only one partition as required for the installation.
• If you are dual-booting Windows XP Professional with an older OS, install Windows XP Professional on a separate partition.

- You can choose from FAT, FAT32, or NTFS filesystems.
- FAT supports only eight-character filenames with a three-character extension, and supports a maximum of a 2 GB partition size in Windows 95, Windows 98, and Windows ME.
- In Windows NT 4.0 and Windows 2000, FAT supports up to 16 GB partitions.
- Fat 32 is supported in Windows 95 (OSR2) and later operating systems, and supports up to 2 TB disk partitions.
- NTFS is the preferred filesystem and has the following benefits:
  — File- and folder-level security.
  — Encrypting File System (EFS).
  — Disk quotas to manage usage of disk space.
  — File compression to save disk space.
  — Dynamic disks to create Dynamic volumes, mounted volumes, and remote storage.
- All disks are initialized as Basic disks.
- You can convert a FAT partition to NTFS without loosing data by using the Disk Management utility or by using the following command:

      convert D: /FS:NTFS

- When dual-booting with older operating systems, you should keep the FAT filesystem.

Installation methods

- Attended installation is performed using the Windows XP Professional setup CD-ROM.
- Installation starts with the Text mode when the basic installation files are copied to the hard disk.
- You can install any third-party device drivers by pressing F6 during this phase.
- You can configure disk partitions and select a filesystem for formatting the selected partition.
- Regional and language options and networking components are installed during the GUI mode.
- You can join a workgroup or a domain during this phase or installation.
- Over the network, installation requires that you should be able to connect to a network file server that holds the necessary installation files.
- You will need to specify the correct path of the \i386 folder.
- You should use the winnt.exe command if you are installing from the MS-DOS operating system.
- You should use the winnt32.exe command if you are installing from the Windows 95, Windows 98, Windows ME, or Windows NT 4.0 operating systems.
- Tables 3-2 and 3-3 list the parameters for the winnt.exe and winnt32.exe commands.

Table 3-2. winnt.exe parameters

Parameter	Function
/r[folder]	Copies and saves an optional folder. The folder is saved after installation.
/rx[:folder]	Copies an optional folder. The folder is deleted after installation.
/s[:sourcepath]	Specifies the location of source files in the format \\server\share\[path].
/t[:tempdrive]	Specifies the temp drive to contain installation files. By default, the drive with most available space is selected.
/u[:scriptfile]	Specifies a script file in case the installation is unattended. This parameter must be used with the /s parameter.
/udf:id[,UDF_file]	Specifies the identifiers that setup uses to see how a uniqueness database file (UDF) modifies the answer file. The parameters given in the UDF file override the parameters given in the answer file. If you do not specify a UDF file, you are prompted to insert a disk containing the $UNIQUE$.UDB file.

Table 3-3. winnt32.exe parameters

Parameter	Function
/checkupgradeonly	Checks the computer only if it can be upgraded to Windows XP Professional.
/cmd:command_line	Specifies a command that should be run immediately after restart of the computer when the text phase is complete.
/cmdcons	Installs Recovery Console as a startup option.
/copydir:foldername	Creates an additional folder with the %systemroot% folder.
/debug[level] [:filename]	Creates a debug file at the specified level from 0 to 4. The default level is 2, and this file collects information about setup warnings. The default debug file is C:\Winnt32.log.
/duddisable	Disables dynamic updates during installation.
/makelocalsource	Specifies that setup should copy all installation files to the local hard drive.
/noreboot	Executes another command before restarting the computer when the text phase is complete.
/s:sourcepath	Specifies the location of source files for the Windows XP Professional installation.
/syspart:[driveletter]	Copies the installation files to the specified drive and makes it active. This parameter must be used with /tempdrive parameter. This command works only on computers running Windows NT4.0, Windows 2000, and Windows XP Professional.
/tempdrive:driveletter	Copies installation files on this temporary drive and installs the operating system on it.
/udf:id[,UDF_file]	Specifies the identifiers that setup uses to see how a uniqueness database file (UDF) modifies the answer file. The parameters given in the UDF file override the parameters given in the answer file. If you do not specify a UDF file, you are prompted to insert a disk containing the $UNIQUE$.UDB file.
/unattend	Upgrades previous versions of Windows 98, Windows ME, Windows NT 4.0, and Windows 2000 without any user input. Also downloads dynamic updates during installation and includes the installation files. Copies all user settings from previous version of Windows.
/unattend[num]:[answer-file]	Used to perform a fresh installation of Windows XP Professional in unattended mode using the specified answer file. The num option specifies the time that must lapse after copying of files before restarting of the computer. Dynamic updates are downloaded and included in installation files.

Upgrading from previous operating systems

- Before upgrading from a previous Windows operating system, check the hardware compatibility by using the following command:

  ```
  winnt32 /checkupgradeonly
  ```

- Make sure that the previous operating system can be directly upgraded to the Windows XP Professional.

  Table 3-4 lists the available upgrade paths.

Table 3-4. Windows XP Professional upgrade paths

Previous operating system	Upgrade
Windows NT 3.1, 3.5, 3.51	Upgrade to Windows NT 4.0 Workstation first. Then upgrade to Windows XP Professional.
Windows 95	Upgrade to Windows 98 first. Then upgrade to Windows XP Professional.
Windows 98	Directly upgrade to Windows XP Professional.
Windows ME	Directly upgrade to Windows XP Professional.
Windows NT 4.0 Workstation	Directly upgrade to Windows XP Professional.
Windows 2000 Professional with SP6 or later	Directly upgrade to Windows XP Professional.
Windows XP Home	Directly upgrade to Windows XP Professional.

Automating the installation

- The following three utilities help in automating the installation of Windows XP Professional for large-scale deployments:

  Setup Manager (setupmgr.exe)
  Used to create answer files for unattended installations.

  System Preparation Tool (sysprep.exe)
  Used to prepare a master or reference computer so that a third-party imaging tool can be used to create an image of the hard disk.

  Remote Installation Service (RIS)
  Used in an Active Directory domain to distribute images to client computers.

- Setup Manager and System Preparation Tool are located in the \Support\Tools folder on the Windows XP Professional setup CD-ROM and must be extracted from the *Deploy.cab* file to the hard disk.

Using Setup Manager

- Setup Manager creates three files named *unattend.txt, unattend.udb* and *unattend.bat*.

- Unattended installation using answer files created by Setup Manager is started using one of the following commands on the target computer:

  From an MS-DOS or Windows 3.x computer, use the following command:

  ```
  winnt.exe [/s:SourcePath][/u:AnswerFile]]/udf:ID[,UDB_File]]
  ```

  From other client operating systems, use the following command:

  ```
  winnt32.exe [/unattend[num]:[AnswerFile][/udf:ID [,UDB_File]]
  ```

- Setup Manager runs a mini-setup wizard on the computer where the unattended installation is performed.

Using System Preparation Tool

- Sysprep is used to prepare a master or reference computer for imaging by a third-party imaging utility.
- As required on target computers, you should install Windows XP Professional and all applications on the master computer.
- Sysprep removes all computer-specific information from the reference computer.
- Table 3-5 lists the parameters that can be used with the sysprep.exe command.

Table 3-5. Sysprep parameters

Parameter	Function
/quite	The user is not prompted for any input
/nosidgen	The utility does not generate any SID after the reboot
/pnp	Forces the Setup to detect PnP devices on destination computers
/reboot	Restarts the master computer after Sysprep is complete
/noreboot	Shuts down the computer without rebooting
/forceshutdown	Forces the computer to complete shutdown

Remote Installation Service (RIS)

- RIS runs on a Windows Server 2003 computer in an Active Directory domain.
- The RIS server is authorized in the Active Directory to distribute disk images to client computers.
- The RIS server can download a preconfigured disk image to the client computer, or the client computer can choose from one of the available images located on the RIS server.
- The following three services must be running in the network to successfully perform RIS installations:

  DNS service
  RIS service depends on DNS service to locate directory service and RIS clients.

  DHCP service
  This service is required by client computers to obtain an initial IP address.

  Active Directory service
  RIS clients use the directory service to locate the RIS server on the network.

- RIS client computers must conform to *NetPC* specifications or should have *PXE* standard network adapters so that they can initially boot from the network.

- For other computers, you can use the Remote Boot Disk Generator utility (rbfg.exe) to create a boot disk.

Post-installation updates

- The Windows XP Professional must be activated within 30 days of installation. The activation can be done over the phone or over the Internet.

- Automatic Updates is used to configure the Windows XP Professional computer to automatically download and install critical system updates.

- Automatic Updates can also be configured in an Active Directory domain where a Windows Software Update Service (WSUS) server downloads all updates for client computers.

- Service packs are collections of several updates in a single file. A service pack can be installed by running the update.exe command once it has been downloaded from the Microsoft web site.

- *Slipstreaming* is the process of combining the installation of service packs with the installation of Windows XP Professional installation.

- Service packs installed using the slipstreaming process cannot be uninstalled.

Troubleshooting failed installations

- If the Windows XP Professional setup CD-ROM does not work, try running it on another CD-ROM drive.

- If setup cannot copy initial setup files from the CD-ROM, you may have insufficient RAM.

- If there is not enough space on the hard disk, add another hard disk.

- If you get an error from a virus scanner saying that an application is attempting to infect the BIOS, disable the virus scanner.

- If a dependency service fails during the GUI phase of the installation, make sure that the network adapter and its settings are correct and that the computer name is unique on the network.

- If the computer cannot connect to a domain controller for joining the domain, make sure that you supplied the correct domain name, the DNS service is running, and your network adapter can communicate on the network.

- You should examine two logfiles generated by the installation process. These files are as follows:

  Setupact.log
  This file contains all the actions performed by setup.

  Setuperr.log
  This file contains all errors generated by setup.

Windows XP Professional startup process

- The startup process starts with the Power-On Self Test (POST) that performs various tests on the computer hardware.

- An appropriate boot device should be located and the master boot record (MBR) should be loaded from the boot device. MBR in turn loads the NTLDR file. In case the computer has a SCSI device, the *NTBOOTDD.SYS* file is loaded.

- The NTLDR switches the boot loader phase to a 32-bit flat memory mode and loads the filesystem driver to load Fat, FAT32, or NTFS partitions.
- The NTLDR reads the *BOOT.INI* file and selects the operating system.
- The NTLDR calls on the *NTDETECT.COM* file to perform the detection of hardware devices.
- The Kernel Load phase begins when NTLDR calls on the *NTOSKERNEL. EXE* file to be loaded. The screen color is changed from black to blue.
- The Kernel creates a registry key known as HKEY_LOCAL_MACHINE\ HARDWARE.
- The Kernel creates a Clone Control Set by copying the control set in the HKEY_LOCAL_MACHINE\SYSTEM\Select subkey of registry.
- The Kernel loads low-level device drivers and filesystems. The devices start initializing as they are loaded. The computer then changes to the GUI mode.
- The system services are started and the logon process starts when the *winlogon* service starts. The Logon To Windows screen is then displayed.
- Once you log on successfully, the Clone Control Set is copied to the Current Control Set in the registry.
- Table 3-6 lists the files that are used in the startup process.

Table 3-6. Windows XP Professional startup files

Filename	Startup phase	Location
NTLDR	Pre-boot and Boot	System Partition Root (usually C:\ drive)
BOOT.INI	Boot	System Partition Root (usually C:\ drive)
BOOTSECT.DOS	Boot (used if MS-DOS is used)	System Partition Root (usually C:\ drive)
NTDETECT.SYS	Boot	System Partition Root (usually C:\ drive)
NTBOOTDD.SYS	Boot (used if a SCSI device is used to boot)	System Partition Root (usually C:\ drive)
NTOSKRNL.EXE	%systemroot%\System32	Kernel Load
HAL.DLL	%systemroot%\System32	Kernel Load
SYSTEM	%systemroot%\System32	Kernel Initialization

The BOOT.INI file

- The *BOOT.INI* file is loaded by the NTLDR and is used to display a menu of operating systems installed on the computer.
- The *BOOT.INI* file consists of two sections: boot loader and operating systems.
- The boot loader section lists the installed operating systems and a timeout value.
- The operating systems section contains Advanced RISC Computing (ARC) paths that direct the boot loader to the correct boot partition where the selected operating system is installed.

- The *BOOT.INI* file can be changed from the System utility in the Control Panel.
- You should click on the Advanced button and then click on the Startup And Recovery button to change the default operating system and timeout value.

Windows Registry

- The Windows Registry is a collection of system configuration settings in a hierarchical datafile.
- The hierarchy is organized into keys and subkeys, each of which can have one or more values.
- The value can be a text identifier, string, binary, word, or extendable string.
- The five main subtrees of the Registry are as follows:

HKEY_CLASSES_ROOT
> This subkey contains Object Linking and Embedding (OLE) data and file associations.

HKEY_CURRENT_USER
> This subkey contains data about the currently logged-on user.

HKEY_LOCAL_MACHINE
> This subkey contains all the hardware-specific configuration data.

HKEY_USERS
> This subkey contains the default set of configuration settings as well as data for each user profile.

HKEY_CURRENT_CONFIG
> This subkey contains data about the currently loaded hardware profile.b

Implementing and Conducting Administration of Resources

This subsection covers the summary of highlights from the "Implementing and Conducting Administration of Resources" section in the Exam 70-270 Study Guide.

NTFS permissions

- Each object on an NTFS has an associated Access Control List (ACL).
- The ACL controls the level of access granted to users or groups.
- The permissions are set either to Allow or Deny.
- The Full Control permission includes all other permissions.
- The Deny permission denies all access to the file or folder
- Table 3-7 lists the NTFS file permissions, and Table 3-8 lists the NTFS folder permissions.

Table 3-7. NTFS file permissions

Permission	Description
Read	Read the file and its attributes, permissions, and ownership.
Read and Execute	Run the file; access granted by Read permission.

Table 3-7. NTFS file permissions (continued)

Permission	Description
Write	Overwrite the file, change file attributes, and view permissions and ownership.
Modify	Modify and delete the file; access granted by the Write and the Read and Execute permissions.
Full Control	All actions permitted by other NTFS permissions, plus this allows the user to change permissions and take ownership.

Table 3-8. NTFS folder permissions

Permission	Description
Read	View the folder's files and subfolders as well as its attributes and permissions.
List Folder Contents	View the names of files and subfolders.
Read and Execute	Move through folders and subfolders; other permissions granted by Read and List Folder Contents permissions.
Write	Create new files and subfolders within the folder and change folder attributes.
Modify	Delete the folder; other permissions granted by the Read and Execute and the Write permissions.
Full Control	Change permissions, delete files and subfolders, and take ownership. Includes all other NTFS folder permissions.

Calculating effective permissions
- A user can be assigned multiple permissions to a resource based on his group memberships.
- The effective NTFS permissions on a resource are the combination of all permissions.
- Permissions can also be inherited from parent folders.
- Individual file permissions override permissions inherited from the parent folder.
- The Deny permission overrides all other permissions.

Copying and moving files and folders
- If a file or folder is *copied* with the same NTFS volume or across NTFS volumes, it gets the permissions are assigned to the destination folder.
- If a file or folder is *moved within* the same NTFS volume, it retains its original permissions.
- If a file or folder is *moved across* NTFS volumes, the permissions are assigned to the destination volume.
- If a file or folder is copied or moved to a FAT/FAT32 volume, all NTFS permissions are lost.

Shared folders
- Folders are shared to allow other users on the network to access your files or folders.
- Individual files cannot be shared.

- *Simple File Sharing* allows everyone on the network to have the same level of access to the folder.
- Simple File Sharing is not available when the computer is a member of the domain.
- *Folder Sharing* allows you to set different levels of share permissions for individual users or groups.
- Shared folders are created either from the Windows Explorer or from the Computer Management console.
- The operating system creates some hidden shares for administrative purposes and is appended with a dollar ($) sign.
- Admin$, C$, D$ and Print$ are examples of hidden administrative shares.
- Hidden shares are not visible when someone browses your computer for shared resources.

Shared Folder permissions

- Shared Folder permissions are effective only when the folder is accessed from the network.
- The Everyone group is assigned Read permissions by default when a folder is shared.
- Share permissions can be assigned to shares on NTFS, FAT, and Fat32 volumes.
- Table 3-9 lists the Shared Folder permissions:

Table 3-9. Shared Folder permissions

Permission	Description
Read	View folder name and attributes, view and execute files, and change folders within the shared folder.
Change	Add files to the folders, create subfolders, change data in files, delete files and folders, and change file attributes. Also, allow the actions that can be performed by Read permission.
Full Control	Take ownership and change permissions of the folder, subfolders, and files within the shared folder. In addition, all permissions assigned by the Read and Change permissions.

Combining NTFS and Share permissions

- Users must have the NTFS permissions on a folder in addition to Share permissions in order to access the folder or files within the folder.
- Effective permissions are calculated as follows:
    a. Calculate the effective NTFS permissions—that is, the sum of all NTFS permissions assigned individually and through group memberships.
    b. Calculate the effective Shared Folder permissions assigned individually or through group memberships.
    c. The most restrictive of the NTFS and Share permissions applies to the user.

Offline files and folders
- The offline files feature allows you to keep working on documents even when you are not connected to the network.
- Fast User Switching must be disabled in order to configure offline files.
- You must first enable offline files from the Offline Files option and configure the synchronization options.
- Offline caching of documents allows you to configure one of the following three settings:
  — Manual Caching of Documents
  — Automatic Caching of Documents
  — Automatic Caching of Documents and Programs
- The Synchronization Manager utility is available in the Accessories folder.
- The Synchronize button forces the synchronization of offline files with their versions on the network file server.
- You can schedule synchronization of files and folders with the following three options:

  Logon/Logoff
      Allows you to synchronize on logon, logoff, or both.

  On Idle
      Synchronizes when the computer is idle and connected to the network.

  Schedule
      Allows you to set a predetermined schedule for synchronization.

Managing print devices
- A *local printer* is the one that is connected directly to one of the ports on the computer.
- A *network printer* is the one that is connected directly to a network port.
- The computer configured to share a print device is known as a *print server*.
- The print server must have sufficient hard disk space and large amounts of RAM to accommodate print jobs submitted by the printing clients.
- A printer installed and shared on a Windows XP Professional computer allows only 10 concurrent connections.
- Printing from Windows, NetWare, and Macintosh clients is supported for shared printers on the Windows XP Professional.
- You must add an LPR port if you want to share printers for Unix clients.

Installing and sharing a printer
- Printers are added and configured from the Printers and Faxes utility.
- The Add Printer Wizard walks you through the installation process.
- You can add the printer to a preconfigured local port such as LPT1.
- You will need to create a new port if you wish to add a printer connected directly to a network port.

- When you share the printer, you can specify the Windows clients that will be using the printer.
- Windows XP Professional will automatically download printer drivers for Windows 2000, Windows NT 4.0, Windows ME, Windows 98, and Windows 95 clients.

Configuring printer properties

- The General tab allows you to specify printer location, set printing preferences, and print a test page.
- The Sharing tab allows you to share the printer or stop sharing it, as well as install additional printer drivers.
- The Ports tab allows you to configure the port connected to the printer. Printer pooling is enabled from this page.
- The Security tab allows you to set printing permissions for local and network users.
- The Advanced tab allows you to configure the availability of the printer and set printer priority and spooling options.
- The Device Settings tab varies from one printer to another and contains device-specific settings.
- The Color Management tab allows you to configure color options so that the displayed and printed colors are consistent.

Printer pooling

- *Printer pooling* helps in sharing the printing load among two or more printers.
- You can enable printer pooling if you have two or more identical printers.
- All printers must use the same printer driver and should be installed to the same port.

Printer priorities

- *Printer priorities* are used to allow users with high-priority jobs to print faster than normal users.
- You must create multiple logical printers for the same physical printer to configure printer priorities.
- Each logical printer is actually connected to the same port.
- Priorities range from 1 to 99, where 99 is the highest priority.
- Printer permissions are assigned separately for each logical printer.

Print permissions

- *Printing permissions* are assigned to control the level of access to local and network users.
- Table 3-10 lists the available print permissions.

Table 3-10. Windows XP Professional print permissions

Permission	Description
Print	Print documents, as well as pause, resume, and cancel user's own documents.
Manage Documents	Pause, resume, and cancel all users' documents. Also provides Print permissions.
Manage Printers	Share a printer, change permissions, delete a printer, and cancel all documents.All actions are permitted by the Print and the Manage Documents permissions.

Managing print jobs
- The Printers and Faxes window lists installed printers on the computer.
- You should double-click on any printer to view the jobs submitted to the printer (print queue).
- The Manage Printers permission allows a user to pause, resume, cancel, or redirect print jobs to another printer in addition to sharing and deleting printers.
- If a printer is having a problem, you can redirect all jobs in the print queue to another printer.
- Individual jobs in the print queue cannot be redirected.

Connecting to an Internet printer
- Internet Information Services must be installed in order to use Internet printing.
- To access a shared printer using a web browser, type *http://PrintServer/PrinterName*.
- To view a list of all available shared printers, type *http://PrintServer/printers*.

Managing Hardware Devices and Drivers

This subsection covers the summary of highlights from the "Managing Hardware Devices and Drivers" section in the Exam 70-270 Study Guide.

Basic disks
- All disks are initialized as Basic.
- Basic disks are organized into partitions.
- A Basic disk can have up to four primary partitions or three primary and one extended partition.
- One of the primary partitions is marked as active and holds the boot files.
- Primary partitions are formatted using the FAT, FAT32, or NTFS filesystem.
- Logical drives are created in an extended partition.

Dynamic disks
- Disks are converted to Dynamic using the Disk Management utility.
- You can create volumes on Dynamic disks to organize files and folders.
- The Dynamic disk is not supported on portable computers.
- Dynamic volumes can be extended on a single disk or on multiple disks.

- You can create Simple, Spanned, and Striped volumes on Dynamic disks.
- Fault-tolerant volumes such as RAID-1 and RAID-5 are supported only on server operating systems.

Simple, Spanned, and Striped volumes

- A Simple volume contains space from a single Dynamic disk.
- Simple volumes can be formatted with Fat, FAT32, or NTFS filesystems.
- Spanned volumes contain space from multiple disks.
- You can create a Spanned volume by combining unallocated space from 2 to 32 Dynamic disks.
- If one of the disks in a Spanned volume fails, the entire volume fails and all data is lost.
- Striped volumes contain unallocated space from 2 to 32 Dynamic disks.
- All disks must be identical and preferably have equal disk space.
- If the space on participating disks is unequal, then only the space equal to the smallest disk is used from each disk.
- Striped volumes offer better performance and more efficient use of disk space.
- Data is written to the Striped volume in 64 KB chunks.
- Striped volumes cannot be extended.
- Striped volumes are not fault-tolerant, and if one of the disks in the volume fails, then the entire volume fails and all data is lost.

Disk Management

- The Disk Management utility is a part of the Computer Management console.
- You can create, delete, and format partitions using Disk Management, as well as assign drive letters.
- You can convert disks from Basic to Dynamic and create Dynamic volumes.
- Converting from a Basic to Dynamic disk is a one-way process and can be done without losing data.
- You must back up all data before converting a Dynamic disk back to a Basic disk.

Mounted volumes

- *Volume Mount Points* are used to extend available disk space without actually extending the size of the volume.
- Volumes can be mounted on existing FAT/FAT32 or NTFS volumes.
- The volume that you wish to mount must be NTFS.

Using Diskpart to manage disks

- Diskpart is a command-line utility for managing disks and volumes.
- Running diskpart.exe at the command prompt starts the diskpart> command interpreter.
- You can list the disks and volumes available on the computer and select a disk or volume to manage.

Disk quotas

- *Disk quotas* are used to effectively use the available space on NTFS volumes.
- Disk quotas are configured on a per-user basis and are not based on groups.
- You can limit the space allocated to a user and set a warning level.
- You can deny disk space to a user when she reaches the configured quota level.
- You can set the same quota for all users or set different quotas for individual users from the Quota Entries button.

Disk Compression

- *Compression* is used in Windows XP Professional to save disk space by compressing files and folders.
- The *Compressed Folders* feature in Windows XP Professional keeps all files compressed in the folder.
- This feature does not work on individual files.
- Disk Compression works on both FAT and NTFS volumes.
- Any new files added to the compressed folder are automatically compressed.
- The *NTFS Compression* is available only on NTFS volumes.
- The NTFS Compression works on individual files also.

Copying and moving compressed files

- If a file from a compressed folder is moved out of the folder, it is automatically uncompressed.
- When a compressed file is copied to another folder on the same NTFS volume or across NTFS volumes, it gets the compression attributes of the destination folder.
- When a file is moved on the same NTFS volume, it retains its compression attributes.
- When a file is moved across NTFS volumes, it gets the compression attributes of the destination folder.
- When a file is copied or moved to a FAT or FAT32 volume, it loses its compression attributes.

Encrypting File System (EFS)

- EFS can be enabled on NTFS volumes to secure files and folders from unauthorized access.
- EFS uses Public Key Cryptography to encrypt the documents.
- Only the person who has the private key can decrypt the document.
- The private key is usually included in the logon credentials of a user.
- When an authorized user opens an encrypted file, it is automatically decrypted and encrypted again when he closes it.
- Encryption is enabled from the Advanced Attributes dialog box of the file or folder properties.

- You can also use the `cipher.exe` command to encrypt or decrypt documents.
- Encryption and NTFS compression are mutually exclusive and cannot be used together.

Maintaining disks

- Hard disks become defragmented when they become aged, when a large number of files are deleted, or when some applications are installed.
- The Disk Defragmenter works by reorganizing files on the disk into contiguous spaces.
- The defragmentation process increases the efficiency of the hard disk.
- The Check Disk (`chkdsk`) utility is used to check for and recover bad sectors on a hard disk.
- Check Disk can also attempt to locate and automatically recover filesystem errors.
- The Disk Cleanup utility helps free up disk space by removing unwanted files from the disk.
- Disk Cleanup removes files in the temp folder and temporary Internet files from the cache memory, and empties the Recycle Bin.

Installing hardware devices

- Most of the PnP devices are automatically detected and configured by Windows XP Professional.
- The Add Hardware Wizard in the Control Panel can be used to install non-PnP devices or PnP devices that are not detected by the Windows XP Professional.
- Before adding hardware, you must first determine the resources, such as I/O port, DMA, and IRQ, that will be assigned to the non-PnP device.
- The System Information utility located in the System applet of the Control Panel allows you to view information about installed devices and resources used by devices, and is very useful when you have resource conflicts or other hardware problems.

Device Manager

- Hardware devices are managed by using the Device Manager utility in Computer Management.
- Undetected or non-PnP devices are listed as Unknown in the Device Manager if an appropriate device driver is not installed.
- You can install a device driver for a non-PnP device from the Device Manager.
- The Device Manager lists the resources used by all hardware devices and also shows whether there are any resource conflicts.
- You can also view the resources used by devices by using Resources By Connection from the View menu.
- The Driver tab in the properties of a device allows you to perform the following actions:

Driver Details
> This page displays information about the device driver.

Update Driver
> You can update the device driver if a newer version is available from the device vendor.

Roll Back Driver
> If an updated device driver does not work as expected, you can roll back the driver.

Uninstall Driver
> You can uninstall a device driver when you wish to remove a device from the system.

Driver Signing

- *Driver Signing* ensures that only device drivers that have been tested by the Windows Hardware Quality Labs (WHQL) are installed on a Windows XP Professional computer.
- All drivers tested by WHQL carry a digital signature.
- There are three options to control how the system responds when a user attempts to install an unsigned device driver:

Ignore
> This option allows installation of unsigned drivers.

Warn
> This option displays a warning but allows installation.

Block
> This option will not allow installation of an unsigned device driver.

- Administrators can make any of the above options a system default by clicking on the Make This Option The System Default button.
- Device driver signatures can be verified by using the sigverif.exe utility from the command prompt.

Hardware profiles

- When you have different hardware configurations for the same computer, you may use hardware profiles.
- Hardware profiles are mostly useful on portable computers.
- Certain devices such as a network adapter or keyboard can be enabled in one hardware profile and disabled in another.
- Hardware profiles are displayed when the system boots, and you can choose one of the profiles to use.
- Windows XP Professional manages hardware profiles dynamically.

Multiple monitors

- Windows XP Professional allows you to add up to 10 monitors to the computer to extend the display.
- All monitors must be identical in resolution, color quality, and display size.
- All display devices must be PCI- or AGP-compatible.

- The integrated display adapter in the motherboard must also support multiple displays and is treated as a secondary display adapter.
- The Extend My Windows Desktop Onto This Monitor checkbox in Display Properties is used for each monitor to configure multiple monitors.

Input/output (I/O) devices

- Windows XP Professional supports most of the available PnP I/O devices.
- Newer PnP I/O devices are automatically detected and installed by the operating system.
- You can attach up to 127 USB devices to the USB ports. Most USB ports support *hot plugging*.
- The keyboard and mouse are either PS2- or USB-compatible and need little configuration.
- Scanners and cameras are usually USB devices and come with their own software.
- You can install scanners and cameras from the Scanners And Cameras utility in the Control Panel. They are detected automatically, and you can install their software when prompted by the operating system.
- Smart card readers are usually the size of a credit card and store personal information.
- Smart cards also carry authentication credentials such as public or private keys that are used in Public Key Cryptography.
- Smart cards need a smart card reader connected to a Windows XP Professional computer and smart card service running on the computer.
- Most internal IrDA, or Infrared devices, are automatically detected and installed when the operating system is installed.
- External IrDA devices must be installed using the Add Hardware utility in the Control Panel.
- Once installed, a Wireless Link utility appears in the Control Panel and can be used to manage these devices.

Power Options

- The Windows XP Professional supports Advanced Power Management (APM) and Advanced Power Interface (ACPI).
- The computer BIOS must support these features.
- APM and ACPI are configured from the Power Options utility in the Control Panel.
- Table 3-11 lists built-in power schemes in Windows XP Professional.

Table 3-11. Power schemes available in Windows XP Professional

Power scheme	Used for	Turn off monitor	Turn off hard disk
Home/Office Desk	Desktop	After 20 minutes	Never
Portable/Laptop	Portable/laptop	After 15 minutes	After 30 minutes
Presentation	Desktop/laptop	Never	Never

Table 3-11. Power schemes available in Windows XP Professional (continued)

Power scheme	Used for	Turn off monitor	Turn off hard disk
Always On	Personal servers	After 20 minutes	Never
Minimal Power Management	Desktops	After 15 minutes	Never
Max Battery	Portable/laptop	After 15 minutes	Never

- If none of the built-in power schemes fit your needs, you can modify one of the schemes.
- The Advanced tab of the Power Options allows you to configure a password when the computer resumes from a standby mode.
- The Advanced Power Management is available in Power Options in only those computers that do not support ACPI.
- In *Standby* mode, Windows XP Professional turns off power to the monitor, the hard disk, and most of the peripherals. When you move the mouse or press a key, the system resumes by turning on all these components.
- In *Hibernate* mode, the operating system saves the information in memory and then shuts down the system. When you turn on the system again, you are returned to the system state that you left idle.

Managing User and Group Accounts

This subsection covers the summary of highlights from the "Managing User and Group Accounts" section in the Exam 70-270 Study Guide.

Local and domain accounts
- The local user and group accounts are available on computers that are stand-alone or part of a workgroup.
- The local accounts allow access to resources located on the local computer only.
- The local accounts are stored in the Local Security Database.
- The domain accounts are created in a domain environment and are stored in the Active Directory database on domain controllers.
- A person with a domain user account can log in to and access resources located anywhere in the Active Directory domain.
- When you log on to the domain, the domain controller creates an access token for your credentials that remains valid until you remain logged on to the domain.

Built-in local user accounts
- The *Administrator* account has full control over the system. You should rename this account and configure a strong password.
- The *Guest* account is used for persons who do not need regular access to the system. This account is disabled by default.

- The *HelpAssistant* account is used by those users who log on to the system using *Remote Assistance.*

- The *InitialUser* account is created when the operating system is installed and is used to activate Windows XP Professional.

- The *SUPPORT_xxxxx* account is the account used by the Help And Support Center.

Guidelines for creating new user accounts

- The user logon names must be unique in the network.

- You can have up to 20 characters in the logon name.

- Some special characters cannot be used in usernames. These are: " / \ [ ] ; : | = , + < > ? and *.

- The passwords can be up to 128 characters long.

- You should implement a policy of strong passwords and let users manage their own passwords.

Creating new user accounts

- The user accounts can be created either from the User Accounts utility in the Control Panel or from the Local Users and Groups utility in Computer Management.

- The User Accounts tool lets you create only two types of accounts: *Administrator* and *Limited Account.*

- The Local Users and Groups utility in Computer Management has two nodes: *Users* and *Groups.*

- You can create, delete, and manage the properties of the user accounts.

- When you create a new user account, the following account options are available:

  User Must Change Password At Next Logon
  This option is selected by default.

  User Cannot Change Password
  Use this option if the first option is not checked.

  Password Never Expires
  Use this option for service accounts.

  Account is Disabled
  The account is disabled when this option is enabled.

- The User Accounts utility also allows you to turn on or off the Fast User Switching feature.

Configuring properties of user accounts

- The following properties of user accounts can be configured:

  General
  You can modify all the properties of a user account except the username and description. You can also unlock a locked-out account from this page.

Member Of
> This page allows you to configure group memberships for the user account.

Profile
> You can specify a path for the user's profile, logon script, and home folder.

Built-in local groups

- The following built-in local groups are available in Windows XP Professional:

Administrators
> Members of this group have full control over the system. The built-in administrator account is a member of this group.

Guest
> The built-in guest account is a member of this group.

Backup Operators
> Members of this group can back up files and directories.

Power Users
> Members of this group can manage user accounts, install devices, and manage shared resources.

Replicator
> This group is used to manage file replication on the computer.

Users
> All local users are members of this group by default.

Built-in system groups

- Built-in system groups can not be deleted, nor can their membership be managed.
- The following built-in local groups are available in Windows XP Professional:

Authenticated Users
> This group represents all users who have user accounts on the computer.

Everyone
> This group represents all users.

Creator Owner
> This group represents those users who become owners of resources that they create.

Network
> This group represents the users who log on to the computer from the network.

Interactive
> This group represents the users who log on locally to the computer.

Anonymous Logon
> This group represents those users who do not have user accounts and cannot be authenticated.

Dialup
> This group represents the users who connect to the computer using dial-up networking.

Managing local groups

- Local groups are managed from the Groups subnode in the Local Users and Groups node in Computer Management.
- You can right-click on a group and delete it or open its Properties dialog box.
- The Members tab allows you to add members to the selected group.
- Deleting a Group does not delete accounts of any users who are members of the group.

System Performance and Reliability

This subsection covers the summary of highlights from the "System Performance and Reliability" section in the Exam 70-270 Study Guide.

Task Manager

- The Task Manager utility is accessed by pressing the CTRL-ALT-DEL key combination or from the Task Bar.
- You can view real-time system performance, stop and start processes, and end applications that are not responding.
- The Processes tab allows you to set the base priority for processes and set the processor affinity for selected processes.
- The Performance tab allows you to view performance objects such as CPU usage, page file usage history, physical memory, and total virtual memory, as used by all processes.
- The Networking tab allows you to view network utilization.
- You can add objects in the Task Manager windows from the View menu.

Performance Console

- The Performance Console utility is located in the Administrative Tools folder in the Control Panel.
- The Performance Console consists of two snap-ins: *System Monitor* and *Performance Logs And Alerts*.

System Monitor

- The *System Monitor* is used to view real-time performance for several components in the computer.
- You can choose from Graph, Histogram, or Report view.
- The following three components make up the System Monitor:

  Object
  : An object refers to a major system component such as CPU, memory, hard disk, etc.

  Counter
  : A counter refers to an aspect of the selected performance object.

  Instance
  : An instance refers to a particular instance of the object.

- The most important components to monitor are as follows:

Processor: %Processor Time
> This counter measures the overall usage of the processor. This value should remain below 90 percent.

Memory: Available Bytes
> A consistent low value of this counter indicates a memory bottleneck.

Memory: Pages/sec
> A number larger than 20 indicates low physical memory in the computer.

Physical Disk: %Disk Time
> If this number is consistently over 50 percent, the disk should be replaced with a faster disk.

Physical Disk: Avg. Disk Queue Length
> A number larger than 2 indicates that the disk is slow.

Logical Disk: %Free Space
> This counter shows the ratio of available free space to the total space on a logical disk.

Performance Logs And Alerts

- The Performance Logs and Alerts snap-in is used to collect performance information so that it can be analyzed at a later time.
- The three parts of this snap-in are as follows:

Counter Logs
> This tool is used to collect performance information for selected objects and counters at regular intervals.

Trace Logs
> This tool is used to log activity for selected counters when some particular events happen.

Alerts
> This tool is used to generate alerts when a performance threshold is reached.

- Alerts can be configured to perform any of the following actions when a performance threshold is reached:
  - Log an entry in the application event log.
  - Send a network message.
  - Start a performance log.
  - Run a program.

Event Viewer

- The Event Viewer console displays error messages, warnings, and other information about application and system events.
- You can view logfiles and search specific entries in logfiles for troubleshooting.

- The following three types of basic logs are displayed in the Event Viewer:

  Application logs
  > This log contains errors, warnings, and other information entries generated by application programs.

  Security logs
  > This log contains entries generated by security-related events such as auditing and logon events.

  System logs
  > This log contains entries generated by system events such as system startup, shut down, services, and devices and drivers.

- You can filter specific events from the View menu.
- Events can be filtered based on event type, event source, category, or event ID.
- Events log files can be maintained as follows:
  — Overwrite Events As Needed
  — Overwrite Events Older Than X Days
  — Do Not Overwrite Events
- If you select Do Not Overwrite Events, you must clear the event logs manually before any new events can be written when the file is full.

Managing services

- The Services Console is located in the Administrative Tools in Control Panel.
- You can configure the type of startup services to automatic or manual, or disable them.
- You can pause, resume, stop, or restart the services for the purpose of troubleshooting.
- The properties of any service allow you to configure the selected service from the following tabs:

  General
  > This page gives you options to configure the service startup type as automatic, manual, or disabled. You can pause, resume, stop, or restart a service from this tab.

  Logon
  > This page specifies the account that the service uses to run. Most of the services run with the Local System Account.

  Recovery
  > You can configure how the system responds when a service fails. The available options for first, second, and consecutive failures are Take No Action, Restart the Service, and Run A Program.

  Dependencies
  > This page displays the services dependent on the selected service as well as the services on which the selected service itself depends.

Backing up and restoring data

- Windows XP Professional includes the Windows Backup Utility that can be run in Wizard mode or Advanced mode.
- Users who have Read, Read and Execute, Modify, and Full Control permissions can back up files and folders.
- Users who have the Backup Files And Directories user rights can back up files and folders.
- Users who have the Restore Files And Directories user rights can restore files and folders.
- Users who have Read, Read and Execute, Modify, or Full Control permissions can back up files and folders.
- Users who have Write, Modify, or Full Control permissions can back up files and folders.
- You can schedule backup jobs from the Schedule tab in the Backup Wizard.
- The Task Scheduler service must be running for scheduled backup jobs.

Backup types

- The following types of backups are supported:

  Normal
  This backup is also known as Full Backup. It backs up all selected files and folders and clears the Archive Bit.

  Copy
  This is similar to the normal backup, but does not clear the archive bit.

  Incremental
  This backs up all files and folders that have changed since the last normal backup. It uses and clears the archive bit. This is the fastest type of backup. To restore, you need the last normal backup and all incremental tapes after the normal backup.

  Differential
  This backs up all files and folders that have changed after the last normal backup. It also uses, but does not clear, the archive bits. To restore, you need the last normal backup and only one differential backup taken after the normal backup.

  Daily
  This type of backup backs up all files changed during the day. It neither uses nor clears the archive bits.

Scheduling backups

- Backup jobs can be scheduled to back up System State and user data during off-peak hours.
- Scheduled backups usually run in unattended mode.
- The Task Scheduler service must be running in order to start the scheduled backup jobs.
- Scheduled backups are configured from the Schedule Jobs tab of the Backup utility.

Restoring data

- The Restore tab of the Backup utility is used to restore data.
- The following options are available to restore files:

Original Location
Files are restored to their original location.

Alternate Location
Files are restored to an alternate location and the folder hierarchy is maintained.

Single Folder
All files are restored to a single folder and the folder hierarchy is lost.

Windows Advanced Boot Options

- The Advanced Boot Options are useful for troubleshooting startup problems.
- Press F8 during startup to invoke the Advanced Boot Options menu.
- The Advanced Boot Options menu has the following boot options:

Safe Mode
This starts the system with minimum services; drivers are needed to start the system.

Safe Mode with Networking
This is basically the Safe Mode with networking support.

Safe Mode with Command Prompt
This starts in Safe Mode, but with the command prompt.

Last Known Good Configuration
this starts the system with the last configuration settings that worked well. This mode is helpful in returning the system configuration to the last working set, even when some configuration changes have resulted in startup problems. This mode is not useful when you have logged on to the system after making changes.

Recovery Console
This option is available only if you have installed the Recovery Console.

Recovery Console

- The Recovery Console is useful in resolving system startup problems, when the Safe Mode and the Last Known Good Configuration Modes do not need help.
- The Recovery Console is installed by using the following command from the Windows XP Professional setup CD-ROM:

      drive: \i386\winnt32.exe /cmdcons

- Once installed, the Recovery Console appears as one of the advanced boot options when you press F8 during the system startup.
- You can replace corrupted critical system files to the hard disk, enable or disable services, and create disk partitions.
- Table 3-12 lists the commands available in the Recovery Console:

Table 3-12. Commands available in Recovery Console

Command	Function
Attrib	Changes the attributes of a file or folder. Options include – to clear the attribute and + to set the attribute. Select c for compression, h for hidden file, r for read-only, and s for system attribute
Chdir or cd	Changes the current working directory or folder.
Chkdsk	Checks a disk for errors.
Cls	Clears the screen display.
Copy	Copies a file. Remember that you cannot copy a file to a floppy disk but copying from a floppy or a CD-ROM to hard disk is permitted.
Delete or Del	Deletes one or more files.
Dir	Displays the contents of a folder and its subfolders.
Disable	Disables a service.
Diskpart	Creates or deletes partitions on the hard disk.
Enable	Enables a disabled service.
Exit	Exits the Recovery Console and restarts the computer.
Expand	Expands a compressed file in a *.cab* folder and copies it to a specified location on hard disk.
Fdisk	Manages partitions on hard disk.
Fixboot	Writes a new boot sector on the system partition.
Fixmbr	Repairs the master boot record on the system partition.
Format	Formats a hard disk with FAT, FAT32, or NTFS. NTFS is used if no filesystem is specified.
Help	Displays a list of all commands available in the Recovery Console.
Logon	Logs on to the operating system.
Listsvc	Displays a list of services.
Map	Displays drive letter mappings.
Mkdir	Creates a new directory (folder).
Rmdir	Deletes a directory (folder).
Rename or Ren	Renames a single file.
Systemroot	Changes the current working directory to the *%systemroot%* folder.

Automated System Recovery

- The Automated System Recovery (ASR) is part of the Windows Backup utility.
- The ASR wizard creates a complete backup of the system partition of the computer.
- The ASR generates a floppy disk that restores the system partitions in the event of a disaster.
- The regular data is restored from regular backups.

Configuring and Troubleshooting the Desktop Environment

This subsection covers a summary of highlights from the "Configuring and Troubleshooting the Desktop Environment" section in the Exam 70-270 Study Guide.

Configuring display properties

- The desktop configuration options include setting display properties, power options, and shortcut menus.
- You can configure display properties to customize your desktop.
- Most of the user-defined settings are stored in user profiles.
- The following display properties can be configured:

Themes
> This option includes desktop background colors, sounds, and icon types.

Desktop
> You can choose a background color for the desktop, and a choice of icons should be displayed on the desktop.

Screen Saver
> When the computer is not in use, a screensaver of your choice can be configured to activate. The default time is 10 minutes. You can set a password if someone else attempts to restore the system back from a screensaver mode.

Appearance
> This tab allows you to configure different windows, color schemes, button styles, and font sizes.

Settings
> Screen resolution, color quality, and adapter-specific settings are configured from this tab.

Configuring display settings

- The following configuration options are available in the settings tab of display properties:

Screen Resolution
> Shows the currently configured resolution for the display adapter listed on this page. The default resolution is 800x600 pixels and can be changed to a larger value to increase the amount of text shown on the monitor.

Color Quality
> Shows the currently configured color quality for the display adapter. The color quality can be changed to its maximum supported value.

Identify
> Used to identify a monitor in multiple display configurations.

Troubleshoot
> Opens the video display troubleshooter.

Advanced
> Displays advanced properties for the display adapter and helps resolve problems related to the display adapter.

User profiles

- The user profiles control the desktop environment for each user of the computer.

- Each user on the local computer has an associated local user profile.
- The user profiles store information about personal preferences, desktop settings, Internet settings, and application preferences.
- Local User Profiles are stored on the local computer.
- Roaming User Profiles are stored on a network file server and are available on any computer where the user logs on.
- A Mandatory User Profile is primarily a roaming profile, but the changes a user makes to her profile are not saved.
- The Default User Profile is a built-in user profile that is used when the user logs on for the first time to a computer system. This profile is modified per the changes made by the user and saved as the user's own user profile.
- The All Users Profile contains settings that apply to all users of the computer.
- Table 3-13 lists the files commonly stored in a user profile.

Table 3-13. Files and folders stored in user profiles

Item	Description
Application Data	This hidden folder contains configuration information about applications.
Internet Cookies	This folder contains cookies used by Internet web sites. Web sites use cookies to store the user's preferences and personal information on the local hard disk.
Desktop	This folder contains files, folders, and desktop shortcuts that the user creates on his Windows XP desktop.
Favorites	When a user stores his shortcuts to favorite locations in Windows Explorer or Internet Explorer, these are stored in the Favorites folder.
Local Settings	This hidden folder contains application data, history, and temporary files. Temporary Internet files are also stored here.
My Documents	This is the folder that appears in the Start menu. Most of the user's documents are stored in My Documents by default.
My Recent Documents	This folder contains shortcuts to recently opened documents. This is also available from the Start menu.
Start Menu	This folder contains the shortcuts to programs that appear in the Start menu.
NTUSER.DAT	This is a part of the Registry that is specific to a particular user. It contains Windows Task Bar and Explorer settings in addition to changes made to the configuration of Control Panel and Accessories settings.

Windows Installer

- The Windows Installer works in conjunction with the installer packages to simplify the installation of applications.
- Each installation package is a file with a *.msi* extension.
- The availability of an application is advertised to the user without actually installing it on the user's computer.
- The user can launch the installation from the interface shown on his computer.
- When an application is *assigned*, it appears as installed on the user's computer as one of the Start menu items. When the user attempts to open the application, it gets installed.

- Applications are also *published* in the Active Directory. A user can locate the application and install it from the Add or Remove Programs utility in the Control Panel.

Files And Settings Transfer Wizard

- The Files And Settings Transfer Wizard is used to transfer user settings and datafiles from an old computer to a new computer.
- This utility is located in the Accessories folder under System Tools.
- You must use one of the built-in serial ports such as the COM port for connecting the old computer and the new computer.
- A *null modem cable* (serial cable) is used to connect two computers.
- Other methods of transferring files and user settings include network file shares and removable media.

User State Migration Tool

- The User State Migration Tool is used in an Active Directory environment.
- It is used to migrate user settings and data files from old computers to new computers in large-scale deployments.
- Two executable files associated with the User State Migration Tool are as follows:

    ScanState.exe
        This file gathers information about user and data settings.

    LoadState.exe
        This file transfers the settings onto the new computer.

- The User State Migration Tool works only with fresh installations of Windows XP Professional.

Implementing, Managing, and Troubleshooting Network Protocols and Services

This subsection covers the summary of highlights from the "Implementing, Managing, and Troubleshooting Network Protocols and Services" section in the Exam 70-270 Study Guide.

IP Addressing

- The IP address is a unique 32-bit address used to identify a computer or host on a network.
- The IP address is written in four 8-bit decimal numbers, according to the *w.x.y.z* notation.
- A part of the IP address represents the network address and the remaining part represents the host address.
- All computers on the same network must have the same network address.
- The *subnet mask* is used to distinguish the *Network ID* from the *Host ID*.
- The IP addresses are divided into address classes as shown in Table 3-14.

Table 3-14. IP address classes

Class	Range of first byte	Number of networks	Hosts per network	Default subnet mask
A	1–126	126	16,777,214	255.0.0.0
B	128–191	16,384	65,534	255.255.0.0
C	192–223	2,097,150	254	255.255.255.0
D	224–239	N/A	N/A	N/A
E	240–255	N/A	N/A	N/A

- This special address (127.0.0.1) is reserved as a *loopback* address for trouble-shooting purposes.
- The IP addresses in the classes A, B, and C are public IP addresses and are assigned to companies.

Private IP addresses

- You can use private IP addresses if your computer is not directly connected to the Internet.
- Private IP addresses can also be used if your network is behind a firewall or proxy server.
- Table 3-15 lists IP addresses reserved for private use.

Table 3-15. Private IP address ranges

Class	Start address	End address	Subnet mask
A	10.0.0.0	10.255.255.255	255.0.0.0
B	172.16.0.0	172.31.255.255	255.240.0.0
C	192.168.0.0	192.255.255	255.255.0.0

Automatic Private IP Addressing (APIPA)

- By default, a Windows XP Professional computer is configured to obtain TCP/IP configuration automatically from a DHCP server.
- If the DHCP server is not available, the APIPA feature automatically configures the TCP/IP properties of a computer.
- The APIPA uses the IP address in the range of 169.254.0.0 to 169.254.255.255 with a subnet mask of 255.255.0.0.
- Computers configured with APIPA continue to look for a DHCP server automatically every five minutes.

Local Area Connection

- All network connections in the Windows XP Professional appear in the Network Connections window.
- The Local Area Connection represents the network adapter installed on the computer.

- You can view the status of the connection and its properties, and rename it or repair it if it is not working.
- You can install clients, services, and protocols for the connection.

Creating a new connection

- The New Connection Wizard gives you the following options:

  Connect To The Internet
  Use this option for connecting to the Internet, checking and sending email, and surfing the Web.

  Connect To A Private Network At Your Workplace
  Use this option for connecting to the business network and using a dial-up or VPN connection.

  Set Up A Small Home Or Office Network
  Use this option for connecting to an existing home or office network.

  Set Up An Advanced Connection
  Use this option for connecting to another computer using serial, parallel, or infrared ports.

Configuring a static IP address

- The minimum information required to configure the TCP/IP properties of a connection are as follows:

  IP address
  This a 32-bit address that must be unique on the network.

  Subnet mask
  This is a 32-bit address that must be the same for all computers on the same network segment.

  Default gateway
  This is the IP address of the router or the gateway when there is more than one segment of the network.

- Open the properties of the Local Area Connection and click on the Internet Protocol (TCP/IP).
- Click the Properties button to open the General TCP/IP properties.
- Click Use The Following IP Address and enter the IP address, subnet mask, and default gateway.

Configuring DNS properties

- The DNS service is used to translate Fully Qualified Domain Names (FQDN) to IP addresses.
- The DNS service in the Windows XP Professional computer is called *DNS Resolver*.
- You can specify one or more DNS servers in the network when configuring the TCP/IP properties.
- The DNS Suffixes decide how the computer responds to unqualified names.
- The DNS Suffixes are configured from Advanced TCP/IP properties.

- The following options can be configured from the DNS tab:

    Append Primary And Connection Specific DNS Suffixes
    This option along with Append Parent Suffixes Of The Primary DNS Suffix is selected by default. The DNS Resolver appends the primary domain name and the DNS name specified in each connection of the TCP/IP properties to the unqualified names.

    Append These DNS Suffixes (In Order)
    You can specify the DNS suffixes and their order.

    Register This Connection's Address In DNS Database
    This option will automatically register its full computer name and IP address in the DNS database.

    Use This Connection's DNS Suffix In DNS Registration
    The computer can use dynamic updates to register its IP address and domain name in the DNS database.

TCP/IP troubleshooting utilities

- The Ping utility is used to test connectivity between two hosts on a network.
- You can ping another computer either by the computer name or by its IP address.
- The Ping 127.0.0.1 tests the TCP/IP configuration of the local computer.
- The Ipconfig command is used to display the TCP/IP configuration of the local computer.
- The Ipconfig /? command displays the switches available with this command.
- The Ipconfig /all command displays the TCP/IP configurations of all network adapters in the computer.
- The Ipconfig /renew command is used to renew the TCP/IP configuration from a DHCP server.
- The Ipconfig /release command is used to release the TCP/IP configuration obtained from a DHCP server.
- The Ipconfig /registerdns command is used to register the computer's IP address with the DNS server.
- The Tracert utility is used to trace the route taken from one host to another, and then check where the connection is broken.
- The Pathping utility is used to check where data packets are being lost on the network path.
- The Net View utility is used to display file and print shares on a network computer.
- Net View requires a proper username and password to use the command.

Repairing a connection

- The Repair utility is used to repair a nonworking connection.
- Right-click on a connection and select the Repair utility from the context menu.

- The following actions are performed:
  - An attempt is made to renew the TCP/IP configuration. This is the same as using the `ipconfig /renew` command.
  - The ARP cache on the local computer is cleared. This is the same as using the `arp -d` command.
  - The NetBIOS name cache is cleared. This is the same as using the `nbtstat -R` and `nbtstst -RR` commands.
  - The DNS cache on the local computer is cleared. This is the same as using the `ipconfig /flushdns` command.
  - The Computer's DNS name is registered with the DNS server. This is the same as using the `ipconfig /registerdns` command.
  - The IEEE 802/1x authentication is restarted for wireless connections.

Dial-up networking

- The dial-up connections are used to connect to the Internet or Remote Access Servers.
- The dial-up connections use the public switched telephone network (PSTN).
- A dial-up computer uses a modem, an ISDN adapter, or a DSL modem.
- A dial-up (or dial-out) connection is configured by using the New Connection Wizard.
- The following properties can be configured:

  General
  Use this to configure modem properties consisting of one or more phone numbers and dialing rules.

  Options
  Use this to configure dialing and redialing options and logon.

  Security
  Use this to configure authentication settings.

  Networking
  Use this to configure the Remote Access Server.

  Advanced
  Use this to configure the Windows Firewall and Internet Connection Sharing (ICS) settings.

Internet Explorer settings

- The dial-up Internet connections require a username and password to connect to the Internet Service Provider (ISP).
- You can configure Internet Explorer from either the Internet Options in the Control Panel or from the Internet Options in the Tools menu within Internet Explorer.
- The Internet Options dialog box has the following configuration tabs:

  General
  With this tab, you can set the home page, delete cookies, and configure how the computer handles temporary Internet files.

Security
> With this tab, you can configure security zones for web sites and security levels for each zone.

Privacy
> This tab has settings to configure how the computer handles cookies and pop-up windows.

Content
> This page has settings to enable the content advisor and configure content ratings according to the RSACi guidelines.

Connections
> With this tab, you can view, modify, or delete dial-up or VPN connections.

Programs
> This tab allows you to configure which programs Windows will use for Internet services.

Advanced
> This tab has additional settings for browsing, multimedia, accessibility, printing, and security.

Internet Connection Sharing (ICS)

- ICS allows you to share a single Internet connection among several users on a small network.
- The computer hosting the ICS service becomes the gateway for other computers in the network.
- ICS serves as a DHCP server and allocates IP addresses in the range of 192.168.0.2 to 192.168.0.254 to other computers and configures itself with the 192.168.0.1 IP address and 255.255.255.0 as a subnet mask.
- ICS can only be used in a small workgroup that is not further subnetted.
- If there are other domain controllers, DNS servers, or DHCP servers on the network, ICS will not work.
- All computers must be configured to obtain an IP address automatically.

Windows Firewall

- The Windows Firewall is automatically installed and enabled when Service Pack2 is installed.
- The Windows Firewall provides the basic protection for the computer from malicious software on the Internet.
- The new Control Panel utility called Security Center appears when SP2 is installed.
- The Windows Firewall is one of the three options in the Security Center. Other options are Automatic Updates and Internet Options.
- The Windows Firewall dialog box has the following three tabs:

General
> This tab enables or disables the Windows Firewall.

Exceptions
> This tab allows or disallows Internet traffic from specific applications and ports.

Advanced
> You can enable or disable this tab for specific connections and configure the ICMP settings for troubleshooting applications. This tab also has settings to configure security logs.

Remote Desktop

- The Remote Desktop allows you to access and control a remote computer from your computer.

- It is helpful when configuring or troubleshooting a remote computer when it is not possible to personally visit the remote site.

- Both the local and the remote computers must be connected to the network in order to establish a connection.

- Terminal services must be running on both local and remote computers.

- The user who wants to use Remote Desktop must be an Administrator or a member of a Remote Desktop users group.

- The Remote Desktop is enabled from the Remote tab of System Properties, and you are allowed to select users to be connected.

- Connection to a remote computer is configured and initialized from the Remote Desktop Connection utility located in the Communications folder in Accessories.

Remote Assistance

- Remote Assistance helps users get help from an expert by sending an invitation to help.

- The Invitation is sent from the Help And Support Center located in the Start menu.

- The invitation can be sent as an email message, from the Windows Messenger, or as a file.

- You can set an expiration date and password so that unauthorized users do not take advantage of this feature.

- The expert, or helper, must open the invitation and accept it to initiate the connection.

- The user sending the invitation is presented with a User Console, while the helper is shown a Helper Console.

- Both the user and the helper can send or receive files as well as chat to resolve the user's problem.

- When any of the users click on the Disconnect button, the session ends.

Configuring, Managing, and Troubleshooting Security

This subsection covers a summary of highlights from the "Installing Microsoft Windows XP Professional" section in the Exam 70-270 Study Guide.

Local Security Policy

- The Local Security Policy applies only to the local computer where it is defined.

- The Administrators can control security settings as Account Policies, User Rights, Security Options, and Audit Policies for the computer.

- The Local Security Policy utility is located in the Administrative Tools of the Control Panel.

Account Policies

- The Account Policies include options for configuring Password Policy and Account Lockout Policy.

- The Password Policy determines how passwords are created and maintained on the computer.

- The Account Lockout Policy determines how accounts are locked out when unauthorized users attempt to access the computer.The following Password Policies are defined:

  Enforce Password History
  This value determines how many passwords are kept in the history so that users cannot use old passwords. A value of 0 means no history is kept. The value can be from 0 to 24.

  Maximum Password Age
  This value determines the maximum number of days a user can keep a password. The default value is 42 days, but can be set anywhere from 0 to 999 days.

  Minimum Password Age
  This value determines how many days a user must keep a password. It prevents users from frequently changing passwords. The default value is 42 days, but it can be set to anywhere between 0 and 999 days.

  Minimum Password Length
  This value determines the minimum number of characters in the password. The value ranges from 0 to 14 characters.

  Passwords Must Meet Complexity Requirements
  These requirements, when enabled, force users to use at least a six-character password, upper- and lowercase letters, and special characters.

  Store Passwords Using Reversible Encryption
  When enabled, this option stores passwords for all users in the domain in reversible encryption. This setting weakens password security.

- The following Account Lockout policies can be defined:

  - Account Lockout Duration: This value determines the number of minutes an account will remain locked out. A value of 0 means the account is locked out indefinitely and an administrator must unlock it.

  - Account Lockout Threshold: This value determines how many invalid logon attempts are allowed before the account is locked out. A value of 0 means that the account will never be locked out.

- Reset Account Lockout Counter After: This value in minutes determines how long it will take to reset the Account Lockout counter.

Local Policies

- The Local Policy contains Security Options, User Rights, and Audit Policy.
- Table 3-16 lists some of the most commonly configured Security Options.

Table 3-16. Most commonly used Security Options

Security Option	Description
Accounts: Administrator Account Status	Enables or disables the Administrator account. This setting does not apply when the system is running in Safe Mode.
Accounts: Guest Account Status	Enables or disables the Guest account.
Accounts: Rename Administrator Account	When enabled, you must specify a different account name for use with the Administrator account.
Accounts: Rename Guest Account	When enabled, you must specify a different account name for use with the Guest account.
Audit: Audit The Use of Backup And Restore Privilege	This works in conjunction with the Audit Privilege Use. When both policies are enabled, an entry is written when files are backed up or restored.
Devices: Prevent Users From Installing Printer Drivers	This policy allows only members of Administrators and Power Users groups to install printer drivers. When disabled, any user can install printer drivers when adding printers.
Devices: Restrict CD-ROM Access To Locally Logged On User Only	When enabled, the CD-ROM drive cannot be accessed simultaneously by locally logged-on user and network user. When disabled, simultaneous CD-ROM access is allowed to the local user and remote user.
Devices: Restrict Floppy Access To Locally Logged On User Only	When enabled, the floppy drive cannot be accessed simultaneously by the locally logged-on user and network user. When disabled, simultaneous floppy drive access is allowed to the local user and remote user.
Devices: Unsigned Driver Installation Behavior	When enabled, this policy determines what happens when someone attempts to install an unsigned device driver. You can set the policy to Block, Warn, or Allow installation of unsigned device drivers.
Interactive Logon: Do Not Display Last User Name	Prevents the Log On To Windows dialog box from displaying the name of the user who was logged on to the system.
Interactive Logon: Do Not Require CTRL+ALT+DEL	When enabled, a user does not need to press the CTRL-ALT-DEL key combination in order to log on to the system.
Network Access: Let Everyone Permissions Apply To Anonymous Users	When enabled, the permissions applied to the Everyone group also apply to the users who log on anonymously.
Network Access: Shares That Can Be Accessed Anonymously	This policy allows you too create a list of network shares that can be accessed by users who log on anonymously.
Recovery Console: Allow Automatic Administrative Logon	This policy determines whether the administrator is required to enter a password when using the Recovery Console. When enabled, the Recovery Console does not prompt for Administrators' password.
Shutdown: Allow System To Be Shut Down Without Having To Log On	When this policy is enabled, the Shut Down option becomes available at the Windows Log On screen. You don't have to log on to the system in order to shut down the system.

User Rights

- *User Rights* are divided into two parts: User Privileges and Logon Rights.
- *Privileges* are User Rights that are assigned to users or groups.
- Privileges also apply to the system as a whole instead of a particular object.
- *Logon Rights* are User Rights that are assigned to a particular user or group account.
- *Logon Rights* control the way users log on to the system.
- Commonly configured Privileges and Logon Rights are shown in Tables 3-17 and 3-18.

Table 3-17. Privileges on Windows XP Professional computer

Privilege	Description	Assigned by default to
Act As Part Of Operating System	When enabled, allows a process to log on like a normal user account. Processes that need this privilege use the LocalSystem account.	None
Add Workstations To Domain	Allows a user to add workstations to domain.	Applicable only on Domain Controllers and is defined in the Default Domain Controller Policy
Backup Files And Directories	Allows a user to back up files and folders even if he does not have permissions.	Administrators and Backup Operators groups
Change The System Time	Allows a user to change the system time.	Administrators and Power Users groups, LocalSystem and NetworkService accounts
Force Shut Down A Remote System	Allows a user to shut down a computer remotely.	Administrators
Load And Unload Device Drivers	Allows users to install or uninstall PnP device drivers. It does not affect non-PnP device drivers.	Administrators
Manage Auditing And Security Log	Allows a user to specify which objects should be audited. Also allows users to manage security logs.	Administrators
Remove Computer From Docking Station	Allows a user to remove a portable computer from a docking station.	Administrators, Power Users, and Users groups
Restore Files And Directories	Allows a user to restore files and folders from backup tapes or other media even if she does not have permissions on destination folders.	Administrators and Backup Operators groups
Shut Down The System	Allows a user to shut down the Windows XP Professional computer.	Administrators, Power Users, Backup Operators, and Users groups
Take Ownership Of Files Or Other Objects	Allows a user to take ownership of files, folders, printers, registry keys, and other system objects such as processes and threads.	Administrators

Table 3-18. Logon rights on Windows XP Professional computer

Logon Right	Description	Assigned by default to
Access This Computer From Network	Allows users to connect to the system from the network.	Administrators, Backup Operators, Power Users, Users, and Everyone groups
Deny Access To This Computer From The Network	Prevents users from connecting to the system from the network.	None
Log On As A Batch Job	Allows users to log on to the system as a batch job.	Administrators group and Anonymous users when IIS is installed on the system
Deny Log On As A Batch Job	Prevents users from logging on to the system as a batch job.	None
Log On As A Service	Allows a user, computer, or service to log on to the system as a service. Services are usually configured to run with LocalSystem, LocalService or NetworkService accounts.	None
Deny Log On As A Service	Prevents a user, computer, or service from logging on to the system as a service.	None
Log On Locally	Allows a user to log on to the system locally or interactively.	Administrators, Backup Operators, Account Operators, Print Operators, and Server Operators groups
Deny Log On Locally	Prevents a user from logging on to the system locally or interactively.	None
Allow Log On Through Terminal Services	Allows users to log on to the system through terminal services. Remote Desktop runs as part of the Terminal Services.	Administrators and Remote Desktop Users groups
Deny Allow Log On Through Terminal Services	Prevents users from logging on to the system through terminal services.	None

Audit Policy

- Auditing is performed in order to monitor access to the system and resources.
- Auditing is a three-step process: enabling the Audit Policy, configuring auditing on objects, and viewing security logs.
- Audit Policy in the Local Security Policy has the configuration options shown in Table 3-19.

Table 3-19. Types of events available for auditing

Event	Description
Account Logon	Not applicable for Windows XP computer.
Account Management	Events related to the enabling, disabling, renaming, creation, deletion, or modification of user or group accounts and resetting passwords.
Directory Service Access	Not applicable for Windows XP computer.
Audit Logon Events	Events related to logging on and logging off on the computer.
Audit Object Access	Events related to access of files, folders, printers, and other resources.

Table 3-19. Types of events available for auditing (continued)

Event	Description
Policy Change	Events related to change in Security Options, user rights assignment, and audit policies.
Privilege Use	Events related to use of User Rights.
Process Tracking	Events related to an action performed by an application or program.
System Events	Events related to system events such as starting or shutting down a computer. Also includes security-related events.

Security Templates

- Security Templates contain predefined security policy settings.
- Different templates are available for the roles of different computers.
- Administrators can select a template, make a copy of it, make required modifications, and apply the template to a computer.
- The following built-in templates are available on a Window XP Professional computer:

  Default Setup Security (Setup Security.inf)
  This template contains the security settings applied to the computer during installation of the operating system.

  Compatible Workstation (Compatws.inf)
  This template contains settings that allow users to run applications certified with the Windows Logon program. Power users can run uncertified applications.

  Secure Workstation (Securews.inf)
  This template is more secure than a compatible workstation.

  Highly Secure Workstation (Hisecurews.inf)
  This template contains security settings for a highly secure workstation. All communications with the computer must be digitally signed.

  System Root Security (Rootsec.inf)
  This template specifies security settings for the system root folder of the computer.

Customizing and applying a Security Template

- The Security Templates snap-in can be added to an empty Microsoft Management Console (MMC).
- Make a copy of the Security Template that closely matches your requirements.
- Modify the copy of the Security Template with your custom security settings.
- Apply the Security Template using the Security Configuration and Analysis snap-in.
- Load the Security Template you customized in the Security Configuration and Analysis snap-in.
- Select Analyze Computer Now to compare the current security settings of the computer to those in the Security Template.

- Select Configure Computer Now to apply the security settings in the template to the computer.

Group Policies

- *Group Policies* are used in the domain environment to apply similar security settings to a large number of computers.
- Multiple Group Policies can be applied to the same computer.
- When multiple Group Policies are applied, the conflicting settings in the Local Security Policies are overridden by the Site Policies.
- The policies applied at the domain level override the policies applied at the site level.
- The policies applied at the Organization Unit (OU) level override the policies applied at the domain level.
- The Resultant Set of Policy (RSoP) snap-in is used to calculate effective policies on a computer when multiple policies are applied.
- The Planning Mode lets you analyze the effective policy before you apply multiple policies.
- The Logging Mode lets you calculate the effective policies that are already applied to the computer.

Exam 70-270 Practice Questions

1. You have a computer with 233 MHz, CPU speed, 256 MB RAM, and about 1200 MB of free hard disk space. The computer has a network adapter for which you have a driver disk. You may wish to install Windows XP Professional on this computer. Which of the following components will you need to upgrade for a successful installation?

   ○ A. CPU

   ○ B. RAM

   ○ C. Hard disk

   ○ D. Network adapter

   Answer C is correct. You need at least 1.5 GB (1500 MB) free hard disk space in order to install Windows XP Professional. You should either add another hard disk or free up some more space in the existing disk.

2. You wish to install Windows XP Professional on a computer that is already running Windows 98. You do not want to remove Windows 98 because some applications will not work with the new operating system. Which of the following filesystems should you choose during installation if the computer will be dual-booting with the two operating systems?

   ○ A. FAT

   ○ B. FAT32

   ○ C. NTFS

   ○ D. Any of the above

Answer B is correct. Windows 98 does not recognize the NTFS filesystem. When you boot the computer using Windows 98, you will not be able to access any partitions that are formatted using NTFS.

3. You installed Windows XP Professional on a new computer. The system worked well for a few weeks and then suddenly stopped working and did not let you log on. What could be the reason?

○ A. You did not accept the licensing agreement during installation.

○ B. You did not enter the correct product key.

○ C. You did not format any partition with NTFS.

○ D. You did not activate the product.

Answer D is correct. The retail versions of Windows XP Professional must be activated within 30 days of installation.

4. Which of the following Windows operating systems cannot be directly upgraded to Windows XP Professional? Select two answers.

❏ A. Windows NT Server 4.0

❏ B. Windows ME

❏ C. Windows 98

❏ D. Windows NT Workstation 3.51

❏ E. Windows NT Workstation 4.0

Answers A and D are correct. Windows NT Server 4.0 can be upgraded either to Windows 2000 Server or Windows Server 2003, but not to Windows XP Professional. Windows NT Workstation 3.51 must first be upgraded to Windows NT Workstation 4.0.

5. Your network administrator has given you the Windows XP Professional CD-ROM and asked you to upgrade your Windows 98 computer to Windows XP Professional. You have located the \i386 folder on the D: drive of your computer (that is, the CD-ROM drive). Which of the following commands can you use to start the upgrade process?

○ A. d:\i386\winnt32.exe

○ B. d:\i386\winnt.exe

○ C. d:\i386\winnt32.exe /upgrade

○ D. d:\i386\winnt.exe /upgrade

Answer A is correct. The winnt32.exe command is used to upgrade Windows 98, Windows NT Workstation 4.0, and Windows ME computers to Windows XP Professional. The winnt.exe command is used for fresh installations from MS-DOS and Windows 3.x computers. The commands given in answers C and D are invalid.

6. Before you start installing Windows XP Professional on your Windows NT Workstation 4.0 computer, you may want to check whether the currently installed hardware and software will be compatible with the new operating system. Which of the following commands can you use to accomplish this?

○ A. `winnt.exe /checkupgradeonly`

○ B. `winnt.exe /checkcompatibility`

○ C. `winnt32.exe /checkupgradeonly`

○ D. `winnt32.exe /checkcompatibility`

Answer C is correct. You can check the compatibility of the existing hardware and software by using the `winnt32.exe` command with the `/checkupgradeonly` parameter.

7. As the network administrator of a small company, you have been asked to deploy Windows XP Professional on 25 new computers. You have also checked that all computers meet the minimum hardware requirements. You may wish to use the Setup Manager to generate answer files for automating the installation process. All users will be installing the operating system themselves by using the answer files that you provide. You do want users to have minimum interaction with the installation process. Which of the following options should you use in the Setup Manager in the User Interaction Level page?

○ A. Provide Defaults

○ B. Fully Automated

○ C. Hide Pages

○ D. Read Only

Answer B is correct. The Fully Automated option in the User Interaction Level page is intended to minimize the user interaction during the unattended installation.

8. The network administrator in your company has asked for your help in installing Windows XP Professional on 50 new computers using the Remote Installation Service (RIS). Which of the following services must be running in the network for RIS-based installations? Select three answers.

❏ A. RIS on client computers

❏ B. Active Directory Service

❏ C. DNS service

❏ D. Internet Information Service (IIS)

❏ E. DHCP service

Answers B, C, and E are correct. RIS installations need Active Directory, DNS, and DHCP services running on the network. Internet Information Services are not required.

9. You configured NTFS permissions on a folder for a group of users and later moved that folder to another partition. Now everyone on the network can access the folder and all files within that folder. What could be the possible reason?

○ A. NTFS permissions are lost when folders are moved.

○ B. The folder has been moved to a FAT partition.

○ C. The folder should have been copied instead of moved.

○ D. Some user has removed all NTFS permissions from the folder.

Answer B is correct. NTFS permissions are lost when a file or folder is moved to a FAT or FAT32 partition.

10. Sarah is a member of HRusers and ACCusers groups. The NTFS permissions for a folder named Directory are Allow Read and Execute for the HRusers group and Allow Modify for the ACCusers group. What are Sarah's effective permissions on the Directory folder?

   ○ A. Read

   ○ B. Read and Execute

   ○ C. Modify

   ○ D. Full Control

Answer C is correct. NTFS permissions are cumulative when a user is a member of more than one group with the exception of the Deny permission, which overrides all other permissions.

11. Allen has been granted Allow Full Control share permission on a network folder named Userfiles. NTFS permissions for the same folder are set to Allow Read and Execute for the HRusers group. Allen is a member of the HRusers group. What are Allen's effective permissions when he tries to access the Userfiles folder from the network?

   ○ A. Full Control

   ○ B. Read

   ○ C. Read and Execute

   ○ D. Deny Full Control

Answer C is correct. The most restrictive of NTFS and share permissions are applied when a shared folder is accessed from the network.

12. Gary wants to share a folder on his computer so that other users on the network can read and make modifications to his work. He wants some users to only read the files and others to read and modify them. When he tries to set permissions for the shared folder, he may not able to do that. What could be the reason?

   ○ A. Gary does not have sufficient rights to set share permissions.

   ○ B. Simple File Sharing is turned on.

   ○ C. Gary is not a member of the Administrators group.

   ○ D. Gary should set NTFS permissions first.

Answer B is correct. You cannot set share permissions when Simple File Sharing is turned on. In Simple File Sharing, everyone gets equal access to the shared folders.

13. Which of the following features in Windows NT Professional allows you to continue working on documents even when you are not connected to the network?

   ○ A. Encrypting File System

   ○ B. Shared Folder Permissions

   ○ C. Fast User Switching

   ○ D. Offline Files

Answer D is correct. Offline Files feature in Windows XP Professional allows you to keep working on documents even when you are not connected to the network. Fast User Switching must be turned off in order to use this feature.

14. You want to add a printer to your computer that is directly connected to a network port. Which of the following procedures must you follow to install the printer?

○ A. Select Local Printer Attached To This Computer and create a New Port when prompted.

○ B. Install as a network printer and then connect it to the network port.

○ C. Use the Automatically Detect My PnP Printer option.

○ D. Install as a Network Printer and select the LPT1 port.

Answer A is correct. When installing a printer that is directly connected to one of the network ports, you should select Local Printer Attached To This Computer and then create a new port by either specifying the printer name or its IP address.

15. You have installed a new color printer in your department. The per-page cost of color printing is very high. You do not want your department's budget to grow due to unwanted color printing. Which of the following options can you use to limit the printing of color pages to selected users only? Select two answers. Each answer is a part of the complete solution.

○ A. Create two ports for the printer, one for black printing and other for color printing.

○ B. Create two user groups for printing, one for black printing and the other for color printing.

○ C. Configure two separate logical printers, one for black printing and the other for color printing.

○ D. Send an email to all users saying that users printing unnecessary color copies will be billed.

○ E. Teach all users how to send color prints and how to send black prints.

Answer C is correct. You should first create two user groups, one that will print in color and the other that will print in black. Then, create two separate logical printers, one for color printing and the other for black printing. When this is done, you should configure permissions separately for each group.

16. The printer used in your office is heavily loaded and your manager has ordered two more similar printers. You have been tasked with the job of installing and configuring these new printers. Which of the following features can you use to share the printing load in your office?

○ A. Install new printers and configure availability hours for each printer.

○ B. Install new printers and configure printer pooling.

○ C. Install new printers and create three identical logical printers.

○ D. Make three equal groups of users and assign each group a separate printer.

Answer B is correct. When you have identical printers, you can share the printing load among several printers using the printer pooling feature in

Windows XP Professional. All printers in the pool must be connected to the same port.

17. You have two identical printers in your office. Paper is jammed in one of the printers and you feel that you will have to call customer service to correct the printer problem. There are about 35 documents in the printer queue waiting to print. What can you do to temporarily resolve the problem so that users can continue to send documents for printing?

○ A. Redirect print jobs to the second printer.

○ B. Ask the users to cancel their documents and send them to the second printer.

○ C. Save the jobs in the spool folder of the print server.

○ D. Change the printer priority to its lowest value.

Answer A is correct. When you have two or more identical printers and one of them stops functioning, you can redirect the faulty printer's print jobs to another, identical printer. This action is transparent to the users and is performed from the print server.

18. You have three disks on a Windows XP Professional computer and you want to take advantage of Striped volumes. What is the first step you should take before you can configure a Striped volume?

○ A. Make sure that all disks have equal free space.

○ B. Convert all disks to Dynamic disks.

○ C. Format all disks with NTFS.

○ D. Make sure that all disks have equal unallocated space.

Answer B is correct. Dynamic disks only offer Simple, Spanned, and Striped volumes. Striped volumes are created by using unallocated space from two or more Dynamic disks. Striped volumes are not fault-tolerant and cannot be extended.

19. Most of the users on your network store documents on your computer, and you have configured file compression on the drive that is used by network users. Since users keep saving unnecessary documents that are not related to their jobs, your manager has asked you to use the disk quota feature to limit usage of disk space. Which of the following is true about disk quotas and file compression? Select three answers.

❏ A. Disk quotas and file compression cannot be used together.

❏ B. Disk quotas can only be configured on NTFS volumes.

❏ C. Disk quotas can be enabled only for user groups.

❏ D. Disk quotas can be enabled only for individual users.

❏ E. Disk quotas take into account the size of the uncompressed files.

Answers B, D, and E are correct. Disk quotas work only on NTFS volumes, are configured on a per-user basis, and the uncompressed size of the files is taken into account when calculating space used by users.

20. Which of the following are features of the NTFS compression in Windows XP Professional? Select two answers.

 ❑ A. Works on FAT volumes

 ❑ B. Works on NTFS volumes

 ❑ C. Works with file encryption

 ❑ D. Individual files can be compressed

 ❑ E. Works only on Dynamic disks

Answers B and D are correct. NTFS compression works only on NTFS volumes and can compress individual files. Folder compression, on the other hand, works on both FAT and NTFS volumes and can compress encrypted files but not individual files.

21. Your computer has a 120 GB hard disk divided into two partitions: drive C is 80 GB and NTFS and drive D is 40 GB and also NTFS. You compressed some files in the Documents folder on the C drive last month. Now, drive C is nearly full and you have moved the files from the Documents folder to the Docscopy folder on drive D, which is not compressed. What will be the compression state of the files after this action?

 ○ A. The files will get uncompressed.

 ○ B. The files will remain compressed.

 ○ C. The files will remain compressed but will uncompress when users open them.

 ○ D. There will be no change in the compression state.

Answer A is correct. When compressed files or folders are moved from one NTFS volume to another NTFS volume, they acquire the compression state of the destination folder. In this case, the destination folder that is not compressed is Docscopy.

22. Your computer is directly connected to the Internet, and you have been surfing the Web ever since you installed Windows XP Professional on it. It seems that there are a lot of temporary and junk files stored in the hard disk of your computer by various web sites. Which of the following utilities is the best to use to clear up the disk space?

 ○ A. Disk Defragmenter

 ○ B. Check Disk

 ○ C. Disk Cleanup

 ○ D. Recovery Console

Answer C is correct. The Disk Cleanup utility removes temporary files from the temp folder of the computer, clears the computer cache, deletes all temporary Internet files, and empties the Recycle Bin.

23. You have installed a second network adapter on your Windows XP Professional computer, but the operating system does not recognize it, although the adapter is a PnP device. How can you properly install the adapter?

○ A. From the update driver in Device Manager.

○ B. From the Add Hardware wizard in Control Panel.

○ C. Restart the computer two to three times more until the operating system detects the adapter.

○ D. Install the driver from "Add or Remove Programs" in the Control Panel.

Answer B is correct. The Add Hardware wizard can be used to install PnP devices that are not automatically detected by the operating system. When prompted, you may supply the driver disk for the adapter to install the device driver files.

24. Your manager received an email from one of your vendors that the newer versions of drivers for the sound cards installed on computers in your office are now available. You follow your manager's orders and download a new driver and install it on your computer first in order to test it. When you restart the computer, the sound card stops working. What are your options?

○ A. Write an email back to the vendor asking for help.

○ B. Use the Update Driver feature to install the driver directly from the vendor's web site.

○ C. Uninstall the sound card and install it again with the old driver.

○ D. Use the Roll Back Driver feature to uninstall the new driver and install the old driver.

Answer D is correct. The Roll Back Driver feature is used to uninstall a newly installed device driver and install the previously installed driver. Remember that this feature is not available for printer drivers.

25. It has come to your notice that some users in your office keep installing untested drivers for the purpose of improving sound quality on their desktops. You have responded to a few calls to address problems where users have installed such drivers. How can you prevent users from installing untested and unsigned device drivers on their computers in the future?

○ A. Define a written company policy so that no one is allowed to install any driver without your permission.

○ B. Configure driver signing options in each computer to block installation of unsigned drivers.

○ C. Configure driver signing options in each computer to warn before unsigned drivers are installed.

○ D. Write a script that will not allow any user to install any device driver on his computers.

Answer B is correct. The driver signing option can be set to block installation of unsigned device drivers on users' desktops. As an administrator, you can make this option the system default on every computer. Another way to prevent this is to take away the Load And Unload Device Drivers user rights from the users.

26. Your company is a marketing enterprise that has 10 telecommuters who carry their laptops with them for presentations. Some of these employees complain

that their monitors turn off too quickly when they are doing presentations. How can you fix the problem?

○ A. Turn off the Hibernate mode on these notebooks.

○ B. Turn off the Standby mode on these notebooks.

○ C. Use the Presentation power scheme.

○ D. Use the Home/Office power scheme.

Answer C is correct. The Presentation power scheme in Power Options does not turn off power to the monitor or the hard disk, so that the notebook remains powered on at all times during the presentation.

27. Which of the following actions are considered good for a secure Windows XP Professional computer?

○ A. Disable the InitialUser account

○ B. Disable the Guest account

○ C. Disable the Administrator account

○ D. Disable the HelpAssistant account

Answer B is correct. The built-in Guest account must be disabled for a Windows XP Professional computer for creating a secure working environment. Although this account is disabled by default, you must make sure that it is not enabled by some previous administrator.

28. When the passwords are required to meet complexity requirements, which of the following criteria must be met when using passwords? Select three answers. Each answer is a part of the complete solution.

❏ A. Passwords must be at least six characters long.

❏ B. Passwords must contain a part of the username.

❏ C. Passwords must contain uppercase letters.

❏ D. Passwords must contain lowercase letters.

❏ E. Passwords must not have any numerals.

Answers A, C, and D are correct. Complexity requirements for passwords means that passwords must be at least six characters long, must contain uppercase letters, lowercase letters, numerals and/or special characters, and must not contain any part of the user's full name or account name. Any three of these criteria should be met in order to maintain complex passwords. In addition to this, password history must be enforced.

29. Your company has received a new accounts application and you are in charge of testing and installing the application on the computers of the accounts department. This application needs a special account to run. You created a new user account for the application. Which of the following passwords options should you select for the application? Select two answers.

❏ A. User must change password at next logon.

❏ B. User cannot change password.

❏ C. Password never expires.

❏ D. Account is disabled.

❏ E. All of the above.

Answers B and C are correct. Passwords for applications that run with a local user account should not expire. You should also select the User Can Not Change Password option.

30. You have installed Windows XP Professional on a computer that already has a Windows NT Workstation 4.0 and is made by the system to dual boot between these two operating systems. The problem is that when you start the system and you are not watching the startup process, Windows NT Workstation 4.0 automatically loads. You want to start the system automatically with Windows XP Professional if you do not get a chance to select the operating system. Which of the following is the safest way to accomplish this?

   ○ A. Open Notepad and change the *BOOT.INI* file. Increase the wait time for Windows NT Workstation 4.0 and decrease the wait time for Windows XP Professional.

   ○ B. Create a second *BOOT.INI* file with only the Windows XP Professional operating system and replace the original *BOOT.INI* file.

   ○ C. Use the Startup And Recovery page in System Properties in the Control Panel and change the default OS to Windows XP Professional.

   ○ D. Use the regedit.exe command to edit registry and change the default operating system.

Answer C is correct. The default operating system in a dual-boot system should preferably be changed from the Startup And Recovery tab that is available in the System Properties page of the Control Panel. It is not recommended that you use any other methods such as editing registry, to change the default operating system.

31. You opened a file in MS Word 2000 and started working on it. You also opened two games to entertain yourself while working on a large, boring file. After a while, the Word file stopped responding and did not allow you to enter any text. How can you get around this problem?

   ○ A. Open Task Manager, locate the MS Word application, and click End Task.

   ○ B. Open System Monitor and try to find out the reason for the problem.

   ○ C. Save the file, close it, and open it again.

   ○ D. Restart the computer.

Answer A is correct. You can use the Task Manager to end an application that is responding. When the application is not responding, you will not be able to save any work or close the file you are working on.

32. One of the Windows XP Professional computers in your small workgroup is configured as a print server. Users are complaining that it takes a long time to get their documents printed, and the print server seems to have become very slow in recent weeks. You now wish to gather performance data on this print server and analyze it whenever you get a chance later in the week. Which of the following options will help you accomplish your goal?

○ A. Open Task Manager to monitor the performance of the print server.

○ B. Use System Monitor to analyze the performance of the print server.

○ C. Use Performance console and use counter logs to collect performance data.

○ D. Use Performance Alerts to generate and send you a network message when the print server slows down.

Answer C is correct. The Performance Logs and Alerts snap-in is used to collect performance data for selected counters so that it can be analyzed at a later time. The Task Manager and System Monitor show real-time performance data.

33. You are now looking at the following performance log data collected in a text file during the past week.

> Processor: %Processor Time-60%
> Memory: Pages/sec-12
> Physical Disk: %Disk Time-75%
> Logical Disk: %Free Space-56%

Which of the following actions should remove the bottleneck in system performance?

○ A. Add a second CPU.

○ B. Add more RAM.

○ C. Replace the hard disk with a faster one.

○ D. Create one more logical partition.

Answer C is correct. A value of more than 50 percent of disk time for the physical disk object indicates that the hard disk is slower than expected and is the bottleneck. You should replace the currently installed hard disk with a faster hard disk.

34. You have enabled auditing for object access on file servers where you suspected that some unauthorized users were attempting to access confidential files. In which of the following Event Viewer logs should you look for auditing entries?

○ A. Application logs

○ B. Security logs

○ C. System logs

○ D. DNS logs

Answer B is correct. Auditing events are written to the security logs. Depending on the events for which you enabled auditing, you should look for entries in security logs to find out unauthorized logons.

35. You took over as the network administrator for a small company last week. While checking security and system logs for one of the file servers, you notice that no entries were written to the logfiles after you took over. What could be the reason?

○ **A.** The logs are configured to overwrite events as needed.

○ **B.** The logs are configured not to overwrite events.

○ **C.** The logs are configured to clear events on the last day of every week.

○ **D.** The logs are configured to overwrite events older than seven days.

Answer B is correct. When the event logs are configured not to overwrite events, the logfiles must be cleared manually. Otherwise, no new entries are written to the logfiles when the file reaches its configured size.

36. A new application installed on a database server in your office is dependent on a service that is installed with the application. The application and its associated service worked well for a week, and then started causing trouble. Users report that the application freezes repeatedly. You suspect that the cause of the problem is failure of the service. You want to get notified immediately if the service stops, so that you can diagnose the problem. How can you configure the service?

○ **A.** Configure the recovery option for the service to run a script that will send you an email.

○ **B.** Configure a performance alert for the service.

○ **C.** Use Task Manager to monitor the application and the service on the database server.

○ **D.** Ask a user to send you an email immediately after the application freezes.

Answer A is correct. The recovery options in the Properties dialog box of the service can be configured to run a program when the service fails. This program can be a script that will send you an email notifying you that the service has failed on the database server.

37. You want Jim to take care of backing up data on one of the file servers but do not want to grant him excessive permissions on the file server. Which of the following is your best option?

○ **A.** Make Jim a member of Administrators group.

○ **B.** Make Jim a member of Power Users group.

○ **C.** Make Jim a member of Backup Operators group.

○ **D.** Make Jim a member of Server Operators group.

Answer C is correct. To enable Jim to back up files and directories, you should make him a member of Backup Operators group. There is no need to make him a member of Administrators group because this will grant him more than the required permissions on the file server.

38. You took a full backup of the file server in your office last Friday night and then took incremental backups on Monday, Tuesday, and Wednesday nights. Today is Thursday and you have taken a differential backup just before installing a new, faster hard disk on the server. After the new hard disk is installed, you find that the server has crashed and you will have to restore the data from backups. Which of the following backup sets will restore the complete data on the file server using minimum tapes?

○ A. Full backup and Wednesday's incremental backup

○ B. Full backup and Thursday's differential backup

○ C. Full backup and incremental backups taken on Monday, Tuesday, and Wednesday

○ D. Just the differential backup taken on Thursday

Answer B is correct. The full backup taken on Friday night along with the differential backup taken on Thursday will restore complete up-to-date data on the file server. The differential backup contains all data that has changed after the last full backup.

39. After installing a new network adapter in one of your test computers, you find that the system boots but stops responding after you log on. Which of the following advanced boot options can help you resolve the problem? Select two answers.

❑ A. Safe Mode

❑ B. Safe Mode with Networking

❑ C. Last Known Good Configuration

❑ D. Recovery Console

❑ E. Directory Services Restore Mode

Answers A and D are correct. You can boot the system in Safe Mode and remove the driver for the new network adapter. You can also use the Recovery Console to resolve the problem. Safe Mode with Networking will not work because the network adapter is causing the problem. The Last Known Good Configuration is useful only if you have not logged on to the system after making configuration changes.

40. You have not installed the Recovery Console on your Windows XP Professional computer. Is there a way to use the Recovery Console without installing it if the system develops a serious problem at a later date?

○ A. Yes, the Recovery Console is installed by default when the OS is installed.

○ B. No, you must install the Recovery Console before you can use it.

○ C. Yes, the Startup And Recovery options in System Properties actually include the Recovery Console.

○ D. Yes, the Recovery Console can be started from the Windows XP Professional setup CD-ROM.

Answer D is correct. You can start the Recovery Console from the Windows XP Professional setup CD-ROM by selecting the Repair option at the Welcome screen. You need not install the Recovery Console in order to use it.

41. You increased the screen resolution of your desktop to maximum and shut down the system for the day. The next morning the system did not boot at all. How can you resolve the problem?

○ A. Reinstall Windows XP Professional.

○ B. Start the system in VGA mode and change the resolution.

○ C. Use Recovery Console to remove the display adapter driver.

○ D. Do nothing. Restart the system two to three times and the problem will be fixed automatically.

Answer B is correct. The VGA mode starts the system in a very basic graphics mode, and you can change the screen resolution to the previous working one. Usually, the system will not allow you to change the resolution to one that is not supported by the display adapter.

42. You are in charge of networking in a very small office that has only 12 Windows XP Professional computers. Only one of the computers is connected to the network, and your manager wants you to configure all computers in such a way that everyone can share the Internet connection. Which of the following IP address ranges will be used in the network once you have configured the Internet Connection Sharing (ICS) on the computer connected to the Internet?

○ A. 192.168.0.1 to 192.168.0.255

○ B. 169.254.0.1 to 169.254.255.255

○ C. 172.16.0.1 to 172.31.255.255

○ D. 10.0.0.1 to 10.255.255.255

Answer A is correct. When ICS is enabled in a workgroup environment, the computer hosting the ICS service runs as a DHCP server also and allocates IP addresses in the range 192.168.0.1 to 192.168.0.255. It assigns the first address 192.168.0.1 for itself. The address range given in Answer B is used in the automatic private IP addressing (APIPA).

43. You are setting up a small network for a branch office of your company. The office will have a proxy server that will serve as a gateway to the Internet for all other computers in the network. You want to use an IP address range that will not conflict with the IP addresses on the Internet. The number of computers in the branch office will never be more than 100. Which of the following IP address ranges should you use for this office?

○ A. 192.168.0.1 to 192.168.0.255

○ B. 169.254.0.1 to 169.254.255.255

○ C. 172.16.0.1 to 172.31.255.255

○ D. 10.0.0.1 to 10.255.255.255

Answer A is correct. Since the number of computers in the branch office will never be more than 100, you can easily use the private IP addresses in class C address range. Although you can use the IP addresses given in answers C and D, it is wise to use the smallest range of addresses whenever possible.

44. You have been asked to analyze a slow connection from your office to one of the branch offices located in another city. Which of the following commands will let you analyze where the data packets that are traveling to and from your computers are being lost on the network path?

○ A. Ping

○ B. Pathping

○ C. Ipconfig

○ D. Tracert

Answer B is correct. Pathping is a TCP/IP troubleshooting utility that helps in finding out the loss of packets on the network path from one location to another. Ping is used to check connectivity, while Tracert is used to trace the route taken by the data packets from one network to another.

45. Even after you configured strong Password Policies in your network and set the appropriate NTFS permissions on company files, you notice that users keep guessing other accounts and passwords to access files that they are not supposed to. What else could you configure in Local Security Policy to prevent users from guessing passwords of authorized users? Select three answers.

❑ A. Enable the Password Complexity Requirements Policy.

❑ B. Ask authorized users to use strong passwords.

❑ C. Set the Account Lockout Policies.

❑ D. Enable auditing for logon events.

❑ E. Disable network access for the file server from the network.

Answers B, C, and D are correct. In order to protect confidential files from unauthorized access and stop unauthorized users from attempting to guess passwords of authorized users, you should enable the auditing of logon events to the file server, ask authorized users to use strong passwords, and set the Account Lockout Policies.

Exam 70-297:
Designing a Microsoft Windows Server 2003 Active Directory and Network Infrastructure

4

Exam 70-297 Overview

Exam 70-297: Designing a Microsoft Windows Server 2003 Active Directory and Network Infrastructure is the first of the two design exams available to complete your MCSE certification journey. If you are not on an MCSE on Windows 2000 track, you must pass one of the two design exams to prove your skills in designing a network infrastructure based on Windows Server 2003 technologies for medium- to large-scale organizations. You will need to review what you learned while preparing for the four core exams, especially the skills covered in Exams 70-293 and 70-294.

If you look at the exam objectives given on the following pages, you will know that the exam will not only test your ability to design a brand-new Windows Server 2003 network infrastructure by gathering information on business and technical requirements of a company, you should also be prepared to be tested on upgrading or migrating an existing network infrastructure to a Windows Server 2003 network. The exam will test you on both the logical and the physical aspects of the Active Directory services and network infrastructure design.

As is evident from its title, this exam does not specifically test your skills on implementation of Windows Server 2003 technologies but instead focuses on your design and planning skills. The exam is based on case studies, and you will need to study the given scenarios carefully in order to assess the current and future needs of the organization before you move ahead and answer the design questions based on these case studies.

In order to be prepared for Exam 70-297, you should have 12 to 18 months prior experience as a Windows Server 2003 administrator in a medium to large organization. You should have recently studied a Windows Server 2003 administrator's book, taken a training course, or completed a self-paced training kit that covers the related areas of study. You will then be ready to use the Exam 70-297 Study Guide in this book as your final exam preparation.

Exam 70-297 is one of the two available design exams required to complete your MCSE certification. The other exam is *Exam 70-298: Designing Security for a Microsoft Windows Server 2003 Network*. This exam is covered in the next part of this book. If you have chosen to specialize in Windows Server 2003 security, you should skip this exam and focus on Exams 70-298 and 70-299 after you have completed the four core exams.

Areas of Study for Exam 70-297

Creating the Conceptual Design by Gathering and Analyzing Business and Technical Requirements

- Analyze the impact of Active Directory on the existing technical environment.
  - Analyze hardware and software requirements.
  - Analyze interoperability requirements.
  - Analyze current level of service within an existing technical environment.
  - Analyze current network administration model.
  - Analyze network requirements.
- Analyze DNS for Active Directory service implementation.
  - Analyze the current DNS infrastructure.
  - Analyze the current namespace.
- Analyze existing network operating system implementation.
  - Identify the existing domain model.
  - Identify the number and location of domain controllers on the network.
  - Identify the configuration details of all servers on the network. Server types might include primary domain controllers, backup domain controllers, file servers, print servers, and web servers.
- Analyze security requirements for the Active Directory service.
  - Analyze current security policies, standards, and procedures.
  - Identify the impact of Active Directory on the current security infrastructure.
  - Identify the existing trust relationships.
- Design the Active Directory infrastructure to meet business and technical requirements.
  - Design the envisioned administrative model.
  - Create the conceptual design of the Active Directory forest structure.
  - Create the conceptual design of the Active Directory domain structure.
  - Design the Active Directory replication strategy.
  - Create the conceptual design of the Organizational Unit (OU) structure.
- Design the network services infrastructure to meet business and technical requirements.
  - Create the conceptual design of the DNS infrastructure.
  - Create the conceptual design of the WINS infrastructure.
  - Create the conceptual design of the DHCP infrastructure.
  - Create the conceptual design of the remote access infrastructure.

- Identify network topology and performance levels.
  — Identify constraints in the current network infrastructure.
  — Interpret current baseline performance requirements for each major subsystem.
- Analyze impact of the infrastructure design on the existing technical environment.
  — Analyze hardware and software requirements.
  — Analyze interoperability requirements.
  — Analyze current level of service within the technical environment.
  — Analyze network requirements.

See "Overview of Active Directory and Network Services in Windows Server 2003" on page 212 and "Analyzing Current Network Infrastructure" on page 229.

Creating the Logical Design for an Active Directory Infrastructure

- Design an OU structure.
  — Identify the Group Policy requirements for the OU structure.
  — Design an OU structure for the purpose of delegating authority.
- Design a security group strategy.
  — Define the scope of a security group to meet requirements.
  — Define resource access requirements.
  — Define administrative access requirements.
  — Define user roles.
- Design a user and computer authentication strategy.
  — Identify common authentication requirements.
  — Select authentication mechanisms.
  — Optimize authentication by using shortcut trust relationships.
- Design a user and computer account strategy.
  — Specify account policy requirements.
  — Specify account requirements for users, computers, administrators, and services.
- Design an Active Directory naming strategy.
  — Identify Internet domain name registration requirements.
  — Specify the use of hierarchical namespace within Active Directory.
  — Identify NetBIOS naming requirements.
- Design migration paths to Active Directory.
  — Define whether the migration will include an in-place upgrade, domain restructuring, or migration to a new Active Directory environment.

- Design a strategy for Group Policy implementation.
    - Design the administration of Group Policy Objects (GPOs).
    - Design the deployment strategy of GPOs.
    - Create a strategy for configuring the user environment with Group Policy.
    - Create a strategy for configuring the computer environment with Group Policy.
- Design an Active Directory service site topology.
    - Design sites.
    - Identify site links.

See "Designing an Active Directory Structure" on page 240 and "Designing a Security Infrastructure" on page 250.

Creating a Logical Design for a Network Services Infrastructure

- Design a DNS name resolution strategy.
    - Create the namespace design.
    - Identify DNS interoperability with Active Directory, WINS, and DHCP.
    - Specify zone requirements.
    - Specify DNS security.
    - Design a DNS strategy for interoperability with Unix Berkeley Internet Name Domain (BIND) to support Active Directory.
- Design a NetBIOS name resolution strategy.
    - Design a WINS replication strategy.
- Design security for remote access users.
    - Identify security host requirements.
    - Identify the authentication and accounting provider.
    - Design remote access policies.
    - Specify logging and auditing settings.
- Design a DNS service implementation.
    - Design a strategy for DNS zone storage.
    - Specify the use of DNS server options.
    - Identify the registration requirements of specific DNS records.
- Design a remote access strategy.
    - Specify the remote access method.
    - Specify the authentication method for remote access.
- Design an IP address assignment strategy.
    - Specify DHCP integration with DNS infrastructure.
    - Specify DHCP interoperability with client types.

See "Designing a Security Infrastructure" on page 250.

Creating a Physical Design for an Active Directory and Network Infrastructure

- Design DNS service placement.
- Design an Active Directory implementation plan.
  — Design the placement of domain controllers and global catalog servers.
  — Plan the placement of flexible operations master roles.
  — Select the domain controller creation process.
- Specify the server specifications to meet system requirements.
- Design Internet connectivity for a company.
- Design a network and routing topology for a company.
  — Design a TCP/IP addressing scheme through the use of IP subnets.
  — Specify the placement of routers.
  — Design IP address assignment by using DHCP.
  — Design a perimeter network.
- Design the remote access infrastructure.
  — Plan capacity.
  — Ascertain network settings required to access resources.
  — Design for availability, redundancy, and survivability.

See "Designing a Name Resolution Structure" on page 285 and "Designing a Network and Routing Solution" on page 302.

5

Exam 70-297 Study Guide

This chapter provides a study guide for *Exam 70-297: Designing a Microsoft Windows Server 2003 Active Directory and Network Infrastructure*. Sections within the chapter are organized according to the exam objective they cover. Each section identifies the related exam objective, provides an overview of why the objective is important, and then discusses the key details you should know about the objective to both succeed on the test and master the objective in the real world.

The major topics covered on Exam 70-297 are:

Creating a conceptual design by gathering and analyzing business and technical requirements
This section is designed to test your knowledge of gathering information on various areas of network design and then creating a conceptual design. These requirements include Active Directory, hardware and software, Domain Name System (DNS), security, and network topology.

Creating the logical design for an Active Directory Iinfrastructure
This section is designed to test your knowledge of creating a logical design for Active Directory infrastructure. Your design should include all aspects of Active Directory, such as OU structure, security, authentication, Group Policies, etc.

Creating a logical design for network services infrastructure
This section is designed to test your knowledge of creating a logical design for a network services infrastructure that includes DNS services, NetBIOS name resolution, remote access, and automation of IP address assignment using DHCP services.

Creating the physical design for an Active Directory and network infrastructure
This section is designed to test your knowledge of creating a physical design for an Active Directory and network infrastructure based on the logical design you create.

The sections of this chapter are designed to reinforce your knowledge of these topics. Ideally, you will review this chapter as thoroughly as you would your course notes in preparation for a college professor's final exam. That means multiple readings of the chapter, committing to memory key concepts, and performing any necessary outside readings if there are topics with which you have difficulty.

You probably will not need a Windows Server 2003 network for this exam because you will be required to apply the knowledge you gained while studying for the four core exams on analyzing business requirements and creating a design for an Active Directory-based network infrastructure using case studies. However, it's not a bad idea to have a two-computer test network just in case you need to practice a few hands-on skills. The two computers can be configured as follows:

- A domain controller running Windows Server 2003 configured with DNS, DHCP, and Routing and Remote Access Service.
- A workstation configured as a member of a workgroup, preferably running Windows XP Professional operating system.

This exam requires that you have good working knowledge of Active Directory and networking technologies in Windows Server 2003. It is strongly recommended that you complete the four core exams before attempting this exam. The first section in this study guide does not relate directly to any exam objective but is provided here to review some key elements that will be helpful in preparing for this exam. These include Active Directory basics, DNS, TCP/IP fundamentals, WINS, and Remote Access Services.

Overview of Active Directory and Network Services in Windows Server 2003

Designing a network infrastructure based on Windows Server 2003 requires that you are conversant with the technologies behind this operating system. Throughout this study guide, you will be dealing with needs assessment, analyzing current and future business requirements, and, based on your knowledge and skills, creating a logical design that can be physically implemented. This section reviews some basic concepts of Active Directory and networking technologies in Windows Server 2003. It starts with an overview of Active Directory and the domain naming system (DNS) that form the backbone of designing the network infrastructure. Some basics about TCP/IP and other networking services, such as NetBIOS name resolution using Windows Internet Name Service (WINS) and remote access, are also covered.

Overview of Active Directory

Active Directory forms the basis of networking in Windows Server 2003 operating system. Active Directory is a collection of network users and resources called *objects* that can be managed from a single point. Active Directory allows you to add, remove, modify, or relocate objects from a centralized location. Users, on the other hand, can easily locate and use the network resources for which they have permissions.

Active Directory is dependent on directory services. A directory is a collection of interrelated objects in a network that is stored centrally and is accessible by users from any part of the network. These objects might include shared files and folders, printers, shared applications, databases, and users themselves. Directory service simplifies the process of storing, locating, and managing these objects. The directory service acts as an administration tool as well as an end-user tool. Users on the network utilize directory services to locate and access the network resources using one or more query procedures.

Features of Windows Server 2003 Active Directory

Directory Services in Windows Server 2003 are known as Active Directory. The following are some of the significant features included in Windows Server 2003 Active Directory:

Centralization
> Active Directory provides a single, centralized storage for all the data in a distributed manner. This allows users to locate and access the data from any location, resulting in easy administration and high availability.

Scalability
> Active Directory offers scalability depending on business requirements. It allows millions of objects per domain while still maintaining the centralized structure.

Extensibility
> The structure of the Active Directory database, known as the schema, can be extended based on business requirements. This feature is not only helpful to administrators but also to application developers.

Manageability
> Active Directory is based on a hierarchical model. This means that it is easy for administrators to keep control of the network as well as for users to locate the network resources.

Integration with Domain Name System (DNS)
> Active Directory is tightly integrated with the DNS. Although these are two separate entities, Active Directory and DNS share an identical structure. DNS zones can be stored in Active Directory, which provides better security for the DNS service. Clients in an Active Directory environment use the DNS service to locate domain controllers.

Security
> Since the Active Directory database contains information about all the objects in the organization, it can be prone to malicious attacks from unauthorized people. Active Directory is integrated with Windows Server 2003 security and provides access control on each object stored in the database. Security policies can be defined at the domain level, site level, Organizational Unit (OU) level, or even on the local computer.

Interoperability with other Directory Services

Active Directory is based on Lightweight Directory Access Protocol (LDAP) version 3, which is the industry standard. It can easily interoperate with other directory services that use the LDAP protocol to share Active Directory information. Digital signatures and encryption secure all LDAP traffic to and from Windows Server 2003 domain controllers.

Logical structure of Active Directory

In the Active Directory, the physical structure of the network is separated from its logical structure. This structure makes it more scalable and easy to administer. The logical structure consists of objects, domains, organization units, trees, and forests, each of which is explained next.

Objects. Active Directory stores network resources as objects. An *object* is the smallest component of the Active Directory that can be administered. Objects are stored in Active Directory in a hierarchical structure in containers and subcontainers. This hierarchy can be thought of like a Windows folder where you find subfolders and files under subfolders. You can modify or scale out this structure to meet the requirements of a growing business.

Object Classes

Objects in Active Directory are made up of *attributes*. The attributes that collectively make up an object are called an *object class*. For example, a user object is made up of attributes such as username, description, password, group membership, etc. Object classes help organize objects based on their attributes. For example, all computers in the network belong to the object class Computers.

Schema

The Active Directory *schema* is a collection of object classes that define how the attributes of an object are to be stored in the database. Like all other objects in Active Directory, the schema is also secured by Windows Server 2003 Access Control Lists (ACLs).

Domains. A *domain* is the core of a Windows Server 2003 Active Directory-based network and is considered the administrative boundary. All objects within this boundary (such as users, computers, and other resources) share the common security database. Each domain stores information only about its own objects. A domain can contain subdomains and can span more than one physical location. Access Control Lists (ACLs) control access to objects within the domain. Security policies, user rights, and permissions defined on objects in one domain are applicable within that domain only.

The naming conventions used in the Windows Server 2003 domain follow the DNS naming structure. For example, a computer named *bookserver* in the domain named *oreilly.com* will have a Fully Qualified Domain Name (FQDN) as *bookserver.oreilly.com*.

The *domain functional level* in the Windows Server 2003 network provides a mechanism that benefits from domain-wide Active Directory features. The following four domain functional levels are available:

Windows 2000 Mixed
> This is the default domain functional level that allows a Windows Server 2003 domain controller to interact with domain controllers running Windows Server 2003, Windows 2000, and Windows NT 4.0 operating systems.

Windows 2000 Native
> This domain functional level allows a Windows Server 2003 domain controller to interact with domain controllers running Windows Server 2003 and Windows 2000 operating systems.

Windows Server 2003 Interim
> This domain functional level allows a Windows Server 2003 domain controller to interact with domain controllers running Windows Server 2003 and Windows NT 4.0 operating systems.

Windows Server 2003
> This domain functional level allows a Windows Sever 2003 domain controller to interact with only those domain controllers that are running a Windows Server 2003 operating system.

The domain functional level of a domain controller running Windows Server 2003 can be raised but cannot be lowered. All domain controllers in the domain must be running appropriate versions of Windows server operating systems to successfully raise the domain functional level.

Organizational units. An *Organizational Unit* (OU) is a container that is used to logically group objects in Active Directory for the purposes of administration. OUs are the smallest units for which you can delegate administrative responsibilities. OUs can contain computers, users, groups, printers and shared folders, etc. You can nest OUs into other OUs within the same domain.

Administrators use OU nesting to organize Active Directory objects in order to simplify and delegate administration. When multiple OUs are nested, all child OUs in the OU hierarchy inherit the permissions assigned to the parent OU. Typically, the structure of an OU will follow the business structure of an organization.

Trees. A *tree* is a hierarchical grouping of one or more domains that is created by adding child domains to an existing Windows Server 2003 parent domain. The first domain you create in your organization is called the root domain. Domains in a tree share a contiguous namespace and a common schema. Windows Server 2003 Active Directory allows you to expand your namespace by adding child domains to existing trees.

For example, the organization *oreilly.com* can name its child domains as *uk. oreilly.com, us.oreilly.com,* and *fr.oreilly.com*. In the *us.oreilly.com*, there could be another child domain named *books.us.oreilly.com*.

Forests. A *forest* represents the outermost boundary of an Active Directory structure. A forest is a hierarchical grouping of one or more domain trees that are completely independent and separate entities. The first domain in the network creates a forest and is called the *Forest Root domain*. The Forest Root domain holds the schema and controls the domain naming for the entire forest. You cannot remove the Forest Root domain without entirely removing the forest itself.

All domains in a forest share a common schema and a *Global Catalog*. These domains are linked by implicit two-way trust relationships. All trees in a forest have different naming structures and operate independently. The forest enables communications across the entire forest.

Physical structure of Active Directory

The two components of the physical structure of Active Directory are *domain controllers* and *sites*. Domain controllers refer to computers running a Windows Server 2003 operating system and running Active Directory services, while sites refer to the physical locations of the organization. These two terms are explained in the following discussion.

Domain controllers. A domain controller is a server running the Windows Server 2003 operating system in the network that is also running the Active Directory services. Domain controllers contain the directory database for the domain. Domain controllers authenticate users' logons and maintain the security policies for the entire domain. All changes to the Active Directory database are done on the domain controllers.

There can be any number of domain controllers in the domain. Multiple domain controllers provide fault-tolerance. When changes to directory objects are made on one domain controller, these changes are replicated to all domain controllers in the domain using the *multimaster replication* model. In this model no single domain controller is the master domain controller. All domain controllers act as peers and hold the same directory database.

There are certain roles of domain controllers that cannot be assigned to more than one domain controller. These roles are known as *operations master* roles. When one of these roles is defined on a domain controller, it performs single-master replication. Operations master roles are classified as one of the following:

Forest-wide operations master roles
> The forest-wide roles include *schema master* and *domain naming master*. Only one domain controller in a forest can be assigned the forest-wide roles.

Schema master
> The schema master role is assigned to the first domain controller in the forest. This domain controller distributes the schema to all other domain controllers in the forest. The domain controller holding the schema master role must be online when changes need to be made to the schema.

Domain naming master
> The domain naming master role is assigned to the first domain controller in the forest. This domain controller controls the addition and deletion of domains in the forest. The domain controller holding the role of domain naming master must be online when adding or removing domains in the forest.

Domain-wide operations master roles
> The following three domain-wide operations master roles are assigned in a domain. Each role can be assigned to only one domain controller per domain.

Relative identifier (RID) master
> The domain controller holding this role assigns blocks of relative identifiers (RIDs) to other domain controllers in the domain. The RID is used with the security identifier (SID) of an object in the domain to create a unique SID for the object.

Primary domain controller (PDC) emulator
> This domain controller acts as a primary domain controller for those clients who do not have the Active Directory client software installed. In other words, the clients that have not migrated to Windows 2000, Windows XP, or Windows Server 2003 use the PDC emulator to log on to the domain.

Infrastructure master
> The domain controller holding this role is responsible for recording any changes made to the domain objects. All changes are first reported to the infrastructure master and then replicated in the domain.

Global Catalog
> Another role that can be assigned to a domain controller is that of a Global Catalog server. This is a catalog service provided by the Active Directory. The Global Catalog server holds information about all the objects in the Active Directory tree or forest. The first domain controller in the forest is assigned this role. You can assign this role to any other domain controller. The Global Catalog server holds the full replica of all object attributes for its host domain and a partial replica of all object attributes for other domains.

Sites. *Sites* in a Windows Server 2003 Active Directory domain are IP subnets that are connected by fast and reliable links. Sites are not part of the Active Directory namespace and contain only computer and connection objects. When users browse for objects in the Active Directory, they see only domains and OUs, and there is no reference to any site. The purpose of sites is to localize as much network traffic as possible. Sites typically have the same boundaries as a local area network. They are primarily created to control replication traffic among domain controllers.

The *replication* process ensures that changes made on one of the domain controllers are passed on to other domain controllers so that users and services are able to access the Active Directory information at any time from any physical location. While replication within a site happens automatically, administrators must manually configure replication between different sites. The information stored in the

Active Directory is logically divided into four categories called the *directory partitions*. These partitions form the major units of the replication process. The following directory partitions are replicated:

Schema partition
> This partition contains information about the objects that can be created in the directory and what attributes these objects can have.

Configuration partition
> This partition contains information about the logical structure of the Active Directory deployment. This data is common to all domains in the forest and is replicated to all domain controllers in the forest.

Domain partition
> This partition contains information about all the objects in the domain. This data is replicated to all domain controllers within the domain only.

Application directory partition
> This partition contains dynamic data that is application-specific. It can contain any type of object except security principles such as users, groups, and computers.

Site replication can be within a site, known as *intrasite replication,* or between different sites, known as *intersite replication.*

Intrasite replication
> Intrasite replication happens automatically between domain controllers within the same site. The data contained in replication traffic is uncompressed because high-bandwidth links are usually available. If changes are made on one domain controller, those changes are quickly replicated to other domain controllers in the site. A Windows service known as Knowledge Consistency Checker (KCC) automatically creates a replication topology among various domain controllers in the site. The KCC checks the replication topology every 15 minutes to ensure that all domain controllers are online. If any of the domain controllers is taken offline, the KCC reconfigures the replication topology.

Intersite replication
> Administrators must configure intersite replication manually, by creating *site links*. A single KCC per site generates all connections between sites. All data is replicated in compressed form. When configuring site links, the administrator provides information about the transport protocol, the cost of the site link, and a schedule for replication. By scheduling replication traffic, the administrator can ensure that replication occurs when the network traffic is low across WAN links.

Trust relationships. A *trust relationship* between two domains ensures that users from the trusted domain are allowed to log on to the trusting domain. Windows Server 2003 uses Kerberos 5 and NT LAN Manager (NTLM) protocols for authentication. Trusts can be *explicit* (created manually) or *implicit* (created automatically). They can be one-way or two-way. The following types of trust relationships can be created:

Tree-root trust

This is implicitly (automatically) established when a new tree root domain is created in a forest. This trust is transitive and two-way.

Parent-child trust

This is implicitly created when you add a new child domain in a tree. This trust is transitive and two-way.

Forest trust

This must be explicitly created by administrators between two Forest Root domains. This trust automatically allows all domains in one forest to trust all domains in the other forest. Forest trusts are available only when you are working in the Windows Server 2003 domain functional level.

Realm trust

This must also be explicitly created by administrators between a non-Windows Kerberos realm and a Windows Server 2003 domain. This type of trust can be transitive or nontransitive and one-way or two-way.

Shortcut trust

This is created explicitly by administrators of two domains in a forest. This type of trust is used to improve logon times when the domains are connected by slow WAN links. This trust is transitive and can be one-way or two-way.

External trust

This is created explicitly by administrators for domains in different forests. This trust can also be created between a Windows Server 2003 domain and a Windows NT 4.0 domain. This trust is nontransitive and can be one-way or two-way.

Overview of a Domain Name System

The Domain Name System (DNS) is a Transmission Control Protocol/Internet Protocol (TCP/IP) service used to resolve Fully Qualified Domain Names (FQDN) to their respective IP addresses. DNS provides user-friendly names instead of complex IP addresses. It provides administrators a method to name computers in a network in a hierarchical fashion. The Active Directory in a Windows Server 2003 domain is integrated with DNS service. Both of these services use a similar namespace. DNS is the locator service for Active Directory objects, and it runs by default on all Windows Server 2003 domain controllers.

DNS namespace

The DNS is organized into a hierarchical namespace, starting with the *root domain*. It ensures that the computer names on the Internet are unique and should resolve to a particular IP address. No two hosts can have the same name within the same domain.

Root domain

The root domain is at the top of the DNS hierarchy. It is represented by a single dot or period.

Top-level domains

Top-level domains are those that we encounter in our everyday Internet surfing. Examples of top-level domains are .com, .net, .biz, .info, .org, .edu, etc.

Second-level domains

The second-level domains are registered for private organizations. The organization that registers the second-level domain name is responsible for managing that domain. It is up to the organization to further create subdomains and child domains under the registered domain name. For example, the second-level domain *oreilly.com* is the registered domain name for the organization named O'Reilly Media, Inc.

A Fully Qualified Domain Name (FQDN) is the name of a particular computer or host in a network that describes the full path of the host in the domain hierarchy. For example, the domain name *books.us.oreilly.com* points to a server named *books* in the *us* subdomain of the second-level domain named *oreilly.com*. The top-level domain is *.com*.

Understanding name resolution

Name resolution refers to the process of resolving a name to its corresponding IP address. DNS servers are used to resolve Fully Qualified Domain Names to IP addresses. The client that needs to resolve a DNS name runs the DNS client service that sends the DNS query to a DNS server and receives the response. DNS queries fall into the following two categories:

Forward lookup query

This is the most common type of DNS query, in which a DNS client needs to resolve a hostname to its IP address. The DNS client sends a name resolution request to its configured DNS server. If the DNS server can resolve the name itself, it sends the resolved IP address back to the DNS client. Otherwise, the DNS server sends queries to other DNS servers until it gets the name resolved. A forward lookup query can be a recursive query or an iterative query.

Reverse lookup query

In this type of query, the DNS client sends a request to its configured DNS server to resolve an IP address to its hostname or domain name. Since the normal DNS zones contain the name to IP address mappings, a reverse lookup zone is created for every DNS zone that contains an IP address to hostname mappings.

Whether a DNS client sends a forward lookup query or a reverse lookup query to its configured DNS server, the query process can take place by either of the following two methods:

Recursive query

In a *recursive query*, the DNS server that receives the name resolution query from a DNS client takes full responsibility for resolving the query for its client. If it knows the IP address of the queried host, it replies with a response. If it does not have any information about the host, it performs additional queries on behalf of its client to other DNS servers until it gets a response. This response is then sent back to the DNS client.

Iterative query

In an *iterative query*, the DNS server that receives the name resolution query checks its own records to resolve the name resolution request. If it does not have any information about the host, it sends a referral back to the DNS client so that the client itself can query other DNS servers.

DNS zones

A DNS *zone* is a database file on a DNS server known as a *name server* that contains resource records on the zone for which it is responsible. These resource records map the IP addresses of the hosts in the domain and other services such as mail servers. A zone contains at least one domain that is known as its root domain. The zone can contain subdomains of the root domain also. When a zone contains domains and subdomains, it must have contiguous domains within the namespace. A subdomain can exist in a zone provided that its parent domain is also contained in the zone.

A zone is primarily an administrative unit that is created on a DNS server to represent a portion of the namespace. You can divide the DNS namespace into multiple zones and host them on a single DNS server, but this is not recommended. On the other hand, it is recommended that you host a zone on multiple name servers. This provides fault-tolerance as well load-balancing among name servers.

Zone types. The following four types of zones are supported in Windows Server 2003, each specifying where the zone database file is stored and what information it contains:

Active Directory-Integrated zone

As the name suggests, the Active Directory-Integrated zone stores the zone database in the Active Directory. When the DNS server is also a domain controller, you can choose to store the zone database in Active Directory. Storing the zone file in Active Directory provides several advantages, such as easy administration, increased security, and conservation of network bandwidth. All zones stored in the Active Directory are *primary zones*. The zone data is automatically replicated along with the Active Directory data.

Standard primary zone

The *standard primary zone* contains the master copy of the zone database. Administrators make changes to the zone's resource records in this copy. The zone data is stored on the DNS server as an ASCII text file. The zone data is replicated to standard secondary zones using the *zone transfers*.

Standard secondary zone

The *standard secondary zone* is a read-only copy of the zone data stored in the standard primary zone. It is not possible to modify any resource record on the secondary zone.

Stub zone

A *stub zone* is a copy of the primary zone that contains only the Start of Authority (SOA), Name Server (NS), and Host (A) resource records for the name server of the zone identified by the stub zone.

Resource records

A zone file is a database file that contains several records, known as *resource records*. A resource record is primarily a hostname to IP address mapping. Table 5-1 lists some of the common resource records:

Table 5-1. Resource records in a DNS zone file

Record	Description
A	Maps a hostname to its corresponding IP address.
CNAME	Creates an alias for the host. More than one hostname can map to a single IP address using the CNAME resource record.
NS	Identifies the DNS server for a particular domain.
SOA	Required as the first record for forward and reverse lookup zones. This record specifies the domain for which the DNS server is responsible.
SRV	Specifies what services are provided by a server and in which domain it serves. Active Directory depends on this resource record.
MX	Identifies the mail server for the domain.
PTR	Maps the IP address to its corresponding hostname in a reverse lookup zone.
WINS	Identifies the WINS server for the DNS domain. In Windows Server 2003, DNS servers are configured to query WINS servers to resolve names that are not contained in DNS database. A WINS server is used to resolve NetBIOS names to IP addresses.

Overview of NetBIOS Name Resolution

NetBIOS names are rarely used in Windows networks these days, but you might have these names in older computers running Windows NT 4.0 or earlier operating systems. You can use either an LMHOSTS file or the Windows Internet Name Service (WINS) to resolve NetBIOS names to their corresponding IP addresses.

LMHOSTS file

LMHOSTS is a static file that contains mappings of NetBIOS names and their IP addresses. This file is usually created manually by administrators and stored either on a local computer or on a network file server. This is a simple text file or a lookup table that contains NetBIOS names and IP addresses. LMHOSTS is suitable only for small networks in a single network segment because it uses broadcast transmission that cannot get past routers.

A sample file is located in the *%systemroot%\system32\drivers\etc* folder of the Windows Server 2003 computer. The following is an example of a small LMHOSTS file:

    192.168.0.1 Mainserver #Main server in office
    192.168.0.10 Intserver # Server providing Internet access
    192.168.0.15 Fileserver #File Server

The best way to use an LMHOSTS file is to create a single file and share it on a network file server. You can then enable LMHOSTS lookup in the WINS tab of TCP/IP properties on a client computer and import the file.

There are several extensions used with entries in the LMHOSTS file. These are as follows:

#PRE
> Preloads an entry into the local cache of the computer.

#DOM:domain
> Associates the computer with the specified domain.

#INCLUDE path
> Used to include another LMHOSTS file into the current file.

#BEGIN ALTERNATE
> Used before the #INCLUDE entry.

#END ALTERNATE
> Used after the #INCLUDE entry.

The following is an example of using the #PRE extension:

```
192.168.0.3 Printserver #PRE Printserver1
```

The following is an example of using the #INCLUDE extension:

```
#INCLUDE \\Fileserver\Adminfiles\LMHOSTS
```

It is important to note that the #PRE entry always comes before the #INCLUDE entry. At least one space is required between the entries in a single line.

WINS servers

A better method of implementing a NetBIOS name resolution solution in your network is to use one or more WINS servers in the network. *WINS servers* prevent broadcast traffic and help conserve the network bandwidth. Once a WINS server is installed in the network, no major configuration is required. A single WINS server is capable of serving about 10,000 clients. In case you have multiple WINS servers, you might want to configure them to replicate the WINS database in order to keep the information up-to-date in each WINS server.

When WINS is deployed in a network, the name resolution takes place in the following order:

1. The local computer cache is checked first.
2. If the name cannot be resolved from the local cache, the computer sends a query to the configured WINS server.
3. If WINS cannot resolve the name resolution query, the computer uses broadcast transmission in the local network segment.
4. If local broadcasts also fail to resolve the name, the computer uses the LMHOSTS file.

WINS replication. When there are multiple WINS servers in a network, you will need to configure *WINS replication* so that all the servers can keep an up-to-date copy of the WINS database. WINS servers can be configured either as pull partners or as push partners. For the WINS replication to work properly, you must configure each WINS server to be both a pull partner and a push partner.

Push partner

The *push partner* sends a notification message to all the WINS servers configured as pull partners whenever there are any changes in the WINS database. The pull partners then request the changes that are sent as an update.

Pull partner

The *pull partner* issues requests to its push partners for WINS database records that have a higher version number.

If you have only two WINS servers in the network, these servers must be both push/pull partners. In case the WINS servers are located across WAN links, the speed of the WAN link is a consideration when deciding the push or pull configuration for replication. When you have a fast WAN link, you should configure the WINS server as a push partner so that it can send updates whenever the WINS database changes. When the WAN link is rather slow, it is better to configure the WINS server as a pull partner so that you can schedule the replication traffic to occur during off-peak hours.

Overview of IP Addressing

The IP Address is a unique address used to identify a computer or a host on the network. This address is made up of 32-bit numbers written in dotted decimal notation in the *w.x.y.z* format. Each block of 8 bits is known as an *octet* or a *byte*. A part of the IP address is known as the *network address* or *network ID*, and the rest of it is known as the *host address* or *host ID*. The network address and the host address are based on the *class* of IP addresses used on the network. All computers on a particular network must have the same number as the network address, while the host address must be unique on the entire network. A second address known as *subnet mask* is used to help identify the part of the network where the host is located.

IP addresses are assigned and controlled by an organization called the Internet Assigned Numbers Authority (IANA). Table 5-2 summarizes the main classes of IP addresses, known as *classful IP address* ranges.

Table 5-2. IP address classes

Class	Range of first byte	Number of networks	Hosts per network	Default subnet mask
A	1–126	126	16,777,214	255.0.0.0
B	128–191	16,384	65,534	255.255.0.0
C	192–223	2,097,150	254	255.255.255.0
D	224–239	N/A	N/A	N/A
E	240–255	N/A	N/A	N/A

The first byte identifies the class of IP addresses used in the network. For example, a host with an IP address 92.137.0.10 is using a class A IP address, and a host with an IP address 192.170.200.10 is using a class C IP address. A special address 127.0.0.1 is used as a *loopback* address for troubleshooting the TCP/IP configuration of the computer.

The IP addresses in the A, B, and C classes are available for public companies and can be assigned by Internet Service Providers (ISP). The class D and class E addresses are reserved for special usage. Another 32-bit binary number known as the subnet mask distinguishes the network ID from the host ID. Its digits are set to 1 and 0, where 1 represents the network portion of the address and 0 represents the host portion. Apart from the IP addresses, the hosts on a network also have a general alphanumeric hostname or Fully Qualified Domain Name (FQDN) in the format *mycomputer.mycompany.com*. Each hostname corresponds to an IP address. The Domain Name System (DNS) is used to translate the IP address of a host to its IP address.

Private IP addresses

Private IP addressing is used when your computer network is not connected to the Internet or if it is located behind a Proxy Server or a Firewall. The IANA has set aside a range of IP addresses in each of the A, B, and C address classes that can be used by private organizations for their internal IP addressing. These addresses are listed in Table 5-3.

Table 5-3. Private IP address ranges

Class	Start address	End address	Subnet mask
A	10.0.0.0	10.255.255.255	255.0.0.0
B	172.16.0.0	172.31.255.255	255.240.0.0
C	192.168.0.0	192.255.255	255.255.0.0

You should not use any of the given private IP addresses if your network is directly connected to the Internet. These addresses ensure that your network is either completely isolated from the Internet or that it is located behind a Firewall or a Proxy Server.

Automatic Private IP Addressing (APIPA)

Usually the IP address is either assigned to a computer statically or assigned through the Dynamic Host Configuration Protocol (DHCP) server. In its default configuration, a Windows XP Professional computer will dynamically obtain its IP address configuration from a DHCP server. When the DHCP server is not available for some reason, the computer can assign itself an IP address automatically. This feature is enabled by default on all Windows XP computers. The automatically assigned address is from the reserved IP address range 169.254.0 to 169.254.255.255. With this address, the computer can connect only to the local network but cannot access any remote network, as only the IP address and subnet mask are assigned.

A computer assigned with APIPA keeps on trying to locate a DHCP server every five minutes in order to obtain a genuine IP address. You can disable the APIPA feature by using the Alternate Configuration. This configuration will be used in case the computer is not able to connect to a DHCP server on startup.

Using DHCP to automate assignment of IP addresses

The DHCP server is used to automate the assignment of IP addresses to client computers in the network. The DHCP server not only assigns an IP address to the client but also supplies other TCP/IP configuration to the client, such as the IP addresses of the DNS servers and routers. In addition to this, it can automatically register and renew the client's DNS name and IP address in the DNS database.

The DHCP runs as a service on one of the servers running the Windows Server 2003 operating system. There should be at least one DHCP server in each network segment. Once the DHCP server is installed, it must be authorized in the Active Directory to service the clients. You must create *scopes* in the DHCP server and activate them. A scope is a pool of addresses that the DHCP server allocates to client computers.

Whenever a TCP/IP client computer boots, it looks for a DHCP server to get a TCP/IP configuration. A DHCP server that has an active scope for the network segment where the client is located assigns an IP address for a specific period of time. This period is called a *lease*. The client must renew its lease when 50 percent of the lease has expired. If the client is successful in renewing the lease, it continues to use the IP address. Otherwise, the client keeps on trying to contact the DHCP server to renew the lease. If the client is not able to renew and the lease expires, the IP address is returned to the address pool and may be assigned to another requesting client.

IP routing

Depending on the size of your network, you may need to divide it into smaller segments. These network segments are known as *subnets*. Network traffic between subnets is carried over by means of IP routers that are either a hardware device or software. *IP routing* refers to connecting small local area network (LAN) segments by means of routers. LAN segments are created to contain the broadcast traffic local to the subnet. Routers do not pass broadcast traffic and thus improve network efficiency. The router acts as a *default gateway* for each client in the subnet.

In most networks, routers are hardware devices. Windows Server 2003 can also be configured as a software router provided that you have at least two network adapters installed on it. The Routing and Remote Access Service (RRAS) provides the routing functions.

When you use subnets in the network, you will need to design an IP addressing solution for the network. If you have a registered IP address, you can divide the available addresses using subnetting. Each computer will then be configured with a subnet mask and a default gateway address in addition to the IP address. The subnet mask will identify the network portion and host portion from the IP address. The DHCP server usually handles all these functions. It is configured with a separate scope for each network segment.

Remote Access

The Routing and Remote Access (RRAS) service in Windows Server 2003 allows remote clients to access the network resources using dial-up networking or Virtual Private Networking (VPN). The two methods of connecting remotely to the network are explained in the following paragraphs:

Dial-up networking
Allows a remote user to connect temporarily to the network using a standard modem and a telephone line or an ISDN line. The client dials a telephone number using her computer modem, which is preconfigured on the remote access server on the network. When authenticated and logged on, the remote user can access the network resources on which she has permissions.

Virtual Private Networking (VPN)
A VPN connection is made through the Internet. This type of connection is called a tunneled connection and is not a direct connection between the remote client and the remote access server. The remote user connects to his ISP and connects to the company network through the Internet. The remote access server, on the other side, is also connected to the Internet. Both create a secure tunnel to establish the connection. VPN has the added advantage that the remote access server is permanently connected to the Internet, and because no modems are required on the server side, a large number of users can connect simultaneously.

Remote access authentication protocols

User authentication in Windows Server 2003 remote access is controlled by a number of authentication protocols and *remote access policies*. The user connecting remotely must present one or more sets of credentials to get access to the remote access server. Access to network resources is further governed and limited by the permissions set on the resources and applicable for the remote user.

Windows Server 2003 supports the following authentication protocols for remote access:

EAP
EAP stands for *Extensible Authentication Protocol*. This is the most secure authentication mechanism that allows you to use a third-party authentication protocol as well as those supplied with Windows Server 2003. These include EAP-MD5 CHAP (Message Digest 5 CHAP), EAP-TLS (Transport Layer Security), and Protected EAP (for wireless networks).

MS-CHAPv2
MS-CHAPv2 stands for *Microsoft Challenge Handshake Authentication Protocol version 2*. This is a password-based authentication mechanism in which both client and server authenticate each other using encrypted passwords. Microsoft recommends using this protocol.

Exam 70-297
Study Guide

MS-CHAP

    MS-CHAP stands for *Microsoft Challenge Handshake Authentication Protocol*. This is an earlier version of MS-CHAP that supports only one-way authentication. This protocol is included to support Windows NT 3.51 and Windows 98 clients that cannot use MS-CHAPv2.

CHAP

    CHAP stands for *Challenge Handshake Authentication Protocol*. This protocol is included to support non-Microsoft clients. It is less secure than MS-CHAP. This protocol requires that passwords be stored using reversible encryption.

PAP

    PAP stands for *Password Authentication Protocol*. This is the oldest and most basic form of authentication in which the username and password are transmitted in clear text over the dial-up network. The transmissions are unencrypted and are not secure. Microsoft does not recommend using this protocol.

SPAP

    SPAP stands for *Shiva Password Authentication Protocol*. This protocol is included to support clients that use Shiva remote access products. It provides very weak encryption for usernames and passwords. All data is transmitted in clear text.

Remote access authorization policies

Once the remote access server authenticates the remote access client, it further tries to authorize the client. The authorization is done using a set of policies known as remote access policies. Each policy contains a set of conditions that the remote client must satisfy. These policies can be configured for an individual user or for a group of users. The components of a remote access policy are as follows:

Policy conditions

    Policy conditions include authentication type, day and time restrictions, data link layer protocol used, tunnel type, and Windows groups that are allowed to connect. A policy can have one or more sets of conditions.

Remote access permission

    The remote client gets permissions to access the remote access server by either satisfying the conditions set in the remote access policies or being explicitly granted access by the administrator.

Remote access profile

    The remote access profile contains dial-in constraints, IP address assignments, multilink features, and authentication and encryption types.

Other ways to configure security for remote access servers is through use of caller ID verification and callback security. The verify caller ID ensures that the remote client is dialing from the authorized telephone number only. The remote access server can be configured to accept or reject the call based on the caller ID. The callback feature serves the same purpose with the added advantage that the telephone charges can be borne by the company.

Analyzing Current Network Infrastructure

The first step in designing a network infrastructure based on Windows Server 2003 Active Directory is to analyze the company, its current network infrastructure, the network topology it is using, and the directory services structure. Each component is important, as it will help you make decisions on several factors that will ultimately affect your design. Analysis of the current infrastructure involves talking to the people who are responsible for administering and maintaining the network, as well as those people who make IT decisions and policies. As you proceed with your analysis, make sure that you keep a record of your findings.

Analyzing the Current Administrative Model

Many companies follow a preset administrative model to minimize administration tasks involved in deploying and maintaining their IT infrastructure. The administration model dictates how network resources are organized and controlled, and how access is secured. Most of the companies follow either the centralized or decentralized model, whereas some companies prefer to keep a hybrid administrative structure.

Centralized administration model

Due to its advantages, the *centralized administration* model is what every company would like to achieve. In this model, the administration of the IT infrastructure is controlled from a central location by a dedicated IT staff. The IT staff has its own hierarchy, starting with the IT manager or IT director and flowing down to network administrators and the IT help desk. The IT staff has control over all aspects of the IT operations in the company's network infrastructure, including design and deployment and even purchase of equipment.

There are two types of centralized administration models. In the first one, both the administration and the resources are centralized. This model is good for companies with a single location but offers very little flexibility when there is more than one geographical location. In the second model, the administration is centralized but the resources are decentralized. It is very much possible with newer administrative tools, such as remote administration and terminal services, to administer the network from a single location. The disadvantage is that the resources, such as servers, are located at a distant location. If something happens to a server, a member of the IT staff will have to personally visit the remote location to fix the problem, which can significantly complicate the support efforts.

The main advantage of the centralized model is that administration is easy and uncomplicated. It is easy to make decisions, as fewer staff members are involved in decision-making. The Active Directory design is simple because you have fewer OUs for delegating administration.

Many companies may not find the centralized model suitable for their requirements because of issues such as limited scalability. When the business grows or the company expands its operations (and the network) to several other geographical locations, it may not be possible to administer it from a single location. Even if that were desirable, the response times would be high.

Decentralized administration model

The *decentralized administration model* is very helpful when the company is spread across several geographical locations and the network infrastructure is very complex. A company using this model will have some sort of IT support staff in each location. Since it may not be possible to administer each and every aspect of the infrastructure from a central location, some administration tasks can be delegated to the local IT staff.

The advantage of the decentralized administration model is that local administrators can respond to problems quickly. This can largely improve response times when there is a problem. It really helps when you have different time zones in different locations.

The disadvantage is that there is cost involved in hiring and training the support staff at each location. It also means that you have to create more domains and/or more OUs so that you can delegate the administration responsibilities to local administrators.

Hybrid administration model

If the centralized administration model seems to be too restrictive and too slow in response and the decentralized model seems to be very expensive, the *hybrid administration model* may be suitable for an organization. You may find that it is very possible to implement a mix of centralized and decentralized models to achieve the overall administration goals. You may keep the major administrative tasks such as resource-planning and security policies and allow the local staff to take care of other issues such as system maintenance, backups, and other smaller support issues.

Another administration approach employed by some companies is to outsource the administrative staff in order to reduce the cost of maintaining the network infrastructure. This helps get skilled staff on an as-needed basis. The advantage is that the company does not have to hire, train, or maintain the IT staff. The disadvantage is that the outsourced staff may lack the dedication you normally find in your own staff. It may also be difficult to trust outsiders when the company deals if secure data.

Documenting your analysis

When you gather information about the current administration model, make sure that you keep a record of your findings. You might have to interview several members of the administration including the local administrators at branch offices. Your documentation must include the following information:

- An organization chart showing different levels of administration, members of IT support staff, and their respective responsibilities.
- The names of persons who make decisions regarding IT projects and control the budget.
- The administration model currently in use. Does the current model allow for future growth?

- Where the IT resources are located How is the administration delegated for geographically dispersed resources?
- Any outsourced services? What are these services?

 Make sure that the documentation you create is simple and accurate. It contains maximum information and still does not consume much of your time. In complex networks, you may need to talk to the main persons responsible for managing the IT services at each location of the company and gather as much information as you think will be important for creating a final design.

Analyzing the Current Geographical Design

From the networking point of view, you will need to know the various geographical locations the company is operating from. The geographical design of the network infrastructure may be limited to a single location or it may be spread across several locations connected with wide area network (WAN) links. The networks in a single location will be linked with high-speed LAN connections while the outer locations may be connected to the head office using a variety of WAN links. Whichever is the case, you will need to gather information about all locations of the company to proceed with your design project.

If the company has a single location, analyzing the geographical model is not a big issue. But when you are dealing with a large corporation, it is important to analyze different geographical locations, the links that connect these locations, and how these locations are administered. Geographical design involves the study of geographical models suggested by Microsoft. Geographical models primarily include local, regional, national, and international models, as explained in the following discussion.

Local model. The *local model* is the simplest of all geographical models, as it is limited to a single physical location. All network resources such as servers, printers, routers, and switches are connected by fast and reliable permanent links. You may find that you are dealing with only one domain at a single site. There is no need to acquire expensive connections for outside connectivity, except for the Internet connectivity. This type of model is easy to design and implement.

Regional model. The *regional model* is one step ahead of the local model where the branches of the company are located outside a single city or town. If you look at the map of the country, the company operations will be located in one particular region spanning a couple of states. The main criteria in designing a network infrastructure for a regional company are the cost and speed of WAN links. In the regional model, a single vendor usually provides the WAN connectivity for all locations.

National model. As the name suggests, the *national model* includes companies that have their locations spread across the entire country. There may be multiple vendors providing the WAN links for connecting various locations of the

Exam 70-297
Study Guide

company. Besides this, all the WAN links may not be of equal speed. Some offices may be connected using fast links such as T1, and others may not have even the slowest dial-up connection. Other considerations include different time zones and different local laws and regulations. Your analysis must include in the documentation all such details that may impact your design.

International model. The *international model* comes into play if the company has one or more offices outside the country. This model needs a detailed study of all the aspects involved, as in the national model. Other things that will need your attention are time zones, language differences, currency regulations, and different laws, such as hiring of employees and software export regulations. A company with international offices may also have multiple branch offices and a large number of employees in each country.

Besides considering the geographical models, you should also take into account any subsidiary offices that the company might have. A subsidiary office is a part of the company but is not necessarily controlled by it. The subsidiary company maintains its own IT infrastructure, but you may be required to analyze any connectivity and resource access issues.

Analyze the current WAN links

It is best to draw a geographical map to document your analysis of the current IT infrastructure. The map should include the type of WAN links between different locations, details of their vendors, and the maximum bandwidth available for each link. When you analyze the WAN links, you should also take into account the current usage levels for each link—what are the complications if the network traffic grows in the future and the WAN links need to be upgraded?

Documenting your analysis

As discussed in the previous section, you should make a map of the geographical model of the company. Your documentation should include the following information:

- The names of the cities where the company offices are located
- The number of users in each location, including the IT support staff
- The types of WAN links connecting the offices, and the link speed, average, and peak usage
- The cost of WAN links and the price structure for each vendor
- If the company has international offices, document details about country-specific information
- Document details about the subsidiary offices of the company, if any

Analyzing the Current Directory Structure

Windows Server 2003 networks are based on the Active Directory, and much depends on how it is implemented. When you analyze the current infrastructure, the next step after analyzing the company and its IT administration model is to check whether the company is already using a domain model and directory services. You will need an analysis of how the domains are implemented and how network resources are located across domains. In case the company has already implemented directory services, you will need information on existing forests, trees, domains, and trust relationships, if any.

Analyzing current Windows 2000 infrastructure

If you are working with a company that has a Windows 2000 network infrastructure, the directory services must also be in place. You will need a careful analysis of how the Active Directory has been deployed in the company. You will most likely be working with the systems or network administrators to gather information on the existing directory structure. The question you need to ask at every step is how the system is implemented and what the rationale is behind the way it is implemented.

Domain structure. You should create a drawing of the domain model that will show the existing domains, trees, and forests. Include in your analysis the full name of each domain, the root domain of each tree, and the name of the root domain of the forest. Find out whether there are any one- or two-way trusts to other Windows 2000 domains or whether there are any one-way trusts to existing Windows NT 4.0 domains. You should also take note of forest level trusts, if any. In any case, you should be clear about the domain structure and how different domains are linked to each other. Figure 5-1 shows a sample domain structure.

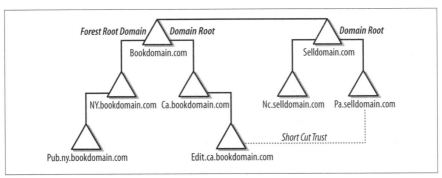

Figure 5-1. Windows 2000 domain structure

As shown in Figure 5-1, you should make a diagram showing the existing domain model. Your diagram should include the following information for each existing Windows 2000 domain:

- The name of each domain
- The name of the root domain of each tree in the domain forest
- The name of the root domain of the forest
- The types of trust relationships between forests, if any
- Any explicit or shortcut trusts created by administrators
- Any explicit trusts created to accommodate Windows NT 4.0 domains

Once you have gathered the above information, you are ready to move down to the OU level.

OU structure. Once you understand how the domain model is implemented, you need to move down to the OU level. Make a diagram for one domain and document the OU structure for the domain. Repeat the process for each domain. The information in your OU analysis documentation should include the following:

- A list of objects included in each OU, including nested OUs.
- A description of permissions assigned to administrators on each OU and objects it contains. Do not forget to include inherited permissions.
- A list of Group Policies linked at each OU.

It is important that you document each piece of information you gather, but at the same time keep your documentation simple. For example, when documenting the OU structure, you could make one diagram for each OU in each domain of the company or use the same diagram for multiple OUs.

Sites and domain controllers. Sites and domain controllers are physical components of the Active Directory. When gathering information on the existing Windows 2000 network directory services, you will need to analyze how the domain is divided into physical sites and how the domain controllers are located in each site. You should do the following and include the information in your analysis:

- When analyzing the domain controllers, check what other roles they are performing. These roles may include operations master roles such as schema master, domain naming master, RID master, infrastructure master, and PDC emulator.
- Find out which domain controller is the Global Catalog server.
- Find out how the Active Directory replication is configured for each site.
- Make a list of the servers that are not domain controllers but perform important network services. These servers might include the DNS server, DHCP server, RRAS server, web server, and messaging server.

Chances are that you will encounter one or two Windows NT 4.0 domains within the Windows 2000 Active Directory infrastructure. Be sure to include analysis of these legacy domains as well. You will need know why these domains have not been upgraded to Windows 2000. Reasons may be monetary but could also relate to certain legacy applications.

Analyzing current Windows NT 4.0 infrastructure

Windows NT 4.0 uses a flat domain model in which each physical location is (ordinarily) under a separate domain. If you are working on a pure Windows NT 4.0 network infrastructure, you will have to do more homework on your analysis. There will be no centralized directory structure in place. In Windows NT 4.0 networks, the highest administrative boundaries are domains and sites that are not available. Primary and backup domain controllers are used for controlling the network services in each physical site. Administrators create two-way trust relationships between domains to enable users from one domain to access resources located in another domain. These trust relationships are nontransitive.

The first thing you need to analyze is why the infrastructure was not upgraded to Windows 2000. What are your choices in upgrading the current Windows NT 4.0 infrastructure to Windows Server 2003? If you decide to upgrade the entire Windows NT 4.0 infrastructure to Windows Server 2003, you can take advantage of newer features such as sites and Organizational Units. The new infrastructure will organize the IT infrastructure in a much better way, and administration of resources will be much easier. Bear in mind that one of the goals of a good directory services design is to simplify administration and lower the cost of ownership. Windows Server 2003 Active Directory services provide these benefits, which were not available with Windows NT 4.0. Figure 5-2 shows how Windows NT 4.0 trust relationships are established.

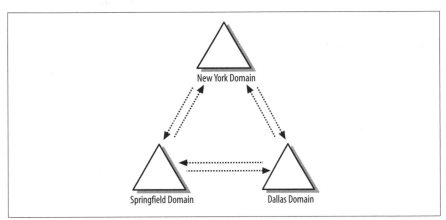

Figure 5-2. Windows NT 4.0 trust relationships

If you decide to keep the current Windows NT 4.0 structure, you may still upgrade the domain objects to the Active Directory model. Other advantages include less time required to implement your design and the retention of old security policies. Users can take advantage of keeping their old passwords and profiles. However, you will not be able to take full advantage of all the features of Windows Server 2003 directory services, and there will be less room for growth.

Your documentation should essentially include the following information:

- The name of each domain.
- The names of the primary domain controller (PDC) and backup domain controller (BDC) in each domain.
- Names of servers providing network services in the domain, including DNS, DHCP, WINS, RAS, IIS, and Exchange servers, along with their IP addresses.
- Types of trust relationships between domains.
- Shared resources in each domain, such as file servers, network printers, etc.
- Names of the domain administrators. These people will help you when you implement your new design.

You will probably need to talk to the top administrators or IT managers to decide who will take over the administrative responsibilities of the new OU structure if the current domain model is restructured to a Windows Server 2003 directory services structure.

Analyzing the Current Technical Environment

After you have gathered information on directory services, the next step is to analyze the current network environment. This includes analyzing the current network equipment, hardware and software issues, and performance requirements. You will need to take inventory of network equipment, such as routers, switches, and hubs, and of computer equipment, such as servers and desktops. Software issues include applications and networking protocols, whereas performance issues include analysis of current performance levels and expectations of the company from the new design.

Servers and desktop hardware

Computer systems, along with the networking hardware such as routers and switches, make up the network. A major task in analyzing the current requirements of the company is to gather as much information as possible about the computer systems in the network, such as servers and desktops. You should take inventory of the entire stock of servers and desktops that are currently in use in the network. Chances are that you will get a ready-made inventory of servers and desktops from one of the administrators in the company. In such a case, it is your responsibility to verify that the information is correct and up-to-date.

At the minimum, your analysis documentation should include the following information:

- The name and make of the computer and its vendor.
- The type and speed of the processor, amount of memory, and number of hard disks and amount of total storage capacity.
- The type and make of the motherboard, its BIOS, and its version number.
- The types of peripherals attached to the computer and their vendors.
- The name of the computer, its location in the network, and its IP address configuration. Some servers might be configured with static TCP/IP configuration.
- The type of networking services running on the computer. Some servers may be configured as DNS servers, DHCP servers, WINS servers, etc., and others might be database servers or email servers.
- A list of operating systems installed on each computer, including service packs installed, if any.
- A list of software installed on the computers, including the name of the application software, its version number, and any service packs or updates installed.
- Shared resources on the computer, such as shared folders or shared printers, as well as the users or groups that have permissions to access the shared resources.
- Users or groups that have permissions to access the computer locally or from the network.

You can divide your inventory into two different groups: one for servers and the other for desktops. The purpose is to clearly understand the current hardware currently in use by the company.

Availability issues. There may be availability issues with the server hardware. Identify which servers need to be available at all times and which ones have been configured as standby servers for the purpose of availability. You might also identify any servers that are being used for load-balancing. If there are no such servers for fault-tolerance or load-balancing, you might need to talk to users or administrators to find out whether there are availability issues with any of the servers. Include all such details in your documentation.

Another issue that will come up during your analysis is the availability of essential network services and critical servers during the upgrade to the newly designed infrastructure. Talk to the network administrators to identify these services and servers so that the upgrade process is trouble free.

Analyzing software requirements

Information on computer and networking hardware is meaningless without information on the software it runs. The software currently used by the company may be packaged software such as Microsoft Office or Microsoft Exchange. There may be, in addition, other software that has been developed in-house by the company's programmers or developers. You will need a careful analysis and documentation of what software is currently in use and how it will be supported in the new design.

Application software. You will need to talk to IT managers, system administrators, software developers, and outside software vendors in order to find out if there are any issues with the current application software. If the company is using packaged software, most of it will also be available for the Windows Server 2003 platform. For the applications that have been developed in-house or outsourced, you will need to address any issues pertaining to their compatibility with the new network environment.

This brings up the issue of training costs involved with the upgrade process. If any parts of the software have been upgraded, users will need to be trained on new or added features. You should document all such issues in your analysis.

Networking software. Networking software includes networking protocols and services. Carefully analyze what networking protocols are in use in each location of the network. You may find that TCP/IP is being used widely; however, you must identify whether any of the legacy clients (such as Windows 95 or Windows 3.x) are still using NetBEUI protocol for networking. If NetBEUI is still in use, there might be applications that require this protocol. Microsoft does not support NetBEUI networking protocol in Windows Server 2003. You can, however, install NetBEUI protocol if it is required, but it is strongly recommended that you replace any such applications that use it.

Be aware that some Novell clients will need implementation of NWLink protocol in the new Windows Server 2003 network. This will enable these clients to operate within the Microsoft network. In case there is any application written to run exclusively on a NetWare server, you will need to check whether the same application or a similar application is available for Microsoft platforms.

Your analysis should include what type of networking services or applications are currently used in the network. These services include Remote Access Service, DHCP for dynamic IP addressing of clients, and DNS and WINS services for name resolution. Besides this, the network might need consistent monitoring for performance issues. You should identify each of these services and how these will be handled in the new infrastructure.

Using too many networking protocols in your network will ultimately result in slowing down network performance. You should try to use as few protocols as possible to avoid performance bottlenecks. It is always wise to avoid using legacy applications that require older networking protocols or services.

Analyzing the current network structure

In the previous section, you analyzed various geographical models. Even if the company has only one office, your network design should include different hardware components used in the LAN and specify the link speeds in each segment or subnet of the LAN. The issue becomes complex when the company has several geographical locations connected by WAN links. You should have a map showing the company locations and analysis of each of the locations and of each LAN within a location. The map should include the following details:

- Number of network segments or subnets, if the LAN is segmented.
- Number of routers, their make and model numbers, and their placement within the network.
- Identify whether the routers are used only to connect LAN segments or for WAN connections as well.
- Check whether there are any hubs or switches used in the network. If yes, note their make and model numbers and their placement within the network.
- Check whether virtual LANs (VLAN) has been implemented.
- Check whether there are any Windows servers being used as routers.
- Identify the type of cabling used in the LAN.
- If the company provides remote access to clients, identify the type of hardware and software used for this purpose.

When you document your analysis, be sure to include as much information as possible. When the company has remote offices, the WAN equipment, link speeds, and their usage issues are of great concern to the IT managers. Include these concerns in your analysis.

IP addressing. For each of the locations, you will need to analyze how the servers and desktop computers are assigned IP addresses. Identify what type of IP addressing method is in use and whether there are any issues with the current method. Your analysis should start with finding out whether the IP address (or address range) is leased by the company from the Internet Service Provider (ISP). Are these addresses from the public address range or is the company using a few public addresses and getting the rest of them are from the private address pool?

The next step is to identify what portion of the address space is reserved for each location. How is the address pool at each location allocated to different subnets in the LAN? Are there any servers or desktops with manual IP address configurations?

The documentation of your analysis should include the following information at the minimum:

- The network ID, subnet mask, and default gateway for the location.
- The name and IP address of the DHCP server or the DHCP Relay Agent.
- The range of IP addresses reserved for the location.
- The names and IP addresses of servers or routers that use statically assigned IP addresses.
- The names of TCP and UDP ports used by any services on the network and the names of servers that use those services.

Once this information is included in your analysis documentation, you will need to refer back to it when deciding on an IP-addressing strategy for your new design.

Analyzing performance requirements

A well-designed network infrastructure should be efficient when it comes to system and network performance. Transfer of information from one location to another between servers and network equipment should take place within a reasonable amount of time. Users should experience minimum delays, whether they are just logging on to the network, accessing a shared resource, or working on a large database file. The network and systems should not only provide good performance but should also be available when required by users or applications.

It is important to analyze current performance levels of the different components in the network infrastructure. Your analysis should include performance of the network, performance of WAN links, and performance levels of each critical server in the network. There are several tools included in Windows Server 2003 to create a performance baseline and to monitor real-time performance. The Performance console (Performance Monitor in Windows 2000) is just one example of performance monitoring tools.

Network performance. You need to talk to network administrators regarding any performance bottlenecks they are currently facing. These bottlenecks or performance issues should be included in your documentation so they can be addressed in your design. You can use the Network Monitor in Windows Server 2003 and Windows 2000 or Microsoft Systems Management Server to identify any performance issues with the existing network. It is always good to compare the network performance at peak usage hours with the baseline created when the network usage is normal.

System performance. System performance can easily be monitored using the Performance console. Systems administrators are the best people to tell you about any outstanding performance issues with existing servers. You can verify several of these issues by sitting down at each server and analyzing the system logfiles. Take some time to examine the logfiles and to identify any performance issues that you or the system administrators are not aware of. If possible, talk to a few users and ask them whether they feel that any server or any shared resource takes an unreasonable amount of time to respond. Document your performance analysis, noting any system or network performance issues and how you plan to address these issues.

Designing an Active Directory Structure

Once you have gathered, analyzed, and documented all necessary information about the current network and directory structure of the company, you need to start working on creating an Active Directory design for the company. The best approach is to start with simple things and maintain room for future growth at the same time. Depending on your analysis of the current infrastructure and present and future business requirements of the company, you might have to design anything from a single domain directory structure to a multiple domain forest structure.

As the designer, it is your responsibility to keep the cost of ownership low, but at the same time, provide better administration of resources and expected security levels. The more homework you do before putting your design on paper, the fewer calls you will get later. It is always good to create the design and review it before implementing it.

In this section, we will look at the available domain and forest functional levels in Windows Server 2003 and then turn our attention to things that need consideration for creating domains, forests, and Organizational Units.

Domain and Forest Functional Levels

A Windows Server 2003 network can operate at four different domain functional levels and three different forest functional levels depending on the types of domain controllers and forests existing in the network. These different functional levels are included in Windows Server 2003 for backward support. When deciding on functional levels, you should consider which functional level you will use during the implementation phase and how that level will be upgraded in the future. You must also keep in mind that these functional levels can be raised but cannot be lowered.

The four *domain functional levels* are as follows:

Windows 2000 Mixed
> This is the default domain functional level that allows a Windows Server 2003 domain controller to interact with domain controllers running Windows Server 2003, Windows 2000, and Windows NT 4.0 operating systems.

Windows 2000 Native
> This allows a Windows Server 2003 domain controller to interact with domain controllers running Windows Server 2003 and Windows 2000 operating systems.

Windows Server 2003 Interim
> This allows a Windows Server 2003 domain controller to interact with domain controllers running Windows Server 2003 and Windows NT 4.0 operating systems. Use this functional level when you are migrating from Windows NT 4.0 to Windows Server 2003.

Windows Server 2003
> This is available only when all domain controllers in the domain are running the Windows Server 2003 operating system. This level offers the highest functionality of all domain functional levels.

The three *forest functional* levels are as follows:

Windows 2000
> This is the default forest functional level. It supports domain controllers running Windows Server 2003, Windows 2000, and Windows NT 4.0.

Windows Server 2003 Interim
> This supports domain controllers running Windows Server 2003 and Windows NT 4.0.

Windows Server 2003
> This is the highest forest functional level available with Windows Server 2003 forests. This is available only when all domain controllers in all domains of the forest are running Windows Server 2003.

Designing a Namespace

Before you start the process of designing the domain and forest structure, it is important to consider the naming structure that will be used in domains and forests. The Active Directory in Windows Server 2003 supports the Lightweight Directory Access Protocol (LDAP) naming structure. This section covers basics of LDAP naming formats, including creating a naming strategy for your design, supporting DNS names, and finally, choosing domain names.

LDAP naming formats

The Active Directory relies on LDAP naming conventions to store objects and their attributes. This allows users and applications to locate resources in the Active Directory network using a wide variety of methods. The Active Directory schema defines object classes, and every class has attributes associated with it. These attributes ensure that every object in the Active Directory has a unique identification. In order to locate a resource or an object in the Active Directory database, you can start your search by using the object name or any of its properties (attributes).

Windows Server 2003 Active Directory supports the following types of name formats.

Relative distinguished name. The *relative distinguished name* (RDN) of an object identifies the object within its parent container. Therefore, this name is relative to other objects in the same container. For most objects, the RDN is the Common Name attribute. The Active Directory automatically creates the relative distinguished name of an object when the object is added to the directory database. No two objects in the same parent container can have the same RDN. The following is an example of a relative distinguished name:

    CN=Myname,CN=Users,DC=Oreilly,DC=com

Whereas CN stands for common name, DC stands for the domain component that is the part of a DNS namespace, such as COM or ORG or NET. The RDN of the parent object in this example is CN=Users.

Distinguished name. A *distinguished name* (DN) uniquely identifies an object by using the relative distinguished name for the object and the names of container objects and domains that contain the object. The distinguished name identifies the object as well as its location in the tree. Every object in the Active Directory has a distinguished name. Distinguished names are unique in the entire forest. You cannot have two objects with the same DN in the forest hierarchy. The following is an example of the distinguished name for an object:

    CN=Myname,CN=Users,DC=Oreilly,DC=com

In this example, the object myname is identified as a user object in the *oreilly.com* domain.

Canonical name. A *canonical name* (CN) of an object is similar to the distinguished name of an object, but it is written in a different syntax. The difference is that the naming starts from the root and goes downward in the hierarchy, and LDAP attributes are not used. The distinguished name given in the previous example will have the following canonical name:

    oreilly.com/Users/myname

User principal name. The *user principal name* (UPN) identifies the user account and the domain in which the account is located. This name looks like an email address and is a standard for logging on to Windows domains. The user principal name for the previous example will read as follows:

    myname@oreilly.com

The part of the UPN after the at (@) sign is known as the *UPN suffix*. Users can log on to the domain using their UPN names, but it is not a requirement.

Designing a naming strategy

The Windows Server 2003 Active Directory is closely linked to the Domain Name System. Active Directory naming follows the DNS naming conventions. Clients use the DNS in the Active Directory domains to locate servers that provide important network services. All Active Directory domains are identified by their domain names as well as with their NetBIOS names.

DNS names start from the root and flow down the DNS hierarchy. The first domain you create in an Active Directory network is designated as the root domain for the forest as well as the root domain for the first domain tree in the forest. The DNS namespace starts from this root domain. For example, a parent domain named *oreilly.com* can have child domains such as *publishing.oreilly.com* and *books.oreilly.com*. These child domains can have further child domains such as *us.publishing.oreilly.com*. Figure 5-3 shows parent and child domains in a DNS namespace hierarchy.

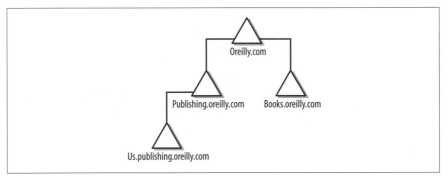

Figure 5-3. Parent and child domains in a DNS namespace

When designing your Active Directory naming strategy, you should consider DNS names as well as NetBIOS names. NetBIOS names are still supported in Windows Server 2003 for backward-compatibility. NetBIOS naming conventions follow a flat namespace unlike the hierarchical structure of a DNS namespace. When you install Windows Server 2003, the operating system automatically creates a NetBIOS name (pre-Windows 2000 name) for the computer. Domain names are also generated in a similar way. In fact, the name you give a computer when installing the operating system is a NetBIOS name. Thus, a single NetBIOS name for any host can also be resolved to its IP address.

With Active Directory, appending the full domain name to the computer name creates the DNS names. For example, if you supply the name *fileserver1* to a computer that is located in the books domain of *oreilly.com*, the operating system will append *books.oreilly.com* to create the DNS name of the computer as *fileserver1.books.oreilly.com*.

When designing a DNS naming convention for your network, make sure to do the following:

- Create names that are easy to remember.
- Create DNS names that are compatible with NetBIOS naming conventions.
- Although DNS names support up to 64 characters in the computer name, limit the names to 15 characters.
- Try to avoid names that create confusion among users.
- Use unique names throughout the organization.
- Make sure the name reflects the purpose of the servers.

Working with registered DNS names. You will most likely be working in an environment where the company has an Internet presence. When this is the case, you will be working with both registered computer names that are accessible from the Internet and unregistered names for computers that are accessible only from inside the network. If the domain name is already registered with the appropriate Internet authority, you will need to design a namespace that will fit well into the registered Internet namespace.

You have the following options for creating the DNS namespace for your design:

Use the same registered DNS names internally and externally.
   Using this method, you will use the registered DNS name of the company as your Active Directory root domain name. This method is recommended by Microsoft and is the easiest to design, implement, and administer.

Use the subdomain of the registered DNS name.
   Using this method, the name of your Active Directory root domain will be a subdomain of the registered DNS name. You will need separate DNS zones to host resource records for internal and external networks. This method provides an additional layer of security for your internal network.

Use different internal and external names.
   In this case, you will need to register two different domain names and maintain two separate namespaces. Unless you have a specific reason to use this strategy, you should not use this method, as this will require more administration and increased cost of ownership.

Choosing domain names. The following guidelines are important when choosing domain names for your design:

* Use names that are short and easy to remember.
* Use only registered domain names for root domains.
* Keep the domain names unique throughout the organization.
* Use only standard characters supported by all DNS platforms to ensure interoperability with non-Windows DNS servers. These include A–Z, a–z, 0–9, and the hyphen (-).
* Keep the internal and external namespaces for the purpose of securing your internal resources. You can, however, base your internal names on external names.

Choosing names for security principals. Users, groups, and computers in a Windows Server 2003 Active Directory network are known as *security principles*. Once you create a design for naming your internal and external domains, you should design naming convention security principals in the organization. It is possible to use the same names for security principals in different domains; however, you should not base your design on these conventions because doing so would cause confusion among users. Your design should provide a strategy to use names in a consistent manner.

When choosing names for users, groups, and computers, follow these guidelines:

- Keep names unique in the domain and use only supported characters.
- Use a maximum of 20 characters for usernames, 63 characters for group names, and 15 characters for computer names.
- Names of security principals cannot include these special characters: #, +, <, >, ", and any leading or trailing spaces.
- Do not use only periods (.), spaces, or the at (@) character for any name.

Designing the Domain Structure

Creating a design for a Windows Server 2003 Active Directory network involves decisions regarding forest and domain structure. This decision further depends on whether you want to create a single domain or multiple domains. When you have multiple domains, you will need to decide on the number of domains as well as the number of domain trees and domain forests.

Creating a single domain

A single Active Directory domain is the simplest one to create and easiest to administer. If possible, you should try to create only a single domain. In many situations, you will find that a single domain will fulfill most of the requirements of the company. A single domain model offers several advantages over multiple domains and is still very scalable.

Some of the advantages of a single domain model include the following:

- It is easy to plan, implement, and administer.
- Since all objects are located in the same security boundaries, there is no need to configure trust relationships.
- Planning user accounts and Group Policies is easier. Account polices and password policies will need to be configured and implemented only once at the domain level.
- You can choose from centralized or decentralized administrative models or use a hybrid administration model.
- There are fewer problems, and less troubleshooting is required.
- The overall cost of ownership is low.

Scalability in a Windows Server 2003 Active Directory domain allows businesses to grow without the need to restructure the domain model. A Windows Server 2003 Active Directory domain can hold up to 1 million different types of objects. You should try to avoid creating complexity at the domain level. Keeping things simple at the top should be the goal of your design.

You can use OUs to achieve further scalability and flexibility in administration. If the organization has multiple geographical locations, you can divide the domain structure into OUs based on locations and delegate the responsibility of these OUs to local administrators. The local administrators can control their respective Ous, and you can still keep the overall centralized control at the head office. This is a better choice than creating multiple domains. Creating the OU structure is covered later in this section.

While OUs are logical partitions of the domain to share or delegate administrative responsibilities, you can create *sites* that physically separate different parts of the domain in order to balance load of replication traffic between domain controllers located at different geographical locations. Creating sites is covered later in the section "Designing a Site Topology."

Creating multiple domains

Unless you have some compelling reason to adopt the multiple domain model, you should avoid using it. Creating multiple domains means there will be more administrative overhead and more cost involved in implementing and maintaining the domain structure. Domain administrators will need to be skilled and should understand the overall Active Directory structure to efficiently manage the network and resources. In some situations, security policies of the organization may force you to adopt the multiple domain model. Other things that might affect your design can include political, technical, or administrative issues.

When using multiple domains, you will need to decide how to define the domain boundaries. Domains can be based on geographical locations or on the departmental structure of the organization. Defining domain boundaries on geographical locations is a better choice because it is unlikely that these locations will change, whereas departments can be added or removed. Figure 5-4 shows multiple domains.

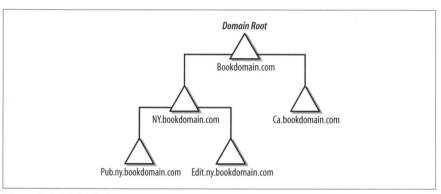

Figure 5-4. Multiple domains

Other issues that will dictate use of multiple domains are as follows:

- When you need to implement decentralized administration of domains located at different geographical locations.
- When you need to implement different security policies at the domain level.
- When you need to provide a different DNS namespace for different departments or different locations of the company.
- When you need to maintain Windows NT 4.0 domains.

- When you need to limit the replication traffic across WAN links that are either slow or unreliable.
- When you need to place the domain controller holding the schema master role in a different domain for security reasons.

 When creating multiple domains, you should try to create domains that are in the same domain tree. Domains in the same tree share a contiguous namespace so that you can reduce administrative overhead as opposed to creating multiple trees.

When you base your Active Directory design on multiple domains, you should be aware that there are several other things involved in implementing and maintaining multiple domains. These are explained as follows:

Cost of domain controllers
Each domain you create will need servers configured as domain controllers. If fault-tolerance is also required, you will need at least two domain controllers at each site. This increases the cost of server hardware and more time will be needed to install and configure the domain controllers.

Creation of trust relationships
Two-way transitive trust relationships are automatically created when you create child domains under parent domains. This results in automatic authentication of users from different domains. However, you might need to create shortcut trusts in order to improve logon times for users who need to log on to domains that are located far away in the domain hierarchy.

Access to resources
With two-way transitive trusts, authentication happens automatically, but this does not mean that users get access to resources automatically. Access permissions will still need to be manually configured so that users can access cross-domain resources.

Group Policies
In Windows Server 2003 domains, a domain is the highest level where Group Policies and access control can be configured. You will need to create these policies for each domain you create.

Administrative access
The Enterprise Admins group is given administrative rights across domains. When you have multiple domains, you will need to add additional administrators to this group.

Designing the Multiple Tree Structure

A domain tree has multiple domains that share a contiguous namespace. It consists of a *parent domain* and *child domains*. A child domain is also known as a *subdomain* of the parent domain. The first domain in the domain tree is always the tree root domain. For example, *us.oreilly.com* is a child domain of *oreilly.com,* and *books.us.oreilly.com* is a child domain of *us.oreilly.com.* In most of these situations, you will not need more than one domain tree, but there may be situations where a single domain tree will not satisfy the requirements of the organization.

One of the main reasons to create multiple trees is that you need more than one DNS namespace in the domain forest. You will need to base your decision on your analysis and other factors, such as future requirements of the organization. Creating more trees simply means that you will need to maintain separate namespaces for each tree and create more domains because each domain tree must have at least one domain.

Designing the Multiple Forest Structure

A *forest* is a group of domain trees that do not share a contiguous namespace. There is always one forest in any Active Directory-based network. This forest is automatically created when you install the first domain controller. The domain you create becomes the Forest Root domain. A forest specifies the outermost security boundary of the network. Administrative control and user access is possible only in the domains within the forest. To extend access to resources outside the forest, you need to create forest trusts. These forest trusts are available only if the forest functional level is Windows Server 2003 and the trusts are not transitive.

Domains in a forest share a common schema, directory partition, two-way transitive trusts relationships between domains, and a common global catalog. As much as possible, you should avoid using multiple trusts and try to contain your design to a single forest. But there may be situations when you will need to consider creating multiple forests. These situations include the following:

Linking two separate organizations
> This situation is very much a reality these days, with a number of mergers and acquisitions taking place. The multiple forests may be needed so that users in one organization can access resources in the other organization.

Creating an autonomous unit
> You may be in a situation where administrators of a forest need independence from the main forest of the organization. For example, a group of developers may need to make changes to the forest schema without affecting the main forest.

Creating an isolated unit
> There may be a situation in which each unit needs to maintain its own security and isolated administration for the forest. Some legal requirements may also require creation of separate forests.

As much as possible, you should try to limit your design to a single forest. With multiple forests, each forest will have to maintain its own schema and directory partition as well as the global catalog. Replication and trust relationships will have to be configured manually. All this means that there are more administrative overheads involved with multiple forests and more complex design is required.

Some of the disadvantages of using multiple forests are as follows:

- Administration overhead increases with more training to administrators and support staff.
- Replication of information between domains of multiple forests must be manually configured.

- DNS name resolution methods must be configured appropriately to resolve names and locate resources across forests.

- Access to resources across forests must be manually configured in each forest.

- Administrators must create separate groups of users in each forest who need access to resources outside their own forest.

- Locating resources in other forests is not as easy as locating resources in a single forest.

- Users must use *user principal names* when logging on to domains in other forests.

Designing Migration Paths to Active Directory

Creating a design for Windows Server 2003 Active Directory network requires that you take into account the existing network, which may consist of Windows NT 4.0 domains, Windows 2000 domains, or a mix of both. You might have gathered information on any existing domains while analyzing the existing structure and the business and technical requirements of the organization. This section explains the ways you can migrate an existing domain structure to Windows Server 2003 Active Directory.

Migrating from Windows 2000 domains

Migrating a Windows 2000 Active Directory domain to Windows Server 2003 is a simple and straightforward process. Windows Server 2003 domains work on the same principles as Windows 2000 domains. Most of the features of the Windows 2000 Active Directory are present in Windows Server 2003 also. It is very possible that a good Active Directory structure is already in place and that you just need to perform a few upgrades. If you get a working Windows 2000 Active Directory domain, you may be able to use the domain structure as it is. But depending on the requirements of the organization, you may have to perform a complete restructuring.

Before you introduce new Windows Server 2003 domain controllers in an existing Windows 2000 Active Directory infrastructure, you will need to use the Active Directory preparation utility adprep.exe. You should also run this utility on any Windows Server 2003 member servers that you want to promote to become domain controllers. The ADPrep utility is located in the \i386 folder of Windows Server 2003 setup CD-ROM. You need to run the adprep /forestprep command followed by the adprep /domainprep command. This prepares the existing Windows 2000 forests and domains, respectively, for the Windows Server 2003 Active Directory by extending the schema to support new object classes and attributes. The existing Windows 2000 permission sets on built-in containers, objects are modified, and administration tools are upgraded.

Migrating from Windows NT 4.0 domains

The Windows NT 4.0 domain structure was entirely different from Windows Server 2003. First of all, there were no sites in Windows NT 4.0. Administrators had to create domains for each geographical location of the organization. The number of domains in large organizations used to be in the hundreds. These domains were not very efficient and had poor scalability. Administrators used to create master user domains to organize users and accounts, and resource domains to organize shared network resources.

If you are working in a situation in which Windows NT 4.0 domains still exist, you will have to consider several options while designing an upgrade or migration strategy for the network infrastructure. You have two options to migrate from Windows NT 4.0 domains. Either you can restructure the entire domain structure or perform an in-place upgrade. If you decide to perform a complete restructuring, you may be able to take advantage of several new features of the Windows Server 2003 Active Directory domain structure. Most of the Windows NT 4.0 multiple domain structures can be incorporated into a single Windows Server 2003 domain. The master account domains and resource domains can be converted to a more efficient hierarchy of sites and Organizational Units.

An in-place upgrade does offer some benefits but is not recommended unless you have some specific reasons for not restructuring. You must consider the in-place upgrade strategy under the following situations:

- When you do not have enough time for analysis, planning, designing, or implementation.
- When you want to keep the changes to the administrative structure to a minimum.
- When you want minimum disruptions of network services during the migration time.
- When you feel that the current Windows NT 4.0 structure will translate well into a Windows Server 2003 Active Structure.

 Windows NT 4.0 domains might have a number of administrators for each domain spread across the locations of the organization. Whether you are performing an in-place upgrade or a complete restructuring, you will need to work with these administrators to ensure that they understand the new structure based on Windows Server 2003 Active Directory services. You should also take into account any issues that these administrators might have with the existing domain structure. A well-documented upgrade plan will always ensure that the plan is implemented as it should be.

Designing a Security Infrastructure

Once you have identified the design structure for domains, trees, and forests, the next step is to design a security structure. The security design of each domain includes designing OUs, accounts for users and computers, and security groups. Administrative control of different parts of the network infrastructure is implemented using Organizational Units, and administrative security policies are implemented using Group Policies. This section covers design of Organizational Units, accounts, and Group Policies.

Designing an OU Structure

Organizational units are the basic units of the administrative security structure. Setting one OU should be your first design step after you are done with the design of a domain structure. Knowledge of different OU models will help you decide how these models can be incorporated into your design. OUs contain users, computers, groups, applications, shared folders and printers, security policies, and other things. The basic reason for creating OUs is to simplify administration. The following discussion explains some of the common reasons for creating OUs within the domain hierarchy.

Purpose of designing OUs

The three primary reasons for creating OUs in each domain are delegation of administration, limiting the visibility of objects, and efficient implementation of Group Policies. The following discussion will look at each of these purposes.

Delegation of administrative control. The foremost purpose of creating OUs is to delegate control of Active Directory objects so that administration can be simplified. OUs based on locations seem to organize things nicely, but this should not be your priority. OUs are not created to look more organized or to allow users to locate objects more easily. The basic purpose of creating OUs is to simplify management of Active Directory objects.

Design of OUs for the purpose of *delegation of control* (also called *delegation of administration*) can be based either on objects or on administrative functions.

Object-based OU design
  In this type of OU, the delegation of control is assigned to administrators according to the types of objects in the Active Directory database. These objects include users, computers, groups, OUs, sites, and domains. To create this type of OU, first place all the objects for which you wish to delegate administration into the OU. Then put an individual administrator or a group into a security group. Once this is done, you can delegate the control of the OU to the security group you created.

Function-based OU design
  In this type of OU, the delegation of control is based on administrative functions assigned to individual administrators or a group of administrators. These administrative functions include account management, defining group policies for the OU, control of group memberships, and resource permissions.

Your OU design will define how precisely you can delegate control of administration, based either on objects or on job functions of administrators. When you choose an OU based on Active Directory objects, you can place all similar objects in a single OU and then define a precise set of permissions for different administrators so that each administrator is responsible for only a particular set of objects. This OU can then have *nested OUs* (child OUs), in which you can define more precise permissions and enable or disable inheritance of permissions.

It is important to emphasize the design of top-level OUs at this point in the discussion. The top-level OUs should be designed so that minimal changes are required at the top level if there are any changes in the organization. You should design the top-level OUs so that not only is the administration simple, but the delegation of control can also be achieved easily. In most organizations, the top-level OUs are based on geographical locations, types of administrative functions, or types of objects in the Active Directory database. Designing top-level OUs essentially means that you are placing your emphasis on a design that is less likely to change, but actually, the design is based more or less on administrative functions in each location. This idea is very helpful when you have dedicated IT administrative staff for each location. When the design is based on administrative functions, it will not change frequently because most common administrative functions usually do not change. When you have a multiple domain model, the top-level OUs should be consistent in each domain. This ensures that administration functions remain similar across all domains.

When designing lower-level OUs or nested OUs, you can decide on more precise control of administrative responsibilities. Lower-level OUs can also be created for the purpose of applying Group Policies. Since Group Policy inheritance will also be effective in this case, you will have to consider the effect of policy inheritance and permissions.

Whatever organizational design you choose, you must always keep in mind that the overall purpose of your design is to make administration simpler. You should avoid using a complex design that makes management more complicated. It is very easy to get into a complex hierarchy of OUs when you sit down and work on your design. Be very careful to create only as many levels of OUs as are actually necessary.

Limiting visibility of objects. Due to security requirement (or for other reasons), some organizations may want to hide certain objects from certain groups of administrators or groups of users. This is something that you cannot achieve using permissions on those objects. Users or administrators who have access to containers of those objects can still view the existence of those objects. One way to hide critical or confidential objects is to place them in a separate OU and then give List Contents permission on the OU to only the authorized users or administrators. This permission effectively hides those objects from unauthorized users.

Effective implementation of Group Policies. Group Policies provide a method to effectively apply uniform security settings and computer configurations to a large number of objects simultaneously. A small example of a Group Policy is defining a uniform Account Lockout and Password Policy and applying it throughout the domain. Group Policies are created using *Group Policy Objects* (GPOs) that are applied at domain, site, and OU levels. Most of the GPOs are applied at the OU level because of different security and computer configuration requirements.

Group Policies travel down from the domain to the site level and then to the OU level. It is a good idea to plan GPOs at the higher level first and then move down to the lower levels. This way, you can apply the Group Policies to a larger number of objects at once. GPO filtering will allow the singling out of objects for which the policies should not be applied at a higher level. Group Policy inheritance also affects your design of the OU structure.

Applying GPOs at the OU level, which is the lowest level where you can do this, gives you more granular control over Group Policy settings. However, it requires the creation of more GPOs. You should try to keep the number of Group Policies to a minimum, because the more policies defined for an object, the longer it takes for the users to access the object. If you need to exclude a group of users from a GPO, create another OU for them instead of using Group Policy filters.

Group Policies are covered later in the section "Designing a Group Policy Structure"

OU design models

The design of the OUs should primarily be based on the administrative structure of the organization. Usually the IT administration staff holds the overall control of resources, irrespective of the parent department in which the resource belongs. This is a kind of centralized approach to controlling the administration of resources of the company, but this model may not suit every organization. This section explains some of the commonly used models on which you can base your OU design.

OU based on location. This model is useful when each geographical location of the organization has its own IT administrative staff. The administration of each location is the responsibility of local administrators. This type of OU is also very helpful when each location has its own administrative requirements that do not correspond with other locations. One major advantage of this model is that the OUs do not change when there are departmental changes in the company because it is unlikely that the locations will also change. Figure 5-5 shows one such model.

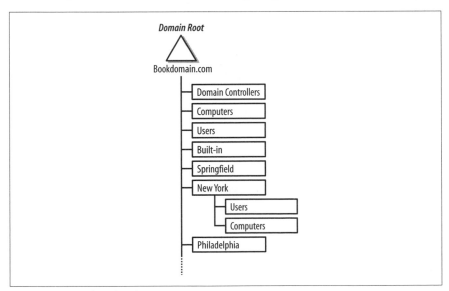

Figure 5-5. OUs based on location

Some of the other advantages of location-based OUs are as follows:

- The central administrative staff can easily implement domain-wide policies.
- Location of resources within the organization can be easily figured out.
- It is simple to create new OUs in the future if the organization expands.

This model also has some disadvantages. First, you will need local administrative staff at each location. Second, the model may not allow you to follow the business structure of the organization.

> An Active Directory site is the same as a separate geographical location. When you base your OU design on the location-based model, you will probably apply Group Policies at the site level.

OU based on organization. This model is useful when the administration of IT infrastructure is based on business units or departments of the organization. Each department or unit should have its own IT administration staff. One major advantage of this model is that each business unit or department can maintain administrative autonomy over the objects it owns. This is independent of other business units or departments of the organization. Figure 5-6 shows one such model.

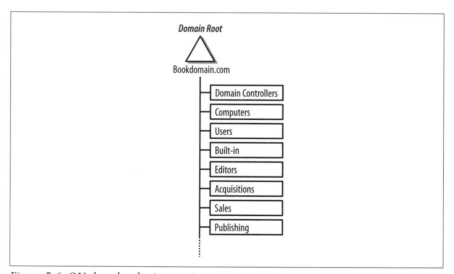

Figure 5-6. OUs based on business units

Some other advantages of business-based OUs are as follows:

- It is easy to create an OU based on organizational structure.
- This model can help business units keep control of their administrative needs.
- This model can accommodate organizational expansion due to mergers or acquisitions.

In spite of some advantages of the organization-based model, one major disadvantage is that the OU structure will be changed when there are changes to the business structure. For example, when a unit or department is added or removed, the OU structure will also have to be modified.

OU based on functions. This model is a good choice for small organizations in which administrative functions span several departments. In this model, the single administrative group is usually responsible for managing the entire network of resources. This group is divided according to business functions within the organization.

One major advantage of this model is that the OU structure does not change when the organization restructures. The disadvantage is that you will have to create several OUs to delegate administration of objects such as users, computers, databases, mail systems, shared folders, and printers.

OU based on location and organization. There are two options for designing hybrid models using both location and organizational models. The first is to design an OU structure that keeps location first and places the organizational structure second. The second option is to design an OU structure that keeps organizational structure first and then places the location. Each of these options is explained in the following list.

Location and then organization
> In this hybrid model, you create the top-level OUs using the location-based model. Then you create lower-level OUs using the organization model. For example, you will first create top-level OUs for different geographical locations of the company. Then, within each top-level OU, you will create OUs for different departments or units of the organization.
>
> The advantages of this model include allowance for departmental growth and defining distinct security boundaries. The disadvantage is that you will have to redesign your OU structure if the administrative staff is reorganized.

Organization and then location
> In this hybrid model, you create the top-level OUs using the organization-based model. Then you create lower-level OUs for each of the locations using the location model. For example, you will first create top-level OUs for different departments or units of the company. Then you will create lower-level OUs for different locations of the company in each top-level OU.
>
> The advantages of this model include delegation of control to local administrators while still maintaining sufficient security between departments. The disadvantage is that the OU structure will need to be redesigned if there is a change in administrative structure.

Built-in containers and OUs in Windows Server 2003. When you install Windows Server 2003 Active Directory on a computer, the following built-in containers and organization units are created by default:

Domain
> This container is the root container for the Active Directory. Permissions applied to this container affect all child containers and objects throughout the

domain. The control of this container is never delegated to anyone. Only service administrators should have permissions on this container.

Built-in container

The built-in default service administrator account is located in this container.

Users container

This is the default container in which all new user accounts are stored. As with the domain container, you should neither change permissions on this container, nor should you delegate the control of this container to anyone. For delegation of control, you should create a separate container for users, and move users from this container to the new container. In case you need to apply GPOs, create a new OU and move the users to the new OU. You must do this because you cannot link GPOs to this container.

Computers container

This is the default container in which all new computer accounts are stored. As with the Users container, you should create a new OU for computers for which you wish to delegate control, assign permissions, or link GPOs to the computer's OU.

Domain controllers OU

This is the default OU where computer accounts for all domain controllers in the domain are located. There is a default set of Group Policies applied to this container, and you should not move the computer accounts from this OU. Not moving the accounts ensures that uniform policies are applied to all domain controllers in the domain. Only the service administrators should have permissions on this container.

Permission inheritance in OUs. By default, all child OUs inherit the permissions assigned to their parent OUs. Similarly, all objects located in each OU inherit the permissions assigned to the parent OU. This inheritance starts from the top-level OU and flows down to the lowest OU and its objects. One major advantage of inheritance is that when delegating control of OUs, administrators can delegate control of the OU. This control is automatically granted for all child objects.

Permission inheritance can also be blocked. In some situations, you may need to assign a set of permissions on a child OU that is different from the parent OU. You can block inheritance of permissions assigned to the parent OU so that they do not apply to the child object where you want a different kind of permission set.

In ideal cases, the permissions assigned at the parent OU should do all the work for you using inheritance. This is possible only if your design reflects a simple OU structure.

Designing a Group Policy Structure

Group Policies are an effective way to control the working environment in an Active Directory network. You can use Group Policies to configure uniform settings for a large number of computers simultaneously. Besides this, you can enforce security policies of the organization as well as control how software is distributed to client computers. This section provides an overview of Group Policies and then discusses the options for implementing a Group Policy structure.

Overview of Group Policy

Group Policy, as the name suggests, is a group of policies that includes several settings that can be enforced on a single computer or multiple computers at once. Each Group Policy is a collection of user and computer configuration settings and is called a Group Policy Object (GPO). This GPO can be linked to the local computer, to an OU, to a site, or to a domain. For a standalone computer, the only GPO applied is the local GPO. When a computer is a part of an Active Directory domain, it can be subject to a number of GPOs coming from a number of sources.

The following two types of Group Policy settings are available with Active Directory:

Computer Configuration
> The settings in these policies apply to specific computer objects regardless of the logged-on user.

User Configuration
> The settings in these policies apply to a specific user regardless of the computer at which she is logged on.

Each of the above policies contains the three types of settings presented in the following subsections.

Software Settings. The settings in this category are used to deploy software to client computers running Windows XP, Windows 2000 (Server and Professional), and Windows Server 2003 operating systems. These computers must be members of the domain. You can specify the software and updates that will be deployed to computers. You can also exclude specific computers that should not get the software. It is also possible to uninstall the software using the settings in this policy.

Software deployment is accomplished by using Windows Installer Packages, which, in turn, use the Windows Installer service.

Windows Installer Packages
> These are self-extracting script files with an *.msi* extension that contain the instructions necessary to install, update, or uninstall the software.

Windows Installer Service
> The Windows Installer Service uses the instructions contained in the Windows Installer Package files to install, update, or uninstall the software.

Software deployment can be carried out in two ways: *assigning* and *publishing*. When a software application is assigned to a user, a shortcut is included in the Start menu of the user's computer. When he opens the shortcut, the installation starts. If the software application is assigned to a computer instead of a user, the installation starts as soon as the computer starts.

When a software application is published, it appears as one of the items in the Add or Remove Programs utility in the Control Panel of the user's computer. The user can install the application whenever needed. Software can only be published to users and not to computers.

Windows Settings. There are a number of Windows Settings that can be changed on a Windows computer to configure the working environment. Table 5-4 lists the settings available for both computer configuration and user configuration.

Table 5-4. Windows Settings in Group Policy

Node	Computer Configuration	User Configuration	Description
Scripts	Yes	Yes	Depending on where you set the scripts, the settings will run when the computer starts or shuts down, or when the user logs on or off the computer.
Security	Yes	Yes	You can configure a number of security settings that can affect the computer or the logged-on user.
Internet Explorer Maintenance	N/A	Yes	These settings are used to customize the Internet Explorer options.
Remote Installation Services	N/A	Yes	These settings are also available for users and are used to manage remote installation service (RIS) on client computers.
Folder Redirection	N/A	Yes	These settings are used to centrally manage users' folders such as My Documents, Start menu, etc., by redirecting them from users' computers to another location.

Administrative Templates. Administrative Templates contain Group Policy settings for both computer and user configuration and are based on the Windows Registry. Table 5-5 lists settings available for both computer and user configurations.

Table 5-5. Settings available in Administrative Templates

Node	Computer Configuration	User Configuration	Description
Control Panel	N/A	Yes	These settings determine which Control Panel utilities should be available to the user.
Desktop	N/A	Yes	These settings control how the user's desktop should appear.
Network	Yes	Yes	These settings control offline files configuration, and network and dial-up connections for the computer or user.
Printers	Yes	N/A	These settings control printer configuration for the computer.
Start menu and Taskbar	N/A	Yes	These settings control how the user can configure the Start menu and the Task Bar.
System	Yes	Yes	These settings are used to configure system startup/shutdown, logon/logoff, and Group Policies.
Windows Components	Yes	Yes	These settings control the configuration of Windows components such as Windows Explorer, Internet Explorer, and Windows Installer.

Multiple Group Policy Objects

Group Policies for computers or users can be applied from multiple sources. You should be aware of how these policies are applied and of how settings in some policies override settings defined in other policies. When GPOs are applied at different levels of the Active Directory hierarchy, they are processed in the following order:

1. All policies configured in the local GPOs are processed and applied first.

2. GPOs linked to the site are processed next. The settings in the site GPO override the conflicting settings in the local GPO. If multiple GPOs are linked to the site, the administrator can control the processing order of these GPOs.

3. GPOs linked to the domain are processed next. The settings in the domain-level GPO override the conflicting settings in the site GPO and the local GPO. If multiple GPOs are linked at the domain level, the administrator can control the processing order of these GPOs.

4. GPOs linked to the parent OU of the computer are processed next. The settings in the OU-level GPO override the conflicting settings in the domain GPO, site GPO, and the local GPO. If the object is in multiple OUs, the GPO linked to the highest-level OU in the Active Directory hierarchy are processed first. If multiple GPOs are linked to the OU, the administrator can control the processing order of these GPOs.

 An easy way to remember the processing order of GPOs is *LSDOU*, which means Local, Site, Domain, and OU. The local GPO is always processed first. This is followed by the GPOs linked to the domain. Site- and OU-level GPOs are processed next.

Group Policy Inheritance

Group Policies can be configured at both the parent and child levels. By default, GPOs linked to the parent level are inherited by all child objects. It is also possible to apply a different GPO at the child level. GPO settings are combined when they are similarly defined at both the parent and the child level. If a setting is not defined at the parent level but is defined at the child level, the child-level setting is applied. This means that any settings in the child object will override the settings in the parent object when there is a conflict.

It is possible to disable the unused computer or user settings in a GPO. This helps reduce the processing time of the GPO since the system must process all settings whether or not they are defined.

Blocking inheritance. Policy inheritance is enabled by default. In some situations you may not want the GPO that is linked to the parent object to be overridden by a GPO linked to the child object. In another situation, you may want to define different settings in a child GPO and block the effect of GPO settings linked to the parent object. This can be done using the No Override and Block Inheritance options that are described in the following list:

No Override
Allows you to prevent settings in a GPO that is linked to the parent object to be overridden by settings in any GPO linked to the child objects.

Block Inheritance

Allows you to block settings in a GPO that is linked to the parent object to be inherited by the child objects. But again, if the No Override option is set on the GPO linked to the parent object, you cannot block inheritance.

It is always better to design Group Policies that are simple and do not call for the use of options such as No Override or Block Inheritance. Your analysis of the security requirements of the organization as well as good documentation will help you decide on a good design. Creating exceptions after linking a Group Policy should be avoided as much as possible.

Filtering GPOs. When you have a large number of users or computers in an OU, it may be difficult to justify the policy settings in a single GPO to be applied to all. In some situations, you may want to exclude a group of users or computers from the GPO settings. A Group Policy needs two permissions to apply to an object: the *Read* permission and the *Apply Group Policy* permission. You can use either of these permissions to exclude the objects for which the Group Policy should not apply.

Prioritizing GPOs. Once again, it is always better to make a good plan instead of creating exceptions. When multiple GPOs need to be linked to an object, you should prioritize the GPOs so that you can control the order of their processing. The object in question can be a site, domain, or OU. Each of these objects can be subject to multiple GPOs. As the GPOs are processed, the GPOs that are linked to the lowest level in the OU hierarchy get the top priority. It is also possible to manually change the order of GPO processing once you have decided on the priority.

Linking Group Policies

As you already know, GPOs can be linked to sites, domains, and OUs. In some situations, you may want to link GPOs to domains and sites, but it is strongly recommended that you link most of the GPOs to the OUs. This way, you can have better control of different aspects of the Active Directory structure. Security settings are an exception to this recommendation because account and password policies are always applied at the domain level. GPOs linked to domains, sites, and OUs are discussed in the following paragraphs.

Linking GPOs to domains. GPOs that are linked to the domain affect all computers and users in the domain. These GPOs cannot be overridden by any other GPOs. When you face a situation in which you need to apply organization-wide standards or policies, you are better off linking GPOs at the domain level. Account Lockout Policies and Password Policies are good examples of such policies. But when you have different account and password policies for different units of the organization, you need to create separate domains. The Account Lockout, Password, and Kerberos Policies are stored in the *Default Domain Policy* and are the same throughout the domain. The advantage is that you have a central point where you can administer these policies. As a rule of thumb, you should keep the GPOs that are linked to a domain to a minimum.

Linking GPOs to sites. In some situations, you may have to link GPOs to sites. This becomes necessary when you have to apply similar settings to a large number of computers in the same physical location. But even then, it is better to create separate OUs for the computers at each location and then create GPOs for each location-based OU. The majority of organizations follow the rule of linking very few GPOs to sites.

Linking GPOs to OUs. It is strongly recommended that you create your GPOs to link them to the OU structure of the Active Directory network. This is the most efficient way to link GPOs. Linking the GPOs at the OU level allows you to efficiently control the GPOs as well as the policies defined in each GPO. This method offers flexibility in the sense that you can design or modify your OU structure to apply Group Policies. It is also easy to move users, computers, or other Active Directory objects between OUs. In addition to this, you can also rearrange or rename the OUs.

Designing an implementation plan for GPOs

With several options for creating OUs and GPOs and linking GPOs to domains, sites, or OUs, it looks like the job of an Active Directory and network designer is extremely complicated. But this is not true. When it comes to designing, you should always start by thinking of a simple and effective design. The simpler you keep the design, the better you can control it. The same rule goes for the design of every aspect of the Active Directory network infrastructure. When you plan Group Polices, think of a simple design. Try to create as few GPOs as possible. Some of the issues that you might face during and after implementation of GPOs include administration, client requirements, and change management. These issues are explained in the following discussion.

Administration of Group Policies. Administration of GPOs is not a problem in small organizations in which a single administrator or a group of a few administrators sit down and decide how the implementation will go and who will manage the GPOs once they are deployed. In larger organizations, the situation may be different. There may be a large group of administrators spread at different geographical locations who will need control of the GPOs. This further depends on the administrative model that is followed by the organization. Your design should clearly identify the administrators, whether the administrators are located centrally or at separate locations, and who will be in charge of different OUs and GPOs linked to them.

When there is a deep hierarchy of administrators at different levels or units of the organization, you will need to determine how administrative control will be equally divided among these administrators. This is where delegation of control comes into play. When deciding the delegation of control for the GPOs, you should keep the following things in mind:

- Control granted at the site level may affect objects in one domain or multiple domains irrespective of the domain in which the GPO is actually located.
- Control granted at the domain level affects all objects in the domain if inheritance is not blocked.

- Control granted at the OU level affects all objects in the OU and other child OUs.
- For better administration and management of permissions for GPOs, you should try to delegate control at the highest-level OU.

Administration of Group Policies includes the following functions, at which the administrators should be proficient:

- Creating GPOs
- Editing settings of an existing GPO
- Importing settings of one GPO into another GPO
- Linking GPOs
- Configuring inheritance and exceptions to inheritance
- Backing up and restoring GPOs
- Using Security Templates
- Using WMI filters

The administrators tasked with the responsibility of managing GPOs should have the following permissions on the GPO:

- Members of Enterprise Admins can edit GPOs linked to sites, domains, and OUs.
- Members of Domain Admins can edit GPOs linked to domains and OUs in the domain. Other users who have the Manage Group Policy Links permission can also link GPOs to domains.
- Members of the Domain Admins Global group can edit GPOs linked to OUs. You can also assign appropriate permissions to other users to edit GPOs linked to OUs.

You should set appropriate guidelines in your design as to who will be responsible for administering and managing GPOs at each level of the Active Directory hierarchy. Your documentation should also specify the best practices for managing GPOs. The best way to implement GPOs is to provide adequate training to users or administrators to whom the delegation of control for the OUs is granted.

Client requirements. In addition to the task of identifying administrative staff who will manage the GPOs, you need to consider which client operating systems can support Group Policies. The first requirement for client computers is that they are members of the Active Directory domain. Group Policies cannot be applied to standalone computers. The following client operating systems support Group Policies:

- Windows XP Professional and Windows Server 2003 support all Group Policies.
- Windows 2000 Professional and Windows 2000 Server support the majority of the Group Policies available in Windows Server 2003. These operating systems do not process any unsupported Group Policy settings.
- Windows NT 4.0, Windows ME, Windows 98, and Windows 95 do not support Group Policies.

It is clear that Windows XP Professional and Windows Server 2003 are the only two operating systems that fully support Group Policies. When you design GPO settings for a group of computers, you should make sure that the settings will apply to the majority of client computers, if not all.

 For computers running Windows NT 4.0, Windows 98, and Windows 95, you have the option of using the System Policy Editor, which has a very limited set of policy settings. Again, this will complicate your work because you will need to work with two different sets of policies.

Managing changes to Group Policies. Another aspect of managing Group Policies is to identify what changes might be allowed in GPOs and how these will be carried out. Appropriate change procedures will need to be defined to specify the circumstances under which changes to GPOs should be made. GPOs are administrative tools and a very critical part of the Active Directory infrastructure. A single change in a GPO linked to a site can affect several thousand computers or users across domains. Similarly, a small change in Password or Account Lockout Policies in the GPO linked to the domain can eventually result in the entire network becoming vulnerable to outside attacks.

It is important to define some rules that govern how changes to GPOs should take place. Whenever a change is required, it should come from the appropriate administrator or a user. No change to any GPO should be carried out without proper approval of the top-level administrative staff. Besides this, there should be a procedure in place to test the effects of the change before it is implemented.

Planning Accounts for Security Principals

Users, computers, and groups are known as security principals in Active Directory. After designing your Organizational Unit structure, the next step is to plan the creation of user, computer, and group accounts. This section discusses some of the best practices that you should follow when planning accounts.

Types of accounts

Windows Server 2003 Active Directory supports five types of accounts. An *account* is a list of attributes that identifies a security principal in the Active Directory. Table 5-6 lists the types of accounts available.

Table 5-6. Types of accounts in Active Directory

Account type	Description
User	The user account in Active Directory is the one that describes the attributes of a person. The user account allows a person to use his credentials to log on to the domain and access resources throughout the domain depending on permissions assigned to the account.
Computer	The computer account represents a physical computer in the Active Directory network. When a computer running Windows Server 2003, Windows XP, or Windows NT 4.0 joins a domain, a computer account is created for it.

Table 5-6. Types of accounts in Active Directory (continued)

Account type	Description
Group	A group account is a collection of users, computers, or other group accounts to which access permissions to resources is assigned. Groups simplify assignment of permissions because you do not have to assign permissions to individual security principals.
InetOrgPerson	The InetOrgPerson account is similar to the user account but allows integration with non-Microsoft-based LDAP directory services.
Contact	A contact represents a person outside the Active Directory network. There are no access permissions associated with it. This account is generally used in mail services and shows up in address books.

When you start the design process of creating accounts, you should first take a look at the accounts that already exist in the network. This will help you understand how accounts are currently created in the network and what policies or conventions are followed. This includes the study of current account naming strategies.

Planning a naming strategy

All accounts, whether they are user, computer, or group accounts, must follow certain predefined naming guidelines so that the naming structure is consistent throughout the Active Directory hierarchy. This makes searching users, computers, groups, or contacts in the directory database easier for the network users. A simple and consistent design allows administrators to easily implement the naming conventions. Your design should clearly define the guidelines for naming accounts.

Naming user accounts. A user's account should obviously identify the user. But how it is to be created depends on how you have defined the guidelines in your design documents. The purpose of creating naming conventions is to standardize the format throughout the organization. Other than the users themselves, the usernames are frequently used by administrators to assign permissions and by other users who send emails to the user.

Some guidelines for naming users in the Active Directory are as follows:

- Every user should have a logon name that is unique within the Active Directory domain. The full name of the user must be unique within the OU where it is created.

- A user logon name should be limited to 20 characters so that it remains compatible with pre-Windows 2000 operating systems.

- Logon names are not case-sensitive.

- Logon names for pre-Windows 2000 computers cannot contain these characters: / \ [ ] < > : ; , + ? * |.

- Your guidelines should clearly identify the method to address identical usernames within a domain. An additional character, such as the middle initial, can be added to avoid a duplicate username.

In spite of solid guidelines, you will run into limitations and have to leave some room for exceptions. There are several conventions that you can follow, but the goal of a good naming convention is to distinguish users from one another, avoid using duplicate names, and at the same time, keep the design simple.

Naming computer accounts. As with the user account name, the computer account names should also be created in such a way that it is easy for users to search for computers in the Active Directory database. A good naming strategy will not only allow a computer to be identified but will also identify its location and purpose.

It is also important to emphasize that there should be different naming conventions for servers and workstations. Naming computers as Computer1 and Computer2 and servers as Server1 and Server2 may work well for a small organization but will not be suitable for large organizations. For example, a server located in New Orleans and configured as database server can be named NO-DB1. Similarly, a client computer belonging to human resources department in a New York office can be named NY-HR1. This helps quickly identify the location and purpose of the computer from its name.

Naming group accounts. The naming conventions used for groups should help identify the group, its *scope,* and its purpose. Groups are used to organize accounts and simplify administration tasks associated with accounts as well as assignment of access permissions. When an administrator is working on access permissions, getting a wrong impression from the name of the group may well lead her to assign a wrong set of permissions. A consistent naming convention will help users and administrators identify the groups easily. The administrators will benefit from simplified tracking of group memberships and assignment of resource permissions.

Some guidelines for naming groups in the Active Directory are as follows:

- The name of the group should be unique within the domain.
- The group name should include its purpose and owner department or unit.
- The group name can contain up to 64 characters.
- Group names are not case-sensitive.
- Group names for pre-Windows 2000 computers cannot contain these characters: / \ [ ] < > : ; , + ? * |.

Whenever you define guidelines, you should make sure that they are enforced. There may be exceptions, but having a uniform group-naming policy throughout the Active Directory network will make searches easy for the users and make administration simpler.

Planning user accounts

User accounts are Active Directory objects that contain information about the user. User accounts provide users a way to log on to a local computer or the domain and access resources for which they have permissions. For administrators, user accounts provide a way to identify users and their group membership, and to control the level of access the users should be granted on network resources. It is worthwhile to say that the administrator account is also a user account but with more powers.

Types of user accounts. There are two types of user accounts in Windows Server 2003 Active Directory:

Local user accounts
> Local user accounts are created on the local computer and are stored in the local security database, and allow the users access to resources located on the local computer only. Local user accounts are usually created when you have a small workgroup network environment. These accounts are available on all client and server computers except domain controllers.

Domain user accounts
> Domain user accounts are created in the Active Directory database and are stored on domain controllers. These user accounts can log on to any computer in the domain and can access resources anywhere in the domain depending on access permissions granted to the user account or to the group of which the user account is a member. Domain user accounts are replicated to all domain controllers in the domain along with other information stored in the Active Directory database.

Built-in user accounts. When you first install Windows Server 2003 on a computer, the operating system creates some built-in user accounts. The two main accounts created by default are *Administrator* and *Guest*.

The *Administrator* user account is the most powerful account on the computer and has full control of the it. This account is a member of the Administrators group on the local computer. The domain administrator is a member of the *Domain Administrators* group by default. This account cannot be deleted but can be renamed.

The *Guest* user account is also created by default, but a very limited set of permissions are associated with it. This account is meant for users who do not need regular access to the computer and will only log on occasionally. This account is automatically made a member of the local Guests group. When working in a domain environment, the Guest account is made a member of the *Domain Guests* group. The Guest user account cannot be deleted, but you can disable it or rename it. For security reasons, it is recommended that you disable the Guest account.

Planning for user authentication

Account policies dictate how users will be authenticated across the Active Directory domain. These policies are a must to safeguard the network and resources from unauthorized access and outside attacks. Account policies control how users use their accounts and how passwords can be used and changed. Other things associated with security are user logon options such as using a pre-Windows 2000 name or a user principal name, and whether or not a smart card is required for logon. This section includes discussion on some of the aspects of user authentication.

Creating Account Lockout Policy. Since the user accounts in a domain are stored in the Active Directory database, the domain controllers must be able to authenticate users who log on to the domain. The authentication process verifies the user's identity and allows access to resources across the domain. The user should use a predefined username and password in order to successfully log on to the domain.

The Account Lockout Policy defines what happens if the user is not able to use his credentials properly. This policy safeguards the domain against unauthorized access by any one who might have obtained a username and is trying to guess the password to get access to the domain. The Account Lockout Policy has three settings that lock the user account after a certain number of unsuccessful logon attempts. These policies are as follows:

Account Lockout Duration
> This policy specifies how long a user account will remain locked out before the system automatically unlocks it. A value of 0 will lock the account until an administrator unlocks it.

Account Lockout Threshold
> This policy specifies how many unsuccessful logon attempts are allowed before the user account is locked out. A value of 0 means that the account will never be locked out.

Reset Account Lockout Counter After
> This policy specifies how long it takes before the counter for unsuccessful logon attempts is reset.

By default, the Account Lockout Policy is not enabled or defined in the Default Domain Policy. Your account policy should define these settings in your design documentation. If these policies are not defined, any outsider can launch an attack on your network. Users should generally be allowed four or five unsuccessful attempts before their account is locked out.

Creating Password Policy. Password Policy defines how users create and change their passwords. The username and password are the primary source of logging on to the domain. This means that Password Policy is the first area that should be given fair consideration when creating an authentication plan. By default, Windows Server 2003 will warn any users who do not use a strong password, and will not allow use of a blank password. In a domain environment, password policies can be created and enforced only at the domain level. Users should be trained to use strong and complex passwords and change them at regular intervals. There are six types of settings available to enforce password policies. These are as follows:

Enforce Password History
> This policy specifies how many passwords the Active Directory will remember so that a user does not use the same password frequently.

Maximum Password Age
> This policy specifies how long a user can keep the same password before she is prompted to change it.

Minimum Password Age
> This policy specifies how long a user must keep a password. This policy prevents users from frequently changing passwords.

Minimum Password Length
> This policy specifies the minimum length of the password for all users in the domain.

Password Must Meet Complexity Requirements
> This policy requires users to create complex passwords. Complexity requirements enforce the use of any three of the following: uppercase letters, lowercase letters, numbers, and special characters.

Store Password Using Reversible Encryption
> This policy stores the user's password in clear text. This policy setting is only used when *digest authentication* is enabled in IIS.

The first five settings are commonly used with Active Directory domains. Although a Windows Server 2003 domain enforces certain Password Policies, you should make it a point to specify the following guidelines for usage of passwords in the domain:

- Passwords must be at least seven characters long.
- Users must retain their passwords for a certain number of days and not change them frequently.
- Passwords must be complex. Users should use a combination of uppercase letters, lowercase letters, numbers, and special characters.
- Users should change their passwords on a regular basis. Microsoft recommends changing passwords every 42 days (6 weeks).
- The Password Policy should be configured to store at least 24 previous passwords of users.

No matter what your design draft suggests, only proper training combined with enforced password policies will create a safe working environment for all.

Logon options. If you have a Windows Server 2003 domain functional level, it does not matter whether the users log on using their username, the user principal name, or any multifactor authentication method. When you are working with lower domain functional levels, you will have to consider other logon options also. The following logon options are available:

Username/password
> This is the most common method of authentication that works with pre-Windows 2000 computers. The Kerberos service validates the username and password with the domain controller.

UPN name/password
> When a UPN name and password are used for logon, a query is sent to the Global Catalog server that provides the username and domain name for the account, which is derived from the UPN name.

Multifactor Authentication
> A username is associated with a digital certificate that provides an additional layer of security for the network. If a smart card is used, the user credentials are read from the smart card, and the user is prompted to enter the Personal Identification Number (PIN) at the logon screen.

Configure logon hours. When you design an authentication policy, you should not forget the logon hours for different users in the organization. Configuring logon hours ensures that users log on to the network during business hours only. This policy should be enforced for local logon as well as domain logon.

Planning computer accounts

Computer accounts allow computers that are members of a domain to authenticate themselves in the domain, but the process remains transparent to the users. You can place computers in Organizational Units and link GPOs to them to enforce Group Policies. This allows you to control security and authentication measures for different types of computers. Computers are usually categorized based on their role in the Active Directory domain.

When creating accounts for computers, you should be careful to grant Add Workstations To Domain rights to authenticated users only. A computer account is usually created automatically when a computer is added to the domain.

Computer accounts should clearly identify the purpose for which the computer is installed in the network. This makes it easy for users and administrators to search computers with specific roles in the Active Directory. Besides this, your design should enforce the naming conventions for new computer accounts, as discussed earlier in this section.

Planning group accounts

Group accounts are created in the Windows Server 2003 Active Directory domain to grant access to resources. Groups simplify administration of accounts and resources. Administrators can assign access permissions to groups instead of assigning permissions to individual objects. There are two types of groups: *local groups* and *domain groups*. Local groups are stored and used only on the computer where they are created. Domain groups are created in the Active Directory database. This section discusses domain groups only.

There are two basic types of groups in Windows Server 2003. These are as follows:

Security groups
> These contain users from the domain or trusted domains. These groups are used to assign permissions to network resources. Administrators create groups and assign permissions to these groups for any number of resources. All members of the group inherit these permissions.

Distribution groups

These are used for email distribution. These groups cannot be assigned permissions to any network resources. Email programs such as Microsoft Exchange use distribution groups as distribution lists.

Security groups are created to club users who have similar needs to access resources. Security groups can be members of distribution lists. You will need to determine what type of group you are creating and how these groups will be named and assigned permissions. Access permissions mainly depend on the type of access the group requires in order to complete its day-to-day jobs. One objective of keeping permissions to a minimum is to ensure that users do not get more permissions than they require to do their jobs properly.

 By default, members of Enterprise Admins, Domain Admins, and Account Operators groups have permissions to create groups. You can add any user to one of these groups to enable him to manage group accounts. It is recommended that you give minimum and limited administrative access.

You might need to create OUs that will hold the groups you create. You can then delegate the control of this OU to a person who will be responsible to maintain groups. Since GPOs cannot be linked to groups, creating an OU is your only choice if delegation of control is to be granted to some one else.

Group scopes. The *scope* of a group determines the objects that can be placed inside it and where the group can be accessed in an Active Directory forest. The scope of a group you can create on a Windows Server 2003 server depends on the domain functional level. The following three group scopes exist:

Domain Local group

Used primarily to grant access permissions to Global groups for resources located in the local domain. This group can contain users and Global groups from any domain in the forest irrespective of the domain functional level.

Global group

Can contain user and computer accounts from only the domain where it is created. These groups can be added to any local group in the domain or forest in order to assign resource permissions to the group. In Windows Server 2003 and Windows 2000 Native functional levels, the group can also contain other Global groups from the local domain.

Universal group

Created primarily to grant resource permissions in multiple domains. These groups are available only when the domain functional level is Windows Server 2003 or Windows 2000 Native. This group can contain users, Global groups, and other Universal groups from any domain in the forest.

Group nesting. *Group nesting* is the process of placing groups inside other groups. But this functionality depends on the domain functional level. Group nesting allows you to simplify the task of assignment of permissions. The more nesting you create in your design, the more complicated you make your design. It is always best to keep nesting to one level.

Table 5-7 summarizes group scopes and nesting for different domain functional levels.

Table 5-7. Group scopes and nesting

Group scope	Objects allowed in Windows Server 2003 and Windows 2000 Native	Objects allowed in Windows 2000 Mixed and Windows Server 2003 Interim
Domain Local	User accounts, Universal groups, Global groups from any domain, and Domain Local groups from same domain; nested Domain Local groups in the same domain.	User accounts and Global groups from any domain. Cannot be nested.
Global	User accounts and Global groups from the local domain; nested Domain Local, global (same domain), and Universal groups.	User and computer accounts from the same domain. Cannot be nested.
Universal	User accounts, Universal groups, and Global groups from any domain; nested Domain Local global or Universal groups.	Not available.

Access requirements for groups. When planning groups, it is necessary to determine the resource access permissions required for these groups and the level of access required. First, you will need to identify the resources, and then the user groups that need access to these resources. The idea behind creating groups is to club users who have similar access requirements for different resources such as folders, printers, and databases. You should try to keep the number of groups to a minimum and also keep the membership limited to only those users who need access to these resources.

The level of access that will be granted to groups should also be considered. Permissions should be enough for the members of the group to do their everyday jobs. Excessive permissions should not be granted in any case. When you need to assign access permissions to different groups for the same resource, you can use group nesting.

Guidelines for creating groups. Your group creation strategy should aim at reducing the administrative functions and not complicating them. The following guidelines will help you design an efficient group plan:

- Do not assign resource access permissions to individual users. Instead, create groups of users with similar resource access requirements.
- Domain Local groups should have members who need access to the resources located in the domain. Access permissions are usually configured for Domain Local groups.
- Global groups should be created to organize users. Place these Global groups inside Domain Local groups.
- Do not place users into Universal groups. Use Universal groups to organize Global groups from different domains that have similar resource access requirements.

Microsoft recommends the following guidelines for creating groups and group nesting, and for assigning permissions:

- User accounts should be placed in Global groups.
- Global groups should be placed in Universal groups.
- Universal groups should be placed in Domain Local groups.
- Resource permissions should be assigned to Domain Local groups.

 An easy way to remember these guidelines is the acronym: *AGUDLP*. Accounts (A) in Global (G) groups, Global groups in Universal (U) groups, Universal groups in Domain Local (DL) groups, and Permissions (P) assigned to Domain Local groups.

Designing a Site Topology

From this point onward, our discussion will focus on the physical design of the Active Directory and network infrastructure. While the logical design of the Active Directory targets effective administration, the physical design revolves around physical components of the network such as sites, domain controllers, name resolution, and remote access. This section focuses on designing a site topology, placement of domain controllers, and planning for the Active Directory replication process.

Planning a Site Topology

One of the main administrative functions is to control the network traffic between different geographical locations of the organization, that essentially is carried over WAN links connecting one location to another. These geographic locations are known as sites. A site is primarily an administrative tool in the Active Directory that is used to keep control of WAN traffic that spans multiple locations. When you install the first domain controller for the domain, a site object is created by default and is known as *Default-First-Site*. If you do not create sites manually, all the domain controllers you install will belong to the Default-First-Site object.

You may recall from our previous discussion that sites in a Windows Server 2003 Active Directory domain are IP subnets that are connected by fast and reliable links. In other words, sites comprise one or more domain controllers that are placed at each location of the organization. And since sites are part of the TCP/IP network of the organization, they follow the same network topology as the network itself. A single site can represent multiple domains or a single domain can span multiple sites. This is because sites are independent of the logical structure of the Active Directory network.

Sites are not part of the Active Directory namespace but contain only computer and connection objects. When users browse for objects in the Active Directory, they see only domains and OUs, and there is no reference to any site. The purpose of sites is to localize as much network traffic as possible. Sites typically have the same boundaries as a local area network. Since sites use the domain name system, it is essential that they be configured with appropriate DNS names.

Designing a site topology is the first step in creating the physical structure of an Active Directory-based network infrastructure. You need a solid understanding of how the sites and site links form the physical network. We will first take a look at the basics of Active Directory sites and explain why sites are created. The following discussion explains the purpose of creating sites.

Controlling authentication traffic. The main purpose of creating sites is to place domain controllers in each site so that local domain controllers can authenticate the clients at the site who are logging on to the network. This prevents the logon traffic from crossing the site boundaries and traveling on WAN links. Domain controllers actually determine clients' IP address and redirect them to the domain controller that is located nearest to them. In case there is no domain controller at the site where the client is located, the client will authenticate using a domain controller located at a site that has the lowest *cost connection* and cache the logon information. This is made possible by SRV resource records in the DNS zone database that provide each site with a preferred domain controller.

Controlling replication traffic. Active Directory stores database information on all domain controllers in the domain. When a change occurs in any of the domain controllers, the same change is replicated to all domain controllers in the domain. This is accomplished using replication technology known as *multimaster replication*, in which all domain controllers store the master copy of the Active Directory database. When domain controllers are located within the same site, replication happens quickly and data is transmitted in uncompressed format. This is because all domain controllers are connected by high-speed LAN links. Replication between sites is carried out differently. A single domain controller in each site is assigned the responsibility of replicating changes to domain controllers in other sites. These updates take a bit longer and are carried across WAN links in compressed format. The replication can be scheduled to happen when the WAN traffic is low during off-peak hours. Later in this section, we will learn how sites can help optimize and control replication traffic across WAN links.

Exam 70-297
Study Guide

Other benefits of creating sites are controlling the *Distributed File System* (DFS) topology and *File Replication Service* (FRS). DFS is used to create a single hierarchy of files and folders on the network regardless of their location. If the file or folder is not located on the same site, the DFS uses Active Directory site information to identify the site and actual file server that is hosting the shared folder. FRS, on the other hand, is a Windows Server 2003 service used to replicate the files in the SYSVOL folder in Active Directory across all domain controllers. The SYSVOL folder contains files that must be replicated throughout the domain. FRS uses site boundaries to manage replication of objects in the SYSVOL folder.

Determining site boundaries

When you start drafting a plan for creating Active Directory sites, you will need to look at your documentation that you prepared during the analysis of current network infrastructure. Creation of sites depends on the physical locations of the organization as well as connectivity details between these physical locations. You will create what is known as *site boundaries* that will largely depend on how you designed your logical administrative structure for the Active Directory network infrastructure.

The information that you will need to have handy before designing the site plan includes the following:

- The geographical locations of different offices of the organization
- Bandwidth and/or speeds of WAN links that connect networks at these locations
- The network layout at each location
- The number of network segments (subnets) in each location
- The speed of LANs at each location

Once you have all this information, you are ready to proceed with the design of Active Directory sites. As a first guideline for creating sites, you should aim at creating as few as possible. For example, if an organization has a large number of very small offices in several cities, it is not worthwhile to create a site for every individual city, even if the locations have very slow WAN links connecting to the main office. This is common with organizations that have a very small number of users or computers in several different locations. When you encounter such a situation, you should create a separate IP subnet for a LAN at the nearest location. Since there is a relatively small number of users at this particular site, the authentication traffic from this location will not be much and should not affect the slow WAN link.

Guidelines for creating sites

Use the following guidelines for your design:

- Create as few sites as possible. Extra sites come with extra cost of administration and overhead.
- Create a site for each physical location of the organization where a domain controller is to be placed.
- Create a site for each LAN or group of LANs that are connected by high-speed backbone links. Even if the LANs are located at different physical locations but connected by high-speed links, you should create a separate site for each location.
- Follow the naming conventions. Names of site objects in Active Directory follow the DNS naming conventions and are stored in the Active Directory. Recall that DNS names use characters A–Z, a–z, 0–9, and the hyphen (-). Avoid using restricted characters.
- Do not forget that the main purpose of the sites is to physically group computers and users so that network traffic across WAN links can be optimized. If you do not see reasons to create a site, do not do so.
- Your design documentation should clearly show the network segment that constitutes the site, its IP address range, and the subnet mask used for the subnet.

- The design documentation should also designate administrators who will be managing the sites once it is implemented. These administrators should be delegated control of the site so that they can manage its change and growth. At the same time, these administrators should be responsible for monitoring the usage of available network bandwidth across WAN links.

Planning for Active Directory Replication

The replication process ensures that each domain controller in the domain has an up-to-date master copy of the Active Directory database. Whenever any change is made to an object in the directory on any domain controller, the change is replicated to all other domain controllers in the domain. A well-designed replication model ensures that domain controllers located at different geographical locations use the available bandwidth of the WAN links efficiently by reducing the network traffic. WAN links usually connect two LANs at different physical locations. When you need to control the way replication occurs across slow WAN links, create additional site links and configure replication manually.

Understanding the replication process

Active Directory handles the replication process differently between domain controllers at the same site and between domain controllers at different sites. These two processes are explained in the following subsections.

How replication takes place. If you look at the Default-First-Site object in the Active Directory Sites and Services snap-in, you will notice that the domain controller in each site is shown as a server object. This server object has a child object known as *NTDS Settings*. The NTDS Settings container has the connection object that further contains the properties of the link between domain controllers for replicating directory information. Each site must have a connection object for replication to happen. A Windows Server 2003 service known as *Knowledge Consistency Checker* (KCC) automatically creates and monitors the replication topology for domain controllers. The KCC service creates different topologies for *intrasite* and *intersite* replication. Whenever domain controllers are added, removed, or moved, KCC automatically adjusts the replication topology.

Intrasite replication. In *intrasite* replication, the directory information is replicated in uncompressed format since high-bandwidth connections between domain controllers are usually available on the LAN. Any changes carried out on one of the domain controllers in the site are immediately replicated to all other domain controllers located at the site. Domain controllers keep polling each other at regular intervals for any changes in the directory database. The Remote Procedure Call (RPC) protocol is used as transport protocol for replication.

Intersite replication. In *intersite* replication, domain controllers are connected by WAN links that may have varying speeds. All replication data is sent in compressed format. Administrators usually configure replication manually so that it happens when the network traffic across WAN links is low. This results in delayed replication to other sites if changes are made to the Active Directory database in one of the sites. Domain controllers that are configured as replication partners poll each other only at specified intervals. Internet Protocol (IP) or Simple Mail Transport Protocol (SMTP) is used as transport protocol for replication.

Table 5-8 lists the differences between the intrasite and intersite replication processes.

Table 5-8. Comparing intrasite and intersite replication

	Intrasite replication	Intersite replication
Data Compression	No.	Yes.
Replication Model	Replication partners notify each other about changes, and then get changes.	Replication partners do not notify each other about changes.
Replication Frequency	Replication partners poll each other periodically for changes.	Replication partners poll each other at specified times only. Updates are replicated at scheduled times only.
Transport Protocols	Remote Procedure Call (RPC).	IP or SMTP.

Replication is triggered by any of the following actions performed on the Active Directory:

- Creating an object
- Deleting an object
- Modifying an object
- Moving an object

Site links

Site links are logical connections between two or more sites in Active Directory that are created to allow replication of the Active Directory database. Once site links have been created, the KCC service automatically creates replication topology by creating connection objects. Site links must be created manually while KCC uses these site links to automatically create connection objects that connect domain controllers. It is also possible to manually create *connection objects*.

Whenever feasible, try to group sites connected by similar WAN links and create a single site link connection. It is possible to create a single site link object to connect domain controllers at multiple sites provided that the WAN links are of the same type, have the same speed, and will be configured with the same replication schedule. This may not be possible in large organizations whose physical locations are connected by different WAN types or speeds. In this situation, you must create site links separately for each pair of sites.

Site link transitivity. All site inks are transitive by default. This means that if site A and site B are linked and site B and site C are linked, then site A and site C are transitively linked. Site link transitivity is based on a particular replication transport protocol. You can disable site link transitivity for a protocol, but it is usually not recommended. When you disable transitivity for a protocol, all site links for that protocol are affected and none remain transitive. In such a situation, you must create site link bridges manually to provide transitive replication.

Figure 5-7 shows transitive site links.

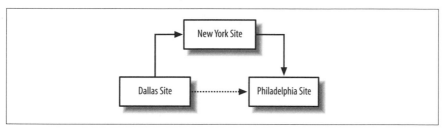

Figure 5-7. Transitive site links

You can disable site link transitivity for a protocol under the following circumstances:

- When you need to have total control over replication traffic patterns.
- When you want to avoid a particular replication path being used heavily.
- When firewalls installed at sites are blocking replication traffic.

 Whether it is more desirable to keep the site link transitivity enabled by default or to disable it depends on the situation you are working with. You must fully understand the effects of disabling the site link transitivity before you do so. Remember that you will have to configure site link bridges if you disable site link transitivity.

Site link bridges. A *Site link bridge* logically connects two or more site links in a transport protocol in which site link transitivity has been disabled for some reason. Since site links are transitive by default, it is very rare to create site link bridges. When the site link transitivity is enabled or left in its default state, creation of site link bridges has no affect on replication between sites.

Bridgehead servers. Once sites and sites links have been created, the KCC service automatically creates *Bridgehead servers* at each site. A Bridgehead server is a single domain controller at each site that is designated as the contact point and is responsible for replication between sites. The KCC service is responsible for automatically creating connection objects between Bridgehead servers. Bridgehead servers are then responsible for initiating the replication process according to a preconfigured schedule.

Although KCC automatically designates a Bridgehead server at each site, you can also manually configure a preferred Bridgehead server if you want a specific domain controller to assume the role of replicating Active Directory information. It is also possible to configure multiple Bridgehead servers at a single site, but only one will be active at a time. Configuring a preferred Bridgehead server prevents the KCC service from providing a failover Bridgehead server automatically if the manually configured preferred Bridgehead server goes offline for some reason. If you do not specify another preferred Bridgehead server or none is available, site replication does not occur.

Site link costs. *Site link cost* is used to determine the preferred links in comparison to other links when more than one link is available for replication. A site link with lower cost is preferred over a site link with higher cost. Site links are configured according to the bandwidth available for the link. By default, all site links are assigned a value of 100 for the site link cost. When more than one link is used for replication, the site link cost becomes cumulative.

Table 5-9 lists the recommended values of site link costs for different available bandwidths.

Table 5-9. Recommended site link costs

Available bandwidth in Kbps	Site Link Cost
4096	283
2048	309
1024	340
512	378
256	425
128	486
64	567
56	586
38.4	644
19.2	798
9.6	1042

You should consult this table before configuring site link costs consistently across the network.

Site link availability. In its default configuration, replication can occur at any time because all site links are always available. To have control over the times when replication should occur, you should change the site link times. It is recommended that replication be scheduled during off-peak hours for large networks where the flow of other network traffic is more important. By default, the intersite replication automatically occurs every 180 minutes. If you set the replication interval too long, you may be able to reduce the WAN usage during peak hours, but replication will be delayed. You need to strike a balance between the two.

Guidelines for creating site links. The Default-First-Site is created by default when you install a domain controller. A default site link object named DEFAULTIPSITELINK is also created for the IP transport. No site link is created for SMTP transport. When creating site links, use the following guidelines:

- Try to use RPC over IP as the transport protocol for all site links unless you have a reason to use SMTP.

- Use uniform naming conventions for site links so that their purpose can be determined from their names.

- Make sure that all sites can connect to each other when you create site links.

- For intrasite replication, configure notification and push replication.

- For intersite replication, configure polling and pull replication between Bridgehead servers.

- Specify the cost of site links carefully.

Planning the Placement of Domain Controllers

Domain controllers are the heart of any Active Directory network. They are the most critical of all servers used in the network. Domain controllers not only provide authenticated access to the network resources but also help the administrators organize users, computers, and resources in the desired way. When designing a network infrastructure based on the Windows Server 2003 Active Directory, it is important to plan the domain controllers, their capacity requirements, their placement across different locations of the organization, and their roles within the Active Directory. This section discusses all of these concerns to help you get ahead with your design.

Capacity requirements for domain controllers

The hardware you choose for your domain controllers must be able to support the number of users in a particular location. Capacity planning means that you must ensure that the server hardware meets recommended guidelines for designating them as domain controllers. It is also recommended that you test the server hardware before starting to install the operating system on it and make sure that vendor support is available in case something goes wrong.

Besides calculating the number of domain controllers required at each site, you will need to identify the specifications of each domain controller at each site separately. Your design documentation should clearly describe these specifications and also keep in mind the future growth of the organization. The number of users that will need logon authentication by the domain controller is the first and most important thing to consider when planning the domain controller hardware, but there are other factors to consider as well. Server hardware can be divided into three main categories: processor, hard disk space, and memory. Table 5-10 lists Microsoft's recommendations.

Table 5-10. Recommended processor, speed, and memory specifications

Number of users	Number of processors	Processor speed	Memory
1–499	1	850 MHz or faster	512 MB
500–999	2	850 MHz or faster	1 GB
1000+	4	850 MHz or faster	2 GB

You should not forget that these are just minimum recommended specifications and are intended for organizations that prefer to use their existing server hardware. In case you are planning for new server hardware, it is recommended that you acquire the fastest possible processor speed and large memory.

 A single 1.6 GHz. processor can support as many users as are supported by two 850 MHz. processors. Similarly, a single 3 GHz. processor can replace two 1.6 GHz. or four 850 MHz. processors. The recommendations listed in Table 5-10 are based on Microsoft calculations; you should memorize them for your exam.

After you have specified the processor and hard disk space, the next component to consider for capacity planning is hard disk. The calculations for determining the required hard disk space are based on roughly 400 MB of disk space for every 1,000 users. This means that for every 10,000 users, you will need 4 GB of disk space. The following guidelines can be used to calculate hard disk space requirements for the domain controllers:

- The drive that holds Windows Server 2003 operating system files needs a minimum of 2 GB space.
- The drive that contains the Active Directory database needs 400 MB of space for every 1,000 users.
- The drive that holds the Active Directory transaction logs needs a minimum of 500 MB of space.
- The drive that holds the SYSVOL folder needs a minimum of 500 MB space.

These calculations will be good if you have planned or created only one domain for your Active Directory structure. The next thing is to check whether the domain controller will also be a Global Catalog server. For a single domain, the Global Catalog will not need extra disk space. In case the domain controller will be a Global Catalog server in a multiple domain forest, look at your forest plan and see how many domains you have created. You will then need to add 50 percent of extra hard disk space for each additional domain.

Placement of domain controllers

There are several things that you need to consider for placement of domain controllers across different locations of the organization. Security, user authentication, and replication are some of the important factors that have to be taken into account. Some factors that you need to determine for placement of domain controllers are discussed here.

The first question that needs to be answered is whether a site really needs a domain controller. To determine this, use the following guidelines:

- If there are a large number of users at a site, it is best to place a domain controller locally for authentication. This will ensure that authentication traffic does not consume the bandwidth of the WAN links. Local domain controllers will ensure that users will be able to log on to the domain even if an unreliable WAN link is down for some reason.

- If the site is connected to several other smaller sites and is acting as a hub for several small geographical locations, you must place a domain controller locally.

- Domain controllers should also be placed at sites that have *site-aware* software applications. Site-aware applications will use the local domain controllers for authentication.

Once you have determined that you need to place a domain controller at a particular site, you must consider the following factors:

Local administrative staff
  Do you have local administrative staff at the site to maintain the domain controllers? If you do not, you will need to maintain these domain controllers using remote administration. You need to make sure that WAN links are reliable for the purpose, and that firewalls and routers are configured to allow remote access to domain controllers.

Physical security
  Are the domain controllers physically secure? You need to ensure that physical security of the domain controllers is given priority so that unauthorized persons do not gain physical access and cause damage to the domain controller or walk away with any hardware component.

Number of domain controllers. The next thing you need to consider is the number of domain controllers require at each site. For smaller organizations, you may well place one domain controller at each site, but you will also have to calculate the exact number of domain controllers at each site. The number of users for each domain in each site is the primary factor affecting this decision. The following guidelines will help you calculate the number of domain controllers:

- You need one domain controller for up to 1,000 users per domain at a particular site.

- You need a minimum of 2 domain controllers if the number of users is between 1,000 and 10,000.

- For every additional 5,000 users, you will need 1 additional domain controller.

- Replication load is another considerable factor. For every 15 replication objects configured in a site, you need 1 extra domain controller.

Placing multiple domain controllers at a site not only provides fault-tolerance but also helps balance the authentication load among them. Another considerable factor is the replication load among domain controllers.

Placement of Forest Root servers. In large organizations where there are multiple domains, you will need to decide on placement of the Forest Root domain controller within a particular site. The first domain that you create in a forest acts as the root domain for the forest. Trust relationships within the domains of a single forest are transitive and usually go through the Forest Root domain. You can also create shortcut trusts if there are multiple domains in a site but the Forest Root domain is located at a remote site. If you have unreliable WAN links, you can add a local Forest Root domain at the local site.

Placement of servers with operations master roles

Although Active Directory supports multimaster replication, the *operations master roles* of domain controllers need fair consideration when you are placing domain controllers across the network sites. Domain controllers with different operations master roles perform specific tasks that not all domain controllers are allowed to perform. The following discussion contains some guidelines for where these domain controllers should be placed.

Forest-wide roles. *Forest-wide roles* are specific for the forest. Only one domain controller in each site can be designated to perform each of these tasks.

Schema master
> The *schema master* role is assigned to one domain controller in a forest that controls the schema. This domain controller is responsible for maintaining and distributing the schema to the entire forest. The domain controller holding this role needs to be online whenever changes to the Active Directory schema are carried out. This role is not used very often. Some applications may require schema modifications and will need the domain controller with this role when these applications are installed. Usually, the domain controller holding the schema master role is placed in a site that contains the largest number of domain controllers and has access to the most skilled administrative staff.

Domain naming master
> Like the schema master, the domain controller with the *domain naming master* role is also rarely used. This domain controller is responsible for recording the additions or deletions of domains to the forest. As with the schema master role, the domain controller holding the domain naming master role should also be placed in a site that contains the largest number of domain controllers and has access to the most skilled administrative staff.

These roles are automatically assigned to the first domain controller installed for a single domain forest. For a multiple domain forest, you can assign these roles to a domain controller that does not host the Global Catalog server role.

Domain-wide roles. *Domain-wide roles* are specific to a particular domain only. These roles are defined for each domain in the forest. As with forest-wide roles, the domain-wide roles can also be assigned to one domain controller in each domain. The roles are as follows:

Relative ID (RID) master
> The *relative ID master* role is responsible for generating and maintaining RIDs and distributing blocks of RIDs to domain controllers in the domain. These RIDs are further used by security principals within the domain. If you are working in a Windows 2000 Native or Windows Server 2003 domain functional level, you should place the domain controller with this role where the administrators will be creating the majority of accounts. In the Windows Server 2003 mixed domain functional level, assign this role to the domain controller that has the PDC emulator role.

Infrastructure master

The domain controller with the *infrastructure master* role records changes to Active Directory objects in a domain. Any changes made to the objects are first reported to the infrastructure master and then replicated to all domain controllers in the domain. The infrastructure master also informs other domain controllers in the forest about changes made to objects within its own domain. Hence, this role is not only important within a single domain forest but also in a multiple domain forest. This role is usually not assigned to any domain controller that is assigned the role of a Global Catalog server unless all domain controllers are Global Catalog servers.

Primary domain controller (PDC) emulator

The *PDC emulator* role is used when you have Windows NT 4.0 backup domain controllers (BDCs) in the domain. This role is used to emulate the Windows NT 4.0 PDC to clients that have not yet migrated to Windows XP or Windows Server 2003. This role is responsible for keeping the Windows NT 4.0 Backup Domain Controller (BDC), Windows 2000 Server, and all Windows Server 2003 domain controllers updated about any changes.

The three domain wide roles are automatically assigned to the first domain controller installed in the domain. When you are working with a large organization that has multiple domain controllers, you should try to assign these roles to separate domain controllers. As with forest-wide roles, you should place the domain controllers with these roles at a site that has the largest number of users and where administrators have easy access to these domain controllers for maintenance.

Placement of Global Catalog server

Global Catalog servers are responsible for maintaining a smaller set of attributes of objects in Active Directory. These servers provide logon for Active Directory clients and also help in locating objects within the domain or the forest. With the Global Catalog server located at a site, the site will experience additional replication traffic because the attributes of all Active Directory objects from the domain as well as from other domains in the forest will be replicated to the local Global Catalog server. Clients can search for objects from anywhere in the forest without contacting the domain controller for that domain.

The domain controller with the role of Global Catalog server basically holds the following information from Active Directory partitions:

Schema partition

There is only one *schema partition* for the entire forest, and it is replicated to all domain controllers in the forest. All information about the attributes of objects in an Active Directory forest is stored in the schema partition.

Configuration partition

There is only one *configuration partition* for the entire forest, and it is replicated to all domain controllers in the forest. All information about the domains, sites, and server objects in an Active Directory forest is stored in the configuration partition.

Domain partition

Each domain in an Active Directory forest has its own *domain partition* that is replicated to all domain controllers in the domain. All information about the objects in the domain is contained in the domain partition.

The first domain controller installed in a domain forest automatically becomes the Global Catalog server. You can assign this role to any number of domain controllers in the forest. The only thing you need to consider is that the domain controller holding the role of infrastructure master should not be made a Global Catalog server. Making a domain controller a Global Catalog server consumes significant resources on the server.

One of the main functions of Global Catalog servers is to facilitate user authentication in a multiple domain forest. If any user logs on to the network using the user principal name (UPN), the name is checked in the Global Catalog server and converted to a normal username. This feature helps users log on to other domains in the forest where their user accounts are not located.

Universal Group Membership Caching. *Universal Group Membership Caching* is an Active Directory feature that works only on Windows Server 2003 domain controllers. This feature is available only in Windows Server 2003 and Windows 2000 Native functional levels. The benefit of this feature is that a domain controller need not be a Global Catalog server in order to have a user provide her Universal group membership when logging on. When the user logs on, the domain controller contacts the Global Catalog server, which may be located at a different site, to get information about the user's Universal group membership. This information is cached in the local domain controller and reduces the logon time when the user logs on next time. But use of this feature is not recommended for sites with a large number of users or where there are several applications that need access to the Global Catalog server. Microsoft recommends that you use this feature for a maximum of 500 users at a site.

The following guidelines will help you decide on placement of Global Catalog servers in the Active Directory network:

- Microsoft recommends that you place at least one Global Catalog server at each site.

- Place a Global Catalog server in a site that has 100 or more users. This will help reduce authentication traffic over WAN links. Use the Universal Group Membership Caching feature for sites with smaller number of users.

- Place a Global Catalog server in a site that has applications that need to search Active Directory objects very frequently. This improves performance of the application. An example of one such application is Microsoft Exchange Server 2003.

- Place multiple Global Catalog servers in a site that has multiple domain controllers. The number of Global Catalog servers should be half of the total domain controllers in a site.

- Check for availability of local administrative staff when placing Global Catalog servers in a site.
- If a domain controller has another demanding role, such as infrastructure master, do not assign it the role of Global Catalog server.
- If you do not want to place a Global Catalog server at a particular site, make sure that the WAN link is reliable so that users can log on to the network without delays and application performance does not suffer.

Designing a Name Resolution Structure

Computers in a network need to communicate with each other. Every computer is given a name that is easy for users to remember. Although these names are unique for every computer, operating systems do not understand names. Computers and other networking equipment use the IP addresses assigned to them as a means of locating and communicating to each other. There has to be a mechanism to translate these names to their corresponding IP addresses.

The focus of this section is to discuss the planning of name resolution strategies for the Active Directory design. These include domain name system (DNS) name resolution and NetBIOS name resolution using Windows Internet Name Service (WINS). WINS is rarely used in Windows networks these days, but you must take into account any older systems or applications that have not been upgraded and still need NetBIOS name resolution.

Designing a DNS Structure

DNS is the preferred method of resolving computer names in a Windows Server 2003 Active Directory network. This is because Active Directory uses the DNS naming conventions and also uses the DNS to resolve these names. Clients and servers use the DNS service to locate other clients and servers in the Active Directory network. The Active Directory domain hierarchy in Windows Server 2003 and Windows 2000 follows the DNS hierarchy. At this point, we encourage you to take another look at the section "Designing an Active Directory Structure," covered earlier in this chapter.

Analyzing the existing DNS structure

Before you start the process of designing a DNS name resolution structure for an organization, you need to examine the existing DNS structure. This includes a close examination of the existing DNS hierarchy and the DNS namespace. Unless you are building the network from scratch, you will need to complete this procedure in most of the situations. The information you gathered while analyzing the Active Directory namespace also will help determine the DNS namespace requirements.

You can use the following guidelines to help you understand the existing DNS structure of the organization:

- Are the DNS services maintained in-house or is a third party, such as an ISP, maintaining it?

- Check the number of DNS servers in the organization and their locations. It is a good idea to draw a map of the DNS servers placed at the company's different locations.

- For each DNS server, find out the role of the server, such as whether it's a primary, secondary, forwarding, or caching only server.

- Check the internal (Active Directory) and external (DNS) namespace. Is the company using the same namespace or different internal and external namespaces?

- What types of DNS zones are used? Are these Active Directory-Integrated zones or standard primary and secondary zones?

- How are the DNS servers and DNS zones secured? What security mechanisms are in place?

- Are there any non-Microsoft DNS servers in the organization? Take a note of any third-party DNS implementations, such as Unix.

Once you have gathered this information, you should examine all aspects of the DNS structure and consult with network administrators about any specific issues they might be concerned with. Also, check whether there are any performance problems they are currently facing with DNS servers.

Designing the DNS namespace

Both internal users and external users will use the DNS namespace that you choose for your organization. By this point, you might have chosen an Active Directory namespace for your design. The DNS names should ideally be identical to your Active Directory domain names. Just in case your design does not fit well with the existing DNS structure, you will have to work with the network administrators to work out a plan for a new DNS namespace. The DNS service in Windows 2000 and Windows NT 4.0 also follow the DNS naming standards. You can either upgrade these DNS servers to Windows Server 2003 or install new DNS servers with Windows Server 2003 Active Directory.

The following actions need to be completed for a good DNS namespace design:

- When deciding on a standard for DNS naming, you will need to take into account the naming conventions selected while designing the Active Directory namespace.

- You should check the name registered by the organization for its Internet presence.

- Check whether your DNS servers will be working completely inside your private network or will be available on the Internet also.

- Check whether the DNS will support the existing Active Directory structure that might already be in place.

The next step is to choose a second-level domain name for your organization, check its availability with the appropriate domain registration authority, and register the selected name. You may choose from any of the top-level domains such as .com, .org, .net, etc., depending on what type of presence the organization wants to have on the Internet. Once this is done, you will create subdomains under the registered second-level domain. The names of these subdomains can be based either on Organizational Units of the company or on geographical locations of the company.

Internal and external namespaces. Selecting domain names for your organization is an important step in the final design of the Active Directory network infrastructure. You will need to decide whether you want to use the same namespace for your external and internal networks or keep internal and external namespaces totally separate.

If you want to keep the same second-level domain name for internal and external purposes, your best bet is to use a subdomain of the external domain for internal purposes. When you use the external domain name for creating subdomains for Internet domains, you need an extra layer for security from outside users for the internal DNS servers and the network form. You will need to protect your internal DNS servers by placing them behind firewalls. Additionally, you will need to add resource records of external DNS servers on internal DNS servers so that internal users can resolve external names in order to use resources that are not located inside the network. For example, if you have registered the domain name *mydomain.com*, you can use *int.mydomain.com* as your internal root domain name.

Although keeping external and internal namespaces entirely separate provides security for your internal DNS servers and the network, this option comes with additional administrative overheads. The disadvantage is that not only will you have to install separate DNS servers for internal and external domains, you will also need to administer and maintain them separately. The decision depends on the size of your organization and how it operates its business. The advantage is that separate DNS servers will handle DNS name resolution requests from external and internal users, and you need not worry about the performance of any of these DNS servers. For example, if you have registered the domain name *mydomain.com* for external Internet users, you can use a different name for your internal domain, such as *myintdomain.com*.

Integration with Active Directory, DHCP, and WINS

For designing a true Windows Server 2003 DNS structure, you need to consider how your DNS design will integrate with other network services such as Active Directory, DHCP, and WINS. This will not only enhance the performance of your network infrastructure but will also simplify administrative tasks. These topics are discussed in the following sections.

Integration with Active Directory. In Windows Server 2003, the Active Directory and DNS work with each other. Active Directory is totally dependent on DNS service, and you cannot install a domain controller (and hence, Active Directory) if you do not have a DNS server running on the network. If the Active Directory does not find a running DNS server when you install a domain controller, you are prompted to install the DNS service on the server where you are performing the installation.

The following are some advantages of integrating DNS with Active Directory:

- When DNS is integrated with the Active Directory, DNS zones are stored in the Active Directory database. You need not create primary and secondary DNS zones or configure zone transfers. The DNS zone data is automatically replicated to other domain controllers along with the Active Directory data.

- Using the Active Directory-Integrated DNS zones improves the security of zone information. Zone databases include complete information about names and IP addresses of all computers in the network and, if compromised, can be dangerous for the organization. With Active Directory-Integrated zones, the zone data replicated is encrypted and is safe from eavesdroppers.

- You can add an additional layer of security for DNS zones by configuring Access Control Lists (ACLs) to DNS objects stored in the Active Directory. One example of this feature is the dynamic updates of the DNS database that can only be performed by client computers that have been configured to send *secure dynamic updates* to the DNS servers.

- When new domain controllers are added to the network, the zone information is automatically updated and no administrative actions are required.

- Administrators do not need to configure or maintain replication for DNS zones across sites because zone data is replicated along with the Active Directory database. This helps with faster and more efficient replication of Active Directory database information as well as DNS zone database information.

Integration with DHCP. DNS servers keep the host (A) and the pointer (PTR) resource records for all DNS clients in the network. Windows Server 2003 DHCP servers can now be configured to update the Windows Server 2003 DNS records servers dynamically whenever a new DHCP-enabled client joins the domain or when a client configuration has changed. DHCP can update any DNS server that accepts dynamic updates, including the Windows Server 2003 DNS servers. This feature improves the DHCP and DNS performance and reduces administrative tasks in maintaining the resource records on DNS servers.

A Windows Server 2003 DHCP server can be configured in the following ways to send dynamic updates to DNS servers:

- Dynamically update DNS A and PTR records if requested by the DHCP clients.
- Always dynamically update DNS A and PTR records.
- Discard A and PTR records when the lease is deleted.
- Dynamically update DNS A and PTR records for DHCP clients that do not request updates.

The first and third options are enabled by default. The last option is for down-level clients such as Windows NT 4.0 and Windows 98. You can configure the DHCP server to always update DNS A and PTR records on behalf of the clients whether or not they request the DHCP server to do so.

By default, post Windows 2000 clients, such as Windows 2000 professional, Windows XP, and Windows Server 2003 clients, will update their own A records with the designated DNS servers but will request the DHCP server to update their PTR records. As another security measure provided with the Active Directory, only those DHCP servers that have been authorized in the Active Directory can serve clients.

Integration with WINS. There may be situations when the organization you are working with has some legacy clients or servers running Windows 98 or Windows NT 4.0 server operating systems that cannot be upgraded or taken offline. These computers might be using NetBIOS names instead of domain names. In such situations, you will need to use Windows Internet Name Service (WINS) for NetBIOS name resolution. For maintaining a uniform name resolution standard across the organization, you will need to direct certain NetBIOS name resolution queries to the WINS servers. This can be done easily by integrating the DNS service with WINS. You can configure the DNS servers with WINS and WINS-R resource records to search the NetBIOS namespace.

WINS resource record
> The WINS resource record is used to instruct the DNS service to use the information in the WINS record to resolve a NetBIOS name that is not found in the DNS zone database. The WINS server in the record is used to resolve the NetBIOS name and send back the result to the DNS server. The DNS service then creates an A record for the NetBIOS host and sends the result of the query to the requesting client or its preferred DNS server.

WINS-R resource record
> The WINS-R resource record is used to instruct the DNS service to use information in the WINS-R record to resolve an IP address to its NetBIOS name. When resolved, the DNS service appends the NetBIOS name to the DNS name and sends the result of the DNS query to the requesting client or its preferred DNS server.

Planning DNS zones

The DNS service stores its resource records in the zone database. DNS zones hold resource records that contain the information about the hosts and services in the zone. Since there are many types of zones available with Windows Server 2003 DNS service, it is good to review them.

Identifying zone types. Different types of zones available with Windows Server 2003 DNS service are standard primary zones, standard secondary zones, Active Directory-Integrated zones, and stub zones. The standard primary and secondary zones store the DNS zone information in files on DNS servers while the Active Directory-Integrated zones store DNS zone data in the Active Directory database. Stub zones are mainly used for delegating control of DNS zones. These zones are discussed in the list that follows.

Standard primary zones

The *standard primary zone* is the traditional type of DNS zone in which master zone data is stored in a file on the DNS server. Changes to the zone data can only be made on the master copy stored in the primary zone database file. The changes are transferred to the secondary DNS servers. In a DNS environment in which dynamic updates are used, all the clients send dynamic updates only to the primary DNS server. This could lead to performance limitations in large organizations in which each client must contact the primary DNS servers for registration. Further, if the primary DNS server is placed across WAN links, the available bandwidth will be used for DNS registrations that otherwise should have been used for other important services. Since there is only one primary DNS server, it can become a single point of failure.

Standard secondary zones

The *standard secondary zone* stores a read-only copy of the standard primary zone. Usually the DNS servers configured as secondary DNS servers are placed close to the clients, or at every site, so that clients can resolve host-names as quickly as possible. This helps reduce the network traffic that might cross the WAN links. A single secondary DNS server can host zones for multiple primary DNS zones. Secondary zones can also be used when the primary DNS servers are not hosted on Microsoft DNS servers. The zone data is replicated from primary DNS servers using a mechanism known as *zone transfers*. Zone transfers are initiated by any of the following instances:

- When the primary DNS server notifies the secondary DNS server
- When a secondary DNS server starts a transfer from the primary DNS server
- When the DNS server service is started on the secondary DNS server
- When the refresh interval configured for the zone has expired

Active Directory-Integrated zones

When the DNS server is installed on a computer that is also a domain controller, you have the option of creating an *Active Directory-Integrated zone*. In this type of zone, the zone information is stored in the Active Directory database and is replicated to other DNS servers along with the Active Directory database. All DNS servers thus become primary DNS servers, and changes can be made to any DNS server. Active Directory zones should be used when you do not have any legacy DNS systems in your network and there are no interoperability issues with non-Microsoft DNS servers. The following are some of the advantages of using Active Directory-Integrated zones:

- The zones' files are stored on domain controllers in the Active Directory database.
- Replication of zones along with the Active Directory is faster than zone transfers that take place when you use standard primary and secondary zones.
- Changes to zone data can be made on any DNS server since all DNS servers are peers.

- Fault-tolerance and load-balancing are automatically provided along with domain controllers.
- Replication is secure since it is encrypted.
- Secure dynamic updates help prevent pollution of zone data.

Stub zones

Stub zones are primarily used for delegating authority of another namespace. They help simplify the administration by updating the delegation zone records every time there is a change in authoritative name servers of the delegated zones. Stub zones contain only the start of authority (SOA), name server (NS), and host (A) records for the name servers. When a stub zone is created, its zone records are populated only with SOA, NS, and A records from the name server authoritative for the zone. Stub zones can also be integrated with Windows Server 2003 Active Directory. Stub zones help improve name resolution performance in the network.

Replication of zone database. The DNS zone database is replicated from one DNS server to others in one of two ways: through zone transfers or through Active Directory replication. It is obvious that only the Active Directory-Integrated zones can take advantage of the Active Directory replication method.

Zone transfers

The standard primary and secondary zones use the *zone transfers* method, which can be either *authoritative zone transfers* (AXFR) or *incremental zone transfers* (IXFR). The AXFR method transfers complete zone database information and can consume a significant amount of network bandwidth. On the other hand, IXFRs transfer only those changes that have occurred since the last zone transfer. In order to keep the bandwidth usage as low as possible for zone transfers, you should make sure that all DNS servers support IXFRs.

Active Directory replication

Active Directory-Integrated zones can take advantage of replication methods used by Active Directory since all zone data is stored in the Active Directory database. The real advantage of Active Directory-Integrated zones can be noticed in networks that span multiple locations and are connected through WAN links. The zone replication traffic is transferred in compressed format with other Active Directory data between domain controllers. You can still control the scope of zone replication by configuring one of the options listed in Table 5-11.

Table 5-11. Zone replication options

Option scope	Description
To all DNS servers in the Active Directory forest	Replicates zone data to all DNS servers running on domain controllers in the Active Directory forest. This option provides the broadest scope of replication. It cannot be selected if you have Windows 2000 DNS servers.
To all DNS servers in the Active Directory domain	Replicates zone data to all DNS servers running on domain controllers in the Active Directory domain. This option cannot be selected if you have Windows 2000 DNS servers.

Table 5-11. Zone replication options (continued)

Option scope	Description
To all domain controllers in the Active Directory domain	Replicates zone data to all domain controllers in the Active Directory domain. This is the default option and is supported on Windows 2000 DNS servers.
To all domain controllers specified in the scope of a specified Active Directory partition	Replicates zone data according to the replication scope of the specified application directory partition. This option is available only when all DNS servers are running Windows Server 2003. You must have enlisted the DNS server hosting the zone in the application directory partition.

Zone delegation and stub zones. Maintaining DNS servers and DNS zones can be a difficult task in large organizations with multiple geographical locations and a large number of users at every location. You can delegate the administrative responsibilities of DNS servers or zones to local administrators. This can be done either by creating subdomains and delegating the control of subdomains to local administrators, or by creating stub zones. When you create stub zones, you create SOA, NS, and A records for the name server that is authoritative for that zone. Stub zones automatically update these records when new name servers are added to that zone.

Stub zones come in handy when you also have Unix BIND DNS servers already running in your network. If the current DNS servers are BIND version 9 or later, the Unix administrators can create stub zones that point to your Active Directory zones. For older versions of BIND, the only option is to create delegation records.

Interoperability options for DNS servers

Windows Server 2003 DNS implementation is designed to support the latest DNS standards so that it can interoperate with other non-Microsoft DNS servers. In addition to this, there are several new features in Windows Server 2003 DNS that are exclusive and may not be supported on other DNS platforms or older version of Windows DNS implementations. When designing a name resolution for your network infrastructure, you will need to take into account all interoperability issues. Table 5-12 will help you recognize some of the important features supported or not supported in several Microsoft and Unix platforms.

Table 5-12. DNS features supported on various platforms

Operating system	SRV records	Dynamic updates	Secure dynamic updates	Active Directory-Integrated zones	Incremental zone transfers	Stub zones	Conditional forwarding
Windows Server 2003	Yes	Yes	Yes	Yes	Yes	Yes	Yes
Windows 2000 Server	Yes	Yes	Yes	Yes	Yes	No	No
Windows NT 4.0 Server	No	No	No	No	Yes	No	No

Table 5-12. DNS features supported on various platforms (continued)

Operating system	SRV records	Dynamic updates	Secure dynamic updates	Active Directory-Integrated zones	Incremental zone transfers	Stub zones	Conditional forwarding
Unix BIND 9.1.0	Yes	Yes	No	No	Yes	Yes	Yes
Unix BIND 8.2	Yes	Yes	No	No	Yes	No	No
Unix BIND 8.1.2	Yes	Yes	No	No			
Unix BIND 4.9.7	No	No	No	No	No	No	No

When you plan the DNS structure for your organization, you will need to see what features are supported on all DNS servers currently running in the organization. If possible, you should plan to upgrade older DNS servers to take advantage of several new and advanced features in Windows Server 2003.

Planning DNS security

DNS servers contain sensitive information about your network, and you should plan to secure them from several types of internal and external threats. In fact, an attacker can get a complete map of your network if he is able to get access to even one of your DNS servers. This section discusses potential attacks on DNS servers and what can be done to secure your DNS servers from these threats.

Potential DNS attacks. The DNS servers may be subject to the following types of attacks:

Footprinting
> A process by which an attacker can use some of the freely available tools on the Internet to transfer entire zones to her computer. The attacker can use this zone data to get information about your network, domain names, hostnames, IP addresses, etc., that may be critical to the functioning of the organization. If the zone transfers are not secure in your network, your network may be prone to footprinting attacks.

Denial of service (DoS)
> This happens when your DNS servers are overwhelmed with name resolution queries launched by an attacker. This type of attack consumes all available resources on the DNS servers, and they are not able to resolve genuine queries.

IP spoofing
> This is also known as *data modification*. The attacker modifies the IP address contained in the packet sent to the DNS server. This IP address looks valid to the DNS server and the DNS server sends the result of an otherwise genuine query to the attacker instead of to the original client sending the name resolution query. If the attacker is initially successful in data modification, he can further launch a DoS attack on one or more DNS servers.

Redirection

This type of attack is also known as a *man-in-the-middle* attack. When a DNS client sends a query to the DNS server, it is actually trying to locate a server or service on the network. Using this type of attack, the attacker is able to redirect the client to a DNS server that is under the attacker's control. The attacker usually carries out such an attack by polluting the zone data on DNS servers.

As you probably noticed from this discussion, if you do not take necessary steps to secure your DNS servers, the business of the entire organization can suffer due to malicious attacks on your network. Your network design should make sure that security is given due importance for all components of the network infrastructure. The next section explains some of the methods that you can implement to secure your DNS servers.

Securing DNS servers. Once you have identified the types of threats that your DNS servers may be exposed to, you need to make sure that the DNS servers are secured against any of these potential threats. A good plan will always ensure that DNS servers have fault-tolerance so that if any one of them is the target of an attack, there is another one to serve the DNS clients. The following guidelines will help you build a secure DNS structure for your network:

- Use different DNS servers for your external and internal namespaces. Configure internal DNS servers to forward Internet queries to the external DNS server.

- Use firewalls to protect your internal DNS servers and, hence, internal namespace from external sources. You can do this by configuring the TCP and UDP ports 53 on the firewalls so that the only communication allowed is between external and internal DNS servers.

- If you are using Active Directory-Integrated zones, configure the DNS servers to accept secure updates only. This prevents DNS servers from accepting dynamic updates from invalid clients.

- Configure the DNS servers to accept queries from only those IP addresses that originate from within your internal network. This will help prevent DoS attacks.

- Disable recursion on DNS servers that are not meant to use recursive queries for resolving hostnames.

- Use the *Secure Cache Against Pollution* feature available on Windows Server 2003 DNS servers so that an attacker may not populate your zone data with invalid resource records. This will help prevent data redirection attacks.

- Restrict zone transfers to the DNS servers that are listed in the NS resource records of the zone. You can also configure the zone transfers to occur for specific IP addresses only.

- DNS Server service allows you to configure Discretionary Access Control Lists (DACL) on DNS objects. You can use these DACLs to allow only authorized administrators to work on DNS servers.

- Make sure that the DNS zones are hosted on NTFS drives only.

Your design should also specify the administrators who will be responsible for maintaining the DNS services in the network. The DNS administrators should be appropriately trained and assigned sufficient permissions so that they are able to manage the DNS service.

 No matter how much security you plan for your DNS servers, the possibility of an outside attack still remains. It is recommended that you regularly monitor DNS service event logs. Sometimes a small mistake by one of your own administrators may leave a loophole in an otherwise secure DNS structure. This may open up the entire DNS structure to outside attack.

Securing zone replication. The information stored in DNS zone databases is replicated to secondary DNS servers across WAN links. It is important that this information be secured so that it is not intercepted during transmission. This needs special attention if this information is transmitted over WAN links using the Internet. If you are using Active Directory-Integrated zones, you need not worry much about this issue because Active Directory replication is already in encrypted form and it is hard to decrypt the data even if it is captured by an attacker. Although it is not impossible, it will take the attacker a long time to make something out of the encrypted data.

To secure zone data replication traveling over the Internet, you should use IP Security (IPSec) encryption. Another way is to use VPN tunneling. In either case, you should plan to use 3-DES—that is, the strongest available encryption algorithm with the Windows Server 2003 operating system. It is always recommended that you plan for using more than one layer of protection for your internal critical data, which may be prone to outside attacks. Never rely on a single method for ensuring security.

Determining number and placement of DNS servers

While designing the physical DNS structure, you will need to specify the DNS server hardware and the number of servers required as well as how these servers will be placed across various locations of the organization. DNS servers will be used not only for DNS name resolution but also for Active Directory services. DNS server deployment plans should make sure that the name resolution process is fast and reliable, and at the same time, the DNS traffic does not take away much of your network bandwidth, especially when the DNS servers are placed across slow WAN links.

Number of DNS servers. The main considerations for determining hardware for DNS servers are the number of users and number of host computers in your organization. Microsoft tests have shown that a Pentium III, 850 MHz server with 512 MB of RAM can support up to 10,000 name resolution queries every second. If you are planning to use your existing hardware, you will need to make your calculations very carefully because some of the existing servers may not be able to support all new features as well as growth in DNS queries when the new network is finally set up. But if you are going to use new server hardware for DNS services, you may well be using much higher processor speeds and/or a higher amount of memory.

Another aspect of capacity planning for DNS servers is whether or not you are using Active Directory-Integrated zones. If this is the situation, the DNS servers will be installed on domain controllers. The domain controllers should have the necessary hardware to support the additional load of DNS services. They should be able to respond to logon requests and DNS queries simultaneously.

You will need to create performance baselines for your DNS servers and compare these baselines with actual performance levels when the servers are most busy. Microsoft has published some guidelines for measuring DNS server performance. The following performance counters should be monitored for each critical DNS server:

- The number of total queries received per second
- The average number of queries received per second
- The total number of responses sent out by the DNS server
- The average number of responses sent by the DNS server per second

You should have your own guidelines for the DNS administrators as to how they can keep the performance of the DNS servers acceptable. Provide some concrete guidelines to administrators regarding monitoring DNS server event logs.

Determining the placement of DNS servers. Efficiency, availability, security, and cost are some of the factors you should consider while planning the placement of DNS servers across the network. If one DNS server is located in each subnet of the network, the clients will be able to get response to queries very efficiently, as a DNS server would be located in their own subnet. But this may be a very costly solution for the organization. You can place one DNS server in each site, but this may not be sufficient for reasons of fault-tolerance. All the factors need due consideration before you can chalk out a final plan.

You can use the following guidelines for placing DNS servers across the network:

- Use multiple DNS servers for fault-tolerance. This is important for a location that has a large number of users. If one of the DNS servers is offline, the other one can respond to client requests for name resolution.
- Use local DNS servers for remote subnets so that DNS traffic does not consume much of the WAN bandwidth. Place at least two DNS servers so that if one server is offline, the second handles the name resolution queries instead of using another DNS server across the WAN.
- For remote locations with a very few number of users, use caching-only DNS servers. Caching-only DNS servers do not host any zones. They improve name resolution by caching the resolved name resolution queries and hence, reduce network traffic.
- Provide load-balancing by placing multiple DNS servers in busy locations. Configure clients with multiple DNS servers so that if one server is busy, the other one can respond to client queries.

- Pay attention to physical security of DNS servers. As with domain controllers, DNS servers should also be out of reach of unauthorized internal or external persons.

 Remember the most important factors in deciding the placement of DNS servers. These are availability, performance, fault-tolerance, and security. When DNS servers are needed across WAN links, make sure that DNS traffic does not consume much of the available WAN bandwidth.

Designing a WINS Structure

Windows Internet Name System (WINS) is used to resolve NetBIOS names to IP addresses. WINS service is needed in those networks where legacy operating systems and applications are still in use. As long as you have computers running operating systems such as Windows NT 4.0 or older in your network, you will need WINS to resolve NetBIOS names. This section discusses some fundamentals of WINS, its components, and planning a secure WINS structure.

NetBIOS name resolution

Before WINS, the NetBIOS name resolution was mainly dependent on broadcast transmissions and LMHOSTS files. NetBIOS clients used to broadcast the local network to locate other clients. Administrators used to create LMHOSTS files on every computer that contained a mapping of NetBIOS names to IP addresses in the network. These methods became obsolete when small networks started to grow into larger routed networks. The limitations of broadcasts and LMHOSTS files started surfacing, and Microsoft came up with a solution known as WINS service.

In a routed network, broadcast traffic is not allowed to pass routers because it causes too much traffic. LMHOSTS files are difficult to maintain because these are text files and must be created and updated manually on each computer. Neither of these solutions are acceptable in larger networks where network traffic must be kept to a minimum and administration must be simplified.

WINS should be implemented in your network for the following reasons:

- To enable NetBIOS name resolution across routed networks
- To reduce broadcast traffic on local network segments
- To simplify and centralize administration of resources that use NetBIOS

Components of WINS structure

WINS structure is basically made up of WINS servers, WINS Proxies, and WINS clients. The functions of each of these are explained in the following sections.

WINS server. The WINS server is the core of a WINS structure. A WINS server enables clients to register, release, and renew their NetBIOS names and IP addresses dynamically as well as resolve NetBIOS name resolution queries. When NetBIOS clients start, they register their names and IP addresses with the WINS server. The WINS server, on the other hand, searches its database when it receives any NetBIOS name resolution request and returns the results of the query to the WINS clients.

As with DNS servers, WINS also has primary and secondary WINS servers:

Primary WINS server

> The *primary WINS server* is the one that holds the master copy of the WINS database. NetBIOS clients register and renew their information with the primary WINS server. This server also responds to NetBIOS name resolution queries from clients.

Secondary WINS server

> The *secondary WINS server* also stores a copy of the WINS database that is replicated from the primary WINS server. It handles NetBIOS name resolution requests when the primary WINS server is not available. NetBIOS clients with Windows 2000 and Windows XP operating systems can be configured with up to 12 secondary WINS servers. If a primary WINS server is not able to resolve a NetBIOS name query, the client attempts to contact other configured WINS servers to resolve the NetBIOS name.

WINS clients use unicast packets instead of broadcast for name resolution queries that are addressed to a single IP address. Hence, routers do not block these requests.

WINS Proxy. *WINS Proxy* is used on network segments where a local WINS server is not available for NetBIOS name resolution. When you have a few non-WINS clients such as Unix or Linux in any network that needs NetBIOS name resolution, you may not need to install a full capacity WINS server at that location. One of the WINS clients can be configured as WINS Proxy to forward NetBIOS name resolution requests from non-WINS clients to the WINS server located in a remote network segment.

When the WINS Proxy receives the NetBIOS name resolution request, it will first check its NetBIOS name cache. If it cannot resolve the name from its cache, it forwards the request to the WINS server that is configured for itself. The WINS server may be located in the local network segment or on a remote segment. Since the request is not a broadcast transmission, routers do not block it.

WINS client. WINS clients are also known as *WINS enabled clients*. These clients register, renew, and release their NetBIOS names with the WINS server. They clients send NetBIOS name queries to the configured WINS server and receive responses. The received responses are stored in the local cache of the client so that it does not have to contact the WINS server again for the same name.

Besides Windows Server 2003, Windows 2000, Windows XP, and several older Microsoft operating systems can be configured to become WINS-enabled clients. These operating systems include Windows ME, Windows 98, Windows 95, all versions of Windows NT, Windows for Workgroups, MS-DOS, and OS/2. Even Unix and Linux clients can use the WINS service through WINS Proxy.

Although Windows XP and Windows 2000 WINS clients can be configured with as many as 12 WINS servers, you should use this feature cautiously because it will ultimately degrade network performance, as the WINS client will continue to contact configured WINS servers one after another if a NetBIOS name is not resolved.

Files in the WINS database

As with DNS, WINS servers also have a database consisting of NetBIOS client names and their corresponding IP addresses. WINS database uses the Joint Engine Technology (JET) database format that provides improved performance and fault-tolerance. The following types of files are used for WINS databases:

WINS.MDB
> This is the main WINS database file. This file contains two tables: one with IP address to owner-ID mappings and the other with NetBIOS name to IP address mappings.

WINSTMP.MDB
> This file is a temporary file created by WINS service.

Logfiles
> WINS transactions are initially stored in logfiles and then written to the database when the system is idle. This helps improve the system performance, as well as provide a backup, in case the system crashes. The size of these logfiles grows very quickly; when one file is full, another is created. You should not delete any of the logfiles until you take a backup of the WINS database.

RES#
> This is a reserved logfile that is used when the WINS sever runs out of disk space.

Checkpoint files
> These files are used during the recovery of a failed WINS server. These files indicate how much data from the transaction logfiles has been written to the WINS database.

Compacting WINS databases. WINS databases keep on growing with an increasing number of WINS clients. When records are deleted from the WINS database, the system does not take back all the free space. To get around this problem, you can compact the WINS database so that the free space unclaimed by the system could be recovered. The WINS database can either be compacted manually or dynamically. If you need to perform a manual compaction, you must stop the WINS server service and take it offline. Dynamic compaction is an automatic process, and WINS server service performs it whenever the system is idle.

Deleting and tombstoning WINS records. With the passage of time, the network keeps on growing, and so does the WINS database. The database might contain obsolete records of those clients that no longer exist on the network. The records for these clients must be deleted from the WINS database file. Selecting the record in the database and deleting it can do a simple deletion of record. But these records can appear in the WINS database again as a result of replication from other WINS servers.

Tombstoning is the process by which a record is marked for deletion in the WINS database. When any client requests the name of the marked record, a negative response is sent to the client. The record remains in the WINS database for some time and is then permanently deleted from all WINS servers in the network.

Planning a WINS structure

The design of the WINS structure will depend on the number of computers and legacy applications that are still in use in the organization. It is very possible that you will not need WINS servers at all if there are no legacy systems in the organization. The plan you make should take into account several things:

- The number of users and applications that need NetBIOS name resolution
- The number of WINS servers needed in the network and their specifications
- The location of WINS servers across the network and across WAN links
- The kind of fault-tolerance you need to provide for WINS servers
- The kind of replication configuration you will need among WINS servers

These considerations are discussed in the following sections.

Number of WINS servers. The number of WINS servers you need across the network mainly depends on the number of users that will need access to WINS servers for name registrations and renewals as well as for name resolution. In a small network, a single WINS server is sufficient to serve up to 10,000 WINS clients for NetBIOS name resolution. But if you are working on a WINS structure design for a large organization, you will need to look into other aspects also, such as performance and fault-tolerance. You should try to get the best performance out of WINS servers by using the following guidelines:

- Install the fastest available processors. If possible, plan for a dual or quad processor server.
- Install as much memory as possible.
- Install fast hard disks and plan for a RAID solution for disk fault-tolerance.
- Install at least a 100 Mbps network adapter.

In case you have to use currently running WINS servers that have older and slower hardware, you should try to replace them with new hardware if the budget permits. Otherwise, you must at least make sure that these servers will be good enough to host the Windows Server 2003 WINS server service when they are upgraded.

Once you have decided about the specifications of WINS servers, you should plan for backup servers as well so that if one of the WINS servers goes down or is taken offline, another is available to service clients. Take into account various locations of the organization that are connected by slow WAN links. If any of the locations have a large number of users that need access to WINS service, you should plan to install at least two WINS servers at the location.

Placement of servers. The plan for placement of WINS servers should aim at providing a highly available solution for NetBIOS name resolution. If you have only one server for a large number of clients, the chances of unavailability increase. If the only WINS server fails, the WINS clients will resort to the broadcast method of resolutions. You never want that to happen, as it can create network bandwidth problems. Hence, it is always better to plan ahead for availability and performance during the design phase.

The WINS server placement plan should take into account the following guidelines:

- Place at least two WINS servers at each location for fault-tolerance.

- Place local WINS servers across slow WAN links so that the WINS traffic does not consume network bandwidth of the WAN links.

- Place a WINS Proxy at any location where you have non-Microsoft clients who need NetBIOS name resolution.

- Even in local network segments where there are a large number of users in each segment, place two WINS servers in each segment so that routers do not have to handle WINS traffic crossing from one network segment to another.

Your network design should take into account all the important aspects of the WINS requirements of the organization and provide a cost-effective and reliable solution.

WINS replication

Once you have decided the specifications and placement for WINS servers, the next step is to plan for replication configurations of each WINS server. As discussed earlier in this section, WINS servers replicate database information to each other in order to keep themselves up-to-date. When some changes occur in any of the WINS servers, these changes are replicated to other WINS servers. You can control how and when the replication between WINS servers takes place. Designing a good WINS replication plan will result in improved performance as well as efficient use of network bandwidth across WAN links. Replication is not a big problem in a small organization that has just a few locations, and each location has one or two WINS servers. In large organizations with multiple locations and multiple WINS servers at each location, you will need to clearly define how replication should be configured.

In smaller networks, you can leave the replication in its default state, where the WINS servers automatically discover other WINS servers and replicate the WINS database information as and when required. In larger networks, administrators will need to choose replication partners for each WINS server at each location and, if required, schedule the replication to occur at off-peak hours when network usage is low. WINS servers can be configured as replication partners in one of the following methods:

Push partner
> The push partner is responsible for notifying its pull partners about any changes that have taken place in its WINS database. You can configure the push partner to wait until a specified number of changes have occurred

before it sends out notification. It is also possible to schedule the notification when any of the WINS client changes its IP address or when the WINS server is shut down and restarted.

Pull partner

The pull partner requests updates from its push partner about any changes in the database of its push partner. You can configure the pull partner to wait for a specific amount of time before it request updates. Pull partners should be configured across slow WAN links.

Push/pull partner

If you do not configure push or pull partners, the WINS server remains in the default configuration of push/pull partners. The WINS servers can request updates from other WINS servers as well as send updates about any changes in its own WINS database.

In most of the cases, you will notice that the push/pull partner configuration is best suited for WINS replication. But this should not be left in its default state. If a WINS server is configured as both a push and pull partner, you will need to decide when it should send notification and when it should request updates. This should normally be configured to occur during off-peak business hours. If the organization is spread into multiple geographical locations with different time zones, you will need to configure WINS servers at different locations with different schedules for WINS replication.

WINS security

As with your DNS structure, the WINS structure also needs to be secured from potential inside and outside security threats. WINS servers may also be exposed to the Internet and to outside persons, and you should make sure that the information in the WINS database is secured at all times. Your design should also take into account the physical security of WINS servers at each location. You should designate only trained and authorized persons to administer the WINS servers. In most of the situations, the DNS administrators should be designated as WINS administrators also, but this may not be true in all cases.

WINS servers may also be prone to attacks such as footprinting, redirection, and denial of service. The WINS replication transmissions that pass through a public medium such as the Internet to remote locations of the organization should particularly be properly secured. You can encrypt the WINS replication data by using either the Internet Protocol Security (IPSec) or Virtual Private Networking (VPN).

Designing a Network and Routing Solution

The next step in designing a Windows Server 2003 Active Directory network infrastructure is to decide on IP-addressing schemes for the network. The first question that needs to be answered is whether you will be using public or private IP addresses, or a combination of both. Once you have decided this, you will need to make a plan for creating sets of IP addresses for different network segments in the organization. After this, you will plan how the assignment of IP addresses will be handled. This section focuses on these and other related issues, including

Internet connectivity for the organization and Network Address Translation (NAT).

Designing an IP Addressing Strategy

IP addresses are grouped into classes A, B, C, D, and E. Out of these, only classes A, B, and C are assigned to organizations. As discussed in the section "Overview of IP Addressing" earlier in this chapter, the class of IP addresses you will need depends on the number of computers in your organization. This number can further be divided into the number of network segments you need and to the number of hosts in each network segment.

If you plan to use public IP addresses, you will need to obtain an IP address for the organization from the Internet Assigned Numbers Authority (IANA). Most of the class A addresses have already been assigned to other organizations, and a very few class B addresses are available. But if you take a look at your requirements, you may not even need a class A address. Class B address space provides IP addresses for more than 65,000 computers on your network. The class C address space provides IP addresses for up to 254 computers. Looking at these figures, a class C address may not be sufficient for your organization, while a class B address space would give too many IP addresses, and many of these would be wasted.

A solution to this problem is to use private addresses for all internal computers in the organization. You can use the public IP address for those servers that should be accessible from the Internet. The internal computers can still access the Internet using Network Address Translation (NAT) or a proxy server. NAT is discussed later in this chapter, in the section "Network Address Translation." Refer back to Table 5-3 earlier in this chapter, which gives a list of IP address ranges available for private use in classes A, B, and C.

 For the exam, you should memorize the public and private IP address ranges, number of networks, and number of hosts supported in each network for each class of IP addresses. Also remember the IP addresses reserved for Automatic Private IP Address (APIPA) assignment.

Once you have decided on the IP addresses you would use, you will need to decide how these addresses will be distributed among various network segments. You will also need to decide on subnet masks for each network segment. Recall that all hosts on a network segment or subnet should have an identical subnet mask. A subnet mask is used to identify the network portion and host portion of an IP address. You can use a scientific calculator to calculate subnet masks for each subnet of the network.

You create subnets in order to efficiently use the available IP address space and manage network traffic. If the organization has multiple locations, and each location has a large number of users and computers, you will also need to divide the LAN at each location into several smaller subnets. This becomes necessary to limit the maximum amount of local network traffic to local segments. In this situation, a simple subnetting scheme may not be effective, as it would result in wasting address space. You might notice that you have to design an IP-addressing scheme in which each subnet has a varying number of computers, and the only option would be to use the *variable length subnet mask* method to efficiently divide your IP address space. You must make sure that IP addresses in the organization do not overlap.

Designing IP Addresses Assignment

IP addresses can be assigned to host computers in a number of ways. These options are explained in the following sections.

Static IP addressing

If the organization is very small, you may configure the IP addresses manually on each computer, and the computers will be said to have *static* IP addresses. These addresses will not change unless the administrator changes them. Static addresses are usually configured on servers that perform critical tasks, such as domain controllers, DNS servers, and DHCP servers. In larger networks, it is not possible to manually assign IP addresses to all computers because of the huge amount of work involved and the chances of errors and duplication of addresses.

Using Automatic Private IP Addressing (APIPA)

The Automatic Private IP Addressing (APIPA) is a reserved address range that, if used on any computer, does not allow the computer to connect to the Internet. The APIPA has a class B address range with IP addresses from 169.254.0.1 to 169.254.255.254, with a subnet mask of 255.255.0.0. This address range is reserved for computers that are configured to use DHCP for address assignment but the DHCP server is not available. Windows 98 and later computers can use APIPA addresses when they are not able to contact a DHCP server on startup. When the DHCP client configures itself with an APIPA address, other options such as default gateway and addresses of DNS and WINS servers are not configured. The client can communicate only with other computers with APIPA addresses. The DHCP-enabled client will keep polling the network for a DHCP server every five minutes by default.

Alternate IP addressing

An alternate IP address is meant for DHCP-enabled computers that will use a static address instead of an automatically configured address from the APIPA address range. The benefit is that if the client is not able to contact a DHCP server when it starts up, it will use the manually configured IP address. With an alternate IP address, you can configure all options, such as addresses of default gateways and DNS and WINS servers, that otherwise would be supplied by the DHCP server. This addressing is beneficial in the following circumstances:

- If the computers were configured manually with alternate addresses that lie in the same scope as those configured on the DHCP server, the client would be able to communicate on the network even if the DHCP server is not available. In this case, the alternate address must be chosen very carefully so that the address does not fall in the address range of any of the DHCP scopes.

- If you have users who work on portable computers at the office or at home, the alternate IP addressing can be used. The clients can use the DHCP-configured address when connected to the office network and use the alternate IP address while connected to the home network.

Dynamic IP addressing with DHCP

Dynamic Host Configuration Protocol (DHCP) is the favored method of allocating IP addresses to client computers in most of the organizations. A DHCP server is configured to allocate IP addresses to DHCP-enabled clients in each network segment. Besides IP addresses, DHCP servers can configure the clients with other IP addresses such as subnet masks, default gateways (routers), DNS servers, and WINS servers. Either a single DHCP server is configured with a scope for multiple network segments or a DHCP server is placed in each network segment. The placement depends on the layout of your network and the number of computer hosts in each segment. Placement of DHCP servers and DHCP server security is discusses later in this section.

Overview of DHCP working. In Windows 2000 and Windows Server 2003 networks, the DHCP servers must be authorized in Active Directory to assign IP addresses to requesting DHCP-enabled clients. An unauthorized DHCP server is known as a *rogue server* and cannot serve clients until it is authorized.

Assignment of an IP address by an Active Directory-authorized DHCP server takes place using the following steps:

1. When a DHCP-enabled client boots up, it sends out a DHCP *Discover* broadcast message on the network. Since routers do not forward broadcast messages, only the DHCP servers on the local network segment can respond.

2. The DHCP server in the local subnet that has a valid IP address scope for the network segment offers an IP address lease to the client. The offer includes the MAC address of the client, the offered IP address, a subnet mask, and a lease period.

3. The DHCP client accepts the lease offer and requests to the DHCP server that the offered address be assigned to it. This message contains the MAC address of the requesting client.

4. The DHCP server that sent the IP lease offer to the DHCP client assigns the IP address to the client for a period that is specified in the lease. The default lease is eight days. This DHCP message is known as *acknowledgement*.

The steps involved in the IP address assignment by a DHCP server are known as Discover, Offer, Request, and Acknowledgement. An easy way to remember these steps is the acronym DORA.

DHCP scopes. A *scope* is a range of IP addresses and other TCP/IP options, such as addresses of routers, DNS servers, etc., that are preconfigured on a DHCP server for a particular network segment. A DHCP server must have at least one scope for every network segment it serves. The scope must be activated before the DHCP server can lease IP addresses to the DHCP clients from this scope. The scope contains the following configuration parameters for the clients:

- The range of IP addresses that can be offered to clients.
- The subnet mask for the network segment where the client is located.
- The period of the lease, which is eight days by default.
- DHCP *scope options* that include IP addresses of the default gateway and DNS and WINS servers.
- *Exclusions* that include the IP address or range of IP addresses that should not be assigned by the DHCP server.
- IP address *reservations*. The reserved addresses are assigned to those clients who should get the same IP addresses every time they request an IP address lease.

When planning the DHCP scopes, remember that the IP addresses you exclude from the scope should not be reserved at the same time. For using reservations, you will need the MAC addresses of all the clients for which you need IP address reservations. You need to be a member of Enterprise Admins, Domain Admins, or DHCP Admins in order to manage DHCP servers in the network.

DHCP scope options. DHCP scope options apply to all DHCP clients that get an IP address from the DHCP server from a particular scope. It should be noted that if any client is configured with a static option, the DHCP option does not apply to that client. Table 5-13 lists some commonly configured DHCP scope options.

Table 5-13. DHCP scope options

Option	Description
003 Router	This is the IP address of the default gateway or the router.
006 DNS Servers	This is the IP address of the DNS server for the client.
015 DNS Domain Name	This option configures the client with DNS domain name.
044 WINS/NBNS Server	This is the IP address of the WINS server for the client.
046 WINS/NBT Node Type	This option specifies the node type for the client. The node type can be b-node, h-node, p-node, or m-node.

DHCP server options. Apart from the scope options, the DHCP server can also be configured with *server options*. The server options apply to all scopes on a particular DHCP server. Server options are used when you have a large number of clients that need identical TCP/IP settings. An example of server options are DNS and WINS server IP addresses that may be identical for all clients at a particular location.

DHCP class options. *Class options* apply to a group of clients that are configured with a class ID. When any client with a specified class ID requests an IP address from the DHCP server, the DHCP server includes the class options with the IP address and other TCP/IP configuration parameters.

DHCP scope reservations. DHCP *reservations* are IP addresses that are reserved for specific clients. These clients should always get the same IP address from the DHCP server. To configure reservations on a DHCP server for a client, you must know the MAC address of the client.

DHCP Relay Agent. In smaller network segments where you do not want to place a local DHCP server for some reason, you can configure a *DHCP Relay Agent* that will forward DHCP messages to the DHCP server located in a remote network segment. For example, if you have only a few client computers in a remote location and you cannot afford to place a DHCP server, you can configure one of the clients as a DHCP Relay Agent. This is because the routers will not allow any broadcast traffic from DHCP clients to pass from one subnet to another. The DHCP Relay Agent can solve this problem by acting as a proxy between the DHCP server and the DHCP clients. Another option is to configure the router to forward BOOTP messages to the remote segment. The second option is useful only if the routers are BOOTP- or RFC 1542-compliant.

 Microsoft frequently tests your knowledge of DHCP Relay Agents and how these are placed across network segments. You must understand the situations where you might need to place a DHCP server in a particular network segment. An alternative to placing a DHCP server is to use a router that is BOOTP- or RFC 1542-compliant.

Integrating DHCP with DNS

DHCP can easily be integrated with DNS servers. The DHCP server can be configured in such a way that each time a client receives an IP address from the DHCP server, the DHCP server registers the host (A) and pointer (PTR) resource records with the DNS server. The default settings of a Windows Server 2003 DHCP server is to update A and PTR resource records of clients if requested by the clients. You can change these DHCP settings to always update the DNS records for DHCP clients whether or not the clients request it. Another default setting is to discard these records whenever the client lease has expired and is not renewed.

DHCP interoperability

When all of your DHCP clients use Microsoft operating systems, there is no specific interoperability issue. It is easy to configure Microsoft clients to use the DHCP server. The situation would be different if you had a mix of Microsoft and non-Microsoft clients in the network. The following guidelines will help you plan automatic assignment of IP addresses for non-Microsoft clients:

- IP addresses for clients that do not support DHCP should be manually configured. When you do so, make sure that these addresses are either not included in any of the scopes or are excluded.

- BOOTP clients do request IP addresses every time they start but do not recognize any lease periods in the DHCP scope.

- Clients that do not have any Microsoft operating systems installed may not support some of the features of Microsoft DHCP servers.

Number and placement of DHCP servers

Your next step is to decide on hardware specifications for DHCP servers and the number of DHCP servers in each network segment. The requirements will differ for different organizations based on the number of client computers, the location of network segments, and the number of computers in each network segment. The choice of server hardware for a single-segmented, nonrouted network is not so difficult, but you may not be the lucky one to work in such a small organization. If this were the situation, you would not be there to design an Active Directory-based network. Consider the following facts when deciding on server hardware:

- The server should preferably have multiple processors.
- The server should have high-performance hard drives. If possible, get hardware-based RAID solution for disk fault-tolerance.
- Install high-speed network adapters, preferably with 100 Mbps speed.

When deciding on placement of DHCP servers, make sure you take into account the availability and performance issues. It is always good to place a DHCP server in each network segment. If this is not possible, you will have to configure DHCP Relay Agents in segments where a DHCP server is not locally available. When you configure DHCP Relay Agents, you may configure routers to forward BOOTP traffic. You should first confirm that the routers are RFC 1542 (BOOTP)-compliant.

It is always good to place DHCP servers locally on network segments that are connected by slow WAN links. The idea is to keep the DHCP-related traffic local to the subnet instead of passing it through slow WAN links.

Configure DHCP servers with the 80/20 rule. The 80/20 rule states that you should configure two scopes on each server in such a way that 80 percent of the addresses in the scope are for the local segment and the rest are for the remote segment. The remote DHCP server should also be configured similarly so that it has 80 percent IP addresses for its own segment and 20 percent IP addresses for the remote segment. This way, if one of the DHCP servers fails, the DHCP server remote to the network segment would be able to allocate limited IP addresses to the other segment.

Securing DHCP servers

As with your domain controllers, DNS servers, WINS servers, and other critical database or mail servers, the DHCP servers should also be secured. One security feature that is built into Windows 2000 Server- or Windows Server 2003-based DHCP servers is to ensure that none of these servers can serve DHCP clients without first being authorized in the Active Directory.

Physical security of DHCP servers is equally important and should be given due consideration. You should place the DHCP server in locked server rooms in which other servers are located. Physical access to DHCP servers should be restricted to authorized administrators only.

Designing an Internet Connectivity Solution

Every organization needs Internet connectivity these days. When you are designing a network infrastructure for your organization, you must create a solid plan for Internet connectivity for the entire organization. When deciding on an Internet connectivity solution, you must take into account several factors, such as connection options, bandwidth requirements, selection of an Internet Service Provider (ISP), and availability. This section focuses on designing Internet connectivity.

Connection options

Connection to the ISP can be done using one of several connection options. The selection depends on the following factors:

- The number of users that need to connect to the Internet simultaneously
- Bandwidth requirements for users and applications that need Internet access
- The budget of the organization for Internet connectivity
- The location of the ISP and the type of connection options available with the ISP

Depending on your location and the level of services provided by the ISP, you may choose from any of the connection options listed in Table 5-14.

Table 5-14. Internet connection options

Type of connection	Type	Speed
Dial-up modem	Circuit Switched	56 Kbps
ISDN	Circuit Switched	ISDN Basic Rate Interface (BRI)-128 Kbps ISDN Primary Rate Interface (PRI)-1.544 Mbps
Cable television (CATV)	Leased Line	Downloads, from 512 Kbps Uploads, from 128 Kbps
Asymmetrical Digital Subscriber Line (ADSL)	Leased Line	Downloads, from 512 Kbps Uploads, from 128 Kbps
T-Carrier (North America)	Leased Line	T-1-1.544 Mbps T-3-44.736 Mbps Fractional T-1, blocks of 64 Kbps
E-Carrier (Europe)	Leased Line	E-1-2.048 Mbps E-2-8.448 Mbps
Frame Relay	Packet Switched	Variable
X.25	Packet Switched	1.544 Mbps
Asynchronous Transfer Mode	Packet Switched	622 Mbps

Bandwidth requirements

Your network design must take into account the bandwidth requirements of the organization for Internet connectivity. When you look at the bandwidth offered by various connection types, you will see that they are the highest theoretical limits, but are never practically achieved. The total bandwidth you need depends on several factors, and none of them should be ignored when you make your calculations. The following paragraphs explain some of the main concerns while calculating the bandwidth requirements.

- Check the number of users who need Internet access. Check whether all users need to access the Internet simultaneously or at random times. A user may just be browsing the Web, reading an email, or downloading a large file.

- Check the operating schedules at different locations of the organization. Some ISPs provide a specific bandwidth at all times, but others may accommodate your bandwidth requirements according to the work schedules of the organization.

- Check the peak usage hours and time zones where the remote offices of the organizations are located. The peak usage timings will not be the same for the entire organization if the offices are located in different time zones.

- Check where the users are located. If all the users are not located at a single site, you will need to decide on placing the Internet connection equipment at different locations.

- Check whether all users need full access to the Internet or whether certain applications will be restricted for some users. It is possible to limit Internet usage in an organization using proxy servers.

- Check what applications need access to the Internet. These applications may include domain controllers, DNS servers, web servers, and email servers. For example, you will need to plan extra bandwidth when domain controllers perform replication.

- Check whether the organization will be using VPN for remote access. You will need to take into account the extra bandwidth required by remote offices connecting to the main office through VPN.

You must remember that all users, services, and applications will share a single Internet connection. You must plan for sufficient bandwidth so that even in peak-usage hours, users do not complain of slow speed and applications do not suffer degraded performance. At the same time, if you have an Internet presence, outside users should not face any slow performance problems because you simply did not plan the bandwidth requirements properly.

Choosing an Internet Service Provider

The selection of an ISP is very critical. You need to consider a number of factors before signing up with an ISP for providing Internet connectivity. There is no doubt that you will depend on your ISP for providing Internet access to the users of your organization, but you will also depend on it for your Internet presence. You must do your homework to make sure that the ISP will be able to handle the requirements of your organization. If you are using VPN for providing network access to remote locations or telecommuters, your dependence on the ISP further increases. The ISP usually maintains its own network and maintains high-speed and redundant links to its higher-level ISPs.

Consider getting answers to the following questions before deciding on an ISP:

- How many other organizations have signed up with the ISP?
- What level of service does the ISP provide?
- What is the percentage of uptime guaranteed?
- How does the ISP handle downtimes in Internet service?
- Does the ISP provide other services such as DNS, web hosting, and email?
- How is the ISP connected to its peers or higher-level ISPs?
- How will the ISP monitor your network bandwidth usage?
- What security features does the ISP provide?

Answers to these questions will definitely help you select a correct ISP for your organization. You should make sure that the ISP has a good reputation among other organizations that use its services.

Network Address Translation

Network Address Translation (NAT) was designed to provide Internet access to an organization that uses private IP addresses for its internal network. If you recall from Table 5-3, the Internet Assigned Numbers Authority (IANA) has reserved certain ranges of IP addresses in each class for private use. If an organization uses any of these addresses for its internal clients, the clients would not be able to access the Internet directly. A solution is to use NAT that hides the internal IP addresses from the Internet. NAT also provides an excellent solution for organizations that have just a few registered IP addresses for their Internet presence but all internal IP addresses are from the private IP address range. One advantage of NAT is that it provides security for small organizations by hiding the internal IP addresses from the outside world.

In order to use NAT with Windows Server 2003, you must install Routing and Remote Access Service (RRAS) or enable Internet Connection Sharing (ICS). While ICS is recommended only for very small organizations, NAT is recommended for most organizations that use private IP addresses.

 NAT can also provide a temporary solution to a fast-growing organization that has fallen short of public IP addresses assigned to it. The organization can use NAT in one of its subnets until it gets a new IP address from the IANA and reorganizes the IP address allocation scheme for the new network segment.

Although NAT is an excellent Internet connectivity and security solution for small organizations, it comes with its own limitations. The following list describes some of these:

- NAT is good only for small organizations that use private IP addresses in a nonrouted network.
- NAT works only on Internet Protocol (IP). It cannot translate other protocols such as SNMP, LDAP, RPC, etc.

- NAT does not support Kerberos 5 protocol. Since Microsoft uses Kerberos 5 protocol for authentication, you cannot use domain controllers located behind NAT servers.

- In spite of its limitations, the Windows Server 2003 NAT supports L2TP/IPSec for VPN connections, a feature that was not available with Windows 2000 Server. This is possible with a new technology known as *NAT Traversal*. When you design a NAT solution for an organization, you must keep in mind that certain features will have to be configured correctly for proper working of NAT. NAT needs an editor if the IP address of an application is included in the IP header. Microsoft's implementation of NAT provides NAT editors for different Internet protocols such as File Transfer Protocol (FTP), Internet Control Message Protocol (ICMP), and LDAP-based Internet Locator Service (ILS)

Planning a NAT solution. If you plan to use NAT for Internet connectivity solutions for an organization, you should consider the following guidelines:

- NAT is suitable only for very small organizations.

- NAT works only in non-routed networks. In other words, the network should not be subnetted.

- Make sure that NAT is the right solution for Internet connectivity. Have a good understanding of its limitations.

- Make an assessment of any applications running on the internal network that NAT will not support.

- Decide whether you want to use a separate DHCP server or whether NAT will be used to allocate IP addresses to internal clients.

- Make an assessment of Internet needs of the organization and decide whether you need multiple connections to the Internet through a NAT server.

- Decide which server will act as a NAT server and how it will be configured. A NAT server should have at least two network interfaces, one for the internal network and the other for the Internet.

- If you would be using multiple public IP addresses to host web and mail servers that must be accessible from the Internet, create a plan for service and port mappings.

Using multiple registered addresses with NAT. When you have registered multiple public IP addresses for your Internet presence, you can configure an *address pool* in NAT to map these addresses to private addresses configured on servers hosting Internet services for outside users. The Address Pool tab of NAT properties allows you to configure these public addresses. This is different from Internet Connection Sharing (ICS) where you can use only a single registered IP address.

Special ports with NAT. NAT can be configured to use *special ports* that map public IP addresses and a port number to private IP addresses on the Internal network. This becomes necessary when certain servers on the internal network are hosting services that must be made available to outside users. An example of this type of mapping is a web server that must be accessible from the Internet. You can map the static IP address of the web server located behind the NAT server with a publicly registered address. When outside users try to access your web server, NAT translates the public address into the private address and opens the specified port for access. The web server in this situation must be configured with a static IP address and a static DNS server IP address from the private address range used on the internal network.

Designing a Perimeter Network

A *perimeter network* protects the internal network of an organization from the Internet. It is also known as a *demilitarized zone* (DMZ). Perimeter networks have their own importance in the overall design of the network infrastructure. Once you decide to use registered IP addresses and host services such as web servers for outside access, the entire network becomes prone to attacks by outside malicious users and professional hackers. A perimeter network allows an organization to keep internal and external resources separated by firewalls so that internal users can access resources on the Internet while outsiders can still access services offered by the organization. The firewall in this case can be a software firewall or a hardware-based firewall. Using a hardware firewall is always recommended, as this equipment is specially made for the purpose and offers many advantages over a software firewall.

Components of a perimeter network

A simple firewall can be configured on routers that connect the internal network to the Internet. Routers allow you to configure access lists that specify what type of network traffic is allowed to pass through the router. You can configure inbound and outbound packet filters on routers to allow only specific traffic to pass through the routers. The filters can be based on IP addresses, ports, or a combination of both.

The following types of firewalls are available:

Packet filtering firewall
> Packet filtering firewalls inspect the incoming and outgoing network packets. Based on certain rules, these networks packets are either allowed or blocked. Packet filtering firewalls are similar to routers where you can configure packet filters.

Application filtering firewall
> Application filtering firewalls inspect the contents of a packet. Based on the application-specific rules, these allow the packets to pass through the firewall, or block them from doing so. An example of an application filtering firewall is Microsoft's Proxy Server.

Stateful inspection firewall
> Stateful inspection firewalls closely inspect the contents of a packet and check for its validity. If a packet seems to be invalid, it is dropped.

Intrusion Detection Systems (IDS). *Intrusion detection systems* continuously monitor the network and warn the administrator if some kind of intrusion has occurred or an outsider has attacked some server or a network resource. There are two types of intrusion detection systems:

Host-based
> The *host-based IDS* is installed on a particular server and continuously monitors the audit logs for traces of an attack.

Network-based
> The *network-based IDS* is installed on the network, and it continuously monitors the data passing through the network. The network traffic is compared to preconfigured signatures or patterns to detect an outside attack.

Firewall options

As you know, a firewall is a hardware device or a software application that controls the network traffic as it passes from one network to another. The most important role of a firewall is to protect your internal network from the Internet. There are a number of options that you can use when designing a perimeter network. These options are explained in the following list:

Bastion host firewall
> A bastion host firewall is a single firewall that connects the internal network to the Internet. This type of firewall is suitable only for small organizations.

Three-homed firewall
> A three-homed firewall has three network interfaces that can be connected to three different networks. One of the interfaces is usually connected to the Internet, and the other two are connected to two different segments for the network. One of these segments hosts the internal servers and computers of the network while the second segment hosts those servers that should be accessible from the Internet.

Back-to-back firewall
> This solution needs two firewalls and creates a true perimeter network or a demilitarized zone. One of the firewalls is connected to the Internet and to the perimeter network. The second firewall connects the perimeter network to the internal network.

Figure 5-8 shows a perimeter network using two firewalls.

The perimeter network usually hosts the web servers, DNS servers, and mail servers for the organization because these servers must be accessible from the Internet. Depending on the size of your organization, you may implement suitable firewall options in the network to secure the internal resources of your organization from outside attacks.

Designing a Remote Access Solution

Remote access is designed for users who want to connect to the company network from remote locations. It enables users to access the resources on the network when they are either working from home or are telecommuting. Remote access can either be granted through dial-up connections or through virtual private

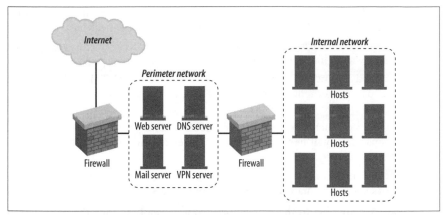

Figure 5-8. Perimeter network using two back-to-back firewalls

networks. In either of these situations, a remote client's access level and permissions are controlled by a combination of the user's Active Directory account permissions and *remote access policies*. This section focuses on designing and implementing a remote access solution for both dial-up and VPN clients.

Remote access design considerations

By allowing remote access to users, you are probably opening up your network or a portion of it to the outside world. There are a number of things that you need to consider so that you can design a highly available and secure remote access structure for the organization. When designing a remote access solution, you need to consider the following:

- How many users will need to access the network remotely? From which location(s) will they be connecting? This will help you figure out the number of user accounts you need to create if they do not already exist.

- Is there a particular time when the users will need to connect? This will help you decide the timing of when the remote access should be allowed.

- How many users will be connecting simultaneously? This will help you decide how much bandwidth you will need for the remote access connection.

- What type of connection will be used for remote access? This will help you decide whether a dial-up connection would be sufficient or whether you need a VPN solution.

- Does the current network infrastructure support remote access? This will help you figure out whether you need to install additional servers and/or routers.

- Do users need to run any applications remotely? If yes, you will have to ensure that the connection bandwidth supports the requirements of these applications.

- If using dial-up lines with modems, you will need to ensure that you have enough modems in the modem bank to support simultaneous connections.

- If using VPN for remote access, you will need to decide on maximum number of ports for L2TP and/or PPTP to support remote connections.

- What type of security policies do you need for remote clients and remote access servers? This will help you design the remote access policies.

- What kind of authentication methods would be used? This will help you decide on an authentication method supported by both ends of remote access.

- What type of encryption should be used for data transmission over public mediums? This will help you decide on an encryption method supported by both ends of remote access.

- What resources will be made available to remote users? What portion of the network should be made available to remote users?

Once you have answers to these questions, you are ready to take the next step in designing the right kind of remote access solution for the organization.

Dial-up remote access

Dial-up remote access to the network uses either public switched telephone network (PSTN) or Integrated Services Digital Network (ISDN) lines. The dial-up client dials a preconfigured number to connect to one of the modems on the network and makes a direct connection to the network. If you are considering a dial-up remote access, you should take into account the following things:

- Dial-up connections are good for users who do not need regular and continuous access to the network and will not be running any applications remotely.

- Dial-up connections needs initial investment in modems, phone lines, and multiport adapters. Besides the cost of equipment, the installation and maintenance charges may also apply.

- Dial-up connections must be verified through callback options or through remote access policies.

Once you have decided that dial-up remote access is the right solution for you, you can decide whether you need PSTN lines or ISDN for the purpose. For a successful connection, the remote access client and the remote access server should be configured with identical telecommunication lines. If you need to support only a few remote users, you may install modems with the remote access servers and configure each server to answer calls from remote servers. In large organizations, you may need to install modem banks or modem pools to support remote access clients.

User account dial-in permissions. Any user who needs to access a Windows Server 2003-based network from a remote location by means of dial-up networking should have appropriate permissions in his user account in the Active Directory. This is the first line of defense for your remote access server and the network from unauthorized outside persons. The following properties can be configured from the Dial-in tab of User Account Properties in Active Directory:

Remote Access Permission (Dial-in or VPN)

You can allow remote access, deny access, or control access through remote access policies. Even when you allow access to a remote user, the access can further be controlled by remote access policies that may be set to allow or deny the connection.

Verify Caller ID

Caller ID verification is used for users who always dial from the same location and use the same telephone number. This setting ensures that only the authorized user is dialing into the remote access server. The telephone number of the user is specified in this option. If the call is not from the specified number, the connection is refused.

Callback Options

You can set this option to No Callback, Set by Caller, or Always Callback to the specified number. This setting provides security because the remote access server can call back the user at a preconfigured telephone number. Another advantage is that the user can thus save the cost of the telephone call if she is calling long distance.

Assign a Static IP Address

This option will cause the remote access server to supply a static IP address to the client once the connection is successful. The administrator can specify a static IP address.

Apply Static Routes

This option will update the routing table of the remote access server. The administrator can define the static routes used for demand dial routing.

VPN remote access

The dial-up remote access solution is good only if you have a small number of users who need to connect to the network remotely. When the number of remote users is large, a VPN solution may be best suited for your needs. A VPN solution will help you reduce the cost of supporting a large number of remote users and provide better security for the network resources. You can also create an *intranet* using VPN technologies to connect a number of geographical locations. Some organizations provide access to their internal networks to other partner organizations by creating *extranets*.

A VPN is a point-to-point network connection between the remote client and the VPN server, and it uses the Internet as a transport medium. This is done by creating a tunnel inside the Internet that carries the data from one computer to another. The data is encrypted by tunneling protocols and cannot be easily decrypted. The Routing and Remote Access Service in Windows Server 2003 supports L2TP and PPTP as tunneling protocols. You can add up to 1,000 ports for each of these protocols to support simultaneous connections.

Some of the advantages of using VPN are as follows:

- VPN supports a larger number of simultaneous connections as compared to dial-up access.

- The cost of implementing a VPN solution is much lower than that of dial-up access.

- VPN supports a number of common network protocols so that users can run different types applications.

- VPN provides enhanced security, as the VPN server can enforce strict authentication and encryption policies.

- Since all data is encrypted while it travels through the Internet, the internal IP addressing scheme is not exposed to any outside persons.

Remote access authentication methods

When designing a remote access solution, you must decide on some kind of authentication method for remote clients. This will ensure that only authorized users get access to the remote access server and network resources located beyond the server. Windows Server 2003 provides a number of options for authenticating remote clients. It is possible to configure multiple authentication methods to support a variety of older Microsoft and non-Microsoft operating systems. Before you decide on a particular authentication method, you must make sure that the remote access server and the remote client have at least one common authentication method.

The following authentication protocols are supported on Windows Server 2003 RRAS servers:

Extensible Authentication Protocol (EAP)
> This is the most secure authentication mechanism that allows you to use a third-party authentication protocol as well as those supplied with Windows Server 2003. These include EAP-MD5 CHAP (Message Digest 5 CHAP), EAP-TLS (Transport Layer Security), and Protected EAP (for wireless networks).

Microsoft Challenge Handshake Authentication Protocol version 2 (MS-CHAP v2)
> This is a password-based authentication mechanism in which both the client and the server authenticate each other using encrypted passwords. Microsoft recommends using this protocol.

Microsoft Challenge Handshake Authentication Protocol (MS-CHAP)
> This is an earlier version of MS-CHAP that supports only one-way authentication. This protocol is included to support Windows NT 3.51 and Windows 98 clients that do not support MS-CHAPv2.

Challenge Handshake Authentication Protocol (CHAP)
> This protocol is included to support non-Microsoft clients. It is less secure than MS-CHAP. This protocol requires that passwords be stored in the Active Directory using reversible encryption.

Password Authentication Protocol (PAP)
> This is the oldest and most basic form of authentication in which both the username and password are transmitted in clear text over the dial-up network. The transmissions are unencrypted and are not secure. Microsoft does not recommend using this protocol.

Shiva Password Authentication Protocol (SPAP)
This protocol is included to support clients that use Shiva remote access products. It provides very weak encryption for username and password and all data is transmitted in clear text.

Remote access policies

Remote access policies ensure that only authorized users connect to the remote access server and the network beyond the remote access server. These policies also ensure that remote clients connect using the appropriate connection type, belong to a designated Windows user group, dial at permitted times, and use an authentication and encryption method that is acceptable to both the remote access server and the remote client. If the client fails to match any of these conditions, the connection will be refused. When studying the remote access requirements of the organization, you must analyze the type of remote access required by the clients and the type of authentication and encryption methods they can support. Your design should consider all these factors when planning remote access policies. Depending on the situation and requirements, you may need multiple policies to be configured and enforced on the network.

Remote access policies are configured on the remote access server or on a *RADIUS* server. When you configure remote access authentication and accounting provider for the remote access server, you have the option of selecting either the remote access server or the RADIUS server for one or both of these purposes. The RADIUS server is usually deployed in large organizations in which multiple remote access servers are installed and centralization of the authentication process is required. RADIUS servers are discussed later in this section.

As discussed earlier, a remote access policy is a set of conditions that the remote client must match before the connection can be granted. The following are three main components of a remote access policy:

Policy conditions. Conditions are a set of attributes that the policy uses to grant or deny permissions to the remote user. If more than one condition is specified in a policy, the client must satisfy all conditions. The following are some of the commonly used conditions:

Authentication Type
Specifies the authentication type configured on the remote client

Day and Time Restrictions
Specifies the day and time of the day when the user is allowed to connect

Framed Protocol
Specifies the data link layer protocol that the remote client must use

Tunnel Type
Specifies the tunneling protocol that a VPN client must use

Windows Groups
Specifies the groups that the connecting user must belong to

Policy profile. The policy profile contains another set of attributes that can be configured to further control access to the remote access server. Some of the commonly configured profile settings are as follows:

Dial-in constraints
> The dial-in constraints include settings such as time limit for the connection, idle time limit before the server will disconnect the user, and hours and days of week when the client can connect.

IP
> These settings allow you to configure whether the client or the remote access server should assign an IP address to the client. You have the option to configure the server to supply a static IP address to the client. You can also configure input and output filters to limit the type of network traffic that should be allowed to flow between the client and the server.

Multilink
> These settings allow the client to use the Windows *multilink* feature so that the client can use multiple telephone lines to increase network bandwidth. If this feature is used, both the server and the client must support multilink.

Authentication
> This setting is used to specify an authentication protocol that the client must use in order to connect. Both the server and the client should use similar authentication protocol for the connection to be successful.

Encryption
> This setting is used to specify an encryption protocol that the client must use in order to connect. Both the server and the client should use a similar encryption protocol. Otherwise, the connection is refused.

 If multiple remote access policies are configured on the remote access server, the client must satisfy all conditions in any one of the policies in order to get connected. The administrator can change the processing order of policies.

Remote access permissions. An administrator can explicitly grant remote access permission to a remote client trying to connect to the remote access server or the client must satisfy all the conditions of at least one remote access policy. Depending on the policy conditions, the client can be allowed or denied connection when she meets all conditions in a policy.

RADIUS server

RADIUS stands for *Remote Authentication Dial-In User Service*. RADIUS servers use the *Internet Authentication Service* (IAS) to authenticate users connecting remotely to the local network. When you have multiple remote access servers in your network and want to simplify the administration and centralize the authentication of remote clients, a RADIUS server is the best choice. RADIUS can be used for dial-up, VPN, and wireless client authentication. The remote access servers can be configured as RADIUS clients to forward an authentication request to the configured RADIUS server.

The following are some of the advantages of using a RADIUS server:

- RADIUS servers provide centralized authentication. Administrators can configure remote access policies on the RADIUS server instead of configuring them on each remote access server.

- RADIUS servers provide centralized accounting for analysis of network usage by remote clients.

- Auditing and logging of remote access servers is centralized.

- Administration and troubleshooting is centralized and simplified. Administrators do not have to visit each remote access server to configure, administer, or troubleshoot authentication problems for remote clients.

Logging for remote access servers

A remote access server running on the Windows Server 2003 operating system supports the types of logging options described in the next sections.

Event logging. Event logging is used for a remote access server that writes events to the system logfiles. By default, only errors and warnings are recorded. You can choose from the following four types of event log options:

- Log errors only
- Log errors and warnings
- Log the maximum amount of information
- Disable event logging

It is recommended that you keep the default event logging option set to record errors and warning events; this is helpful in resolving a majority of problems with remote access servers. If you configure the remote access server event logs for maximum information, you should make sure that the logfiles are large enough and that there is plenty of free disk space on the server.

Authentication and accounting logging. This logging feature enables you to collect information on local authentication attempts as well as information on usage of Remote Access Services on the local remote access server.

RADIUS-based logging. If you are using a RADIUS server for authentication and accounting purposes in the organization, you should consider configuring logging options on the RADIUS server. The advantage of collecting and checking event logs on the RADIUS server is that you get information at a central point. You don't have to check authentication logs for all remote access servers in the network. A majority of ISPs use RADIUS servers and RADIUS-based authentication. The RADIUS-based logging will help you track authentication attempts from all the client remote access servers.

6

Exam 70-297 Prep and Practice

The material in this chapter is designed to help you prepare and practice for *Exam 70-297: Designing a Microsoft Windows Server 2003 Active Directory and Network Infrastructure*. The chapter is organized into four sections:

Preparing for Exam 70-297
    This section provides an overview of the types of questions on the exam. Reviewing this section will help you understand how the actual exam works.

Exam 70-297 Suggested Exercises
    This section provides a numbered list of exercises that you can do to gain experience in the exam's subject areas. An in-depth study of practice case scenarios will help you prepare better for the exam.

Exam 70-297 Highlighters Index
    This section compiles the facts within the exam's subject areas that you are most likely to need another look at—in other words, the areas of study that you might have highlighted while reading the Study Guide. Studying the highlights is useful as a final review before the exam.

Exam 70-297 Practice Questions
    This section includes a comprehensive set of practice questions to assess your knowledge of the exam. The questions are more or less similar in format to the exam. After you've reviewed the Study Guide, read the questions and see if you can answer them correctly.

Before you take Exam 70-297, review the exam overview and take another look at the Highlighters Index. Many online web sites provide practice tests for the exam. Duplicating the depth and scope of these practice exams in a printed book isn't possible. Visit Microsoft's Certification site for pointers to online practice tests (*http://www.microsoft.com/learning/mcpexams/prepare/practicetests.asp*).

Preparing for Exam 70-297

Exam 70-297 is a computer-generated exam. This exam is different from the core exams in the sense that it contains four or five mini-exams known as *testlets*. You will have limited time for completing each testlet. An onscreen timer clock displays the amount of time remaining on the exam. Most questions on each testlet of the exam are multiple-choice. Multiple-choice questions are either:

Multiple-choice, single answer
> A radio button allows you to select a single answer only.

Multiple-choice, multiple answer
> A checkbox allows you to select multiple answers. Usually the number of correct answers is indicated in the question itself.

Typically, the test environment will have Previous/Next and Mark For Review options. You can navigate through the test using the Previous/Next buttons. You can click the Mark For Review checkbox to flag a question for later review. At the bottom of the screen is a calculator button.

Other formats for questions are used as well, including:

List prioritization
> Pick the choices that answer the question and arrange the list in a specified order. Lists initially appear on the right side, and you have to click << ADD to add them in the correct order to the list on the left side. For example, you might have to list the steps for creating a local user from the Computer Management Console.

Hot area
> Indicate the correct answer by clicking one or more areas of the screen or dialog box provided with the question. For example, you might be asked to click an appropriate tab on the Display Properties to configure screen resolution.

Select and place
> Using drag-and-drop, pick answers from the given set of choices and place them in an appropriate spot in a dialog box or diagram. For example, you might be asked to select local users or groups who have the rights to backup files and folders.

Active screen
> Use the dialog box provided to configure the options correctly or perform the required procedure. For example, you might be asked to click an appropriate option from the local policies in order to configure Account Lockout Policy.

Simulation
> Use the simulated desktop environment provided to perform a specific task or troubleshoot. For example, you might be asked to configure a static IP address for a given network adapter.

Exam 70-297 is a design exam. It is obvious that the exam is based on case-scenario-type questions, followed by a set of multiple-choice questions. There are usually four or five case scenarios or case studies (known as testlets). Each of these testlets spans multiple pages of information, some of which is relevant and some of which is irrelevant to the case. You are required to study the information on all these pages before you can answer 10 to 12 questions based on the information. If you have not practiced properly, the information may seem confusing at times. It is important that you do not skip any part of the information so that you can correctly answer the questions in the testlet.

While many of the questions on Exam 70-297 are multiple-choice, hot area, select and place, and active screen, the simulation type of questions are being used increasingly by Microsoft to ensure the testing process more accurately reflects actual hands-on knowledge rather than rote memorization. With the exception of multiple-choice, single-answer questions, all of the other questions can have multiple answers or multiple required procedures to obtain full credit. If all of the expected answers or procedures are not performed, you will only get partial credit for the answer. This is usually indicated in the question itself.

Exam 70-297 Suggested Exercises

Exam 70-297 expects you to have a sound knowledge of what you have learned during the preparation for Windows Server 2003 core required exams. It is suggested that you take this exam after you have completed the four core exams. All the skills you learned for the four core exams will be required for this exam. You are expected not only to be a good administrator in these areas, but also to have the solid planning skills of a network designer. The measured skills are extended to include many new areas of study, including analysis of an existing Active Directory and network infrastructure, business and technical requirements of an organization, and, based on your analysis, design of the logical and physical network infrastructure for an organization.

You will need plenty of planning and design experience to pass the exam. This design will be based on your skills in analyzing the given information in a case study. You'll need to review the Study Guide closely, paying special attention to any areas with which you are unfamiliar. This section provides a numbered list of exercises that you can do to gain experience in the exam's subject areas. Performing the exercises will help ensure that you have plenty of planning and design experience with all areas of the exam.

You probably will not need a Windows Server 2003 network for this exam because you will be required to apply the knowledge you gained while studying for the four core exams. The exam tests your planning and designing skills instead of any hands-on skills. The case scenarios presented in the exam will require you to have an in-depth knowledge of Windows Server 2003 technologies and how they can be applied when you are creating a design for an Active Directory-based network infrastructure. However, it's not a bad idea to have a two-computer test network just in case you need to practice a few hands-on skills.

Before you take Exam 70-297, we strongly recommend that you review key features of Windows Server 2003 Active Directory and network services. You might have studied these features while preparing for the four core exams. The companion book *MCSE Core Required Exams in a Nutshell*, Third Edition (O'Reilly), covers all four core exams.

Analyzing the Current Administrative Model

1. Determine whether the company is following a centralized, decentralized, or hybrid administrative model.
2. Find out why a particular model is being followed.
3. Interview administrators and IT managers.
4. Determine whether a different administrative model would be more productive and cost-effective.
5. Document your findings, noting all details.

Analyzing the Current Geographical Design

1. Determine how many locations the company is operating from.
2. Draw a map showing different locations of the company.
3. Determine how networks of these locations are interconnected.
4. Determine the types of WAN links and their bandwidth for each location.
5. Determine whether there are any issues with WAN connectivity.
6. Determine how many locations have local administrative staff.
7. Document your findings.

Analyzing Current Windows 2000 Infrastructure

1. Determine the current logical structure of the Windows 2000 Active Directory.
2. Determine how many domains, trees, and forests have been implemented.
3. Determine the implicit and explicit trust relationships between domains.
4. Note the names of all domains, trees, and forests.
5. Determine whether there are any performance issues with the current network or directory structure.
6. Determine whether there will be any issues during migration to Windows Server 2003.
7. Make a diagram of the current domain and forest structure.

Analyzing Current Windows NT 4.0 Infrastructure

1. Determine the number of locations of the company.
2. Determine the number of domains for each location.

3. Determine the types of trust relationships between domains.

4. Determine why the current infrastructure was not upgraded to Windows 2000.

5. Determine whether all applications will support migration to Windows Server 2003.

6. Determine how the current domains will translate into the Windows Server 2003 Active Directory structure.

7. Make a diagram of the current Windows NT 4.0 structure.

Analyzing the Current Network Structure

1. Determine the server and network hardware installed at each location.

2. Make lists of names of servers and desktops.

3. Find out the capacity of servers, as well as their makes and models.

4. Note the names of servers that provide critical network services.

5. Find out whether there are any outstanding performance issues with servers or network segments.

6. Determine what software applications are running on the network.

7. Determine whether all packaged applications will be supported in the Windows 2003 platform.

8. Determine the number of applications that are developed in-house.

Analyzing Current Subnets and IP Addressing

1. Make a drawing showing network segments and how they are connected.

2. Find out the IP address allocation for each subnet.

3. Find out the subnet mask, default gateway, DNS, and WINS servers for each subnet.

4. Determine the make and models of routers.

5. Determine how many DHCP servers are in each subnet for automatic IP addressing.

6. Interview network administrators and a few users regarding any outstanding performance issues.

7. Document your findings.

Designing a Naming Strategy

1. Determine what kind of naming conventions will be used for user accounts, computers, and groups.

2. Determine how user accounts will be named.

3. Determine whether any clients will be using UPN names for logging on to the network.

4. Determine how users locate objects in the Active Directory.

5. Document your guidelines to apply uniform naming conventions throughout the domain.

Choosing Domain Names

1. Determine whether the company will be using the same registered names externally and for the Active Directory domain.
2. Determine how external and internal namespaces will be designed.
3. Determine whether the internal namespace will be based on the external registered namespace.
4. Determine whether the internal and external namespaces will be entirely separate and independent.
5. Prepare your naming design based on the above factors.

Designing a Domain Structure

1. Determine whether a single domain will fulfill the requirements of the organization.
2. Determine whether security policies will be uniform for all parts of the network.
3. Determine whether any units of the company need a separate set of password or account policies.
4. Determine the number of administrators available for maintaining domains.
5. Determine whether multiple domains will be required for different units of the organization.
6. Prepare a single- or multiple-domain structure based on your analysis.

Designing an OU Structure

1. Determine the type of OU structure best suited for the organization.
2. Determine whether location-based, function-based, or organization-based OUs will be used.
3. Determine whether a mix of location-based and organization-based OU designs will be suitable.
4. Design an OU structure for multiple locations of the organization.
5. Design top-level and lower-level OUs based on your analysis.
6. Determine how delegation of control will be granted to administrators.
7. Make a diagram of the OU structure.
8. Name the OUs, following naming conventions.
9. Determine how permissions will be inherited in nested OUs.
10. Document your design and include all details.

Designing a Group Policy Structure

1. Determine what Group Policies will be required at domain, site, and OU levels.
2. Determine how Group Policy inheritance will work.

3. Determine whether any Group Policies will be blocked or overridden by other policies.
4. Determine the types of settings required for each Group Policy.
5. Design an Account Policy for the domain.
6. Design a Password Policy for the domain.
7. Determine how Group Policies will be processed in case of multiple policies.
8. Document your design.

Planning Accounts for Security Principals

1. Create a design for computer accounts.
2. Create a design for user accounts.
3. Create a design for group accounts.
4. Determine how group nesting will be done.
5. Determine how resource access permissions will be granted.
6. Determine naming conventions for accounts.
7. Document your design.

Planning a Site Topology

1. Draw a map of different locations of the company.
2. Determine whether any sites will act as a hub for nearby smaller sites.
3. Determine site boundaries and design site links.
4. Determine how site replication will be configured.
5. Determine how site cost links will be configured.
6. Determine whether preferred Bridgehead servers will be configured at any site.
7. Document your site plan.

Placement of Domain Controllers

1. Determine the number of domain controllers required at each site.
2. Calculate the capacity requirements of domain controllers.
3. Determine how domain controllers will be physically secured at each location.
4. Determine which domain controllers will hold operations master roles.
5. Determine which domain controllers will be Global Catalog servers.
6. Determine the placement of Forest Root servers.
7. Draw a map of the network and show the number and placement of domain controllers.

Analyzing the Existing DNS Structure

1. Determine what kind of DNS servers are currently working in the network.
2. Determine whether any DNS servers are experiencing performance problems.
3. Determine how DNS servers are placed across different locations of the network.
4. Determine the names and location of primary, secondary, forwarding, and caching-only servers.
5. Determine how zones are configured on DNS servers.
6. Determine how zone replication is configured.
7. Document your findings.

Designing the DNS Namespace

1. Determine whether the same DNS namespace will be used externally and internally.
2. Determine whether the internal namespace will be based on the external namespace.
3. Determine whether external and internal namespaces will be entirely separate and independent.
4. Determine the administrative overheads and cost of hardware before deciding on a DNS design.
5. Document the naming conventions for domains, subdomains, and other hosts.
6. Determine how DNS will be integrated with Active Directory, DHCP, and WINS.
7. Create a DNS design based on your analysis.
8. Document your design.

Planning DNS Zones

1. Determine the requirements for creating DNS zones.
2. Determine whether Active Directory-Integrated or standard primary and secondary zones will be configured.
3. Determine how zone transfers will be configured in case of standard zones.
4. Determine whether you need to create stub zones for delegation of control.
5. Determine how zone transfers will be secured from external attacks.
6. Create a DNS zone design based on your analysis.
7. Document your plan.

Determining Number and Placement of DNS Servers

1. Determine interoperability issues with third-party DNS servers.
2. Determine the number of DNS servers required at each location.

3. Determine how DNS servers will be physically secured.

4. Determine which administrators will be responsible for maintaining DNS servers.

5. Prepare a plan for number and placement of DNS servers.

6. Document your plan.

Planning a WINS Structure

1. Determine whether any legacy applications or clients need NetBIOS name resolution.

2. Determine whether all locations need WINS servers.

3. Determine the number of WINS servers at each location or each subnet.

4. Determine how servers will be placed across the network.

5. Determine whether push or pull replication will be required between WINS servers.

6. Determine how WINS servers will be physically secured.

7. Document your design taking account of all factors.

Designing IP Addresses Assignment

1. Determine the number of registered IP addresses required by the company.

2. Determine how the registered IP address space will be divided into different locations.

3. Determine the portion of IP addresses for each location.

4. Calculate a subnet mast for each subnet of the network.

5. Determine the servers that need registered IP addresses for Internet presence.

6. Design an IP address allocation plan.

Dynamic IP Addressing with DHCP

1. Determine the number of DHCP servers required for all locations of the network.

2. Determine how DHCP servers will be configured with scopes.

3. Determine what scope and server options will be configured.

4. Determine the servers that need address reservations.

5. Determine which smaller subnets will need DHCP Relay Agent.

6. Determine where the DHCP servers will be placed and how they will be secured.

7. Design a complete DHCP solution based on your analysis.

8. Document your plan.

Designing an Internet Connectivity Solution

1. Determine the number of users that need Internet access.
2. Determine whether the company needs an Internet presence.
3. Determine the locations from where Internet access is required.
4. Calculate the total bandwidth requirements for Internet connectivity.
5. Determine which connection option is best suited for the company.
6. Check various ISPs and the services they offer.
7. Design an Internet connectivity plan based on your analysis.
8. Document the complete plan.

Network Address Translation (NAT)

1. Determine whether NAT is the right solution for Internet connectivity.
2. Determine whether users just need to surf the Web or to run applications also.
3. Determine any special ports to be used by applications.
4. Determine whether the company needs multiple registered IP addresses.
5. Determine the capacity and placement of the NAT server.
6. Design a NAT solution and prepare documentation.

Designing a Perimeter Network

1. Determine whether the network requires security from external sources.
2. Determine how many firewalls are required.
3. Determine whether an intrusion detection system is also required.
4. Determine which servers will be placed inside the perimeter network.
5. Determine how internal users will connect to the Internet.
6. Determine how external users will access the Web and mail servers.
7. Document your design specifying all aspects of your plan.

Remote Access Design Considerations

1. Determine the number of users that require remote access.
2. Determine whether everyone needs to use dial-up remote access.
3. Determine whether the existing remote access server needs to be upgraded.
4. Determine what remote access protocol is supported by all users.
5. Determine the days and times when remote access is required.
6. Determine the locations from where the remote clients will be connecting.
7. Design and document your dial-up remote access plan.

VPN Remote Access

1. Determine whether a large number of users need remote access.
2. Determine whether VPN will be a cost-effective solution for remote access.
3. Plan for Internet access for VPN servers.
4. Calculate the total number of L2TP and/or PPTP ports required on VPN servers.
5. Determine what authentication methods should be used.
6. Document your VPN access plan.

Design Remote Access Policies

1. Determine how many polices are required by company security policies.
2. Determine what policy conditions are required.
3. Determine authentication and encryption supported by various types of remote clients.
4. Document the requirements.
5. Design one or more policies and specify their processing order.

Logging for Remote Access Servers

1. Determine what level of event logging is required.
2. Determine the size of logfiles based on selected logging options.
3. Determine when the log will be analyzed.
4. Determine when the logfiles should be checked.
5. Document the logging plan you create.

RADIUS Server

1. Determine the number of remote access servers required in the organization.
2. Determine whether centralization of authentication and accounting is required.
3. Determine whether a RADIUS server is required, based on the number of remote access servers.
4. Determine whether remote access policies will be configured on remote access servers.
5. Determine whether authentication and accounting logging should be done on the RADIUS server.
6. Document the placement and configuration requirements of the RADIUS server.

Exam 70-297 Highlighters Index

In this section, we've attempted to compile the facts within the exam's subject areas that you are most likely to need another look at—in other words, the areas of study that you might have highlighted while reading the Study Guide. The title of each highlighted element corresponds to the heading title in the Exam 70-297 Study Guide. This way, if you have a question about a highlight, you can refer back to the corresponding section in the Study Guide. For the most part, the entries under a heading are organized as term lists with a Windows Server 2003 feature or a component as the term, and the key details for this feature or configuration listed next.

Overview of Active Directory and Network Services in Windows Server 2003

This subsection covers a summary of highlights from the "Overview of Active Directory and Network Services in Windows Server 2003" section in the Exam 70-297 Study Guide.

Active Directory
- *Active Directory* is a centralized and searchable collection of objects.
- Users, computers, and applications can search objects in Active Directory.
- It is a scalable, manageable, and secure form of storing information.
- Active Directory is integrated with DNS service.
- It is based on Lightweight Directory Access Protocol (LDAP).
- The logical structure of Active Directory is separate from its physical structure.
- Objects, domains, trees, forests, and Organizational Units form the logical structure.

Objects
- Network resources are stored as objects in Active Directory.
- Objects in Active Directory include users, computers, and shared resources in the network.
- Each object is made up of attributes.
- Object classes help organize objects based on their attributes.
- A *schema* is a collection of object classes.
- A schema defines how the attributes of objects can be defined.

Domains
- A *domain* is the administrative boundary of a network.
- All objects in a domain share a common security database.
- The Active Directory database in each domain stores information about objects in its domain only.
- Access to objects in a domain is controlled by Access Control Lists (ACLs)

- Security policies defined on objects in a domain are applicable only within the domain.
- Naming conventions in a domain follow the DNS naming structure.

Domain functional levels

- Windows 2000 Mixed (default) allows interaction with Windows 2000 and Windows NT domain controllers.
- Windows 2000 Native allows interaction with Windows 2000 domain controllers only.
- Windows 2003 Interim allows interaction with Windows NT 4.0 domain controllers only.
- Windows Server 2003 can have only Windows Server 2003 domain controllers.
- Windows Server 2003 allows interaction with other Windows Server 2003 domain controllers only.

Trees

- A *tree* is a hierarchical grouping of domains.
- All domains in a tree share a contiguous namespace.
- The first domain you create becomes the tree root domain.
- A tree is created by adding child domains to the parent domain.

Forests

- A forest is the hierarchical grouping of domain trees.
- A forest is the outermost boundary of the Active Directory structure.
- The first domain you create becomes the Forest Root domain in a forest.
- All domains in a forest share common schema, domain naming, and Global Catalog.
- Domains in a forest are linked by implicit two-way trust relationships.

Forest functional levels

- Windows 2000 (default) supports interaction with Windows 2000 and Windows NT 4.0 domains.
- Windows Server 2003 Interim supports interaction with Windows NT 4.0 domains only.
- Windows Server 2003 supports interaction with other Windows Server 2003 domains only.

Organizational units (OUs)

- An *OU* is a container used to logically group objects in Active Directory.
- An OU is the basic administrative unit in Active Directory.
- An OU is the smallest unit for which delegation of control can be assigned.
- Nesting of OUs is used to organize objects and simplify administration.
- When multiple OUs are nested, all child OUs inherit the permissions of the parent OU.
- Typically, the structure of an OU follows the business structure of the organization.

Physical structure of Active Directory

- Domain controllers and sites are two components of the physical structure of Active Directory.
- Domain controllers hold the Active Directory database for the domain.

Domain controllers

- Domain controllers are servers running the Windows Server 2003 operating system.
- Active Directory is installed on domain controllers.
- All changes to directory objects are done on domain controllers.
- There can be any number of domain controllers in a domain.
- Multiple domain controllers are used for fault-tolerance and performance.
- Domain controllers authenticate users and computers across the domain.
- They are used to apply security policies across the domain.

Operations master roles

- All domain controllers are peers and take part in multimaster replication to keep the directory database up-to-date.
- Operations master roles are assigned to individual domain controllers for specific functions.
- Each role can be assigned to only one domain controller in the forest or domain, depending on the role.
- The forest-wide operation master roles work at the forest level.
- The domain-wide operations master roles work at domain level.

Forest-wide operations master roles

- The schema master role is responsible for distributing schema to all domains in the forest.
- The first domain controller in the forest is assigned the schema master role.
- The domain controller with schema master must be online when changes to the schema are made.
- The domain naming master role is responsible for addition or deletion of domains in forest.
- The first domain controller in the forest is assigned the domain naming master role.
- Only one computer can be assigned the role of schema master and domain master in a forest.

Domain-wide operations master roles

- The Relative ID (RID) master role is responsible for distributing blocks of RIDs to other domain controllers in the domain.
- The Primary Domain Controller (PDC) emulator role is responsible for logons for clients that do not support Active Directory.
- The Infrastructure master role is responsible for recording changes to objects in Active Directory.

- All changes in Active Directory objects are first reported to the domain controller with Infrastructure master and then are written to the directory database.
- Each domain-wide role is assigned to only one domain controller in the domain.

Global Catalog

- The Global Catalog is a catalog service provided by Active Directory.
- The Global Catalog server holds information about all objects in the forest or tree.
- The Global Catalog holds a full replica of all objects in its parent domain and a partial replica of all objects in other domains in the forest.
- The first domain controller in the forest is assigned this role.

Sites

- Sites are IP subnets connected by fast and reliable links.
- Sites are not part of the Active Directory namespace.
- Sites contain only computers and connection objects.
- The purpose of creating sites is to localize as much network traffic as possible.
- Sites typically have the same boundaries as the local area network.
- Sites help control replication traffic between domain controllers.

Replication

- Replication is the process of keeping all domain controllers up-to-date with Active Directory information.
- Changes in one domain controller's database are transmitted to all other domain controllers by replication.
- Information is stored in directory partitions on domain controllers.
- Schema partition, configuration partition, domain partition, and application directory partition are included in replication.
- Replication between domain controllers at the same site (intrasite) happens automatically.
- Replication between domain controllers at different sites (intersite) must be configured manually.

Intrasite replication

- Intrasite replication happens automatically whenever changes to directory objects are made.
- Data is transmitted in uncompressed format.
- The Knowledge Consistency Checker (KCC) service automatically creates replication topology.
- KCC automatically checks for topology changes every 15 minutes.
- Domain controllers keep polling each other for changes and then make changes.

Intersite replication

- Administrators manually configure intersite replication.
- Site links are created to configure intersite replication.
- Site link cost is defined between different sites.
- A single KCC per site generates all connections between sites.
- Data is transmitted in compressed format to save WAN bandwidth.
- Administrators usually schedule replication to happen during off-peak hours.

Trust relationships

- *Trust relationships* ensure that uses in one domain can access resources in other domains.
- Trust relationships can be one-way or two-way, and can be transitive or non-transitive.
- Trust can be implicit (automatic) or explicit (created manually).
- A tree root trust is established implicitly when a new tree root domain is added to the forest.
- A parent-child trust is created implicitly when a new child domain is added to the domain tree.
- A forest trust is created manually (explicitly) between two Forest Root domains.
- A realm trust is created manually between the Windows domain and the non-Windows Kerberos realm.
- A shortcut trust is created manually between two domains in a forest to improve logon performance.
- An external trust is created manually for domains in different forests.

DNS namespace

- The *DNS namespace* is hierarchical starting from the root domain.
- The DNS namespace ensures that computer names on the Internet are unique.
- The Root Domain is at the top of the hierarchy and is represented by a dot (.).
- Top-level domains are those that we use for everyday Internet surfing, such as .com, .net, .org, etc.
- Second-level domains are registered to private organizations.
- A Fully Qualified Domain Name (FQDN) describes the full path of a host in the DNS hierarchy.

Name resolution

- *Name resolution* is the process of translating a FQDN into an IP address.
- The client that sends a name resolution query to a DNS server runs the DNS client service.
- The DNS server resolves the name into an IP address and returns the IP address to the client.

Prep and Practice

Name resolution queries

- A forward lookup query consists of resolving a name to its IP address.
- A reverse lookup query consists of resolving an IP address to its name.
- In a recursive query, the DNS server either resolves the name for the client or gets it resolved from other DNS severs.
- In an iterative query, the DNS server resolves the query; otherwise, it sends a referral to the client.

DNS zones

- DNS servers store information in zone files.
- A *zone file* contains resource records of the zone for which it is responsible.
- A *zone* is the primary administrative unit for a DNS namespace.
- A zone must contain at least one domain that is known as the zone's root domain.
- A zone can also contain subdomains of the root domain.
- A zone can have multiple domains.

Zone types

- Zones can be standard primary, standard secondary, or Active Directory-integrated.
- Zone data in standard primary and secondary is stored in text files.
- The primary zone contains the master copy of the zone data, and all changes are made to this zone.
- Secondary zones contain a read-only copy of the zone data.
- Zone transfers replicate zone data from primary zones to secondary zones.
- Active Directory-integrated zones store the zone database in Active Directory.
- Active Directory-integrated zones are secure, and they simplify administration and replication.
- All zones stored in Active Directory are primary.
- A stub zone is a copy of the primary zone for a delegated zone.
- It contains only SOA, NS, and A records for the name server authoritative for the zone.

Resource records

- The records in a zone file are known as *resource records*.
- Table 6-1 lists types of resource records in a zone file.

Table 6-1. Resource records in a DNS zone file

Record	Description
A	The resource record that maps the hostname to its corresponding IP address.
CNAME	The canonical name record that creates an alias for the host. More than one hostname can map to a single IP address using the CNAME resource record.
NS	The Name Server record that identifies the DNS server for a particular domain.

Table 6-1. Resource records in a DNS zone file (continued)

Record	Description
SOA	The Start of Authority record that is required as the first record for forward and reverse lookup zones. This record specifies the domain for which the DNS server is responsible.
SRV	The Service record specifies what services are provided by a server and in which domain it serves. Active Directory depends on this resource record.
MX	The Mail Exchange record that identifies the mail server for the domain.
PTR	The Pointer record that maps the IP address to its corresponding hostname in a reverse lookup zone.
WINS	The Windows Internet Name Service record that identifies the WINS server for the DNS domain. In Windows Server 2003, DNS servers are configured to query WINS servers to resolve names that are not contained in a DNS database. A WINS server is used to resolve NetBIOS names to IP addresses.

NetBIOS name resolution

- *NetBIOS name resolution* is the process of resolving NetBIOS names to IP addresses.
- Broadcast transmissions, LMHOSTS files, or WINS servers can be used for this purpose.
- An LMHOSTS file is created manually on each computer or stored centrally on a file server.
- An LMHOSTS file contains static mappings of NetBIOS names and IP addresses.
- It is difficult to create, maintain, or administer LMHOSTS files in a large network.

WINS servers

- *WINS* resolves NetBIOS names and prevents broadcast traffic in the network.
- WINS servers contain mappings of NetBIOS names and IP addresses in the WINS database.
- Clients send NetBIOS queries to the WINS server.
- Clients register and renew their information with the WINS server.
- A single WINS server can serve up to 10,000 clients.
- Multiple WINS servers are used for fault-tolerance and performance.
- WINS servers replicate the changes in the WINS database to each other.

WINS replication

- WINS servers perform replication as push partners, pull partners, or both push and pull partners.
- Push partners send notification to pull partners when there is a change in their database.
- Pull partners poll push partners for changes in their database.
- Replication is configured according to available WAN link bandwidth.

IP addressing

- An IP address is a unique address used to identify a host on a network.
- An IP address is made up of 32 binary numbers.
- Each block of eight numbers is called an octet written as a decimal number.
- A 32-bit subnet mask identifies the network address and host address from the IP address.
- All computers on the same subnet share a common subnet mask.

IP address classes

- IP addresses are divided into class A, B, C, D, and E.
- Only addresses from classes A, B, and C are assigned to organizations.
- Table 6-2 summarizes IP address classes, the number of hosts in each class, and default subnet masks.

Table 6-2. IP address classes

Class	Range of first byte	Number of networks	Hosts per network	Default subnet mask
A	1–126	126	16,777,214	255.0.0.0
B	128–191	16,384	65,534	255.255.0.0
C	192–223	2,097,150	254	255.255.255.0
D	224–239	N/A	N/A	N/A
E	240–255	N/A	N/A	N/A

- Address 127.0.0.1 is reserved for loopback testing.
- Addresses in class D and E are reserved for special purposes.

Private IP addresses

- Private addresses can be used if the network is not directly connected to the Internet.
- The network can connect to the Internet using a proxy server or a firewall.
- These addresses are used only for internal networks.
- Table 6-3 summarizes the private address ranges and their default subnet masks.

Table 6-3. Private IP address ranges

Class	Start address	End address	Subnet mask
A	10.0.0.0	10.255.255.255	255.0.0.0
B	172.16.0.0	172.31.255.255	255.240.0.0
C	192.168.0.0	192.255.255	255.255.0.0

Automatic Private IP Addressing (APIPA)

- The APIPA range is from 169.254.0.0 to 169.254.255.255, with a subnet mask of 255.255.0.0

- A client uses APIPA when it cannot find a DHCP server on startup.
- A client configured with APIPA can only communicate with another client with APIPA.
- APIPA supplies only the IP address and subnet mask.

Automating IP address allocation using DHCP

- The *DHCP server* automates allocation of IP addresses and other TCP/IP configurations.
- The DHCP server can also automatically register client information with DNS servers.
- The DHCP server is configured with a scope for every network segment.
- The *DHCP scope* contains a pool of IP addresses, address leases, and addresses of the default gateway (router) and the DNS servers.
- The client must renew the lease before it expires, or else the IP address is returned to the address pool.

IP routing

- Large networks are divided into smaller segments known as subnets.
- The IP address space is divided to accommodate hosts in each subnet.
- A subnet mask is used to identify the subnet where the client is located.
- Routers connect different network segments and use routing protocols.
- Local network segments are connected by high-speed links.
- Remote network segments are connected by wide area network (WAN) links.

Remote access

- Remote access is provided either through dial-up or virtual private networking (VPN).
- Dial-up allows a remote user to connect temporarily.
- A telephone line and a modem are used to dial a remote access server.
- The remote access server authenticates the user before granting access to the network.
- VPN is good for a large number of remote users.
- The user connects to her ISP and the connection is established by creating a tunnel through the Internet.
- L2TP and PPTP protocols are used as tunneling protocols.

Remote access authentication

- Remote users are authenticated either by the remote access server or by a RADIUS server.
- Remote access dial-in permissions for a user define which users can connect remotely.
- Users are further authenticated by remote access policies.
- Remote access policies contain conditions that the user must satisfy.
- A policy profile contains authentication protocols and encryption methods that the user must use.

Analyzing Current Network Infrastructure

This subsection covers a summary of highlights from the "Analyzing Current Network Infrastructure" section in the Exam 70-297 Study Guide.

Centralized administrative model

- Administration of an IT infrastructure is controlled from a central location.
- The IT staff has its own hierarchy, starting from the IT manager.
- The IT staff makes design, implementation, and purchase decisions.
- Companies with a single location have centralized administration and resources.
- Large companies may centralize administration but decentralize resources of remote locations.
- Administration is easy, and a few members can make decisions quickly.
- Active Directory logical design is simple.
- The disadvantage is that if the company grows, administration may not be possible from a central location.
- This model offers limited scalability and is not good for large companies with multiple locations.

Decentralized administrative model

- Good for large organizations with multiple geographical locations.
- Each location has its own IT administration staff.
- Administration is delegated to the local staff for local resources.
- Local problems can be resolved quickly.
- Response times are improved.
- The disadvantage is that the cost of hiring IT staff at each location may be high and more domains must be created.

Hybrid administrative model

- Most organizations follow the hybrid administrative model.
- Major administrative tasks, such as designing, planning, and security policies, are centralized.
- Resource management is delegated to the local IT staff at different locations.
- Local administrators can perform regular maintenance, backups, etc.

Documenting your analysis

- Make an organizational chart showing the different levels of administration.
- Note the name of the person responsible for making IT decisions.
- Note the administrative model currently in use.
- Note the location of major resources in the organization.
- Note how administration is delegated to the local IT staff.
- Check whether any services are outsourced.
- Keep your documentation simple but informative.

Analyzing geographical models

- In a Local model, the company is located in a single city, and there is only one domain.
- A Regional model can span several cities in several nearby states.
- Different locations may be linked by WAN links usually provided by a single vendor.
- A National model spans several states across the entire country.
- Different locations may be connected by WAN links of varying speeds.
- More than one vendor may be involved in providing WAN links and Internet connectivity.
- Different locations may be working in different time zones.
- The company has an International model when it is operating from two or more countries.
- There may be different laws and regulations governing software exports, hiring manpower, etc.
- Multiple locations in an International model may have different working hours due to time zones.

Analyzing multiple locations and WAN links

- Make a drawing showing each location of the organization.
- Note the WAN types and the WAN link bandwidths of each location.
- Note the name of the vendor for WAN connectivity.
- Check whether there are any bandwidth issues or performance problems with the current WAN links.
- Note the cost of each WAN link.
- Note the average and peak usage of the available WAN bandwidth.
- Note the contact details about local administrative staff at each location.
- If the company has international offices, get details on country-specific information.

Analyzing a current Windows 2000 domain structure

- Analyze how domains are implemented.
- Analyze how resources are located across various locations.
- Ask the administrators questions about the deployment of Active Directory and the domain model.
- Make a diagram of the current directory structure.
- Note the name of each domain and the name of the root domain of each tree in the forest.
- Note the name of the root domain of the forest and trust relationships.
- Check whether there are any shortcut trusts or explicit trusts created by administrators.
- Check whether there are any Windows NT 4.0 domains within the Windows 2000 structure.

Analyzing a current Windows 2000 OU structure

- Get a list of all objects in each OU, including nested OUs.
- Get a list of permissions granted to administrators on OUs.
- Check inherited permissions.
- Make a list of Group Policies linked to each OU.

Analyzing Windows 2000 sites and domain controllers

- Make a list of all sites at different locations.
- Check the number and location of domain controllers at each site.
- Check the operations master roles assigned to domain controllers.
- Note how site links are created.
- Note how replication is configured between domain controllers at different locations.
- Find out which domain controllers are Global Catalog servers.
- Make a list of servers that are not domain controllers.
- Make a list of servers that are performing other network services, such as DNS, DHCP, WINS, RRAS, web servers, email servers, etc.

Analyzing a current Windows NT 4.0 infrastructure

- Windows NT 4.0 uses a flat domain model.
- There are no sites in a Windows NT 4.0 domain model.
- Each location is usually under a separate domain.
- Check why the network was not upgraded to Windows 2000.
- Documentation should include the names of all locations and domains.
- Check whether there is more than one domain in any location.
- Note the names of primary and backup domain controllers at each location.
- Note the names of servers providing other network services, such as DNS, DHCP, WINS, RRAS, web servers, email servers, etc.
- Note the trust relationships created by administrators.
- Note the shared resources in each domain, such as file and print shares.
- Take contact details of the local administrators.

Analyzing the current technical environment

- Analyze the current servers and desktop hardware.
- Check whether there is any performance issue with critical servers.
- Check whether there is any performance issue with the network.
- Talk to administrators about availability of essential services during the upgrade.

Server and desktop hardware

- Check whether any hardware needs replacing.
- Documentation should include the make, model, and vendors of each computer.

- Check the speed of the processor, memory, hard disks, and total capacity.
- Check the motherboard, its BIOS, and its version number.
- Check the types of peripherals and their vendors.
- Check the location of computer in the network, IP address configuration.
- Check whether some servers are configured with static TCP/IP configuration.
- Check the type of networking services running on the computer.
- Check the operating system installed on each computer and service packs installed, if any.
- Check the list of software installed on the computers, including the name of the application, its version number, and installed service packs.
- Check the shared resources on the computer and list of users or groups that have permissions to access these resources.

Analyzing software requirements

- Software may be packaged software or developed in-house.
- Check how the currently running software will be supported in the new infrastructure.
- Check what costs will be involved for training users on new software.
- Check networking software and protocols used in the network.
- Check whether there is any legacy software currently in use.
- Check whether the legacy software will be replaced or rewritten.
- Check whether the network needs to support other non-Microsoft clients such as Novell or Unix.

Analyzing the current network structure

- Make a diagram of the current network structure.
- Note the number of LANs in each location.
- Note the number of network segments or subnets, if the LAN is segmented.
- Note the number of routers, their make and model numbers, and their placement within the network.
- Identify whether the routers are used to connect only LAN segments or for WAN connections.
- Check whether there are any hubs or switches used in the network. If yes, note their make and model numbers and their placement within the network.
- Check whether virtual LAN (VLAN) has been implemented.
- Check whether there are any Windows servers being used as routers.
- Identify the type of cabling used in the LAN.
- If your company provides remote access to clients, identify the type of hardware and software used for this purpose.

IP addressing

- Analyze the type of IP addressing currently in use.
- Check whether there are any issues with the current IP addressing scheme.

- Check what portion of the address space is used with each location.
- Note the network ID, subnet mask, and default gateway for the each location.
- Note the name and IP address of the DHCP server or the DHCP Relay Agent for each location.
- Note the range of IP addresses reserved for the location.
- Note the names and IP addresses of servers or routers that use statically assigned IP addresses.
- Note the names of TCP and UDP ports used by any services on the network.
- Note the names of servers or other computers that use special ports services.

Analyzing performance requirements
- Analyze current performance levels for the servers and network.
- Check whether any of the critical servers are performing as expected.
- Talk to administrators about any issues with network performance.
- Check whether all parts of the network are performing as expected.
- Check event logs of critical servers for any issues not known to administrators.
- Use the Systems Management server for monitoring network performance.
- Use the Performance console for monitoring individual system performance.
- Talk to users to find out whether they know of any performance issues with servers or the network.
- Prepare documentation of your analysis.

Designing an Active Directory Structure

This subsection covers a summary of highlights from the "Designing an Active Directory Structure" section in the Exam 70-297 Study Guide.

LDAP naming formats
- Active Directory relies on LDAP naming conventions to store objects and their attributes.
- This allows users to locate objects in a variety of ways.
- An object can be searched based on its name or its attributes.
- The Relative Distinguished Name (RDN) identifies the object within its parent container.

Relative Distinguished Name (RDN)
- RDN is relative to other objects in the same container.
- An example of RDN is CN=Myname,CN=Users,DC=Oreilly,DC=com
  Distinguished Name (DN).
- DN uniquely identifies the object by using the RDN and names of container objects and domain names.
- DNs are unique in the entire forest.
- An example of DN is CN=Myname,CN=Users,DC=Oreilly,DC=com.

Canonical name (CN)

- CN is similar to the RDN but written in a different syntax.
- Naming starts from root and goes down the hierarchy.
- An example of CN is oreilly.com/Users/Myname.

User principal name (UPN)

- UPN defines the user account and its domain.
- UPN looks like an email address.
- An example of UPN is myname@oreilly.com.
- The @ sign is known as UPN suffix.

Designing a naming strategy

- Active Directory naming follows DNS naming standards.
- Clients use the DNS service to locate other clients and services.
- DNS names start from the root and flow down the hierarchy.
- Windows Server 2003 automatically creates pre-Windows (NetBIOS) names for computers.
- DNS names are created by appending the full domain name to the computer name.

Guidelines for naming conventions

- Create names that are easy to remember.
- Create DNS names that are also compatible with NetBIOS conventions.
- DNS names can be up to 64 characters, but try to limit the names to 15 characters.
- Try to avoid names that create confusion among users.
- Use unique names throughout the organization.
- The name should reflect the purpose of the servers.

Using the same internal and internal registered names

- You can use registered names for your external and internal network.
- This method is recommended by Microsoft.
- This method is easiest to design, implement, and administer.

Using the subdomain of the registered name

- You can create a subdomain of the registered name for the internal network.
- You will create separate DNS zones for external and internal namespaces.
- More security will be required for the internal network.

Using separate external and internal names

- You can keep external and internal names entirely separate.
- Two separate namespaces will have to be maintained.
- This method involves more administration and more cost of ownership.
- Do not use these methods unless you have specific reasons to do so.

Choosing domain names

- Use names that are short and easy to remember.
- Use only registered domain names for root domains.
- Keep the domain names unique throughout the organization.
- Use only standard characters supported by all DNS platforms.
- Keep the internal and external namespaces for the purpose of securing your internal resources.

Choosing names for security

- Keep names unique in the domain and use only supported characters.
- Use a maximum of 20 characters for usernames and up to 63 characters for group names.
- Computer names can have up to 15 characters.
- You cannot include these special characters: #, +, <, >, ", and any leading or trailing spaces.
- Do not use only periods (.), spaces, or the @ character for any name.

Creating a single domain

- This is easy to plan, implement, and administer.
- Single domains are scalable and still manageable.
- All objects are located in the same security boundaries.
- There is no need to configure trust relationships.
- Planning user accounts and Group Policies is easier.
- Account polices and Password Policies are configured only once at the domain level.
- You can choose from centralized or decentralized administrative models.
- There are less problems and less troubleshooting is required.
- The overall cost of ownership is low.

Creating multiple domains

- Whenever possible, keep the design to a single domain.
- More administration and cost of ownership is involved in multiple domains.
- You will need to decide on domain boundaries.
- You should try to create domains that are in the same domain tree.
- Multiple domains in a tree should share a contiguous namespace.

Reasons to create multiple domains

- When decentralized administration of domains located at different locations is required.
- When different security policies are required at the domain level.
- When you need different DNS namespaces for different departments.
- When you need to maintain Windows NT 4.0 domains.
- When you need to limit the replication traffic across slow WAN links.
- When you need to place the schema master domain controller in a different domain.

Implications of creating multiple domains

- The cost of one or more domain controllers has to be considered.
- Two-way trust relationships will be automatically created.
- Access permissions across domains will need to be configured.
- Group Policies will need to be planned for each separate domain.
- Administrative access is automatically granted to the Enterprise Admins group across all domains.

Designing a multiple tree structure

- Create multiple trees when you need to maintain more than one DNS separate namespace.
- You will need to create more domains.
- Cost of ownership will increase.
- More administration will be required.
- Multiple trees can exist under a single domain forest.

Designing a multiple forest structure

- A *forest* is a group of domain trees that do not share a contiguous namespace.
- Domains in a single forest share a common schema and directory partition.
- Domains also share a common Global Catalog.
- Unless you have a reason to do so, limit the forest structure to a single forest.

Reasons for creating multiple forests

- When you need to link two separate organizations.
- In situations where two companies have merged.
- When you need to create an isolated unit that needs a separate security infrastructure.
- When there are legal requirements.

Disadvantages of multiple forests

- Administration overheads increase.
- Replication between domains of multiple forests must be manually configured.
- Name resolution must be configured to locate resources across forests.
- Access to resources across forests must be manually configured in each forest.
- Separate groups of users must be created in each forest to access resources outside their own forest.
- Users must use user principal names when logging on to domains in other forests.

Migrating from Windows 2000 domains

- The Windows 2000 directory structure is similar to Windows Server 2003.
- You must use the `adprep.exe` command on domain controllers to prepare upgrades to Windows Server 2003.
- The `Adprep.exe /forestprep` command prepares the forest for upgrades.

- The `Adprep.exe /domainprep` command prepares the domain for upgrades.
- The `Adprep` command prepares the Windows 2000 Active Directory for new features.

Migrating from Windows NT 4.0 domains

- Windows NT 4.0 uses a flat domain structure.
- Options for migrating include complete restructuring and in-place upgrade.
- Complete restructuring offers many benefits of Windows Server 2003 Active Directory.
- Consider an in-place upgrade when you do not have enough time for analysis, design, and implementation.
- Consider an in-place upgrade when you need to retain user accounts and passwords.
- Many new features of Active Directory will not be available if an in-place upgrade is planned.
- You must make sure that the current structure will translate well into Windows Server 2003 after an in-place upgrade.

Designing a Security Infrastructure

This subsection covers a summary of highlights from the "Designing a Security Infrastructure" section in the Exam 70-297 Study Guide.

Purpose of Organizational Units (OU)

- *OUs are basic units of administration.*
- OUs contain users, computers, shared resources, and other OUs.
- Delegation of control, limiting visibility of objects, and implementation of Group Policies are main reasons for creating OUs.

Delegation of control

- Delegation of control is either object- or function-based.
- Simplifies administration of objects within the Active Directory.
- In object-based OUs, the delegation of control is assigned according to types of objects.
- Similar objects are placed in an OU, and permissions are assigned on the OU.
- In function-based OUs, the delegation of control is assigned based on administrative functions.

Limiting visibility of objects

- Some objects may need to be hidden from certain users for security reasons.
- Visibility of Active Directory objects cannot be limited by using simple NTFS permissions.
- All confidential objects are placed in a single OU.
- List Contents permission on the OU is given only to authorized users or groups.

Implementing Group Polices

- An OU is the smallest unit where Group Policies can be applied.
- Group Policies are used to apply uniform security or other settings to a large number of users or computers.
- Group Policies are applied at the domain, site, and OU level.
- Applying Group Policy Objects (GPOs) at the OU level provides granular control over a group of objects.

OU based on location

- This model is useful when each location of the company has its own administrative staff.
- Each location is placed under one OU.
- Users, computers, and local resources are placed in child OUs.
- Delegation of control is assigned to local administrators.
- This model is also used when the administrative responsibilities of locations do not match.
- The advantage is that the OU design does not change when the departmental changes occur in the organization.
- Locations of resources within the organization can be easily figured out.

OU based on organization

- This model is used when administrative functions are divided according to the business units of the organization.
- Each unit or department has its own IT administrative staff.
- Each unit is placed under a separate OU.
- The advantage is that this OU structure is easy to create.
- Each department or unit can keep control of its IT resources.
- This model can accommodate organizational expansions due to mergers or acquisitions.
- The disadvantage is that this OU structure will change if departments are added or removed.

OU based on functions

- This model is good for small organizations.
- A single administrative staff looks after several departments of the organization.
- The advantage is that the OU structure does not change if departmental changes occur in the organization.
- The disadvantage is that several OUs should be created to delegate administration of different IT functions.

OU based on location and organization

- There are two hybrid models that suit several organizations.
- OUs can be designed based on location first and then organization.
  - The top-level OUs consist of different locations of the organization.
  - The lower-level OUs consist of different units of organization.

- OUs can also be created based on organization first and then location.
  - The top-level OUs consist of different units of the organization.
  - The lower-level OUs consist of different locations of organization.

Built-in containers and OUs in Windows Server 2003

- The *domain* is the root container for the Active Directory.
- The built-in container contains the default service account for the domain.
- The users container contains all user accounts created in the domain and is not used for delegation of control.
- The computers container contains all computer accounts created in the domain and is not used for delegation of control.
- The Domain Controllers OU contains computer accounts for all domain controllers in the domain; a default set of Group Policies is applied to this container.
- To delegate control, you should create separate OUs for users and computers.
- Domain controllers should not be moved out of the Domain Controllers OU.

Permission inheritance in OUs

- By default, all permissions assigned to the parent OU are applied to child OUs.
- Objects in an OU inherit permissions applied to the parent OU.
- Inheritance starts from the top-level OU and flows down to the lowest level of OUs.
- Permission inheritance can be blocked when you need to assign a different set of permissions to a child container.
- The advantage of inheritance is that when delegation of control is granted to one OU, it applies to all child OUs.

Overview of Group Policies

- Group Policy contains several settings that can be applied to a users or computers.
- Group Policies simplify administration of users, computers, and resources.
- Group Polices are defined in Group Policy Objects (GPOs).
- GPOs can be applied at the domain, site, or OU level.
- For a standalone computer, only the local GPO is applied.
- Each Group Policy contains computer configuration and user configuration settings.
- Computer configuration settings apply to computers or groups of computers.
- User configuration settings apply to users or groups of users.
- Each policy contains software settings, Windows Settings, and Administrative Templates.

Software settings in GPO

- These settings are used to control installation of software on multiple computers.

- These policies apply to Windows XP Professional, Windows 2000, and Windows Server 2003 computers.
- Windows Installer packages are used to deploy software and updates on client computers.
- The Windows Installer service uses instructions in installer packages for software installation.
- Software installation is carried out in two ways: assigning and publishing.
- An assigned software application is installed from the Start menu of a client computer.
- An assigned software application is installed from the Add or Remove Programs in Control Panel.
- You can also exclude certain computers that should not get the software.

Windows Settings

- Table 6-4 lists different settings and whether they apply to computers, users, or both.

Table 6-4. Windows Settings in Group Policies

Node	Computer configuration	User configuration	Description
Scripts	Yes	Yes	Depending on where you set the scripts, they will run when the computer starts or shuts down, or when the user logs on or off the computer.
Security	Yes	Yes	You can configure a number of security settings that can affect the computer or the logged-on user.
Internet Explorer Maintenance	N/A	Yes	These settings are used to customize the Internet Explorer options.
Remote Installation Services	N/A	Yes	These settings are also available for users and are used to manage remote installation service (RIS) on client computers.
Folder Redirection	N/A	Yes	These settings are used to centrally manage users' folders such as My Documents, Start Menu, etc., by redirecting them from users' computers to another location.

Administrative Templates

- Table 6-5 lists the settings in the Administrative Templates of Group Policy.

Table 6-5. Settings available in Administrative Templates

Node	Computer configuration	User configuration	Description
Control Panel	N/A	Yes	These settings determine which Control Panel utilities should be available to the user.
Desktop	N/A	Yes	These settings control how the users' desktops should appear.

Table 6-5. Settings available in Administrative Templates (continued)

Node	Computer configuration	User configuration	Description
Network	Yes	Yes	These settings control offline files configuration and network and dial-up connections for the computer or user.
Printers	Yes	N/A	These settings control printer configuration for the computer.
Start Menu and Task Bar	N/A	Yes	These settings control how the user can configure the Start menu and the Task Bar.
System	Yes	Yes	These settings are used to configure system startup/shutdown, logon/logoff, and Group Policies.
Windows Components	Yes	Yes	These settings control the configuration of Windows components such as Windows Explorer, Internet Explorer, and Windows Installer.

Multiple Group Policy Objects (GPOs)

- Group Policies for users and computers can be applied from multiple sources.
- All policies configured in the local GPOs are processed and applied first.
- GPOs linked to the site are processed next and override the conflicting settings in the local GPO.
- GPOs linked to the domain are processed and override conflicting settings in the site GPO and the local GPO.
- GPOs linked to the parent OU of the computer are processed next and override conflicting settings applied at the domain-, site-, and local-level GPOs.
- If the object is in multiple OUs, the GPO linked to the highest-level OU in the Active Directory hierarchy is processed first.
- If multiple GPOs are linked at the domain level, site level, or OU level, the administrator can control the processing order of these GPOs.

Group Policy inheritance

- Group Policies applied at the parent level apply to all child objects.
- If a policy is not defined at the parent level but defined in the child level, the child level policy applies.
- If a policy setting is defined at both the parent and the child level, the settings defined at the child level are applied.
- It is possible to disable unused policy settings to improve performance.

Blocking and filtering GPOs

- No Override option is used to prevent a parent-level GPO setting from applying to the child container.
- The Block Inheritance option is used to apply GPO settings to all child objects in the parent container.

- Policies can be filtered to exclude a group of computers or users from getting policy settings.
- The Apply Policy and Read Group Policy permissions are used to filter GPOs.

Prioritizing GPOs

- When multiple GPOs are applied to an OU, the administrator can change the processing order.
- The GPO at the lowest place in the list is processed first.

Linking GPOs to domains

- GPOs linked to a domain apply to all objects in the domain.
- Security policies are usually applied at the domain level.
- These GPOs cannot be overridden by other GPOs.
- You can centralize the administration of Group Policies.
- Kerberos, Password, and Account Policies are stored in Default Domain Policy GPO.
- Only a few GPOs should be linked to domains.

GPOs linked to sites

- GPOs are linked to sites when a large number of computers or users in a site need similar configuration settings.
- A better way is to create OUs for different sites and apply GPOs to these OUs.
- If you have to link GPOs to sites, keep them to as few as possible.

GPOs linked to OUs

- The preferred method of applying GPOs is at the OU level.
- It is the most efficient way to apply Group Polices.
- This method offers maximum flexibility.
- It is easy to move users and computers from one OU to another.
- You can also rearrange or rename OUs for applying GPOs.

Administering Group Policies

- Administering Group Policies is important in organizations with a deep OU structure.
- Administration depends on the administrative model used in the organization.
- Administrative control should be equally delegated.
- Administrators at different geographical locations should be granted delegation of control for local OUs.

Delegation of control

- Control granted at the site level may affect objects in one domain or multiple domains, irrespective of the domain where the GPO is actually located.
- Control granted at the domain level affects all objects in the domain if inheritance is not blocked.

- Control granted at the OU level affects all objects in the OU and other child OUs.
- For better administration and management of permissions for GPOs, you should try to delegate control at the highest-level OU.

Client requirements for Group Polices

- Windows XP Professional and Windows Server 2003 support all Group Policies.
- Windows 2000 Professional and Windows 2000 Server support a majority of the Group Policies but do not process any unsupported Group Policy settings.
- Windows NT 4.0, Windows ME, Windows 98, and Windows 95 do not support Group Policies.

Types of accounts

- Users, groups, and computers are known as security principals.
- Table 6-6 lists the types of accounts in Windows Server 2003 Active Directory.

Table 6-6. Types of accounts in Active Directory

Account type	Description
User	Describes the attributes of a person. The user account allows a person to use his credentials to log on to the domain and to access resources throughout the domain depending on permissions assigned to the account.
Computer	Represents a physical computer in the Active Directory network. When a computer running Windows Server 2003, Windows XP, or Windows NT 4.0 joins a domain, a computer account is created for it.
Group	Is a collection of users, computers, or other group accounts to which access permissions to resources are assigned. Groups simplify assignment of permissions because you do not have to assign permissions to individual users.
InetOrgPerson	Is similar to the user account but allows integration with non-Microsoft-based LDAP directory services.
Contact	Represents a person outside the Active Directory network with no access permissions associated with it. This account is generally used in mail services and shows up in address books.

Naming user accounts

- User accounts identify the user.
- You should create guidelines for naming user accounts in the network.
- Every user should have a unique logon name within the Active Directory domain.
- Logon names should be limited to 20 characters for compatibility with pre-Windows 2000 operating systems.
- Logon names for pre-Windows 2000 computers cannot contain these characters: / \ [ ] < > : ; , + ? * |
- Your guidelines should clearly identify the method to address identical usernames within a domain.
- An additional character such as the middle initial can be added to avoid a duplicate username.

Naming computer accounts

- Computer names should make it easy for users to locate computers.
- A computer name should identify its location and purpose.
- There should be different naming conventions for servers and desktops.

Naming group accounts

- The name of the group should be unique within the domain.
- The group name should include its purpose and owner department or unit.
- The group name can contain up to 64 characters.
- Group names are not case-sensitive.
- Group names for pre-Windows 2000 computers cannot contain these characters: / \ [ ] < > : ; , + ? * |

Types of user accounts

- Local user accounts are stored and used on a local computer only.
- Domain user accounts are stored in the Active Directory and can be used anywhere in the domain or in trusted domains.
- The Administrator account is the most powerful built-in user account.
- The Guest account is created to grant temporary access to users without a regular user account.

Creating Account Lockout Policy

- Account Lockout Policy is applied at the domain level.
- These policies define what happens if a user does not use the account properly.
- Account Lockout Duration specifies how long the account remains locked.
- Account Lockout Threshold defines how many bad logon attempts are permitted before the account is locked out.
- Reset Account Lockout Counter After defines when the account lockout counter will be reset.
- By default, the Account Lockout Policy for the domain is defined in the Default Domain Policy.

Creating Password Policy

- *Password Policy* defines how users create and maintain their passwords.
- Password Policy is applied at the domain level, throughout the domain.
- By default, Active Directory will not allow weak passwords or blank passwords.
- Enforce Password History specifies how many passwords the Active Directory will remember to prevent repetition of passwords.
- Maximum Password Age specifies how long a user can keep the same password.
- Minimum Password Age specifies how long a user must keep a password.
- Minimum Password Length specifies the minimum length of the password for all users in the domain.
- Password Must Meet Complexity Requirements specifies that users should use complex passwords.

- Store Password in Reversible Encryption policy stores the user's password in clear text. This policy setting is only used when digest authentication is enabled in IIS.

Password guidelines

- Passwords must be at least seven characters long.
- Users must retain their passwords for a certain number of days.
- Users should use a mix of uppercase letters, lowercase letters, numbers, and special characters.
- Users should change their passwords every 42 days (6 weeks).
- The Password Policy should be configured to store at least 24 last passwords of users.

Logon options

- When username/password is commonly used for logging on to the domain, a domain controller authenticates the user.
- When UPN name/password is used for logging on to the domain, a query is sent to the Global Catalog server.
- Multifactor authentication may include options such as biometric authentication, smart card, digital signatures, etc.

Planning computer accounts

- Computer accounts allow computers to authenticate in the domain.
- Computer accounts are placed in OUs for applying GPOs.
- Users with Add Workstations to Domain rights can create computer accounts.
- This right should be given only to authenticated users.
- A computer account should clearly identify the computer, its location, and its purpose.
- Different account guidelines should be used for servers, desktops, and portable computers.
- Naming conventions should be clearly defined in the design.

Planning group accounts

- Groups are used to club users to grant access to resources.
- Groups simplify administration of user accounts and the permissions associated with them.
- Security groups contain users from the domain or trusted domain.
- Resource access permissions are granted to security groups.
- Distribution groups are used in mailing lists.
- Security groups can be members of distribution groups.
- You should create OUs that hold groups to simplify administration.

Group scopes and nesting

- The *scope* of a group determines the objects that can be placed inside it.

- The scope of a group specifies where the group can be accessed in the Active Directory.
- The scope of a group depends on the domain functional level.
- *Group nesting* is the process of placing groups within groups.
- Group nesting allows you to simplify assignment of permissions.
- Table 6-7 summarizes group scopes and nesting.

Table 6-7. Group scopes and nesting

Group scope	Objects allowed in Windows Server 2003 and Windows 2000 Native	Objects allowed in Windows 2000 Mixed and Windows Server 2003 Interim
Domain Local	User accounts, Universal groups, Global groups from any domain, and Domain Local groups from same domain; nested Domain Local groups in the same domain.	User accounts and Global groups from any domain. Cannot be nested.
Global	User accounts and Global groups from the local domain; nested Domain Local, Global (same domain), and Universal groups.	User and computer accounts from same domain. Cannot be nested.
Universal	User accounts, Universal groups and Global groups from any domain; nested Domain Local global or Universal groups.	Not Available.

Guidelines for creating groups and nesting
- Do not assign resource access permissions to individual users.
- Create groups of users with similar resource access requirements and assign permissions to groups.
- Domain Local groups should have members who need access to the resources located in the domain.
- Global groups should be created to organize users.
- Use Universal groups to organize Global groups from different domains that have similar resource access requirements.
- User accounts should be placed in Global groups.
- Global groups should be placed in Universal groups.
- Universal groups should be placed in Domain Local groups.
- Resource permissions should be assigned to Domain Local groups.

Designing a Site Topology

This subsection covers a summary of highlights from the "Designing a Site Topology" section in the Exam 70-297 Study Guide.

Planning sites
- Sites and domain controllers are physical components of the Active Directory.
- Sites are IP subnets connected by fast and reliable links.
- A site contains one or more domain controllers at a single location.

- A Default-First-Site is created when the first domain controller is installed.
- Sites are used to control replication and authentication traffic across WAN traffic.
- Sites are used to localize as much network traffic as possible.
- Sites are not part of the Active Directory namespace.

Determining site boundaries

- Site boundaries depend on the physical locations of the organization.
- Note the bandwidth of WAN links.
- Draw a diagram of the network layout at each location.
- Check the number of network subnets in each location.
- Check the speed of LANs at each location.

Guidelines for creating sites

- Create as few sites as possible, as more sites mean more administration.
- If you do not see reasons to create a site, do not create it.
- Create a site for each physical location where a domain controller will be placed.
- Create a site for each LAN or group of LANs connected by high-speed backbone links.
- Follow the naming conventions.
- Allocate the IP address range and subnet mask for the site.
- Designate administrators who will be delegated control of the site.

Planning for replication

- Intrasite replication happens automatically between domain controllers at a single site.
- Intersite replication is configured by administrators.
- Table 6-8 lists the differences between intrasite and intersite replication.

Table 6-8. Comparing intrasite and intersite replication

	Intrasite replication	Intersite replication
Data Compression	No.	Yes.
Replication Model	Replication partners notify each other about changes, and then pull changes.	Replication partners do not notify each other about changes.
Replication Frequency	Replication partners poll each other periodically for changes.	Replication partners poll each other at specified times only. Updates are replicated at scheduled times only.
Transport Protocols	Remote Procedure Call (RPC).	IP or SMTP.

Site links

- *Site links* are created manually to form logical connections between sites.
- KCC creates connection objects using site links.
- Sites should be grouped by similar WAN links.

Site link transitivity
- Site links are transitive by default.
- If you disable site link transitivity, you must create site link bridges manually.
- Disable site link transitivity in order to:
  — Have total control over replication traffic patterns.
  — Avoid a particular replication path being used heavily.
  — Allow replication to pass through firewalls.

Bridgehead servers
- KCC automatically creates Bridgehead servers at each site.
- You can manually designate preferred Bridgehead servers.
- If multiple Bridgehead servers are designated, only one is active at a time.

Site link cost
- *Site link cost* is used to determine the preferred links when multiple links are available.
- Site link cost depends on the speed of the WAN link.
- Table 6-9 lists recommended values of site link costs.

Table 6-9. Recommended site link costs

Available bandwidth in Kbps	Site link cost
4096	283
2048	309
1024	340
512	378
256	425
128	486
64	567
56	586
38.4	644
19.2	798
9.6	1042

Guidelines for creating site links
- Try to use RPC over IP as the transport protocol for all site links.
- Use uniform naming conventions for site links.
- Make sure that all sites can connect to each other.
- For intrasite replication, configure notification and push replication.
- For intersite replication, configure polling and pull replication between Bridgehead servers.
- Specify the cost of site links carefully.

Capacity planning for domain controllers

- The most important factor is the number of users logging on to the domain.
- Calculate the number of domain controllers at each site.
- Table 6-10 lists recommendations for processor speeds and memory.

Table 6-10. Recommended processor, speed, and memory specifications

Number of users	Number of processors	Processor speed	Memory
1–499	1	850 MHz. or faster	512 MB
500–999	2	850 MHz or faster	1 GB
1000+	4	850 MHz or faster	2 GB

Number of domain controllers

- You need one domain controller for up to 1,000 users per domain at a particular site.
- You need a minimum of 2 domain controllers if the number of users is between 1,000 and 10,000.
- For every additional 5,000 users, you will need 1 additional domain controller.
- For every 15 replication objects configured in a site, you need 1 extra domain controller.

Placement of domain controllers

- Place a domain controller locally if there are a large number of users at a site.
- If the site is acting as a hub for several small sites, you must place a domain controller locally.
- Domain controllers should also be placed at those sites that have *site-aware* software applications.
- Make sure that domain controllers are physically secure.
- Make sure that local administrative staff is available.

Placement of Global Catalog server

- You should place at least one Global Catalog server at each site.
- Place a Global Catalog server in a site that has 100 or more users.
- Place a Global Catalog server in a site if applications frequently search Active Directory objects.
- The number of Global Catalog servers should be half of the total domain controllers in a site.
- Check for availability of local administrative staff.
- Do not assign the role of Global Catalog server to an infrastructure master.
- If you do not place a Global Catalog server at a site, make sure that the WAN link is reliable.

Placement of servers with operations master roles

- The schema master and the domain naming master should be placed at a site in which there are a large number of domains.

- The RID master should be placed at a site in which administrators create or modify objects.

- The infrastructure master should be placed in a site in which there are a large number of users.

- The PDC emulator should be placed in a site in which you have Windows NT 4.0 clients.

Designing a Name Resolution Structure

This subsection covers a summary of highlights from the "Designing a Name Resolution Structure" section in the Exam 70-297 Study Guide.

Analyzing the existing DNS structure

- Make a diagram of the DNS server placed at different locations of the company.

- Are the DNS services maintained in-house or by the ISP?

- How many DNS servers are installed in the organization and what is their location?

- For each DNS server, find out the role of the server, such as primary, secondary, forwarding, or caching-only.

- Check the internal and external namespace. Is the company using the same namespace or different internal and external namespaces?

- What types of DNS zones are used? Are they Active Directory-Integrated zones or standard zones?

- How are the DNS servers and DNS zones secured?

- Are there any non-Microsoft DNS servers in the organization?

- Make a note of any third-party DNS implementation, such as Unix.

Guidelines for DNS namespace design

- Take into account the naming conventions selected while designing the Active Directory namespace.

- Check the name registered by the organization for its Internet presence.

- Determine whether the DNS servers will be working completely inside your network or will be available on the Internet.

- Check whether the DNS will support the existing Active Directory structure that might already be in place.

Advantages of DNS integration with Active Directory

- DNS zone data is automatically replicated to other domain controllers with the Active Directory.

- Replication of zone data is encrypted and safe from eavesdroppers.

- You can configure Access Control Lists (ACLs) to DNS objects stored in the Active Directory.

- Secure dynamic updates are available only with Active Directory integration.

- Zone information is automatically updated to new domain controllers.
- Replication is faster and efficient.

DNS integration with DHCP

- DNS integration with DHCP improves performance.
- It reduces administrative overheads.
- It improves security of DNS zones.
- By default, the DHCP server dynamically updates A and PTR records only if requested by the DHCP clients.
- You can also configure the DHCP server to always dynamically update the A and PTR records.
- By default, A and PTR records are discarded when the client lease expires.
- DHCP can dynamically update DNS A and PTR records for legacy clients.
- You can configure the DHCP server to always update the DNS A and PTR records of the clients.

DNS integration with WINS

- DNS integration with WINS allows clients to resolve NetBIOS names through the DNS server.
- DNS zones can be configured with WINS and WINS-R resource records.
- The DNS server sends queries to configured WINS servers and receives a response.
- The response is sent to the DNS client.

Standard primary zone

- Stores resource records for one or more domains.
- Stores the master copy of the zone database.
- Changes to zone data are done on standard primary zones.
- It is less secure than the Active Directory-Integrated zone.

Standard secondary zone

- Standard secondary zones store a read-only copy of zone data.
- These zones are used to improve DNS name resolution performance.
- Zone data is replicated using zone transfers.
- Secondary DNS servers get notification from the primary DNS server about changes in zone data.
- Zone transfers are initiated when the refresh interval expires or when the primary DNS server notifies the secondary DNS server.

Active Directory-Integrated zone

- The zone files are stored on domain controllers in the Active Directory database.
- Replication of zones—along with the Active Directory is faster than zone transfers that take place when you use standard primary and secondary zones.

- Changes to zone data can be made on any DNS server, since all DNS servers are peers.
- Fault-tolerance and load-balancing are automatically provided along with domain controllers.
- Replication is secure, since it is encrypted.
- Secure dynamic updates help prevent pollution of zone data.

Zone transfers

- Zone transfers are either authoritative (AXFR) or incremental (IXFR).
- AXFR transfers complete zone data from primary to secondary.
- IXFR transfers only change data since the last transfer.

Zone replication options

- Zone replication occurs along with Active Directory replication.
- All data is encrypted and secure.
- Only updated zone data since the last replication is transmitted.
- Replication is fast and consumes less bandwidth than zone transfers.
- Table 6-11 lists the options available for zone replication.

Table 6-11. Zone replication options

Option	Description
To all DNS servers in the Active Directory forest.	Replicates zone data to all DNS servers running on domain controllers in the Active Directory forest. This option provides the broadest scope of replication. This option cannot be selected if you have Windows 2000 DNS servers.
To all DNS servers in the Active Directory domain.	Replicates zone data to all DNS servers running on domain controllers in the Active Directory domain. This option cannot be selected if you have Windows 2000 DNS servers.
To all domain controllers in the Active Directory domain.	Replicates zone data to all domain controllers in the Active Directory domain. This is the default option and is supported on Windows 2000 DNS servers.
To all domain controllers specified in the scope of a specified Active Directory partition.	Replicates zone data according to the replication scope of the specified application directory partition. This option is available only when all DNS servers are running Windows Server 2003. You must have enlisted the DNS server hosting the zone in the application directory partition.

Interoperability of DNS servers

- You should try to upgrade old DNS servers.
- Windows Server 2003 DNS supports several of the latest standard features.
- It works well with several non-Microsoft DNS implementations.
- Table 6-12 lists the DNS features supported on various DNS platforms.

Table 6-12. DNS features supported on various platforms

Operating system	SRV records	Dynamic updates	Secure dynamic updates	Active Directory-integrated zones	Incremental zone transfers	Stub zones	Conditional forwarding
Windows Server 2003	Yes	Yes	Yes	Yes	Yes	Yes	Yes
Windows 2000 Server	Yes	Yes	Yes	Yes	Yes	No	No
Windows NT 4.0 Server	No	No	No	No	Yes	No	No
UNIX BIND 9.1.0	Yes	Yes	No	No	Yes	Yes	Yes
UNIX BIND 8.2	Yes	Yes	No	No	Yes	No	No
UNIX BIND 8.1.2	Yes	Yes	No	No			
UNIX BIND 4.9.7	No	No	No	No	No	No	No

Potential attacks on DNS servers

- In a *footprinting attack*, the attacker can use some freely available tools on the Internet to transfer entire zones to her computer.

- A *denial of service* (DoS) attack happens when your DNS servers are overloaded with name resolution queries launched by an attacker.

- With an *IP-spoofing* or *data-modification* attack, the attacker modifies the IP address contained in the packet sent to the DNS server.

- In a *Redirection* or *Man-in-the-Middle* attack, the attacker is able to redirect the client to a DNS server that is under the attacker's control.

Securing DNS servers

- Use different DNS servers for your external and internal namespaces.

- Configure internal DNS servers to forward Internet queries to the external DNS server.

- Use firewalls to protect your internal DNS servers.

- Use the Active Directory-Integrated zone, if possible.

- Use Secure Updates only with Active Directory-Integrated zones.

- Configure the DNS servers to accept queries from IP addresses within your internal network.

- Disable recursion on DNS servers that are not meant to use recursive queries.

- Use the Secure Cache Against Pollution feature available on Windows Server 2003 DNS servers.

- Restrict zone transfers to the DNS servers that are listed in the NS resource records.

- Use discretionary Access Control Lists (DACL) on DNS objects.
- Make sure that the DNS zones are hosted on NTFS drives only.

Determining number of DNS servers

- The number of DNS servers depends on the number of users in a subnet.
- If using Active Directory-integrated zones, DNS servers will be hosted on domain controllers.
- If planning to use old server hardware, make sure they are good in performance.
- DNS servers should accommodate future growth in queries.
- You should create baselines for DNS performance.
- Performance should be monitored for total queries received and total responses sent by the DNS server.

Guidelines for placement of DNS servers

- Use multiple DNS servers for fault-tolerance.
- Use local DNS servers for remote subnets to limit the use of WAN bandwidth.
- For remote locations with a very few number of users, use caching-only DNS servers.
- Provide load-balancing by placing multiple DNS servers in busy locations.
- Configure clients with multiple DNS servers for improved performance.
- Pay attention to the physical security of DNS servers.
- DNS servers should be out of the reach of unauthorized persons.

Designing a WINS structure

- WINS is used for NetBIOS name resolution.
- Some legacy clients and applications may need WINS.
- WINS reduces broadcast traffic in the network by using unicast transmissions.
- The WINS database contains NetBIOS name to IP address mappings.
- The primary WINS server hosts the master copy of the WINS database.
- The secondary WINS server hosts the read-only copy of the WINS database.
- WINS replication keeps the WINS database up-to-date.

WINS clients and WINS Proxy

- WINS clients send NetBIOS resolution queries to WINS servers.
- WINS clients are also known as WINS-enabled clients.
- Windows Server 2003, Windows 2000 and Windows XP, Windows ME, Windows 98, Windows 95, all versions of Windows NT, Windows for Workgroups, MS-DOS, and OS/2 can be WINS-enabled clients.
- WINS searches its database and returns the results to clients.
- The WINS Proxy is used for non-Microsoft clients.
- One of the WINS clients is configured as the WINS Proxy.

WINS database

- The WINS database contains mappings of NetBIOS names and IP addresses.
- Clients register, renew, and update their information in the WINS database.
- Transactions to the WINS database are stored in logfiles first.
- The WINS database can be compacted to free up disk space.
- Tombstoning records permanently deletes them from WINS database.

Planning a WINS structure

- Consider the following factors:
  — The number of users and applications that need NetBIOS name resolution.
  — The number of WINS servers needed in the network and their specifications.
  — The location of WINS servers across the network and across WAN links.
  — The kind of fault-tolerance you need to provide for WINS servers.
  — The kind of replication configuration you will need among WINS servers.

WINS server hardware

- A single WINS server can serve up to 10,000 clients.
- Install multiple servers for performance and availability.
- Install the fastest available processors, preferably a dual or quad processor.
- Install as much memory as possible.
- Install fast hard disks and RAID solution for disk fault-tolerance.
- Install at least a 100 Mbps network adapter.

Placement of WINS servers

- Placement of WINS servers should aim at high availability and performance.
- Place at least two WINS servers at each location for fault-tolerance.
- Place local WINS servers across slow WAN links to prevent WINS traffic across WAN links.
- Place a WINS Proxy where you have non-Microsoft clients such as Unix and Linux.
- Place two WINS servers in each subnet of the local network so that routers do not have to deal with WINS traffic.

WINS replication

- WINS servers exchange database information through replication.
- Servers can be configured to push, pull, or push/pull replication.
- Push partners notify their pull partners about changes in the WINS database.
- Pull partners pool push partners for changes in the WINS database.
- By default, all WINS servers are push/pull partners.
- Push partners should be configured for fast network links.

- Pull partners should be configured for slow WAN links.
- WINS replication can be scheduled for off-peak hours.

Designing a Network and Routing Solution

This subsection covers a summary of highlights from the "Designing a Network and Routing Solution" section in the Exam 70-297 Study Guide.

IP address assignment

- IP addresses configured manually are known as *static IP addresses*.
- Automatic IP address assignment works on DHCP clients that do not find a DHCP server on startup.
- The APIPA IP address range is 169.254.0.0 to 169.254.255.254.
- Clients configured with APIPA poll for a DHCP server every five minutes.
- APIPA clients cannot connect to the Internet.
- Alternate IP addressing is used in place of APIPA.
- Alternate IP addressing is usually configured on portable computers.

Automatic IP addressing with DHCP

- DHCP severs are used to automatically assign IP addresses to clients.
- The DHCP server must be authorized in Active Directory to serve clients.
- A DHCP client sends out a DHCP Discover broadcast message on the network.
- The DHCP server with a valid IP address scope offers an IP address lease to the client.
- The DHCP client accepts the lease offer and requests the IP address from the DHCP server.
- The DHCP server that sent the IP lease offer to the DHCP client assigns the IP address to the client for a period that is specified in the lease.
- The default lease is for eight days.

DHCP scope

- Every DHCP server has at least one active scope.
- The scope contains the following configuration for the clients:
  — The range of IP addresses for clients.
  — The subnet mask for the network segment.
  — The period of the lease, which is eight days, by default.
  — DHCP scope options that include the addresses of the default gateway, the DNS server, and the WINS server.
  — The exclusions range that specifies the IP addresses not to be assigned by the DHCP server.
  — The reserved IP addresses for clients who should get the same IP addresses every time.

DHCP scope options

- DHCP scope options apply to all clients in the subnet.
- Table 6-13 lists commonly used scope options.

Table 6-13. DHCP scope options

Option	Description
003 Router	This is the IP address of the default gateway or the router.
006 DNS Servers	This is the IP address of the DNS server for the client.
015 DNS Domain Name	This option configures the client with the DNS domain name.
044 WINS/NBNS Server	This is the IP address of the WINS server for the client.
046 WINS/NBT Node Type	This option specifies the node type for the client. The node type can be b-node, h-node, p-node, or m-node.

DHCP Relay Agent

- The DHCP Relay Agent is placed in smaller subnets where the DHCP server cannot be placed.
- One of the DHCP clients is configured as the DHCP Relay Agent.
- The DHCP Relay Agent receives messages from DHCP clients and forwards them to the DHCP server.
- BOOTP-compliant (RFC 1542) routers can be used in place of DHCP Relay Agents.

Number and placement of DHCP servers

- DHCP servers should preferably be placed in every network segment.
- DHCP servers should be placed locally on locations connected with slow WAN links.
- The number of DHCP servers depends on the number of clients on the network.
- Multiple DHCP servers should be installed for fault-tolerance.
- The DHCP server should have high-speed processors and fast network adapters.
- Hard disks of DHCP servers should be fast and reliable.
- DHCP servers should be physically secured.
- Only authorized administrators should be granted access to the DHCP servers.

Internet connection options

- Table 6-14 lists connection options for Internet.

Table 6-14. Internet connection options

Type of connection	Type	Speed
Dial-up modem	Circuit Switched	56 Kbps
ISDN	Circuit Switched	ISDN Basic Rate Interface (BRI)-128 Kbps
		ISDN Primary Rate Interface (PRI)-1.544 Mbps

Table 6-14. Internet connection options (continued)

Type of connection	Type	Speed
Cable Television (CATV)	Leased Line	Downloads, from 512 Kbps Uploads, from 128 Kbps
Asymmetrical Digital Subscriber Line (ADSL)	Leased Line	Downloads, from 512 Kbps Uploads, from 128 Kbps
T-Carrier (North America)	Leased Line	T-1-1.544 Mbps T-3-44.736 Mbps Fractional T-1, blocks of 64 Kbps
E-Carrier (Europe)	Leased Line	E-1-2.048 Mbps E-2-8.448 Mbps
Frame Relay	Packet Switched	Variable
X.25	Packet Switched	1.544 Mbps
Asynchronous Transfer Mode	Packet Switched	622 Mbps

Calculating bandwidth requirements
- Check the number of users who need Internet access.
- Check whether all users need full access to the Internet.
- Check the operating schedules at different locations of the organization.
- Check the peak-usage hours and the time zones where the remote offices are located.
- Check whether the users are located in a single site or in multiple sites.
- Check whether certain applications will be restricted for some users.
- Check what applications need access to the Internet
- Check whether the organization will be using VPN for remote access.
- Check whether you need to install a proxy server or NAT for Internet access.

Choosing an Internet Service Provider (ISP)
- An ISP provides the gateway for Internet connectivity.
- Check how many other organizations have signed up with the ISP.
- Check the level of service provided by the ISP.
- Check the percentage of uptime guaranteed.
- Check how the ISP handles downtime.
- Check whether the ISP provides other services such as DNS, web hosting, and email.
- Determine how the ISP is connected to its peers or higher-level ISPs.
- Determine how the ISP will monitor your network bandwidth usage?
- Check what security features the ISP provides.

Network Address Translation (NAT)
- NAT is designed to provide Internet access to small organizations that use private IP addresses.
- NAT hides the internal IP addresses of the network.

- NAT cannot be used on subnetted networks.
- NAT does not support Kerberos protocol, and you cannot use domain controllers behind NAT servers.
- NAT is enabled from the Routing and Remote Access Services in Windows Server 2003.

Considerations for a NAT solution

- NAT is suitable only for very small organizations.
- NAT works only in non-routed networks.
- Understand the limitations of NAT and make sure it is the right solution.
- Check whether any applications running on the internal network are not supported by NAT.
- Decide whether NAT will be used for automatic IP addressing or whether you will use a DHCP server.
- Decide whether you need multiple connections to the Internet through the NAT server.
- Decide which server will act as a NAT server.
- Decide how the NAT server will be configured.
- Create a plan for service and port mappings if you need to host services on the Internet.

Components of a perimeter network

- A *perimeter network* separates the internal network from the Internet.
- Perimeter networks are used for securing private networks.
- Servers that should be accessible from the Internet are placed inside the perimeter network.
- Firewalls are used to separate internal and external networks.
- The perimeter network is also called *demilitarized zone* (DMZ).
- Firewalls can be hardware equipment or software-based.

Intrusion Detection Systems (IDS)

- IDS monitors a host or the entire network for possible attacks.
- A host-based IDS monitors a single computer.
- A network-based IDS system monitors the network.
- IDS compares network traffic to preconfigured patterns to see whether an attack has occurred.
- IDS sends alerts to the administrators if an attack occurs.

Remote access design considerations

- How many users will need to access the network remotely?
- From which location(s) will they connect?
- Is there a particular time when the users will need to connect?
- How many users will be connecting simultaneously?
- What type of connection will be used for remote access?

- Does the current network infrastructure support remote access?
- Do users need to run any applications remotely?
- For dial-up, how many modems do you need in the network for simultaneous connections?
- For VPN access, you will need to decide on maximum ports for L2TP and/or PPTP protocols.
- What type of security policies do you need for remote clients and remote access servers?
- What kind of authentication and encryption methods will be used?
- What resources will be made available to remote users?
- What portion of the network should be made available to remote users?

Dial-up remote access

- Dial-up connections are good for a small number of users who need temporary access.
- Dial-up access requires an investment in modems and other equipment.
- Dial-up connections should be verified using callback.

User account dial-in permissions

- Users must have appropriate permissions in their user accounts for remote access.
- Remote access permission can be allowed or denied for a user.
- Caller ID can be verified for security reasons.
- Callback options are also used for security.
- The remote computer can be assigned a static IP address by the remote access server.

Advantages of VPN remote access

- VPN supports a large number of simultaneous connections.
- The cost of implementing a VPN solution is much lower than the cost of dial-up access.
- VPN supports a number of common network protocols.
- Users can run different types of applications remotely.
- VPN provides enhanced security through strict authentication and encryption policies.
- All data is encrypted while it travels through the Internet.

Remote access authentication methods

- Remote access in Windows Server 2003 supports several authentication protocols.
- EAP is the most secure of all and provides support for smart cards and wireless connectivity.
- MS-CHAPv2 is a two-way authentication protocol that uses encryption in transmissions.
- MS-CHAP can be used by older Windows clients.

- CHAP can be used to support non-Microsoft clients.
- PAP is not very secure and transmits the username and password in plain text.
- SPAP is supported for clients that use Shiva software products.

Remote access policies

- Remote access policies are defined on remote access servers for authenticating users and securing networks.
- Policies can also be defined on RADIUS servers for centralization of administration.
- Policies consist of policy conditions, remote access permission, and policy profiles.
- Multiple policies can be defined on a single remote access server.
- The remote client must satisfy all conditions in at least one policy to connect successfully.

Policy conditions

- The Authentication Type specifies the authentication type configured on the remote client.
- Day and Time Restrictions specify the day and time when the user is allowed to connect.
- The Framed Protocol specifies the data link layer protocol that the remote client must use.
- The Tunnel Type specifies the tunneling protocol that a VPN client must use.
- The Windows Groups specifies the groups to which the connecting user must belong.

Policy profile settings

- Dial-in constraints include settings such as time limit for the connection, idle time limit before the server will disconnect the user, and hours and days of the week when the client can connect.
- IP settings allow you to configure whether the client or the remote access server should assign an IP address to the client.
- Multilink settings allow the client to use the Windows multilink feature so that the client can use multiple telephone lines to increase network bandwidth.
- The authentication setting is used to specify an authentication protocol.
- The encryption setting is used to specify an encryption protocol that the client must use in order to connect.
- Both the server and the client should use at least one common encryption and authentication protocol.

Advantages of using RADIUS servers

- RADIUS servers provide centralized authentication.
- Administrators can configure remote access policies on the RADIUS server for all remote access servers.

- RADIUS servers provide centralized accounting for analysis of network usage.
- Auditing and logging of remote access servers is centralized.
- Administration and troubleshooting is centralized and simplified.

Remote access event logging

- Events related to remote access are stored in system logs.
- By default, errors and warning events are recorded.
- Other options include errors only, warnings only, and maximum amount of information.
- Auditing authentication and accounting helps with troubleshooting and analyzing unauthorized access attempts.

Exam 70-297 Practice Questions

1. A company has six offices across the country, and each office has administrators who look after system maintenance and backups. The major IT decisions, such as domain panning, purchases, and security policies, are made at the head office. What kind of administrative model is the company following?

   ○ A. Centralized

   ○ B. Decentralized

   ○ C. Hybrid

   ○ D. Outsourced

   Answer B is correct. When there is local administrative staff at remote locations but major IT decisions are taken at the head office, a decentralized model is in use.

2. A company has four different offices located in four cities in California and nearby states. Each office is independently managed by the local IT staff. What type of geographical model is in place?

   ○ A. Local

   ○ B. National

   ○ C. Regional

   ○ D. International

   Answer C is correct. When a company is located in several nearby states, it uses a regional geographical model.

3. You have started the analysis of the current network infrastructure of a company and are in the process of preparing analysis documentation. The company has 16 offices located across the country. Which of the following would be the most important factor when analyzing the network performance of the interoffice connectivity?

   ○ A. Number of subnets in each office

   ○ B. Number of users in each office

   ○ C. Speed of LAN connections

   ○ D. Speed of WAN links

Answer D is correct. When a company is spread across the country, different vendors may be involved in providing WAN connectivity. The type and speed of the WAN links is an important factor when analyzing the interoffice connectivity.

4. You need a Windows-based tool that can be used to monitor the network performance of each critical server individually. You do not have time or budget to purchase any other software application for this purpose. Which of the built-in tools is best suited for analyzing network traffic to and from each server?

   ○ A. Performance Console

   ○ B. Network Monitor

   ○ C. Task Manager

   ○ D. System Monitor

   Answer B is correct. The built-in Network Monitor can be used to analyze traffic to and from a single Windows 2000 or Windows Server 2003 server. If you need to monitor the entire network from a single server, you will need the full version of Network Monitor included with Microsoft Systems Management Server.

5. When analyzing the IP addressing scheme used on the current network infrastructure, which of the following is the least important consideration?

   ○ A. IP address range in each subnet

   ○ B. Subnet mask for each subnet

   ○ C. Names of DNS servers for each subnet

   ○ D. Default gateway in each subnet

   Answer C is correct. When you are analyzing the IP-addressing scheme, the names of servers providing network services, such as DNS and WINS, are not as important as determining how IP address space has been divided to accommodate IP subnets.

6. You are analyzing the current Windows Server 2003 network for an organization. The organization has two Unix servers in one of the network segments. The development department uses these servers for testing software applications. The servers are placed in their own separate domain. What type of trust relationship might exist between the Windows domain and the Unix domain?

   ○ A. Realm trust

   ○ B. External trust

   ○ C. Forest trust

   ○ D. Shortcut trust

   Answer A is correct. A realm trust is created between Windows Server 2003 Active Directory domain and a non-Microsoft domain that uses Kerberos 5 as security protocol.

7. You are the systems administrator for your company, which deals with development of software products. The company is expanding and wants to open new offices in London, England, and Singapore. The company will initially be

exporting its products from the head office in the United States. Local staff will independently handle the new domains once they are implemented. The local country managers will make decisions about account and password policies. You have been asked to analyze the design requirements of the Active Directory domains for the new offices, which will be connected to the head office. Which of the following is your best option for designing new domains?

○ A. Create a new forest for each of the new locations.

○ B. Add the new domains to the existing domain tree.

○ C. Create new domains as subdomains of the head office.

○ D. Create new sites for the domain at the head office.

Answer B is correct. It is best to create new domains in the existing domain tree. Since there is no need for a new separate forest, the existing domain structure can be expanded by adding new domains to the domain tree. You should try to keep the Active Directory structure to a single forest as much as possible.

8. You have been asked to design an Active Directory structure for a fast-growing company that is planning to open six offices across the country. You were talking to the IT manager, who indicated that he wants each office to have its own Security policies. He was not sure whether it calls for a different domain or a different forest for each location. Which of the following is a good reason to create a new forest? Choose two answers.

❑ A. When you have different security policies

❑ B. When local administrators are available

❑ C. When you need an isolated unit within the company

❑ D. When each business unit needs independent control of resources

❑ E. When two companies have merged but each wants to retain autonomy over its networks

Answers C and E are correct. As much as possible, you should keep the forest structure to a single forest. A new forest should be created only when some unit of the company needs isolation from the rest of the company. A different forest may also be a good choice when two companies have merged and each wants to retain autonomy over its IT infrastructure.

9. Which of the following is not an advantage of keeping the Active Directory network to a single domain?

○ A. A single domain is scalable and manageable

○ B. Centralized administration is possible

○ C. Organizational units can be used to delegate administration

○ D. Business units can be isolated according to their security needs

Answer D is correct. If you need to isolate business units for reasons of security requirements or granting autonomy over their respective resources, it is better to create separate domains for each business unit.

10. You have been asked to upgrade an existing Windows 2000 Active Directory domain to a Windows Server 2003 domain. Which of the following utilities

should be run before the upgrade process can actually start? Select two answers.

❑ A. adprep /forestprep

❑ B. adprep /domainprep

❑ C. adprep /dnsprep

❑ D. adprep /gcprep

❑ E. adprep /schemaprep

Answers A and B are correct. The Active Directory Preparation Tool adprep.exe should be run on Windows 2000 domain controllers to prepare them for Windows Server 2003 Active Directory. The adprep /forestprep command adds new features to the forest schema. The adprep /domainprep adds domain-specific features to the Windows 2000 domain.

11. You have finalized the design of the Active Directory domain structure for a company and are now in the process of designing the OU structure. The IT manager wants you to create a separate OU for each location of the company, but the resources at each location should be grouped according to the departments of the company. Which of the following OU models should you choose?

○ A. Location-based

○ B. Function-based

○ C. Organization-based

○ D. Location-, then organization-based

Answer D is correct. The IT manager is asking you to follow the "location, then organization" model for creating OUs. The top-level OUs should be based on locations of the company. Beneath each location-based OU, you should create OUs for each department of the company.

12. Which of the following is the main purpose of creating Organizational Units?

○ A. Delegation of control

○ B. To grant resource access permissions

○ C. To create Active Directory sites

○ D. To localize network traffic

Answer A is correct. The main reason for creating Organizational Units is to delegate control of these units to local administrators. Remember that an OU is the smallest administrative unit for which you can delegate control. Other reasons for creating OUs are limiting visibility of objects in the Active Directory and implementing Group Policies effectively.

13. The network you are analyzing contains Window NT 4.0 and Windows 2000 domain controllers. You want to install Windows Server 2003 domain controllers and create two new domains. The existing domain controllers will remain in the network. Which of the following domain functional levels can you have?

○ A. Windows 2000 Mixed

○ B. Windows 2000 Native

○ C. Windows Server 2003 Interim

○ D. Windows Server 2003

Answer A is correct. The Windows 2000 Mixed domain functional level allows a Windows Server 2003 domain controller to interact with Windows 2000 and Windows NT 4.0 domain controllers.

14. Which of the following operations master roles is required for creating and deleting domains from a forest?

○ A. PDC emulator

○ B. Schema master

○ C. Domain naming master

○ D. Relative ID master

○ E. Infrastructure master

Answer C is correct. The domain controller holding the role of domain naming master must be online when domains are added or removed from a forest.

15. You are designing a solution for cross-forest resource access for a Windows Server 2003-based Active Directory network. The network consists of three forests, and trust relationships have already been created. Which of the following logon options should be used by users to log on to trusted forests?

○ A. Universal principal name

○ B. Username and password

○ C. Username and domain name

○ D. Domain name and password

Answer A is correct. Users need UPN names to log on to domains in trusted forests. The UPN name of a user contains the user account name and the domain name. It looks like an email address—for example, myname@mydomain is a UPN name.

16. You want to design Universal groups to allow users from one domain to access resources in another trusted domain. When you ask one of the administrators to create a Universal group for testing, he reports that this option is not available on any of the six domain controllers in the network. What could be the reason?

○ A. The administrator does not have rights to create Universal groups.

○ B. The domain functional level is not Windows Server 2003 or Windows 2000 Native.

○ C. The forest functional level is not Windows Server 2003.

○ D. Universal groups are available only in forests that are not in domains.

Answer B is correct. Universal groups are available only if the domain functional level is either Windows Server 2003 or Windows 2000 Native.

Windows 2000 Mixed or Windows Server 2003 Interim levels do not support Universal groups.

17. You have created a diagram showing different servers that will host Internet services for your organization. Two firewalls will separate these servers from the internal network and the Internet. How should you assign IP addresses to these servers?

○ A. Through APIPA addressing

○ B. By placing a DHCP server in the perimeter network

○ C. By using alternate IP address configuration

○ D. By manually configuring IP addresses

Answer D is correct. All critical servers that host Internet services, such as a web server, DNS server, mail server, etc., should be configured with static (manual) IP addresses. This is because these servers usually need registered IP addresses.

18. A Windows Server 2003 computer is designated as a file server in the Active Directory domain. This server is located in the FileServ OU. The FileServ OU is part of the NY domain located at a New York site. Group policies are linked to the domain, site, and NY OU. The file server itself has a GPO linked to it. Identify the correct processing order of GPOs.

○ A. Local, domain, site, and OU

○ B. Domain, site, local, and OU

○ C. Local, site, domain, and OU

○ D. OU, site, domain, and local

Answer C is correct. Local GPO is processed first, followed by site, domain, and Organizational Unit GPOs. The GPO linked to the site overrides the conflicting settings in the local GPO. Similarly, the GPO linked to the domain overrides conflicting settings at the site level. Domain settings are overridden by settings in the GPO linked to the OU.

19. What happens if an OU is linked to multiple GPOs from several sources?

○ A. Only the first GPO is processed.

○ B. The administrator can choose which GPO should be processed.

○ C. The GPO with maximum settings is processed.

○ D. All GPOs are processed starting from the lowest GPO in the list.

Answer D is correct. When multiple GPOs are linked to the OU, all GPOs are processed, starting from the lowest GPO. However, the administrator can change the processing order of the GPOs.

20. According to Microsoft recommendations, which of the following groups should be used to assign resource access permissions?

○ A. Domain Local

○ B. Global

○ C. Universal

○ D. Any of above

Answer A is correct. Microsoft recommends that resource access permissions should be assigned to Domain Local groups. Users should be placed in Global groups, Global groups should be placed in Universal groups. and Universal groups should be placed in Domain Local groups. This simplifies administration of resources and helps troubleshoot resource access problems.

21. One of the departments in your organization wants to design its own account policies due to security requirements for its development projects. Which of the following is the best option to accomplish this?

    ○ **A.** Place the department in a separate OU

    ○ **B.** Place the department in a separate domain

    ○ **C.** Place the department in a separate site

    ○ **D.** Create a new forest for the department

    Answer B is correct. Account policies are applied at the domain level and are effective in the entire domain. You cannot have two different account policies in a single domain. Creating a new forest can also solve the problem, but there is no reason to do so.

22. Which of the following networks can use Network Address Translation for Internet connectivity?

    ○ **A.** A network with 1 subnet, 120 client computers, 2 domain controllers, a DNS server, a web server, and a mail server

    ○ **B.** A network with 2 subnets, 60 client computers in each subnet, 2 domain controllers, and 2 DNS servers

    ○ **C.** A network with 3 subnets, 80 client computers in each subnet, 4 domain controllers, a DNS server, and a WINS server

    ○ **D.** A network with 4 subnets, 45 client computers in each subnet, 2 domain controllers, a DNS server, a web server, and a mail server

    Answer A is correct. Network Address Translation can be used only for small organizations that do not have any network segments. Web servers, DNS servers, and mail servers can exist behind NAT servers and still be visible from the Internet using registered IP addresses.

23. A US-based company has registered a second-level domain name as catsupplies.com. This domain will be available for public access on the Internet. The company wants to keep its internal Active Directory domain structure entirely separate from the external domain. Which of the following DNS names should you choose for the internal network of the company?

    ○ **A.** int.catsupplies.com

    ○ **B.** us.catsupplies.com

    ○ **C.** catsupplies.net

    ○ **D.** internal.catsupplies.com

    Answer C is correct. All other names are subdomains of the registered domain name. If you want to keep internal and external namespaces separate, the only option from the given choices is catsupplies.net.

24. A junior administrator assigned with the task of managing account policies is trying to figure out where the Account and Password Policies are stored on the domain controller. Can you tell her where these policy settings are configured?

○ A. Default domain controllers policy

○ B. Default forest policy

○ C. Default domain policy

○ D. Default site policy

Answer C is correct. Password and account policies for the domain are located in the default domain policy GPO. These policies are applied to all objects in the domain and cannot be overridden by other policies.

25. You are designing a plan for controlling replication of the Active Directory database between two domain controllers located in separate locations connected by WAN links. What do you need to create? Select two answers.

❏ A. Sites

❏ B. Site links

❏ C. IP subnets

❏ D. Subnet links

❏ E. Bridgehead servers

Answers A and B are correct. You need to configure sites and site links for controlling replication between domain controllers at remote locations connected by WAN links. You can configure replication to occur when other network traffic is low.

26. What needs to be configured if you disable site link transitivity between remote sites?

○ A. Site link costs

○ B. Bridgehead servers

○ C. Site link bridges

○ D. Preferred Bridgehead servers

Answer B is correct. Site link transitivity is enabled by default. If you disable site link transitivity for a replication protocol, you will need to configure site link bridges between sites. Site link transitivity should be disabled in rare circumstances.

27. Which of the following should be considered a good reason to place a Global Catalog server in a site? Select all correct answers.

❏ A. When there are less than 100 users at a site

❏ B. When there are more than 100 users at a site

❏ C. When some applications need to query the Global Catalog

❏ D. When the sites are connected by slow WAN links

❏ E. When there are a number of domain controllers at a site

Answers B, C, D, and E are correct. A site needs a Global Catalog server if any of these is correct. Besides this, the number of Global Catalog servers should be half the number of domain controllers at a site. This calculation is important for sites that have multiple domain controllers and a large number of users at a single, large site.

28. Your IT manager wants you to choose a server from the existing server hardware to install the Windows Server 2003 operating system. You need to calculate the processor requirements for a site with nearly 900 users. Which of the following processor configurations can be used?

   ○ A. One 850 MHz Processor and 512 MB RAM

   ○ B. One 850 MHz Processor and 1 GB RAM

   ○ C. Dual 850 MHz processor and 1 GB RAM

   ○ D. Quad 850 MHz processor and 2 GB RAM

   Answer C is correct. Microsoft recommends that for 500 to 999 users, you should use a dual processor server with a minimum of 850 MHz speed and at least 1 GB RAM.

29. What is the best place to install domain controllers within a site?

   ○ A. At a place where a large number of users are working

   ○ B. At a place that is physically secure

   ○ C. At a place that is easily accessible by all users

   ○ D. At a place that is difficult to reach

   Answer B is correct. Domain controllers and other servers that provide critical network services should be placed in physically secure locations. Physical security is one of the main reasons behind creating server rooms or Network Operations Centers (NOCs).

30. You are designing the DNS structure for a company. The company needs maximum protection for its DNS zone data so that it is difficult for hackers and attackers to get information about names and IP address used inside the company. Which of the following types of DNS zones should you suggest?

   ○ A. Active Directory-integrated zones

   ○ B. Standard primary zones

   ○ C. Standard secondary zones

   ○ D. Stub zones

   Answer A is correct. Active Directory-Integrated zones offer maximum possible security for DNS zone data. The zone data is stored in the Active Directory on domain controllers and replicated in encrypted form along with other Active Directory information.

31. You have decided to analyze the current performance levels of the existing DNS servers in the network. Which of the following performance counters should you monitor? Select all correct answers.

   ❏ A. Total queries received per second

   ❏ B. Total responses sent per second

   ❏ C. Average queries received per second

   ❏ D. Average responses sent per second

Answers A, B, C, and D are all correct. The Performance console includes the given counters for the DNS object. You should create a performance log and analyze the logs to see whether any of the existing DNS servers are experiencing performance bottlenecks.

32. You are designing an Active Directory infrastructure for a medium-sized organization that wants to have an Internet presence. You are currently working on the IP address allocation plan. How should you define scopes on DHCP servers for allocating IP addresses to file servers, print servers, and printers so that they get the same address every time they are started?

○ A. By assigning static IP addresses

○ B. By DHCP scope reservations

○ C. By DHCP scope options

○ D. By using alternate addresses

Answer B is correct. The servers and other equipment configured to get IP addresses from the DHCP server should have address reservations on the DHCP server so that they always get the same IP address.

33. You are designing an Active Directory infrastructure for a small organization that has nearly 120 computers in a single network segment. You are currently working on the IP address allocation plan. How can you ensure that the clients will continue to communicate on the network and use the Internet even if the DHCP server is not available?

○ A. By using DHCP server options

○ B. By using address reservations

○ C. By using Automatic Private IP Addressing

○ D. By using alternate addressing

Answer D is correct. Alternate IP addressing is used when the clients are configured to use a DHCP server for IP address assignment and it is not available. The client will use the IP address configured as the alternate address. The alternate addresses are usually in the same subnet range that has been configured in the DHCP scope.

34. Which of the following should you specify in your guidelines for naming computer accounts for servers? Select two answers.

❏ A. The name should identify the server and its purpose.

❏ B. The name should identify the parent domain and OU of the server.

❏ C. The name should identify the administrator of the server.

❏ D. The name should identify the location of the server.

❏ E. The name should identify the domain controller where the account exists.

Answers A and D are correct. The account names for servers should identify their location and purpose. For example, a print server located in a San Francisco office can be named as SFPrint1 (which stands for San Francisco Print server 1).

35. While designing a remote access solution for a large company, you are planning to use the Internet as the medium. Your plan includes installing VPN servers so that long-distance telephone charges can be saved for remote users. The IT manager has asked you about some advantages of VPN over dial-up? Which of the following is not an advantage of using VPN?

○ A. Support for large number of users

○ B. Additional processing overheads

○ C. Internet is used as the medium

○ D. Scalability is better than dial-up

Answer B is correct. Remote access using VPN adds additional processing overheads for servers because the server has to perform encryption and decryption of data packets sent and received from the Internet. If you are planning to use older hardware as VPN servers, you should carefully determine the processing needs for the VPN server.

36. You are designing a DNS infrastructure for a company that already has a mix of Windows and Unix DNS servers in place. The company wants to retain all the existing DNS servers, including the Unix DNS servers. Security of zone data is the main concern for the company. Which of the following DNS servers will support secure dynamic updates for DNS zones?

❑ A. Windows Server 2003

❑ B. Windows 2000

❑ C. Windows NT 4.0

❑ D. UNIX BIND 9.1.0

❑ E. UNIX BIND 8.2

Answers A and B are correct. Only Windows Server 2003 and Windows 2000 DSN implementations support secure dynamic updates. Secure dynamic updates are supported in the Active Directory-integrated zone that is available only in Windows Server 2003 and Windows 2000.

37. Several users in the network have reported in the last hour that when they try to connect to the database server, they get connected to an unknown web site on the Internet. What kind of DNS attack has been launched against your DNS servers?

○ A. Footprinting

○ B. IP Spoofing

○ C. Denial of service

○ D. Man in the Middle

Answer D is correct. The Man-in-the-Middle attack happens when an attacker is able to redirect DNS queries to another DNS server that is under the attacker's control. The attacker launches this type of attack by modifying some of the resource records in the zone database. The zone is actually "polluted" with invalid resource records.

38. You want to design a remote access solution for a large company that will be using several remote access servers. You want to centralize authentication of remote users. How can you draft the plan?

○ A. Use one of the domain controllers to authenticate remote clients

○ B. Use a RADIUS server for authentication

○ C. Designate one of the remote access servers as authentication server

○ D. Configure one of the domain controllers as RADIUS client

Answer B is correct. Authentication of remote access clients can be centralized using a RADIUS server. Remote access policies can be configured on a RADIUS server for all remote access servers. Remote access servers are configured as RADIUS clients.

39. People who want to connect to the remote access server are using a variety of Windows operating systems. While you have denied access to users who still have Windows 95 and Windows for Workgroups, the company policy states that unless there is a security risk, users should be allowed to connect. You want to finalize MS-CHAP2 as the authentication protocol. Which of the following operating systems will not support this protocol? Select three answers.

❑ A. Windows XP

❑ B. Windows 2000 Professional

❑ C. Windows NT 4.0 SP 4

❑ D. Windows 98

❑ E. Windows NT 3.51

❑ F. Windows 95

Answers D, E, and F are correct. Windows 95, Windows NT 3.51, and Windows 98 do not support MS-CHAP2 authentication protocol.

40. You have been tasked to design a remote access solution for a company that deals with highly confidential data. You plan to use the most secure authentication protocol for authentication of remote clients. Which of the following is the most secure of all authentication protocols available with Windows Server 2003?

○ A. EAP

○ B. MS-CHAPv1

○ C. MS-CHAPv2

○ D. CHAP

○ E. PAP

Answer A is correct. The Extensible Authentication Protocol (EAP) is the most secure of all authentication protocols available with Windows Server 2003. One of the requirements of this protocol is that the remote access server must be a member of an Active Directory domain.

Exam 70-298:
Designing Security for a Microsoft
Windows Server 2003 Network

7

Exam 70-298 Overview

Exam 70-298: Designing Security for a Microsoft Windows Server 2003 Network, is one of Microsoft's capstone exams with a focus on network security in a Windows Server 2003 environment. The exam is intended to measure a candidate's proficiency and understanding of Windows security design.

Exam 70-298 is one of two exams that satisfy the core exam design requirement for the Windows 2003 MCSE (the other is *Exam 70-297: Designing a Microsoft Windows Server 2003 Active Directory and Network Infrastructure*) and is a required core exam to obtain the MCSE: Security certification for Microsoft Windows Server 2003. By just passing this exam, you become a Microsoft Certified Professional (MCP).

In order to be prepared for Exam 70-298, Microsoft recommends that you should have at least one year of experience in designing network infrastructures and implementing and administering a Windows desktop operating system in a network environment with the following characteristics:

- 250 to 5,000 (or more) users
- Three or more physical locations
- Three or more domain controllers
- Network services and resources such as messaging, database, file and print, proxy server, firewall, Internet, intranet, remote access, and client computer management
- Connectivity requirements from branch offices and individual users in remote locations to the corporate network

To pass this exam, it is very helpful, though not required, to have passed the Windows Server 2003 MCSE core exams and to have a hands-on understanding of the various security features available in Microsoft Windows Server 2003, including:

- Group Policy and Security Templates
- Certificate Services
- Software Update Services (SUS) (but don't be surprised if Windows Server Update Services (WSUS) gets tested soon).
- IP Filters
- Encrypting File System (EFS)
- IPSec
- 802.1x authentication on wireless networks
- Internet Information Server (IIS) and Secure Sockets Layer (SSL)
- Active Directory Delegation
- File, Folder, and Registry Security
- Routing and Remote Access Services (RRAS)
- Internet Authentication Services (IAS)

Areas of Study for Exam 70-298

Here are Exam 70-298 objectives as listed by Microsoft Learning at *http://www. microsoft.com/learning/exams/70-298.asp*.

Creating the Conceptual Design for Network Infrastructure Security by Gathering and Analyzing Business and Technical Requirements

- Analyze business requirements for designing security. Considerations include existing policies and procedures, sensitivity of data, cost, legal requirements, end-user impact, interoperability, maintainability, scalability, and risk.
  - Analyze existing security policies and procedures.
  - Analyze the organizational requirements for securing data.
  - Analyze the security requirements of different types of data.
  - Analyze risks to security within the current IT administration structure and security practices.
- Design a framework for designing and implementing security. The framework should include prevention, detection, isolation, and recovery.
  - Predict threats to your network from internal and external sources.
  - Design a process for responding to incidents.
  - Design segmented networks.
  - Design a process for recovering services.
- Analyze technical constraints when designing security.
  - Identify capabilities of the existing infrastructure.
  - Identify technology limitations.
  - Analyze interoperability constraints.

See "General Network Security Framework" on page 396 and "Security Infrastructure Technologies" on page 415.

Creating the Logical Design for Network Infrastructure Security

- Design a public key infrastructure (PKI) that uses Certificate Services.
  - Design a certification authority (CA) hierarchy implementation. Types include geographical, organizational, and trusted.
  - Design enrollment and distribution processes.
  - Establish renewal, revocation, and auditing processes.
  - Design security for CA servers.
- Design a logical authentication strategy.
  - Design certificate distribution.
  - Design forest and domain trust models.
  - Design security that meets interoperability requirements.
  - Establish account and password requirements for security.

- Design security for network management.
  - Manage the risk of managing networks.
  - Design the administration of servers by using common administration tools. Tools include Microsoft Management Console (MMC), Terminal Server, Remote Desktop for Administration, Remote Assistance, and Telnet.
  - Design security for Emergency Management Services.
- Design a security update infrastructure.
  - Design a Software Update Services (SUS) infrastructure.
  - Design Group Policy to deploy software updates.
  - Design a strategy for identifying computers that are not at the current patch level.
- Create the Physical Design for Network Infrastructure Security.
- Design network infrastructure security.
  - Specify the required protocols for a firewall configuration.
  - Design IP filtering.
  - Design an IPSec policy.
  - Secure a DNS implementation.
  - Design security for data transmission.
- Design security for wireless networks.
  - Design public and private wireless LANs.
  - Design 802.1x authentication for wireless networks.
- Design user authentication for Internet Information Services (IIS).
  - Design user authentication for a web site by using certificates.
  - Design user authentication for a web site by using IIS authentication.
  - Design user authentication for a web site by using RADIUS for IIS authentication.
- Design security for Internet Information Services (IIS).
  - Design security for web sites that have different technical requirements by enabling only the minimum required services.
  - Design a monitoring strategy for IIS.
  - Design an IIS baseline that is based on business requirements.
  - Design a content management strategy for updating an IIS server.
- Design security for communication between networks.
  - Select protocols for VPN access.
  - Design VPN connectivity.
  - Design demand-dial routing between internal networks.
- Design security for communication with external organizations.
  - Design an extranet infrastructure.
  - Design a strategy for cross-certification of Certificate Services.

- Design security for servers that have specific roles. Roles include domain controller, network infrastructure server, file server, IIS server, terminal server, and POP3 mail server.
  — Define a baseline Security Template for all systems.
  — Create a plan to modify baseline Security Templates according to role.

See "Securing Network Communications" on page 441 and "Secure Active Directory Design" on page 467.

Designing an Access Control Strategy for Data

- Design an access control strategy for directory services.
  — Create a delegation strategy.
  — Analyze auditing requirements.
  — Design the appropriate group strategy for accessing resources.
  — Design a permission structure for directory service objects.
- Design an access control strategy for files and folders.
  — Design a strategy for the encryption and decryption of files and folders.
  — Design a permission structure for files and folders.
  — Design security for a backup and recovery strategy.
  — Analyze auditing requirements.
- Design an access control strategy for the registry.
  — Design a permission structure for registry objects.
  — Analyze auditing requirement.

See "Secure Active Directory Design" on page 467.

Creating the Physical Design for Client Infrastructure Security

- Design a client authentication strategy.
  — Analyze authentication requirements.
  — Establish account and password security requirements.
- Design a security strategy for client remote access.
  — Design remote access policies.
  — Design access to internal resources.
  — Design an authentication provider and accounting strategy for remote network access by using Internet Authentication Service (IAS).
- Design a strategy for securing client computers. Considerations include desktop and portable computers.
  — Design a strategy for hardening client operating systems.
  — Design a strategy for restricting user access to operating system features.

See "Data Access Control Strategies" on page 479.

Microsoft exam objectives are subject to change at any time without prior notice.

Chapter 8 will address each point and provide the detailed information needed to prepare for the exam. Chapter 9 will provide several scenarios and dozens of questions similar to the real exam.

8

Exam 70-298 Study Guide

This chapter provides a study guide for *Exam 70-298: Designing Security for a Microsoft Windows Server 2003 Network*. Sections within the chapter are organized according to the exam objective they cover. Each section identifies the related exam skill objective, provides an overview of why the skill is important, and then discusses the key details you should know about the objective to both succeed on the test and master the skill in the real world.

The major topics covered on Exam 70-298 are:

Creating the Conceptual Design for Network Infrastructure Security by Gathering and Analyzing Business and Technical Requirements
This section exists to measure your ability to rank various general security solutions and design security frameworks, as well as develop processes for detecting, isolating, and recovering from security incidents, guided by stated business requirements. Questions in this section will often have multiple "right" answers, and the candidate will be tasked with selecting the most appropriate choice.

Creating the Logical Design for Network Infrastructure Security
This section focuses on Microsoft Certificate Services, Windows trust models, Password Policy, patch management, remote administration, Terminal Services, and securing Emergency Management Services (EMS).

Creating the Physical Design for Network Infrastructure Security
This objective covers network infrastructure security. You will be required to make firewall configuration decisions, implement IP filtering, enable appropriate IPSec policies, secure DNS, implement secure data transmission, secure wireless networks, select the appropriate Internet Information Services (IIS) Security Options, select the appropriate VPN access protocols, and use Security Templates for role-based servers.

Designing an Access Control Strategy for Data
This section tests your knowledge of directory services permissions, access control strategies, Active Directory delegation, auditing, group strategies, Encrypting File System (EFS), and file, folder, and registry permissions.

Creating the Physical Design for Client Infrastructure Security
This objective covers infrastructure security for client connections, including Routing and Remote Access Services (RRASs), Internet Authentication Service (IAS), and hardening client operating systems.

The sections of this chapter are designed to reinforce your knowledge of these topics using case studies with follow-up questions. The 70-298 exam focuses on larger design concepts. While the test candidate must be familiar with the various options and features available in each tested security infrastructure component, the exam usually does not ask any questions in enough detail to require memorizing or using a specific tool interface.

However, when preparing for this exam, it helps to have a firm understanding of the exact options and components you will be tested on so that covered terminology and concepts are not unfamiliar. When preparing for 70-298, you can prepare two computers to assist in reviewing the related concepts.

The two computers can be configured as follows:

- A domain controller running Windows Server 2003 configured with DNS, DHCP, Routing and Remote Access Service (RRAS), IAS, IIS Windows Software Update Services (WSUS), and Certificate Services.

- A workstation running the Windows XP Professional operating system.

This exam requires that you have good working knowledge of Active Directory and networking technologies in Windows Server 2003. It is strongly recommended that you complete the four core exams before attempting this exam.

General Network Security Framework

Microsoft wants to ensure that you are familiar with basic security framework categories. Many exam questions will contain multiple solutions that could be used to solve a particular problem, but only one will meet the security requirements with a minimum of manual effort, and maximize the benefits over the cost.

Security Framework

Security policies and procedures focus on prevention, detection, isolation, and recovery.

Prevention
Most security practices and policies focus on preventing malicious, adverse events from occurring. Prevention can be accomplished using numerous security mechanisms, including Access Control Lists, authentication, and encryption. The majority of Windows security mechanisms focus on prevention.

Detection

Detection is the act of noticing and recording an adverse event. If you can't prevent an adverse event from happening, detection at the earliest opportunity is the next best goal. In Windows, this is most often accomplished using logfiles. Exam 70-298 focuses on security auditing using the Security log as seen in the Event Viewer and IIS logging.

Isolation

Isolation includes two objectives: preventing one adverse event from causing additional damage to the current system or network, and preventing additional events in other systems by limiting access between systems. This can be accomplished using many methods, including Access Control Lists, network devices, and network traffic isolation (e.g., VPNs).

Recovery

Recovery focuses on returning an asset damaged by an adverse event back to normal operations as soon as possible. This is accomplished using redundant service mechanisms, backup solutions, and effective incident response planning.

An effective security policy covers all four aspects of operational security and measures the benefits of the policy against the cost. An administrator must analyze the internal and external risks threatening computer assets to design security policies. When developing policies or when modifying existing security policies, the administrator must analyze the business requirements of the entity she is protecting. Considerations include sensitivity of data, proposed threats and risks, cost of policies, operational impact, legal requirements, technological limitations, interoperational issues, scalability, existing policies, and management requirements. Systems and data should be appropriately protected with sufficient security policies.

When taking Exam 70-298, a scenario's business requirements should be treated as absolutely required. If the proposed solution cannot completely fulfill the stated business requirements, the solution should not be chosen as an answer. Business requirements are not optional.

Segmenting Networks

Segmenting networks into the appropriate security domains is a common task for an administrator. In a nutshell, network traffic should only be allowed to and from the source and destination networks and hosts where the data is authorized to be used. Segmentation is commonly accomplished using the following:

- Router
- Ethernet Switch
- Firewall
- Network Address Translation
- IP Filters
- Virtual Private Network

Router

Routers work at the Internetwork protocol layer (called the Network Layer in the OSI model). In a TCP/IP network, data packets are routed from source to destination using host Internet Protocol (IP) addresses. An administrator can segment network traffic based upon source and destination IP addresses (and often transport protocol port numbers). Routers are most often used to separate boundary networks (e.g., private LAN from the Internet), but can be used to separate internal networks and wide area networks. Additionally, routers do not pass broadcast packets by default. Routers are excellent security devices for separating security domains, but normally do not have the capability of upper-layer protocol analysis or data content inspection. A Windows server with multiple network cards can perform routing. The Routing and Remote Access Service (RRAS) allows granular control of routing with a choice of multiple routing protocols (e.g., RIP, OSPF, etc.)

Ethernet Switch

Ethernet switches are Layer 2 bridge devices that work using host physical Ethernet (i.e., MAC) addresses and are the most common network devices for connecting multiple hosts in an internal network. A switch treats each node as belonging to its own separate collision domain, although broadcast traffic is sent to all nodes on the same switch (unless configured otherwise). Ethernet Switches can provide a minimal layer of security between hosts, as most hosts can only "see" traffic headed to and from themselves, along with the broadcast packets. Switches prevent intruders from easily eavesdropping on (i.e., sniffing) other host unicast traffic. However, a malicious intruder can use various Layer 2 spoofing methods to circumvent the normal security domain protection afforded by the switch. For that reason, an Ethernet Switch should not be seen as a trustworthy security device for separating networks.

Hosts on the same network segment (i.e., connected by an Ethernet Switch, bridge, or hub) can be given different higher-layer network addresses to create more than one logical network. Hosts belonging to separate logical networks will behave as if there were a router placed between them. This allows additional security domains to be created on a single physical network segment, although it is not considered a strongly secure solution. As with Ethernet network switches, malicious hackers can easily circumvent logically separated networks.

Firewall

A *firewall* is an intelligent device or software program that allows network traffic to be filtered between security domains using information from multiple network layers. Firewalls can block and allow traffic using IP addresses, transport protocol numbers, domain names, and data content. The most sophisticated firewalls can analyze data packets for anomalous information and detect attacks by specific characteristics.

Every firewall should have a deny-by-default rule, meaning that all traffic not specifically allowed should be blocked by default. Firewalls must be configured to allow the appropriate network protocols to traverse between authorized hosts and networks. Common ports that need to be open on a Windows host include: Kerberos, LDAP, RPC, ICMP, and SMB.

Firewalls are among the best solutions for separating security domains. Windows XP Pro comes with a host-based software called Windows Firewall (called Internet Connection Firewall prior to XP Pro Service Pack 2), as does Windows Server 2003 Service Pack 1 and later.

Network Address Translation

Network Address Translation (NAT) is a service provided by many network devices (e.g., routers, firewalls, etc.) and RRASs. Network Address Translation converts one or more private host IP addresses (e.g., 10.x.x.x, 172.16.x.x, 192.168.x.x) to one or more public IP gateway addresses. Network Address Translation was initially developed because of the dwindling number of freely available public IP addresses, but NAT solutions also provide an additional layer of protection against malicious attacks because a malicious attacker (or malware program) cannot easily convert a NAT-generated public IP address back to its original private IP address. However, a NAT solution should not be relied upon to provide significant security protection to any environment. Most client-side attacks will readily traverse NAT-protected networks and be able to pass their malicious behaviors to and from the impacted host with little impedance.

IP Filters

The Windows TCP/IP Filters feature in Microsoft's Internet Protocol network protocol can block unauthorized inbound traffic based upon transport protocol port or Internet Protocol number (see Figure 8-1). First available in NT 4.0, and still available in XP Pro and Windows Server 2003, IP Filters is considered a low-technology security solution and has been replaced by the more functional Windows Firewall. Still, it may appear as a valid or invalid solution on Exam 70-298, especially if the scenario involves NT 4.0 or Windows 2000. A major weakness of IP Filters is that any configured settings affect all network adapters. Additionally, IP Filters is *nonstateful*, meaning that it cannot automatically open new dynamic inbound ports based upon authorized outbound traffic. IP Filtering can be used for inbound static filtering, but is probably insufficient for computers needing dynamic port features.

Virtual Private Network

Virtual Private Networks (VPNs) allow private data to be securely transported (encrypted and/or authenticated) across public, untrusted networks (such as the Internet). VPNs across the Internet are often used when private data networks are cost-prohibited. Windows comes with multiple built-in VPN protocols, including L2TP, PPTP, IPSec, SSL, and TLS. This chapter will cover these protocols in more detail later. Among the various solutions for segmenting networks, firewalls are considered the most security trustworthy, but also the most complex to configure. Routers can be used for basic—but efficient—packet filtering, but do not normally have the more sophisticated filtering options of a firewall. Ethernet switches can provide a minimal level of security protection on internal networks

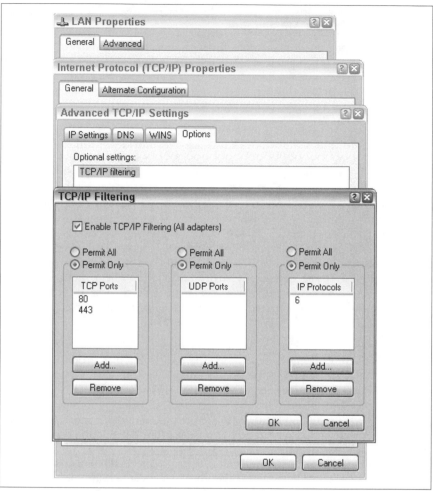

Figure 8-1. Windows TCP/IP Filtering configuration dialog box

by not allowing hosts to see other host's unicast network traffic, but malicious hackers can easily circumvent this protection. NAT is often enabled on many network devices or in RRAS, and it provides only a minimal level of protection against external intruders. IP Filters can be used for inbound blocking and may be the only default choice for legacy clients. VPNs are often used to protect confidential data traveling across untrusted networks.

Encryption

Encryption is a cryptographic process that prevents unauthorized parties from reading confidential information. Encryption is used in many areas of Windows, including EFS, HTTPS, Terminal Services, secure email, WEP, and as a component of most VPN protocols. Encryption algorithms are either symmetric or asymmetric.

Symmetric encryption ciphers

Symmetric encryption algorithms use the same secret key to encrypt the data as to decrypt it. With symmetric encryption, all intended authorized parties normally share the same secret key (which also prevents authentication of the sender). Symmetric encryption is usually stronger than asymmetric encryption for the same key size, but its number one problem is the inherent issue of how to securely transport the secret key to all participating parties.

Common Windows symmetric encryption algorithms, in increasing order of protection, are Rivest Cipher 4 (RC4), Data Encryption Standard (DES), strengthened DES (DESX), Triple DES (3DES), and Advanced Encryption Standard (AES). XP (SP1 and above) and Windows Server 2003 use AES with EFS by default. Nonservice-packed versions of XP use DESX with EFS by default, but switch to the stronger 3DES if the "Use FIPS compliant algorithms for encryption, hashing, and signing security" option is enabled. However, if the FIPS option is enabled on XP Pro SP1 or later or in Windows Server 2003, it actually downgrades the cryptographic protection from AES to 3DES. If FIPS is enabled, it increases Remote Desktop Protocol (RDP) encryption from RC4 to 3DES and requires that client or server to use TLS versus SSL for secure web transactions.

Asymmetric encryption ciphers

Asymmetric encryption always uses a private/public key pair for encryption and authentication. It uses one key to encrypt and another different but related key to decrypt. What one key encrypts, the other can decrypt. Each participating user keeps their private key confidential—never sharing. Theoretically, any other person in the world can have the user's public key.

A user wishing to encrypt something to another user must use the destination user's public key to encrypt the data. The receiver then uses his related private key, which only he has, to decrypt the encrypted data.

In most cases of asymmetric encryption, asymmetric ciphers are only used to securely transport the symmetric cipher key that was used to do the actual data encryption. With asymmetric encryption, a one-time (or session) symmetric encryption key is used to securely encrypt the data. The symmetric encryption key is then encrypted using the receiver's public asymmetric key. Both the encrypted data (encrypted by the session encryption key) and the encrypted session key are sent to the receiver. The receiver unlocks the encrypted session encryption key, which is then used to decrypt the encrypted data. This is an important point to understand and is the basis of much of today's popular encryption solutions (e.g., SSL, TLS, PKI, S/MIME, EFS, etc.).

Because only one user in an asymmetric cipher exchange has her unique legitimate secret key, any data that is encrypted by the sender's (also known as the *publisher's*) secret key, and subsequently decrypted later by the receiver using the legitimate related public key, can be authenticated as having been signed by the sender.

Table 8-1 illustrates encryption key uses.

Table 8-1. Asymmetric encryption key use

To do this	Sender uses	Receiver uses
Encryption	The receiver's public key to encrypt	His private key to decrypt
Authentication	Her private key to sign	The sender's public key to verify

Authentication

For our purposes, *authentication* is the process of verifying that an identity (i.e., an identity label such as a user account name) belongs to a particular person or computer. When the person or computer using a particular identity supplies the correct "secret" (e.g., a password) that only they should know, it proves ownership of the identity—i.e., authentication.

Supplying one of these three types of "secrets" can authenticate a user or computer's identity:

- Something only they know (e.g., password, PIN, etc.)
- Something only they are (i.e., biometrics)
- Something only they have (e.g., cryptographic key fob, smart card, etc.)

Each of these is known as an *authentication factor*. If a user or computer is asked for two of the three types of factors to authenticate, it is known as *two-factor authentication*. If the user or computer is asked for all three types of authentication to prove their identity, it is known as *multi-factor authentication*. Two-factor authentication is normally considered more secure than single-factor authentication, and multi-factor authentication is considered the most secure type of authentication (all other factors being equal). Environments requiring high security should use two- or multi-factor authentication for logon security.

The most common type of authentication in Windows is a logon password, although increasing smart card and two-factor support gets added to every new version of Windows. Windows XP Pro and Windows Server 2003 can natively support smart card authentication. In order to use a smart card, a logon user must have access to a smart card reader device.

Windows passwords

Windows passwords can be up to 127 characters long and be composed using any supported Unicode character, although the vast majority of Windows users include only letters, numbers, and other keyboard symbols in their passwords.

Windows passwords are stored in the Windows authentication databases (i.e., either the Security Accounts Manager or Active Directory databases) as cryptographic password hashes. Windows stores all passwords in two hashed forms: LAN Manager (LM) and NT hashes. The LM hash is very weak and easily crackable (i.e., convertible to the plain-text equivalent). The NT hash is a secure cryptographic hash, but is still subject to the normal password-cracking attacks. The NT hash is natively supported in Windows NT 4.0, Windows XP Pro, and Windows Server 2003 and later. To support NTT hashes, Windows 9x operating systems need to be fully patched, and the Directory Services Client Extension software needs to be installed. Most environments should consider disabling LM password hash storage if all necessary clients and servers support NT hashes. LM hash storage can be disabled by enabling the "Do not store LAN Manager hash on next password change" Security Option and changing all current passwords.

Authentication protocols

Windows uses various challenge-response authentication protocols to authenticate a user. Windows 2000 and later supports the following authentication protocols: LM, NTLM, NTLMv2, and Kerberos. Of the four protocols, only the latter two (NTLM version 2 and Kerberos) are considered secure. Authentication protocols are used when a user or computer attempts to authenticate during a Windows logon, and for other logon attempts with other protocols (e.g., Integrated Authentication with IIS, etc.).

Windows NT 4.0 and Windows 9x operating systems do not support Kerberos and can only support NTLMv2 if fully patched. Windows 9x clients must also have the Directory Services Client Extension software installed to support NTLMv2. Windows 2000, XP Pro, and Windows Server 2003 and above will use Kerberos to connect to Windows 2000 and above domain resources. For local logons or non-2000 and above domain resources, Windows will use one of the other three authentication protocols. Secure environments should disable the LM and NTLM (version 1) authentication protocols. This can be done by appropriately configuring the "LAN Manager authentication level" Security Option (see Figure 8-2) located in Group Policy or Local Computer Policy under Computer Configuration → Windows Settings → Security Settings ▸ Local Policies ▸ Security Options.

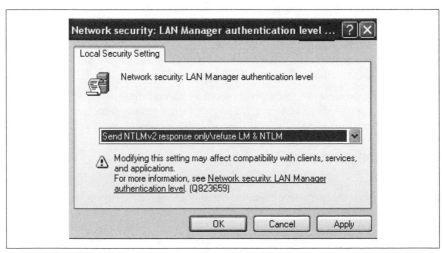

Figure 8-2. LAN Manager authentication level dialog box

Kerberos is considered a Single Sign-On (SSO) solution for Windows.

Trusted for Delegation

Although not commonly known by most users, all interactions between a user (or other security principal, such as a computer or group) and a Windows object occurs through a process called *impersonation* or *delegation*. When a user accesses an object, it does so using software (e.g., Windows Explorer, Microsoft Office, Internet Explorer, etc.). The involved software "takes" the user's security credentials and hands them to the security manager process, which then compares the user's credentials and identity against the resource's list (i.e., Access Control List) of what security principals should have access to a particular resource and what those allowed permissions are.

When software uses a security principal's credentials to access a local resource, the process is called *impersonation*. When software uses a security principal's credentials to access a network object, it is called *delegation*. In Windows 2000, only Kerberos authentication can be delegated. In Windows XP Pro and Windows Server 2003, other authentication protocols such as NTLMv2 can be used in delegation.

Some programs and services, such as EFS, require that the involved users or computers be trusted for delegation in order for the service or application to work correctly. For instance, EFS will not work on remote computers (EFS is inherently a local process) or between laptop users and their remote home file servers, unless the remote server computer account where the EFS files are stored is trusted for delegation. This is a common test question on Exam 70-298. A computer or user can be trusted for delegation by adding the account to the "Enable computer and user accounts to be trusted for delegation" user rights assignment option (see Figure 8-3). This special privilege should not be given lightly. An attacker compromising a trusted for delegation account can possibly compromise the involved account or service and use passed credentials maliciously.

In secure environments, sensitive accounts that should never be allowed to be used in delegation should specifically have their delegation ability disabled. This can be done in the account's User Account Properties (see Figure 8-4) by enabling the "Account is sensitive and cannot be delegated" option.

Windows environments requiring high security should disable the storage of LM password hashes, disable LM and NTLM authentication protocols, and review any user or computer account that is trusted for delegation.

Public Key Infrastructure

Asymmetric cryptography is an excellent option for encryption and authentication, as long as the private/public key pair can be relied upon as legitimate. Assuming the owner of the private/public key pair keeps his private key confidential and protected, the larger issue is how can anyone else be assured that a stated public key really is the legitimate public key? What is to prevent a malicious attacker from claiming to be the private key party, creating her own bogus private/public key pair, and distributing the forged public key to everyone else?

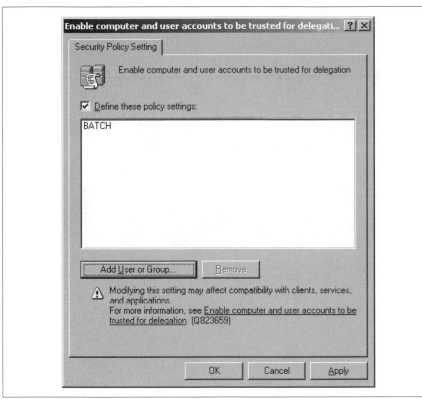

Figure 8-3. Enabling an account to be trusted for delegation

Public Key Infrastructure (PKI).

Public Key Infrastructure requires that a trusted third party (usually called the *Certification Authority*) verify and attest to the validity of the public keys used in an asymmetric transaction. Each user with a private/public key pair who wants to have a higher level of trust submits his public key to the Certification Authority (CA), who then verifies the legitimacy and ownership.

Usually, the CA asks for proof of ownership of the submitted public key in the form of additional authenticated material. A Windows CA may only require that the user already have an existing, authenticated user or computer account. When the user correctly logs on and gets authenticated during normal Windows logon authentication, it is enough proof for the Windows CA. External, public CAs (we will cover this later) might require a valid credit card number, Articles of Incorporation, or other public document attestation.

Digital certificate

When the public key submitter has successfully proven his authenticity as well as his key's authenticity to the CA, the CA will sign the submitted public key with the CA's private certificate signing key. This creates a *digital certificate*. A digital

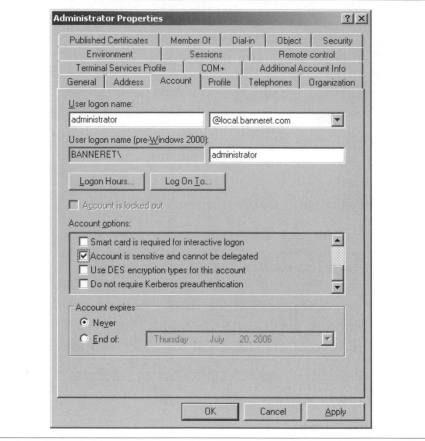

Figure 8-4. Ensuring that a particular account cannot be trusted for delegation

certificate is a user's (or computer's) public key signed, as verified by the CA. When a receiver wants to use another user's signed public key, she must first verify the legitimacy of the sender's public key by verifying the CA's signing. Because a sender's digital certificate is signed by the CA's private key, the receiver must have the CA's public key. This is often already preinstalled in Windows (and is called a *Trusted Certification Authority*), or the user must newly accept the CA's public key as trusted. The user then uses the CA's public key to verify the signed digital certificate (i.e., the user's public key signed, by the trusted CA). Once the sender's public key is verified, the receiver can use the user's public key to encrypt data to the user or verify anything signed and sent by the user.

As noted in the previous paragraph, digital certificates are usually given to users or computers (the latter is often called a *machine certificate*). When investigating various forms of asymmetric encryption and authentication, it is important to pay attention to the type of certificate. Some cryptographic programs, such as WEP, are only interested in machine authentication. Others, such as EFS, are interested in user authentication and protection. Not knowing the difference might lead an administrator to choose the wrong type of cryptographic solution.

When a PKI domain is in place, it is essentially stating that the participating user's (or computer's) public keys have been verified and signed by a mutually trusted third-party CA, and that it can be relied upon. This is different from self-signed applications, such as Pretty Good Privacy (PGP), where each receiver has to individually trust each sender's public key. In theory, the use of a PKI system means the participating public keys can be trusted more than with self-signed applications.

Certification Authority creation decisions

When a new PKI infrastructure is put in place, three major decisions need to be made about the Certification Authority server(s):

- Root or subordinate
- Offline or online
- Public or private

Every PKI domain starts with a *root* CA server. The first CA server in a PKI hierarchy is always the root. The root CA server contains a self-signed root CA certificate that begins the hierarchy of trust. In most cases, the root CA server does not hand out or verify individual digital certificates to other users and computers. Instead, one or more additional *subordinate* CA servers are created, and each of their personal signing certificates are signed by the root CA server. This, in effect, passes the root CA's signing authority down to the additional subordinate servers. The subordinate child CA servers may be limited in what, for who, and how long, they can sign. This is known as *qualified subordination*, and it's a new feature in Windows Server 2003 Certificate Services.

You can have one or more root CAs, although there is only one per PKI hierarchy. Each root CA is the king of its PKI domain. When more than one root CA is used, it is to create more than one PKI domain hierarchy. Separate root CAs are desirous when greater levels of security are needed between PKI domains. For instance, one root CA may be needed to handle digital certificate requests for a top secret web server project, and another used for securing web services and email for an entirely separate exchange project. Both projects might be within the same company and require PKI, but neither project has anything to do with the other. Separate root CAs may also be needed for geographical and organizational purposes as well. Of course, using more than one root CA within a company means more operational overhead and management.

The *child subordinate* CA servers are the ones that issue individual digital certificates to the participating users or computers. Subordinate servers in this role are known as *issuing* CA servers. Not all subordinate CA servers are issuing CAs. Depending on the overall PKI design, there may be one or more subordinate CA servers under the single root CA, and each eventually flows down into child-issuing CA servers that do the real digital certificate work. Figure 8-5 shows what is known as a *three-tier* PKI CA infrastructure. If the PKI project had a root CA, and then an immediately issuing CA, it would be known as a *two-tier* infrastructure. Although it is common in the real world to see a single CA server servicing the entire PKI domain, acting as both a root CA and an issuing CA, a *one-tier* infrastructure is considered very insecure.

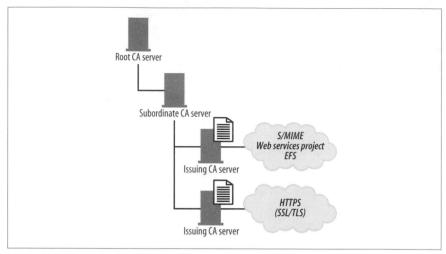

Figure 8-5. Example of a three-tier PKI domain.

This is because the root CA needs to be heavily secured, and in most cases made an *offline* root CA. An offline root is physically or logically disconnected from the PKI network in which it serves. In most cases, it is necessary for the root CA to be online so that it can issue new certificate signing authority certificates for lower child subordinates, and for other periodic housekeeping duties, such as publishing a certificate revocation list. The root CA is brought back online when needed, but is otherwise kept offline. Keeping the root CA offline significantly decreases the risk of malicious attack. Issuing CAs are usually online and operational, so that certificate requests and distributions can occur as required.

So the standard PKI domain includes an offline root CA and one or more online subordinate CA servers. All participating CAs need to be highly secured. If one of the CA servers becomes compromised, a malicious individual could create and assign rogue digital certificates and essentially break the trust of all digital certificates previously issued.

When setting up a PKI domain, another decision that needs to be made is whether or not the root CA and/or subordinates will issue publicly trusted digital certificates. A *public* CA is one that is widely trusted by the computing world and is usually previously installed as a *trusted root* CA in a wide number of computers. Publicly trusted CAs include Verisign, Thawte, and Microsoft. For instance, Microsoft Windows comes preinstalled with dozens of publicly trusted CAs (see Figure 8-6).

Publicly trusted PKI systems are almost mandatory for asymmetric solutions that will be accessed by the general public. For instance, if a company plans to have a web server with an SSL/TLS certificate, it is very advantageous for the company to use a web server digital certificate signed by a widely trusted public CA. Then when a user or computer connects to the web server and begins secure transmissions, the web server's digital certificate will already have been verified by the public CA as being legit and valid. Participating users will still need to decide

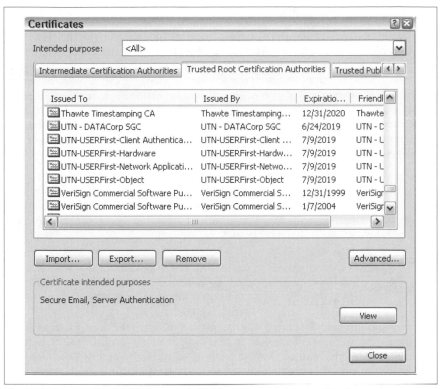

Figure 8-6. Example of publicly trusted Certification Authorities in Windows

whether they will trust the digital certificate, but the public CA's automatic attestation means that the user can at least trust that the submitted digital certificate is from who it claims to be from. Publicly validated certificates usually have a cost premium associated with them.

Private CAs are used frequently as well, especially for internal projects and internal employee needs. Any Windows server (NT 4.0 with option pack, Windows 2000 Server, and Windows Server 2003) comes with a built-in Microsoft PKI service called Certificate Services. It can be installed and configured to serve the internal enterprise. An administrator can use Group Policy to install the internal, private CA as a trusted CA, but it will never be considered a public CA. The idea is that internal employees, and others relying on a private CA, already have a previously established trust with the enterprise that is using the private CA. These individuals don't need a third-party trust entity to verify the legitimacy of the private digital certificates. Practically, using a private CA means a user relying on a digital certificate signed by the private CA may get an additional prompt to also trust the CA that issued the digital certificate. Using a public CA removes this additional PKI decision.

Exam 70-298
Study Guide

Certification Authority revocation

Certification Authority managers have a handful of duties, including accepting digital certificate requests, evaluating the request, issuing and renewing digital certificates, and revoking compromised or invalid certificates. If a user's private/public key becomes compromised, the CA server manager can *revoke* the digital certificate—a process called *revocation*. When a certificate is revoked, the CA manager adds the digital certificate's serial number to the issuing CA's *certificate revocation list (CRL)*. Participating programs and browsers involved in the PKI domain can request a CRL from the CA server, in order to verify that any given digital certificate issued by the CA has not been revoked.

In some cases, it might make more sense for a root CA to revoke a subordinate CA's signing certificate. For instance, suppose an issuing CA was dedicated to a programming project that was discontinued. The root CA could revoke the issuing CA's signing certificate, which would have the effect of revoking any certificate the issuing CA had ever issued.

 In theory, revocation works well, but in practice, many programs and browsers do not check for certificate revocation, so that revoking a certificate might not have the intended desired consequence.

PKI domains are an excellent way of establishing public key trust and are becoming more popular. PKI is used in many applications, including secure email, wireless security, EFS, and software publishing. Understanding PKI and Microsoft Certificate Services will become essential for most administrators as more security technologies begin to rely upon it. Microsoft Certificate Services will be covered in more detail later. It is a heavily tested topic on Exam 70-298.

Auditing

Auditing refers to the collection of events and conditions—adverse and otherwise—that allow event tracking and security analysis. Although Windows has many different logfiles (e.g., IIS, RRAS, installation logs, etc.), most Windows security events are logged to the *Security log* and are readily viewable in the *Event Viewer* application. In order for the Security log to collect information, one or more Windows audit categories must be enabled. The audit categories are:

- Audit account logon events
- Audit account management
- Audit directory service access
- Audit logon events
- Audit object access
- Audit policy change
- Audit privilege use
- Audit process tracking
- Audit system events

Each audit category (see Figure 8-7) can be enabled for the success or failure of an event. If a security principal (i.e., user or computer) attempts to perform an audited action and is successful, it will be recorded as a success event. If a security principal attempts to perform an audited action and is unsuccessful, it will be recorded as a failure event. For example, if a user tries to change the system time but does not have the user privileges to do so, it will be recorded as a failure event. Often, failure events are just as important as success events. In another example, if a malicious attack attempts a brute force password attack, there will likely be many more failure events than success events, and the sheer number of failure events should arouse the suspicions of the administrator.

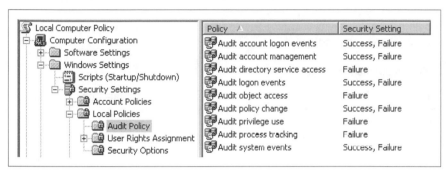

Figure 8-7. Available audit categories

Audit account logon events enables auditing domain account logons and authentication events. Audit object access records registry, files, and printer access. Audit Policy changes tracks changes to audit policies and security policies. Privilege use auditing tracks the success or failure of user rights assignments (also known as *user special privileges*). Audit process tracking logs messages each time a process starts, stops, or has a status change. Audit system events logs major OS happenings such as a startup, shutdown, or system time changes. Using Audit Policy, some audit categories can only be enabled or disabled for all users. Others can be enabled or disabled on a per-user or group basis.

 Per User Selective Auditing, introduced in Windows XP Pro SP2 and Windows Server 2003 SP1, allows any audit category to be enabled or disabled on a per-user basis. Per User Selective Auditing is interfaced using the Auditusr.exe executable and is not accessible through the normal Audit Policy tools or methods. Per User Selective Auditing is a new feature and so far has not been tested on the exam. Candidates should act as if it doesn't exist when answering exam questions.

The following sections describe each audit category in more detail.

Audit account logon events

If enabled on a domain controller and domain accounts are used, Audit account logon events are logged on the authorizing domain controller no matter which computer gets logged on or authenticated to. This audit category tracks domain account authentication events and logon behavior. Account logons are tracked when a user logs on to a computer or when a security principal accesses a resource (such as file or printer share). Audit account logons can only be enabled or disabled for all users in normal audit policy.

Audit account logon events were introduced in Windows 2000. On Windows NT, Audit logon events were the only possible choice for tracking security principal logon and authentication events. This necessitated visiting each computer in a network to enable logging and going back to check the logs when trying to track a malicious hacker across a network. Having Audit account logon events means going to every domain controller computer in a domain (at most) when tracking malicious logons versus visiting every computer in the domain (as long as domain accounts were involved).

Audit account management

Enabling Audit account management tracks when a user account or group is created, changed, or deleted. It also tracks when a password is set or changed, or when group membership is modified. Audit account management can only be enabled or disable for all users in regular Audit Policy.

Audit directory service access

Audit directory service access records the event of a user accessing an Active Directory object. It can track hacker activities during a compromise, but creates a lot of uninteresting "noise." This means that when this category is enabled, lots of event log entries will be created even for legitimate traffic. So much so that determining what is and isn't authorized can be difficult to figure out. Still, if a malicious event involves Active Directory, this category can provide lots of valuable data. It can be enabled on a per-user or group basis in normal Audit Policy.

Audit logon events

This category records logons and authentication events at the computer where a resource is accessed and tracks domain account logons on the computer where a logon event is happening. This is the opposite effect of Audit account logons. Audit logon events can also track local account logons. Audit logons can only be disabled or enabled for all users in normal Audit Policy.

Audit object access

This category tracks success or failure of a security principal (user, group, service, or computer account) trying to access a file, folder, registry key, or printer. After the category is enabled, auditing must be turned on by selecting the individual object and security principal to be tracked in Windows Explorer. This latter step is often forgotten by security administrators, leading to blank security logs.

When enabled, object accesses will generate multiple event messages for a single object access—one for each accessed requested. Most object accesses will create four to eight event messages for a single object access event. Audit object access can be enabled or disabled on a per-user or group basis in normal Audit Policy.

Audit Policy change

Audit Policy change tracks any change to user rights assignment, audit, or trust policies. It might catch a hacker attempting to elevate privileges. Audit Policy change can only be enabled or disabled on a global basis in normal Audit Policy.

Audit privilege use

Audit privilege use tracks use or attempted use of user rights assignment privileges. Privileges allow a user, group, computer, or service to do something across a wide range objects not explicitly given by regular security permission (e.g., Logon as service or Logon as a batch job). Audit privilege use can only be enabled or disabled on a global basis in regular Audit Policy and across most user privileges at once. However, three user privileges (i.e., Backup files and directories, Restore files and directories, and the access of global system objects) require additional enabling under Security Options in Group Policy to enable auditing. This is because enabling those three would create so much noise that the logs would be useless. For instance, the nightly tape backup would likely create hundreds of thousands of events from doing the normal backup.

Audit process tracking

Audit process tracking stores detailed tracking information for events such as program activation, process exit, handle duplication, and indirect object access. Like auditing directory access, this audit category is very noisy, but will reveal every program and command a malicious hacker tried or used. On standalone domain controllers and other servers in which new programs are not stopping and starting all the time, this category will not produce as many events as auditing directory access. This category can only be enabled or disabled globally for all security principals in normal Audit Policy.

Audit system events

Audit system events tracks when a security principal restarts or shuts down the computer or when an event occurs that affects either the system security or the Security log.

Auditing success or failure and which accounts

Exam 70-298 will often test your knowledge of when to enable success or failure events. In general, audit both success and failure events when told to audit all events or when told to audit a computer or resource for malicious use. Otherwise, read the test question for more clues on what type of event(s) to enable. Usually these types of test questions are more about reading comprehension than product knowledge.

For audit categories that allow individual users or groups to be monitored, choose the Everyone group if asked to track all users. Add the Anonymous null session user (if offered on the test) if a malicious hacker is suggested.

Log rotation

Security logs should be collected and rotated frequently enough that data is not overwritten. It is important that logs be rotated on a regular basis in order to balance accuracy and usability. Logs can quickly become overly large. A monitored computer can easily have daily logs tens to hundreds of megabytes in size. If the logfiles are not ended and new logs started (i.e., rotated) frequently enough, the logfiles will grow too large to handle easily during the data analysis portion. Smaller logs offer better performance. The offsetting problem is in losing accuracy because similar malicious events may be spread across two or more logs. Thoughtful decision making must accompany logfile rotation and archiving.

The Event View application allows an administrator to set various log rotation settings (see Figure 8-8).

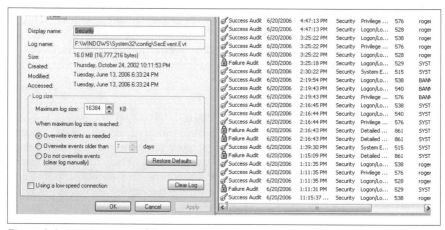

Figure 8-8. Event Viewer with log rotation options

The three main log rotation options are:

- Overwrite events as needed
- Overwrite events older than x days
- Do not overwrite events (clear log manually)

You can only choose one log rotation option. If one of the two latter choices is enabled, and the logfile meets its maximum logfile size indicated in the dialog box (as shown in Figure 8-8), new events will not be added to the log until something is corrected. With the latter option, the administrator can optionally choose to halt the system (i.e., blue screen) if the logfile becomes full. Although halting used to be the default option, now this option requires enabling a second Security Option called "Shutdown system immediately if unable to log security audits."

Centralized event collection

In most networks, individually checking each security log manually on every PC almost guarantees that the security logs won't be checked routinely. Smart administrators collect security events to a centralized database and monitor only for significant events worth additional consideration. Microsoft provides several programs for centralized collection, including Microsoft Audit Collection System, Log Parser, SMS, and MOM. The latter two options are occasionally mentioned in Exam 70-298. *Microsoft Systems Management Server* (SMS) is an encompassing host and network management tool that has dozens of significant capabilities, along with collection of security log data and alerting on significant events. *Microsoft Operations Manager* (MOM) is a server-installable program that is preconfigured to collect and alert on significant audit events. MOM is very useful because Microsoft's own experts define what events are and aren't critical. The exam might also mention System Monitor, which can enable many different types of system counters, but System Monitor's counters are not very useful for security auditing.

Exam 70-298 also tests IIS logging, which is covered in a separate section on IIS later in this chapter.

Security Infrastructure Technologies

Microsoft provides several significant infrastructure technologies to run and manage a Windows network. This section of the chapter will cover securing infrastructure servers, certificate services, patch management, remote administration tools, terminal services, and Windows trust models.

Securing Infrastructure Server

Infrastructure servers are the servers that handle the large administrative tasks in a Windows network: Active Directory domain controllers, DNS, DHCP, WINS, etc. Infrastructure servers, by their very nature, contain useful enterprise information and must be widely available on the network. This makes them attractive to attackers. All infrastructure servers should be strongly secured. Following are some general recommendations to harden infrastructure servers:

- Restrict physical access.
- Minimize who can log into the server locally and remotely.
- Mandate long and complex passwords for infrastructure server administrators.
- Uninstall or disable unneeded services and applications.
- Do not install IIS, Microsoft Office, or other high-risk applications, if possible.
- Do not browse to untrusted sites using Internet Explorer; limit Internet browsing as much as possible.
- Separate server roles where possible (e.g., try not to let a domain controller also be the DNS server as well, don't let the Certificate Services server run IIS for web enrollment, etc.).
- Provide redundant servers for critical services (e.g., Active Directory, DNS, etc.)
- Manage infrastructure servers using their own high-security GPOs
- Keep server security patches up-to-date

- Consider enabling a host-based firewall to minimize unneeded port connections
- Use IPSec to minimize traffic connections
- Disable booting on anything besides the primary hard drive, and password protect the BIOS to prevent boot priority changes
- Implement a thorough auditing policy, recording as much activity as possible in case it is needed for forensic investigations

Infrastructure servers should be among the highest-secured computers in any environment.

Secure DNS design. DNS infrastructure servers deserve special attention. The strongest security decision a DNS administrator can make is to ensure that internal DNS domains are not commingled with externally reachable DNS domains. DNS administrators want to make sure that private IP addresses and internal hostnames are not reachable by external, unauthorized users. Every entity should have separate internal and external DNS domains, and where appropriate, separate DNS servers for internal and external domains.

DNS servers should be configured to ensure secure zone transfers between primary (Active Directory-Integrated or standard) and secondary DNS servers. This is configured in the DNS server and ensures that only predefined servers can receive DNS zone information (see Figure 8-9).

DNS servers should be configured to require secure dynamic updates (see Figure 8-10). By default, Windows 2000 and later computers will attempt to register their IP address and DNS hostname with the DNS server listed in their primary DNS field in the Internet Protocol properties dialog box. Secure dynamic updates (a default Windows DNS server setting) requires that the host attempting to submit the hostname and IP address already be logged on and authenticated before attempting the registration.

 Don't confuse Secure zone transfers with Secure Dynamic Updates.

DNS servers should be configured to prevent cache pollution. Cache pollution is when an unauthoritative DNS server responds with a host IP address that does not belong to one of its controlled zones. Attackers can use this to redirect users to spoofed locations. Disabling cache pollution is the default on Windows DNS servers, but can be disabled in the DNS server configuration dialog box (see Figure 8-11).

All infrastructure servers, including DNS, need to be securely configured.

Certificate Services

Microsoft Certificate Services is heavily tested on Exam 70-298. Most test candidates encounter multiple scenarios involving this topic. Certificate Services is Microsoft's Certification Authority component for Windows PKI. Available since

---

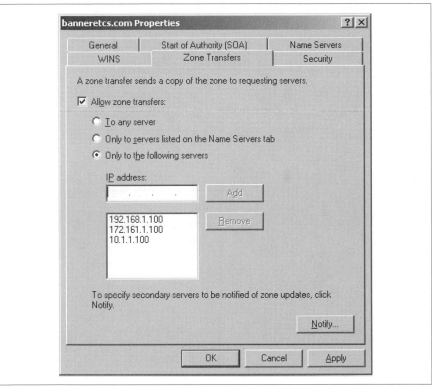

Figure 8-9. Configuring secure zone transfers

Windows NT 4.0, Certificate Services is a full-fledged and mature product competing with other CA technologies. Exam 70-298 will not usually test on the details, as they will be presented below, but understanding how Certificate Services works will help candidates handle any proposed test questions.

Once you have a PKI domain infrastructure, you can use the CA server wherever you need asymmetric cryptography (accounting for public versus private needs). Microsoft networks commonly use Certificate Services for the following applications:

- EFS
- IPSec
- Code signing
- HTTPS
- S/MIME and Exchange
- Wireless security
- Smart cards

Several of these applications will be covered in the following sections.

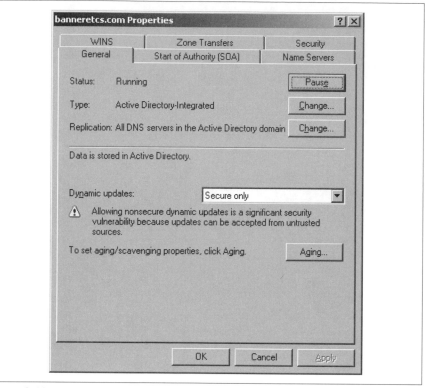

Figure 8-10. Requiring secure dynamic updates

Installing Certificate Services

Certificate Services is not installed by default, but can be added under Add/ Remove Programs, Windows Components. In most cases, administrators will install the IIS web component of Certificate Services as well, during the install.

The first major decision is whether the CA server will be a root or subordinate CA server. The first CA server in any PKI domain must be a root CA. After authorizing one or more subordinate issuing CA servers, the root CA server can be taken offline until needed.

Enterprise or standalone CA? Certificate Services also asks the installer if the CA server should be an enterprise CA (i.e., integrated with Active Directory) or standalone. If the users or computers interacting with the CA server are (or are to be) located in Active Directory, it's probably best if the CA server is installed as an enterprise CA. If the CA server will not be interacting with Active Directory users and computers, it should be installed as a standalone CA server. Here are the issues and benefits of an enterprise CA:

- Requires AD and DNS (and IIS as well for web enrollment), but does not have to be installed on a domain controller
- Should be used when dealing with users and computers in the company

---

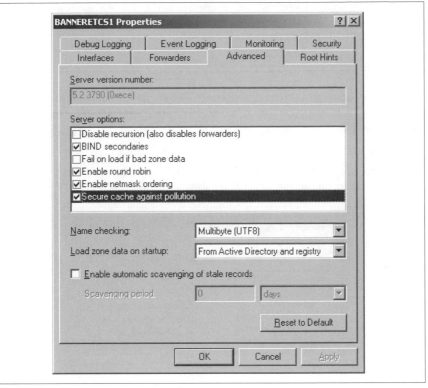

Figure 8-11. Preventing DNS cache pollution

- Can automatically verify user's identity in AD, and auto-enroll or auto-approve certificates
- When installed, uses Group Policy to propagate its digital certificate to the Trusted Root Certification Authorities store for all users and computers in the local domain
- Allows CA managers to use certificate templates
- Can publish certificates and certificate revocation lists to Active Directory
- Allows auto-enrollment (covered later in this chapter)
- Allows auto-approval (standalones only have manual approval)
- Allows auto-mapping certificate to user or computer accounts
- Can create and use wireless and smart card certificates (standalones cannot)
- Allows control over certificates and the certificate process using GPOs

When an enterprise CA is installed, a copy of its root certificate is placed in Active Directory as a Trusted Root Certification Authority. Other CAs' (standalone or commercial) certificates might have to be added manually.

In order for an enterprise CA to publish certificates to an Active Directory domain, it (i.e., its computer account) must be part of the *Cert Publishers* group in the domain it wishes to publish or issue certificates. This happens automatically for all enterprise CAs in the domain in which the CA runs, but must be done manually in all other domains.

Standalone CAs are used for external needs or non-AD:

- Must run on a member or standalone server
- Can be used as a Trusted Offline Root when the extranet or Internet is involved
- Doesn't have certificate templates; users must give additional identifying info
- Can't do smart card or wireless certificates for logging on to AD

Once Certificate Services is installed, it is accessed through the Certification Authority administrator tool or MMC snap-in (see Figure 8-12).

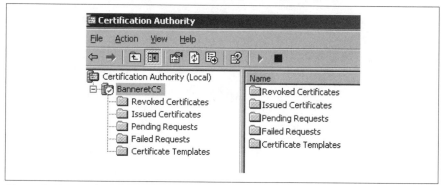

Figure 8-12. Certification Authority console

Windows Server 2003 Certificate Services allows a certificate manager to do the following:

Publish certificates
    Create and publish certificates to Active Directory, IIS, or another location where users, computers, and applications can retrieve them

Enroll clients
    When the client requests a certificate approve request and then issues a certificate

Renew certificates
    Can renew expired or nearly expired certificates

Revoke certificates
    Publish revoke certificates to a CRL at regular intervals

Certificate templates

Digital certificates are created by approving and publishing certificate templates to the Certification Authority. Certificates contain different information for different PKI uses (e.g., user, logon authentication, smart card, computer authentication, EFS recovery agent, etc.). An IPSec certificate contains different information than a EFS certificate. For this reason, Microsoft Certification Authorities use certificate templates to create certificates. Each template contains predefined fields of information (e.g., username, email address, etc.) that are required to approve and publish a digital certificate.

Every certificate request is issued against a particular certificate template. Certificate templates are accessed through a Certificate Templates MMC console or by right-clicking the *Certificate Templates* container object in the Certification Authority console and choosing *Manage* (see Figure 8-13).

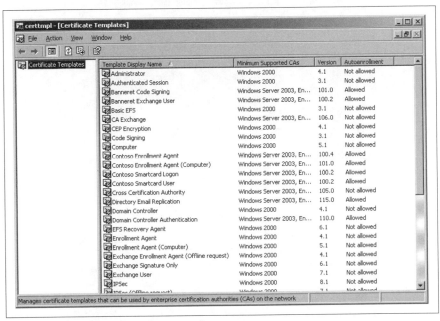

Figure 8-13. Certificate Templates console

The digital certificate publishing process includes the following steps:

1. Using the Certificate Templates console, the certificate administrator creates or modifies a certificate template.

2. Configure appropriate fields in the Certificate Template (see Figure 8-14).

3. Permissions are assigned to the template (covered in the next section), including what users and groups can request certificates based upon the certificate template, whether or not auto-enrollment is enabled, and who can manage the certificates based on the certificate template.

4. The certificate manager than publishes the certificate template to the Certification Authority.

5. The user or computer requests (or auto-enrolls) a particular certificate.

6. The Certification Authority matches the request against a particular certificate template.

7. The request is either manually approved by a certificate manager or auto-approved by the Certification Authority, if the certificate template was configured that way and the submitted information meets the request.

8. If approved, the user or computer gets the new certificate and can then install it.

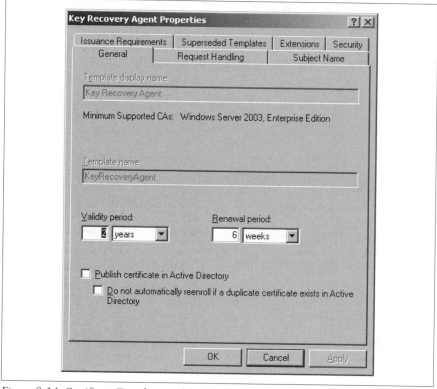

Figure 8-14. Certificate Template modification example

Certificate template permissions

Each certificate template has the following permissions (see Figure 8-15), which can be allowed or denied:

- Full Control
- Read
- Write
- Enroll
- Autoenroll

Usually, only certificate managers have Full Control. A user requesting a certificate must have Read and Enroll permissions to the Certificate Template that her request is based upon. If the Auto-enroll permission is enabled, it ensures that Active Directory will automatically initiate the certificate request when the user or computer logs on. The certificate request must still be approved (either manually or automatically).

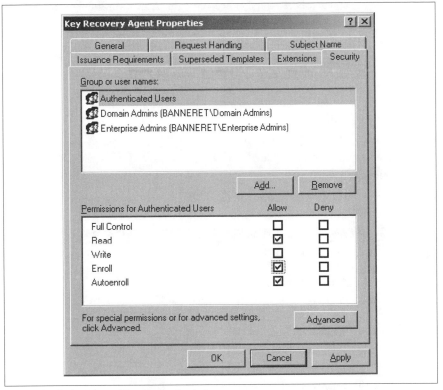

Figure 8-15. Certificate Template permissions

Here are the issues and requirements of auto-enrollment:

- Works only on certificates from a Microsoft Windows Server 2003 enterprise CA
- Works only on XP Pro and Windows Server 2003 computers, but not on Windows 2000 computers
- Works only with version 2 Certificate Templates (which are new to Windows Server 2003)
- Is enabled by default in Group Policy at the \Windows Settings\Security Settings\ Public Key Policies leaf under Computer Configuration or User Configuration leaf objects
- A user or computer account needs Read, Enroll, and Autoenroll permissions to the certificate template for auto-enrollment to work

Do not confuse auto-enrollment with *Automatic Certificate Request Settings* (ACRS). ACRS is also available, and works with Windows 2000 and later computer accounts. But ACRS works only with version 1 certificate templates—of which there are only a limited number of types—and with domain computer accounts and certificates.

Manual certificate requests

If the Autoenroll permission is not enabled, the user must manually request the certificate. A manual certificate request can be done many different ways, including:

- Through the Certificates console
- With a certificate request file
- Through web enrollment

Users can request certificates using the Certificates console (see Figure 8-16).

Figure 8-16. Manually requesting a new certificate using the Certificates console

A user can also create a certificate request file. It usually ends with an *.Inf* file extension, but its contents and format are beyond the scope of this book. The Certreq.exe utility can then be used to submit the request to the Certification Authority.

Web enrollment. Perhaps the easiest way to submit a certificate request is using web enrollment. Web enrollment can be installed as an optional component of Certificate Services. When installed, it creates a new virtual directory called CertSrv in IIS. Users can access it by typing in the web server's name or IP address followed by \CertSrv. The web enrollment interface is shown in Figures 8-17 and 8-18. Figure 8-17 shows the main web enrollment web site home page, and Figure 8-18 shows some of the advanced options that can be selected while requesting a certificate.

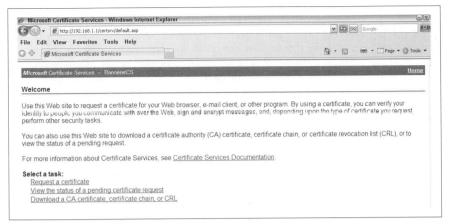

Figure 8-17. Web enrollment home page

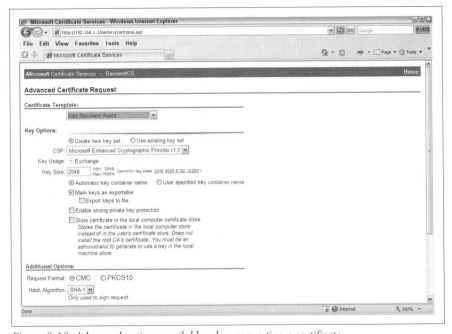

Figure 8-18. Advanced options available when requesting a certificate

For security reasons, the web enrollment web site should not be located on the same server as Certificate Services.

No matter how the certificate is requested, when approved, it will become available for pick up in a predefined location (if a nonenterprise CA is used) or sent automatically to the user's desktop to install (if an enterprise CA is involved). The user must usually manually install the certificate by completing the Certificate Install wizard.

If laptops require machine certificates to participate wirelessly (i.e., 802.1x), they cannot get the certificate wirelessly to begin with because they don't have the certificate they need to connect to the wireless network. The laptop user must obtain the certificate by connecting to the LAN or have the certificate imported manually via a floppy disk or alternative method.

Auto-mapping and client-mapping

Microsoft enterprise CAs can also use Active Directory to automatically associate an approved certificate with a user or computer account. This is known as *auto-mapping*. Any time a certificate is associated with an Active Directory user or computer, it is called *client-mapping*. In IIS, an administrator can require that all connecting HTTPS users have a client-side certificate to prove their identity to the server. Client-mapping is also known as *Directory Services Mapping*.

Key archival

Without exception, the single most important concept to understand when implementing a PKI solution is key archival. The asymmetric encryption used in a PKI solution is normally very secure. If the end user or computer loses the private key (which decrypts the encrypted data), then unless their private key is backed up elsewhere, the data could be lost forever.

An administrator should not implement PKI or any technology that relies upon asymmetric encryption (e.g., EFS, secured email) without first instituting a rock solid key archival plan.

Unfortunately, Microsoft Windows stores the user's or the computer's PKI private key within their user or local machine profile. User profiles are notorious for being lost, damaged, and abandoned. And an administrative action as simple as resetting a user's password may make their PKI private key unavailable. Administrators and users must assume that the original copy of their private key will be lost or unavailable at some future point in time.

End users can be allowed to manually back up their private keys. A setting in the Certificate Template called "Allow private key to be exported" (see Figure 8-19) must be enabled prior to the issuing of the certificate to the user. Backed-up private keys are normally password-protected, and should be stored in two physically separate, secure locations. It is not unusual for the backup private key to be corrupted or lost, so make two copies and store them in two different locations.

A better choice is to enable automatic key archival on the CA (see Figure 8-20). This is a new feature in Windows Server 2003 Certificate Services, but if implemented, it nearly guarantees that a copy of every private key issued by the CA server will be available if needed in an emergency recovery event. Enable the "Archive subject's encryption private key" option (as shown in Figure 8-19) for each certificate template you wish to have the private key automatically backed up on. Next, enable the "Archive the key" option on the CA server Recovery Agent tab under the CA server Properties (see Figure 8-20). Then add one or more recovery agents.

Contoso Enrollment Agent (Computer) Properties   ? X

| Issuance Requirements | Superseded Templates | Extensions | Security |
| General | Request Handling | Subject Name |

Purpose: [Signature and encryption ▼]

☐ Archive subject's encryption private key

☐ Include symmetric algorithms allowed by the subject

☐ Delete revoked or expired certificates (do not archive)

Minimum key size: [1024 ▼]

☑ Allow private key to be exported

Do the following when the subject is enrolled and when the private key
associated with this certificate is used:

● Enroll subject without requiring any user input

○ Prompt the user during enrollment

○ Prompt the user during enrollment and require user input when the
   private key is used

To choose which cryptographic service providers
(CSPs) should be used, click CSPs.   [CSPs...]

[OK]   [Cancel]   [Apply]

Figure 8-19. Allowing private key to be exported

Recovery agents are selected user accounts given a Recovery Agent certificate. If a users (or computer's) private key is lost, the recovery agent can log on, extract the backed-up private key, and republish it to the original recipient. Key recovery is not an overly easy process and requires several steps. You can require that it take more than one recovery agent to recover an archived key.

In high-security environments, the Recovery Agent user is a special user account made just for recovering lost private keys. The user account is created, a Recovery Agent certificate is installed, the recovery agent's private key is then exported and removed from the network, and the Recovery Agent user account is disabled until needed. When a data recovery event happens, the administrator can re-enable the Recovery Agent's user account, re-import the private key, and then let the user perform the key recovery process and re-disable it afterward.

Key Recovery Agents should not be confused with the EFS Recovery Agent. A Key Recovery Agent recovers other user's private keys, which the original user (or other specified agent) then uses to recover the encrypted files. An EFS Recovery Agent always gets a backup copy of the file's symmetric encryption key and can directly recover the related encrypted files without the original user's private key.

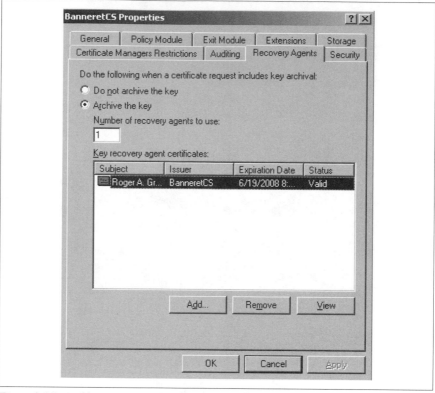

Figure 8-20. Enabling automatic key archival on the CA

Certificate Revocation List

A CA server should print an updated Certificate Revocation List (CRL) at regular intervals. Windows Server 2003 introduced the concept of dynamic CRLs. Before, every CRL contained every revoked certificate serial number. Dynamic CRLs contain just the list of newly revoked certificates. A Windows Server 2003 CA will publish normal (i.e., complete) CRLs at longer, predefined time intervals, and small, dynamic CRLs at more frequent time intervals. Dynamic CRL updates improve revocation lookup times and allow the CRL to be published more frequently.

CA roles and administrative groups

Windows Server 2003 allows a Certificate Services server to have securely defined administrative roles. The idea is to give different administrators different rights and roles so that no one user has all the roles and permissions.

Roles and groups	Security permission	Description
Local Administrator	Install Certificate Services	Only the local administrator can install application software, including installing Certificate Services.
		Membership in the local Administrators group on the CA is required to renew the CA certificate. Members of this group are considered to be all powerful on the CA, with administrative authority over all other CA roles.
CA Administrator	Manage CA permission	This is a CA role and includes the ability to assign all other CA roles, renew the CA's certificate, create CRLs, configure and maintain the CA, and read certificates. Does not allow request approval.
		Local Administrators, Enterprise Admins, and Domain Admins are CA Administrators by default on an Enterprise CA.
		Only local Administrators are CA Administrators by default on a standalone CA. If the standalone CA is logged on to an Active Directory domain, Domain Admins are also CA Administrators.
Certificate Manager	Issue and Manage Certificates permission	Approve, revoke, unrevoke, and renew certificates. This is a CA role. This role is sometimes referred to as CA Officer.
Enrollees	Authenticated Users	Enrollees are clients who are authorized to request certificates from the CA as well as to request CRLs. This is not a CA role. A user must have Read and Enroll permissions on a certificate template to request a certificate based on that template.

All CA roles are assigned and modified by local administrators, enterprise admins, and domain admins using the Security tab on the CA Server console's Properties tab.

Users can have multiple roles unless "role separation" is enforced. The CA Administrator and Certificate Manager roles can be assigned to either Active Directory users or local users in the Security Accounts Manager (SAM).

Secure email. PKI domains are frequently used to secure email transmissions, both encrypted and authenticated. Microsoft Certificate Services and Exchange both support Secure MIME or S/MIME. You can secure many Exchange services, including SMTP, POP, IMAP, NNTP, and Outlook for Web Access (Server 2003 only). For email to external customers, it is strongly suggested that you use a public CA.

Generally, the steps used to configure secure email for use in Outlook or Outlook Express are:

1. Enable and publish the Exchange User or Exchange (Signature Only) Certificate Templates.
2. Install the resulting Exchange certificate to the client computer.
3. Install the certificate in Outlook or Outlook Express.
4. Select the Encrypt or Sign button in Outlook or Outlook Express (see Figure 8-21).

In order to encrypt a message to someone else, you must have already installed his public key.

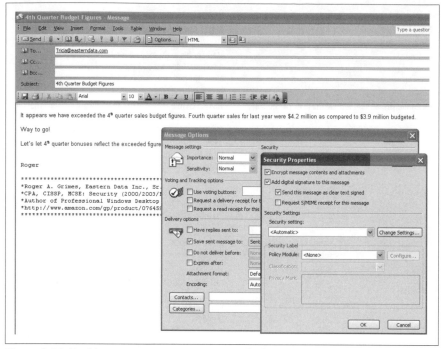

Figure 8-21. Enabling encryption or signing in Outlook

Smart cards. Smart cards are physical credit-card-sized security tokens that hold a user's (or computer's) asymmetric private and/or public keys. The user can put her smart card into a smart card reader and type in her PIN to authenticate to Windows.

Although smart card support is native in Windows XP Pro and Windows Server 2003, it requires a significant amount of planning and setup. You need the following components:

- Certification Authority (CA)
- Smart Card Certificates
- Active Directory
- Smart cards
- Smart Card Readers/Writers
- Smart Card Software (to interface to the reader/writer)
- Windows 2000 and later clients

Further, to deploy smart cards in a Windows 2000 or Windows Server 2003 Active Directory environment, the following requirements must be met:

- All domain controllers and computers in the Active Directory forest must trust the root CA of the Smart Card certificate's certificate chain.

- The CA that issues the Smart Card certificate must be included in the Active Directory NT Authority (NTAuth) store.
- Kerberos authentication must be used.

The general steps for installing a smart card are as follows:

1. Install Smart Card Readers/Writers and accompanying software to all involved computers, including the CA.
2. Install Internet Information Services (IIS) to support web enrollment.
3. Install and configure Certificate Services as an enterprise CA, if needed.
4. Include a web enrollment component.
5. Configure and publish the following templates to the Certificate Services CA:
   a. Enrollment Agent
   b. Enrollment Agent (computer)
   c. Smart Card Logon
   d. Smart Card User
6. Establish an Enrollment Agent.
7. Configure the web enrollment web site to be in the Local Intranet security zone on Enrollment Agent and/or the user's computer(s).
8. Allow Enrollment Agent to request Smart Card Certificates on behalf of other users.
9. Now authorized users can request a Smart Card Certificate from the web enrollment web site:
   a. Click on "Request a certificate link."
   b. Click on "Or, submit an advanced certificate request."
   c. Click on "Create and submit a request to this CA."
   d. Choose the correct Smart Card Certificate type in the Certificate Template field and click on the Submit button at the bottom of the page. Type in the PIN, if requested.
   e. After the certificate request is approved, install the Smart Card Certificate.

Enrollment workstation. When using smart cards, most CA administrators set up an *enrollment workstation*, where a trusted employee (called the *Enrollment Agent*) requests a Smart Card Certificate on behalf of the intended smart card user (see Figure 8-22). The eventual smart card user shows up at the enrollment workstation, inserts his smart card, types in his new associated PIN, and retrieves the created Smart Card Certificate to his smart card that is now inside the reader. Windows Server 2003 has an Enrollment Agent and Enrollment Agent (computer) Certificate Templates that must be used to create the enrollment workstation.

New features of Windows Server 2003 Certificate Services

Windows Server 2003 Certificate Services has several improved features over Windows 2000 Certificate Services:

- User auto-enrollment (must have XP or above)

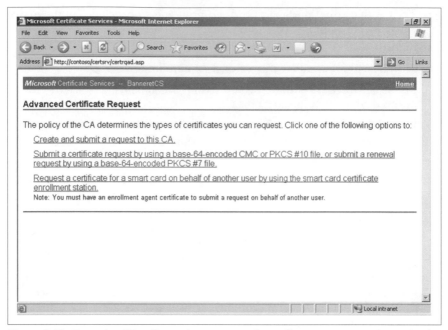

Figure 8-22. Example of Enrollment Agent using web enrollment to request a Smart Card Certificate on behalf of another user

- Version 2 Certificate Templates
- Improved key recovery
- Delta CRLs (just the changes since the last full CRL)
- Qualified subordination
- New command-line utilities

In a Windows 2000 domain, an administrator might have to upgrade the schema to support Windows Server 2003 Certificate Services using ADPREP /FORESTPREP. The primary symptom is that a new Windows Server 2003 Certificate Server has been installed in an existing Windows 2000 network, and the new features listed above are not available.

Backing up a CA server

A CA server can back up and restore a CA database by doing the following:

- Using Backup and Restore in the Certification Authority console
- Using Certutil.exe with the –backup and –restore parameters
- System State backup or restore

Alternately, you can restore a corrupted CA database by doing an *Automated System Restore* (ASR). The ASR backs up the local System State, which contains the CA database, the CA server configuration, and the CA server's private key.

Microsoft Certificate Services is a highly functional and versatile PKI solution.

Patch Management

Keeping Windows and other hosted applications up to date with all required security patches is one of the single best security defenses an administrator can implement. Manually patching each computer can be a time-consuming process that more than likely leads to missed and slow patching. This section will cover Microsoft's most popular patch management solutions, including Microsoft Baseline Security Analyzer, Windows Update, Automatic Update, Software Update Services, and other enterprise options.

Microsoft Baseline Security Analyzer

Microsoft Baseline Security Analyzer (MBSA) is a free patching and vulnerability detection tool from Microsoft. It must be downloaded from Microsoft's web site and installed on Windows 2000 and above computers, although it can analyze Windows NT 4.0 computers as well. It comes in both GUI and command-line (i.e., Mbsacli.exe) forms and can be run against one or more computers. It requires that the operator either run it locally or have an administrator-level password to access remote computers. It will detect missing patches on Microsoft's operating systems and most popular server applications (e.g., Internet Explorer, Outlook, Exchange, SQL, etc.), and report on a small list of critical vulnerabilities (e.g., no administrative password, no password expiration date, etc.). MBSA cannot patch computers; it can only report on missing patches.

Windows Update/Microsoft Update

Windows Update (called *Microsoft Update* in the latest versions) is a free ActiveX control application that can be accessed through Internet Explorer or the Help and Support application. It can only be run manually, and the user running it must be logged in with administrative-level permissions. Windows Update will detect missing Windows patches and install them. The newer version of Windows Update, called Microsoft Update, will also check for and install missing patches for Microsoft's most popular applications (Internet Explorer, Outlook, Exchange, SQL, etc.). Windows Update/Microsoft Update is a poor choice for centralized patch management because it must be run manually on each computer, the executing user must be logged in as an administrator, and it provides no centralized control or reporting.

Automatic Updates

Automatic Updates (AU) is a free client-side patch management service that can be installed on Windows 2000 and later workstations and servers. It can check for and install missing Windows and popular Microsoft application patches and apply them. AU runs with the LocalSystem context, so the logged-in user does not need to be an administrator. AU can be set to check for new patches on a weekly or daily basis, and can be configured to allow the user to review the patches before downloading or applying them. AU's client behavior can be controlled using Group Policy or Registry edits. AU is a mediocre choice for centralized patch management because it lacks sophisticated bandwidth management mechanisms and provides no centralized reporting.

Software Update Services

Software Update Services (SUS) is the most frequently tested patch management exam topic. It has been renamed Windows Server Update Services (WSUS) and given increased functionality in 2006, but so far only the less functional SUS has been tested on Exam 70-298. The biggest difference between SUS and WSUS is that WSUS gives the administrator more granular control over what computers and groups receive particular patches. With either product, the exam questions should be the same, focusing on SUS/WSUS server placement.

 Just in case Exam 70-298 begins to focus on WSUS, candidates should become familiar with the basic functionality of WSUS and how it differs from SUS. If WSUS does appear on the exam, Microsoft is likely to test the candidate's knowledge on the key differences between SUS and WSUS.

SUS/WSUS is a free server service that can be installed on Windows 2000 and later servers. It uses an IIS management interface, so IIS must also be installed; and WSUS additionally installs an MS-SQL (or MSDE) database backend. SUS/WSUS servers can download Microsoft software patches directly from Microsoft and then redistribute them to participating clients or other SUS/WSUS servers. The client-side software is Automatic Updates (discussed earlier) and must be configured to download from a participating SUS/WSUS server, using either Group Policy or Registry edits.

The SUS/WSUS server downloads Microsoft patches and then waits for the SUS/WSUS administrator to approve each patch. An enterprise can use multiple SUS/WSUS servers to spread out the bandwidth requirements. Each enterprise location can have its own SUS/WSUS server, which downloads updates directly from Microsoft, or each remote location can point to another parent SUS/WSUS server (to conserve Internet bandwidth).

Most SUS/WSUS exam questions focus on where to place the SUS/WSUS servers, either to conserve bandwidth to Microsoft and the Internet, or to conserve internal bandwidth to the corporate office. To conserve Internet bandwidth, have each remote SUS/WSUS office download from a centralized SUS/WSUS server using internal networks. To conserve internal bandwidth, have each remote SUS/WSUS office download its patches directly from Microsoft.

Because SUS/WSUS relies upon AU for its client-side software, it does not work with Windows 9x and Windows NT 4.0. Otherwise, SUS/WSUS is an excellent, free patch management solution for the Windows operating system and popular Microsoft applications. It allows centralized control, patch testing before deployment, centralized reporting, and bandwidth management.

Active Directory Software Installs

Another way to install patches is by using the Active Directory Software Installs feature (see Figure 8-23). Software Installs allows any type of program file to be installed. Using an Active Directory Group Policy, the administrator defines an installation package, which contains the necessary files and instructions to install the patch. Software Installs can be configured to install as soon as the computer starts up and logs on, when the user logs on, or with some other predefined event (e.g., the user clicks on a file attachment that needs the related application to open). The user can also install packages using the Add/Remove applet.

An administrator can install any software patch or update, not just Microsoft patches. Software Installs uses the local Windows Installer service, which normally runs with the LocalSystem context, to install software, so that the local logged-on user does not need to be logged in with administrator privileges for software to install.

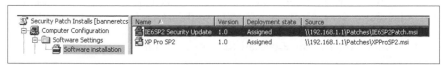

Figure 8-23. Installing patches with Active Directory Software Installs

You may be tested on the various file extension types that Software Installs works with:

- MSI
- MST
- MSP
- ZAP

Active Directory Software Installs works best with Microsoft Software Installation (MSI) packages, which the local Windows Installer service then installs. MSI files contain all the necessary files, registry edits, and instructions needed to automatically install the file. Unfortunately, most software patches do not come as .*MSI* files so the administrator needs to either create custom MSI files or use MSP or ZAP file types.

Microsoft Transform (MST) files can only be used when installing MSI software and for the purpose of modifying an MSI installation during the install. The .*MSI* file installs the application, and the related .*MST* file custom configures the MSI application just after it is installed. .*MST* files are never installed alone or separately.

Microsoft Patch (MSP) files were commonly created by Microsoft for installing software patches and updates, but have become less popular. ZAP files are essentially text files used to install any other type of file that isn't an MSI, MST, or MSP (e.g., Setup.exe). The administrator creates a custom ZAP with the necessary commands and formatting needed to install the application or patch. The drawback of ZAP files is that they are not installed by the Windows Installer service, and hence, the local logged-on user would have to be logged on as an administrator to allow Software Installs to install most programs. Also, ZAP files cannot be automatically uninstalled (as is possible with the other choices).

Although patches can be installed using Software Installs, it is a cumbersome way of doing it. Although Software Installs allows most software to be uninstalled with a click of a button, the uninstallation process doesn't work well with service packs and other types of patches. And like some of the other less than optimal methods previously mentioned, Software Installs lacks easy bandwidth control, auditing, and centralized reporting. Active Directory Software Installs will not usually be the correct answer for a patch management solution on the certification exam.

Systems Management Server

Systems Management Server (SMS) was covered earlier in this chapter in the section "Centralized event collection." It is a holistic host and network management solution. It can allow very granular control of software patching and even be used to install non-Microsoft patches. It is an excellent way to install security patches. Unfortunately, it is a commercial and very complex product (although you'll never see either of those two points tested on the exam). SMS might be a viable solution on the exam, especially for very large enterprises.

Distributed File System

Distributed File System (DFS) allows DFS-enabled shares to be distributed across one or more Windows file servers. Microsoft patches can be delivered using DFS and some other related scripts, but this solution is complex and is not usually the answer. Its biggest problem, as a patch management solution, is that it does not allow granular control without a lot of additional programming and does not have centralized patch management reporting. DFS was created to allow distributed file sharing, and not specifically for patch management.

Commercial solutions

As good as SUS/WSUS and SMS are as patch management solutions, dozens of other third-party vendors offer excellent patch management solutions. However, this is a Microsoft certification exam and third-party products are rarely mentioned or tested.

Most exam questions will focus on SUS patch management and SUS server placement. Most candidates will encounter at least one question regarding SUS.

Remote Administration Tools

XP Pro and Windows Server 2003 come with many tools designed for remote management. The most popularly tested tool is Remote Desktop, but Microsoft likes to test on less popular choices such as Telnet and Emergency Management Services.

Remote Desktop

Remote Desktop allows administrators to connect remotely to administer and manage Windows 2000, Windows XP Pro, and Windows 2003 servers, using the Remote Desktop Protocol (RDP) over TCP 3389. A connecting administrator can manipulate the system as if he was locally logged on, and map local drives and printers as mounted drives and printers on the remote server. This allows the administrator to copy data to and from the remote server (even the Clipboard feature works between the remote and local box) and to send print jobs to their local printers. Connections are encrypted by default.

At the time of this writing, the encryption used with RDP can easily be broken; for that reason, RDP should not be used without being tunneled inside another, more secure VPN. This, of course, will never be tested on the exam. For certification purposes, RDP should be thought of as a secure remote administration method.

Up to two simultaneous connections can be established at one time to Windows server products, and any currently logged-in local administrators will not be kicked out (contrast this to XP Pro's Remote Desktop, which will kick out the currently logged-in user and allow only one remote connection). Remote connections can be made over the internal network or across the Internet. The remote connecting client needs to use a Remote Desktop connection or Terminal Services client.

Remote Desktop is installed by default, but disabled. To use, administrators must enable the service (see Figure 8-21) by enabling the "Enable Remote Desktop on this computer" option in the System applet, as well as be a part of the local Administrators group. Nonadministrators must be added as members to the Remote Desktop Users group in order to be able to use Remote Desktop for Administration. This can be done in Active Directory Users and Computers or by selecting the Select Remote Users button, as shown in Figure 8-24. For securely administering servers, Remote Desktop will often be the correct choice on the exam.

Remote Desktop Web Client

Remote Desktop Web Client can be installed as an optional component of IIS's World Wide Web service using Add/Remove Programs. It installs a new Remote Desktop virtual directory in IIS and allows a remote user to connect to an IIS web site and establish a Remote Desktop connection. When the remote user connects to the Remote Desktop Web Connection web site, it pushes and installs a new Remote Desktop web client in the form of an ActiveX control. After the control is installed, the web site immediately connects the user to the normal RDP TCP port 3389. It's important to remember this fact. Although this type of connection starts out over HTTP port 80, the eventual connection is made over TCP port 3389. This could be a firewall configuration question on the exam.

Remote Assistance

Remote Assistance is another option available under the System applet (see Figure 8-24). It is installed and enabled by default. Remote Assistance allows a local "novice" to invite an "expert" to assist with a desktop support issue. It uses RDP over port 3389 and allows the expert to either view the current session or actively participate, at the novice's choice. Novices must "invite" the experts to connect. Invitations can be sent via email, file attachment, or instant messaging. Remote Assistance is not normally a correct answer choice on the exam, but may be offered as a potential solution.

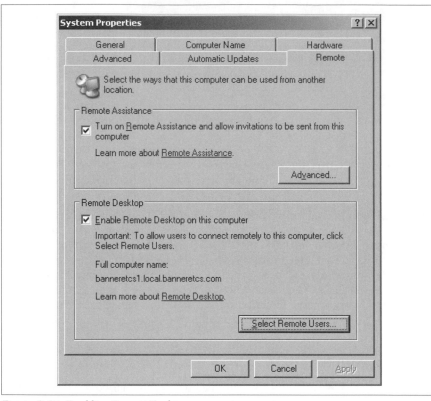

Figure 8-24. Enabling Remote Desktop

Remote Administration (HTML)

Remote Administration is an optionally installed component of IIS's World Wide Web service. It installs a new virtual directory and allows administrators to connect over HTTPS to the IIS server to do common administrative tasks. When installed, the Remote Administration service must be configured with both an HTTP and HTTPS port, although only the HTTPS port allows remote administration. Both ports are installed at high, nondefault ports (i.e., they are usually not installed on 80 and 443). To connect remotely, the administrator connects to the IIS server on the new SSL port—for example:

```
https://192.168.1.1:8088
```

The Remote Administration (HTML) tool is not a fully featured remote management tool, but it allows administrators to do many common server tasks, such as modify user accounts, shut down the server, configure existing services, and start new services.

 Occasionally, Microsoft exams mention custom HTML administrative tools, written by a third party. Custom applications may or may not be secure. It is up to the administrator to determine whether the custom application is secure enough to use for remote administration.

Telnet

If the *Telnet* server services is enabled (it's available, but not active in Windows 2000, XP Pro, and Windows Server 2003), administrators can connect remotely over TCP port 21 to establish a command-line interface. There, administrators can run any command-line-based tool—and in the newer versions of Windows, there are dozens. Although normal Telnet uses only plain-text logons and communications, if the Windows Telnet client is used to connect to a Windows Telnet server, Telnet can use the NTLM protocol for authentication (when used on the local network connecting to other domain resources). This prevents the user's password from being sent in clear text, but the password, in challenge-response form, can still be sniffed and an attempt to crack it can be made. If NTLM authentication cannot be negotiated, the user's logon name and password will be sent in clear text. Either way, all other communications after the logon are sent in clear text. Telnet is a viable remote administration tool, but it lacks GUI capabilities and is not always secure.

Many other test preparation guides and example exams assume Telnet always uses plain-text logon names and passwords. This isn't the case with Windows Telnet, when connecting to Microsoft Telnet servers belonging to the same domain and network as the user logging on. Microsoft exams know that NTLM authentication can be used instead of plain-text logons. However, because all the communications after the logon are sent in plain text, Telnet isn't a very secure remote administration choice.

Microsoft NetMeeting Remote Desktop Sharing

The *NetMeeting Remote Desktop Sharing* service is installed but disabled by default in Windows Server 2003. When enabled, a remote user can use the NetMeeting client software to connect to the server. NetMeeting will allow the connecting user to view and manipulate the server's shared desktop. Although NetMeeting can be used to manage remote servers, it is not a recommended solution in most cases.

Emergency Management Services

Emergency Management Services (EMS) was added in Windows Server 2003 as a way for local and remote administrators to recover from and diagnose critical system crashes (i.e., blue screens or problems so bad the system won't boot). EMS works using a Telnet-like service over serial ports. If a terminal server (this is a COM port hardware device and has nothing to do with Microsoft Terminal Services) or COM port concentrator device is connected to the affected server, it may be possible for a remote administrator to connect to the COM port device over an IP network, and then connect into the affected server. Essentially, EMS allows a special command-line session (called the *Special Administration Console*, or SAC) to be established to a crashed server without a locally attached keyboard or monitor. The terms "out-of-band" management and "headless" operations are frequently associated with EMS. EMS is not normally used to administer servers.

Because an EMS and SAC console session does not require a logon name or password, administrators must make sure EMS is secured either physically or by addressing security at the connecting terminal. The former sentence is a valid exam objective.

Terminal Services

Terminal Services allows one or more remote users to connect to a Windows server running the Terminal Services service (in NT 4.0, you had to install a special edition of NT called Terminal Service Edition) in order to run one or more hosted applications. Even DOS users, using a DOS-based version of the Terminal Services client, can connect to a Terminal Services GUI session. Terminal Services uses RDP and supports encryption in Windows 2000 Server and later (if clients are running the newer client versions as well).

There are frequent exam questions on Terminal Server security and settings (see Figure 8-25).

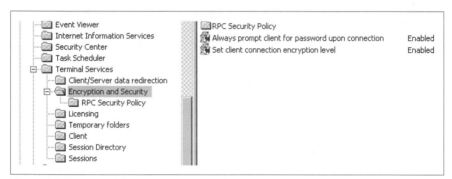

Figure 8-25. Terminal Service encryption and security settings

Terminal Services encryption can be set to three levels:

* High Level
* Low Level
* Client Compatible

High-Level encryption means that RDP communications will be protected by the maximum encryption key size supported by the server. If clients cannot also accept this key length, it will not be allowed to connect. *Low-Level* and *Client-Level encryption* means that RDP communications will be protected by the maximum key size supported by the client. In high-security scenarios, the administrator will want to ensure that the encryption level is set to High Level. Terminal Services has dozens of other settings, some of which could impact security indirectly. You should be familiar with all of the configuration choices available in Group Policy for Terminal Services.

Older Terminal Services versions came with Terminal Services Advanced Client Web Client, which could be activated through IIS. Remote Desktop Web Client replaced it.

Terminal Services can be used to remotely administer a file server, but it would be a poor choice for doing this since it exists to let multiple remote users run hosted applications. It would be better for an administrator to use Remote Desktop to manage a server, rather than Terminal Services.

 Terminal Services, Remote Desktop for Administration, Remote Assistance, and Remote Desktop all use RDP over default TCP port 3389, and rely on similar Windows components.

Remote Desktop, Remote Assistance, Remote Admin (HTML), NetMeeting, Terminal Services, EMS, and Telnet can all be used to remotely administer servers. The single best choice is normally Remote Desktop. However, the exam will frequently ask you to choose another choice when the preferred choice isn't possible. Exam candidates should be familiar with all the choices and the reasons to use each.

Windows Trust Models

Every domain in a Windows 2000 and later forest trusts every other domain in the forest with a two-way transitive trust. If multiple domain trees are present in a single forest, the two-way transitive trusts are between the parent domains of each domain tree. With Windows Server 2003, you can even have trusts between forests, as long as all the participating domain controllers are Windows Server 2003 and the forest is in Windows Server 2003 Native mode. If one of the forests is not a Windows Server 2003 forest, the trust between the forests would have to be an external trust.

What does a Windows trust mean for Windows security? A user belonging to one domain will automatically belong to the Everyone and Authenticated Users group in any other domain in the forest. In a multidomain forest, it is likely that at least one of the domains is weaker than the others. A knowledgeable attacker could use this knowledge to become a user in the weakest domain, and then leverage his newly gained domain memberships in attacking the stronger domains.

Securing Network Communications

A major portion of the 70-298 exam covers securing network communications. This section will cover IPSec, securing IIS web sites, RRAS, IAS, and securing wireless networks.

IPSec

The Internet Protocol Security (IPSec) protocol is one of the most common VPN protocols used today. It protects (authenticates and/or encrypts) IP packets only, providing end-to-end host security, from origination source to destination host. Originally introduced in Microsoft Windows 2000, it can be used in previous versions of Windows if the appropriate patches and IPSec client software are applied. IPSec is commonly used to secure the following:

- LAN
- WAN connections (router to router, gateway to gateway)
- VPN connections (e.g., RRAS)

IPSec works by examining every IP packet passing through a particular host's network adapter. The IPSec filter examines the network packet to see whether its contents meet predefined rules (known as *filters*). If the network packet meets one of the predefined filters, IPSec performs additional actions upon the packet. Depending on the predefined action that was related to the filter, IPSec can do the following:

- Secure the traffic between source and destination (require IPSec and turn on authentication and/or encryption). IPSec can require that the traffic be secured between source and destination, and either drop the packet if the destination host cannot use IPSec or decide it is unnecessary if the client cannot do it (i.e., request security).
- Block and drop the packet; in this way, it can act as a packet filtering firewall.
- Pass it in clear text, unauthenticated and unencrypted.

Microsoft Windows comes with three built-in, but initially disabled, IPSec policies. Only one IPSec policy can be enabled at one time on any particular host. Both IPSec hosts using the IPSec connection must agree on the rules as well as the actions and protocols used to allow IPSec to be used between endpoints.

Creating an IPSec policy

Administrators can create, modify, and apply IPSec policies using command-line tools (i.e., Netsh.exe or IPsecpol.exe) or using the IP Security Policy console. Creating an IPSec policy involves the following steps:

1. Create an IPSec policy.
2. Create one or more IPSec Rules to attach to a particular policy. Each rule is tied to an IP filter. Rule properties are as follows:
   - AH or ESP (packet header authentication or data integrity/encryption)
   - Computer Authentication Method (Kerberos, Certs., Preshared Secret) (one or more)
   - Connection Type (All, LAN, RRAS) (one per rule)
   - Perfect Forward Secrecy (enable or disable)
   - Filter Action (block, permit, negotiate) (one per rule)
   - Tunnel endpoint IP address (optional)
3. Create an IP Filter (only one per rule) and attach it to a rule:
   - Filter which IP packet to catch
   - Source and Destination IP address
   - Source and Destination Port
   - Protocol Type (ICMP, TCP, UDP, etc.)

Essentially, one or more IP Filters are made, each describing the IP header characteristics that would trigger IPSec into action (i.e., a packet headed from a particular host). Each filter is tied exactly to one rule. The rule determines what happens to the packet (i.e., secured, dropped, passed) and what protocols are used. The collection of filter-based rules makes up the IPSec policy. Figure 8-26 shows the IPSec component relationship.

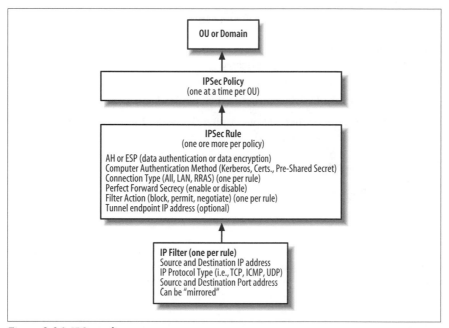

Figure 8-26. IPSec policy components

IPSec authentication

IPSec allows three authentication methods for each IPSec rule. A single IPSec rule can have one or more methods with an order of preference. The three authentication methods are:

- Kerberos (the default method)
- Certificate (must have a trusted Certification Authority available)
- Pre-shared Secret (manually exchange secret keys)

In a single-forest Windows network, Kerberos is the easiest authentication method to use. If your computer is joined to the domain (i.e., authenticated), this is the easiest method to implement. Kerberos authentication does not work well or easily outside of the same forest. Using digital machine certificates is one of the most secure ways to authenticate IPSec; the administrator must setup a trusted CA for both of the IPSec hosts to use and have previously distributed IPSec machine certificates to each involved IPSec host. Although using digital certificates is the most complex method of IPSec authentication, it can work across forest boundaries and even the Internet (if the correct IP ports are allowed through any filtering devices). The least secure method is to use a previously manually exchanged Pre-Shared Key (PSK) between the two participating end points. If you use the PSK method, use a long and complex PSK.

AH versus ESP

IPSec has two protocols that can be chosen in each IPSec rule to determine whether secured traffic is authenticated and/or encrypted. The two IPSec protocols are:

Authentication Header (AH)
    Data and packet header authenticated

Encapsulated Security Payload (ESP)
    Authentication and/or encryption of data payload

For the exam, remember that AH just authenticates and ESP encrypts (as well as authenticates the payload if chosen).

Tunnel versus Transport mode

IPSec has two modes:

* Tunnel
* Transport

Tunneling encapsulates the whole IP packet and passes it from source to destination. Tunneling is often used to create an IPSec tunnel between two network devices. Transport mode protects only the payload data. Transport mode is often used between individual computer hosts to each other. A good way to remember Transport versus Tunnel mode may be the following: "The dump truck transport vehicle only protects its payload, but the entire dump truck can pass through a tunnel."

Default IPSec policies

Microsoft provides three default IPSec policies (see Figure 8-27):

Client (respond only)
    If the server requests security, the client will enable IPSec but will otherwise communicate in clear text.

Server (request security)
    The server always requests IPSec to be used, but doesn't require it if the connecting client cannot use IPSec.

Secure Server (require security)
    The server does not allow non-IPSec communications.

Server and client designations do not mean that a particular policy can only be used by workstation or server versions of Windows. Every Windows host has both server and workstation functionality (i.e., the Server service and the Workstation service). For example, even Windows 2000 Workstation can run a Telnet server and function as a "server." These IPSec policies apply to that concept of

Console Root	Name	Description	Policy Assigned
IP Security Policies on Local Comp	Client (Respond Only)	Communicate normally (unsecured). Use the default...	No
	Require IPSec to Access Intranet Web Server	Require IPSec to Access Intranet Web Server	Yes
	Secure Server (Require Security)	For all IP traffic, always require security using Kerbe...	No
	Server (Request Security)	For all IP traffic, always request security using Kerb...	No

Figure 8-27. IPSec policy console

client and server. Only one policy can be active (i.e., assigned) at one time per host.

In real-world networks, the default three policies are hardly ever used. They are not granular enough for most networks. They cover all IP and ICMP traffic, regardless of port, purpose, or destination. Implementing the require security policy would cause problems in most environments. However, these are the three policies you will most likely be tested up on the 70-298 exam, so know them well. Also, because IPSec has the ability to drop IP traffic based upon IP and port addresses, it can function as a basic firewall packet filter.

 Remember that IPSec does machine authentication only. The user's identity cannot be made part of the IPSec equation.

Securing Internet Information Services (IIS) Web Sites

Internet Information Services (IIS) is one of Microsoft's most attacked products. Administrators must take great care to secure IIS web sites. To secure IIS, it is essential to understand how its security works. There are five major permission and security-related contexts in play during every web server request:

- IIS permissions
- Web User Authentication
- NTFS permissions
- Execute permissions
- Web Application Pool Identity

IIS permissions

The IIS Server has its own security permissions separate from Windows and the normal NTFS file and folder permissions (see Figure 8-28). The IIS permissions are:

- Script source access
- Read
- Write
- Directory browsing

These IIS permissions can be specifically configured for each IIS server, IIS web site, virtual directory, web page, and web site file. An IIS administrator can set IIS permissions to be as granular as she wants. Permissions set at the highest level (the parent container) are inherited down below to the lower containers, unless otherwise contradicted at the lower level.

The "Script source access" permission determines whether a user browsing to that object should be able to see the source code behind the displayed web page or object. In most cases, an administrator would not want to enable this permission, as an attacker may be able to review the source code and find vulnerability. The Read permission must be given in order for a web site object or page to be displayed to an end user.

The Write permission, if not contradicted by other permissions, would allow a user to create new files, delete files or objects, or modify existing files and objects. If this permission is allowed, it opens up a potential avenue of attack for a malicious intruder. Unfortunately, the permission must be given if a user is to save or upload any information or objects, which a large percentage of web servers allow. Administrators should only assign this permission when necessary.

If enabled, "Directory browsing" tells the web server to list the files in directory listing instead of rendering the files and objects in HTML. This is an easy way to list files and to allow users to download and upload files.

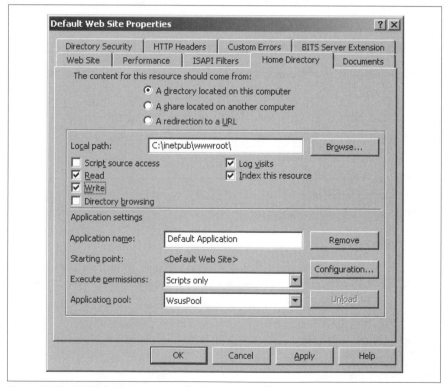

Figure 8-28. IIS Web Site Properties displaying available permissions

Not all IIS permissions are available at every level (e.g., "Directory browsing" is not a displayed permission when the focus is a single file or object.

Web User Authentication

Each web request made to an IIS web site is made through a user context. Either the request is made through an authenticated user (that exists in Active Directory or the local SAM file) or the IIS anonymous user (*IUSR_machinename*) is used. Authentication type (covered below) can be set differently per web server, per web site, per virtual directory, per web page, or per web file or object—and the authentication setting follows normal inheritance rules.

This is a very important point, because each web object requires a particular authentication type and a particular user security context. If authenticated users are not required, then IIS uses the security context of the *IUSR_machinename* user account, which belongs to the Everyone and Authenticated Users group. An IIS administrator can allow the IIS anonymous access to certain files and folders and require authenticated access for others.

NTFS permissions

NTFS permissions can override every other permission type. Every Windows file and object has a security Access Control List, and that list defines which security principals (users, computers, and groups) can access it, and if they can, with what permissions. Using NTFS permissions, an IIS administrator can specifically determine which users have access to which objects, including web server objects. For instance, the web server administrator can take away the NTFS permissions from the *IUSR_machinename* account to access any files in a high-security web site. If the *IUSR_machinename* account is denied access, any user trying to access that object would have to authenticate first. Using the appropriate (i.e., least privilege) NTFS permissions on IIS files and objects is one of the best ways to secure a web server.

Execute permissions

Every IIS web site, folder, and virtual directory has additional IIS permissions that determine whether scripts and executables can run (see Figure 8-28). The Execute permissions can be set to:

- None
- Scripts Only
- Scripts and Executables

If the Execute permission is set to None, no scripts or executables can run, but other types of files can be read or displayed. If Scripts Only is set, only scripts can run, but no executables (or DLLs) or applications. If the Execute permission is set to Scripts and Executables, then all file types can run and execute. Contrary to what many resources say, only Scripts Only is needed if you want to run a regular script file. Some sources say wrongly that Scripts and Executables are needed for script files.

Web Application Pool Identity

All web sites run in a web application pool security context (see Figure 8-28). By default, all web applications share a single application pool called *DefaultApp-Pool*. Additional application pools can be defined. Each application pool is assigned an *identity*. An identity is a user or service account used to provide the security context of the application pool. If an intruder "breaks out" of a web server or its application, he will be limited to seeing what is in the application pool, and further limited by the security context of the application pool's identity account. If an IIS web server hosts more than one web site, the IIS administrator should consider placing each unrelated web site in a different application pool.

The combination of the IIS permissions, web user authentication, NTFS permissions, Execute permissions, and the application pool identity permissions determines the effective security permissions of any web server object. Each of these permissions must be configured to its least privilege setting to minimize vulnerabilities.

 NetBIOS file shares and Share permissions have no effect on IIS or its effective permissions.

IIS authentication

What user context IIS allows the remote web user to use is of primary importance to IIS's effective security permissions. The possible IIS authentication choices are as follows (see Figure 8-29):

- Anonymous
- Integrated Windows
- Digest
- Basic
- .NET Passport

Anonymous. As discussed earlier, when Anonymous is chosen, the web user request will be executed in the security context of the *IUSR_machinename* user account. The IIS anonymous user (which has no relationship to the anonymous null session account used in NetBIOS) belongs to the Everyone and Authenticated Users group.

This means that if a malicious intruder can "break out" of the web server and into Windows behind the scenes, they will be able to do anything the Everyone and Authenticated Users group can do. At the very least, this usually means that web server intruders may be able to get Read and Execute permissions to most files found on the server (as Read and Execute permissions are the most common permissions given to the Authenticated Users group on the server by default). This is why it is important to make sure IIS and its applications are appropriately configured.

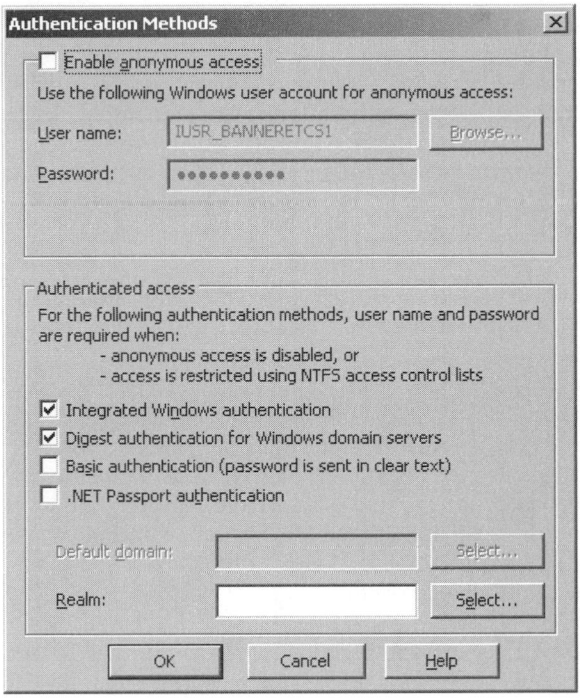

Figure 8-29. IIS authentication choices

Integrated Windows. Integrated Windows authentication is generally meant for intranet web sites. It can use any authentication protocol: LM, NTLM, NTLMv2, or Kerberos. If the web server connected to it is defined as being on the user's intranet (in Windows, any web server located on the same IP subnet as the user is automatically placed in the user's intranet browser zone), Windows will first attempt to connect anonymously, but then pass the user's current logon name and password if Integrated Windows authentication is requested. For web servers not located in the currently defined intranet zone, Internet Explorer will prompt the user for her logon name and password. This is to prevent external malicious web sites from requesting the valid logon credentials of the user.

In order for Integrated Windows authentication to work, the user's logon account must be stored in Active Directory or the local SAM file on the server. Logon credentials passed using Integrated Windows authentication are considered secure, although if a remote attacker can trick the user's computer into sending LM authentication (and hence the user's LM password hash), the user's plain-text password can be trivially cracked. However, this latter point is almost never tested on the exam. For exam purposes, consider all Integrated Windows authentication communications to be secure.

Digest. Digest authentication requires that the user's logon account be located in Active Directory or the local SAM database, but it does not use one of the

Exam 70-298
Study Guide

Windows logon authentication protocols (i.e., LM, NTLM, NTLMv2, or Kerberos) to communicate the user's logon name and password. The user will always be prompted for his logon name and password, which are then protected using a digest hash algorithm. This option always requires that the user's password be stored in easily reversed hash form. Under the user's logon account or in Group Policy, the following "Store password using reversible encryption" setting must be enabled for each user wishing to use Digest authentication in IIS. Digest authentication is considered to be weakly secure, but better than plain-text, authentication method.

 Reversible encryption is required for CHAP authentication in RRAS and IAS as well.

Basic. Basic authentication sends the user's logon name and password in near plain-text conditions. The user's credentials are slightly obscured using Base64, but this is easily converted back to plain text. Basic authentication requires that the user's logon account be stored in Active Directory or in the local SAM. Computers or browsers that don't support Digest or Integrated Windows authentication (e.g., Macintosh, Unix, or Linux computers) can use this option. Basic authentication is considered insecure.

.NET Passport. .NET Passport was intended to be a universal, SSO web site authentication solution, but it never took off as much as Microsoft had hoped. Web sites using .NET Passport authentication work this way:

1. The user creates a .NET Passport identity and password on a Microsoft Passport web server. This additional Microsoft-owned server is never the same as the eventual web server.

2. When a user wants to access a web server requesting .NET Passport authentication, the web site redirects them to a Microsoft Passport authentication server.

3. The user logs on to her Microsoft Passport account on the Microsoft Passport authentication server.

4. The Microsoft Passport authentication server passes a successful authentication token back to the original web site that the user was trying to enter.

The idea behind Microsoft Passport was that the user would only need to log in once to access multiple participating web sites, and the user's Passport logon credentials would never be passed to the participating web servers. So if the web server became compromised, it wouldn't affect the user's security, because the user's logon name and password were never stored there in the first place.

Microsoft Passport support is waning. However, on the exam, Microsoft Passport is a valid option for external, Internet-facing web servers, and its authentication is considered secure.

Authentication can be chosen on a per-web-server, per-web-site, per-virtual-directory, per-folder, per-file basis. If multiple authentication choices are selected, the client can choose which method to use. If anonymous authentication and an authenticated method are selected at the same time, the anonymous method will be used. This is because most browsers connect anonymously first, and only send or prompt for other authentication credentials if the anonymous connection fails first.

Installing and using SSL/TLS

Web server traffic can be authenticated and encrypted using Secure Sockets Layer (SSL) or Transport Layer Security (TLS) protocols. TLS is the next version of SSL. SSL will be phased out in the near future, and only TLS will be used to create HTTPS communication streams. Both protocols require that the web server (and optionally the client) have digital certificates. Installing SSL/TLS requires the following general steps:

1. The web server administrator generates an asymmetric key pair and submits the public key to a (usually public) CA.

2. The CA verifies the pubic key and signs it, creating a web server digital certificate. The certificate is tied to the web server URL address.

3. The web server administrator installs the Web Server Certificate and configures IIS to use the certificate whenever a user connects to the HTTPS-enabled port(s).

Follow these steps when requesting a Web Server Certificate in IIS:

1. In IIS Manager, right-click the web site name.

2. Choose Properties.

3. Click the Directory Security tab.

4. Click on the Server Certificate button.

5. Follow the wizard to Create a New Certificate (see Figure 8-30).

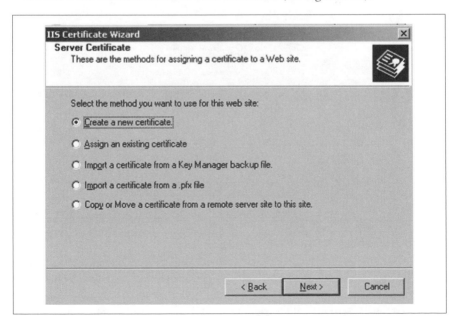

Figure 8-30. Installing an SSL/TLS Certificate in IIS

When a user connects to an SSL port, the following happens:

1. The server sends the client its web server digital certificate attesting to its identity and authenticity.
2. If the client accepts the digital certificate as authentic, the client and the web server begin to negotiate a symmetric encryption algorithm to use.
3. The client creates a session symmetric encryption key and sends it to the server, using the server's digital certificate to encrypt the new key during transmission to the server.
4. The server and the client begin using a session symmetric key to encrypt communications back and forth between each other.

Client certificate mapping. Normally, SSL/TLS is used to authenticate the web server to the client and to encrypt communications thereafter. But the server can also request that the client have a digital certificate as well to authenticate the client to the server. This is known as *client certificates*. Client certificates can be required by configuring IIS (see Figure 8-31) to require them, using the corresponding radio button found on the Secure Communications tab. Click "Enable client certificate mapping" to tell IIS to use the client certificates already stored in Active Directory. Client certificate mapping is a very secure way to protect web server data streams.

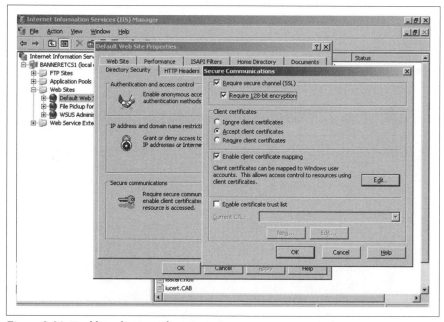

Figure 8-31. Enabling client certificate mapping

URLScan

IIS contains an incoming HTML parser (`Http.sys`) that strips out many malicious HTML commands. In fact, IIS 6 contains a lot of the HTML parsing functionality that could only be obtained by installing an additional Microsoft product, URLScan, in IIS 4 and 5. Many IIS administrators mistakenly believe that they no longer need URLScan, since its functionality is now in IIS 6 by default.

However, only some of URLScan's functionality was placed in the IIS 6 HTML parser. Web administrators wishing to have higher levels of security or gain greater levels of granularity in what is or isn't allowed should still install Microsoft's free URLScan ISAPI filter. URLScan is configured by modifying its accompanying *Urlscan.ini* file. There administrators can choose what HTML commands are allowed and not allowed in great detail and granularity. Dropped HTML requests are logged to a separate URLScan log and are not logged in the normal IIS logfiles.

IIS logging

All web servers should have active and detailed logfiles about legitimate and malicious activity. IIS comes with built-in logging. Most IIS logging is done to the logfile(s) specified under the IIS Web Site tab (see Figure 8-32).

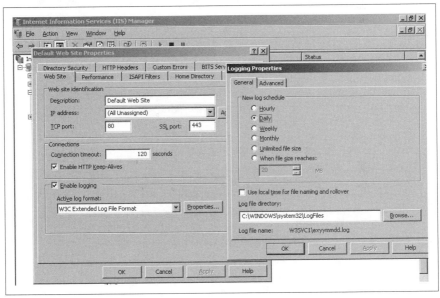

Figure 8-32. Configuring IIS logs

The information saved depends on the logfile format and the selected fields. IIS has four default log types:

- Microsoft IIS Log File format
- NCSA Common Log File format
- ODBC Logging
- W3C Extended Log File format (the default logging option)

Microsoft IIS Log File format. The Microsoft IIS Log File format is a fixed ASCII text-based format that cannot be customized. It records the following fields: client IP address, username, date, time, service and instance, server name, server IP address, time taken, client bytes sent, server bytes sent, service status code, Windows status code, request type, target of operation, and any script parameters.

NCSA Common Log File format (IIS 6.0). The NCSA Common Log File format is an older, uncustomizable, fixed ASCII text-based format for HTTP, SMTP, and NNTP services. The NCSA Common Log File format records the following data: remote host address, remote log name (always blank), username, date, time, GMT offset, request and protocol version, service status code, and bytes sent.

ODBC Logging. ODBC Logging allows IIS logging to be recorded to any ODBC-compliant database, such as Microsoft SQL Server, Oracle, or Microsoft Access. ODBC Logging saves the following data fields: client host, username, log time, IIS service, machine name, server IP address, processing time, bytes received, bytes sent, service status, Windows status, operation, target, and passed parameters.

In order to use ODBC Logging, the administrator has to first configure an ODBC-compliant database table with the fields indicated in the previous paragraph. The administrator configures the ODBC logon authentication dialog box that interfaces with the ODBC-compliant server, including database instance, table name, username, and password used to authenticate with the server (see Figure 8-33). Having to supply the ODBC connector with the username and password is considered a security risk. It goes without saying that you should not use the well-known SQL Server administrator account name, SA, for ODBC logging. ODBC Logging can significantly slow down an IIS server due to the *Http.sys* cache being disabled. However, this is a common option and a correct answer choice on the exam.

W3C Extended Log File format. W3C Extended Log File format is an IIS Log File format that allows you to choose which fields to log (see Figure 8-34). W3C, with all fields selected, is considered an optimal IIS Log File format because it maintains decent performance and records the most information.

You should examine the field options available in each IIS logging file format and note the differences, strengths, and weaknesses. This is one of the areas in which Exam 70-298 often asks for detailed answers.

Web Service Extensions

IIS 6 installs with basic HTML functionality only. In order to run scripts, ASP pages, ISAPI filters, CGI scripts, BITS, WebDAV, and other processes giving more functionality, they must be approved as Web Service Extensions (see Figure 8-35). Securing IIS servers means disabling any unnecessary Web Service Extensions.

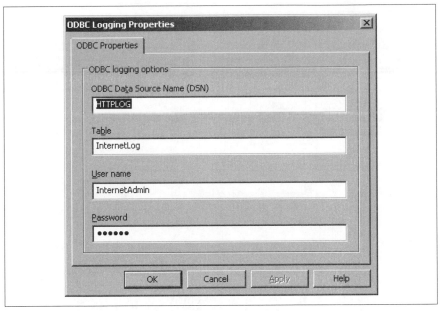

Figure 8-33. IIS ODBC Logging options

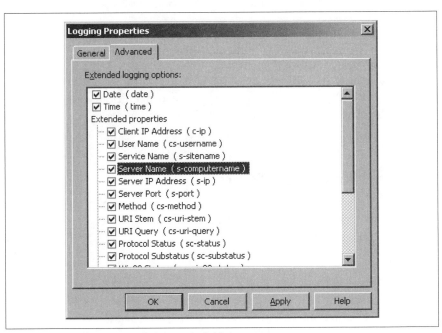

Figure 8-34. IIS W3C Extended Log File field options

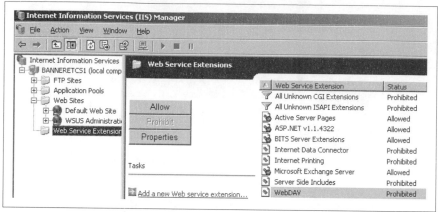

Figure 8-35. IIS 6 Web Service Extensions

WebDAV

Web-based Distributed Authoring and Versioning (WebDAV) is an open Internet standard with the goal of allowing users to save and retrieve files to and from web servers (among other goals). IIS supports WebDAV as a Web Service Extension. When enabled (it is disabled by default), it will allow computers with WebDAV clients to save and retrieve files from WebDAV-enabled web sites.

Windows 2000 and Office 2000 and later support WebDAV. In Windows, the WebDAV client is enabled through the Web Client service; however, if the user has a recent version of Microsoft Office installed, the Web Client service is not needed. WebDAV is a frequent exam topic. Using WebDAV along with SSL/TLS is a good way to secure web-based communications to and from the server. Used with EFS, WebDAV is an excellent way to guarantee that files are encrypted when stored on the web server and during network transmission.

Exam 70-298 will almost certainly have one or more questions dealing with IIS security.

Routing and Remote Access Service

Chapter 5 covered RRAS and its options in detail. Exam 70-298 focuses on the RRAS security issues, particularly VPN types, authentication protocols, and IAS.

There are two basic VPN protocols in RRAS:

- L2TP
- PPTP

Of the two, L2TP, used in conjunction with IPSec, is significantly more secure than PPTP. PPTP was an earlier VPN protocol invented by Microsoft that can be used with legacy clients. Windows 9x and Windows NT 4.0 need the latest patches and the latest Microsoft VPN client software to use L2TP. When in doubt about which RRAS VPN protocol to use on the test, choose the L2TP/IPSec combination.

RRAS authentication protocols

There are six RRAS authentication protocol choices that can be made in each Remote Access Policy (see Figure 8-36). From most secure to least secure, these are:

- EAP
- MS-CHAPv2
- MS-CHAP
- CHAP
- Unencrypted authentication (PAP, SPAP)
- Unauthenticated access

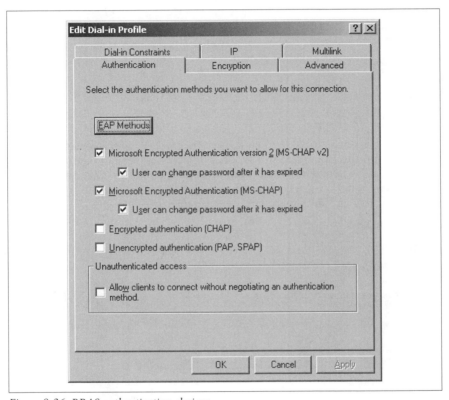

Figure 8-36. RRAS authentication choices

Extensible Authentication Protocol (EAP) is the most secure protocol, and likely to be the only one used in the future (although there are dozens of flavors). We'll cover EAP more in the next section. MS-CHAPv2 is the most secure authentication protocol for clients who cannot support EAP. MS-CHAPv2 supports two-way authentication and is considered a relatively secure protocol. MS-CHAP is a legacy protocol with some minor issues and is considered to be a weakly secure protocol. Only use this when you have to.

Exam 70-298 Study Guide

CHAP is another legacy protocol that should only be used when it must be (i.e., Macintosh, Linux, Unix clients). It is considered very weak security-wise—just a notch above plain-text authentication. Unencrypted authentication protocols, such as PAP and SPAP, send logon credentials in plain text and should only be used when they are the only protocols that the clients support. Unencrypted authentication protocols are not considered secure. Although Unauthenticated access is the weakest authentication choice and is not secure when used by itself, it may be an appropriate protocol if the network communication's stream is securely protected by another protocol or device. For example, if RRAS traffic uses an external VPN tunneling device, selecting unauthenticated access may prevent the user from being prompted twice for logon credentials. If multiple authentication protocols are selected, the client can choose, and will often choose the weakest.

 Most RRAS authentication types (EAP can be the exception) are user authentication methods. If a user is prompted for a username and password, it is user authentication. Other protocols such as IPSec, which never prompt the user for a logon name or password, are computer authentication. It is important to understand which type of authentication you need (if not both), for a particular solution.

EAP authentication. Extensible Authentication Protocol is a very secure form of authentication. It can be used in user or computer authentication, and comes in dozens of flavors (although Windows only natively supports a few). In Windows, EAP can be used with usernames and passwords or with digital certificates and smart cards. EAP in Windows comes in three flavors (see Figure 8-37):

- Protected EAP (PEAP)
- EAP-TLS (also known as "Smart Card or other certificate")
- EAP-MD5 (also known as MD5-Challenge)

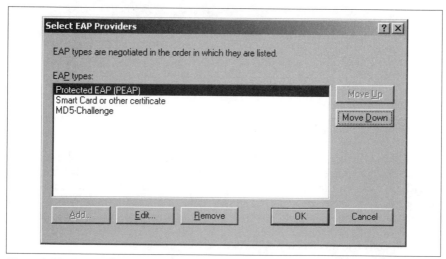

Figure 8-37. EAP authentication choices

PEAP works by first establishing a secure VPN tunnel before transmitting the EAP certificates used to secure the session. PEAP is used in Windows for 801.x security, so associate PEAP with wireless security when taking Windows certification exams. EAP-TLS also uses digital certificates (this should be easy to remember, as TLS web sites use digital certificates), often stored on a smart card. So, if the exam talks about using Smart Card authentication over VPNs, think EAP-TLS. EAP-MD5 is a very secure password challenge response authentication choice.

 RRAS authentication choices are also available in IAS.

Windows Basic Firewall

Enabling RRAS disables Internet Connection Firewall/Windows Firewall, if indeed a host-based firewall is enabled. RRAS contains basic IP filtering (see Figure 8-38) that can be used instead. Using RRAS IP filters (also known as the RRAS Windows Basic Firewall) located in Remote Access Policies, you can specify which transport protocol port numbers and IP addresses are allowed into and out of the RRAS server.

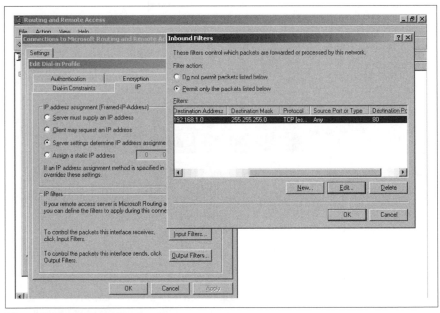

Figure 8-38. RRAS IP Filtering

CMAK. Client-side VPN connection definitions (i.e., connection profiles) can be simplified and automated by the administrator using the Connection Manager Administration Kit (CMAK). The administrator can create all the connection profile settings into a single installable file and send it to the remote user. The remote user simply executes the CMAK connection file, and it automatically—and appropriately—configures the user's remote connection session.

Internet Authentication Service

Internet Authentication Service (IAS) is Microsoft's implementation of RADIUS. IAS can be used to manage one or more RRAS servers. If you have multiple RRAS servers (called *RADIUS clients* or *network access servers* in RADIUS terminology), IAS can allow the administrator to configure one set of Remote Access Policies (with authentication choices, etc., configured) and manage multiple RRAS servers with a common, shared configuration (see Figure 8-39).

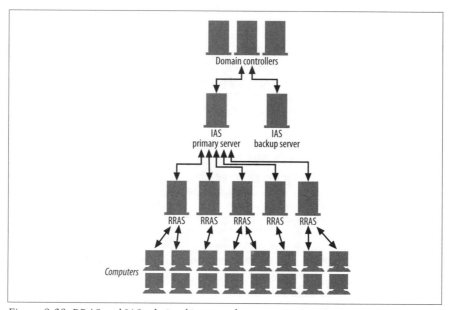

Figure 8-39. RRAS and IAS relationship example

How IAS works (a simplified scenario)

The following steps explain how IAS works:

1. When a remote VPN user connects directly to the RRAS server, the RRAS server (acting as a RADIUS client) forwards the request to the IAS server.

2. The IAS server checks the user's credentials on the domain controller, and checks to see whether the user is allowed to connect remotely. IAS server must be part of the RAS and IAS Servers group to be able to query the DC.

3. RADIUS Remote Access Policy (just like RRAS policy) is evaluated against the user, and the user is allowed or denied.

4. IAS sends acceptance or denial of user authentication to the RRAS server.

Figure 8-40 has a graphical representation of how IAS works.

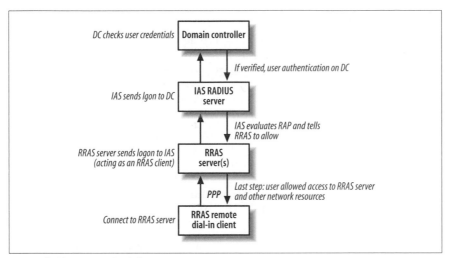

Figure 8-40. How IAS works

In order for IAS to work, each RRAS server must be configured to use the IAS RADIUS services (see Figure 8-41).

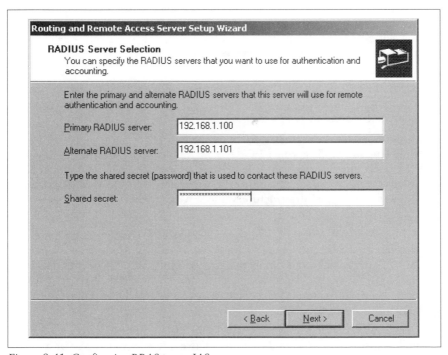

Figure 8-41. Configuring RRAS to use IAS

IAS and RRAS are frequent subjects on Exam 70-298.

Securing Wireless Networks

Wireless networks are among the toughest networks to secure. Starting with Windows XP, Microsoft offered the Zero Wireless Configuration Service. It attempts to make wireless networking as easy as possible, even if it means creating more security problems. To begin to understand wireless security, you need to be familiar with basic wireless networking terminology.

802.11

802.11 is a family of specifications for *wireless local area networks* (WLANs) developed by a working group of the Institute of Electrical and Electronics Engineers (IEEE). The five most popular specifications in the family are: 802.11, 802.11a, 802.11b, 802.11g, and 802.11i. All five use the *Ethernet* protocol and CSMA/CA (carrier sense multiple access with collision avoidance) for path sharing.

802.1x

802.1x is a newer networking security standard covering wireless authentication (also known as *network access control*) to LANs and wireless networks. EAP and PEAP VPNs are part of the 802.1x standard.

802.11i

IEEE 802.11i is the newest and most secure wireless networking standard, covering both authentication and encryption. It specifies EAP for authentication and WPA2 encryption for confidentiality. Wireless networks using 802.1x authentication and WPA/WP2 encryption are considered very secure, especially compared to legacy WEP wireless protection.

Wireless Access Point

A Wireless Access Point (WAP) is the network device that a wireless node connects to in order to join the wireless network or to establish a wireless network connection.

Infrastructure Mode

Infrastructure Mode is when a WAP is a terminating network device designed to support multiple wireless nodes at once (much like a wired hub), and often interfaces the wireless network to the wired network. Most WAPs that you buy at the store are Infrastructure Mode WAPs.

Ad-hoc Mode

Ad-hoc Mode WAPs are peer-to-peer connections. Usually, every computer that has a wireless network card can act as an Ad-hoc Mode WAP. Windows XP Pro clients will often connect to Ad-hoc Mode WAPs, even though most users only intend to connect to Infrastructure Mode WAPs. A secure wireless client should only connect to Infrastructure Mode WAPs (see Figure 8-42).

Wired Equivalent Privacy (WEP)

WEP is an older, legacy wireless VPN protocol, focusing on data encryption and integrity that was found to be very flawed. It is considered to be an insecure VPN protocol, but is better than using wireless networking in plain text. It will stop casual wireless network eavesdropping.

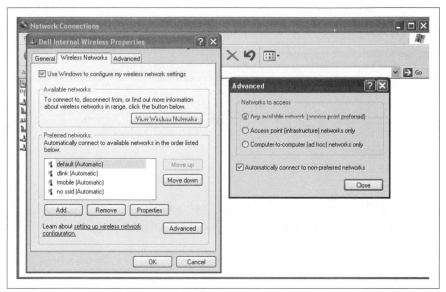

Figure 8-42. Choosing Ad-hoc versus Infrastructure Mode in the Windows wireless client

Wi-Fi Protected Access (WPA/WPA2)
> WPA (and the newer version, WPA2) is a newer, more secure, wireless VPN protocol, for both authentication and encryption, designed to replace weaker WEP. WPA2 is part of the 802.11i standard and is considered very secure. WPA2 is better than WPA, and eventually WPA will go away completely. However, WPA2 is so new that so far it has not been tested on Exam 70-298.

SSID
> Service Set Identifiers (SSIDs), or Extended Service Set Identifiers (ESSIDs), are labels used to identify wireless networks. The SSID is normally broadcast frequently so wireless nodes can locate WAPs.

Common wireless vulnerabilities

There are many wireless network vulnerabilities, including the following:

- By default, data on wireless networks is sent as clear text. If an additional VPN protocol supporting encryption, such as WEP, WPA/WPA2, SSL, or IPSec, isn't used, the data can be sniffed. Every WAP acts like an Ethernet hub, and each wireless node can eavesdrop on the other.

- Malware injection or denial of service (DoS) attacks are possible because wireless networks lack any authentication by default. Rogue wireless nodes can inject malicious packets and generate DoS attacks.

- Unauthorized (rogue) WLANs and WAPs can be installed, allowing users to bypass required networking security controls. Plus, the administrator of an unauthorized WLAN can look on other people's traffic and implement Man-in-the-Middle attacks.

All of these attacks are possible because wireless networks are unauthenticated and unencrypted by default.

Common wireless Security Options

To combat these vulnerabilities, administrators can implement one of the following common Security Options, listed from least to most secure:

- 802.11x Legacy Wireless security
- RRAS VPN protocols
- WEP
- IPSec
- WPA2
- WPA2-802.1x with EAP and Dynamic Encryption keys
- 802.11i (usually not tested)

802.11x Legacy Wireless security recommendations

In the past, the following security recommendations were often given to wireless network administrators.

- Require User Authentication passwords
- Change Default SSID
- Turn off SSID broadcasting
- Change WAP's default administrator password
- Enable MAC filtering
- Enable WEP or WPA encryption
- Consider disabling DHCP

While each of these options can provide some security, each of them is easily bypassed. Test questions will often involve replacing one or more of these methods with one of the newer wireless VPN protocols.

Wi-Fi Protected Access (WPA)

After WEP was cracked (over and over), wireless security experts created a new encryption protocol called Wi-Fi Protected Access (WPA). WPA (see Figure 8-43) and its newer variant, WPA2, are considered significantly stronger than WEP. WPA2 supports 802.1x EAP with dynamic key distribution or pre-shared secrets. A wireless network using WPA is considered fairly secure encryption. A wireless network using WPA2 is considered very secure.

Figure 8-43 shows WPA with the Pre-Shared Key (PSK) option enabled. The other options are Open, Shared, and WPA (alone without a PSK). There is another option called "The Key is provided to me automatically." When enabled, Windows will expect the key to be given to the client over the network or to be stored on the local network card adapter. Choosing WEP or WPA will encrypt the data across the wireless network, but the issue of how wireless nodes authenticate still needs to be solved.

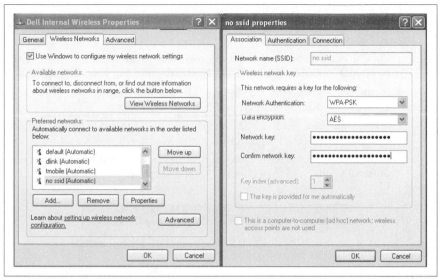

Figure 8-43. Enabling WPA in the Windows wireless client

802.1x wireless security

802.1x security addresses the authentication problem. It uses EAP (PEAP or smart cards) along with IAS and/or RRAS, and a backend PKI server (i.e., Certificate Services). Windows 9x and later (even Pocket PCs) can use 802.1x security. It's an add-on client to W2K and before, and standard on XP and above.

If EAP-TLS (i.e., smart cards) is used, it requires certificates on the client and on the IAS or RRAS server. EAP-TLS is transparent to the user, but it provides machine and user authentication. PEAP requires the user to input her logon name, password, and a server-side certificate to create an encrypted channel, but it doesn't require client-side digital certificates.

Steps to enable 802.1x authentication. The following describes how to enable 802.1x authentication:

1. Give *RAS and IAS Server* certificates to IAS/RRAS server(s).
2. Add IAS and RRAS server(s) to the RAS and IAS Servers group.
3. Create custom template from *User Signature* Certificate Template.
4. Add a custom application policy called *<Organization> Wireless User* if you want to require it for extra security. Must use Organization's OID arc.
5. Modify the custom template to not require user input during enrollment if you want auto-enrollment to work.
6. Give Read, Enroll, and Auto-enroll permissions to appropriate wireless users.
7. Configure Remote Access Policy on IAS or RRAS server to require "Smart card or other certificates" for authentication.
8. Configure a wireless client:

Exam 70-298
Study Guide

a. Install the new cert on appropriate wireless nodes.

b. In the Network Connections window, right-click on Wireless Adapter and click on Properties.

c. On the Wireless Networks tab, choose the appropriate Service Set Identifier (SSID) option in the Preferred Networks box and choose Properties.

d. In the SSID Properties dialog box, choose the Authentication tab (see Figure 8-44). Choose Properties.

e. Enable the "Enable IEEE 802.1x authentication for this network" option, and then choose the Properties button below it.

f. Enable the "Use a certificate on this computer" option or one of the other valid choices. Then choose OK and save the new settings.

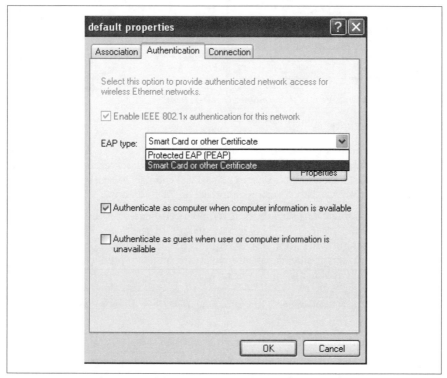

Figure 8-44. Enabling 802.1x Wireless security with certificates

Most wireless security topics on the 70-298 exam test your knowledge of WPA and 802.1x, and how to move a client from less secure WEP or other legacy solutions. Remember that other nonwireless-specific VPN options, such as SSL, IPSec, etc., can also be used to secure wireless networks.

Exam 70-298 frequently tests your knowledge on protecting network data streams. A Windows administrator can use SSL/TLS (IIS needed), IPSec, WebDAV (IIS needed), RDP, 802.1x (wireless), RPC over HTTPS, SSH (not a default Windows program), WPA/WPA2, 802.1x, and other programs to encrypt and authenticate. A successful exam candidate will understand the requirements, strengths, and weaknesses of the various data communication protocols.

Secure Active Directory Design

This section of the chapter will covers Secure Active Directory design, Active Directory delegation, and Group Design.

Creating an Active Directory design with security in mind takes lots of planning. Essentially, administrators use Active Directory containers and OUs to manage resources and to provide efficient security. In general, for good secure design, the following should be true:

- All Active Directory security design should be focused on role-based security—that is, who needs what security given the particular role they have in the organization? This is a huge concept to understand and underlies the rest of the security design.
- Use separate forests when separate security and management is absolutely needed between two entities.
- Typically, you don't want internal corporate users in the same forest as external public Internet users.
- Use separate domains when you want various entities to have their own autonomy, but when centralized control is still required.
- Some Group Policy settings, such as Password Policy and Account Lockout Policy, can only be made at the domain level. If two different policies are required, separate domains will also be required.
- Separate entities by OUs when centralized control is desired.
- Create a new OU any time a collection of security principals (users or computers) have common security needs not already met by the current structure.
- Apply common security settings as far up in the Active Directory structure as is operationally feasible—although, don't go above the domain level (i.e., applying site-level GPOs) unless it is a requirement. Site-level GPOs face replication and other issues that complicate secure design.

Active Directory security works by applying security settings configured in Group Policies to OUs. OUs should contain users or computers linked by their common roles. Group Policies can only be applied to OUs (and site containers) and apply only to the user and computer objects in the OU.

To repeat and clarify:

1. Define the various roles needed for your users and computers.
2. Create separate role-based OUs for both users and computers (see Figure 8-45).
3. Place the various users and computers into their appropriate role-based OUs.
4. Create role-based GPOs for both users and computers.
5. Link the role-based GPOs to the role-based GPOs.

This is the essence of secure Active Directory design. You can go one step further by creating role-based Security Templates and importing them into the role-based GPOs (see Figure 8-46).

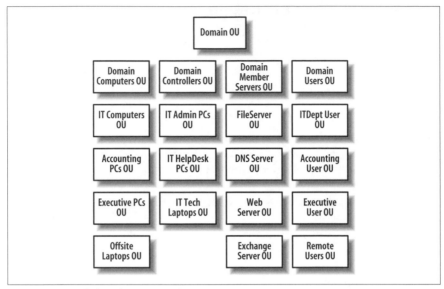

Figure 8-45. Role-based OU example

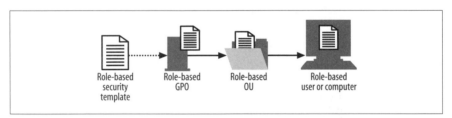

Figure 8-46. Role-based Active Directory security

When the 70-298 exam asks you to design a secure Active Directory infrastructure, follow the five steps just listed. Define the unique roles and unique security needs first. Then design role-based OU and GPO structures to support the user and computer roles.

Active Directory Delegation

Windows Server 2003 Active Directory was created with role delegation in mind. The idea is that an administrator can give a group of mid-level administrative users (e.g., Help Desk, Desktop Tech Support) granular control over any Active Directory container or OU. If the mid-level administrator shouldn't have all the powers and rights of a true Administrator, then an administrator can delegate various common administrative roles (e.g., password changes, etc.) to the user without giving the user all the rights of an Administrator.

Administrators can start the Delegation of Control wizard by right-clicking on any container or OU in Active Directory Users or Computers and choosing the Delegate Control option. Figure 8-47 shows some of the available delegation options. Most 70-298 candidates are tested on Active Directory delegation, so you should review the full list as partially displayed in Figure 8-47.

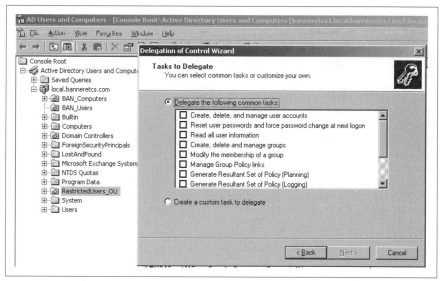

Figure 8-47. Delegation of Control Wizard

Group Design

Security permissions should always be assigned to groups and not individual users. There is an effective way to leverage Windows security groups to maximize efficiency and security. As covered in previous chapters, there are three major group scopes:

- Domain Local (or local)
- Global (domain-wide)
- Universal (forest-wide)

Users should always be placed into role-based groups based upon the least privilege needed security permissions. Security can be maximized if a few basic rules are followed:

1. Resource (e.g., file, folder, printer, etc.) permissions should always be assigned to a Domain Local group.
2. Users should be placed in Global groups.
3. Global groups should be placed into the Domain Local groups.

    Alternatively, Global groups can be placed into Universal groups, and the Universal groups placed into the Domain Local groups.

This strategy is known as AGLP or AGULP.

- Accounts should be placed in Global groups.
- Global groups should be placed in Universal groups (if needed) or Domain Local groups.
- The Domain Local groups should be given the resource Permissions.

 The AGULP method is known as AGLP if Universal groups are not involved. In general, only groups should be added to Universal groups.

Although the AGLP/AGULP method of assigning permissions may seem foreign to many exam candidates, for many reasons it is truly the most efficient and effective way of assigning security permissions in a Windows network. This is not some theoretical model that doesn't work well in the real world. It is the best— and should be the only way—administrators assign permissions. And to give it further credibility, most candidates will be tested on the AGLP/AGULP method in Exam 70-298. When given a permission question regarding users and groups, if you pick an answer choice that does not always support the AGLP/AGULP method, you will be wrong. The AGLP/AGULP method even minimizes Active Directory replication.

Secure Active Directory design focuses on role-based security. Role-based GPOs are created and placed into role-based OUs and containers, which hold role-based users and computers. The Windows Server 2003 Active Directory delegation feature allows mid-level administrators to be given pseudo-supervisory roles without giving them full Administrator privileges. The AGLP/AGULP method of group design ensures efficient and effective security design.

Client Hardening

This section of the chapter will focus on client-side GPO settings and other security settings for particular client roles. It will discuss GPO application order, the most popularly tested GPO settings, Password Policy, and kiosk security, as well as summarize Security Templates, Windows Firewall, and discuss legacy client automation options.

GPO Application Order

Group Policy Objects (GPOs) apply Windows configuration settings that could otherwise be applied manually or using registry edits. GPOs make Windows enterprise networks easier to manage. GPOs are linked to Active Directory containers or OUs and can be applied to user and computer objects.

If multiple GPOs exist, as is usually the case, the last applied GPO usually wins in the cases of conflicted settings. If no settings conflict, then all the applied GPO settings are implemented. Here is the GPO application order:

1. Local Computer Policy is applied when the computer starts up and the user first logs on, if there are any defined settings.

2. Site-level GPOs are applied next.

3. Domain-level GPOs are applied next.

4. OU-level GPOs are applied last, and the lower a GPO is linked in the Active Directory infrastructure, the later it is applied (i.e., GPOs applied to child OUs will be applied after parent OU GPOs).

 The mnemonic LSD...OU is often used by exam candidates to remember the GPO application order.

If multiple GPOs are applied at the same level, the GPO's order of precedence determines what gets applied last. A GPO with a higher priority will win in cases of conflicted settings. The higher the priority, the later it is applied.

Ways to override normal GPO application order

The normal GPO application order assumes that no GPOs applied earlier are marked as Enforced or "No override." Enforced GPOs will be applied last and win in the cases of conflicted settings. The application order is as follows:

1. Use Set Block Policy Inheritance to block a GPO's natural downward inheritance. Can only be applied at an OU level or container level. When enabled, this will block all above GPOs from applying at the block level or below.

2. Use the Set Disabled option (whole GPO) per GPO per OU to inactivate.

3. Use Set Disable User settings or Disable Computer Settings per GPO.

4. Use Set No Override (also called Enforced in the Group Policy Management console) per GPO per OU. When set on GPO, downstream OUs and containers can't block inheritance. It will be the dominant GPO.

5. Use the "Enable loopback processing" mode to set on a per-GPO basis. A GPO with loopback is always re-applied last.

6. Use Deny Read or Apply Group Policy permissions of a particular GPO to a user, group, or computer so that GPO doesn't apply to them. Security takes precedence.

Kiosk computers. Loopback processing is set under Computer Configuration container → Administrative Templates → System → Group Policy. It ensures that computer-defined settings apply to a specific PC, regardless of user permissions. Loopback processing is intended for special use computers, such as kiosk machines. (See MS KB 231287.) Exam 70-298 frequently mentions or tests how to securely configure kiosk computers. The correct answer choices will almost always include either Security Templates, GPOs, or loopback processing.

Popularly Tested GPO Settings

This section will focus on the most popularly tested GPO topics on the 70-298 exam.

Startup and Shutdown scripts

An administrator can push user- and computer-based scripts using GPOs. A script can be run when a computer logs on (i.e., using a Startup script) to the domain or when it logs off (i.e., using a Shutdown script); or when a user logs on (i.e., using a Logon script) or when the user logs off (i.e., using a Logoff script). Any type of script, command, or batch file that the host computer can process can be placed in a GPO script. Scripts are run in the LocalSystem context, so that the logged-in user does not have to be an administrator to have all of the script settings apply (as is the case with most registry edits). VBScripts and JScript files are processed by the `Wscript.exe` or `Cscript.exe` programs located on the local Windows system.

Password Policy

Password Policy is frequently tested on the 70-298 exam. You should be familiar with all the Password Policy settings available in a GPO (see Figure 8-48). Password Policy, Account Lockout Policy, and Kerberos policy can only be set at the domain-level and take affect in an Active Directory Domain GPO. Password Policy and Account Lockout Policy can be set at a local level as well, but only affect local accounts. If users log into a domain, the domain-level policy will apply.

Figure 8-48. Password Policy settings

The "Enforce password history" setting ensures that users will not use a previously used password, at least for a certain number of password changes. Windows will remember, and won't allow the user to re-use, the last 24 previous passwords by default. "Maximum password age" is the maximum number of days a password can be used before expiring. This should be set to a reasonable interval to offset the potential threats of password guessing and cracking. Normally, a maximum password age of 45 days is considered fairly secure. "Minimum password age" determines how long a user must use a new password before he can change to a new one. This setting is to prevent users from trying to circumvent the "Enforce password history" setting. Normally, it is set to one to two days.

"Minimum password length" is the minimum length a password can be. Longer passwords are more secure. Unfortunately, currently, the longest maximum minimum password length is 14 characters. Today's environments need longer minimum password sizes. A 15-character password automatically disables the storage of the LM password hash, which is the single best thing an administrator can do to stop Windows password cracking. The "Password must meet complexity requirements" setting ensures that all newly created Windows logon passwords created or changed through the normal GUI contain nondictionary words or phrases. According to Microsoft, if this policy is enabled, passwords must meet the following minimum requirements:

- Must not contain all or part of the user's account name
- Must be at least six characters in length
- Must contain characters from three of the following five categories:
  - English uppercase characters (A through Z)
  - English lowercase characters (a through z)
  - Base 10 digits (0 through 9)
  - Nonalphanumeric characters (e.g., !, $, #, %)
  - Unicode characters (not represented in the previous categories)

 It's unfortunate that we cannot mandate longer minimum password lengths, as increased password length beats password complexity character for character.

Restricted groups

Local group membership can be restricted (see Figure 8-49). Once a particular group's membership is defined in a GPO, if any unauthorized members (i.e., not added in the Restricted Groups section of the GPO) are added or deleted, they will be removed or re-added when the GPO next applies.

Service control

Exam 70-298 frequently tests candidates' knowledge of controlling Windows services using GPOs. With a GPO, you can control what services can start, and who can manage them (see Figure 8-50).

Software Restriction Policies

Software Restriction Policies (SRP), also known as *SAFER*, allow an administrator to control what applications can and can't run on a Windows XP Pro and later computer. Windows 2000 has a smaller subset of features similar to SRP, but these features are not nearly as granular. The SRP management console is accessed using Group Policy or Local Computer Policy.

The first decision to make is whether SRP is going to deny all software by default, except that which is allowed, or allow all software to run by default, except that which is denied (the default when SRP is turned on). Once the overall rule is set, exceptions to the major rule are defined. Hence, if you decide to implement the deny-by-default rule as the major rule, every program you want to run is then defined as an exception to the default rule.

The deny-by-default rule is called *Disallowed* in SRP. The other choice—that is, to allow all software to run except that which is explicitly denied—is called *Unrestricted*. This major SRP setting, called Security Levels, is made under the Security Settings leaf object.

Exam 70-298
Study Guide

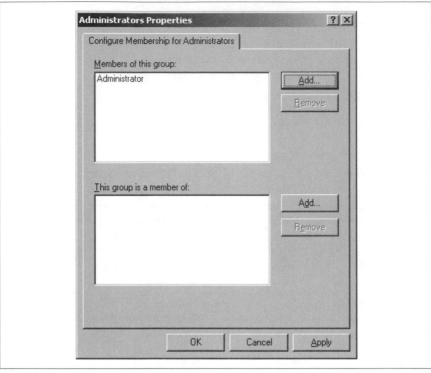

Figure 8-49. Example of restricted groups

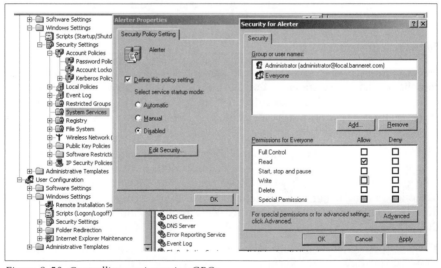

Figure 8-50. Controlling services using GPOs

SRP exception rules. After that default decision is made, the administrator goes about setting exceptions. Exceptions are policy rules that either allow specific software (when using the Disallowed main setting), or deny specific software (when using the Unrestricted setting). There are four different types of exception rules:

- Certificate rules
- Hash rules
- Internet Zone rules
- Path rules

Certificate exception rules allow an administrator to deny or allow software digitally signed by a specific digital certificate. For example, an administrator can deny all JavaScript files except those signed by an internal private digital certificate. Hash rules allow you to input a valid MD5 or SHA1 file hash value (i.e., digital fingerprint). Like Certificate rules, it allows an administrator to deny or allow a particular file or program regardless of where the program is or what it is named.

The Internet Zone rule will allow or deny all software installed and executed in a particular Internet Explorer Zone, but only if the file was installed with a Windows installer (MSI) file. Since most Internet-installed software programs do not install with an MSI file, it has become practically the rule class almost worthless. Path rules allow an administrator to define exceptions using folder or registry paths. Figure 8-51 shows some example exception rules.

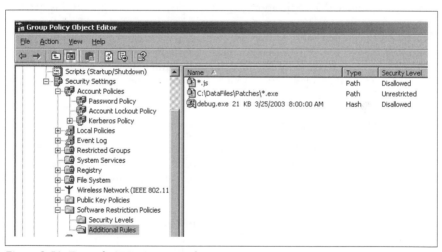

Figure 8-51. Example SRP exception rules

Setting up a deny-by-default SRP takes some planning and work. None of the rule exceptions work perfectly by themselves, but all four types used together can roughly enforce what software is and isn't allowed to run on a Windows XP and later computer.

Unfortunately, there appear to be many ways to bypass each particular exception rule. Most users won't be able to guess how to hack around SRP, but it can be done. Of course, this is never tested on the exam. If an administrator needs absolute security in real life, he should rely upon NTFS permissions instead.

Although SRP doesn't work on Windows 2000, Group Policy had SRP-like policies. In a GPO, choose User Configuration\Administrative Templates\System. There are two similar settings called "Run only allowed Windows applications" and "Don't run specific Windows applications." Exam 70-298 has been known to test on the latter options as well as the newer SRP.

Folder redirection

By default, a user's My Documents folder is stored in her user profile. If the user has a roaming profile, the contents of her My Documents directory is copied down from a server every time she logs in, and up to the server every time she logs out. As her My Documents directory grows larger, it can start to take a significant amount of time for her to log on and log off. An administrator can use GPOs to redirect her My Documents folder to a shared network drive instead of to her local drive. When folder redirection is enabled, it essentially changes the link and storage location of the user's My Documents directory, and more importantly, no longer stores them with her profile.

WMI filtering

Windows XP Pro introduced the WMI Filtering feature in GPOs. WMI filtering allows XP Pro and later computers to be analyzed by an administrator-defined WMI script, and GPO applications to be skipped if certain conditions are not met. For example, a WMI script in a Software Install GPO may query the user's local hard drive and ensure that there is enough space to load a new application. If disk space is low, the WMI filter can cause the GPO not to install the new software program, as it normally would if the WMI filter didn't exist. WMI filters don't work against Windows 2000, so a WMI filter will never make a GPO skip a Windows 2000 computer.

Confirming Group Policy settings

GPOs are a wonderful tool for centralizing the management and configuration of Windows XP Pro and later computers. Microsoft has several tools that can be used to report on the effective Group Policy settings applied to a user or computer, including RSOP and Gpresult.

RSoP. *Resultant Set of Policies* (RSoP) is a graphical tool that allows an administrator to view the current effective GPO settings applied to a particular user or PC, and that also allows the administrator to run "what-if" scenarios (i.e., to be in *Planning mode*). If an administrator is planning to move a user or computer to another container or OU in Active Directory, or add the user or computer to another group, he can run the RSOP tool in Planning mode and discover what the new effective settings would be before the change is made.

Gpresult. Gpresult.exe is a command-line tool that summarizes the groups and Group Policies that apply to a user and computer. If run with the /v parameter, it will display every enforced GPO setting, and list which GPO applied the setting. Gpresult.exe /v is an excellent way to document effective GPO settings on a particular user or computer.

Gpresult.exe should not be confused with Gpupdate. Gpupdate can be used to force Group Policy refreshes prior to the predefined Group Policy refresh interval.

Security Templates

Security Templates let an administrator make portable the security settings she could otherwise set manually or with a GPO. The settings can be directly applied against a particular computer (using the Security Configuration and Analysis tool or using Secedit.exe), or imported into a GPO. If a Security Template is applied locally, it "tattoos" the registry, creating a permanent registry edit that persists (i.e., lives through reboots). An administrator can import more than one Security Template into a GPO. If any settings conflict, then the last one imported wins.

Common Security Templates

Windows 2000 and later comes with pre-installed Security Templates. They are:

Setup Security.inf
Security as defined when system was set up, including all file permissions. Contains hundreds of settings; it's very large.

Default*.inf
The same as Setup Security.

Rootsec.inf
Specifies default user permissions on the root directory of the system drive, some of which are inherited on down.

Hisec*.inf
Requires the SMB packet signing communications, among other things (prevents connections to legacy clients).

Secure*.inf
Requires complex passwords and removes all users from Power Users group among its options.

Compatws.inf
Relaxes C:\Program Files permissions so that users can read and write, as is the need with some older applications (such as MS-Office 97). Also removes all users from the Power Users group using a Restricted Group with nobody defined.

Security Configuration and Analysis tool. The Security Configuration and Analysis tool can be used to compare (i.e., analyze) a computer against a particular Security Template and note the differences. It can also be used to apply (i.e., configure) Security Template settings.

Secedit.exe. Secedit.exe is essentially the command-line version of the Security Configuration and Analysis Tool. Secedit actually came first and was released in Windows NT 4.0 SP 4. It can be used to compare and apply Security Template settings against a PC. The command-line version is especially useful in scripting and automation scenarios. The Windows Server 2003 version of Secedit has a /generaterollback option, which is especially useful for recovering back to the original security settings when the newly applied security settings cause problems.

Historically, on average, the Exam 70-298 candidate has had at least one question on Security Templates.

Windows Firewall

Windows XP Pro and Windows Server 2003 come with a host-based firewall called Windows Firewall (it was called Internet Connection Firewall in XP Pro pre-SP2 releases). Windows Firewall, when enabled, will block all incoming requests not initiated by a preceding related outbound network connection, unless an inbound exception is configured (see Figure 8-52). Exceptions must be created for any authorized service process (e.g., NetBIOS drive share, DHCP server, DNS server, etc.). Enabling Windows Firewall without any planning for actively used server services will almost ensure legitimate service interruptions.

Figure 8-52. Example of Windows Firewall Exceptions

Legacy Clients

Microsoft security exams frequently mention legacy clients (i.e., pre-Windows 2000) and how they would be secured. You should be familiar with how to secure and manage legacy clients in a Windows Server 2003 environment. The following sections cover some commonly mentioned files and programs for legacy computers.

Ntuser.dat

Ntuser.dat holds the user's profile. The profile is all the user's desktop settings (e.g., screensaver, background, etc.), his user-specific security settings, and his My Documents folder (among other things). When a user logs on with his name and password, Windows accesses his user profile and changes his desktop environment.

If the user has a roaming profile, the profile file is stored on a network share. When the user logs into the computer, the computer copies down his profile from the network share and places it on the local hard drive. When he logs out, it copies his profile and any changes back up to the network share. If his profile file is called *Ntuser.man*, it means the user profile is mandatory and can't be modified. Any changes the user makes to his desktop environment will be lost when he logs off the computer.

Ntconfig.pol

The *Ntconfig.pol* was the precursor to Group Policy and Security Templates in Windows NT 4.0 and Windows 9x. An administrator could create the *Ntconfig.pol* file using the System Policy Editor (`Poledit.exe`) and then apply it. NT 4.0 SP4 first released Security Templates and the `Secedit.exe` utility to apply them.

Active Directory Client Extensions

Windows 9x and Windows NT 4.0 require the Active Directory Client Extension software (it's called slightly different names—AD Client Extension, DS Client, *DSClient.exe*, etc.—in different test questions) to connect to Active Directory. It allows legacy clients to authenticate to Active Directory (and using the newer NT password hashes and NTLMv2 authentication protocols), but does not allow GPOs to be applied.

To prepare for the 70-298 exam, you should refamiliarize yourself with the details of Group Policy and popular GPO choices. While the 70-298 exam is not nearly as operationally detailed as some of the earlier workstation and server exams, it often mentions specific Group Policy settings, and you must know which choices are valid and which are invalid, given a particular set of business requirements.

Data Access Control Strategies

This section focuses on protecting data and programs on the local hard drive. It will cover Windows security permissions and EFS.

Windows Security Permissions

Microsoft Windows NTFS partitions contain very granular security permissions in the form of Share and NTFS permissions. Nearly every Windows object on an NTFS partition has security permissions, including files, folders, printers, and registry entries.

Share permissions

All Windows computers have Share permissions, even non-NTFS volumes (i.e., FAT partitions). Share permissions apply only to users or computers accessing resources over NetBIOS shares. If the same resources are accessed locally (not using a NetBIOS share), the Share permissions don't apply. The three possible Share permissions are:

- Full Control
- Change
- Read

All newly created shares on XP Pro and Windows Server 2003 have the default rights of Everyone Allow-Read. Contrast this with NT 4.0 and Windows 2000's Everyone Allow-Full Control. The Full Control allows anyone with the permission to modify, delete, rename, and otherwise manipulate the resource to the fullest extent possible. Users with Full Control to a resource can change the permissions configured on the resource, even taking permissions way from the Administrator (although, luckily, the Administrator can always take ownership of the resource and reset the permissions).

The Change permission is much like the NTFS Modify permission. It allows a security principal to add, modify, move, rename, or delete a resource. The Read permission allows a security principal to view, copy, and print (if possible) a resource.

Permissions set above in parent containers are normally (but not always) inherited below, unless inheritance is disabled. Inheritance can be controlled on a per-user and per-object basis. An administrator can allow inheritance to apply to one user and not another.

Many resources, including Microsoft, recommend always setting the Share permissions to Full Control, and letting the underlying NTFS permissions handle the effective security. In practice though, Share permissions should be set to their least privilege setting. If a security principal doesn't need Full Control permissions, don't give them.

NTFS permissions

NTFS permissions apply to nearly ever object on an NTFS partition, whether the object is accessed over a Share or locally. There are 14 granular NTFS permissions (see Figure 8-53), each of which can be Allowed or Denied. Many administrators are only familiar with the seven "summary" NTFS permissions as they are presented by default in Windows Explorer. These permissions are:

- Read
- Write

- List (folders only)
- Read and Execute
- Modify
- Full Control
- Special Permissions (any combination of the underlying 14 granular permissions)

Again, any security principal given Full Control permissions has absolute control over the resource. Normal inheritance rules apply.

It is important that a Windows administrator know what granular permissions make up the summary permissions. Table 8-2 shows how the 14 "advanced" permissions make up the summary permissions. And a good Windows security administrator often uses the more granular permissions to ensure that least privilege policies are being followed.

If a Deny permission is set at the same level as an Allow permission for a given user, the Deny permission will override the Allow permission. However, if the Allow permission is set explicitly on an object and the Deny permission is inherited from a parent container or folder above, the explicitly set Allow permission will override the inherited Deny permission.

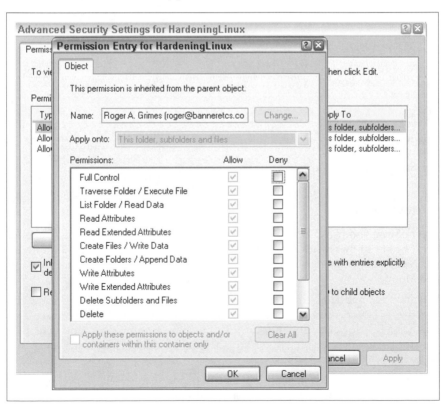

Figure 8-53. NTFS advanced permissions

Table 8-2. NTFS Summary versus Advanced permission settings

Permission	Full Control	Modify	Read and Execute	List	Read	Write
Traverse Folder/ Execute File	X	X	X	X	–	–
List Folder/ Read Data	X	X	X	X	X	–
Read Attributes	X	X	X	X	X	–
Read Extended Attributes	X	X	X	X	X	–
Create Files/ Write Data	X	X	–	–	–	X
Create Folders/ Append Data	X	X	–	–	–	X
Write Attributes	X	X	–	–	–	X
Write Extended Attributes	X	X	–	–	–	X
Delete Subfolders and Files	X	–	–	–	–	–
Delete	X	X	–	–	–	–
Read Permissions	X	X	X	X	X	X
Change Permissions	X	–	–	–	–	–
Take Owner- ship	X	–	–	–	–	–
Synchronize	X	X	X	X	X	X

Effective permissions

If both Share and NTFS permissions apply to an object, the least permissive set of permissions apply. For example, if the Share permissions give Full Control and the NTFS permissions give Read and Modify, the effective permissions are Read and Modify.

Windows XP and later contain a Windows Explorer feature that will show the effective NTFS permissions for a given security principal to an object (see Figure 8-54). However, the Effective Permissions feature does not take into account Share permission effects and a host of other potentially impacting features (such as EFS, for instance).

An administrator needs to take all the following features into account when accessing the effective permissions given to a user or computer:

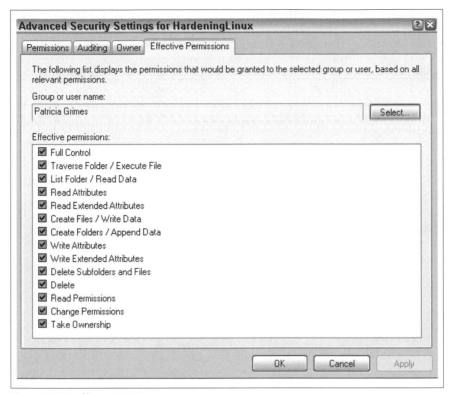

Figure 8-54. Effective NTFS permissions

- Object's Access Control Entries (ACE) permissions
- Disk subsystem type-FAT or NTFS
- Share permissions (if they apply)
- NTFS permissions (if they apply)
- Account permissions
- Group Membership and Permissions
- Inheritance
- Windows trusts (cross-domain access)
- Encryption (EFS)

In real life, and for the exam, make Windows security permissions as restrictive as possible (i.e., least privilege). Whenever possible, assign permissions to groups, following the AGLP/AGULP method previously discussed.

Encrypting File System (EFS)

Windows Encrypting File System (EFS) was introduced in Windows 2000 and improved in Windows XP Pro and Windows Server 2003. EFS encrypts files stored on local or remote NTFS partitions using public key cryptography (with asymmetric and symmetric keys). When a user encrypts a file (see Figure 8-55), a session symmetric encryption key is created (called the *File Encryption Key* or FEK). The FEK is then used to encrypt the file. Every file has a unique FEK. The FEK is then encrypted using the user's asymmetric public EFS encryption key. Additional copies of the same FEK are encrypted for every user who has EFS access to the file (XP Pro and Server 2003 allow EFS-protected files to be shared), which usually includes one or more EFS Data Recovery Agents (DRAs). When the user needs to access an EFS-protected file, the file's FEK is decrypted by the user's private EFS key (which is stored in the user's profile).

EFS encryption and decryption happens transparently to the user. Files copied across network links are sent decrypted by default. If the file should be encrypted during network transmission, a network encryption protocol (e.g., SSL, WebDAV, IPSec, etc.) should be used as well.

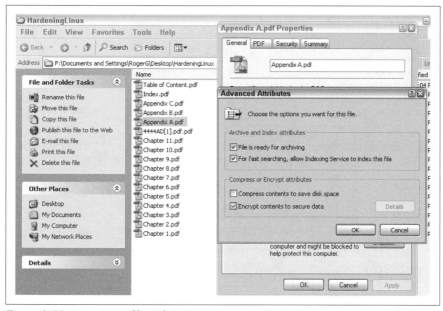

Figure 8-55. Protecting a file with EFS

By default, Windows chooses the local (or domain in a domain environment) Administrator to be the EFS Data Recovery Agent, except on standalone versions of XP Pro workstation, where no EFS Recovery Data Agent is enabled by default. If an EFS Data Recovery Agent is enabled, it means that if the user's private EFS key is ever lost, the EFS Data Recovery agent can recover the files for the user (or her administrative representative).

 Note that EFS and Compression cannot be turned on at the same time despite featuring two checkboxes (instead of the more GUI-correct radio buttons). This has been a mistake in the GUI since Windows 2000.

EFS is globally turned on by default, and as such, any user can encrypt any file located on any NTFS partition. It is important that an EFS Data Recovery Agent or DRA (or Key Recovery Agent [KRA] in Certificate Services) be defined and used. If a DRA or KRA cannot be defined, the administrator should strongly considered disabling EFS globally. If the user loses his EFS private key, his protected files could remain encrypted forever.

When Certificate Services is not used, EFS uses a self-signed, 100-year certificate created on the user's local machine. If Certificate Services is used, EFS will automatically locate the CA server and the resulting EFS certificate will only be good for two years, but can be renewed.

Here are some other important EFS points:

- EFS works with WebDAV.
- EFS works with offline folders and files (XP Pro and later).
- XP Pro and later supports EFS file sharing.
- The Cipher.exe command-line utility can be used to review EFS-protected files and their related certificates.
- Remote servers holding EFS-protected files need their server account enabled with the Trusted for Delegation option.

EFS is strong file encryption. A data or key recovery plan must be tested and implemented before allowing users to use EFS.

Exam 70-298 tests your knowledge of various Microsoft security technologies from a planning consultant's point of view. Common topics include Certificate Services, network data encryption, secure Active Directory design, SUS, IPSec, wireless security, remote administration, IIS, RRAS, IAS, and VPN technologies. To be successful, you must master each of these technologies and be able to define the strengths and weaknesses of various proposed solutions. Most exam questions are high-level, focusing on management and design, but many questions expect you to understand the details of each of these technologies (although not normally the interface). Chapter 9 will test your understanding of the issues covered in this chapter and further prepare you for the 70-298 exam.

9

Exam 70-298 Prep and Practice

The material in this chapter is designed to help you prepare and practice for *Exam 70-298: Designing Security for a Microsoft Windows Server 2003 Network*. The chapter is organized into four sections:

Preparing for Exam 70-298
> This section provides an overview of the types of questions on the exam. Reviewing this section will help you understand how the actual exam works.

Exam 70-298 Suggested Exercises
> This section provides a numbered list of exercises that you can follow to gain experience in the exam's subject areas. An in-depth study of practice case scenarios will help you prepare better for the exam.

Exam 70-298 Highlighters Index
> This section compiles the facts within the exam's subject areas that you are most likely to need another look at—in other words, the areas of study that you might have highlighted while reading the Study Guide. Studying the highlights is useful as a final review before the exam.

Exam 70-298 Practice Questions
> This section includes a comprehensive set of practice questions to assess your knowledge of the exam. The questions are more or less similar in format to those on the exam. After you've reviewed the Study Guide, read the questions and see whether you can answer them correctly.

Before you take Exam 70-298, see the exam overview and take another look at the Highlighters Index. Many online web sites provide practice tests for the exam. Duplicating the depth and scope of these practice exams in a printed book isn't possible. Visit Microsoft's Certification site for pointers to online practice tests (*http://www.microsoft.com/learning/mcpexams/prepare/practicetests.asp*).

Preparing for Exam 70-298

Exam 70-298 is a scenario-based design exam. Candidates are typically given four to six design scenarios (called *testlets*) followed by multiple questions related to each scenario. Each of these testlets spans multiple pages of information, some of which is relevant and some of which is irrelevant to the case. You are required to study the information on all these pages before you can answer the questions based on the information. If you have not practiced properly, the information may seem to be confusing at times. It is necessary that you do not skip any part of the information so that you can correctly answer the questions in the testlet.

Most questions are the simple multiple-choice format, but several questions will contain graphical representations that you'll have to analyze and interpret.

While many of the questions on Exam 70-298 are multiple-choice, there are also hot area, select and place, active screen, and simulation types of questions that are being used increasingly by Microsoft to ensure that the testing process more accurately reflects actual hands-on knowledge rather than rote memorization. With the exception of multiple-choice, single-answer questions, all of the other questions can have multiple answers or required multiple procedures to obtain full credit. If all of the expected answers or procedures are not performed, you will only get partial credit for the answer. This is usually indicated in the question itself.

Typically, each testlet will have Previous/Next and Mark For Review options. A candidate can navigate through the questions in a testlet using the Previous/Next buttons, but only within each exam testlet. The candidate can click the Mark For Review checkbox to flag a question for later review, but again, only within each testlet. Once the candidate has finished answering and reviewing the questions in a particular testlet, he cannot go back. Therefore, it's important you completely finish each testlet before heading on to other scenarios, while still considering the overall time constraints for finishing the entire exam.

Exam 70-298 Suggested Exercises

Exam 70-298 expects you to have a sound knowledge of what you have learned during the preparation of Windows Server 2003 core required exams, plus an understanding of Chapter 8. It is suggested that you take this exam after you have completed the four core exams, plus *Exam 70-297: Designing a Microsoft Windows Server 2003 Active Directory and Network Infrastructure*. Exam 70-298 contains a fair amount of Active Directory design and organizational unit placement that can only be made easier by passing Exam 70-297 first.

You are expected not only to be a good administrator in these areas, but also to have the solid planning skills of a network and security infrastructure designer. The measured skills are extended to include many new areas of study, including analysis of an existing Active Directory and network infrastructure, business and technical requirements of an organization, and, based on your analysis, design of the security infrastructure for an organization.

You will need plenty of planning and design experience to pass the exam. This design will be based on your skills in analyzing the given information in a case study. You'll need to review the Study Guide closely and focus on any areas with which you are unfamiliar. This section provides a numbered list of exercises that you can follow to gain experience in the exam's subject areas. Performing the exercises will be useful to help to ensure that you have plenty of planning and design experience with all areas of the exam.

The exam tests your planning and design skills instead of any hands-on skills. The case scenarios presented in the exam will require you to have an in-depth knowledge of Windows Server 2003 technologies and how they can be applied when you are creating a design for an Active Directory-based network infrastructure. It is not bad idea, however, to have a Windows XP Pro client computer and Windows Sever 2003 enterprise server test network just in case you need to practice a few hands-on skills.

 Before you take Exam 70-298, we strongly recommend that you review key features of Windows Server 2003 Active Directory and the network services that you studied while preparing for the four core exams. The companion book *MCSE Core Required Exams in a Nutshell*, Third Edition, by William Stanek (O'Reilly), covers all four core exams.

In addition to understanding the material in Chapter 8 and in the "Exam 70-298 Highlighters Index" later in this chapter, you should also be experienced in the network and Windows Server 2003 technologies and applications that are discussed in the next sections.

Segmenting Networks

1. Understand the differences between a router, Ethernet switch, firewall, NAT device, IP filtering, and VPNs.
2. Given a particular business scenario and requirements, understand which device or feature is most appropriate to segment network traffic.

Encryption and Authentication

1. Understand the two different types of cryptographic encryption—symmetric and asymmetric—and when each should be used.
2. Understand the difference between encryption and authentication, and which cryptographic technology supports which cryptographic features.
3. Understand which key is used when in asymmetric encryption and authentication.
4. Understand which Microsoft technologies use encryption and authentication.
5. Understand what is Federal Information Processing Standard (FIPS) is and why it is required in some environments.
6. Know the difference between one-factor, two-factor, and multi-factor authentication.

7. Understand the difference between a Windows password hash and a Windows authentication protocol.

8. Be able to choose which Windows password hash type and which Windows authentication protocols are subject to trivial cryptographic attacks, and which Group Policy setting can disable them.

9. Understand the need for and difference between impersonation and delegation.

10. Be able to describe the Windows technologies that commonly need delegation enabled.

11. Understand what EFS protects and when.

12. Understand what VPN protocols (e.g., PPTP, L2TP, IPSec, SSL, SSH, RDP, etc.) protect and when.

13. Understand Public Key Infrastructure (PKI) and why it is needed.

14. Describe and understand the following PKI components: Certification Authority, key pair, digital signature, digital certificate, trusted CA, trusted root CA, revocation, and certificate revocation list.

15. Describe the three major decisions for each created certification authority.

16. Explain the difference between a one-tier, two-tier, and three-tier PKI hierarchy.

17. Understand the difference between a user certificate and a machine certificate.

18. Explain the term *self-signed* and why it is considered less trustworthy than PKI solutions.

Auditing

1. Name the nine different audit categories and know what security event types they track.

2. Understand when each type of audit category should be enabled and tracked.

3. Be able to configure the audit log duration and rotation policies.

4. Be able to design a centralized auditing collection solution.

Security Infrastructure Technologies

1. Explain the basic steps needed to secure any infrastructure server.

2. Understand how to design a secure DNS infrastructure for both internal and external use.

3. Understand the difference between DNS secure zone transfers and secure dynamic updates.

4. Explain when each of the following network communication security protocols can be used: IPSec, RDP, SSL, and SSH.

Certificate Services

1. Understand the new features in Windows Server 2003 Certificate Services.
2. Be able to install Certificate Services, as either enterprise or standalone, root or subordinate, public or private, online or offline, as the business requirements demand. Be able to decide when each type of CA is needed.
3. Be able to explain the benefits of an enterprise CA.
4. Know the difference between auto-enroll, auto-approve, and auto-mapping.
5. Be able to explain the entire Certificate Services process—from configuring the Certificate Template, to enrollment, approval, distribution, and revocation.
6. Understand the need for Certificate Templates, what can be configured on each Template, and how Templates are made available in Certificate Services.
7. Describe and explain the different Certificate Template permissions and when they are needed.
8. Describe the different certificate request enrollment methods.
9. Understand the requirements needed for auto-enrollment.
10. Be able to discuss and design the various key archival/recovery methods.
11. Explain the need for a Key Recovery Agent.
12. Be able to configure a Key Recovery Agent in Certificate Services and also for a particular Certificate Template.
13. Be experienced in web enrollment and its various options and functions.
14. Explain the difference between auto-mapping and client mapping.
15. Explain the various CA roles.
16. Describe in general terms how Certificate Services is used in the following applications: secure email, smart cards, IPSec, and SSL.
17. Explain what a Smart Card is and what it contains.
18. Be able to configure a Smart Card enrollment agent and workstation.
19. Describe multiple methods for backing up Certificate Services data.

Patch Management

1. Know when to use the various Microsoft patch management solutions: Microsoft Baseline Security Analyzer, Windows Update, Automatic Update, Software Update Services, and other enterprise options.
2. Be able to install, use, and configure SUS/WSUS services.
3. Be able to design a SUS/WSUS distribution strategy to meet various business and network bandwidth requirements.
4. Understand Active Directory software installs and the four different file types: MSI, MST, MSP, and ZAP.

Remote Administration Tools

1. Be able to design and choose among the various remote administration options: Remote Desktop, EMS, Remote Assistance, Remote Administration (HTML), Telnet, and NetMeeting Remote Desktop Sharing.
2. Understand the difference between Remote Desktop Protocol (RDP) and the protocols that use RDP.
3. Understand when each remote admin tool can be used, and the strengths and weaknesses of each.

Terminal Services

1. Understand why Terminal Services might be used.
2. Know the various Terminal Service Security Options available in Group Policy.

Windows Trust

1. Understand what a Windows trust is and what effect it has upon security.
2. Understand the various types of Windows trusts, and when each can be used.

IPSec

1. Understand when IPSec can be used.
2. Describe the components of an IPSec policy.
3. Know the difference between the AH and ESP protocols.
4. Be able to design and implement various IPSec policies depending on the business requirements.
5. Describe the three default Microsoft IPSec policies and when each would be used.

Securing IIS Web Sites

1. Explain the majority components for securing an IIS web site and how they all interoperate with each other.
2. Explain the effect of NetBIOS Share permissions on an IIS web site.
3. Describe the various IIS permissions and what each allows.
4. Explain the various IIS authentication methods and when each is needed.
5. Understand the need for a web application pool and the web pool identity.
6. Understand how to install SSL/TLS and what it accomplishes.
7. Describe client-side certificate mapping and why it is needed.
8. Explain URLscan, what it does, and why it is needed.
9. Explain the various IIS logging file formats and what each contains.
10. Explain web service extensions.
11. Describe WebDAV, why it is needed, and how to implement it.

RRAS and IAS

1. Explain the two RRAS VPN protocols and when each should be used.
2. Describe the six RRAS VPN protocols and when each should be used.
3. Describe the CMAK tool.
4. Describe the RRAS access policies and how they are used.
5. Explain RADIUS and RADIUS terms (e.g., RADIUS client).
6. Explain IAS and when it should be used.
7. Explain IAS and RRAS interaction.

Securing Wireless Networks

1. Understand various basic wireless terminologies.
2. Understand the difference between Ad-hoc and Infrastructure Mode.
3. Describe the various wireless vulnerabilities.
4. Know when to implement the various wireless security technologies: 802.11x Legacy Security, RRAS VPN Protocols, WEP, IPSec, WPA2, and WPA2-802.1x with EAP and Dynamic Encryption Keys.
5. Describe the legacy 802.11x security technologies.
6. Understand the differences between WEP and WPA encryption.
7. Describe how to implement 802.1x wireless security, both from a client and server point of view.

Secure Active Directory Design

1. Describe the main objective of secure Active Directory design.
2. Understand when separate forests, domains, and OUs are required.
3. Explain how security is applied in an Active Directory environment.
4. Explain Active Directory application order and how Group Policy is applied.
5. Explain the various GPO override methods and where each applies.
6. Explain why Security Templates are used.
7. Describe Active Directory delegation.
8. Know the various options of the Delegation of Control wizard.
9. Know the various Windows security group scopes, and when each is needed.
10. Explain the appropriate way to use nested groups when applying Windows security permissions.

Client Hardening

1. Explain the concept of a kiosk computer and how it should be secured.
2. Explain Startup and Shutdown scripts.
3. Know the Password Policy settings and where they must be applied to be effective.

4. Explain Restricted groups and where they apply.

5. Understand the ways to control a Windows service using Group Policy.

6. Explain software restriction policies and the four exception rule types.

7. Explain folder redirection and why it would be used.

8. Explain WMI filtering, where it can be used, and why it would be used.

9. Explain the various methods to confirm Group Policy application.

10. Define the default Windows Security Templates and when each would be used.

11. Decide when to use the Security Configuration and Analysis console tool instead of Secedit.exe.

12. Explain the Windows Firewall, its default settings, and when exceptions are needed.

13. Describe methods for securing legacy clients.

Data Security Strategies

1. Understand the difference between Share and NTFS permissions, and when each applies.

2. Understand, in detail, the various Share and NTFS permissions.

3. Know the 14 "advanced" NTFS permissions and which ones make up the seven "summary" higher-level permissions that most users normally work with.

4. Explain what the Full Control permission gives a user when all other permissions are given except for Full Control.

5. Explain when a Deny permission does not override an Allow permission.

6. Explain inheritance.

7. List the various mechanisms that can have an impact on Windows security permissions.

8. Explain the NTFS Effective Permissions tab and what is reported there.

Encrypting File System

1. Explain how EFS works.

2. Explain the differences in EFS when used with Microsoft Certificate Services.

3. List the new features in EFS in Windows XP Pro and Windows Server 2003, as compared with Windows 2000.

4. Describe when delegation is needed for EFS.

5. Explain the various methods to protect EFS files when they are being transferred across a network.

Exam 70-298 Highlighters Index

In this section, we've attempted to compile the facts within the exam's subject areas that you are most likely to need another look at—in other words, the areas of study that you might have highlighted while reading the Study Guide. The title of each highlighted element corresponds to the heading title in the Exam 70-298 Study Guide. This way, if you have a question about a highlight, you can refer back to the corresponding section in the Study Guide. For the most part, the entries under the headings are organized as term lists with a Windows Server 2003 feature, or with a component as the term and the key details for this feature or configuration listed next.

Segmenting Networks

This subsection is a summary of highlights from the "Segmenting Networks" section in the Exam 70-298 Study Guide.

Router

- Routers work at the OSI Network layer (layer 3). They use logical network addresses (e.g., IP addresses) to route information from source to destination hosts. Routers do not care about MAC addresses or frame types.

- Routers use routing protocols to route network traffic. RRAS supports RIP and OSPF routing protocols. In general, RIP is low administration used for small networks, and OSPF is high administration (but more efficient) used for large networks.

- Routers do not normally pass broadcast network traffic from one network to another.

- A dual-homed Windows server can act as a router, as can a RRAS-enabled server with more than one network interface.

- Routers are a good way to segment networks, and are often used to prevent unauthorized external Internet traffic from reaching internal networks.

- Network traffic is blocked or allowed on a router by defining the router's Access Control List (ACL).

Ethernet switch

- Ethernet switches are OSI layer 2 devices, moving network traffic according to MAC addresses and frame types.

- Ethernet switches normally allow only a connected host to "see" traffic headed to and from itself, plus broadcasts (i.e., a switch passes broadcast packets). This logically isolates one host's unicast traffic from others on the same switch.

- Malicious hackers can use multiple techniques (e.g., ARP spoofing, ARP flooding, etc.) to bypass the normal unicast segmentation given to hosts on a switched network.

- Ethernet switches are the most common LAN concentrator device for connecting multiple computer hosts.

- All computers on the same switch are usually on the same IP subnet, but additional IP subnets can be created to logically separate computer hosts on the same network segment. This would be sufficient for segmentation on a low-security network.

Firewall

- Security administrators can use firewalls to restrict network traffic based upon source and destination IP addresses, domain names, transport port numbers, and data content. Firewalls usually have the features of a router (i.e., multiple network segments that do not pass broadcast traffic).
- Firewalls are a great choice for segmenting network traffic. They are often used to segment two networks or more from each other (e.g., Internet and private internal LAN), but can be used to segment internal network segments.
- Firewalls can be network devices placed on a network chokepoint or be host-based and placed on an individual host.
- Windows XP Pro and Windows Server 2003 SP1 come with a Microsoft-provided, host-based firewall called Windows Firewall (or Internet Connection Firewall in previous versions).

NAT

- Network Address Translation devices or software converts public IP addresses to private (and vice-versa). NAT allows one or more private IP addresses to share a single (or multiple) public IP address.
- Firewalls, routers, and other network segmentation devices often contain NAT functionality.
- Although NAT is not considered a solid network security device, it does provide some network segmentation and security because external intruders cannot easily determine internal private IP addresses. It can be used to provide an additional layer of security to Internet-accessible devices residing on an internal private network.

IP Filters

- Windows NT and later versions have a feature called IP Filters that can be enabled to prevent authorized inbound traffic on specific transport port numbers or IP protocol numbers.
- When enabled, it applies to all network interfaces at once.
- Although it can still be used, it has been replaced by the much more functional Windows Firewall.

VPN

- Virtual Private Networks are used to securely transport (encrypted and/or authenticated) confidential network traffic over untrusted networks.
- Windows comes with multiple built-in VPN protocols, including L2TP, PPTP, IPSec, SSL, TLS, and RDP, which authenticate and/or encrypt network traffic.

Encryption and Authentication

This subsection is a summary of highlights from the "Encryption" and "Authentication" sections in the Exam 70-298 Study Guide.

Cryptography types

- To encrypt data, symmetric encryption uses the same encryption key as was used to encrypt it. Most encryption involves symmetric encryption keys.
- Common Windows symmetric ciphers include DES, 3DES, DESX, and AES.
- Asymmetric cipher algorithms use two related, but different, keys (called a *key pair*) to encrypt or authenticate data. The private key is only known by one user (or computer), but the public key can be known by anyone.
- The private key can decrypt whatever the public key has encrypted. The public key can decrypt whatever the private key has encrypted. The receiver's public key is used for encrypting data to the receiver. The sender's private key is used for signing data to be sent to a receiver.
- Common Windows asymmetric ciphers include RSA and Diffie-Hellman.
- With most asymmetric encryption, a one-time symmetric encryption key (called the *session key*) is used to encrypt the data. The asymmetric key pair is used to encrypt the session key and securely transport it between source and destination.
- Asymmetric cryptographic algorithms can also be used for authentication purposes. Authentication is the process of verifying a user's identity or data's integrity between two network hosts. Authentication ties the source user's identity to the data's integrity.
- Most of today's popular cryptographic authentication/encryption routines use asymmetric keys (e.g., SSL, TLS, SSH, 802.1x, S/MIME, smart cards, etc.).
- When using asymmetric encryption, the sender uses the receiver's public key to encrypt the data. When using asymmetric authentication (i.e., signing), the sender uses her private key to sign the data.
- *Federal Information Processing Standards* (FIPSs) are government standards covering information processing. This includes encryption, which must be followed by most government agencies (and often, contractors). FIPS can be enabled in Windows by enabling a Group Policy setting called "Use FIPS compliant algorithms for encryption, hashing, and signing." The FIPS option was added to allow administrators to use more secure encryption and hashing standards. If FIPS is enabled, it increases Remote Desktop Protocol (RDP) encryption from RC4 to 3DES, and requires that client or server to use TLS over SSL for secure web transactions. However, if the FIPS option is enabled on XP Pro SP1 or later, or in Windows Server 2003, it actually downgrades the cryptographic protection from AES to 3DES.
- Authentication (i.e., proof of identity ownership) can be proven by the following:
  — Something only the user knows (e.g., a password, PIN, etc.).
  — Something only the user has (e.g., smart card, USB token, etc.).
  — Something only the user is (e.g., biometrics, fingerprint, hand geometry, written signature, etc.).

- Authentication can be one-factor, two-factor, or multi-factor, depending on how many different types of authentication (of the three just listed) are used. All other things considered even, two-factor is more secure than one-factor, and multi-factor is considered more secure than two-factor.

- Two of the same factor (e.g., prompting a user for two different passwords) is not considered two-factor and is also not considered as secure as using different factors for authentication.

Password hashes versus authentication protocol

- Windows stores all Windows logon passwords as password hashes in the authentication database (i.e., SAM or Active Directory).

- By default, Windows stores all passwords as two types of password hashes: LAN Manager (or LM) and NT (also known as NTLM hash).

- The LM hash is used with the LM authentication protocol only and is considered very insecure. It is only needed in legacy systems (Windows 9x unpatched). It should be disabled, when possible, by enabling the "Do not store LAN Manager password hash on next password change" Group Policy setting and forcing password changes.

- The NT hash is considered very secure and is used with the NTLM, NTLMv2, and Kerberos authentication protocols.

- When a user (or computer) authenticates to Windows, the challenge-response authentication process is handled by an authentication protocol. The authentication protocol ensures that neither the plain-text password nor the hash is transmitted across the network. Instead, a client response is created, using the password hash sent. This is to prevent network eavesdropping hackers from easily retrieving the user's password or password hash from the communication's stream.

- There are four types of authentication protocols that can be used by Windows during a normal logon: LM, NTLM, NTLMv2, and Kerberos.

- Only Windows 2000 and later computers can use Kerberos, and then only in a domain environment when accessing domain resources. Windows 9x and Windows NT 4.0 cannot use Kerberos.

- Windows NT 4.0 can use NTLM and NTLMv2 (when fully patched). Windows 9x can use NTLM and NTLMv2 when fully patched.

- The Kerberos authentication protocol is always used between Windows 2000 and later computers when connecting to Windows 2000 and later domain resources. Otherwise, one of the other three authentication protocols is used.

- The LM and NTLM authentication protocols are considered weak. Unfortunately, Windows 2000 and later computers can use all four authentication protocols by default, and it is possible for an attacking computer to request that an attacked computer use the weaker protocols. Therefore, administrators should disable the LM and NTLM authentication protocols, when possible, by enabling the "LAN Manager authentication level: Send NTLMv2 response only\refuse LM and NTLM" option.

Impersonation versus delegation

- Impersonation is used when a Windows program, service, or process accesses a local Windows resource on behalf of the user or computer (i.e., Windows Explorer opening a file for a user). Delegation is a Windows program, service, or process accessing a remote network resource on behalf of the user or computer. The user, service, or computer account that is trying to access a resource on behalf of another user or computer must be *trusted for delegation*.

- Kerberos, NTLM, and IIS Digest and SSL client mapping can be used in delegation in Windows Server 2003 (in Windows 2000, only Kerberos could be delegated). By default, domain controllers are trusted for delegation—other computers, services, and users are not.

- Many services, such as EFS, require that the remote computer be trusted for delegation. If EFS is not working on a remote computer, check to make sure the "Account is trusted for delegation" option is enabled in the remote computer's account in the Active Directory Users and Computers console. Only Enterprise Admins and Domain Admins can modify the delegation option.

- User, computer, and services accounts that definitely should not be used for delegation should have their "Account is sensitive and cannot be delegated" option enabled.

Public Key Infrastructure (PKI)

- PKI is a cryptographic asymmetric (also called *public key cryptography*) authentication and encryption solution for enabling greater levels of trust between two or more parties. Each participating party has a key pair: private and public keys.

- A Certification Authority (CA) is used to verify and attest to the validity of each participating party's public key. A PKI solution enables multiple parties to have a great level of trust to each other when conducting cryptographic authentication and encryption activities with each other.

- A digital signature is a piece of data (e.g., content or hash) signed by the publisher's (or sender's) private key. Because the digital signature is created by using the sender's private key, which only he has, the digital signature ties the signed data to the signer's identity. If the digital signature is verified at the receiver (by using the signer's public key), it can be believed that the data did not change between the signer and the receiving location.

- A digital certificate is a publisher's public key signed by a CA. A digital certificate is a public key attested to by an independent third party. It essentially says that the publisher's public key can be relied upon as having come from the publisher who it says it is from. Of course, the latter sentence only makes sense if the receiver trusts the CA to verify the identity of the public key's owner.

- A digital certificate used by a user account is called a user certificate. A digital certificate used by a computer is known as a machine certificate.

- A *trusted CA* is a CA that is trusted by the receiver. Any digital certificates signed by the trusted CA will automatically be accepted as a valid public key that belongs to the publisher who it says it belongs to. Trusted CAs are already preinstalled in Windows or must be accepted as an additional trusted

CA by the receiver. If a trusted CA signs a digital certificate, it doesn't mean the receiver will automatically trust the publisher. It just means that the receiver accepts the identity of the digital certificate's publisher.

- A trusted root CA is the top CA in a PKI hierarchy of trust, from which all other CA trusts come. Every PKI hierarchy will have a root CA (which is always self-signed). The other CAs in the PKI hierarchy are known as Intermediate CAs.

- *Revocation* is the process of declaring an otherwise valid digital certificate as invalid because of trust compromise (i.e., the publisher's private key was compromised). If a trust compromise has occurred, the CA is contacted (if not already notified), and the CA places the digital certificate's serial number on the CA's *certificate revocation list* (CRL). The CRL is placed in a location (called the *CRL distribution point* or *CDP*), where the receiver that is receiving a publisher's digital certificate can check for revocation.

Certification Authority creation decisions

- When creating a new Certification Authority, three decisions must be made. Table 9-1 describes the decisions and the reasons for the outcome of each.

Table 9-1. Certification Authority creation decisions

Decision	First option	Second option
Root or subordinate	The first CA in any PKI hierarchy must be the root. All other CAs are subordinate.	The CAs that issue the digital certificates (i.e., *issuing CAs*) are subordinate to the root.
Offline or online	Root CAs should usually be offline and only brought online to issue CA certificates to subordinates and to update CRLs.	Issuing CAs should be online.
Public or private	Public CAs are needed when the digital certificates they create will be relied upon by previously unrelated third parties or when a highly recognized trusted CA is desired. Public CAs are often used on Internet web sites accessed by the general public or to sign software that will be distributed to the general public.	A private CA is fine for most internal company needs, even when two previously unrelated business parties begin to do business together.

- Most root CAs should be offline to prevent a malicious attack.

- PKI hierarchies can be described as one-tier, two-tier, or three-tier. When the root CA is also the online issuing CA, it is considered a one-tier PKI hierarchy. One-tier hierarchies are considered very insecure, because the root CA is online and subject to malicious attack. A two-tier hierarchy has an offline root and an online issuing CA, and is considered relatively secure. The most secure PKI hierarchy is called three-tier, where the additional middle CA is administrative or policy CA.

- In theory, PKI hierarchies, because they involve third-party attestation of the identities of the participating parties, allow more default trust between the participating parties. Self-signed applications (e.g., PGP) do not have the third-party verification of identities, and as such are considered less trustworthy.

Auditing

This subsection is a summary of highlights from the "Auditing" section in the Exam 70-298 Study Guide.

Audit categories

- There are nine security audit categories in Windows. Table 9-2 summarizes the categories and what they track.

Table 9-2. Audit categories and what they audit

Audit category	Description/purpose
Audit account logon events	Tracks domain controller authentication events and logon behavior. Account logons are tracked when a user logs on to a computer or when a security principal accesses a resource (such as file or printer share).
Audit account management	Tracks when a user account or group is created, changed, or deleted. It also tracks when a password is set or changed or when group membership is modified.
Audit directory service access	Records the event of a user accessing an Active Directory object.
Audit logon events	Audits logons and authentication events at the computer where resource is accessed. Tracks domain account logons on computer where the logon event is happening. This is the opposite effect of Audit account logons. Audit logon events can also track local account logons.
Audit object access	Tracks success or failure of security principal (user, group, service, or computer account) trying to access a file, folder, registry key, or printer. After the category is enabled, auditing must be turned on by selecting the individual object and by choosing the security principal to be tracked in Windows Explorer.
Audit Policy change	Tracks any change to user rights assignment, audit, or trust policies. It might catch a hacker attempting to elevate privileges.
Audit privilege use	Tracks use or attempted use of user rights assignment privileges. Privileges allow a user, group, computer, or service to do something across a wide range of objects not explicitly given by regular security permission (e.g., Logon as service or Logon as a batch job).
Audit process tracking	Stores detailed tracking information for events such as program activation, process exit, handle duplication, and indirect object access.
Audit system events	Tracks when a security principal restarts or shuts down the computer or when an event occurs that affects either the system security or the security log.

- In general, audit both success and failure events when told to audit all events or when told to audit a computer or resource for malicious use. Otherwise, read the test question for more clues on what type of event(s) to enable. Usually, these types of test questions are more about reading comprehension than product knowledge. For audit categories that allow individual users or groups to be monitored, choose the Everyone group if asked to track all users. Add the Anonymous user (if offered on the test) if a malicious hacker is suggested.

Log rotation

- Security logs should be collected and rotated frequently enough that data is not overwritten. It is important that logs be rotated on a regular enough basis to balance accuracy and usability. The three main log rotation options are:
  - Overwrite events as needed
  - Overwrite events older than x days
  - Do not overwrite events (clear log manually)

- You can only choose one log rotation option. If one of the two latter choices is enabled, and the logfile meets its maximum logfile size, new events will not be added to the log until something is corrected. With the latter option, the administrator can optionally choose for the system to halt (i.e., blue screen) if the logfile becomes full. Although halting used to be the default option, now a second Security Option called "Shutdown system immediately if unable to log security audits" must be enabled.
- Microsoft provides several programs for centralized collection, including Microsoft Audit Collection System, Log Parser, SMS, and MOM.

Security Infrastructure Technologies

This subsection is a summary of highlights from the "Security Infrastructure Technologies" section in the Exam 70-298 Study Guide.

Steps to secure any infrastructure server

- Restrict physical access to the server(s).
- Minimize who can log into the server locally and remotely.
- Mandate long and complex passwords for infrastructure server administrators.
- Uninstall or disable unneeded services and applications.
- Do not install IIS, Microsoft Office, or other high-risk applications.
- Do not browse to untrusted sites using Internet Explorer; limit Internet browsing as much as possible.
- Separate server roles where possible (e.g., try not to let the domain controller also be the DNS server, don't let the Certificate Services server run IIS for web enrollment, etc.).
- Provide redundant servers for critical services (e.g., Active Directory, DNS, etc.).
- Manage an infrastructure server using its own high-security GPOs.
- Keep server security patches up to date.
- Consider enabling a host-based firewall to minimize unneeded port connections.
- Use IPSec to minimize traffic connections.
- Disable booting on anything besides the primary hard drive.
- Implement a thorough auditing policy, recording as much activity as possible in case it is needed for forensic investigations.

Securing DNS

- Internal DNS domains should not be commingled with externally reachable DNS domains. DNS administrators want to make sure that private IP addresses and internal hostnames are not reachable by external, unauthorized users. Every entity should have separate internal and external DNS domains, and where appropriate, separate DNS servers for internal and external domains.
- DNS servers should be configured to ensure secure zone transfers between primary (Active Directory-Integrated or standard) and secondary DNS

servers. This is configured in the DNS server and ensures that only pre-defined servers can receive DNS zone information.

- DNS servers should be configured to require secure dynamic updates. By default, Windows 2000 and later computers will attempt to register their IP address and DNS host name with the DNS server listed in their primary DNS field in the Internet Protocol properties. "Secure dynamic updates" (a Windows DNS server default) requires that the host attempting to submit the name already be logged on and authenticated before attempting the registration.

Network communication protocols

- There are many communication protocols that can be used to protect network traffic. Table 9-3 lists several.

Table 9-3. Network communication protocols

Protocol	Description and use
Remote Desktop Protocol (RDP)	RDP is a proprietary Windows protocol that is used with Terminal Services, Remote Desktop, and Remote Assistance. Works by default over TCP port 3389. Provides (weak) encryption for logon password and all data. Can be used to administrate computers, provide help desk support, or to run applications in Terminal Server. Excellent choice for remote administration (ignoring the encryption issues as they are ignored on the test). Authenticates user.
SSL/TLS	Open standard supported by many vendors. Asymmetric encryption and authentication. SSL/TLS certificate must be installed on the server; can be required on the client optionally. Works over TCP port 443. Is considered very secure and easy to use. A great choice for protecting network communications between a server and client. Normally authenticates server computer.
IP Security (IPSec)	Open standard supported by many vendors. Introduced in Windows 2000; can work on NT 4.0 and Windows 9x if updated software is installed. Can be used to encrypt and authenticate traffic between two endpoints. Can use Kerberos, a Pre-Shared Key, or a machine digital certificate for authentication. Is machine authenticated. Considered fairly complex to manage and troubleshoot, especially when mixing between different vendor platforms. An excellent choice for internal network connections, between network access devices, and as a firewall on a single host.
Secure Shell (SSH)	Common, open standard supported by many vendors, but not available from Microsoft. Works across TCP port number 22 by default; can use symmetric or asymmetric cryptography. Can be used as a secure Telnet session or as a VPN tunnel in which to tunnel nearly any other protocol or service.

Certificate Services

This subsection is a summary of highlights from the "Certificate Services" section in the Exam 70-298 Study Guide.

New Certificate Services features in Windows Server 2003

- The new Certificate Services features in Windows Server 2003 are:
  - User Auto-enrollment (must have XP or above)
  - Version 2 Certificate Templates
  - Improved key recovery
  - Delta CRLs

- — Qualified subordination
- — New command-line utilities
- In a Windows 2000 domain, an administrator might have to upgrade the schema to support Windows Server 2003 Certificate Services using ADPREP/ FORESTPREP. The primary symptom is that a new Windows Server 2003 Certificate Server has been installed in an existing Windows 2000 network, and the new features just listed are not available.

Enterprise or standalone

- Microsoft Certificate Services can be installed as an enterprise CA or as a standalone. An enterprise CA has many benefits over a standalone CA; however, a standalone CA may be all that is needed. Here are the benefits of an enterprise CA over a standalone CA:
    - — Requires AD and DNS, but does not have to be installed on a domain controller
    - — Should be used when handling digital certificates belonging to users and computers in the company
    - — Can automatically verify user's identity in AD, and auto-enroll or auto-approve certificates
    - — When installed, it uses Group Policy to propagate its digital certificate to the Trusted Root Certification Authorities store for all users and computers in the local domain
    - — Allows CA managers to use Certificate Templates
    - — Can publish certificates and certificate revocation lists to Active Directory
    - — Allows Auto-enrollment
    - — Allows Auto-approval
    - — Allows Auto-mapping certificate to user or computer account
    - — Can create and use wireless and smart card certificates
    - — Allows control over certificates and the certificate process using GPOs
- A standalone CA should be used when these features are not desired or when the users or computers it will be supporting are not located on the internal domain or forest.

Automatic Certificate Services

- *Auto-enrollment* allows a user or computer to automatically request a digital certificate simply because he belongs to a particular group that has the auto-enroll permission to a certificate template.
- *Auto-approval* is a setting in Certificate Services that allows a certificate request to be automatically approved without manual intervention, because the certificate candidate meets a predefined condition.
- *Auto-mapping* is when Certificate Services automatically places a user or computer's digital certificate in the Active Directory associated with her account services (e.g., SSL), relying on the client's certificate to find it without asking the client. If the certificate is automatically or manually saved to the user or computer's Active Directory account, it is called *client-mapping*.

Certificate Services pathway

- To be able to issue digital certificates to participating users or computers, the CA manager must perform the following steps:
    a. Install Certificate Services, deciding whether the CA is to be root or subordinate, public or private, enterprise or standalone, and online or offline.
    b. Enable one or more Certificate Templates to be published to the CA.
    c. Configure each enabled Certificate Template with its various attributions and requirements.
    d. Configure key archival solution.
    e. Configure each enabled Certificate Template with necessary groups and corresponding certificate permissions (e.g., Read, Write, Enroll, Auto-enroll).
    f. Publish to CA.
    g. Approve appropriate certificate requests or turn on auto-approval.
    h. Distribute approved digital certificates or allow them to be picked up (e.g., IIS web enrollment).
    i. Revoke certificates if compromised or when no longer needed.

Certificate Templates

- Certificate Templates are digital certificate templates that are created by Microsoft or the CA manager and that facilitate creating and issuing digital certificates to users and computers. They ultimately define what requirements a user or computer must meet in order to request a certificate or to get approval, contain the certificate permissions given to particular users, groups, or computers, and, in a nutshell, make creating and distributing digital certificates easier.

 You should review the individual fields available in a Certificate Template.

Certificate Template permissions

- Each Certificate Template has the following permissions:
    — Full Control
    — Read
    — Write
    — Enroll
    — Auto-enroll
- A user or computer must have Read and Enroll permissions to request a certificate. A CA manager must have Full Control permissions to manage a Certificate Template. A requester must have Auto--enroll permissions on the Certificate Template in order to be auto-enrolled.

Certificate request enrollment methods

- There are multiple ways for a user or computer to request a digital certificate.
    — Auto-enrollment
    — Certificates console
    — Certificate request file
    — Web enrollment

 You should be familiar with web enrollment and the various selectable options in the web site.

Auto-enrollment requirements

- In order to enable auto-enrollment, the following things must be true:
    — Certificate Services must be installed as an enterprise CA.
    — Clients must use Windows XP Pro or Windows Server 2003 computers.
    — Works only with Version 2 Certificate Templates (which are new to Windows Server 2003).
    — Must be enabled in Group Policy (which it is by default).
    — User or computer account needs Read, Enroll, and Auto-enroll permissions to the Certificate Template.

Key archival methods

- It is critical that a key archival solution be enacted prior to issuing any digital certificates. Without key archival, if the user or computer loses her private key, the data it encrypted may be lost forever. There are two major ways to accomplish key archival:
    — Automate key archival in Certificate Services and choose one or more Key Recovery Agents.
    — Allow user to manually back up his private keys.

- The former method is more reliable. If you rely on users to back up their own keys, you can almost be assured that one or more users will not do it, or will lose their keys. If you allow the manual method, the users should back up their private keys and store them in two or more independent, but protected, locations. Either method requires that the key archival solution be defined in the Certificate Template. The manual method requires that the "Allow private key to be exported" option be enabled. To enable automatic key archival, the "Archive subject's encryption private key" option needs to be enabled.

- When the Certificate Services key archival is defined, one or more users are defined as Key Recovery Agents (KRAs). Then, when Certificate Services issues a new digital certificate and key pair, a backup of the private key is automatically created and stored in Active Directory. A KRA can recover the key and restore it to the original owner (or his agent), if needed.

CA roles

- Table 9-4 shows the various CA roles.

Table 9-4. CA roles

Roles and groups	Security permission	Description
Local Administrator	Install Certificate Services	Only the local administrator can install application software, including installing Certificate Services.
		Membership in the local Administrators group on the CA is required to renew the CA certificate. Members of this group are considered to be all powerful on the CA, with administrative authority over all other CA roles.
CA Administrator	Manage CA permission	This is a CA role and includes the ability to assign all other CA roles, renew the CA's certificate, create CRLs, configure and maintain the CA, and read certificates. Does not allow request approval.
		Local Administrators, Enterprise Admins, and Domain Admins are CA Administrators by default on an Enterprise CA.
		Only local Administrators are CA Administrators by default on a standalone CA. If the standalone CA is logged on to an Active Directory domain, Domain Admins are also CA Administrators.
Certificate Manager	Issue and Manage Certificates permission	Approve, revoke, unrevoke, and renew certificates. This is a CA role. This role is sometimes referred to as CA Officer.
Enrollees	Authenticate Users	Enrollees are clients who are authorized to request certificates from the CA as well as request CRLs. This is not a CA role. A user must have Read and Enroll permissions on a Certificate Template in order to request a certificate based on that template.

Using Certificate Services in applications

- Certificate Services can be used in many applications, including email, smart cards, IPSec, and SSL. In general, the appropriate Certificate Template must be enabled, and the user or computer issued a certificate that is then imported into the related application. Review Chapter 8 for more details.

Smart cards

- A smart card is a credit-card-sized cryptographic storage device that holds and cryptographically protects a user's cryptographic identity information (i.e., private and public keys). Smart cards are often placed in smart card readers and used in two-factor authentication solutions (e.g., in conjunction with a PIN) to authenticate users to an application or to log on to Windows. Windows XP Pro and Windows Server 2003 natively support smart cards.

 You should be able to configure a smart card enrollment agent and workstation.

Backing up Certificate Services

- In a Certificate Services environment, the data it creates and issues is critical to those people and applications that rely upon it. Accordingly, Certificate Services configuration data and the data it issues should be backed up frequently. You can back up Certificate Services using one of the following methods:
  - As part of your normal server backup (make sure to include metadata)
  - Using Backup and Restore in the Certificate Authority console
  - Using Certutil.exe with the –backup and –restore parameters
  - Using System State backup or restore
- No matter how you do it, it should be done regularly.

Patch Management

This subsection is a summary of highlights from the "Patch Management" section in the Exam 70-298 Study Guide.

Microsoft patch management tools

There are many Microsoft patch management tools that can be used to apply patches to Windows and many common Microsoft applications. Table 9-5 summarizes them.

Table 9-5. Microsoft patch management tools

Microsoft tool	Description
Microsoft Baseline Security Analyzer	Free download. Detects missing patches and common misconfigurations and vulnerabilities. Does not apply patches. Comes in both GUI and command-line versions.
Windows Update/Microsoft Update	Accessible in Internet Explorer or the Help Center. Can identify missing security patches and apply them. The user must be logged in as an Administrator to run, and must be connected to Microsoft's Internet site. Not a good solution for centralized patch management.
Automatic Updates	Free service that can be set to automatically check for and download appropriate patches. Can do everything automatically, or can be set to ask user for permission to download and/or apply patches. The end-user does not need to be logged on as an administrator. Available on Windows 2000 and above.
Active Directory Software Installs	Not a preferred software patch solution, but, using the Software Installs feature of Active Directory, patches can be applied to Windows 2000 and later machines. Uses the Microsoft Windows Installer service to install software locally. In most cases, does not require that the end user be a local administrator. Lacks sophisticated patch management features.
Software Update Services/WSUS	Free download. Microsoft's preferred patch management solution for small and mid-sized businesses. SUS/WSUS servers download and install patches that must be approved by the administrator. Allows a fairly high degree of control. Client-side software is the Automatic Updates service, which installs approved patches locally. Placement of one or more SUS/WSUS servers determines bandwidth usage. The most frequently tested patch management solution on the exam.
SMS	A commercial solution (which can do a lot more than just patch management), allows a very granular control of which patches are applied and when. Microsoft's preferred solution for large businesses.

Prep and Practice

You should be able to configure Active Directory Software Installs and understand the four file types used: MSI, MST, MSP, and ZAP.

SUS/WSUS server distribution

- SUS/WSUS servers can download Microsoft software patches directly from Microsoft and then redistribute them to participating clients or other SUS/WSUS servers. An enterprise can use multiple SUS/WSUS servers to spread out the bandwidth requirements. Each enterprise location can have its own SUS/WSUS server, which downloads updates directly from Microsoft, or each remote location can point to another parent SUS/WSUS server (to conserve Internet bandwidth). To conserve Internet bandwidth, have each remote SUS/WSUS office download from a centralized SUS/WSUS server using internal networks. To conserve internal bandwidth, have each remote SUS/WSUS office download its patches directly from Microsoft.

 You should be able to install, use, and configure SUS/WSUS services.

Software Install extensions

- You may be tested on the various file extension types that Software Installs works with:

  MSI
  > For installing programs with *.MSI* files.

  MST
  > For modifying programs installed with *.MSI* files.

  MSP
  > For installing patches with an *.MSP* file extension (not common anymore).

  ZAP
  > For installing everything else; requires that the end user be a local administrator.

Remote Administration Tools

This subsection is a summary of highlights from the "Remote Administration Tools" section in the Exam 70-298 Study Guide.

- There are many different remote admin tools that a Windows administrator can use, including those discussed in Table 9-6.

Table 9-6. Microsoft remote administration tools

Remote admin tool	Discussion
Remote Desktop	Uses RDP protocol over TCP port number 3389 and gives the remote user the desktop of the user account they logged in with. XP Pro allows a single connection, while Windows Server 2003 allows two concurrent connections. XP Pro will kick any currently logged-on local users out, while Windows Server 2003 will allow the current logged-on local users to stay. The Remote Desktop user can do anything that a regular user can, plus he can map printers, drives, and serial ports on the Remote Desktop host to the remote client (therefore allowing remote printing, file copying, etc.). RDP is (weakly) encrypted by default. Remote Desktop is installed by default, but disabled. It must be enabled in the Control Panel System applet. By default, members of the Administrator group can use Remote Desktop when enabled, but all other Remote Desktop users must be added to the Remote Desktop Users group. Remote Desktop is an excellent remote management tool.
	Remote Desktop also has an IIS component that can be loaded. The remote user connects to the IIS virtual site, downloads a Remote Desktop ActiveX web client, and then connects to TCP port 3389 like regular Remote Desktop clients.
Remote Assistance	Remote Assistance also uses the RDP protocol over default port TCP 3389 and allows a locally logged-in user (i.e., the novice) to invite another user (i.e., the expert) to share a desktop. The local user can invite the expert via email, IM, or a file attachment. The local user can also determine whether the remote expert can only view or whether she can control the desktop. Remote Assistance is normally turned on by default. Remote Assistance isn't really for remote management, although it can be used that way if the remote user doesn't mind having to wait for an invitation.
Remote Administration (HTML)	Administrators can also install a remote admin console option in IIS that allows basic server tasks (managing users, adding printers, changing permissions, etc.) to be done over an SSL connection. The port number is randomly chosen, but usually is at TCP port 8000 or above. The Remote Administration (HTML) console is a good choice for remote administration, but works only for some common predefined tasks.
NetMeeting Remote Desktop Sharing	NetMeeting is an older method of accomplishing remote management. It requires the NetMeeting client, which then can connect to the NetMeeting Remote Desktop Sharing client. Although it does allow a desktop environment to be shared and viewed on the server, it is not preferred over Remote Desktop. The NetMeeting Remote Desktop Sharing service is installed by default on Windows Server 2003, but is disabled.
Telnet	XP Pro and Windows Server 2003 both come with a Telnet server service. Remote administrators can connect to it over TCP port 23. However, it does not encrypt data communications by default and allows only the remote user to run non-GUI tools. It's not the preferred method of remote administration, but it can be used to run non-GUI tools and commands.
Emergency Management Services (EMS)	EMS is used for emergency recovery operations only. Once loaded, it can be connected through to a serial terminal or concentrator. The remote administrator is given a special EMS terminal console with a limited number of command-line commands. EMS is not normally used for remote administration, unless it is needed.

Terminal Services

This subsection is a summary of highlights from the "Terminal Services" section in the Exam 70-298 Study Guide.

Terminal Services

- Terminal Services is used to allow multiple remote users connect to a Windows server to run one or more applications. It is not normally used for remote administration, but could be used this way in a pinch. Terminal Services also uses the RDP protocol over default TCP port number 3389.

Terminal Services Security Options

- The 70-298 exam often discusses Terminal Services Security Options. Most questions focus on the encryption settings, which can be set to three levels:
  — High Level
  — Low Level
  — Client Compatible

- High-Level encryption means that RDP communications will be protected by the maximum encryption key size supported by the server. If the client cannot also accept this key length, it will not be allowed to connect. Low-Level and Client-Level encryption means that RDP communications will be protected by the maximum key size supported by the client. In high-security scenarios, the administrator will want to ensure that the encryption level is set to High Level.

 Terminal Services has dozens of other settings, some of which could impact security indirectly. You should be familiar with all of the configuration choices available in Group Policy for Terminal Services.

Windows Trust

This subsection is a summary of highlights from the "Windows Trust Models" section in the Exam 70-298 Study Guide.

Windows trust security

- By default, every domain in a Windows 2000 and above domain trusts every other domain in the same forest. Various types of trusts (e.g., forest, external, etc.) can be established manually. Every authenticated user in a domain is automatically added to the Everyone and Authenticated Users group in every other domain in the same forest. This gives users (or intruders) in one domain rights and permissions in the other domains that they would normally not have otherwise.

IPSec

This subsection is a summary of highlights from the "IPSec" section in the Exam 70-298 Study Guide.

IPSec in general

- The open standard, IPSec, can be used fully patched in Windows 9x and later, but was introduced initially in Windows 2000. It can only be used to authenticate and encrypt TCP/IP traffic, as its name indicates.

- IPSec has two protocols: Authentication Header (AH) and Encapsulated Security Payload (ESP). AH ensures authentication of the IP header, verifying source and destination addresses, as well as the integrity of the entire packet (with a few necessary exceptions). ESP can authenticate and/or encrypt the network packet's payload data, but does not protect the data's IP header.

IPSec components

- An IPSec policy includes the following components:
  - IP Filter (which asks which packets are to be covered by IPSec) includes source and destination IP addresses, port numbers, and protocol types. They're can only be one IP filter per rule.
  - IP Rule (which asks what to do with a packet that meets the IP Filter characteristics) includes AH versus ESP treatment, and action (e g , pass, discard, secure). There can be one or more rules per IPSec policy.
  - Authentication type: Kerberos, Pre-Shared Key, Digital Certificate.
- In order for IPSec to be used between two endpoints, the two endpoints must share similar (or compatible) settings in their IPSec policies.

Default Microsoft IPSec policies

- Microsoft has three default IPSec policies:

  Client (respond only)
  If the server requests security, this will enable IPSec; but if it is not requested, it can communicate clear text.

  Server (request security)
  The server always asks for IPSec, but doesn't require it.

  Secure Server (require security)
  This does not allow non-IPSec communications.

- The exam frequently tests a candidate's knowledge of these three policies.

IPSec modes

- IPSec has two modes:
  - Tunnel
  - Transport
- Tunnel mode is usually used between two network endpoint devices (e.g., router to router or gateway to gateway). Transport mode is the normal mode between two computer hosts using IPSec.

Securing IIS Web Sites

This subsection is a summary of highlights from the "Securing Internet Information Services (IIS) Web Sites" section in the Exam 70-298 Study Guide.

IIS web site security

- IIS has several components for securing web sites, which include:
  - IIS permissions
  - Web User Authentication
  - NTFS permissions
  - Execute permissions
  - Web Application Pool Identity

IIS permissions

- The IIS permissions are:
  - — Script source access
  - — Read
  - — Write
  - — Directory browsing

- IIS permissions can be specifically configured for each IIS server, IIS web site, virtual directory, web page, and web site file. Permissions set at the highest level (the parent container) are inherited down below to the lower containers unless otherwise contradicted at the lower level.

- The "Script source access" permission determines whether or not a user browsing to that object should be able to see the source code behind the displayed web page or object.

- The Read permission must be given for a web site object or page to be displayed to an end user.

- The Write permission, if not contradicted by other permissions, would allow a user to create new files, delete files or objects, or modify existing files and objects.

- "Directory browsing" tells the web server to list the files in directory listing, instead of rendering the files and objects in HTML.

Web User Authentication

- Every web request made to an IIS web site is made through a user context. Either the request is made through an authenticated user (that exists in Active Directory or the local SAM file) or the IIS anonymous user (*IUSR_machinename*) is used. Web User Authentication can be set per web server, per web site, per web page, per virtual directory, per folder, or per file: The IIS authentication types are:
  - — Anonymous
  - — Integrated Windows
  - — Digest
  - — Basic
  - — .NET Passport

- These IIS authentication methods are covered in more detail here:

  Anonymous authentication

  - When Anonymous is chosen, the web user request will be executed in the security context of the *IUSR_machinename* user account.

  - The IIS anonymous user belongs to the Everyone and Authenticated Users group.

  Integrated Windows authentication

  - Integrated Windows authentication is generally meant for intranet web sites.

  - It can use any authentication protocol: LM, NTLM, NTLMv2, and Kerberos.

- If the web server connected to is defined as being on the user's intranet, Windows will first attempt to connect anonymously, but then pass the user's current logon name and password if Integrated Windows authentication is requested.
- In order for Integrated Windows authentication to work, the user's logon account must be stored in Active Directory or the local SAM file on the server.

Digest authentication

- Digest authentication requires that the user's logon account be located in Active Directory or the local SAM database, but it does not use one of the Windows logon authentication protocols (i.e., LM, NTLM, NTLMv2, or Kerberos) to communicate the user's logon name and password.
- The user will always be prompted for her logon name and password, which is then protected using a digest hash algorithm.
- This option always requires that the user's password be stored in easily reversed hash form. Under the user's logon account or in Group Policy, the setting "Store password using reversible encryption" must be enabled for each user wishing to use Digest authentication in IIS.
- Digest authentication is considered to be a weakly secure, but better than the plain-text authentication method.

 Reversible encryption is required for CHAP authentication in RRAS and IAS, as well.

Basic authentication

- Basic authentication sends the user's logon name and password in near plain-text conditions.
- Basic authentication requires that the user's logon account be stored in Active Directory or in the local SAM.
- Computers or browsers that don't support Digest or Integrated Windows authentication (e.g., Macintosh, Unix, and Linux computers) can use this option.
- Basic authentication is considered insecure.

.NET Passport

- .NET Passport requires that each participating user have a .NET Passport account.
- Once the user has authenticated to a .NET Passport server, his authentication token is sent to the original intended .NET Passport web site.
- .NET Passport is considered a very secure authentication method.

Prep and Practice

NetBIOS Share permissions have no effect on an IIS web site.

Web application pools

- Each web site runs in a web application pool and its related identity. Each application pool is assigned an *identity*. An identity is a user or service account used to provide the security context of the application pool.
- If an intruder "breaks out" of a web server or its application, she will be limited to seeing what is in the application pool and further limited by the security context of the application pool's identity account.
- If an IIS web server hosts more than one web site, the IIS administrator should consider placing each web site in a different application pool.

SSL/TLS

- SSL/TLS is used to authenticate a server's identity to a client, encrypt and authenticate data to and from the server and optionally, a client's identity to a server.
- It uses asymmetric cryptography and requires that the SSL digital certificate be installed on the participating web server.

URLScan

- URLScan is a free, optional component that can be downloaded and installed to make IIS more secure. IIS 6 contains some of the earlier functionality of URLScan, but the latest version has even more functionality than the included version, such as HTTP Verb control, URL string parsing, maximum URL string length settings, etc. When installed as an ISAPI filter, URLScan gives an IIS even more security control over its web sites.

IIS logging

- IIS comes with built-in logging. Most IIS logging is done to the logfile(s) specified under the IIS web site Home Directory tab. The information saved depends on the logfile format and the selected fields. IIS has four default log types:
  — Microsoft IIS Log File format
  — NCSA Common Log File format
  — ODBC Logging
  — W3C Extended Log File format (the default logging option)
- You should become familiar with the specific fields in each Log File format, as discussed in Chapter 8.

Web Service Extensions

- By default, IIS 6 can only display plain HTML code. To allow more advanced web technologies to run, additional functionality must be added in the form of Web Service Extensions. By default, all web service extensions are prohibited. An IIS administrator can add additional web extensions (e.g., Web-DAV, Active Server Pages, ISAPI filters, etc.) and mark them as Allowed.

WebDAV

- Web Distributed Authoring and Versioning (WebDAV) is an open standard allowing remote web clients to save and manage documents on WebDAV-enabled web sites.

- WebDAV is a web service extension that must be marked Allowed in order to run. WebDAV clients must be running a WebDAV client. Windows 2000 and later can use the Web Client service or use the built-in functionality that comes with Microsoft Office.

- WebDAV can be utilized with EFS to allow encrypted documents on both the web server's hard drive and while the files are transferred over the network.

RRAS and IAS

This subsection is a summary of highlights from the "Routing and Remote Access Service" and "Internet Authentication Service" sections in the Exam 70-298 Study Guide.

Routing and Remote Access Service

- Exam 70-298 focuses on the RRAS security issues, particularly the VPN types, authentication protocols, and IAS. There are two basic VPN protocols in RRAS:
  - L2TP
  - PPTP

- Of the two, L2TP, used in conjunction with IPSec, is significantly more secure than PPTP. When in doubt on the test, choose the L2TP/IPSec combination.

- PPTP was an earlier VPN protocol invented by Microsoft, and it can be used with legacy clients.

- Windows 9x and Windows NT 4.0 need the latest patches and the latest Microsoft VPN client software to use L2TP.

RRAS authentication protocols

- There are six RRAS authentication protocol choices that can be made in each Remote Access Policy, from most secure to least secure:
  - EAP
  - MS-CHAPv2
  - MS-CHAP
  - CHAP
  - Unencrypted authentication (PAP, SPAP)
  - Unauthenticated access

- Extensible Authentication Protocol (EAP) is the most secure protocol. It can be used in user or computer authentication. In Windows, it comes in three flavors:
  - Protected EAP (PEAP)
  - EAP-TLS (also known as Smart Card or other certificate)
  - EAP-MD5 (also known as MD5-Challenge)

- PEAP works by first establishing a secure VPN tunnel before transmitting the EAP certificates used to secure the session. PEAP is used in Windows for 801.x security, so associate PEAP with wireless security when taking Windows certification exams.

- EAP-TLS also uses digital certificates, often stored on a smart card. So, if the exam talks about using Smart Card authentication over VPNs, think EAP-TLS.

- EAP-MD5 is a very secure password challenge response authentication choice.

- MS-CHAPv2 is the most secure authentication protocol for clients who cannot support EAP. MS-CHAPv2 supports two-way authentication and is considered a relatively secure protocol.

- MS-CHAP is a legacy protocol with some minor issues. MS-CHAP is considered to be a weakly secure protocol. Use only when you have to.

- CHAP is another legacy protocol that should only be used when it has to be (i.e., Macintosh, Linux, Unix clients). It is considered very weak security-wise—just a notch above plain-text authentication.

- Unencrypted authentication protocols, such as PAP and SPAP, send logon credentials in plain text and should only be used when they are the only protocols the clients support. Unencrypted authentication protocols are not considered secure.

- Although Unauthenticated access is the weakest authentication choice and is not secure when used by itself, it may be an appropriate protocol if the network communication's stream is securely protected by another protocol or device.

Connection Manager Administration Kit (CMAK)

- The CMAK can be used by administrators to predefine remote access connection profiles, which are then sent to end users who install and use them. It prevents end users from having to manually define complicated connection profiles.

 You should be familiar with RRAS access policies, how they are configured, and what the configuration choices are.

Internet Authentication Service

- Remote Authentication Dial In User Service (RADIUS) is an open standard used to authenticate and track remote users.

- Microsoft's implementation of RADIUS is called Internet Authentication Service (IAS).

- RADIUS servers normally work in conjunction with one or more network access servers (e.g., RRAS), which are known as RADIUS clients.

- RADIUS/IAS servers can be used to centralize the control and Remote Access Policies of multiple RRAS servers.

How IAS works (a simplified scenario)

1. When a remote VPN user connects directly to RRAS server, the RRAS server (acting as a RADIUS client) forwards the request to the IAS server.

2. The IAS server checks the user's credentials on the domain controller, and checks to see whether the user is allowed to connect remotely. The IAS server must be part of the RAS and IAS Servers group to be able to query the DC.

3. RADIUS Remote Access Policy (just like RRAS policy) is evaluated against the user, and the user is allowed or denied.

4. IAS sends acceptance or denial of user authentication to RRAS server.

Securing Wireless Networks

This subsection is a summary of highlights from the "Securing Wireless Networks" section in the Exam 70-298 Study Guide.

802.1x

- 802.1x is a newer networking security standard covering wireless authentication. 802.1x VPN tunnels are considered secure, especially compared to legacy WEP wireless protection. EAP and PEAP VPNs are part of the 802.1x standard.

Infrastructure Mode

- Infrastructure Mode is when a WAP is a terminating network device designed to support multiple wireless nodes at once (much like a wired hub), and often interfaces the wireless network to the wired network.

Ad-hoc Mode

- Ad-hoc Mode WAPs are peer-to-peer connections. Usually every computer that has a wireless network card can act as an Ad-hoc Mode WAP. Windows XP Pro clients will often connect to Ad-hoc Mode WAPs, even though most users only intend to connect to Infrastructure Mode WAPs. A secure wireless client should only connect to Infrastructure Mode WAPs.

Wired Equivalent Privacy (WEP)

- WEP is an older, legacy wireless VPN encryption protocol that was found to be very flawed. It is considered to be an insecure VPN protocol, but is better than using wireless networking without any encryption.

Wi-Fi Protected Access (WPA)

- WPA and WPA2 are two newer, more secure wireless VPN protocols designed to replace the weaker WEP. WPA2 is part of the 802.11i standard and is considered very secure. WPA2 is better than WPA; eventually, WPA will go away completely.

SSID

- Service Set Identifiers (SSID), or Extended Service Set Identifiers (ESSID) are labels used to identify wireless networks. The SSID normally is frequently broadcast so wireless nodes can locate WAPs.

Common wireless vulnerabilities

- There are many wireless network vulnerabilities, including:
  — Network communication eavesdropping/sniffing
  — Malware injection or denial of service (DoS) attacks
  — Unauthorized (rogue) WLANs and WAPs
- All of these attacks are possible because wireless networks are unauthenticated and unencrypted by default.

Common wireless Security Options

- To combat the previously mentioned vulnerabilities, administrators can implement one of the following common Security Options, listed from weakest to most secure:
  — 802.11x Legacy Security
  — RRAS VPN Protocols
  — WEP (commonly on test as something to replace)
  — IPSec
  — WPA/WPA2 (commonly used to replace WEP)
  — WPA2-802.1x with EAP and Dynamic Encryption Keys (most secure option usually tested, requires RRAS/IAS and/or digital certificates)
  — 802.11i (not usually tested)

802.11x Legacy Security

- In the past, the following security recommendations were often given to wireless network administrators.
  — Require User Authentication passwords
  — Change Default SSID
  — Turn off SSID broadcasting
  — Change WAP's default administrator password
  — Enable MAC filtering
  — Enable WEP or WPA encryption
  — Consider disabling DHCP
- While each of these options could provide some security, each of them is easily bypassed. Most of today's networks should be secured using 802.1x security (or 802.11i when possible).

Active Directory Design

This subsection is a summary of highlights from the "Secure Active Directory Design," "Active Directory Delegation," and "Group Design" sections in the Exam 70-298 Study Guide.

Secure Active Directory design

- In general, good secure design meets the following requirements:
  — It should be focused on role-based security. Users and computers should be placed in role-based groups and OUs. Role-based GPOs should be linked to the role-based OUs.

— Use separate forests when separate security and management is absolutely needed between two entities.

— Typically, you don't want internal corporate users in the same forest as external public Internet users.

— Use separate domains when you want various entities to have their own autonomy, but when centralized control is still required.

— Some Group Policy settings, such as Password Policy and Account Lockout Policy, can only be made at the domain level. If two different policies are required, separate domains will be required.

— Use separate entities by OUs when centralized control is desired.

— Create a new OU any time a collection of security principals (users or computers) have common security needs not already met by the current structure.

— Apply common security settings as far up in the Active Directory Services Structure as is operationally feasible, although don't go above the domain level (i.e., applying site-level GPOs) unless it is a requirement. Site-level GPOs face replication and other issues that complicate secure design.

Active Directory Delegation

• Using the Delegation of Control wizard, users can be given various "subadministrative" duties and control on an OU and the objects in that OU. Active Directory Delegation was invented so that a group of mid-level administrators could be given some administrative-like duties (e.g., password changes, creating groups, managing users, etc.) without making them full administrators.

 You should familiarize yourself with the options available on the Delegation of Control wizard.

Group Policy application order

1. Local Computer Policy is applied when the computer starts up and the user first logs on, if there are any defined settings.

2. Site-level GPOs are applied.

3. Domain-level GPOs are applied.

4. OU-level GPOs are applied; the lower a GPO is linked in the Active Directory infrastructure, the later it is applied (i.e., GPOs applied to child OU's will be applied after parent OU GPOs).

GPO override methods

• GSet Block Policy Inheritance blocks a GPO's natural downward inheritance. Can only be applied at an OU level or container level. When enabled, it will block all GPOs above the block from applying at the block level or below.

• Set Disabled option (whole GPO) per GPO per OU to inactivate.

• Set Disable User settings or Disable Computer Settings per GPO.

- *Set No Override* (also called *Enforced* in Group Policy Management console) is set per GPO per OU. When set on GPO, downstream OUs and containers can't block inheritance. It will be the dominant GPO.
- Use "Enable loopback processing mode" to set on a per-GPO basis; a GPO with loopback is always re-applied last.
- Deny Read or Apply Group Policy permissions of a particular GPO to a user, group, or computer so that the GPO doesn't apply to them. Security takes precedence.

Security Templates

- Security Templates allow the security settings and options that could otherwise be set in a Group Policy or registry edit to be set in a portable Security Template file.
- Security Templates can be imported into a Group Policy Object. If multiple Security Templates are imported and there are any settings in conflict, the last one imported wins.
- Security Templates can also be applied locally using the Security Configuration and Analysis tool or Secedit.exe.
- Locally applied Security Template settings will remain in effect until otherwise changed (unlike Group Policy settings, which will stop applying if the GPO no longer applies).

Default Security Templates

- Windows 2000 and later comes with preinstalled Security Templates. They are as follows:

Setup Security.inf
Security as defined when the system was set up, including all file permissions. Contains hundreds of settings and is very large.

Default*.inf
This is the same as Setup Security.

Rootsec.inf
Specifies the default user permissions on the root directory of the system drive, some of which are inherited on down.

Hisec*.inf
Requires the SMB packet signing communications, among other things (prevents connections to legacy clients).

Secure*.inf
Requires complex passwords and removes all users from the Power Users group, among other things.

Compatws.inf
Relaxes C:\Program Files permissions so that users can read and write, as is the need with some older applications (such as MS-Office 97). Also removes all users from the Power Users group using a Restricted Group with nobody defined.

Security Configuration and Analysis tool

- The Security Configuration and Analysis tool can be used to compare (i.e., analyze) a computer against a particular Security Template, to note the differences, and to apply (i.e., configure) Security Template settings.
- Secedit.exe is essentially the command-line version of the Security Configuration and Analysis tool.
- The Windows Server 2003 version of Secedit has a /generaterollback option, which is especially useful for recovering back to the original security settings when the newly applied security settings cause problems.

Windows security groups

- Security permissions should always be assigned to groups and not individual users. There is an effective way to leverage Windows security groups to maximize efficiency and security. As covered in previous chapters, there are three major group scopes:
  - Domain Local (or Local)
  - Global (domain-wide)
  - Universal (forest-wide)
- Users should always be placed into role-based groups, based upon the least privilege needed security permissions. Security can be maximized if a few basic rules are followed:
  - Resource (e.g., file, folder, printer, etc.) permissions should always be assigned to a Domain Local group.
  - Users should be placed in Global groups.
  - Global groups should be placed into the Domain Local groups.
  - Alternatively, Global groups can be placed into Universal groups, and the Universal groups placed into the Domain Local groups.
- This strategy is known as AGLP or AGULP (if Universal groups are used). Accounts should be placed in Global groups. Global groups should be placed in Universal groups (if needed) or Domain Local groups. The resource permissions should be assigned to the Domain Local group.

Client Hardening

This subsection is a summary of highlights from the "Client Hardening" section in the Exam 70-298 Study Guide.

Kiosk computers

- Microsoft security exams often test on the concept of kiosk computers (computers that are available to the general public, but that should be highly resistant to change or tampering).
- Normally, kiosk computers are locked down using Group Policy or Security Templates.
- Particularly, the loopback processing Group Policy option ensures that the computer policies will override any user policies no matter who logs in.

Startup and Shutdown scripts

- An administrator can push user and computer-based scripts using GPOs. A script can be run when a computer logs on (i.e., using the Startup script) to the domain or when she logs off (i.e., using the Shutdown script); or when a user logs on (i.e., using the Logon script) or when she logs off (i.e., using the Logoff script).

- Any type of script, command, or batch file that the host computer can process can be placed in a GPO script.

- Scripts are run in the LocalSystem context, so that the logged-in user does not have to be an administrator to have all of the script settings apply.

Password Policy

- Candidates should be familiar with all the Password Policy settings available in a GPO.

- Password Policy, Account Lockout Policy, and Kerberos policy can only be set at the domain level and take effect in Active Directory.

- Password Policy and Account Lockout Policy can be set at a local level as well, but affect only local accounts. If users log into a domain, the domain-level policy will apply.

- The "Enforce password history" setting ensures that users will not use a previously used password, at least for a certain number of times.

- The "Maximum password age" setting is the maximum number of days a password can be used before expiring.

- The "Maximum password age" setting should be set to a reasonable interval to offset the potential threats of password guessing and cracking. Normally, a maximum password age of 45 days is considered fairly secure.

- The "Minimum password age" setting determines how long a user must use a new password before he can change to a new one. This setting is to prevent users from trying to circumvent the "Enforce password history" setting. Normally, it is set to one to two days.

- The "Minimum password length" setting is the minimum length a password can be. Longer passwords are more secure.

- The "Password must meet complexity requirements" setting ensures that all newly created Windows logon passwords created or changed through the normal GUI meet a few minimum requirements and do not contain simple dictionary words or phrases.

Restricted Groups

- Restricted Groups is a GPO option that allows an administrator to define Local Group membership.

- Once a particular group's membership is defined in a GPO, if any unauthorized members (i.e., not added in the Restricted Groups section of the GPO) are added, they will be removed when the GPO next applies.

- And conversely, if a group member is removed from a restricted group (without removing them from the GPO Restricted Groups section of the GPO), the GPO will add them back during the next group policy refresh.

Windows Service Control

- GPOs allow a Windows service to be controlled and managed. It can control which services are allowed to start, and who has what permissions to them.

Software Restriction Policies

- *Software Restriction Policies* (SRP) allow an administrator to control what applications can and can't run on a Windows XP Pro and later computer.
- Windows 2000 has a smaller subset of features similar to SRP, but they are not nearly as granular.
- The SRP management console is accessed using Group Policy or Local Computer Policy.
- SRP has two main modes when enabled:

  Disallow
  Deny by default, allow execution by exception.

  Unrestricted
  Allow by default, deny by exception.

- After that default decision is made, the administrator goes about setting exceptions. There are four different types of exception rules:

  Certificate Rules
  Executables are signed by a particularly digital certificate

  Hash Rules
  Executable only with a specific hash value

  Internet Zone Rules
  Only applications installed by an MSI file located in a specific Internet Explorer security zone (e.g., Internet, Intranet, Local Computer, etc.)

  Path Rules
  Applications determined by directory or registry path

Folder redirection

- By default, a user's My Documents folder is stored in her user profile.
- If the user has a roaming profile, the contents of the My Documents directory is copied down from a server every time the user logs in, and up to the server every time she logs out. As the user's My Documents directory grows larger, it can start to take a significant amount of time for the user to log on and off.
- An administrator can use GPOs to redirect the user's My Documents folder to a shared network drive instead of to her local drive. When folder redirection is enabled, it essentially changes the link and storage location of the user's My Documents directory, and more importantly, no longer stores them with the user's profile.

WMI filtering

- WMI filtering allows XP Pro and above computers to be analyzed by an administrator-defined WMI script, and skipped if the GPO should not apply to the computer.

- For example, a WMI script in a Software Install GPO may query the user's local hard drive and confirm whether there is enough space to load a new application.
- WMI filters don't work against Windows 2000 or earlier computers, so a WMI filter will never make a GPO skip a Windows 2000 computer.

Confirming Group Policy settings

- Several tools can be used to measure effective GPO settings on a particular user or computer:
  — RSOP
  — Gpresult

RSoP

- Resultant Set of Policies (RSoP) is a graphic tool that allows an administrator to view the current effective GPO settings applied to a particular user or PC, and also allows the administrator to run "what-if" scenarios.
- If an administrator is planning to move a user or computer to another container or OU in Active Directory or add the user or computer to another group, he can run the RSOP tool in Planning mode and discover what the new effective settings would be before the change is made.

Gpresult

- Gpresult.exe is a command-line tool that summarizes the groups and Group Policies that apply to a user and computer.
- If run with the /v parameter, the Gpresult.exe tool will display every enforced GPO setting, and list which GPO applied the setting. Gpresult.exe /v is an excellent way to document effective GPO settings on a particular user or computer.

Windows Firewall

- Windows XP Pro and Windows Server 2003 come with a host-based firewall called Windows Firewall (it was called Internet Connection Firewall in XP Pro pre-SP2 releases).
- When enabled, Windows Firewall will block all incoming requests not initiated by a preceding related outbound network connection, unless an inbound exception is configured.
- Exceptions must be created for any authorized server process (e.g., NetBIOS, DHCP server, DNS server, etc.) or else remote users will not be able to connect.

Configuring Legacy Clients

This subsection is a summary of highlights from the "Legacy Clients" section in the Exam 70-298 Study Guide.

Ntuser.dat

- Ntuser.dat holds the user's profile. The profile is all the user's desktop settings (e.g., screensaver, background, etc.), his user-specific security settings, and his My Documents folder (among other things). When a user logs on with his name and password, Windows accesses his user profile and changes his desktop environment.

- If the user profile file is called *Ntuser.man*, it means the user profile is mandatory and can't be modified. Any changes the user makes to his desktop environment will be lost when he logs off the computer.

Ntconfig.pol

- The `Ntconfig.pol` tool was the precursor to Group Policy and Security Templates in Windows NT 4.0 and Windows 9x. An administrator could create the *Ntconfig.pol* file using the System Policy Editor (`Poledit.exe`) and then apply it. NT 4.0 SP4 first released Security Templates and the `Secedit.exe` utility to apply them.

Active Directory Client Extensions

- Windows 9x and Windows NT 4.0 require the Active Directory Client Extension software (it's called slightly different names in different test questions, including AD Client, DS Client, and DSClient.exe) to connect to Active Directory. It allows legacy clients to authenticate to Active Directory (and using the newer NT password hashes and NTLMv2 authentication protocols), but does not allow GPOs to be applied.

Data Security Strategies

This subsection is a summary of highlights from the "Data Access Control Strategies" section in the Exam 70-298 Study Guide.

Share permissions

- Share permissions apply only to users or computers accessing the resource over the network NetBIOS shares. The three possible Share permissions are:
  — Full Control
  — Change
  — Read
- All newly created shares on XP Pro and Windows Server 2003 have the default rights of Everyone Allow-Read.
- The Full Control permission allows anyone with the permission to modify, delete, rename, and otherwise manipulate the resource to the fullest extent possible. Users with Full Control to a resource can change the permissions configured on the resource, even taking permissions away from the Administrator (although, luckily, the Administrator can always take ownership of the resource and reset the permissions).
- The Change permission is much like the NTFS Modify permission. It allows a security principal to add, modify, move, rename, or delete a resource.
- The Read permission allows a security principal to view, copy, and print (if possible) a resource.
- Permissions set above in parent containers are normally (but not always) inherited below, unless inheritance is disabled.
- Inheritance can be controlled on a per-user and per-object basis. An administrator can allow inheritance to apply to one user and not another.

- Many resources, including Microsoft, recommend always setting the Share permissions to Full Control and letting the underlying NTFS permissions handle the effective security. In practice though, Share permissions should be set to their least privilege setting. If a security principal doesn't need Full Control permissions, don't give them.

NTFS permissions

- NTFS permissions apply to nearly ever object on an NTFS partition, whether the object is accessed over a share or locally. There are 7 summary permissions made up of 14 more granular NTFS permissions, each of which can be Allowed or Denied. The NTFS summary permissions are:

  — Read
  — Write
  — List (folders only)
  — Read and Execute
  — Modify
  — Full Control
  — Special Permissions (any combination of the underlying 14 granular permissions)

- Table 9-7 shows the fourteen granular NTFS security permissions and how they make up the seven summary permissions.

Table 9-7. NTFS Advanced permission settings

Permission	Full Control	Modify	Read and Execute	List	Read	Write
Traverse Folder/ Execute File	X	X	X	X	-	-
List Folder/Read Data	X	X	X	X	X	-
Read Attributes	X	X	X	X	X	-
Read Extended Attributes	X	X	X	X	X	-
Create Files/ Write Data	X	X	-	-	-	X
Create Folders/ Append Data	X	X	-	-	-	X
Write Attributes	X	X	-	-	-	X
Write Extended Attributes	X	X	-	-	-	X
Delete Subfolders and Files	X	-	-	-	-	-
Delete	X	X	-	-	-	-
Read Permissions	X	X	X	X	X	X
Change Permissions	X	-	-	-	-	-
Take Ownership	X	-	-	-	-	-
Synchronize	X	X	X	X	X	X

- Again, any security principal given Full Control permission has absolute control over the resource. Normal inheritance rules apply.
- If a Deny permission is set at the same level as an Allow permission for a given user, the Deny permission will override the Allow permission. However, if the Allow permission is set explicitly on an object and the Deny permission is inherited from a parent container or folder above, the explicitly set Allow permission will override the inherited Deny permission.

Effective permissions
- If both Share and NTFS permissions apply to an object, the least permissive set of permissions apply.
- For example, if the Share permissions give Full Control, and the NTFS permissions give Read and Modify, the effective permissions are Read and Modify.
- Windows XP and later contains a Windows Explorer feature that will show the effective NTFS permissions for a given security principal and object. However, the Effective permissions feature does not take into account Share permission effects and a host of other potentially impacting features (such as EFS).
- In real life and for the exam, make Windows security permissions as restrictive as possible (i.e., least privilege). Whenever possible, assign permissions to groups, following the AGULP method discussed earlier in the section "Active Directory Design."

Encrypting File System

This subsection is a summary of highlights from the "Encrypting File System (EFS)" section in the Exam 70-298 Study Guide.

EFS in general
- EFS protects files enabled with EFS protection while they are stored on a disk. EFS does not encrypt files as they are copied across a network. Therefore, to encrypt EFS-protected files as they are copied across a network, a remote user should use an additional VPN protocol, such as IPSec, SSL, SSH, or WebDAV.
- EFS is enabled globally by default on all Windows 2000 and above computers. To enable EFS on a file or folder, a user right-clicks the resource, chooses Properties and then the Advanced button, and enables the "Encrypt contents to secure data" option.
- You cannot encrypt and compress a file or folder at the same time.

EFS and Certificate Services
- If Certificate Services is not installed, the first time a user enables EFS on her first file or folder, EFS will generate a self-signed EFS digital certificate good for 100 years.
- If Certificate Services is reachable and the EFS certificate template active and published, Certificate Services will generate the user's EFS digital certificate. It will only be good for two to three years, but will auto-renew if needed.

New EFS features in Windows XP Pro and Windows Server 2003

- File sharing
- Easy key backup
- Works with WebDAV
- Works with Offline Folders and Files
- Has stronger encryption

Important EFS points

- Here are some other important EFS points:
    — EFS works with WebDAV.
    — EFS works with Offline Folders and Files (XP Pro and later).
    — XP Pro and later supports EFS file sharing.
    — The Cipher.exe command-line utility can be used to review EFS-protected files and their related certificates.
    — Remote servers holding EFS-protected files need their server account enabled with the "Trusted for Delegation" option.
    — EFS is strong file encryption. A data or key recovery plan must be tested and implemented before allowing users to use EFS.

Exam 70-298 Practice Questions

This section will test you on the previous concepts and familiarize you with the Exam 70-298 testlet formats. Four testlet scenarios will be covered, each with 10 or more questions to answer.

Testlet #1: Temptation Winery

Overview

Temptation Winery operates several Napa Valley vineyards and a wine and wine accessory global distribution operation. The company recently acquired 15 new wineries and 6 new warehouses throughout North America. Temptation winery recently hired a new CEO, Tricia Lovell, a hands-on technology leader, to take them to the next level.

Physical locations

The company's main office is located in Napa Valley, California. Temptation Winery has a total of 18 wine vineyard locations and 12 distribution warehouses. Most are located in North America, but a few of the vineyards and physical locations are located in Italy and Paris. Each winery has between 20 and 100 full-time employees, but only a handful of employees at each location perform executive functions.

Planned changes

The following changes will be made within the next year:

- The company will expand the branch office in Paris. The Paris office will support French operations, plus the other offices and facilities in Italy. The Napa Valley headquarters will directly support the North American operations and facilities, and has executive approval over the Paris and Italy operations.

- All servers in all locations are either Windows Server 2003 or will be upgraded in the next three months.

- All client computers are Windows XP Pro or will be upgraded in the next three months.

- All computers in the current Windows NT 4.0 domain must be migrated to the new Active Directory infrastructure.

- Two new Windows Server 2003 file servers called TWFS1 and TWFS2, respectively, will be installed and configured. One will be placed at the Napa Valley headquarters and the other in Paris.

- Each winery will have several kiosk computers for visitors to learn about the winery and be able to order wine and wine accessories.

- Field supervisors at each winery and distribution warehouse will use laptop computers and a wireless network to connect to the main network.

Business process

The main IT department is located in the Napa Valley office and manages all servers and computers in North America. There are small IT teams (one to two people) at each winery and warehouse, as well as in Italy and Paris. The small teams have administrative access to local resources. The main North American IT team has final approval and guidance on all IT issues no matter where the resource is located. IT staff members in the Napa Valley headquarters frequently travel to the other locations to perform advanced management skills, upgrades, and new installs.

The non-U.S. facilities all report to Paris, which accumulates information and reports it to the Napa Valley office.

The wine production executive team uses a custom-made, web-based database application named *ops.tempwine.com* that holds and provides confidential information on the growing of the grapes and production of the wine. The database is considered extremely important and is the reason why Temptation's wines are so coveted around the world for their consistency and quality. If the information were to leak out, it would be considered disastrous for the company. The application uses IIS 6 and ASP.NET. It is hosted on an IIS 6 web server in Napa Valley. Supervisors can access the database application from anywhere in the world where they have Internet access or access to the private company network.

There is a second web-based database application called *sales.tempwine.com*, which allows local and Internet visitors to buy wine and wine-related apparel. It also holds information on each winery location. Web cams update pictures of the grapes on the vine and workers every minute for visitors to see. It uses ASP.NET,

ADO.NET, and Microsoft SQL Server running on IIS 6 servers. It is accessible on the local company network or on the Internet.

Directory Services structure

The company uses an Active Directory forest root domain called tempwine.com for the North American operations. The Napa Valley IT team administers the domain. The Paris office runs on a domain called paris.tempwine.com. Italy runs on an NT 4.0 domain called it.tempwine.com. Each physical location contains one or more domain controllers and file servers. All employees and company computers, with the exception of the kiosk computers, have accounts in Active Directory or the Windows NT 4.0 domain.

All North American servers are either Windows 2000 or Windows Server 2003, but all will be upgraded to Windows Server 2003. All client computers in North America are running Windows XP Pro, but many of the European computers are Windows 2000.

Employee interviews

The following contains the content of interviews with the company employees.

CEO

Securing our corporate databases and data is mission-critical. We keep all of our grape and winery confidential information online. We must make sure this data never gets to unauthorized users.

The company must be able to share data between operation offices, the wineries, and the warehouses.

Our public web sites must use publicly trusted SSL certificates. Customers must be able to access our web sites, both locally and over the Internet, to buy wine and accessories. They must be assured of the authenticity of our servers and the confidentiality of their transactions, with a minimum of interruptions. All web servers have security logs that record every transaction and access. If someone violates our standing security policy or if a malicious intrusion is noticed, I must be notified immediately so an incident response team can respond.

All information must be encrypted when stored and transferred across the network. Any employee caught with unencrypted information on a portable device or media will be fired upon discovery.

IT team leader

VPNs using the public Internet are used instead of our previously used private T-1s. The cost savings has been tremendous, but at the same time, we are worried about reliability and security.

We currently use several custom legacy applications to manage the wineries and warehouses. They require administrative access to run. Within the next two years, the legacy applications will be replaced, but for now they are mission-critical.

We want a centralized patch management strategy, but patch approval must be decided at the Napa Valley location. Patches should be downloaded from Napa Valley's headquarters and not over the Internet directly from vendors.

We need to automate routine administrative tasks in the local and remote offices. I want to minimize manual tasks as much as possible.

Our CEO requires that we log all transactions and accesses on our network. While this is understandable, it has lead to information overload. We get so many log events that we basically ignore our logs. We need a better way to manage our logs.

All accesses and transactions to all servers must be recorded and logged, even for administrators. Logs must be saved and rotated. We have a corporate security officer who is supposed to review the logs, but I'm fairly confident that the overwhelming amount of information has made him less likely to catch the important stuff.

Only IT staff and help support staff should have administrative access to user desktops; however, the users with the legacy applications also have administrative access. This violates corporate security policy.

Kiosk computers must be highly resistant against tampering.

We have two web servers, one that the public must access and the other that is used to store confidential information. Unauthorized users should never be able to access the confidential information database.

Each employee must use two-factor authentication (wireless smart card and a PIN) to access the corporate network. We have a private PKI infrastructure to support this requirement.

Customer requirements

Company employees must be able to access the wireless network.

Kiosk computers can only be used to access the company's public web server.

Customers can register themselves with our public web server application to receive newsletters and discounts, and so we can track their purchasing history. Their account information must be stored in Active Directory, for ease of use, and all their information protected both when stored and when transferred over the network.

Active Directory requirements

Each North American physical location in the North American domain must contain one top-level OU for each company location. Accounts for all employees must be located in the OU for their primary location.

All IT and Help Desk staff must be members of the ITMembers group. IT Management is also a member of the ITExecs group. Senior support staff members are member of the ITLevelII group, and less experienced team members are part of the ITLevelI group.

All client computers in the forest must be part of a common desktop environment specification to maximize security and efficiency.

IT client support technicians at each physical location must be able to reset their own users' passwords and manage printers.

Network infrastructure

All IT staff members use RDP to access remote servers.

After TWFS1 and TWFS2 are deployed, all users in the TWFAllUsers group must be able to access a shared folder located on the servers.

Only members of the WebAdmin group should be able to make changes to the web sites and the web servers.

All remote admin traffic must be authenticated and encrypted.

Questions

1. You are designing the company's Active Directory structure. Your solution must meet the CEO and IT team leader's requirements for the public web server. Which design should you use?

   ○ A. Single domain forest for the entire company with all OUs inside the single forest root domain.

   ○ B. Two separate forests, each with its own domain. The public web server is one forest, while all other company resources are in another forest, with a one-way forest trust between the two forests.

   ○ C. Three separate forests, each with its own domain. One forest for North America, one for Europe, and one for the public web server. All forests have a two-way external trust.

   ○ D. Single forest with multiple domains. One domain for North America, one domain for Europe, one domain for the public web server.

   The correct answer is B. The scenario clearly states that the North American headquarters has final control over the European divisions. This can best be done by placing both North America and European divisions in the same forests. Who controls what in management determines Active Directory structure. The second forest is needed because external public web servers should never share the same Active Directory infrastructure as the internal company—that would mean too much risk. The only way to minimize risk is to create separate forests. The one-way forest trust will allow the IT team to administrate the second forest, while preventing the pubic forest's users from accessing the corporate forest.

2. The kiosk computers at each physical location need to be secured against unauthorized tampering and modification. You have made them physically secure, and now you need to secure them logically with a minimum amount of administrative effort needed for the lockdown and for long-term management. How should you do it?

○ A. Join the kiosk computers to the corporate domain and place the kiosk computers in a kiosk-specific OU. Use a kiosk-specific Group Policy to push down the local computer security settings. Enable loopback policy processing.

○ B. Install one kiosk computer and manually lock down. Clone the kiosk computer's hard drive and copy to the remaining kiosk computers.

○ C. Install one kiosk computer and use a specially configured Security Template to lock down. Clone the kiosk computer's hard drive and copy to the remaining kiosk computers.

○ D. Don't join the kiosk computers to the domain. Create a local Security Template with the appropriate security settings and install it in the computer's *Autoexec.bat* file so that each time the computer is rebooted, the local Security Template is applied.

The correct answer is A. The requirement of the least amount of administrative effort essentially means the kiosk computers must be managed using Group Policies. While joining the kiosk computers to the corporate domain takes some additional effort and increases risk to the corporate domain, it will allow minimal management effort to fulfill the requirements.

3. The kiosks computers at each physical location need to be secured against unauthorized tampering and modification. You have made them physically secure, and now you need to secure them logically, maximizing security risk to the corporate forest first and secondarily using a minimum amount of administrative effort needed for the lockdown and for long-term management. How should you do it?

○ A. Join the kiosk computers to the corporate domain and place the kiosk computers in a kiosk-specific OU. Use a kiosk-specific Group Policy to push down the local computer security settings. Enable loopback policy processing.

○ B. Install one kiosk computer and manually lock down. Clone the kiosk computer's hard drive and copy to the remaining kiosk computers.

○ C. Install one kiosk computer and use a specially configured Security Template to lock down. Clone the kiosk computer's hard drive and copy to the remaining kiosk computers.

○ D. Don't join the kiosk computers to the domain. Create a local Security Template with the appropriate security settings and install it in the computer's *Autoexec.bat* file so that each time the computer is rebooted, the local Security Template is applied.

The correct answer is B. Minimizing the security risk to the corporate forest rules out connecting the kiosks to the corporate domain, so answers A and D are not correct. Answer D would not work. To allow the *Autoexec.bat* file to install the Security Template each time the computer is rebooted, the logged-in user would have to be a local Administrator. This is not what you would want on a kiosk computer.

4. You are designing a SUS infrastructure for the company. You need to decide where to place the SUS servers to minimize direct connections to Microsoft's web site.

○ A. Place a single SUS server at the North American headquarters and instruct all forest computers to download their updates from the single SUS server.

○ B. Place a SUS server at each physical location. Configure each to download their updates from Microsoft.

○ C. Place two SUS servers at each physical location. Instruct one to download updates from Microsoft and the other to download its updates from the first.

○ D. Place a single SUS server at each physical location. Configure the SUS server in the North American forest root domain to download updates from Microsoft. Tell all other SUS servers to download updates from the forest root domain SUS server.

Answer D is correct. Only choices A and D would minimize connections to Microsoft. Answer A would be a second choice because a single SUS server would not perform as well as several distributed SUS servers, still accomplishing the same goal.

5. You need to design an IPSec policy for the private web server in the Napa Valley headquarters. You need to decide which policy settings to use. What should you choose?

○ A. An IPSec policy that will allow only HTTP and HTTPS to and from corporate computers and deny all other traffic.

○ B. An IPSec policy that will allow HTTPS to and from corporate computers, plus allow RDP traffic from anywhere. Deny all other traffic.

○ C. An IPSec policy that will allow HTTP and HTTPS from corporate computers, HTTPS traffic from external computers, and RDP traffic from anywhere. Deny all other traffic.

○ D. An IPSec policy that will allow HTTPS from anywhere, and only RDP traffic from the corporate computers. Deny all other traffic.

The correct answer is B. Corporate security policy clearly states that all network traffic must be encrypted, thus any solution with HTTP allowed must be rejected, ruling out answers A and C. Answer D would potentially allow external users to access the private web server, which is against corporate policy.

6. You need to design an IPSec policy for the public web server in the Napa Valley headquarters. You need to decide which policy settings to use. What should you choose?

○ A. An IPSec policy that will allow only HTTP and HTTPS to and from corporate computers and deny all other traffic. Deny all other traffic.

○ B. An IPSec policy that will allow HTTPS to and from corporate computers, plus allow RDP traffic from anywhere. Deny all other traffic.

○ C. An IPSec policy that will allow HTTP and HTTPS from corporate computers, HTTPS traffic from external computers, and RDP traffic from anywhere. Deny all other traffic.

○ D. An IPSec policy that will allow HTTPS from anywhere, and only RDP traffic from the corporate computers. Deny all other traffic.

The correct answer is D. Corporate security policy clearly states that all network traffic must be encrypted, thus any solution with HTTP allowed must be rejected, ruling out answers A and C. Answer B doesn't allow external traffic to reach the public web server.

7. You are designing a security strategy for the infrastructure and file servers (i.e., not web servers) at each physical location to prevent unauthorized access from the Internet.

   O A. Use Windows Firewall to prevent unauthorized traffic from the Internet from connecting to the servers.

   O B. Place all servers in a private IP subnet with NAT devices to connect them to the Internet.

   O C. Use IPSec to allow only communications to and from each file server from other file servers.

   O D. Configure local computer policy to use IP filtering.

The correct answer is A. Windows Firewall allows network connections to be defined by subnet, IP address, port number, and IP packet type. It would perform well in this scenario. Answer B would work, but NAT doesn't completely remove the risk of remote connections to private resources. Answer C would not allow normal client computers to access the file server. Answer D is wrong because IP filtering cannot be defined by IP address.

8. You need to design the best wireless security strategy you can to protect the company's wireless network from unauthorized access. What should you do?

   O A. Configure the wireless network nodes to use 802.1x security with digital certificates.

   O B. Configure the wireless access point with a host-based firewall to prevent access to unauthorized ports.

   O C. Require client-side certificates for all SSL/TLS connections.

   O D. Change all wireless access point SSIDs, disable SSID broadcasting, and disable DHCP on the wireless access point.

The correct answer is A. Choice B would not prevent unauthorized computers connecting to allowed ports. Answer C would only apply to connections made to web servers. The solutions in answer D are not considered very effective. 802.1x security with digital certificates is the best choice.

9. You need to design the best wireless security strategy you can to protect the company's wireless network from unauthorized access using EAP authentication. You want the most effective EAP choice that requires a username and password. Which EAP choice is best?

   O A. PEAP

   O B. EAP-TLS

   O C. EAP-MD5

   O D. .NET Passport

The correct answer is C. Choices A and B do not ask for user names or passwords. They use digital certificates. Answer D has nothing to do with EAP.

10. You need to design an access control and permission strategy for the mid-level admins located at each remote location so they can manage their own local users and printers. You place all the sub-admins in their own local group. How can you accomplish this using a minimum of administrative effort?

　○ A. Create a sub-admin OU. Create a role-based Security Template, link it to a role-based OU, and then link that to the sub-admin OU.

　○ B. Add the sub-admins to the Domain Admins group of each of their local domains.

　○ C. Give the sub-admins Full Control to all user and printer objects in their local domains.

　○ D. Use the Delegation of Control wizard to give the sub-admins group management rights over their local users and printers.

The correct answer choice is D. The Delegation of Control wizard was made for just such a purpose. Answer choice A might work, but contains more administrative effort than the former. Answer choice B would give the sub-admins too much control and control over more objects than just user and printer accounts. Answer choice C might work but is not the Microsoft recommended method.

11. You need to design a permission structure that allows legacy applications to run on computers without giving the end-users full Administrative permissions.

　○ A. Create an application shortcut with the RunAs feature. Make the legacy application start with the local Administrator's context. Give the local Administrator's password to the end users, but don't tell them it's the local Administrator's password. Instruct them to enter the password you give them when they run the legacy application using the RunAs shortcut.

　○ B. Find out what registry settings and file locations are needed by the legacy application. Create a Security Template with the appropriate Full Control permissions to those locations. Import the Security Template into a GPO that will be applied to all users needing access to the legacy application.

　○ C. Give the computer accounts running the legacy applications Full Control permissions to the legacy application's registry and folder locations.

　○ D. Create a GPO. Link the GPO to the OUs that contain the users needing access to the legacy application. Use the GPO to make all legacy application users local Administrators.

The correct answer is B. Answer A would not be good because you never want to give the local Administrator's password to regular end users. Answer C would allow any user on a particular computer to access the legacy application, but the permissions would not follow the user. Answer D would make all legacy application users local Administrators, which is denied by security policy.

12. The Temptation Winery company is creating a new application to replace the legacy applications previously mentioned. The CEO wants PKI and temporary certificates to be used to only allow involved programmers and selected users to access the new application. Once the new application is up and running, the CEO wants—as quickly as possible—to revoke the previously issued PKI digital certificates used during the programming phase and force end users to use existing certificates already stored on their smart cards. What is the PKI solution that should be set up to quickly expire the temporary keys?

○ A. Get all involved programmers and end users public certificates. When the project is over, ask the public CA to revoke all purchase certificates.

○ B. Use an existing private CA-issuing server to issue new certificates to involved programmers and users. When the project is over, revoke each existing certificate.

○ C. Using an existing private CA-issuing server, create a new subordinate CA. Issue involved programmers and users certificates from the new subordinate CA. When the project is over, go to the parent CA and revoke the subordinate's CA issuing CA certificate.

○ D. Create a new private online root CA. Issue certificates with daily expiring certificate expiration dates. Set the CA to allow certificate auto-renewal. When the project is over, remove the new online root CA.

The correct answer is C. A is the wrong answer because a public CA is not needed. B is incorrect because it has too much administrative overhead. Answer C is faster for quickly revoking certificates at the end of the project. Answer D is wrong because root CAs should not be online, and setting daily auto-renewals would probably lead to problems.

13. The CEO wants to require more security for users accessing the internal confidential database web server. Currently, users are required to use a smart card and PIN number to log on. How can security best be increased?

○ A. Require a longer PIN to be used with the smart card.

○ B. Require a second PIN to be used with the smart card.

○ C. Require a biometric retinal scan instead of the smart card and PIN.

○ D. Require a smart card, PIN, and fingerprint scan.

The answer is D. Only answer D is multi-factor. The other choices are either one-factor or two-factor solutions. In general, to increase authentication security, increase the number of factors.

14. The IT leader indicated that current security logging is inadequate. What is the best solution?

○ A. Collect all security logs to a central database location and run predefined queries to extract only the important events.

○ B. Customize each security log so that only critical information is collected, and then save to a centralized security log database.

○ C. Turn off security logging on noncritical machines.

○ D. Increase the size of the maximum security logfile and decrease the maximum number of days a security log is retained.

The correct answer is A. This is the only solution that works and fulfills the security policy requirements. Answer B would decrease the amount of security log events collected. It's always best to grab everything you can and query out the important stuff later. All the events may be needed in an important forensic investigation, so collect everything you can. Answer C violates security policy by not collecting security audits on some computers. Answer D would have no impact on the problem.

15. Confidential data transferred over the network from all file and web servers must be encrypted to internal computers. Choose the best solution.

   ○ A. Enable IPSec with the AH protocol for all traffic.

   ○ B. Enable IPSec with the ESP protocol for all traffic.

   ○ C. Enable EFS and WebDAV.

   ○ D. Enable EFS and Offline Folders and Files.

   The correct answer is B. Answer A would not encrypt the data. Answer C is only applicable for web servers. Answer D is only applicable for remote computers with Offline Folders and Files Shares and would not protect all traffic.

Testlet #2: Sunshine Surf Apparel

Overview

Professional surfer Kathleen Alice runs a large surf shop business with over 400 locations in 40 countries. It sells surfboards, surf trips, and all sorts of surfing apparel. There are many different departments at each location including: surfboards, clothing, travel, security, and administration.

Physical locations

The company's main office is located in Florida. It has three branch offices in:

- California
- Hawaii
- Australia

All of Sunshine Surf Apparel's client computers are XP Pro and the servers are Windows Server 2003.

Planned changes

Sunshine Surf Apparel is entering into a joint venture with Blue Water Bathing Suits. The Blue Water Bathing Suits company consists of a single Windows 2000 Active Directory domain. Blue Water Bathing Suits does not plan to upgrade any of its computer infrastructure, including its Windows 2000 server and workstations.

The network communications between the two companies will happen over the Internet using VPN protocols. Users from both companies will access data stored in a shared directory named Data, located on a Sunshine Surf Apparel server.

Directory Services structure

Sunshine Surf Apparel's Active Directory structure consists of a single forest with the following domains: sunshinesurf.com (for the continental U.S. locations), au.sunshinesurf.com (for the Australian branch office), and hi. sunshinesurf.com (for the Hawaiian branch office).

Network infrastructure

The headquarters and all branch offices run one or more domain controllers and file servers, all running Windows Server 2003. An IIS 6 web server is located at the Florida headquarters. The four offices connect to each other as follows:

Office location	Connection type/speed
Florida headquarters to California branch office	Dedicated T1 link
California branch office to Australia	512 KB link to the Internet, both sides
California branch office to Hawaii	384 KB private link, both sides
Hawaii to Australia	128 KB private link, both sides

The company has an existing private PKI infrastructure using Microsoft Certificate Services.

Problem statements

Some nonadministrative users have been making unauthorized registry and file resource changes to workstations and servers.

It is difficult to maintain all client computers with the latest patches.

Some computers are running old versions of application software. The company is unsure whether it is in complete software license compliance.

Access to file and share resources is assigned per user, which must be changed to make it more manageable.

Employee interview

The following interview discusses the situation.

Chief Information Officer
> We need to prevent both internal and external threats. Recently, a trusted database administrator was arrested for stealing credit card identities from our customers and making unauthorized purchases. She was recently fired, but it made us realize the significant threat we face from trusted insiders. Also, the CEO is constantly worried about confidential information leaking to the public or the media. Unfortunately, we have very little money budgeted for new security equipment and software this year.

Business requirements

All remote admin must be encrypted and authenticated. But because RDP is not strongly secure, RDP cannot be used to access company resources off the local network.

Security patches must be installed with a minimum of corporate WAN bandwidth use.

Each branch office is responsible to test software patches before deploying them within its environments.

All private company information must be kept confidential when stored and transferred, and its access tracked. Of course, the normal public company information (i.e., brochureware) is available on the company's publicly accessible web site.

All web server content updates must be encrypted and authenticated.

All email sent to business partners must be encrypted and authenticated by default.

All employees and business partners must have digital certificates to access company resources.

Questions

1. You need to design an access control strategy all users in each company department that meets the security requirements. Your solution must minimize forest-wide replication.

   ○ A. Create a Global group for each department and a Global group for each location. Add users to their respective department groups as members. Place departmental Global groups with the location Global groups. Assign the location Global groups to Active Directory resources in their respective domains, and then assign permissions for those resources by using the location Global groups.

   ○ B. Create a Global group for each department and add the respective users as members. Create Domain Local groups for resources. Add Global groups to their respective Domain Local groups. Then assign permissions to resources by using the Domain Local groups.

   ○ C. Create a local group on each local file server and add department users as members. Assign the appropriate permissions of each resource to the local groups.

   ○ D. Create a Universal group for each location and add the respective users as members. Assign the Universal group to the resources. Then assign resource permissions by using the Universal groups.

   The correct answer is B. It is the only answer that follows the preferred AGLP permission assigning method.

2. You need to design a remote administration solution for servers on the internal network, when accessing them from remote, external locations. Which solution meets the business and security requirements?

○ A. Use EMS over a serial connection.

○ B. Use Telnet with IPSec enabled for the connection.

○ C. Use Remote Desktop for Administration.

○ D. Use the RDP web client.

The correct answer is B. Answer A is only used for emergency recovery operations. Answer B requires IPSec to be used since Telnet passes logon information in plain text, and without IPSec would not be the correct answer choice. Answers C and D are disallowed because they are not allowed by the security requirements.

3. You need to design a method to encrypt confidential information. What is the best choice?

○ A. Require encrypted connections to all server computers.

○ B. Require encrypted connections to all server and client computers.

○ C. Require EFS on all servers and portable computers.

○ D. Require EFS on all client and server computers and IPSec to encrypt all communications.

The correct answer is D. Only answer D protects the information while stored and while transferred.

4. You need to design a solution to update the content on your web server. What is the best choice?

○ A. Use EFS.

○ B. Use FTP.

○ C. Use EFS and WebDAV over SSL.

○ D. Use IPSec with the AH protocol.

The correct answer is C. EFS would not protect information transferred over a network. FTP has no encryption or authentication by default. IPSec with the AH protocol enabled does not encrypt data.

5. You need to design a security Audit Policy to track accesses to the shared Data folder. How can you do that?

○ A. Audit for Directory Access.

○ B. Audit for Logon Events.

○ C. Audit for Logon Account Events.

○ D. Audit for Object Access.

The correct answer is D. Directory Access auditing would not access shared folder accesses. Audit for Logon Events and Logon Account Events would not audit all accesses to the shared folder.

6. You need to design a security Audit Policy to track logon attempt successes and failures using domain accounts. How can you do that?

○ A. Audit for Directory Access.

○ B. Audit for Logon Events.

○ C. Audit for Logon Account Events.

○ D. Audit for Object Access.

The correct answer is C. Audit Logon Account Events tracks domain account logons.

7. Security policies are pushed to client computers using Group Policies. What tools can be used to check the local effectiveness of applied security settings using Group Policies, to ensure that the appropriate Group Policy settings are being applied? (Choose two. Each answer is a complete solution.)

❑ A. Gpupdate

❑ B. Gpresult

❑ C. Security Configuration and Analysis tool

❑ D. Netsh

The correct answers are B and C. Gpupdate refreshes Group Policy because doesn't tell you the exact settings that applied. Netsh has nothing to do with Group Policy.

8. You are designing a SUS infrastructure for the company. You need to decide where to place the SUS servers to minimize company WAN bandwidth use.

○ A. Place a single SUS server at the Florida headquarters and instruct all forest computers to download their updates from the single SUS server.

○ B. Place a SUS server at each physical location. Configure each to download its updates from Microsoft. Configure the computers at each physical location to download their updates from their local SUS server.

○ C. Place two SUS servers in Florida. Instruct one to download updates from Microsoft and the other to download its updates from the first. All computers should download their updates from the second SUS server.

○ D. Place a single SUS server at each physical location. Configure the SUS server in Florida to download updates from Microsoft. Tell all other SUS servers to download updates from the Florida SUS server. All computers should then download updates from their local SUS server.

Answer B is correct. It is the only choice that would minimize corporate WAN bandwidth (while maximizing Internet bandwidth requirements).

9. Secure email is needed between Sunshine Surf Apparel and Blue Water Bathing Suits. How can this be accomplished?

○ A. Use existing PKI infrastructure to issue S/MIME digital certificates to all participating parties. Have Blue Water Bathing Suits add Sunshine Surf Apparel's PKI server as a trusted CA server. Then each party should use its S/MIME certificate to send secure email.

○ B. Install Outlook for web access. Require Blue Water Bathing Suits employees to send confidential email to the email addresses accessible in Outlook for web access.

○ C. Use PGP to encrypt email. Have each user add the other user's private key to the PGP keyring.

○ D. Use IPSec with the ESP protocol to encrypt all communications to and from Sunshine Surf Apparel's email server. Block all non-IPSec traffic.

Answer A is the correct choice. Nothing in B indicates that email would be encrypted or authenticated. Answer C is wrong because users should exchange public keys, not private keys. Answer D would cut off all nonsecure email, which would stop all non-IPSec email from reaching the email server.

10. How can Sunshine Surf Apparel be assured that all internal corporate employees have digital certificates?

    ◯ A. Enable auto-mapping.

    ◯ B. Use IIS web enrollment.

    ◯ C. Enable auto-enrollment.

    ◯ D. Enable auto-approval.

The best answer choice is C. Answer A indicates that when the user is issued a certificate, it will be linked to her Active Directory account, but it does not guarantee the user will get a certificate. Answer B requires manual work by the user. Answer D would automatically approve the certificate, but only after it is requested. We need to make sure each user requests a certificate.

Testlet #3: Lee Teaching Supplies Company

Overview

Lee Teaching Supplies is an industry leader in teaching supplies and textbooks on the east coast of North America.

Physical locations

Lee Teaching Supplies has three offices, in New York, Washington, D.C., and Georgia.

Business processes

The IT staff in New York uses client computers to remotely administer all Lee Teaching Supplies file servers, web servers, infrastructure servers, and domain controllers. Employees use their company-supplied laptops to access business information, which is stored on a Microsoft SQL Server with an IIS 6 web frontend.

Directory Services structure

The company has a single Active Directory domain named leeteaching.com. Each physical location has its own OU. Each physical location OU has child OUs representing the various departments located at each physical location.

All servers run Windows Server 2003. All IT administration is done in the central headquarters located in New York.

Network infrastructure

All client computers run Windows XP Pro, and all server computers run Windows Server 2003, with the exception of the newly acquired Georgia office. The Georgia office consists mostly of Windows 9x computers.

Lee Teaching Supplies company uses a two-tier private PKI solution with a subordinate issuing CA.

Each branch office has both wired and wireless networks for desktop, server, and laptop computers. The wireless infrastructure uses RADIUS, RRAS, IAS, and wireless access points that support 802.1x security, WEP, and WPA.

Problem statements

Ever since roaming profiles were initiated, users logging on to and off of the network encounter substantial delays.

Windows security groups often end up with unauthorized and missing members.

Lee Teaching Supplies is heavily reliant on EFS to protect stored data. There are two remote file servers where EFS has been enabled, but where it doesn't appear to be working.

Employee interview

The following interview discusses the situation.

Chief Information Officer
> Selling teaching supplies is my company's primary concern. Mine is security, and although management supports that objective, we must improve security on all computer resources using existing tools. We need a more secure Password Policy.
>
> We also have several Windows 9x legacy systems, which we would like to authenticate to Active Directory.
>
> Access to all servers must be logged, especially on IIS servers. We would like to track all IIS server access to a Microsoft SQL database log.
>
> We must be able to deploy security settings from a central location.
>
> We need to control what services and applications are running on each computer and server.
>
> Our law consultants are telling us we need logon message banners to warn unauthorized users against accessing our computer systems.
>
> We need a better, automated patch management solution for our entire enterprise. Right now, we reply on Automatic Updates—although it works, we are never sure what computers have what patches applied, and we are never given a chance to test patches before applying them. And when Automatic Updates goes off on every computer at 2 A.M., it overwhelms our limited network bandwidth.

We need to better track administrative tasks (e.g., adding and deleting users, modifying rights, etc.).

We must use the most secure wireless protection methods available.

Questions

1. You need to design a PKI certificate distribution method that meets the requirements of the CIO. Your solution must use minimum administrative effort. What should you do?

   ○ **A.** Use auto-enrollment and auto-approval for all computers.

   ○ **B.** Use IIS web enrollment for all computers.

   ○ **C.** Ask all users to use certificate requests files.

   ○ **D.** Use auto-enrollment where you can and IIS web enrollment where you have to.

   Answer D is correct. The company has Windows 9x legacy clients that cannot use auto-enrollment. Thus, the next best choice is IIS web enrollment.

2. Design a security solution to roll out logon messages.

   ○ **A.** Turn on logon messages using Group Policy. Apply to all computers.

   ○ **B.** Disable the Ctrl-Alt-Del key press requirement.

   ○ **C.** Configure the logon message text on all screensavers using a GPO.

   ○ **D.** Enable Logon Account Event auditing.

   The correct answer is A. The last three answers will not enable logon messages.

3. You need to design a security Audit Policy that will track when administrators modify local user and computer accounts on servers and domain controllers. What should you do?

   ○ **A.** Enable System Event auditing.

   ○ **B.** Enable Process Tracking auditing.

   ○ **C.** Enable Account Management auditing.

   ○ **D.** Enable Privilege Use and Object Access auditing.

   The correct answer is C. Account Management auditing would be the correct choice to monitor local user and group modifications.

4. You need to design a security Audit Policy that will track whether computers have been shut down or restarted. What should you do?

   ○ **A.** Enable System Event auditing.

   ○ **B.** Enable Process Tracking auditing.

   ○ **C.** Enable Account Management auditing.

   ○ **D.** Enable Privilege Use and Object Access auditing.

   The correct answer is A. When a Windows computer is shut down or restarts, it records these events in the system log only if System Event auditing has been enabled.

5. You instructed an administrator to track all accesses to a file share called Data. The administrator enabled Audit Object Access for successes and failures, but cannot figure out no event messages are being written when users access the share. What is wrong?

   ○ A. Forgot to enable "Trust this account for delegation."

   ○ B. Forgot to enable Audit Logon Accounts.

   ○ C. Forgot to give the Everyone group Allow-Full Control to the share.

   ○ D. Forgot to enable object access auditing in Windows Explorer.

   The correct answer is D. Enabling Object Access is a two-step process. First the Audit Object Access must be enabled globally, then the administrator must select the objects to monitor in Windows Explorer and enable auditing for selected users, groups, and computers.

6. It appears that a user or program is making unauthorized changes to its registry. What security audit category should be enabled to track registry changes?

   ○ A. System Events

   ○ B. Object Access

   ○ C. Special Privileges

   ○ D. Policy Change

   The correct answer is B. Audit Object Access tracks changes to selected files and registry settings.

7. You need a patch management tool to ensure all servers in your environment are in current patch compliance on all existing critical security patches. You don't want to take the chance that a patch management tool used will accidentally apply the patch. Which tool should you use?

   ○ A. Microsoft Baseline Security Analyzer

   ○ B. Windows Update

   ○ C. SUS/WSUS

   ○ D. RSoP

   The correct answer is A. MBSA will detect missing patches, but not apply them.

8. You need to design a patch management strategy that meets the security requirements of the company. Which should you do?

   ○ A. Use Microsoft Baseline Security Analyzer.

   ○ B. Migrate Windows Update users to Microsoft Update.

   ○ C. Use SUS/WSUS.

   ○ D. Use Active Directory Software Installs.

   The correct answer is C. SUS/WSUS is the Microsoft preferred solution for installing critical security patches.

9. You need to design a security solution to protect wireless networking according to the business requirements of the company. Which solution should you use?

○ A. Create a wireless network policy that uses data encryption and dynamic key assignments. Create a GPO with the new wireless policy and link it to the domain OU.

○ B. Use MAC filtering.

○ C. Use WPA encryption.

○ D. Require that all laptop users install SSL client certificates.

The correct answer is A. This describes 802.1x security, which is among the best wireless security solutions available. Answer B is a legacy option that is easy to bypass. Option C would be a good option if WPA2 or answer A weren't available. Answer D would only work when connecting to web servers.

10. You need to design a security log strategy that meets the requirements of the company. Which should you choose?

○ A. Enable logging on the company web site and select ODBC logging.

○ B. Enable logging on the company web site and configure URLScan logging.

○ C. Enable logging on the company web server and use the NCSA Common Log File format.

○ D. Enable IPSec and enable IPSec logging.

The correct answer is A. It is the only answer that meets the business requirements.

11. You need to design a method to deploy security configuration settings to servers and workstations with the least amount of long-term administrative effort. What should you do?

○ A. Run the RSoP Planning wizard and choose the appropriate Security Template.

○ B. Log on remotely to each server and configure the Local Computer Policy.

○ C. Create role-based OUs for each type of computer and place the respective computers inside the appropriate OU. Create role-based Security Templates and attach them to role-based GPOs. Then link the role-based GPO to the role-based OUs.

○ D. Create a role-based Security Template, log on locally to each computer, and apply the template using the Secedit.exe program.

The correct answer is C. This is the correct way to deploy security settings in an Active Directory environment. The RSoP Planning wizard would not configure security settings. Answers B and D might work, but require too much administrative effort in the long run.

12. You need to design a Windows security group strategy for deploying security permissions to local resources. How do you do it?

○ A. Give resource permissions to the Domain Local groups. Put users in Global groups. Place those Global groups in the Domain Local groups.

○ B. Give resource permissions to Global groups. Put the members in the Global groups.

○ C. Give resource permissions to Universal groups. Place the Universal groups in Global groups. Place the users in the Global groups.

○ D. Give the resource permissions to individual users. Place the users in Global groups. Place the Global group as a member of the Domain Local group.

The correct answer is A. It is the only answer that follows the AGLP (or AGULP) method of assigning security permissions.

1. EFS is enabled across all servers and workstations. On two file servers, EFS does not seem to be working. What is a common solution?

○ A. Enable the NT password hash.

○ B. Install Certificate Services and publish the EFS Certificate Template to the CA server.

○ C. Require FIPS-based encryption algorithms.

○ D. Enable the file server computer accounts to be trusted for delegation.

The correct answer is D. File server computer accounts must be trusted for delegation for EFS to work remotely. Answers A, B, and C have nothing to do with the possible solution.

2. Even since roaming user profiles were enabled, various users have complained of extremely long logon and logoff times. How can you best fix the problem?

○ A. Disable roaming profiles.

○ B. Enable folder redirection using a Group Policy.

○ C. Delete documents in the My Documents folder that have not been used in over one year.

○ D. Enable the user's account to be trusted for delegation.

The correct answer is B. When roaming profiles are enabled, the user's profile, which includes his My Documents folder, must be copied up to the network and down to the local machine when the user logs on or off a computer. If the user's My Documents folder is big, this can create extremely long logon or logoff times. Folder redirection can be used to keep the user's My Document folder on the network file server.

3. The administrator wants to prevent any unauthorized applications, programs, or scripts from being executed by end users. What technology should you deploy?

○ A. Use Share permissions.

○ B. Use Folder Redirection.

○ C. Use Software Restriction Policies.

○ D. Use Active Directory Software Installs.

The correct answer is C. The other answer choices could not be used to stop unauthorized software execution.

4. The CIO wants to change the company's Password Policy for domain logons. Where must the Password Policy be changed?

○ A. At the Site OU

○ B. In Local Computer Policy

○ C. In Default Security Template

○ D. At the domain container

The correct choice is answer D. Although the Password Policy can be modified at any OU or contain level, it must be modified at the domain level to take affect.

5. The local Administrators Group is constantly getting unauthorized members who really don't belong there. Often well-meaning administrators who are trying to rule out permission problems with an application error have caused this problem. They throw the user with the application error into the Administrators group to see whether the application error goes away, but then they forget to remove the user. What Group Policy feature can be used to remedy this situation?

○ A. Restricted Groups.

○ B. Software Restriction Policies.

○ C. Password Policy.

○ D. Enable the "This account is sensitive and cannot be delegated" option.

The correct answer is A. GPO's Restricted Groups feature is the only choice that would remove unauthorized members from the local Administrators group.

Testlet #4: Elizabethan Broadway Productions

Overview

Elizabethan Broadway Productions is a producer of Broadway plays, which run on Broadway and elsewhere. Besides producing plays, they sell scripts, write screenplays, and sell acting props and set materials.

Physical locations

Elizabethan Broadway Productions is headquartered in New York, with 16 retail locations on the east and west coasts of North America.

Planned changes

The company wants to add two new VPN servers to allow mobile users and remote locations to connect to the corporate headquarters' network. The previous single VPN server is overworked with remote client connections. All client computers are Windows XP Pro. There is an existing web server on the network for production applications, and a second web server for testing and development.

Business processes

Elizabethan Broadway Production has the following departments:

- Management
- Information Technology
- Accounting
- Productions
- Script Writing
- Retail Sales

Internet users must register with a username and password with Elizabethan Broadway Productions to purchase scripts and props from the company's public web site. Customer information is stored in a Microsoft SQL Server database with an IIS 6 frontend.

After web customers place orders, the data is stored in a shared folder called Data, and the Retail Sales department is responsible for fulfilling the order and shipping it. The Accounting department is responsible for financial collections and balancing the books on a monthly basis.

Directory Services structure

The network consists of a single Active Directory domain. Each department has its own OU.

All servers run Windows Server 2003. All client computers run Windows XP Pro.

Network infrastructure

The New York office has a high-speed connection to the Internet. A single Microsoft Internet Security and Acceleration Server (ISA) protects the internal network.

Remote users connect to the corporate network over the Internet using a VPN tunnel.

The New York office has a private offline root CA installed. No user or computer certificates have been issued. Management wants to use digital certificates, but the IT team is too overworked to manually distribute the certificates.

The accounting department has a very popular accounting application that requires Administrator access to run.

The New York office also has a wireless network.

Employee interview

The following interview discusses the situation.

Chief Information Officer
    There is currently no automated patch solution.

We have a problem with users installing unauthorized software and modifying their local registries.

The New York Internet connection has been over-utilized and slow for over a year now. Therefore, no new applications or solutions can be added that put additional strain in the Internet connection.

Only local laptop users should be using the wireless network. Wireless security consists of enabling WEP encryption and MAC filtering.

Confidential data stored on portable computers, transferred from the web site, and located in the shared Data folder must be encrypted.

The accounting department needs a two-factor authentication solution for accessing its computers.

Questions

1. Design an authentication strategy for the account department. Your solution must meet the business requirements.

   ○ A. Install wireless 802.1x security.

   ○ B. Disable the storage of LM password hashes.

   ○ C. Activate the PKI infrastructure, install smart card readers, and let Accounting use smart cards with a PIN.

   ○ D. Run the RSoP wizard in Planning mode.

   The correct answer is C. Management wants employees to use digital certificates for authentication, which requires smart cards and an active PKI domain.

2. Elizabethan Broadway Productions now has three VPN servers. Where should the VPN servers be terminated to decrease security risks?

   ○ A. In the DMZ, just after the firewall but before the internal LAN

   ○ B. Just before the firewall on the external Internet segment

   ○ C. Inside the network, past the firewall

   ○ D. On the wireless network, past the firewall

   The correct answer is A. VPN tunnels are famous for allowing malicious traffic and malware to slip past the firewall. For that reason, all VPNs should be terminated outside the local network. A good location is in the DMZ.

3. Elizabethan Broadway Productions has three VPN servers. It takes additional administrative effort to manage both servers. What is a good solution to minimize management overhead?

   ○ A. Buy a super server and consolidate all VPN servers into one master VPN server.

   ○ B. Add more memory to the first VPN server, and turn off the second and third.

   ○ C. Use IAS server to manage all VPN servers.

   ○ D. Put the VPN servers on a round-robin access server to evenly distribute the workload.

The correct answer is C. IAS is made to manage multiple VPN servers more easily. Answers A and B aren't good solutions because they remove the service redundancy given by multiple servers. Answer D would not decrease VPN management overhead.

4. Elizabethan Broadway Productions has three VPN servers. A new business partner wants to connect to the VPN servers, but the several connecting computers are very old Macintosh computers. How can the VPN servers be modified to accept older Macintosh authentication?

   ○ A. Configure RRAS to use PPTP.

   ○ B. Configure RRAS to use L2TP/IPSec.

   ○ C. Configure RRAS to allow CHAP or Basic authentication.

   ○ D. Configure RRAS to allow MS-CHAP and MS-CHAPv2 authentication.

   The correct answer is C. Legacy Macintosh computers do not use MS-CHAP or MS-CHAPv2 authentication (Mac OS X 8.5 and later can use MS-CHAP), but can use CHAP or Basic authentication.

5. You need to design a better security solution for the web servers. Your solution must address company requirements and provide a granular way to parse incoming web requests. What should you do?

   ○ A. Enable WebDAV.

   ○ B. Enable Windows Integrated Authentication.

   ○ C. Enable HTTPS.

   ○ D. Install and configure URLScan.

   The correct answer is D. Only URLScan allows incoming web requests to be parsed on a granular basis.

6. One of the most common IT support issues is dealing with wrongly configured VPN connections. How can the IT support staff decrease support calls related to incorrectly configured VPN connections?

   ○ A. Use the Connection Manager Administration Kit (CMAK) to make and distribute VPN connection profiles.

   ○ B. Disable IPSec/L2TP security and require only PPTP connections.

   ○ C. Enable unauthenticated access in RRAS.

   ○ D. Require 802.1x security.

   The correct answer is A. The CMAK utility was made so that administrators could create and predefine VPN connection profiles and send them to users to install and use.

7. How can IT prevent unauthorized software from being installed or executed?

   ○ A. Use Software Restriction Policies.

   ○ B. Use the CMAK application.

   ○ C. Configure Internet Explorer settings to prevent software downloads.

   ○ D. Block all file downloads on the ISA server firewall.

The correct answer is A. Answer B is for remote VPN connections. Answer C could prevent software downloads from the Web, but would not affect downloads elsewhere (e.g., FTP, IM, etc.) and would not prevent local installs. Answer D would not prevent local installs.

8. How can Elizabethan Broadway Productions' PKI solution be fixed, leveraging existing infrastructure?

○ A. Install a new online enterprise root CA.

○ B. Install a new offline issuing CA.

○ C. Use the existing offline root CA to create an online issuing CA.

○ D. Use the existing offline root CA to create an online root CA.

Answer C is the correct answer. The company already has an offline root CA. The best option is to use the existing offline root CA to create a new subordinate online issuing CA. Answers A and B would ignore the existing root CA. Answer D would just create another root CA, when what we need is an issuing CA.

9. Management wants internal employees to be able to authenticate to the internal web server using their Active Directory accounts, but without having to manually log on to the web server. What is the best choice?

○ A. Disable anonymous access.

○ B. Enable Windows-Integrated authentication.

○ C. Enable .NET Passport authentication.

○ D. Use RDP.

The correct answer is B. Answer A would have no effect upon the solution. Answer C would not be using the user's already existing Active Directory account. Answer D is used for remote server management, not general web server authentication.

10. On the public web server, the first few introduction web pages should be available to any user, without any authentication needed. Then there are several web pages that external users should have to authenticate in order to see. How can you accomplish this?

○ A. Create two separate web sites. On the first web site, allow anonymous connections and post the web pages not needing authentication. On the second web site, require authentication.

○ B. Enable both anonymous connections and authenticated access on the web server.

○ C. Use NTFS permissions and allow the anonymous user to access the public web pages, but enable Deny-Full Control to Authenticated Users on the pages requiring authentication.

○ D. Set anonymous authentication, which is needed on the public web pages that do not need authentication. Then disable anonymous authentication and require authenticated access on the web pages and directories requiring authenticated access.

Prep and Practice

The correct answer is D. Answer A would work but would be overkill. Answer B would allow anonymous users to connect to the web site's pages requiring authentication. Answer D would prevent authenticated users from seeing pages marked with Deny-Full Control.

Index

We'd like to hear your suggestions for improving our indexes. Send email to *index@oreilly.com*.

I

IANA (Internet Assigned Numbers
Authority), 224
IAS (Internet Authentication
Service), 460, 492, 515, 516
ICF (Internet Connection Firewall), 13,
495
(see also Windows Firewall)
ICS (Internet Connection Sharing), 119,
181
IDSs (Intrusion Detection
Systems), 313, 372
IIS (Internet Information Server), 117,
445–456, 491
authentication, 448–452
authentication methods, 512
client certificate mapping, 452
execute permissions, 447
IIS logging, 453–454
log file format, 454
logging, 514
NTFS permissions, 447
permissions, 445
securing, 511–515
SSL/TLS installation and use, 451
URLScan, 452
web application pool identity, 448
web printing and, 52
Web Service Extensions, 454, 514
Web user authentication, 447
WebDAV, 456
impersonation, 404, 498
implicit trusts, 218
infrastructure master, 217
infrastructure Mode, 462, 517
infrastructure servers, 415
Input/Output (I/O)
devices, 68, 164
ports, 64
Integrated Installation, 31
Integrated Windows
authentication, 449, 512
international geographical model, 232
Internet Assigned Numbers Authority
(IANA), 224
Internet Connection Firewall (see ICF)
Internet connection options, 370
Internet Connectivity, 309–313, 331
Internet Explorer, 14, 116, 180
Internet Information Servier (see IIS)

Interrupt Requests (IRQs), 64
intersite and intrasite replication, 218,
336, 337
Intrusion Detection Systems
(IDSs), 313, 372
IP addresses and addressing, 105,
224–226, 340
address assignment, 369
address classes, 105, 177, 340
alternate IP addressing, 304
analyzing, 326
APIPA (Automatic Private IP
Addressing), 225, 340
assignment of addresses, 330
classful IP address ranges, 224
DHCP, 226, 305, 330, 369
automation via, 341
IP routing, 226
private address security, 416
private IP addresses, 225, 340
static address configuration, 109,
178
subnets, 226
IP Filters, 495
IP routing, 341
Ipconfig command, 112, 179
IPSec (Internet Protocol
Security), 441–445, 491, 502,
510
AH and ESP protocols, 444
authentication, 443
built-in policies, 442
components, 511
default policies, 444, 511
modes, 511
Tunnel and Transport modes, 444
IP-spoofing attacks, 366
IrDA (Infrared) devices, 164
wireless devices, 69
IRQs (Interrupt Requests), 64
ISPs (Internet Service Providers),
choosing, 371
Iterative queries, 221
IUSR_machinename accounts, 447, 448

K

Kerberos, 403, 497
policy, 522
keyboards, 68

N

About the Authors

Pawan K. Bhardwaj, an independent technical trainer and author, is MCSE, MCSA, Security+, Network+, I-Net+, and A+ certified. He teaches Windows Administration and Networking classes and also provides consulting to training institutions. He has authored or contributed to 12 certification books and served as technical reviewer for the best selling titles *MCSE Windows 2000 Exams in a Nutshell* and *MCSE 2003 Core Exams in a Nutshell*, both published by O'Reilly.

Roger A. Grimes (CPA, CISSP, CEH, MCSE: Security) is a 19-year Windows security veteran who has written 6 books and over 150 national magazine articles on the subject. Roger is a three-time Microsoft MVP in Windows Security (and MVP of the Month in December 2005). He participated in the Microsoft Windows Server 2003 Learning curriculum and was an Early Achiever of the Windows Server 2003 MSCE: Security designation. Roger has written advanced Windows security courses for Microsoft, Foundstone, and SANS.

Colophon

The animal on the cover of *MCSE Core Elective Exams in a Nutshell* is a water buffalo. Not to be confused with the American bison, the water buffalo is native to Africa and Asia and is also found in parts of Europe as well as Pakistan and Afganistan. It spends its time in grassy swamplands, where it can spend copious amounts of time wallowing in mud and water while finding much vegetation to eat. The water buffalo likes to spend most of its time submerged almost completely in the water. This offers the water buffalo a natural protection against insects and parasites that can plague it. It is mainly nocturnal, especially in areas heavily populated with humans.

The water buffalo is a massive animal, standing over 6 feet and weighing over 2,000 pounds. Both males and females have long horns that begin at the top of the head and reach back. These horns can be curvy or straight and can reach lengths of six feet. Its hair is dark gray, coarse, and short. Its diet consists of grass, tree bark, sticks, and other vegetation.

The cover image is from *Riverside Natural History*. The cover font is Adobe ITC Garamond. The text font is Linotype Birka; the heading font is Adobe Myriad Condensed; and the code font is LucasFont's TheSans Mono Condensed.

Better than e-books

Buy *MCSE Core Elective Exams in a Nutshell*
and access the digital edition FREE on
Safari for 45 days.

Go to www.oreilly.com/go/safarienabled
and type in coupon code B6K8-I2ZJ-4XAL-G6JM-WLRX

Search
thousands of
top tech books

Download
whole chapters

Cut and Paste
code examples

Find
answers fast

Search Safari! The premier electronic reference
library for programmers and IT professionals.

Related Titles from O'Reilly

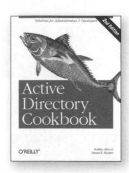

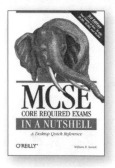

Windows Administration

Active Directory Cookbook, *2nd Edition*

Active Directory, *3rd Edition*

DNS on Windows Server 2003

Essential Microsoft Operations Manager

Essential SharePoint

Exchange Server Cookbook

Learning Windows Server 2003, *2nd Edition*

MCSE Core Elective Exams in a Nutshell

MCSE Core Required Exams in a Nutshell, *3rd Edition*

Monad

Securing Windows Server 2003

SharePoint Office Pocket Guide

SharePoint User's Guide

Windows Server 2003 in a Nutshell

Windows Server 2003 Network Administration

Windows Server 2003 Security Cookbook

Windows Server Cookbook

Windows Server Hacks

Windows XP Cookbook